Why Do You Need This New Edition?

This comprehensive business communication text focuses on core principles and skills with an emphasis on leadership for today's global workplace. Here are six good reasons to buy this new edition:

1. *Increased Emphasis on Leadership.* The new edition builds on the popular leadership theme introduced in the first edition, expanding the discussion and application of leadership in every chapter—with an emphasis on how effective communication skills can enhance one's ability to lead and influence others. The leadership focus is further developed by new chapter-opening scenarios that profile successful real-world business leaders, and with new boxes called *Leaders on Leadership*, which provide practical advice and insights from contemporary business leaders.

2. *Stronger Emphasis on Technology.* The new edition includes new and expanded discussions of the impact of new communication technology on the global workplace. New *Communication for a Digital Age* boxes further extend the technology coverage by describing technological tools and how to apply them in the workplace.

3. *New Pedagogical Aids to Enhance Learning.* This edition introduces expanded chapter-opening scenarios profiling successful

business leaders. These narratives are followed by provocative *Leading Questions* to give students something to ponder and look for as they read the chapter. In addition to other study aids—such as learning objectives, internal "Recap" summaries, and a running marginal glossary—this edition includes new chapter *Wrap-Ups*, which review key concepts, and *The Principle Points* sections, which summarize the five communication principles as they apply to chapter content.

4. *Numerous New Examples and Boxes Throughout.* Figures, cartoons, examples, and boxes have been replaced and updated throughout to reflect technological trends and key developments. In addition, *Communication Ethics @ Work* boxes offer a penetrating look at recent events such as David Letterman's "office romance" or the recent issues surrounding Greg Mortensen's alleged fabrication of information related to his foundation and fundraising efforts to build schools in Pakistan and Afghanistan.

5. *Updated and Expanded Research Base.* This edition expands the contemporary research base in communication studies and related fields, including new findings related to generational differences in the workplace.

6. *Streamlined Coverage.* Recognizing the need to keep the book at a manageable length while still capturing the changing world of communication in the global workplace, we have made every effort to streamline the text, removing outdated and redundant information. The result is a more concise text.

PEARSON

Business and Professional Communication

Principles and Skills for Leadership

Second Edition

Steven A. Beebe
Texas State University—San Marcos

Timothy P. Mottet
Texas State University—San Marcos

PEARSON

Boston Columbus Indianapolis New York San Francisco Upper Saddle River
Amsterdam Cape Town Dubai London Madrid Milan Munich Paris Montréal Toronto
Delhi Mexico City São Paulo Sydney Hong Kong Seoul Singapore Taipei Tokyo

DEDICATED TO

Sue Beebe
—SAB

Rick Gonzalez
—TPM

Editor-in-Chief, Communication: Karon Bowers
Senior Acquisitions Editor: Melissa Mashburn
Director of Development: Eileen Calabro
Development Editor: Hilary Jackson
Editorial Assistant: Megan Hermida
Marketing Manager: Blair Zoe Tuckman
Associate Development Editor: Corey Kahn
Senior Digital Editor: Paul DeLuca
Digital Editor: Lisa Dotson
Project Manager: Anne Ricigliano

Project Coordination, Text Design, and Electronic Page
   Makeup: Cenveo Publisher Services
Senior Cover Design Manager/Designer: Nancy Danahy
Cover Image: © Corbis Flirt/Alamy
Text Permissions: Robyn Feller
Photo Research: Marta Johnson, PreMediaGlobal
Manufacturing Buyer: Mary Ann Gloriande
Printer/Binder: Courier/Kendallville
Cover Printer: Courier/Kendallville

Credits and acknowledgments borrowed from other sources and reproduced, with permission, in this textbook appear on the appropriate page within text or on pages 409-428 and 436.

Library of Congress Cataloging-in-Publication Data

Beebe, Steven A.
  Business and professional communication : principles and skills for
leadership / Steven A. Beebe, Timothy P. Mottet. — 2nd ed.
       p. cm.
  Includes bibliographical references and index.
  ISBN 978-0-205-02899-3 (alk. paper)
  1. Communication in management.   2. Business communication.
  3. Leadership.   4. Communication.   I. Mottet, Timothy P. II. Title.
  HD30.3.B42 2013
  658.4'5—dc23

                                                        2011047398

10 9 8 — CRK — 15 14

www.pearsonhighered.com

ISBN 0-205-02899-3
ISBN 978-0-205-02899-3

Brief Contents

Detailed Contents

PART II Relationship Skills

PART III   Collaboration Skills

To be effective in the twenty-first century workplace, you need to be able to communicate and influence others in positive and ethical ways. We agree with James Hume's well-crafted epithet: "The art of communication is effective leadership." Consequently, this book is about two things: communication and leadership. Communication and work go hand-in-hand; it's hard to talk about the workplace without also talking about the communication that makes work happen, from developing relationships with co-workers to building work teams and making presentations. Closely linked to any discussion of workplace communication is the art and science of leading others. As with our successful first edition, the purpose of this revision is to prepare readers for the communication and leadership demands of the modern workplace. We do this by presenting key communication principles and skills and emphasizing how to apply those principles and skills in order to lead and be successful in business and professional settings.

What's New in This Edition

We are grateful to both students and faculty who have provided excellent confirming comments and constructive suggestions to enhance this book. Responding to their suggestions, we've made the following revisions to this new edition:

- STRONGER EMPHASIS ON LEADERSHIP As suggested by the subtitle, *Principles and Skills for Leadership*, the principles and skills discussed focus on enhancing students' leadership talent. Although leadership was a strong emphasis in the first edition, we've developed and enhanced our leadership focus more fully in text discussions and new features in this new edition.

  - Each chapter now opens with a *narrative* that illustrates how communication and leadership principles resulted in business and professional success for an actual business leader and organization. We follow each narrative with *Leading Questions*, a series of provocative questions that encourage students to think about and apply the leadership principles described in the opening scenario to the subsequent chapter discussions.

Although you probably do not recognize the name Indra Nooyi, you're probably familiar with many of the products she is responsible for producing, including Pepsi, Gatorade, and Fritos. Nooyi is CEO of PepsiCo, which is responsible for Pepsi products as well as Tropicana, Frito Lay, Gatorade, and Quaker Oats products. In 2010 she was named number 1 on *Fortune*'s list of the "50 Most Powerful Women" and number 6 on *Forbes*'s list of the "World's 100 Most Powerful Women."

leading questions

1. Nooyi attributes much of her success to being grounded and knowing who she is as a person. How do you see self-awareness being related to leadership effectiveness?

2. How do you see self-awareness and mindfulness being similar and different?

- NEW *Leaders on Leadership Boxes* further reinforce the leadership theme by presenting practical advice about communication and leadership from seasoned real-world leaders. Although these leaders are at the peak of their profession, they offer down-to-earth advice that students will find applicable to their own career path. Students learn what these leaders have learned—that communication is critical to one's ability to be effective in the workplace.

Listen Up[56]

When you talk you expect other people to listen to you. So does your boss. In fact, one of Sheila Lirio Marcelo's sources of frustration as a leader is people who don't listen to her. As the founder and chief executive officer of Care.com, she assumed that her followers would listen to her. But even as CEO, she found her employees not listening. When asked, "What are your pet peeves?" she said, "Having to repeat myself more than three times." Having one of her employees tune her out is only one of her concerns. Another concern she has is "people who jump to conclusions with one observation. I'm a big believer in getting a few data points of observable behavior before you give somebody the gift of feedback on something. And I typically will say: 'Look, I've observed this two or three times. Let's have a conversation about it.'"

Marcelo emphasizes listening by giving employees a new perspective. She does this by asking her employees to do another person's job for a while. "I give them a new seat at the table. And people don't have a choice where they sit; we rotate them. . . . You sit with somebody else from a different team so you get to know their job. What are they doing? What are they saying on the phone? How do they tick? It forces people to listen."

In this chapter we've emphasized what Marcelo and other leaders consider to be a weakness in new employees. Listening strategies that have been detailed include turning off competing messages, listening with your eyes, and linking both major ideas and details together. A number of responding strategies were also reviewed, including how to respond with empathic messages as well as responding by adapting to gender and cultural differences.

Whether you're listening to your boss, your colleagues, a client or a customer, make sure that you are listening at peak proficiency so that your listening behavior won't become a pet peeve of others—especially your boss's pet peeve.

- **INCREASED EMPHASIS ON TECHNOLOGY** Recognizing the ongoing impact of new technological tools, including social networking, microblogging, video conferencing, and interviewing, and presentation software on the global workplace and on our communication, we have increased our coverage of digital communication and its influence.

  - NEW *Communication Skills for a Digital Age boxes* explore the latest communication technology, such as making organizational websites "culturally-friendly" and the "Do's and Don'ts of Using Facebook at Work," and then offer tips for how to incorporate and manage such tools in your workplace communication.

Communication Skills FOR A Digital Age

Making Organizational Websites Culturally Friendly

"I'm lovin' it." You may quickly recognize this popular slogan and jingle, used by McDonald's restaurants. The fast-food chain has been very successful in spreading this message of "love" for their people and products around the globe. Have you ever considered how they do that so successfully? One major consideration is their company's web presence. McDonald's executives and web designers have taken a careful and thoughtful approach to developing web presence that is relatable among various cultures.[31] They consider cultural values, such as high and low context, when determining color, content, layout, image choice, and the interactive nature of the site. In higher context cultures, images and content tend to focus on the value of a product to bring people together, and in low-context cultures they tend to market

selection played a major role in the likelihood that users would report positive impressions of a site. Put simply, the organizations that took cultural considerations into account were more likely to have their website rated positively by a diverse audience. And following McDonald's lead, diverse websites can certainly enhance a product or organizations' image in a global marketplace, translating to more opportunities for growth.

Applying Your Skills[35]

- *Analyze your audience.* When considering the cultural implications of your website, first identify your target audience. You can make better judgments about the cultural implications of many items on your site if you first know

- NEW text discussions highlight technological developments, including such topics as: the impact of text messaging on verbal communication in the workplace (Chapter 3); electronic brainstorming (Chapter 10); the effective use of technology and email in the workplace (Chapter 14); and tips for how to develop effective writing skills in the digital age—this age of "informal communication" (Chapter 14).

- **UPDATED AND EXPANDED RESEARCH BASE** Each chapter includes numerous references to the latest communication and leadership research. New research helps students apply each of the five communication principles to their own workplace experiences.

- **COMPLETE CHAPTER ON BUSINESS WRITING** Recognizing the importance of effective writing skills in today's workplace, we have expanded the former Appendix on written communication to a complete chapter, covering basic business writing skills, using technology and email thoughtfully, and writing business letters and specific documents.

- **STRIKING NEW DESIGN AND VISUALS** One of the principles we teach is that *Information is not communication*. We want to go beyond merely explaining key principles and concepts, so we provide numerous examples, boxes, photos and cartoons to help engage the reader in the material and illustrate core concepts.

  - A new design and color palette keep the book fresh and contemporary-looking.

  - Examples, photos, cartoons, and boxes have been replaced and updated throughout to make this new edition as current as possible and to reflect trends and key events.

- **STREAMLINED COVERAGE AND REDUCED LENGTH** Recognizing the multiple demands on students' time, we have made this edition more concise and streamlined, while maintaining the breadth and depth of coverage that readers valued in the first edition.

Plan of the Book

Our comprehensive text focuses on core communication principles and skills, with an emphasis on leadership for today's global workplace. Beginning in Chapter 1, we introduce students to key leadership approaches and then explicitly discuss how communication principles and skills are integral to being an effective and ethical leader.

- **A FOCUS ON LEADERSHIP** Although some students may aspire to an influential leadership role, such as being CEO at a large company, many others are simply trying to figure out their vocational calling. Yet regardless of how firm a student's professional goals are (whether they aspire to be the next Donald Trump or Oprah Winfrey or simply get a job to pay the bills), students in the contemporary workplace will influence colleagues and co-workers with their communication skills. A person need not be anointed "the leader" to be a leader in the workplace. Regardless of how students perceive themselves, they will influence others as they communicate with their colleagues, which is the essence of leadership.

  Every chapter of the text is infused with discussions related to principles and skills for leadership. Although most business and professional communication textbooks include a discussion of leadership, we have woven discussion and application of leadership *into each chapter*, from the opening scenarios that profile successful leaders to tips and guidelines for how to communicate and lead effectively in boxes and text discussions throughout.

- **A FOCUS ON COMMUNICATION SKILL APPLICATIONS** Rather than merely listing and describing communication skills, our approach is designed to help students apply communication skills to the workplace. The second edition strengthens and expands our application of communication skills to business and professional settings, from the chapter opening narratives and "*Leading Questions*" to practical tips and guidelines to the skill-building activities at the end of chapters.

  In business and professional contexts there are four primary communication skill sets that lead to success: relating, collaborating, presenting, and writing. We offer specific recommendations on how to develop these competencies, drawing upon the latest communication research and wisdom from seasoned leaders.

  - *Relationship Skills.* Relationship skills are essential in working with others in a variety of business and professional settings. In addition to helping students understand how professional relationships are established and maintained, we focus on specific skills, such as how to interview others as well as how to be interviewed and how to manage interpersonal conflict.

  - *Collaboration Skills.* Working in groups and teams, and attending and leading meetings occupies a considerable amount of time in the contemporary workplace. Whether collaborating face-to-face or in electronically-mediated situations, today's workers must understand how to work together effectively and appropriately. How to solve problems and make decisions as a team, as well as learning how to unleash the creative potential of groups during meetings, are key skills that are emphasized in Chapters 9 and 10.

- *Presentation Skills.* In addition to relating and collaborating, contemporary workers are frequently called on to present their ideas to others. Whether one-on-one, during meetings, or to a larger audience, effectively presenting information to others as well as persuading others are essential communication and leadership competencies.

- *Writing Skills.* Although our emphasis in this book remains on developing oral skill competence, being able to communicate ideas in writing is important when relating, collaborating, and presenting to others. We've expanded our former appendix about business and professional writing skills into a fully developed new chapter, Chapter 14.

- **A FOCUS ON COMMUNICATION PRINCIPLES** We've organized our study of business and professional communication around five fundamental communication principles that can enhance communication skill and leadership abilities. Together, these five principles provide readers with a useful framework for understanding how leaders can become effective communicators. The five principles are:

    Principle One: Leaders are **aware** of their communication with themselves and others

    Principle Two: Leaders effectively use and interpret **verbal** messages

    Principle Three: Leaders effectively use and interpret **nonverbal** messages

    Principle Four: Leaders **listen** and respond thoughtfully to others

    Principle Five: Leaders appropriately **adapt** messages to others

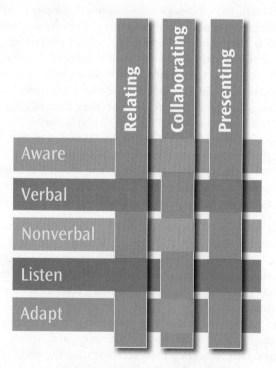

FIGURE 1.2 Communication Principles and Skills for Leadership

In most business and professional communication texts, communication principles are introduced early in the book and then rarely explicitly mentioned. In our text, these core communication principles are clearly integrated into our discussion of business and professional communication skills throughout the book.

In addition to making explicit references to each principle in our discussions, **NEW** summaries, called *The Principle Points*, connect the principles to specific chapter content.

The Principle Points sections appear at the end of each skill development chapter and not only help readers see how the principles relate to the chapter material, but also serve as a helpful summary feature to confirm students' understanding of key communication and leadership principles.

The Principle Points

Principle One: Be aware of your communication with yourself and others.

- Be aware of how others perceive you in terms of interpersonal attraction, similarity, and status.
- Be aware of the types of communication you use in your various workplace relationships with supervisors, subordinates, coworkers, and customers.
- Be aware of your own and others' conflict styles when relating in the workplace.

Principle Two: Effectively use and interpret verbal messages.

- To delegate effectively, use verbal messages that follow the DRGRAC method: stating desired results, establishing guidelines, providing resources, clarifying accountability, and describing consequences.

Overview of the Book

The opening chapter provides the prelude to the study of business and professional communication by explaining fundamental communication models and concepts. We then introduce the five communication principles and show how those principles are linked to the critical skills of relating, collaborating, presenting, and writing. We also describe leadership approaches and how leadership has been studied during the past century.

Chapters 2 through 5 present each of the five communication principles in more detail. Chapter 2 discusses Principle 1, being aware of self and others, noting how a person's social style reflects his/her self-concept as well as how he/she perceives others. Helping students understand their own approach to leadership and the role of organizational culture also enhances their awareness of themselves and others. Chapter 3 presents the key principles of using and interpreting both verbal messages (Principle 2) and nonverbal messages (Principle 3). Our use of verbal and nonverbal symbols constitutes the messages we both send and receive. Chapter 4 describes Principle 4, the process of listening and responding to others. Chapter 5 helps students adapt to others (Principle 5) by understanding how one's personality, culture, and gender influence how we send and interpret messages.

The remaining chapters apply the principles of communication to the three most important skill sets used in business and professional contexts: relating, collaborating, and presenting. We first apply the five communication principles to the skills of relating to others. Chapter 6 describes different types of workplace relationships and emphasizes how to understand and manage conflict at work. Chapters 7 and 8 cover essential information to help students relate to others during interviews. Chapter 7 emphasizes core principles and skills of interviewing, while Chapter 8 identifies the most common types of interviews encountered in business and professional settings: information gathering interviews, job interviews, and appraisal interviews.

Building upon the skill of relating to others in interpersonal contexts we turn our attention to collaborating with others. Chapter 9 helps students apply the five principles to a variety of group and team situations and understand how teams work. Chapter 10 focuses on the ubiquitous business meeting and how to make meetings effective. Skills for enhancing decision making, problem solving, and conducting creative meetings are presented along with skills for facilitating meeting discussion, avoiding groupthink, and reaching consensus.

The next three chapters discuss the vital professional skill of presenting messages to others. Chapter 11, a combination of the first edition's Chapters 11 and 12, explains how to develop a message, including how to find and use interesting and appropriate supporting material and organize a message for maximum clarity and impact. Chapter 12 focuses on how to deliver a message and use a wide array of technological tools to add visual and auditory support to a presentation. Chapter 13 offers tips and strategies for informing, persuading, and presenting special kinds of speeches in professional settings. Special emphasis is placed on developing business briefings and reports, as well as on how to use persuasive strategies to sell products and services to others. The last chapter is a primer on writing skills. A unique "time management" appendix offers strategies to help students communicate efficiently by managing their time and improving their work productivity by applying five key time-management and communication-management strategies.

Special Features to Help Students Learn

To help students interact with the material, we've incorporated several pedagogical features to connect the book's content to student's professional lives. These special features make interactive connections between fundamental communication principles and skills and students' business and professional careers, by continuously applying key concepts to real-life situations.

- **PRINCIPLES MODEL** Introduced in Chapter 1, we illustrate the importance of the five communication principles with a layered model that provides the over-arching structure for the book. The colorful model, which reappears in several chapters to reinforce the five principles, gives students a clear visual model to help the principles stick in their minds and inform their practice. New *The Principle Points* summary sections at the end of the chapter further review how the five principles apply to the specific chapter content.

- **COMMUNICATION ETHICS @ WORK BOXES** A study of communication and leadership without an emphasis on ethics could lead students to presume that the goal of one's professional career is to win at all costs using any method that achieves results. We believe that effective communicators are ethical communicators and that ethical behavior and communication are crucial to becoming successful leaders. Ethics boxes in every chapter relate chapter content to an ethical issue or question. These boxes can be used for student reflection, class discussion, or assignments to help students see relationships between not only doing well but also doing good.

Communication Ethics @ Work

Apple Investors' Interests versus Steve Jobs' Health: Where Should the Lines Have Been Drawn?

On August 25, 2011, the late Steve Jobs resigned from his position as CEO of Apple. Although the message did not come as a surprise, his January 17, 2011 message that he was taking a medical leave of absence did surprise some investors and his communication even became an ethical issue. Jobs stated, "I will continue as CEO and be involved in major strategic decisions for the company . . . . I love Apple so much and hope to be back as soon as I can. In the meantime, my family and I would deeply appreciate respect for our privacy."[81]

Although the news didn't come as a surprise to many investors, there was a concern about what this would mean for the future

specificity and precision. Had he disclosed the diagnosis and prognosis, employees, investors, and customers would have been less anxious. Shareholders did not know whether he was leaving to undergo a procedure that might dramatically improve his health. They did not know whether he was seeking another unusual treatment. They had no idea whether he was on the verge of death. And they had no idea what would happen to Apple without Jobs at the helm.

However, Former U.S. Securities and Exchange Commission Chairman Arthur Levitt said the company had disclosed enough about Steve Jobs's health.[84] Levitt, who headed the SEC in the late 1990s, claimed the severity of Jobs's cancer

- **INTEGRATED RECAP AND SUMMARY FEATURES** Educational theorists confirm that students learn with repetition. To make sure the key content is reinforced, periodic Recap boxes summarize and review key chapter concepts. We also provide a bulleted summary of key information at the end of every chapter in a business-like summary called *Wrap-Up* to help students review and master the material.

- **GLOSSARY AND CHAPTER-END KEY TERM REVIEW**   To help students master key terms we've included a new section called *Reviewing Key Terms* at the end of each chapter. Page references to key terms and their marginal definitions give students a quick way to review their understanding of essential content. We've also included all key terms that appear in boldface throughout the book in an alphabetized glossary at the end of the book.

- **APPLYING YOUR SKILLS**   Each chapter concludes with an activities section, *Applying Your Skills*, which includes a wealth of activities, assignments and resources to apply the chapter content to students' daily lives, and to help them practice key skills.

Comprehensive Learning Resources

In addition to the built-in array of learning features and resources described above, we offer an array of instructional resources to help students learn and instructors teach communication principles and skills for leadership.

Name of Supplement	Available	Instructor or Student Supplement	Description
Instructor's Manual and Test Bank	Online	Instructor Supplement	The instructor's manual includes a sample syllabus, chapter summaries, learning objectives, lecture outlines, class discussion questions, and an experiential classroom activity for each chapter. The Test Bank contains multiple-choice, true/false, and essay questions referenced by page number and skill level. Available for download in our Instructor's Resource Center, www.pearsonhighered.com/irc (access code required).
MyTest	Online	Instructor Supplement	This flexible, online test-generating software includes all questions found in the test bank, allowing instructors to create their own personalized exams. Instructors can also edit any of the existing test questions and even add new questions. Other special features of this program include random generation of test questions, creation of alternate versions of the same test, scrambling of question sequence, and test preview before printing. Available at www.pearsonmytest.com (access code required).
PowerPoint™ Presentation Package	Online	Instructor Supplement	The textbook-specific **PowerPoint™ Presentation Package** provides lecture slides for each chapter of the book, containing lecture outlines as well as figures and photos from the text. Available for download at www.pearsonhighered.com/irc (access code required).
Pearson's Business and Professional Communication Study Site	Online	Student Supplement	This open-access student website features business and professional communication study materials including a complete set of practice tests (multiple choice, true/false, and essay questions) for all major course topics. Students will also find weblinks to valuable sites for further exploration of major topics. The site can be accessed at www.abbpcomm.com.
MySearchLab with eText (text packaged with MySearchLab) ISBN: 020586550X; Standalone access code card ISBN: 0205250211	Online	Instructor & Student Supplement	**MySearchLab with eText** features access to the EBSCO ContentSelect database and step-by-step tutorials offering overviews of the writing and research process. **MySearchLab with eText** also includes our video upload tool, MediaShare, chapter assessments, and flashcards. See the next page for more details.

MySearchLab®

Proven. Engaging. Trusted.

MySearchLab with eTEXT provides engaging experiences that personalize learning, and comes from a trusted partner with educational expertise and a deep commitment to helping students and instructors achieve their goals. This online study and research tool features access to the EBSCO ContentSelect database, and step-by-step tutorials which offer complete overviews of the entire writing and research process. Additionally, **MySearchLab** offers **course specific** tools to enrich learning and help students succeed.

eTEXT: Identical in content and design to the printed text, the Pearson eText provides access to the book wherever and whenever it is needed. Students can take notes and highlight, just like a traditional book. The Pearson eText also is available on the iPad for all registered users of MySearchLab.

MediaShare: A cutting edge video upload tool that allows students to upload presentations, interviews, role plays, and group assignments, for instructors and classmates to watch (whether face-to-face or online) and provide online feedback and comments. Customizable rubrics can be attached for further evaluation and grading purposes. Grades can be imported into most learning management systems. Structured much like a social networking site, MediaShare can help promote a sense of community among students.

MyOutline: This valuable tool provides step-by-step guidance and structure for writing an effective outline, along with a detailed help section to assist students in understanding the elements of an outline and how all the pieces fit together. Students can download and email completed outlines to instructors, save for future editing or print—even print as notecards. Instructors can choose from our templates or create their own structure for use.

Video Clips: Videos related to key text content are included on the site. These clips will allow students to gain a deeper, more nuanced understanding of basic communication principles.

Online Quizzes: Chapter quizzes test student comprehension, are automatically graded, and grades flow directly to an online gradebook.

Chapter-specific Content: Each chapter contains Learning Objectives and Flashcards. Flashcards review important terms and concepts from each chapter online. Students can search by chapter or within a glossary and also access drills to help them prepare for quizzes and exams. Flashcards can be printed or exported to your mobile device. These chapter resources can be used to enhance comprehension, help students review key terms, prepare for tests, and retain what they have learned.

A **MySearchLab with eTEXT** access code is no additional cost when packaged with new print copies of this text. [To order use this ISBN: 020586550X.] Contact your local Pearson Publisher's Representative at www.pearsonhighered.com/replocator.

Acknowledgments

Although our two names appear on the cover, any book is a team project involving many people. We are grateful to the many individuals who helped us make this book a reality. We are indebted to the scholars and practitioners whose research and ideas inform the principles and skills that constitute the content of this book. We also are thankful for our students, past and present, who have helped us shape our approach to teaching. A textbook reflects both our role as scholars and educators; our students continue to enrich our lives with questions, feedback (both encouraging and constructive), and their very presence in our classrooms make us better authors.

We are especially thankful for the outstanding editorial support we have received from our colleagues and friends at Pearson. Karon Bowers, Editor-in-Chief, Communication, continues to be an important friend and mentor who is always there with needed support, information, and inspiration. Jeanne Zalesky, our Acquisitions Editor for the first edition, provided exceptional encouragement and insight that shaped our approach to this project. Melissa Mashburn, our Senior Acquisitions Editor on this edition, provided similar support and encouragement. A great gift to both of us is our continued partnership with our Development Editor, Hilary Jackson. As with the first edition, she has infused this book with intelligent creativity, a wealth of ideas, and considerable knowledge about writing and editing. We are indebted to Diana Ivy, a cherished friend, whose work informs this project as we drew upon the five communication principles that also appear in the book she has co-authored.

We appreciate the many excellent educators and teachers who read the manuscript and helped us polish our prose and our ideas. We thank the following individuals for sharing their teaching skill, subject-matter expertise, and vast experience to make this a better book:

Shae Adkins, Lone Star College

Cin Bickel, Laredo Community College

Lisa Collins, Trinity Valley Community College

Michele S. Foss-Snowden, California State University-Sacramento

Edwin Ray Flowler, El Paso Community College

Kim Gatz, Northern Illinois University

Valerie Manno Giroux, University of Miami

Stacey D. Gish, Western Kentucky University

Bob Harrison, Gallaudet University

Jackqueline Irwin, California State University-Sacramento

Amy Tilton Jones, Del Mar College

Jennifer Karchmer, Western Washington University

Brendan B. Kelly, University of West Florida

Jacqueline Layng, University of Toledo

Diane Matuschka, University of North Florida

Kelly Petkus, Austin Community College

Jeffrey Pomeroy, Southwest Texas Junior College

Rob Rostoni, Geneva College

Jessica Samens, Minnesota State University-Mankato

Timothy Steffensmeier, Kansas State University

Amy Veuleman, McNeese State University

Elizabeth J. Vick, Northern Virginia Community College

Shirley H, Washburn, Roosevelt University

Mark Zampino, University of Hartford

Robert Zetocha, Southeast Community College-Nebraska

We each have been influenced by colleagues, friends, teachers, and family members who have offered their support and inspiration for this project. Timothy is grateful for his many colleagues, graduate students, friends, and family members who have supported him throughout this book project. He is fortunate for his colleagues at Texas State University–San Marcos and former colleagues at The University of Texas–Pan American (UTPA). At Texas State, Timothy would like to give special thanks to Richard Cheatham, Sue Hall, Marian Houser, and Phil Salem who were particularly supportive of this book project. At The University Texas–Pan American, Tim would like to thank Dahlia Guerra, Sharon Valdes,

Cory Cunningham, Liz Parker-Garcia, Jessica Parker-Raley, Marisa Saavedra, Dora Saavedra, and Kimberly Selber.

Timothy would also like to thank his UTPA research assistants: Monica Mercado, Gil Castillo, Andrea Fuentes, Rebekah Sepulveda, and Pablo de la Rosa. Timothy is particularly grateful to Katrina Newell, a very gifted researcher and writer, who served as his primary research assistant on this book project and completed the first draft of Chapter 14. Timothy's friendship with Steve and Sue Beebe, Jim McCroskey, Virginia Richmond, Marilyn and Robert Root, Mary Hoffman, Steve Houser, DC and Renee Cowan, and Jane and Chris Brayton serve as a constant source of encouragement and guidance. Timothy is grateful for the love of his family—his parents, Carol and Joe Mottet and other family members including Julie and Rob Johnson, Dan and Barb Mottet, Doug and Jane Mottet, Maria and Alfredo Gonzalez, and Anita and Alfredo Gonzalez. Finally, Tim would like to extend a very special thanks to Rick Gonzalez for his love, patience, understanding, and support. Tim is most appreciative of the inspiration he receives from Rick and for the education he has received from him.

Steve is grateful for many friends and colleagues who have offered support and encouragement for this project. His colleagues at Texas State University–San Marcos in the Department of Communication Studies continue to be supportive of his research and writing endeavors. Steve is especially grateful for co-authors on other book projects—John Masterson, Mark Redmond, Diana Ivy, David Roach, and Sue Beebe—for influencing his ideas on this project. Steve is especially thankful for the friendship and collaboration with Tim Mottet on this project; it is a special joy in life to have someone be both cherished friend and valued colleague. He is also thankful to his friend and research colleague Kosta Tovstiadi for providing research support for this book. Consulting partners and friends Laurie Romig, Dennis Romig, and Jim Bell have significantly influenced this project through their skill in transforming research conclusions into practical applications. Sue Hall, Senior Administrative Assistant in the Department of Communication Studies and Steve's "right hand"; Meredith Clayton, Administrative Assistant; Bob Hanna, technology specialist; and graphic designer Malinda Murray have each provided outstanding support and skilled, professional assistance that has made this project a reality. Finally, Steve is grateful for the enduring support and love of his family. His sons, Mark and Matthew Beebe, have made the business of being a dad the most important life-profession a person could have. Steve's new daughter-in-law, Brittany, enriches his life with sunshine and joy. Steve's in-laws, the late Herb Dye and Jane Dye, have been a source of gentle graciousness and generous support for over 40 years. And his parents, Russell and Muriel Beebe, have offered a lifetime of ethical lessons and love through seven decades of marriage (and now beginning their eighth decade together) to demonstrate the power of a loving partnership. Finally, this book or any other book Steve has written would not be possible without the support, editorship, encouragement, and thoughtful commentary provided by his life traveling companion, best friend, and loving wife, Sue Beebe.

Steven A. Beebe
Timothy P. Mottet

1

Communicating and Leading at Work

chapter **outline**

After reading this chapter, you should be able to

- Define communication and describe why communication is important.
- Define leadership and explain the relationship between leadership and communication.
- Compare and contrast leading, managing, and following.
- Identify and describe each of the five major communication principles.
- Identify and describe six approaches to leadership.
- Explain the three major communication skill sets: relationship skills, collaboration skills, and presentation skills.

He grew up in the 1950s and had a variety of jobs, including tossing papers on his paper route, working in a knitting factory, and becoming a furrier. Vowing to escape the vocational history of his parents—not much pay, no benefits, and no job security—after college, he worked at Xerox and then for Hammerplast, a Swedish housewares company. But his career path took an interesting and lucrative turn when one of his housewares customers bought lots of drip-brewing thermoses.[1] Although you're probably not familiar with the name Howard Schultz, you are familiar with Starbucks. The company Schultz leads is the world's largest coffee retailer.[2] His ability to lead and influence others has made him one of the world's most innovative leaders. He bought Starbucks in 1987 when the company had only six stores; within five years Starbucks had 150 stores. At the beginning of the second decade of the twenty-first century, there were over 16,000 Starbucks stores worldwide.

Schultz attributes his leadership success to his communication skills, which he developed as a communication major at Northern Michigan University.[3] Rather than communicating to employees, shareholders, and customers through advertising and mediated messages, Schultz prefers face-to-face communication. According to Schultz, Starbucks is successful not because of its high-gloss and expensive Madison Avenue advertising campaigns, but because of its grassroots word-of-mouth advertising based on the relationships that Starbucks employees form with customers. He even states, "Word of mouth, we discovered, is far more powerful than advertising."[4] Although Starbucks has had its ups and downs as a company, it has a founding leader who knows the importance of communication in helping Starbucks remain competitive. He believes leadership is anchored in developing relationships with people.

How do you take your coffee? Howard Schultz takes his with both excellent communication skills and visionary leadership. In summarizing his success as a communicator, Schultz notes, "We're not in the coffee business serving people, but in the people business serving coffee."[5]

leading **questions**

1. Howard Schultz uses a personal relational style of leading his employees. How would you evaluate *your* relational leadership skills? What would you like to learn that would enhance your communication and leadership skills?

2. Schultz had a variety of jobs before becoming CEO. How have the jobs you've held contributed to developing your communication and leadership skills?

3. What do you think Schultz means when he says, "We're not in the coffee business serving people, but in the people business serving coffee"?

Communication and Leadership

This book is about two things: communication and leadership. Specifically, it's about how you can apply communication skills to lead in the workplace. Communication and work go hand in hand; it's hard to talk about the workplace without also talking about the communication that makes work happen. And closely linked to any discussion of workplace communication is the art and science of leading others. Leaders develop relationships, build teams, and make presentations before groups of people, using effective communication principles and skills. One study found CEOs rated leadership and communication as the top job skills needed in business and professional settings.[6]

To be effective in the workplace, you need to be able to communicate effectively and appropriately to influence others in positive and ethical ways.

Communication and You

Would you be surprised if we told you we know precisely what you will do for a living? Perhaps you've known what your vocational goal was since you were in elementary school. Or you may still be uncertain as to what your specific career track will be. Regardless of whether your career goals are clear or fuzzy, we know what you will *do*. You will communicate. Research has consistently found that you will spend from 80 to 90 percent of your typical day communicating with others.[7] To live is to communicate. To work is to communicate. You can't help it. You *will* communicate with others.

> *"The art of communication is the language of leadership."*
>
> — **James Humes**

A number of recent studies underscore the need for and importance of communication skills for the twenty-first-century workplace. Research supports two important conclusions: If you possess effective communication skills, you are much more likely to be successful. Without communication skills, you are less likely to be successful.

- *Communication is the most valued workplace skill.* In a recent survey of recruiters from companies with more than 50,000 employees, communication skills were cited as the single most important decisive factor in choosing managers.[8] The survey, conducted by the University of Pittsburgh's Katz Business School, points out that communication skills (including written and oral presentations), as well as an ability to work with others, are the main factor contributing to job success.[9] Temporary job service agencies, such as Kelly and Manpower, report that they are selecting and placing job candidates with better communication or interpersonal skills than candidates with higher degrees.[10]

- *Without effective communication skills your career may suffer.* In a national survey of employers, the lack of basic oral/written skills and effective business communication skills appeared to be a major stumbling block for new entrants into the job market.[11] Employers also ranked the leadership skills of four-year college graduates as deficient, noting their inability to collaborate, work in teams or groups, and problem-solve.[12]

  A study conducted by the research firm Robert Half Technology reports that information technology (IT) workers need more than technical abilities—they also need to be well-rounded business professionals. Nearly 45% of respondents said their IT staff members must improve their project management skills and could improve verbal and written communication abilities. Organizational and interpersonal skills also were listed as underdeveloped skill sets needed by information technology workers.[13]

Why is there so much evidence that communication skills are important to your business and professional work success? It's because regardless of what your job title is, you'll spend most of your time communicating with others. These research conclusions, about both the prevalence and importance of communication, should reassure you that you're investing your time and energy wisely by studying business and professional communication.

When he was chairman of General Electric, Jack Welch said the key characteristic he looked for in a leader was her or his ability to communicate well. Specifically, he wanted "someone who is comfortable talking to *anyone—anybody* in the world, in New Delhi, Moscow, Cairo, Beijing—*anywhere!*"[14] Warren Buffett, one of the richest persons on the planet, once announced to MBA students at his alma mater, Columbia University, that he would offer $100,000 to any student in the audience in return for 10 percent of future earnings. He then added that if the student would take a communication skill development course or public speaking training, he would increase his offer to $150,000. Buffet is a major advocate of communication skill training and has noted that taking a communication training course was one of the best investments he had ever made.[15]

When you complete your study of business and professional communication, you will be able to include a set of communication skills on your resume that can enhance your career success. Communication skills are leadership skills. These essential skills will immediately make you competitive in a global marketplace.

People who communicate effectively do well on the job. Others find the communication demands of the job challenging.[16] This book will prepare you for the communication and

Donald Trump's success in business has a great deal to do with his communication skills and his ability to influence others, as well as the power to "hire and fire." His leadership skills are evident on his show, "The Apprentice."

leadership demands of the modern workplace by introducing you to key communication principles and skills to help you be successful at work.

Leadership and You

You may think you're not really interested in being a leader; you may just want to get a job and enjoy a productive life. You don't want to be the boss; you just want to work. Or you may aspire to a major leadership role such as being a corporate chief executive officer at a large company. You've dreamed of being a captain of industry and seeing your photo on the cover of *Fortune* magazine. Regardless of your professional goals, and even if you don't aspire to be the next Donald Trump or Oprah Winfrey, you *will* influence others through the way you communicate with people.

There is a difference between being a leader and exerting leadership influence. You don't have to be anointed "the leader" to use leadership skills. You can't help but use them. Whether you perceive yourself as a leader or not, regardless of your job title or current vocational goals, you *will* influence others through the way you communicate with them.

Simply stated, to lead is to influence others. You influence others through your communication. This is why leadership and communication are connected. Your very presence in an organization, regardless of your job description or level within the organization, will influence others. By enhancing your communication competence you will also enhance your leadership abilities. To help you accomplish your professional goals—whether working in a large corporation, a small business, or in a profession such as law, medicine, or education—this book can enhance what you'll spend most of your time doing at your job: communicating and influencing others.

Communication: Making Sense and Sharing Sense

Jet Blue Airlines, a low-cost airline from New York, apologized to its customers after it mismanaged an ice storm where customers were required to remain on a JetBlue aircraft for 11 hours. JetBlue used their website as well as YouTube to offer their apology to the traveling public.[17] However, many of their customers never saw the apology. What JetBlue learned was that just placing a message on a website doesn't mean that communication has occurred. Communication happens not when a message is crafted and sent, but when the message has helped create meaning for someone.

terms & definitions

Communication the process of acting on information.

The Nature of Communication

Reduced to its essence, **communication** is the process of acting on information.[18] Someone does something or says something, and there is a response from someone else in the form of an action, a word, or a thought. As JetBlue Airlines learned, presenting information to others

leaders on leadership

The Leadership-Communication Link

Because of the relationship between communication and leadership principles, in each chapter we feature leadership advice from chief executive officers or other experienced leaders from a variety of organizations. Although you may wonder whether the advice offered by leaders at the upper echelon of power applies to you, we assure you that it does. Communication and leadership principles have a universal application, regardless of level of responsibility.

When asked about his key principles of leadership, chief executive officer of the Container Store, Kip Tendell, offered specific communication strategies for developing a positive, productive work climate. To him, both leadership and communication are inextricably linked to explain and predict what it feels like to work in an organization. How do you create a positive and productive work climate? Here's what Tindell suggests:

> The way we create a place where people do want to come to work is primarily through two key points. One of our foundation principles is that leadership and communication are the same thing. Communication is leadership. So we believe in just relentlessly trying to communicate everything to every single employee at all times, and we're very open. We share everything. We believe in complete transparency. There's never a reason, we believe, to keep the information from an employee, except for individual salaries.[19]

His key message: It's important to study both communication and leadership principles.

- Because of the communication-leadership connection, regardless of your level of leadership aspirations, when you study communication, you're also learning how to lead others.

- It's through communication that you influence an organization's work climate. Positive communication messages result in a supportive work climate, where workers are more productive and they feel comfortable sharing their concerns and ideas.

- Possessing good communication skills can help you make authentic connections to others—to be transparent, honest, and real.

So regardless of the group, team, or organization in which you participate, communicating well and being open to create transparency are leadership behaviors that will serve you well.

does not mean that there is communication: *Information is not communication.* "I put it in the memo. Why didn't you do what I asked?" "It's in the company policy statement." "It's on the website!" These expressions of exasperation assume that if you send a message, someone will receive it. Communication does not operate, however, in a linear, input-output process. What you send is rarely what others understand. Human communication is more sophisticated than simply sending and receiving messages. **Human communication** *is the process of making sense out of the world and sharing that sense with others by creating meaning through the use of verbal and nonverbal messages.*[20] Let's examine the key elements of this definition.

COMMUNICATION IS ABOUT MAKING SENSE We make sense out of what we experience when we interpret what we see, hear, touch, smell, and taste. To make sense out of a message we look for patterns or structure. We relate what happens to us at any given moment to something we've experienced in the past. An effective communicator attempts to learn as much as possible about his or her listeners so that the message crafted makes sense to them.

COMMUNICATION IS ABOUT SHARING SENSE We share what we experience by expressing it to others and to ourselves. We use words as well as nonverbal cues (such as gestures, facial expressions, clothing, music) to convey our thoughts and feelings to others. It's through the process of sharing our understanding of our experiences that we connect to other humans.

COMMUNICATION IS ABOUT CREATING MEANING Meaning is created in the hearts and minds of both the message source and the message receiver. We don't send meaning by sending a letter to someone; we *create* it based on our experiences, background, and

terms & definitions

Human communication the process of making sense out of the world and sharing that sense with others by creating meaning through the use of verbal and nonverbal messages.

culture. Succinctly stated, *meanings are in people, not in words.* A word or a nonverbal expression triggers meaning within us. The only meaning a word has is when you ascribe meaning to what you read and see. When, for example, you hear a rumor that there may be companywide layoffs you may think, "My job is safe; I'm a hard worker"; but someone else may hear the rumor and think, "Yikes, I may get fired!" The same rumor creates different meaning in different people.

When we communicate with another person who is physically present, the communication is **transactional**, meaning that messages are sent and received simultaneously. As you talk to someone and create meaning, you respond to that person's verbal and nonverbal messages even as you speak.[21] Whether in a brief visit in someone's office, or during a lengthy meeting, even if you remain silent or embarrassingly nod off to sleep, your nonverbal behavior provides information to others about your emotions and interest, or lack of interest. The transactive nature of communication suggests that you cannot *not* communicate. People interpret your communication even when you are not intentionally expressing an idea or feeling. Here's another way to summarize this idea: Ultimately, people judge you by your behavior, not by your intent. And because you behave in some way (even when you are asleep), there is the potential for someone to make sense out of your behavior.

Leaders more typically communicate using transactive communication assumptions. When a team member is going through a difficult time, effective leaders stop what they're doing and spend time listening and talking to the team member. Leaders who are paying close attention to the team members' nonverbal messages and are carefully listening can adapt their communication accordingly to meet team members' communication needs without team members having to ask for help. Leaders and team members together create messages and meanings by closely paying attention to each other's verbal and nonverbal messages and by adapting their communication accordingly.

COMMUNICATION OCCURS THROUGH VERBAL AND NONVERBAL MESSAGES
Words and nonverbal behaviors are symbols you use to create meaning that makes sense to you. A **symbol** is something that represents a thought, concept, object, or experience. The words on this page are symbols that you use to derive meaning that makes sense to you. Some symbols are nonverbal, such as your use of gestures, posture, tone of voice, clothing, and jewelry. Nonverbal messages primarily communicate emotions—our feelings of joy or sadness, likes and dislikes, or our interest or lack of interest in others.

Our definition of human communication suggests that the message we express is not always the message that is interpreted as we'd intended it. Making sense and sharing sense with others is a fragile process. It's also a transactional process that occurs both live-and-in-person, as well as via mediated channels such as text message or email.

The Components of Communication

The most basic components of communication include the source, message, channel, receiver, noise, feedback, and context. Understanding these elements can help you analyze your own communication with others. Let's explore these elements in greater detail.

- *Source.* The **source** of the message is the originator of the ideas and feelings expressed. The source puts a message into a code that can be understood by a receiver. Putting ideas, feelings, and thoughts into a code is called **encoding**. Just the opposite of encoding is the process of **decoding**; this occurs when the receiver interprets the words or nonverbal cues.

- *Message.* The **message** is the information being communicated by the source. As you transactively communicate with others, it's important to understand two key dimensions of human communication message: the content and relational dimensions that are present during every communication episode.

    The **content** of a communication message is the new information, ideas, or suggested actions the speaker wishes to express. Another name for the content dimension

terms & definitions

Transactional occurring simultaneously.

Symbol a word, sound, visual image, gesture, or object that represents a thought, a concept, another object, or an experience.

Source the originator of a thought or emotion, who puts it into a code that can be understood by a receiver.

Encoding the process of translating ideas, feelings, and thoughts into a code.

Decoding the process of interpreting ideas, feelings, and thoughts that have been translated into a code.

Message written, spoken, and unspoken elements of communication to which people assign meaning.

Content the new information, ideas, or suggested actions that a speaker wishes to express.

that may be more appropriate for the workplace is **task dimension**. Leaders, including managers, supervisors, or those who take charge of a particular project, communicate content messages with others to accomplish certain tasks, to get work completed.

The **relational dimension** of a communication message is usually more implied; it offers cues about the emotions, attitudes, and amount of power and control the speaker feels toward others.[22] The relational dimension focuses more on nonverbal messages and conveys relational cues. Another way of distinguishing between the content and relational dimensions of communication is to consider that the content of a message refers to *what* is said. The relational cues are provided in *how* the message was communicated. Although your supervisor may say "great job," about a project you've been working on, her lack of eye contact, monotone vocal inflection, and lackluster enthusiasm may actually suggest she is not all that pleased with your work.

- *Receiver.* The **receiver** of the message is the person or persons who interpret the message. When communicating with others, it's the receiver that will ultimately determine if your message was successful—whether it was understood and was appropriate. Effective communicators are receiver oriented; they understand that the listener is the one who ultimately makes sense of the message you express. If you're selling a product, for example, your prime focus should be on whether the customer understood your message.

- *Channel.* The **channel** is the means by which the message is expressed to the receiver. If you're typical, you receive messages from a variety of channels. Increasingly, in business and professional settings (as well as in all communication situations), you are receiving messages via a mediated channel such as text messages, email, phone, video conference, or even a Facebook post or tweet.

- *Noise.* **Noise** is anything that interferes with the message being interpreted as it was intended. As we've emphasized, what we express isn't always interpreted as we intend. Noise happens. If there were no noise, then all of our messages would be interpreted accurately. But noise is always present. It can be literal—such as beeps coming from a BlackBerry or computer that tells you that you have incoming email—or it can be psychological, such as competing thoughts, worries, and feelings that capture our attention.

- *Feedback.* Another element integral to communication is feedback. **Feedback** is the response to a message. Without feedback, communication is less likely to be effective. When your boss says, "Would you please give me a copy of the Williamson proposal?" you may say, "Is that the James Williamson proposal or the Kyra Williamson proposal?" Your quest for clarification in response to the request is feedback. Feedback can seek additional information, or simply confirm the message has been interpreted: "OK, I'll have the Williamson proposal on your desk by this afternoon."

- *Context.* One final component of communication is **context**—the physical, historical, and psychological communication environment. As the saying goes, everyone has to be somewhere. All communication takes place in some context. A meeting held in the executive boardroom in comparison to a brief conversation held around the water cooler is likely to have different communication expectations. The context of the designer-decorated executive boardroom will likely result in more formal communication exchanges than conversation with people standing around a workroom water cooler. The physical environment has an effect on how people communicate.

The communication-as-transaction perspective acknowledges that when we communicate with another, we are constantly reacting to what our partner is saying and expressing. As Figure 1.1 illustrates, we send and receive messages at the same time. Even as we talk, we are also interpreting our partner's nonverbal and verbal responses. Transactive communication also occurs within a context; and noise can interfere with the quality and accuracy of the meaning of messages. As we send messages, we monitor the degree to which the other person understands our message.

terms & definitions

Task dimension a form of content dimension in the workplace; leaders, including managers, supervisors, or those who take charge, communicate content messages to accomplish certain tasks.

Relational dimension the dimension of communication that offers cues about the emotions, attitudes, and amount of power and control a speaker feels in relation to listeners.

Receiver the person who interprets a message.

Channel the means by which a message is expressed to the receiver.

Noise interference, either literal or psychological, that hinders the accurate encoding or decoding of a message.

Feedback the response to a message.

Context the physical, historical, and psychological environment in which communication occurs.

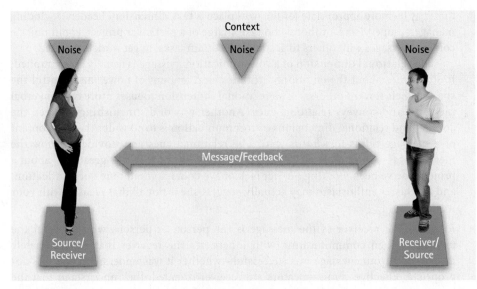

FIGURE 1.1 Communication as Transaction

Leadership: Influencing Others Through Communication

Postcards were all the rage in the early twentieth century in David City, Nebraska, yet J. C. Hall knew he needed a bigger market than a small Nebraska town in which to sell his imported postcards. So in 1910 he hopped on a train to Kansas City with a couple of boxes of postcards under his arm and a vision for making money. He started a mail-order postcard business from his Kansas City YMCA room. After some initial success, however, he found that people weren't buying postcards like they used to. He needed to change the focus of his business. His brother Rollie joined him in 1915, and together they started making their own greeting cards. Things were going well until a fire destroyed their entire greeting card stock. Having listened to his customers' needs, J. C. decided to hire an illustrator to make Christmas cards. Good move: Business boomed. J. C.'s other brother, William, joined the business and under J. C.'s leadership, the brothers continued their success. In 1928 they started printing the word "Hallmark" on the backs of the cards. When J. C. died in 1982, he left $100 million to charity. Today Hallmark Cards has annual sales of more than $4 billion.[23]

J. C. was successful for two reasons. First, he was a master communicator. He knew what his customers wanted; he listened to them. He used his communication skills to adapt to a changing marketplace. He crafted messages that connected to people. Second, he knew how to lead others. Whether it was working with his brothers to build the family business or being an innovative leader in establishing the greeting card industry, J. C. successfully influenced others. Can you learn the same principles and skills of leading others that J. C. Hall

used to establish a $4 billion company? We believe the answer is an unequivocal *yes*. As the chapter-opening quote from James Humes proclaims, "The art of communication is the language of leadership."

Whether it's who comes out on top on *American Idol* or who becomes the next president of the United States, we're often fascinated with who emerges as number one. More specifically, we're interested in who becomes a leader, what a leader does, and how a leader maintains his or her leadership position. Typically it's the leader who both sets the tone of an organization or a team and establishes the work agenda.

A key question we explore in this book is what are the underlying communication principles that enhance leadership? As we noted earlier, to lead is to influence. Here's a complete definition of leadership: **Leadership** *is the process of influencing others to achieve goals through verbal and nonverbal messages.* Researchers have emphasized several different perspectives on leadership.

An effective leader influences others through both verbal and nonverbal communication and with strong presentation skills.

- *Leaders help make something happen.* James MacGregor Burns, in his classic book *Leadership*, described leadership this way: "Leadership is leaders inducing followers to act for certain goals that represent the values and the motivations—the wants and needs, the aspirations and expectations—of both leaders and followers."[24]

- *Leaders create the extraordinary.* According to Alan Keith, "Leadership is ultimately about creating a way for people to contribute to making something extraordinary happen."[25]

- *Leaders are ethical.* Leaders can make something extraordinary happen by influencing others through either ethical or unethical means. An ethical leader doesn't try to coerce others through brute force or knowingly using inaccurate or inappropriate appeals to fear.

We believe that what each of these perspectives have in common is that *leadership occurs through communication*, both verbal messages (what a leader says) and nonverbal messages (what a leader does). We also emphasize that leadership is not something only one person does. In most teams, groups, and organizations, there are many people who influence others. In fact, each team member undoubtedly influences what the group does or does not achieve.[26] So it's likely that you will provide leadership even though you may not be formally designated as "the leader." In an effectively led team, team members feel greater satisfaction, are more productive, and are less likely to be absent.[27] The quality of leadership influences virtually every aspect of what it feels like to be in any organization.

Leading Versus Managing

There are differences between being a leader and being a manager. A **manager** is someone who has been appointed to coordinate and facilitate, whereas a leader influences others even if he or she has not been designated to assume a specific leadership role. Metaphorically speaking, a manager's job is to keep the trains running on time; the leader's job is to design the trains. Managers keep things organized and emphasize accomplishing the task. Leaders are focused not just on short-term accomplishments but also on how the team,

The story of 33 Chilean miners trapped underground in a collapsed mine for 69 days—and shown here being rescued in October 2010—exemplifies "servant leadership," where the team worked together to set up routines and ensure its survival.

group, or organization will accomplish its goals over the long term. A manager coordinates the work; a leader influences the major changes in designing and implementing the work.

Can a manager also be a leader? Yes, a good manager can also become a leader when influencing others. The typical function of a manager is to influence the more routine, mundane, and repetitive elements of the work. A manager becomes a leader when he or she takes on more innovative tasks and influences the group or organization in new and creative ways. The same person can both lead and manage.

Although a boss may have legitimate power to be the leader, even those not in a leadership role can influence team or organizational behavior. A leader is someone who has an ability to influence others regardless of whether she or he has been given the title "leader."

Leading Versus Following

The relationship between leaders and followers is symbiotic: A leader can't lead unless there are those who follow her or him; you can't have one without the other. If the key role of a leader is to influence others through communication, the prime task of a follower is to respond ethically and appropriately to the influence of a leader.

The word *follower* sometimes connotes a person who may wait to be told what to do rather than move forward on his or her own initiative. Without effective followers, however, little would get accomplished. So followers have more power and influence in organizations than they may perceive they have.

An effective follower does more than respond to a micromanaging leader; good followers use their own ideas and strategies to achieve their work goals. Precisely what do effective followers do? One researcher found that skilled followers engage in two activities: (1) They are independent and critical thinkers rather than passive and noncritical thinkers, and (2) they actively engage in the work, rather than waiting to be told what to do.[28] In most situations, the best followers are those who rate highly on both of these important attributes.

In 2010 when thirty-three miners in Chile were trapped underground for over two months, some of the miners became leaders to ensure their survival. But if all thirty-three miners assumed forceful leadership roles at the same time it would have hampered their efforts to be rescued. Some needed to lead while others needed to follow. Yet even when following suggestions from the leaders, the "followers" were not merely passive bystanders; they used their own critical thinking skills to ensure their survival. Followers collaborate with leaders while keeping an eye on the goal.

Although we've suggested that the best follower is someone who is both an independent and critical thinker and actively engaged in the task, the best follower style ultimately depends on the nature of the task; the trustworthiness, credibility, and ethics of the leader; and the specific situation. If the task is routine, doesn't violate sound ethical principles, and is well conceived, it may be best to simply do the work assigned. It may be a job that doesn't call for much independent thought, such as taking customer orders at a fast-food restaurant—the work simply needs to be done. Yet for more complicated tasks—such as helping a customer design a new computer system—independent, critical thinking may be what is needed.

Leadership Approaches

Are people born with traits that make them leaders, or can anyone be taught to lead? What are the key functions and styles of leadership? Scholars who study how to develop leaders approach the study of leadership in several different ways. Although you may now have a clearer sense of what leadership is and how leaders are different from managers and followers, at the beginning of our study of communication and leadership it is useful to understand how the study of leadership has been approached. Knowing different approaches to studying and developing leaders can help you identify and enhance your own leadership skills. We'll identify six approaches for classifying and developing leaders: (1) trait, (2) functional, (3) styles, (4) situational, (5) transformational, and (6) servant leadership.

TRAIT APPROACH The question of whether leaders are born to lead is the focus of the trait approach to leadership. The **trait approach** to leadership suggests that there are certain psychological and physical attributes or traits that make leaders effective. According to this approach, if you are born with these traits, or if you cultivate specific leadership skills, then you will be a good leader. So those who subscribe to a trait approach to leadership will select someone to be a leader who possesses those traits. Over the course of several years of study, leadership researchers have identified intelligence, confidence, social skills (including communication skills), administrative skills, and enthusiasm as some of the traits effective leaders typically possess. One research study found that across several cultures, the most admired qualities of a leader are honesty, being forward-looking, competence, and being inspirational.[29] Another study found that leaders who had good argumentation skills and were not afraid to speak up were more likely to be effective than those who were not as skilled in asserting their ideas and who were apprehensive about speaking up.[30]

Historian Doris Kearns Goodwin identified a list of traits she believes are attributes of great American presidents. Her list of top leadership traits includes the courage to stay strong, self-confidence, an ability to learn from errors, a willingness to change, and emotional intelligence.[31]

But are we saying that if a person possesses these specific traits she or he will be a good leader? Additional research suggests that although many leaders do seem to have traits or special skills that can enhance their ability to influence others, *just having these traits does not necessarily mean a person will be an effective leader.* Many of the attributes that researchers have identified may be important but are not sufficient to make a leader effective. One pair of classic research studies critically examined dozens of research investigations that claimed to identify specific leadership traits. The results of these studies were inconclusive.[32] The researchers concluded that no single set of traits or characteristics predicts who will be a leader. Leadership is more complicated than that. The situation, the motivation and talents of the group or team members, and other factors determine which leadership approach is best.

THE FUNCTIONAL APPROACH The **functional approach** to leadership suggests that leaders exist to perform essential functions or behaviors that help an organization or team achieve its goals. Rather than identifying personality characteristics or other traits, the functional approach to leadership divides the essential leadership behaviors or functions that enhance the workings of a group into two categories: (1) task functions and (2) process functions.

Task functions are those behaviors that help the team or organization get the work done. Whether the leader is appointed or elected, one of his or her responsibilities is to ensure that the task the group is undertaking is completed. But don't get the idea that only one person performs these specific functions. Several different people can perform task functions. Sometimes the functions are explicitly assigned to people, and at other times the functions are accomplished as sensitive and skilled people become aware that these task functions need to be performed.

terms & definitions

Trait approach an approach to leadership that focuses on the psychological and physical attributes or traits that make leaders effective.

Functional approach an approach to leadership that suggests that leaders perform essential functions, tasks, and processes that help an organization or team achieve goals.

Task functions behaviors that help a team or organization get work done.

One of the key task functions of a leader is to organize the work; groups and organizations need procedural leaders to help get the job done. What leaders say, how effectively they listen, and how they adapt messages to others help them effectively ensure that the following common procedural tasks get done:

- Setting the agenda
- Recording what is accomplished
- Determining when a meeting begins and ends
- Distributing information before a meeting

Besides organizing the work, leaders also help get the work done by carrying out some of the following tasks:

- Initiating or proposing new ideas
- Seeking information and opinions
- Giving information
- Elaborating on the ideas of others
- Evaluating ideas

In most organizations and teams, many if not most people assume task roles. A team member who rarely helps with any of these tasks often earns the undesirable title of "slacker."

Process functions are the second major kind of behaviors that leaders assume in groups. Leaders who enact process functions help maintain a harmonious climate by encouraging amiable relationships among people. To attend to process functions, leaders listen and respond to others. They seek to maintain a friendly environment that also promotes honest, frank discussion. Conflict is a normal and expected part of working with others. It would be unusual if there were no conflict among people in groups. Process leaders focus on managing relationships. Specific process roles include the following:

- Encouraging reticent members to talk
- Mediating conflict
- Compromising or helping other to compromise
- Gatekeeping: monitoring and acting to ensure some members don't talk too much and others don't talk too little

One person may perform both task and process functions. But just as with task leadership, several people will likely help maintain a group or team's process. Some colleagues may be good encouragers but let someone else perform the gatekeeping function, for example. In most organizations these process roles are not formally assigned, whereas some of the task functions may be assigned ("Daria, would you make copies of this report?"). It is unlikely that you will start a team meeting by saying, "OK. Mamie, you're in charge of making sure that Jack and Linda talk more during this meeting." Process roles are assumed when needed. Skilled leaders remain alert to when these process functions need to be performed and adapt accordingly. These roles usually emerge, based on the needs of the group or organization and the personalities, skills, sensitivity, and past experiences of the people who are present.

terms & definitions

Process functions functions performed by leaders that help maintain a harmonious climate by encouraging amiable relationships among others.

Authoritarian leaders leaders who influence by giving orders and seeking to control others.

THE STYLES APPROACH A leadership style is a preferred way of behaving to influence others. The styles approach to leadership suggests that leaders use one of three primary styles when attempting to accomplish the work of the team or the organization: (1) authoritarian, (2) democratic, or (3) laissez faire. The strategies used to influence people usually fall into one of these broad categories.[33]

Authoritarian leaders influence by giving orders and seeking to control others. Military officers assume this leadership style; so do dictators like Hitler. But you don't have to be in the military or in a dictator-ruled country to experience an authoritarian leadership

style. Perhaps you've been in a group and wondered, "Who put her in charge?" Or, maybe you noted that action needed to be taken, so you asked someone to do what you thought needed to be done.

Democratic leaders, as you might suspect from the name, consult with others before issuing edicts. This type of leader seeks to join in the process of influencing without bulldozing the group into action it may resent. Sometimes formal votes are taken, but the leader or leaders will gauge the reaction of the group through dialogue and by reading nonverbal cues. Democratic leaders are aware of the needs of the team or organization rather than focused on achieving their own personal agenda. In addition to just being aware of what is needed, they adapt their behavior to respond to the needs of the team. They are more likely than the authoritarian leader to listen and thoughtfully respond to the wishes of the team. Their verbal and nonverbal messages are based on awareness of both the task at hand and the feelings of team members.

Most North Americans are usually more satisfied with their participation in a team if it is led by a democratic leader than if it is led by an authoritarian leader. Evidence indicates that people led by an authoritarian leader spend more time on task, getting the work done; but this occurs only when the leader is present. When the authoritarian leader is absent, the workers work less.

Laissez-faire leaders take a hands-off, laid-back approach to influencing others. *Laissez-faire* is a French phrase that implies noninterference. This leadership approach is based on the assumption that the less direction provided by the leader, the better. In many ways this type of leader shies away from actively influencing the group. He or she influences only when pushed to lead.

This type of leadership is easiest to spot in an elected or appointed leader who won't lead. In some cases a laissez-faire leader fears making a mistake. In other cases this type of leader just wants to be liked and doesn't want to ruffle anyone's feathers. But as the slogan goes, not to decide is to decide. The laissez-faire leader is influencing the group by his or her silence or inactivity. The group may be bewildered and have high uncertainty, but the laissez-faire leader is reluctant to act. Although there are times when teams and organizations like the freedom that comes with a laissez-faire leader, over time such a hands-off approach can result in chaos. In general people seem to prefer democratic leaders more than laissez-faire nonleaders.

After learning about the different styles of leadership the question many people ask is, "Which style works best?" The answer: *It depends*. The effective leader adapts his or her style to fit the needs of the organization and the task at hand. Because teams and organizations are open systems, and because things change, a skilled leader takes many things into consideration when enacting his or her leadership style, which gives rise to the situational approach to leadership.

THE SITUATIONAL APPROACH During a crisis, people need a quick-thinking, decisive leader who can orchestrate what needs to be done. During more routine situations, the

terms & definitions

Democratic leaders leaders who consult with the group before issuing edicts.

Laissez-faire leaders leaders who take a hands-off, laid-back approach to influencing others.

The situational leadership approach was exemplified by Mayor Rudy Giuliani, who adapted quickly to respond to the dire situation in New York City following the 9/11 attacks in 2001.

leader may just need to back off and let others "do their thing." And at still other times a leader needs to play a more active role in gathering ideas and information from people. Because leadership style is not a one-size-fits-all concept, a skilled leader adapts to the situation. The **situational leadership approach** views leadership as an inter-active process that links a particular style of leadership with such factors as culture, time limitations, group member personalities, and the work the group needs to do. Sometimes a group needs a strong, authoritarian leader to make decisions quickly so that the group can achieve its goal. After the September 11, 2001, attacks on the World Trade Center in New York City, Mayor Rudolf Giuliani received high praise for his quick, decisive action to cope with the devastation and the city's emotionally battered population. The city needed a strong leader to help restore order in the chaos. Although most groups prefer a democratic leadership style, leaders sometimes need to be more assertive.

Groups with clear, highly structured goals and a high level of stress may work best with a more authoritarian leadership style. For example, for workers on an assembly line making microwave ovens, the task is to produce as many ovens as possible in a short amount of time; in this high-stress situation, more directive, authoritative leadership may be needed. But if a team of advertising executives is trying to develop ideas for new ways to sell micro-wave ovens, a less authoritarian, more nondirective democratic or even laissez-faire leader-ship style may be best. The less structured nature of the task calls for a less structured, less strict leadership approach. So, according to the situational leadership approach, the answer to the question "What's the best leadership style?" is "It depends."

One simple rule for determining the appropriate leadership style is this: When the leader emerges naturally from the group or is leading a group that exists to carry out a single task, the group will permit him or her to be more directive. If the group will be together for some time and the quality of group relations is important to the functioning of the team, a more participative democratic leadership style is in order.[34]

terms & definitions

Situational leadership an approach that views leadership as an interactive process that links a particular style of leadership with such factors as culture, time limitations, group member personalities, and the work the group needs to do.

Transformational leadership the process of influencing people to see the future in new ways.

TRANSFORMATIONAL LEADERSHIP APPROACH To transform something is to change it from what it is now to something new and different. **Transformational leadership** is the process of influencing people to see the future in new ways. The transformational leader influences the team or organization by giving the team a glimpse of the future, energizing or realigning the culture, or giving the organization a new structure.[35] The leader influences by helping team members see all of the possibilities within the team, including those that may not yet be visible.[36] Microsoft founder Bill Gates challenged existing ways of thinking and developed the world's largest software development com-pany. Michael Dell transformed the way computers were marketed in the late twentieth and early twenty-first centuries. Entrepreneur Mark Zuckerberg, founder of Facebook, transformed the way people make social connections using the Internet. Each of these leaders helped to transform the people they lead by building a shared vision, challenging existing ways of thinking, and thinking holistically, from a systems perspective.

Three fundamental skills of transformational leadership have been identified by author Peter Senge:

1. *Build a shared vision.* Don't impose a vision, but listen to team members and then help them shape the future together, rather than just announcing what the future will be.

2. *Challenge existing ways of thinking.* A transformational leader pushes and prods the team or organization to think in new ways.

3. *Be a systems thinker.* Transformational leaders are aware of the interconnectedness of people, plans, resources, inputs, and outputs.[37]

Communicating a vision that people can support is one of the most important functions of a transformational leader. An authoritarian leader would just announce, "Here's your vision: now get it done." The democratic leader would ask, "What vision do you want?" The laissez-faire leader would do nothing about developing a vision unless asked to create a vision by someone else. The situational leader would say, "Let's see what type of team I'm leading and then I'll determine how to articulate and share a vision." The transformational leader paints a vivid picture of the future based on an understanding of both individual members and the culture of the entire organization. The transformational leader understands the needs, goals, hopes, and fears of individuals and is able to develop a collective vision that draws on this knowledge of the people whom he or she leads. Listening skills, interpersonal skills, conflict management skills, and feedback skills are essential competencies for transformational leaders. Such leaders also provide inspiration, motivation, and intellectual stimulation for the team. In addition, they consider the cultural backgrounds of those whom they lead. Research supports the important role of culture in determining the best way to transform a team or organization.[38]

SERVANT LEADERSHIP APPROACH To be a servant is to support, nurture, and assist others. Several researchers have identified a leadership style, known as **servant leadership**, in which the leader explicitly views himself or herself as being of service to the group or team.[39] Robert Greenleaf, one of the first researchers to develop the concept of servant leadership, described it this way:

> It begins with the natural feeling that one wants to serve, to serve first. Then conscious choice brings one to aspire to lead. The difference manifests itself in the care taken by the servant—first to make sure that other people's highest priority needs are being served. The best test is: Do those served grow as persons; do they, while being served, become healthier, wiser, freer, more autonomous, more likely themselves to become servants?[40]

To be a servant leader is to work actively to meet the needs of others while keeping an eye on the needs of the entire group, team, or organization that the leader is influencing.

What do servant leaders do? Leadership researcher Larry Spears, building on the initial idea of servant leadership, suggested that among the key actions of a servant leader were listening, empathy, and healing.[41] Underlying these behaviors is the notion that a servant leader has a high concern for people, relationships, and team member satisfaction—servant leaders desire to serve others; they wisely think about the future and strive to leave the organization better than they found it.

As you read through the description of a servant leader, you may be thinking, "This person sounds too good to be true." We're not suggesting that a servant leader always makes the best choices or is indeed a perfect leader. But a servant leader is one who is motivated both to *do good* and *do well*. For a servant leader, the ends do not justify the means. What matters is not only the outcome that is achieved but also the manner in which the team acts to achieve the outcome. For example, if you noted that your team needed additional background statistics, you decide quietly and quickly to do the needed research to help the team. The servant leader is comfortable being in the background and working to achieve the goals of the team rather than drawing attention to his or her own efforts.

terms & definitions

Servant leadership a style of leadership in which the leader explicitly views himself or herself as being of service to the group or team.

RECAP

Leadership Approaches

Approach	Description
Trait	Effective leaders possess certain traits or characteristics that contribute to their effectiveness.
Functional	Leaders influence others by performing two primary functions: • Task functions, which help accomplish the work. • Process functions, which help establish a positive climate.
Styles	Leadership is enacted in three primary styles: • Authoritarian leaders direct and control others. • Democratic leaders solicit input from others and seek to lead by involving others in the decisions. • Laissez-faire leaders intentionally influence others only when asked or directed by others to lead.
Situational	Leadership is an interactive process in which a leader adapts his or her approach based on the needs of the group. • More structured tasks in high-stress situations call for more directive leadership. • Less structured tasks in situations in which positive interpersonal relationships are important call for more democratic, collaborative approaches to leadership.
Transformational	A leader influences others by • Developing a shared vision. • Using listening and relationship-building skills to create a climate of trust.
Servant	A leader influences others by • Being altruistic: sacrificing for others. • Being an emotional healer: listening, supporting, empathizing. • Being wise: thinking about the future as well as the present. • Being persuasive: using arguments, reasoning, logic, and information to convince others rather than demanding change. • Being an organizational steward: striving to leave the organization better than he or she found it.

Leading Others: Applying Communication Principles at Work

As you begin your study of business and professional communication and glance at the table of contents, the number of terms, ideas, and skills to learn about leadership and communication may seem overwhelming. To help you make sense out of the many ideas and the information that we present, we frame our study of business and professional communication around five fundamental principles that can enhance your communication skills and leadership abilities.[42] Together, these five principles provide you with a framework for understanding how communication works at work:

Principle One: Leaders are aware of their communication with themselves and others

Principle Two: Leaders effectively use and interpret verbal messages

Principle Three: Leaders effectively use and interpret nonverbal messages

Principle Four: Leaders listen and respond thoughtfully to others

Principle Five: Leaders appropriately adapt messages to others

You may be taking a course in business and professional communication with the hope of just getting a good job and keeping it. Or you may already have a job and you have visions of someday climbing a bit higher on the corporate ladder. We've encouraged you to consider your professional career not only as just getting and keeping a job but also recognizing your potential to influence others using your leadership skills. These five principles can serve as a useful framework for assessing your communication and leadership skills regardless of your specific career objective. We briefly introduce each of the principles here and discuss them in greater detail in the chapters that follow.

Principle One: Leaders Are Aware of Their Communication with Themselves and Others

The first principle is to be aware of your interactions with others while at work. Effective communicators who skillfully lead others are conscious or "present" when communicating. Ineffective communicators mindlessly or thoughtlessly say and do things they may later regret. Being aware of your own (and others') communication involves two important processes. First, it's important to be aware of what motivates or drives a person to communicate. For example, if you know that one of your colleagues is going through a divorce, you may want to cut your coworker some slack when she or he seems a bit edgy or tense during a staff meeting. Becoming aware of what motivates you and others to communicate will help you adapt your communication to make it more effective, which is the focus of our fifth communication principle.

Second, it's important to be aware of how people perceive or see situations differently. No two people perceive a situation similarly. You may see a situation one way and a person who works for you sees it differently. For example, if you have no children but a colleague does have a child, you may not be interested at all in the new child-care facility that will be opened near your work, but your coworker is ecstatic not to have to pick up his daughter across town. Often perceptual differences result in a number of communication problems at work simply because of differences; people can view the same situation with different interpretations. In Chapter 2 we present skills to help you become more aware of why you and others communicate the way you do, as well as skills to help you check your perceptions, which can improve communication accuracy and understanding. To be an effective leader or follower, regardless of the type of work involved, it's important to be aware of your own thoughts, assumptions, and communication behavior, and the behavior of others as well.

Principle Two: Effectively Use and Interpret Verbal Messages

The second principle we introduce here and elaborate on in Chapter 3 is to effectively use and interpret verbal messages. We communicate through a **language**, which consists of symbols and a system of rules that makes it possible for people to understand one another. As we noted earlier, symbols are words, sounds, visual images, or even gestures that represent thoughts, concepts, objects, or experiences. The effective communicator both encodes and decodes messages accurately; he or she selects appropriate symbols to form a message and interprets carefully the messages of others. The words on this page are symbols you use to derive meaning that makes sense to you.

Because a number of today's organizations are global, with offices located throughout the world, it's becoming more important for employees to be bilingual. People who are bilingual can read and write at least two languages. As a leader you will have ample opportunity to instruct others in how to complete a particular task. It's essential that your followers understand your verbal messages and that you understand their verbal messages. Mastering the principle of effectively using and interpreting verbal messages will enhance your role as a VIP—a *verbally* important person who understands the power of words to influence others.

terms & definitions

Language a system of symbols and rules for their use that make it possible for people to understand and communicate with one another.

Principle Three: Effectively Use and Interpret Nonverbal Messages

Nonverbal communication is communication other than written or spoken language that creates meaning for someone. Unspoken messages can communicate powerful ideas or express emotions with greater impact than mere words alone. Understanding and interpreting nonverbal messages are especially important in the workplace. A survey of more than 550 managers from fifty businesses and organizations found that 92 percent of respondents indicated that nonverbal communication was either important or very important in a variety of business situations.[43] A leader patting an employee on the back or an employee slamming shut an office door not only conveys a message but also communicates emotions. Our emotions are communicated primarily through our use of nonverbal messages. If you have ever said, "It's not what he said that bothered me, but it's how he said it that bothered me," then you already understand the power of nonverbal communication. You may have a potential customer telling you that she will call you next week (the verbal message). However, you know she will not call you because her message was lacking sincerity (the nonverbal message). Again, it's not *what* she said ("I will call you next week") but *how* she said it (insincere voice, lack of eye contact, or fidgeting) that created and conveyed the meaning to you. We continue our discussion of nonverbal messages along with verbal messages in Chapter 3, as well as provide you with skills to help you put into practice this communication principle for leadership.

Principle Four: Listen and Respond Thoughtfully to Others

Although effective leadership requires people to develop and send messages to others that are meaningful, it is equally if not more important for leaders to listen and receive messages from others. Listening involves being **other-oriented**, which is when we consider the needs, motives, desires, and goals of others. A crucial part of leadership is being able to meet the needs of the people you lead. There is evidence that the skill of being other-oriented or empathic is decreasing. One study found that college students in the early part of the twenty-first century are 40 percent less empathic than college students in the 1980s and 1990s—empathy skills seemed to drop off after about 2000.[44] Listening to others is essential to being empathically other-oriented. The only way you know what people need, is to listen to them. What are they telling you? What are they not telling you? Listening is so important to leadership that Stephen Covey, a well-known leadership expert, features listening as one of his seven habits of highly effective people. Covey noted, "Seek first to understand, then to be understood."[45]

Listening is a process. It not only involves receiving messages, but it also includes responding thoughtfully to what others are saying. Responsive messages involve asking questions related to what the person is talking about, restating in your own words what you hear the other person saying, and being nonverbally responsive by leaning forward, making eye contact, and nodding your head. Responsive messages are affirming. They communicate to other people that they have been listened to and that you understand them. Chapter 4 discusses in greater detail how you can enhance your leadership effectiveness by developing your listening skills.

Principle Five: Appropriately Adapt Messages to Others

Leading others requires you to develop and use communication that is appropriately adapted to the people you lead. When you adapt a message to others you make choices about how best to develop a message to achieve your communication goal. The workplace is full of diversity; a one-size-fits-all approach to communication doesn't work in the twenty-first century. For messages to have an impact, they must be tailored to the people receiving them. Chances are that you will be working with people from all over the globe. Even men and women don't always understand

terms & definitions

Nonverbal communication any communication, other than written or spoken language, that creates meaning for someone.

Other-oriented focused on the needs, motives, desires, and goals of others in one's communication.

Communication Ethics @ Work

What's Your Ethics Credo?

Ethics are the beliefs, values, and moral principles by which we determine what is right or wrong. An ethical communicator is one who considers the thoughts, feelings, and considerations of the people with whom a communicator is interacting. The National Communication Association has developed a Credo for Communication Ethics to emphasize the importance of being an ethical communicator:

> Ethical communication is fundamental to responsible thinking, decision making, and the development of relationships and communities within and across contexts, cultures, channels, and media. Moreover, ethical communication enhances human worth and dignity by fostering truthfulness,

fairness, responsibility, personal integrity, and respect for self and others.[46]

In the workplace it's especially important to be mindful of your ethical principles because of the trust others place in you, especially when managing other people's money or having access to private information such as medical or financial records.

What's your personal ethics credo? As you work with others in business and professional contexts, what are key ethical principles that guide you in communicating with others? Imagine you are being interviewed for a job and the interviewer asks you what your ethical principles are. What would you say?

each other because of gender differences in communication. Your ability to lead and influence others effectively depends on your ability to adapt messages appropriately to others.

Another way to tailor your communication is to adapt to another person's personality. Some people are talkative; others are quiet. Some people enjoy a good argument; others find arguing upsetting. Your ability to adapt and adjust your communication makes others more comfortable and enhances understanding. In Chapter 5 we discuss this principle in greater detail by discussing how you can lead more effectively by adapting to personality, culture, and gender differences.

Leading Others: Applying Communication Skills at Work

terms & definitions

Ethics the beliefs, values, and moral principles by which we determine what is right and wrong.

In the workplace you communicate—make sense and share sense with others—to achieve specific work objectives. You achieve those objectives through three sets of communication skills: you relate, you collaborate, and you present messages to others. Communication in the interpersonal context helps develop and manage workplace relationships. Communication in

RECAP

Communication Principles for Leadership

Communication Principle	Description
Principle One: Be **aware** of your communication with yourself and others.	Be mindful of your communication and conscious of what motivates you and others to communicate.
Principle Two: Effectively use and interpret **verbal** messages.	Select appropriate symbols to clearly communicate messages to others, and decode others' messages carefully.
Principle Three: Effectively use and interpret **nonverbal** messages.	Use unspoken symbols to communicate the emotional and relational aspects of your message.
Principle Four: **Listen** and respond thoughtfully to others.	Actively listen to others, using responses to ensure and demonstrate you have understood the message correctly.
Principle Five: Appropriately **adapt** messages to others.	Customize messages to enhance message clarity; consider the personal, social, and cultural characteristics of listeners.

teams allows people to collaborate with others. Finally, communication in the public context takes place through effective business and professional presentations. Although each context is different, the communication principles remain the same. You use the same five principles to develop and manage relationships as you do to make effective sales presentations to potential customers. What's different is how the communication principles are applied. You will see how the five communication principles are woven throughout the three contexts (interpersonal, team, and public) and how the context determines how the principles are applied to achieve communication goals as you assume leadership roles. In the model in Figure 1.2 you'll note that the same five principles are present regardless of whether the skill is relating, collaborating, or presenting. In each context, you draw on all five fundamental principles.

Relating to Others: Interpersonal Communication

A **relationship** is an ongoing connection we make with others through interpersonal communication.[47] To relate to someone is to give and take, listen and respond, act and react. When we talk about a good or positive relationship with someone, we often mean that we are together, or "in synch." You will develop and manage relationships with your manager, your coworkers, with the people you lead, and with your customers and clients. Communication allows the relationships to develop. Without communication, there are no relationships. To relate to others effectively, you should be aware of your communication, effectively use verbal and nonverbal messages, listen and respond, and appropriately adapt your messages to others in interpersonal situations.

Interpersonal communication occurs when at least two people interact with each other to mutually influence each other, usually for the purpose of developing and managing their relationship. You engage in interpersonal communication when you interview for a job or visit with a colleague. You communicate with an interviewer with the hope of influencing the person and developing a relationship—convincing him or her that you're the most qualified for the position. When talking with a colleague, you may be swapping office stories or just talking about the weather.

Yet true interpersonal communication occurs not simply when you interact with someone, but when you treat the other person as a unique human being. Think of all human

terms & definitions

Relationship an ongoing connection developed with another person through interpersonal communication.

Interpersonal communication communication that occurs when two people interact to mutually influence each other, usually for the purpose of managing relationships.

Media richness theory theory that a communication medium is rich if it has (1) potential for instant feedback, (2) verbal and nonverbal cues that can be processed by senders and receivers, (3) natural language, and (4) a focus on individuals.

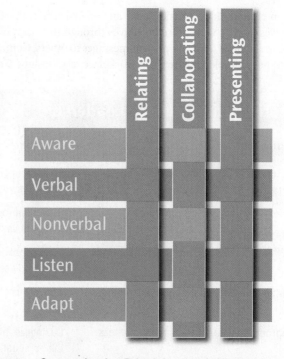

FIGURE 1.2 Communication Principles and Skills for Leadership

Communication Skills FOR A **Digital Age**

Matching Your Media to Your Message

In the movie *Up in the Air*, Ryan Bingham, played by George Clooney, has the job of firing people. He chooses to handle this difficult and delicate task in person. A new colleague thinks it would save money to fire people via video conference. The movie ultimately makes the point that live-and-in-person is a better, kinder way of sharing such profound news.

Technology has made it easier to share information quicker and easier with many people in an organization. You can just as easily be e-connected to your colleagues in the next room or in the next continent because of the Internet and a vast array of technological tools. Because of the ease in using technology, coupled with the increasing likelihood that you will be communicating with people from other cultures, you may need to decide when you need to share news face-to-face and when it may be more efficient to communicate virtually, such as using text messages, email, instant messaging, Skype, YouTube, Facebook, or other electronic means.

One practical theory, called **media richness theory,** helps explain when it is best to communicate in person rather than participate in mediated communication. A method or channel of communication is said to be rich if it has the following characteristics:[48]

1. There is the possibility of instant feedback.
2. Both verbal and nonverbal cues can be processed by senders and receivers.
3. There is natural, informal use of language rather than formal language.
4. Messages are customized to individuals rather than communicated to a mass of people.

Face-to-face communication is media rich; writing a memo that goes out to all employees is media lean. The continuum of media-rich and media-lean methods of communication are presented here.

When should you use more media-rich methods of communication (which may involve travel and the expense of gathering in one place at one time), and when is it acceptable to use more efficient media-lean communication approaches? Here are a few tips.

Use media-rich methods if:

- Your message is likely to be misunderstood because it's highly detailed and complex.

- Your message is important to people (such as about their compensation).
- There is a high potential for interpersonal conflict.
- You want to know immediately how people will respond to your message.

Use media-lean methods if:

- The information is routine and noncontroversial, such as announcing the time and place of a meeting.
- You will follow up the presentation of detailed information with a face-to-face meeting later.
- You want to communicate a simple message to many people quickly, such as the closing of a street or a parking garage for repairs.
- You already have a good interpersonal relationship with your intended audience because you have spent time in face-to-face collaboration on other projects.

Applying Your Skills

Given the principles of media richness theory, consider how best to collaborate with team members in the following situations:

1. You've had an e-meeting via the Internet with your colleagues. It's your job to distribute the minutes of the meeting. Should you use a media-rich or media-lean method of communicating the minutes to your coworkers?

2. As project manager, you've noticed increased conflict and relational tension between the team working in Houston, Texas, and the team based in Mexico City. During the last conference phone call it was clear the tensions were escalating between the two groups. To manage the conflict, should you use a media-rich or media-lean context? Specifically, what would be a good forum to help manage the conflict?

3. Because of the aging baby boomers in the organization, the human resources department has developed a new retirement policy for the company. The new policy is somewhat complicated because of the various formulas for calculating retirement benefits. Workers in the organization are assigned to project teams. It's your job to communicate the new policy to project team members. Should you use a media-rich or media-lean method of communicating to the employees?

Communication allows interpersonal relationships to develop, as individuals engage in a simultaneous process of creating meaning and influencing each other.

communication as occurring on a continuum ranging from impersonal communication to interpersonal communication.

Impersonal communication occurs when you treat people as objects, or when you respond to their roles, such as responding impersonally to a sales clerk or server, rather than to the unique person.

People who are skilled interpersonal communicators are able to establish quality relationships with others, know how to manage conflict effectively and appropriately, and connect with people from all walks of life including those who may have a different cultural or ethnic background. As we noted at the beginning of this chapter, Howard Schultz is an effective leader because of the quality interpersonal relationships he establishes with both his coworkers and his customers.

Collaborating with Others: Team Communication

Another set of skills comes to the fore in collaborating with others. To collaborate is to work with other people to achieve a specific outcome. In business and professional settings you typically collaborate with others when working in groups and teams. **Group communication** is the verbal and nonverbal message transaction that occurs among three to about fifteen people who share a common purpose or goal, who feel a sense of belonging to the group, and who exert influence on others.[49] You experience group communication when you facilitate a meeting with the people you lead or when you attend a staff meeting with your coworkers.

Skilled collaborators are those who can help manage the relationship dynamics of a group or team. Because of their skill in listening and relating to others, they help a group maintain a positive, supportive climate. Skilled group members also facilitate getting the work accomplished. They have skills that help the team solve problems, make decisions, and reach agreement.

Two attributes distinguish group communication from other forms of communication.

- First, groups have a common goal, something members all would agree is the reason for their existence. Members of a small group need to be able to identity with the group and its purpose; they should sense it is *their* group.

- Second, group members exert influence on each other. Each person potentially influences the actions and responses of others. Even if a group member sits silently, his or her silence has the ability to influence others and is a powerful form of nonverbal communication. Each group member, by virtue of being a member of the group, has the potential to exert leadership on—and thus, to lead—the group.

A **team** is a *coordinated* group of individuals who collaborate to achieve a specific common goal, such as making a product or completing a long-term project. A team is more highly structured and organized than a group. Teams have evolved to have clearly defined roles, duties, and responsibilities for team members. We elaborate on the distinction between a group and a team in Chapter 9.

Because you'll spend so much of your work time collaborating with others on the job, Chapter 9 will allow you to see how groups and teams work. Chapter 10 will provide you with specific strategies for improving team meetings. As we examine group communication and discuss how to build teams, we will apply each of the five communication principles for leadership.

Presenting to Others: Public Communication

Public communication occurs when a speaker addresses a gathering of people to inform or persuade and even sometimes entertain them. This type of communication tends to cause anxiety for some because it requires developing, organizing, and delivering a presentation to an audience. Public communication tends to be more formal and more structured than interpersonal or team communication. As a leader you will have ample opportunities to make presentations before business and professional colleagues. In Chapters 11, 12, and 13, we will apply the five principles of communication to a number of different types of business presentations: informative briefings, reports, public relations presentations, sales presentations, introductions, and ceremonial presentations (presenting an award, making a toast).

Of the three communication contexts (interpersonal, group, public), public communication has the distinction of being the one that has been formally studied the longest. In 333 B.C. Aristotle wrote his famous work called *The Rhetoric*, which was the first fully developed treatment of the use of speech to convince an audience. He defined **rhetoric** as the process of discovering the available means of persuasion in a given situation. Today, many communication departments have several courses that focus exclusively on how to persuade others, design and deliver both informative and persuasive messages, and evaluate the messages of others. Although we have certainly advanced in our understanding of informing and persuading others in the past two millennia, much of what Aristotle taught has withstood the test of both time and scholarly research.

Wrap-Up

Communication is essential for leadership. At its most basic level, human communication is the process of making sense out of the world and sharing that sense with others by creating meaning through verbal and nonverbal messages.

Leaders influence others through communication. You use communication skills to relate to others, collaborate with others, and present information to others. There are six approaches to leadership:

- The trait leadership approach: Leaders possess certain traits or characteristics that make the leader effective.

- The functional leadership approach: Considers two elements of leadership—task functions that help accomplish the work, and process functions that help establish an overall positive climate.

- The styles approach: Identifies three primary leadership styles: authoritarian (which emphasizes directing and controlling others), democratic (which is a participative leadership style), and laissez-faire (in which a leader only leads when asked or absolutely needed).

- The situational approach: Views leadership as an interactive process, in which a leader adapts his or her leadership style based on the needs of the group.
- The transformational approach: A leader influences others by developing a shared vision while listening and relating to those people the leader leads.
- The servant leader approach: Emphasizes that a leader's key function is to serve, facilitate, and help the organization or group achieve its full potential.

Reviewing Key Terms

The Principle Points

Five communication principles are fundamental to enhancing leadership and business and professional communication skills. We refer to these principles throughout the book as a way of organizing the skills and applications of human communication.

- *Leaders are aware of their communication with themselves and others.* Being mindful of your communication is important to help you improve your communication.
- *Leaders effectively use and interpret verbal messages.* Words are powerful and influence our thoughts, our actions, and our relationships with others.
- *Leaders effectively use and interpret nonverbal messages.* Unspoken cues provide important information about our emotions, feelings, and attitudes.
- *Leaders listen and respond thoughtfully to others.* Being able to interpret accurately the messages of others enhances comprehension and relational empathy.
- *Leaders appropriately adapt messages to others.* It is important to adapt messages to others to enhance both understanding and empathy.

Applying Your Skills

1. Keep a conversation journal for one day. Take note of the times you are aware of a message sent not equaling the message received. Who was normally blamed for the miscommunication? The source? The receiver? Why do you think that is?

2. Comparing Leadership Styles. Divide the class into several groups. One person in each group should be appointed to lead a group discussion to answer the following question: What should be done to lower the cost of college textbooks? Each group leader should enact a different leadership style. One group leader should be instructed to use the democratic leadership style, another group leader should use a laissez-faire leadership style, and another should use an authoritarian style. Following the group discussion, each group should discuss the pros and cons of the specific leadership style enacted in their group.

3. What are your best leadership attributes and what leadership skills should you work to enhance? Make a list of your best leadership attributes, as if you were being considered for a leadership role in a business or professional setting. Make a second list of the leadership skills and competencies you'd like to enhance. Note the role and function of communication in your two lists.

2

Being Aware of Self and Others

chapter **outline**

After reading this chapter, you should be able to

- Describe what it means to be mindful in communication with others, and explain why self-awareness is important.

- Define social style and discuss the effects of social style on communication behaviors.

- Identify and describe each of the four social styles.

- Discuss strategies for adapting your communication to others' social styles.

- Differentiate between the three approaches to motivation: classical, human relations, and human resources.

- Explain the importance of understanding organizational culture and how to use cultural knowledge to enhance leadership.

- Discuss how written rules, stories, metaphors, ceremonies, and artifacts contribute to the culture of an organization.

- Identify and apply strategies for managing the ethical challenges of deceit, responsibility, and consistency.

Although you probably do not recognize the name Indra Nooyi, you're probably familiar with many of the products she is responsible for producing, including Pepsi, Gatorade, and Fritos. Nooyi is CEO of PepsiCo, which is responsible for Pepsi products as well as Tropicana, Frito Lay, Gatorade, and Quaker Oats products. In 2010 she was named number 1 on *Fortune*'s list of the "50 Most Powerful Women" and number 6 on *Forbes*'s list of the "World's 100 Most Powerful Women."

Although Nooyi considers herself a normal person, who juggles being a corporate leader with being a mother, a wife, a daughter, and a daughter-in-law, much of her success is grounded in her awareness of who she is as a person and her awareness of others, which was cultivated through her relationship with her paternal grandfather who taught her to be a thoughtful and mindful person. My grandfather "taught me to be a lifelong student. Don't ever think you've arrived, and remember that what you don't know is so much more than what you do."[1] Being grounded and self-aware of her strengths and weaknesses has allowed Nooyi to be more open to new ideas, learning and growing as a person. Through this self-awareness, she has become a more mindful person.

Nooyi's keen self-awareness and mindfulness of others is how she attracts and retains her best employees. She invests time in developing the people who work for her. "We look at a 10- to 15-year development plan for our high-potential people," says Nooyi. "This looks at their children, their schools, their spouse's job, aging parents—anything that affects where they will be comfortable working. That way we can build opportunities to develop their careers in tandem with their personal lives."[2]

Another example of Nooyi's mindfulness is when she wrote to the parents of 29 of her senior executives' parents to inform them of what a great job they did in raising their child. She informed the parents of how much their now-grown child had contributed to the success of PepsiCo. In these personal letters, she considered each senior executive a gift. According to Nooyi, this letter-writing activity "unleashed emotions that were unbelievable, creating an emotional bond among executives, their parents, and me."[3]

leading **questions**

1. Nooyi attributes much of her success to being grounded and knowing who she is as a person. How do you see self-awareness being related to leadership effectiveness?

2. How do you see self-awareness and mindfulness being similar and different?

3. Within the past five years, have you become a more thoughtful person? If so, how? Who has influenced your thoughtfulness?

4. What do you think motivated Nooyi to send thank you letters to her senior executives' parents? Why not send the letter to the senior executives?

As we noted in Chapter 1, the first principle that guides the communication and leadership skills in the workplace is to *become aware of your communication with yourself and others.* Figure 2.1 illustrates where Principle One fits into our model of Communication Principles and Skills for Leadership. You will notice that becoming self-aware is at the top of the model, suggesting that effective workplace communication begins with self-awareness. Being self-aware typically occurs in two steps. First, you become aware of how you and others communicate. Second, you determine if the way in which you communicate with yourself and others is effective. By being self-aware you can answer the question, Am I meeting my goals? You can also determine if the people with whom you interact are achieving their goals. If not, what's going wrong? Adhering to our first principle of communication is central to monitoring your own accomplishments and how you communicate with other people.

"Don't bother just to be better than your contemporaries or predecessors. Try to be better than yourself."

—William Faulkner

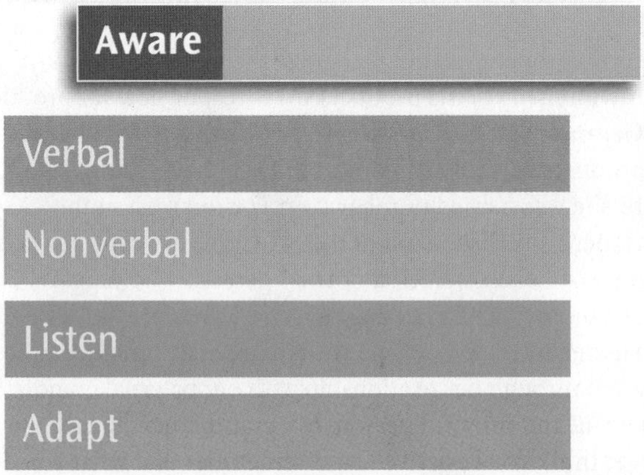

FIGURE 2.1 **Communication Principles and Skills for Leadership**

Mindfulness is awareness of your own and others' thoughts, actions, and motivations.[4] It is your ability to get out of your own head and into others' heads. Being mindful is the process of actively paying attention not only to how you communicate and relate to your customers, employees, colleagues, or superiors, but also to how they communicate with you. If the saying "open mouth, insert foot" immediately comes to mind after you said something you wish you hadn't, then you already understand the importance of being mindful in your communication with others and how difficult mindfulness is to achieve.

This chapter explains how to become more aware of your own communication and the communication of others. Some leaders have a way of making their communication fit with others' communication styles. For example, if your client is task oriented and driven to reach goals, then he's probably not interested in small talk and discussing weekend plans. So you adapt your communication style to fit your client's style. You become task oriented as well, and you keep your communication focused on helping your client reach his goals.

Mindful communicators are also aware of three other important aspects of leadership: leadership assumptions, organizational culture, and ethics. If you assume a leadership role, you may be guided by a set of beliefs about what motivates people to behave. Some leaders believe that followers are motivated by rewards and punishments. Other leaders believe that followers are motivated by becoming active participants in the leadership process. What about you? What assumptions do you have about followers— and are they accurate?

Leaders are mindful of organizational culture and how it's created through communication. Organizational culture is always changing and evolving and includes multiple factors, such as traditions, stories, metaphors, ceremonies, and artifacts. Effective leaders are plugged into the culture of their organization and know how to use their communication to influence that culture.

Finally, are you aware of the role that ethics play in leadership and communication? Your ethics are revealed through your communication, and your communication ultimately reinforces your ethics. Being aware of ethical issues will begin to prepare you for the ethical challenges that you will face as a leader.

Be Aware of Social Styles

Awareness begins with an understanding of how you communicate with others and how others communicate with you. Your **social style** is a pattern of communication behaviors that others observe when you interact with them.[5] A manager who immediately gets up from her desk and greets you with a warm smile and a handshake, compliments you on your appearance, and asks you about your family has a social style that is noticeably different from that of a manager who greets you without eye contact while completing an email, then asks you numerous questions about the status of the project you're leading (and grumbles about the answers you give). Your social style is similar to your signature—your handwritten signature is unique. Similarly, your social style is unique; no one has a social style that

terms & definitions

Mindfulness awareness of your own and others' thoughts, actions, and motivations.

Social style a pattern of communication behaviors that others observe when you interact with them.

Communication Skills FOR A Digital Age

Using Technology Appropriately When Communicating with Others

You don't need to be an expert in communication to know that technology is changing the way you communicate and how you interact with others in the workplace.[6] Not everyone is pleased with how people are using technology to communicate. For example, have you ever been in a face-to-face conversation with someone who is chatting online or interrupts your conversation to take a call on his or her cell phone? If you have ever been in this situation, you know how frustrating it is to try to communicate with others when they're using technology. Below are some ways you can be more mindful when using technology to communicate.

Applying Your Skills When Using Cell Phones[7]

- *Excuse yourself before taking a call.* The call may be important to you, but realize that you are also important to the person in front of you. Taking a call signals that the person you are with is less important than the person calling. If that's not the impression you want to give, don't take the call. The caller can always leave you a voicemail.

- *Don't talk on your cell phone in front of someone who expects your attention.* Administrative support staff members and cashiers in the company cafeteria deserve the respect of having your attention.

- *Don't yell while talking on your cell phone.* Have you noticed how some people scream when using the cell phone? Lower your voice or move to a quieter place to continue the call.

- *When in close distance to others, such as in an airplane, office, or elevator, keep it short.* Call the person back when you have more privacy.

Applying Your Skills When Using Social Networking Site[8]

- *Refrain from having a face-to-face conversation while also chatting online.* Give the other person your full attention. Make sure you're following your company's policy regarding using social networking sites while at work.

- *Make sure that your content is suitable for the eyes of your employer and employees.* Your employers or prospective employers may be checking you out. What will

your employees learn about you from viewing your Facebook page? Is this appropriate?

- *Be as careful when you chat online about your work, personal life, or social events as you would when talking to a stranger.* Your posts on newsgroups and online communities may be publicly available in archives where they can be found years later.

- *Make only comments about a named individual that would be acceptable if made face to face.* Laws on bullying, stalking, and defamation all apply online, and the penalties can be severe.

- *Be careful when discussing details of your whereabouts.* It is important, for your own safety, that you keep private where you are planning to go and when you will not be at home or in the office.

perfectly matches your own. Becoming a mindful communicator and leader involves becoming aware of your own social style and the social styles of others. This awareness allows you to more effectively adapt your communication to others.

Identifying Your Social Style

Your social style is a combination of two primary dimensions: assertiveness and responsiveness. **Assertiveness** is the capacity to make requests; to actively disagree; to express positive

terms & definitions

Assertiveness an individual's capacity to make requests, actively disagree, express positive and negative personal feelings, and stand up for himself or herself without attacking another.

Those in service professions, like this doctor and nurse, tend to be amiables. Their social style is characterized by responsiveness to others.

or negative personal feelings; to initiate, maintain, or disengage from conversations; and to stand up for oneself without attacking another.[9] **Responsiveness** is the capacity to be sensitive to the communication of others, to be seen as a good listener, to make others comfortable in communicating, and to recognize the needs and desires of others.[10] To assist you in becoming more self-aware of your own social style, we encourage you to complete the self-report measure in Rating Scale 2.1. Depending on your self-reported levels of assertiveness and responsiveness, your social style will fall into one of the following four quadrants: amiable, analytical, driver, or expressive.[11]

AMIABLE   If you're an **amiable**, you are a relationship specialist and are high on responsiveness and low on assertiveness. Adjectives used to describe amiables include *conforming, unsure, pliable, dependent, awkward, supportive, respectful, willing, dependable,* and *agreeable.* Amiables seem to be most comfortable working in environments where they can provide services and be supportive and helpful in their relationships with others. Such people are often drawn to careers in teaching, human resources, social work, psychology, and other helping professions.

ANALYTICAL   If you're an **analytical**, you are a technical specialist and are low on both responsiveness and assertiveness. The adjectives used to describe analyticals include *critical, indecisive, stuffy, picky, moralistic, industrious, persistent, serious, exacting,* and *orderly.* Professions such as science, engineering, construction work, accounting, and certain aspects of law often have a high proportion of people with this style. Some research suggests that analyticals are more likely to be apprehensive about communication and thus more withdrawn and quiet.[12] As a result, analyticals may be less effective communicators than others and more resistant to interacting with others.

DRIVER   If you're a **driver**, you are a control specialist and are low on responsiveness and high on assertiveness. Among the adjectives used to describe drivers are *pushy, severe, tough, dominating, harsh, strong-willed, independent, practical, decisive,* and *efficient.* These people might be small-business owners, top managers, production managers, administrative personnel, politicians, or in other decision-making positions. Because of their ability to take responsibility and direct others, top management often puts these individuals into positions of control.

EXPRESSIVE   If you're an **expressive**, you are a social specialist and high on both responsiveness and assertiveness. The adjectives used to describe expressives include *competent, excitable, versatile, reacting, ambitious, stimulating, enthusiastic, dramatic,* and *friendly.* Persons with an expressive social style are often found in sales, entertainment, and advertising; or they may be artists, musicians, or writers. These people know how to use their communication skills to gain recognition and attention, and they like being seen and noticed by others.

terms & definitions

Responsiveness an individual's capacity to be sensitive to the communication of others, be seen as a good listener, and to make others comfortable in communicating.

Amiable a social style characterized by high responsiveness and low assertiveness. People with this style are considered relationship specialists; they enjoy working in supportive and helpful roles.

Analytical a social style characterized by low responsiveness and assertiveness. Individuals with this social style are considered technical specialists; they enjoy working in technical positions.

Driver a social style characterized by high assertiveness and low responsiveness. Persons with this social style are considered control specialists; they often enjoy working in leadership and management positions.

Expressive a social style characterized by high assertiveness and responsiveness. Individuals with this social style are considered social specialists; they are able to use their communication skills to gain recognition and attention, and enjoy being noticed by others.

RATING SCALE 2.1   Identifying Your Social Style[13]

Following is a list of twenty personality characteristics. Please indicate the degree to which you believe you display each characteristic while interacting with others by marking whether you (5) *strongly agree* that you exhibit the characteristic, (4) *agree* that you exhibit it, (3) are *undecided*, (2) *disagree* that you exhibit the characteristic, or (1) *strongly disagree* that it applies. There are no right or wrong answers. Work quickly; record your first impression.

_____ 1. Helpful

_____ 2. Defend my own beliefs

_____ 3. Independent

_____ 4. Responsive to others

_____ 5. Forceful

_____ 6. Have strong personality

_____ 7. Sympathetic

_____ 8. Compassionate

_____ 9. Assertive

_____ 10. Sensitive to the needs of others

_____ 11. Dominant

_____ 12. Sincere

_____ 13. Gentle

_____ 14. Willing to take a stand

_____ 15. Warm

_____ 16. Tender

_____ 17. Friendly

_____ 18. Act as a leader

_____ 19. Aggressive

_____ 20. Competitive

Scoring instructions:

Add your ratings for these characteristics to determine your Assertiveness score:

2 + 3 + 5 + 6 + 9 + 11 + 14 + 18 + 19 + 20

Add your ratings of these characteristics to determine your Responsiveness score:

1 + 4 + 7 + 8 + 10 + 12 + 13 + 15 + 16 + 17

Scores above 34 indicate high assertiveness or responsiveness. Scores below 26 indicate low assertiveness or responsiveness. Scores between 26 and 34 indicate moderate levels of assertiveness or responsiveness.

Now map your assertiveness and responsiveness scores on the graph below to determine your social style. First, find the point on the vertical axis that corresponds to your assertiveness score, and draw a horizontal dotted line in from that point on the axis. Then find the point on the horizontal axis that corresponds to your responsiveness score, and draw a vertical dotted line up from that point on the axis. Place a dot at the point where these two lines intersect; the quadrant in which the dot falls indicates your social style. For example, if you scored 35 on assertiveness and 46 on responsiveness, you would fall within the "Expressive" quadrant.

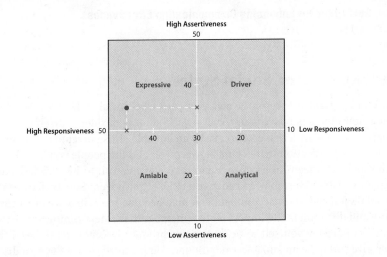

One of the ways you can make you awareness of social styles work for you is to style flex.[14] To style flex, follow three steps: (1) identify your social style, (2) identify the other person's social style, (3) use the following style-flexing strategies and communication skills.

If You Have an Amiable Social Style

When communicating with an **Analytical** person	When communicating with an **Expressive** person	When communicating with a **Driver**
• Be punctual, focus on the task, use a formal tone • De-emphasize feelings: minimize eye contact, avoid touch • Be systematic: develop a plan, follow the rules • Be organized: prepare in advance, use specific details in presentations	• Increase your speed, respond and decide promptly, minimize paperwork • Increase your energy: stand up straight, use expressive gestures and eye contact, talk louder, faster, and with more intensity than you might normally • Focus on the big picture: prioritize topics and focus on those of highest priority; avoid specific details • Initiate conversations, avoid tentative language, disagree tactfully	• Set realistic goals and develop a plan • Prioritize topics and focus on those of highest priority; avoid the details • Be organized: present options, anticipate questions and prepare answers, focus on results • Avoid tentative language • Identify problems; disagree tactfully

If You Are a Driver

When communicating with an **Analytical** person	When communicating with an **Expressive** person	When communicating with an **Amiable** person
• Slow down: analyticals react negatively to pressure to be speedy; avoid pushing • Listen more: drivers tend to want to talk; invite the person to speak, and paraphrase what she or he says • Minimize expressive gestures and monitor your speech; speak more slowly and with less intensity than you might normally • Prepare thoroughly; gather all necessary details and information to build credibility	• Be aware of and acknowledge the other person's feelings; be warm and enthusiastic • Allow for fun and joking; pay attention to and comment on the other person's physical space (office decorations, photos) • Be confirming: recognize the other's contributions; be supportive; provide incentives • Be flexible with your time; listen and respond; practice patience	• Be genuine: engage in personal conversation and offer appropriate self-disclosure • Be supportive: be a good listener, paraphrase what the other person says and respond appropriately; be appreciative and helpful • Focus on feelings: pay attention to the other person's nonverbal cues; amiables will not always voice their unhappiness • Slow down: as a driver, you often speak fast because you like to get things done; relax deadlines and avoid rushing

FIGURE 2.2 **Style Flexing Guidelines for Enhancing Communication Effectiveness**

Identifying Others' Social Styles

Although it's important for you to be aware of your own social style, what may be more important is how others perceive your social style. You may consider yourself to be a driver when others you work with perceive you to be an amiable. This perceptual difference may influence the communication that occurs between you and the people you lead. For example, if you supervise a team of lifeguards and they perceive you to be very laid back and easygoing (an amiable), they may consider you to be a "pushover." Rather than you supervising them, they may supervise you, and you may become frustrated at your inability to take control and direct them. It's important to remember that others communicate not with the person *you* perceive yourself to be, but with who *they* perceive you to be. If the lifeguards perceive you to be an amiable, even though you perceive yourself to be a driver, the lifeguards will communicate with you as though you were an amiable. Effective leadership begins with understanding this important perceptual difference.

If You Have an Expressive Social Style

When communicating with an **Analytical** person	When communicating with a **Driver**	When communicating with an **Amiable** person
• Be task-focused, punctual, formal • Be systematic: follow the rules, have a plan • Prepare thoroughly, focus on facts and specific details, provide evidence • Minimize expressiveness; avoid dramatic gestures and vocal intensity	• Be task-focused, punctual, formal • Plan your work: determine specific goals and objectives • Be organized: prepare thoroughly and know what you intend to say; use facts and be results-oriented • Avoid power struggles: both Expressives and Drivers are assertive; make an effort to listen more; slow down and be willing to negotiate	• Allow the other person to speak more; paraphrase what you hear • Be supportive: make the other person feel understood; listen with empathy • Minimize expressiveness, use tentative or provisional language ("possibly," "maybe," and "could") • Slow your speech, relax deadlines, avoid rushing; amiables tend to take longer to make decisions

If You Have an Analytical Social Style

When communicating with an **Expressive** person	When communicating with a **Driver**	When communicating with an **Amiable** person
• Be warm, build rapport, offer appropriate self-disclosure • Speak more rapidly than you might normally; react quickly • Say what you think: speak up, disagree tactfully, identify problems rather than ignoring them • Be flexible; improvise, relax the rules, be encouraging	• Prioritize your information and share the most important points; avoid subpoints or details unless asked • Be results oriented and practical • Say what you think • Present options, but allow the person to determine his or her own objectives and goals; relax the rules	• Be genuine; build rapport; offer appropriate self-disclosure; be loyal • Provide structure: define the job, assist in planning • Avoid logical appeals; focus on main points and leave out details • Be supportive and helpful; make the other person feel understood; recognize his or her contributions

FIGURE 2.2 (continued)

To become more aware of how others perceive you as well as of how you perceive others' social styles, we encourage you to complete Rating Scale 2.1 again. This time, however, we suggest using the measure in a couple of different ways. First, you may want to ask a classmate or someone you work with to use the measure to evaluate you. This way, you can become more aware of how others perceive your social style and you can compare those perceptions with your own self-perception. This information will also help you better understand why others communicate with you in a particular manner. For example, maybe you have always wondered why some people seem to be scared of you or appear threatened by you. It may be because they perceive you to be a driver, but what they may not know is that you're really an analytical.

Second, you may also want to complete the measure while focusing on a real-life workplace relationship that is important to you and could benefit from more effective communication. What you do with the feedback is important. The next section of this chapter provides you with some practical skills to help you put your new self-awareness of social styles to work for you.

Adapting to Social Styles

Being aware of your social style and the social styles of others allows you to adapt your communication, which enhances your ability to be effective. **Style flexing** is a process of adapting your communication to how others communicate. For example, if you're an analytical leader who is working with a team of drivers, you will enhance your leadership effectiveness if you communicate more like a driver. This would include being direct with members of the team, focusing on outcomes, and allowing them the freedom to determine goals and objectives. Again, this is not your preferred way of communicating with others, but it's how drivers communicate. Figure 2.2 suggests ways to help you style flex to others' social styles.

terms & definitions

Style flexing the process of adapting your communication to how others communicate.

According to management communication consultants Robert and Dorothy Bolton, style flexing is a way of tailoring communication to another person's processes.[15] When you style flex, you maximize the fit between you and another person. Most men have their suits tailored to ensure that they fit perfectly. When your suit fits you perfectly, you look and feel better. When workplace relationships fit, you're more productive and effective.

Becoming aware of your own and others' social styles gives you important information that you can use to lead others more effectively. Another source of information that will enhance your ability to lead others is awareness of the beliefs and assumptions that you hold about leadership.

Be Aware of How to Motivate Others

Becoming a mindful communicator and leader involves becoming aware of the beliefs you have about what motivates people to follow leaders. Why do you believe people would follow you, and how do these beliefs ultimately influence your leadership style and ability to lead? Researchers have identified a number of different approaches to how organizations function and how the people within the organizations are motivated to work and follow others. Three of these approaches include classical, human relations, and human resources.

Using the Classical Approach

The **classical approach to motivation** is based on the principle of reward and punishment. Put simply, workers are motivated to work hard when they are rewarded for good work and not rewarded for poor work. The classical approach to organizations also assumes that there is one best way for a team or organization to perform a given task. The leader's job is to influence the workers to behave in ways that help them produce goods or services in the most efficient and effective way possible. Fredrick Taylor's 1911 book *The Principles of Scientific Management* was influential in helping leaders structure work so that it could be done in effective and efficient ways.[16] Max Weber is another author who wrote about classical approaches to looking at bureaucracies or formal organizations.[17] Weber noted that organizations are structured by rules and regulations and driven by people who have legitimate authority to control and direct people's behaviors.

Under the classical approach, work is organized to be performed with no wasted motions. Time is money, and the more quickly the work can be accomplished, the better. Most fast-food restaurants organize their teamwork using classical assumptions of leadership. The manager assumes that she is in charge and that her team will perform and follow her. When you place your order for a hamburger, the people who make your meal don't typically huddle and say, "Well, what's the best way to make this hamburger?" The manager or the organization has already

Communication between manager and employees at a fast-food restaurant chain is focused on completing specific tasks in an efficient manner.

decided this for them. The procedure has been established, and the team members' job is to produce the hamburger as fast as possible, following this procedure. An organization or team that operates with a classical assumption about leadership has identified a clear leader who is expected to keep things running like clockwork, and team members have accepted that they're fulfilling the role that is needed. Work is organized like an assembly line in which each person has been trained to do his or her part in producing whatever it is that the team is creating.

Communication in organizations that operate using classical leadership assumptions is typically downward; the leader is a person with the power and authority to tell the others in the organization or team what to do. Team members are not expected to spend much time collaborating with others to figure out how to do their jobs. They have been trained to do their work with little variation. Communication is usually about the task at hand; there is little attention focused on relationships. "Just do it" might be the slogan that summarizes a classical leadership approach. Tacked onto that slogan would be the charge to "do it quickly" and "do it efficiently."

Using the Human Relations Approach

The **human relations approach to motivation** is based on the idea that people are influenced not just by power and position, but they have their own motivations for working hard or not. You can't just tell people what to do and expect that they will do it. In fact, humans are influenced by their working conditions and how they are treated in the workplace. The human relations approach motivates people by providing them with such perks as free ice cream in the company cafeteria or introducing casual-dress Fridays to create a more positive work climate.

Abraham Maslow's well-known theory of human needs being organized into a hierarchy of five levels also helped management and leadership theorists understand how to enhance employee motivation. Maslow's five needs, arranged from most basic to higher-level needs, are (1) physiological needs (for food, water), (2) safety needs (to feel secure and safe), (3) affiliation needs (to belong to a group and have friendships with others), (4) self-esteem needs (to feel positive about oneself), and (5) self-actualization needs (to become the best possible person you can be).[18] Although management researchers have not found consistent support for the precise theory Maslow described (the needs may not operate as a hierarchy; we sometimes need several things at the same time), his research continues to have intuitive appeal and has served as a framework for basic assumptions about how people behave in relationships as well as the workplace.

One breakthrough large-scale research project had a major impact on our understanding of motivation in the workplace. Research conducted by Elton Mayo and Friz Roethlisberger at the Hawthorne plant of the Western Electric Company between 1927 and 1932 revealed what became known simply as the *Hawthorne effect*.[19] These studies found evidence that the way people are treated has an impact on their work. When trying to test whether changes in working conditions (such as improvements in the workroom lighting) had an effect on work productivity, the Hawthorne researchers found that just paying attention to workers and asking for their input on the working conditions influenced work output and work climate. In other words, it's not just directing people to do a job that influences the amount and quality of work that gets accomplished. People are motivated by their own desire for recognition and their need to feel positive about what they are doing. The research also documented the important role of communication in establishing a positive work climate, such as leaders listening to employees' concerns and asking for their input.

Another influential management researcher, Fredrick Herzberg, suggested two levels of motivators that influence how people respond to their work: their working conditions and leadership from others.[20] Herzberg called the first level of motivators **hygiene factors**. These are basic aspects of one's job that simply have to be there for a worker to feel satisfied. Hygiene factors include salary, working conditions, and the quality of supervision workers receive. If the hygiene factors are present, that's good—but these factors alone won't necessarily motivate a worker to work harder, faster, or better. The second level of motivators, which Herzberg called motivation factors, will, if present, actually motivate a worker to do a better job. **Motivation factors** include how interesting the work is, whether a worker

terms & definitions

Human relations approach to motivation an approach to motivation based on the idea that people are influenced not just by power and position but also have their own motivations for working hard.

Hygiene factors basic aspects of a job that have to be there for a worker to feel satisfied about the work, including salary, working conditions, and supervision.

Motivation factors aspects of a person's job that motivate the person to do better.

receives recognition for a job well done and opportunities for promotion, and the amount of job responsibility a person has. As with Maslow's research, there has not been consistent research support for Herzberg's model. But leaders and managers continue to use Herzberg's assumptions to attempt to motivate and lead others.

Communication based on the human relations approach to leadership concerns both task and relationship issues. Communication is not always directed downward, telling people what to do; it can take the form of conversations with colleagues about how to best do whatever job confronts the team. And communication based on the human relations approach is more informal than that based on the classical approach, which emphasizes doing things according to company policy and standard operating procedures. With the human relations approach, it's okay to allow exceptions to policy and procedures if they keep people happy. People will be more motivated if they have some influence over how the job is done. People have influence through communication. So, rather than limiting communication among workers, the human relations approach encourages communication.

Using the Human Resources Approach

The **human resources approach to motivation** views people as resources who can be full partners in enhancing a team or organization. As noted earlier, the human relations leadership approach views people as needing positive encouragement rather than just direction; however, some people view the human relations approach as a way to manipulate people by being nice to them so that they work harder. This third approach, the human resources approach, seeks to empower people to participate in the work of the organization or team. In contrast to the human relations approach, a human resources approach asks workers and team members what they like or dislike and gives them more control over work processes, rather than just trying to manipulate them with pleasantries. For example, PepsiCo's Nooyi has created a workplace where she hopes her employees are motivated and thrilled to come to work every day. "We have an empowering culture that is constructively competitive," she adds. "In the past, when you said, 'Move,' they moved. Now they say, 'Let me do this.'"[21] It is this personal empowerment that motivates employees when using the human resources approach.

The human resources approach to motivation views all people in the team or organization as individuals who have feelings and emotions and also have intellectual resources to accomplish the task. The approach emphasizes both the task at hand and the people who do the work. With the classical approach, leaders motivate through their title, status, and power. They provide employees with rewards or they withhold rewards. With the human relations approach, leaders motivate others by paying attention to the work environment and meeting the needs of employees. With the human resources approach, leaders motivate by making employees partners at work and giving them more decision-making and problem-solving responsibilities.

Leadership researchers Robert Blake and Jane Mouton's book *The New Managerial Grid* describes various management styles that draw on the various theories of motivation we've discussed.[22] The grid, shown in Figure 2.3, has two dimensions: (1) a concern for people and (2) a concern for production. These two dimensions are similar to the task and relationship roles that we discussed in the last chapter, and they combine to produce five different management or leadership styles. First is the impoverished leader (1, 1 on the grid), who has little concern for people or work productivity. Second is the country club leader (1, 9 on the grid); this leader motivates others by emphasizing comfort and a positive climate but does little to focus on work productivity. Third is the middle-of-the-road leader (5, 5), who leads by compromise. In the upper-right-hand corner of the grid is the team management leader (9, 9), who has a high concern for both people and the task. This leader motivates others by viewing people as resources to work with rather than colleagues who should be manipulated with pleasantries or forced to do the work with threats and punishments. Last is the authoritative leader (9, 1), the leader who says, "It's my way or the highway. Do what I say or you're gone."

The communication in a group, team, or organization that uses a human resources paradigm flows not just from the top down or horizontally, but from all directions, with a special emphasis on upward communication. Information is shared in many channels, including face-to-face. As suggested by Blake and Mouton's managerial grid, the content of the communication stems from concerns about both people and productivity.

terms & definitions

Human resources approach to motivation an approach to motivation that views employees as resources who can be full partners in enhancing a team or organization.

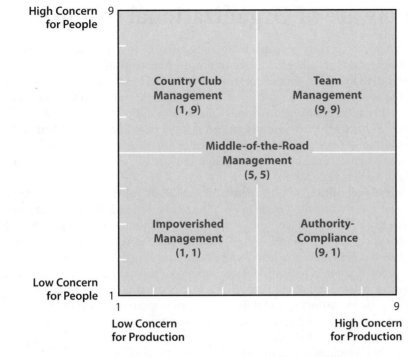

FIGURE 2.3 **The Managerial Grid**

RECAP

How to Motivate Others

Approach	Description	Communication Flow
Classical	• Workers are motivated by leaders who provide rewards and punishment. • There is one best way to accomplish the task efficiently; work should be structured by someone in authority.	Communication is typically directed from the top down.
Human Relations	• People are motivated by their individual needs. • Rewards are better than punishment in motivating others; leaders enhance employee self-motivation by providing employees with a positive, pleasant work climate to achieve maximum worker productivity.	Communication between individual workers is encouraged. Some upward communication is encouraged. Downward communication is intended to maximize worker productivity.
Human Resources	• Workers are motivated by leaders who include and involve them in decision-making processes that impact their work. Leaders treat employees as partners who take responsibility for problem solving. • Rather than manipulating workers with only positive messages, leaders share information with workers and involve them in both the work procedures and work outcomes.	Upward communication is emphasized as well as horizontal communication. Worker involvement in decisions is fostered. Downward communication reflects the point of view of workers.

Be Aware of Organizational Culture

We've emphasized that there are many things to be aware of as you communicate with others in business and professional settings: your own perceptions of yourself as well as how you are perceived by others, your social style and the social styles of others, and underlying assumptions about leadership. A key factor that has a pervasive influence on each of these elements is the culture of an organization.[23] Culture is a concept that anthropologists use to describe the distinctive beliefs, values, assumptions, and rules that distinguish one group of people from another group. A culture is revealed to others in a number of different daily routines and practices, ranging from how people interact and treat each other to how they spend their free time and money.

Organizational culture is the learned pattern of beliefs, values, assumptions, rules, and norms that are shared by the people in an organization. Organizational culture includes what it feels like to be in an organization; whether the organization maintains a rigid, do-it-by-the-book approach or is a more relaxed, informal place to work. The culture of an organization also affects all aspects of how the work is accomplished. Your shopping experience at Walmart, for example, is probably different from your shopping experience at an upscale department store like Nordstrom. Both sell shirts, socks, and shoes, but what it feels like to shop at each place is distinctive and different from the experience at the other retail establishment. The stores have a different organizational culture in terms of how employees interact with customers. You are met at Wal-Mart by a greeter who shoves a shopping cart your way; at Nordstrom you receive more individual attention (and pay higher prices).

Why is it important to be aware of organizational culture? Because it influences how you communicate with others. If you're not aware of the organizational culture and so fail to adapt to either implicit or explicit cultural expectations, you may create conflict and stress. Imagine that your first job was at Google, where you enjoyed an open and flexible organizational culture, and then you changed jobs and worked for another software company that had a more traditional and rigid organizational culture. If you couldn't adapt to the change in culture, you'd likely experience anxiety and uncertainty. Or if you're working in an organization that has a strict dress code, you clearly need to be aware of those rules. But other rules and assumptions may be less obvious and less formal, such as whether you address your boss as Ms. Valdes or Sharon.

The culture of an organization influences more than just such superficial choices as what style of clothes you wear or what you call your boss. The culture influences the way you do your work. How closely you adhere to deadlines, how quickly you respond to email messages, and how you observe unwritten rules (such as whether it's acceptable to hang out in the coffee room when the supervisor is there) may influence whether you get a pay raise or not, or even whether you'll keep your job. To be aware of more than just surface features of organizational culture, it's important to understand how organizational culture is developed and evolves.

Understanding Organizational Culture

Organizational culture experts Tom Peters and Robert Waterman identified sixty-two "excellent" organizations during the 1980s and discussed these organizations in their book *In Search of Excellence*.[24] Peters and Waterman identified the cultural factors that they believed made these companies outstanding. They noted that the companies focused on emphasizing good customer relations, taking quick and decisive action to solve problems, encouraging positive and supportive coworker relationships, and focusing on what the company did best (whether it was making sticky notes or hamburgers). Many of these same ideas were reflected two decades later in Jim Collins's book *Good to Great*.[25] Collins's comprehensive study examined the qualities that allow some companies to transition from good to great in terms of financial performance. Although both of these books have influenced how leaders think about and develop organizational culture, not all of the excellent or great companies profiled endured. Some, such as electronics superstore Circuit City, struggled financially and eventually went bankrupt in 2009. What the authors of these research studies documented with the passage of time is that there is no one perfect organizational culture. Organizational cultures are complicated and complex, for several reasons: Organizational cultures emerge through communication, are expressed both explicitly and implicitly, include many factors that shape the culture, are multilayered, and change over time.

ORGANIZATIONAL CULTURE IS CREATED THROUGH COMMUNICATION What it feels like to be in an organization, as well as the way things get done there, are ultimately rooted in how people communicate with other people. The rules (explicit requirements), roles (who does what), assumptions (underlying beliefs about the nature of work and human relationships), and values (what is good and what is bad) don't just happen; the forces that contribute to organizational culture are created through interaction among the people there. Some aspects of the culture may be explicitly spelled out in writing. But most cultural aspects are not; instead, people learn them by observing as well as by talking with other people. You learned the organizational culture at your school not just by reading the student handbook, but also by observing other students and talking with them.

There is considerable research about how we are socialized to a particular job or organization. To be "socialized" means to understand what is expected of us when we work in an organization.[26] It is through our communication with others—whether it's our boss, our colleagues, or our customers—that we truly understand the culture of an organization.

ORGANIZATIONAL CULTURE IS COMMUNICATED BOTH EXPLICITLY AND IMPLICITLY Sometimes organizational culture is explicitly spelled out in written policies and verbal directives; and in other instances, the culture is conveyed indirectly through the example set by others. Maybe you've worked in an organization that had explicit rules prescribing when you should arrive at work and take breaks; perhaps you had to punch a time clock. Yet in another organization, rules were more relaxed—you didn't have to report in at a precise time and you could come and go as you liked as long as the work got done. There were no written rules about work time; new workers just followed the example set by others. Employees at Google, for example, have a relaxed culture that includes free gourmet meals, exercise rooms, and even laundry and dry cleaning services. These perks are not included in a contract. However, they are an aspect of the corporate culture at Google that was explicitly established by Google's founders—and they are part of what people who work at Google have implicitly come to expect from the organization.

ORGANIZATIONAL CULTURE INCLUDES MULTIPLE FACTORS There is not just one factor that contributes to what it feels like to be in an organization, but many factors. The forces that contribute to the organizational culture include what you see, what you read, and what you hear when you visit an organization. What should you observe to get a sense of organizational culture? Here are a few of the factors that simultaneously shape and reflect organizational culture:

- *Written rules and policies:* As we've noted, sometimes organizational culture is explicitly expressed in written polices. These rules and policies may be found on a website or in a handbook or presented during orientation sessions. But if you only looked at the written policies, you'd miss a lot of the forces that shape the culture. It's often more informal communication channels that give you the most important clues about organizational culture.

- *Stories:* "Hey, did you hear what happened to Marciale last night?" Not only will such an opening line get your attention, but the story itself can offer clues to the culture of an organization. The stories and gossip that circulate in an organization reveal information about the values and expectations of the organization. Are supervisors valued or made fun of? Are staff members respected? Do people express genuine warmth for others, or are suspicion and mistrust embedded in the tales that are told? Listening to the stories and how they are expressed (whether with playful humor or mean spirits) can help you identify organizational culture.

Cartoon © Mark Parisi, printed with permission, www.offthemark.com

Physical space in an organization often defines the organizational culture, such as the open floor plan of the Facebook corporate offices in Palo Alto, California.

- *Metaphors:* Noting the metaphors—the comparisons or analogies that are used to describe the organization—can provide clues about organizational culture. "We're all like family here," says your new coworker. That metaphor sends a different message than someone saying, "Welcome to the crazy house."

- *Ceremonies:* Noting organizational rituals and what gets celebrated and rewarded can give you insights into what is valued. If employees get awards for perfect attendance or for achieving high work output, then those achievements are clearly valued by the organization. If people get recognition for working ten, twenty, or thirty years at the organization, then you know that longevity is valued and rewarded. Do colleagues frequently go out to lunch together to celebrate birthdays? What gets celebrated and the behaviors that are spotlighted provide significant clues about organizational culture.

- *Artifacts and decor:* Do people have cubicles or private offices? Is there matching furniture, or do people have a hodgepodge of chairs and desks in their workspace? The attention given to what the physical space in the organization looks like is another clue that helps decode the organizational culture. Fine art on the office walls rather than tattered and torn posters suggests that top management wants to create an inviting work experience. For example, Facebook's corporate offices in Palo Alto, California, reflect an organizational culture that promotes cooperation. Rather than working in offices, Facebook staff members work in large open spaces or in conference rooms, which are called aquariums because they are glassed cubes within a room. One reporter described it this way: "No cubicles, no offices, no walls, just a rolling tundra of office furniture."[27] The appearance of an organization can give you insight into whether it's an austere, serious work environment or a place where people are encouraged to have fun and be innovative.

ORGANIZATIONAL CULTURE IS MULTILAYERED AND MULTIFACETED When we talk about the culture of an organization, don't get the idea that there is only one culture per organization. There are many layers and pockets of organizational culture within a single organization. People in upper management may operate in a formal, structured organizational culture, but the custodial staff may have a more relaxed, joking, and informal culture. Employees may go out for drinks after work or socialize after hours with each others' families. Middle managers, however, may never socialize outside of work. Even at the same level of an organization, there may be different cultural expectations. For example, perhaps in a company's Software Development department, everyone jokes with their colleagues and tells silly stories, and people laugh a lot. But in the Information Technology department, there is a more serious, get-down-to-business approach to work. Although both departments are at the same level in the organization, there are organizational cultural differences that are due to tradition and the personalities and social styles of the workers. As organizational culture expert Judith Martin has noted, "Some aspects of the culture will be shared by most members . . . other aspects . . . will be interpreted differently by different groups, creating subcultures that overlap and nest within each other."[28]

There is no one single culture that defines a single organization. Subcultures—cultures that emerge within a more dominant culture—add to the complexity of the fabric of the overall culture. Even in a small organization such as a fast-food restaurant, there can be different cultures within the larger culture. One work crew may be somber and approach

Being Aware of How Others See Us[29]

Dan Rosenweig, president and chief executive of Chegg, is a powerful person. He is in charge of a large online textbook rental company with hundreds of people who report to him, yet he wants to increase his awareness of how he can be a better leader and a better person. He realizes that other people have insights about him of which he's often unaware. To increase his awareness of how others view him, he often asks his employees a simple question:

"If you had my job, other than giving yourself more vacation and a raise, what's the first thing that you would do that you don't think we're doing yet?" I try to make it comfortable when you do the review process by asking people: What do you need more of from me? What do you need less of from me? What is it that I'm doing that you would like me to stop doing completely? And

what is it that I'm not doing enough of that you'd like some more of? From there, it becomes a much more comfortable conversation.

How can you apply Rosenweig's question to enhance your own work effectiveness and increase your awareness of your communication skill? To learn how others view you, consider asking a trusted friend or colleague, "What are things that I should be doing that you don't think I'm doing?" Or, "What is something you think I need to know, but don't know about the way I communicate with others?" No, we're not suggesting that you ask such questions of everyone indiscriminately. But asking people you trust and who know you, such as a close friend, for perceptions about yourself that you may not be aware of can increase your self-awareness. With a better perception of how others see you, you can work on the skills that can enhance the quality of relationships you have with others.

their work with dread, while another crew may playfully enjoy the work of serving customers and making sandwiches.

ORGANIZATIONAL CULTURE CHANGES The culture of an organization today may not be the culture of the organization next month. Organizational cultures morph and evolve based on a number of factors, including the people who join or leave the organization, the adoption of new policies or the discarding of old policies, new technology, new leadership, and a host of other factors. Because organizational culture is fluid, it's sometimes hard to pin down the organizational culture once and for all. It was Greek philosopher Heraclitus who said, "You can never step in the same river twice." One constant element in our lives, as well as in our work, is change. The pace of life and the development of new technological tools that are being introduced into the workplace support Heraclitus's notion that, because of change, the "river" that was here yesterday is different than the "river" here today. The organizational culture of yesterday is not the organizational culture of today or tomorrow.

Using Organizational Culture to Lead

We've noted why it's important to be aware of organizational culture as a general concept, but it's especially important to understand the culture of an organization as you develop leadership experience. Such awareness can help you understand your role as both a leader and a follower. "Why is she doing this now?" asks an exasperated team member. Or, "What is the reason for this new policy? Don't we have enough to do without filling out new forms on the web?" asks a frazzled coworker. Understanding the role of organizational culture can give you insight into the "Why" questions that you and others may ask when working in business and professional settings, especially when a leader proposes a new idea. A new policy, procedure, or ritual may be instituted not because of the whim of the leader (although that certainly may be the case), but as a result of the leader's understanding of the organizational culture. Rather than trying to interpret the action of a specific leader microscopically, in isolation from the larger culture of the organization, viewing leadership behavior from the broader perspective of organizational culture may provide new insights as to why new initiatives are suggested.

Leaders influence the culture of an organization by the symbols they use, both verbal symbols (what leaders say) as well as nonverbal symbols (what leaders do). Organizational culture expert Edgar Schein has identified five ways leaders communicate organizational culture through the symbols they use: (1) what they focus on and pay attention to; (2) how they react to major events and crises; (3) their actions as role models, coaches, or teachers; (4) the criteria they use to reward others; and (5) the criteria used to recruit, promote, and "excommunicate" others from the group.[30] Each of these ways of transmitting culture to an organization involves using symbols to communicate which behaviors in an organization should increase or decrease. As business expert Stanley Davis has noted, "Caring for the culture cannot be delegated. It can be shared but not left for someone else to do. The leader is the fountainhead. . . . If the leader is a great person then inspiring ideas will permeate the corporation's culture."[31] As we've emphasized, leadership is not always embodied in one person—many people influence others through communication. So many people within an organization who influence or lead have the potential to influence the organizational culture. And with the power of influencing the culture of an organization comes certain ethical obligations and responsibilities.

Be Aware of Ethical Leadership Challenges

Mindful leaders are aware that ethics play an important role in the leadership process. **Ethics** are the beliefs, values, and moral principles by which we determine what is right and wrong. Being sensitized to ethical communication and becoming aware of how to lead in an ethical manner will, we hope, prevent you from being seduced into unethical leadership practices.

A recent survey by the Ethics Resource Center found that 43 percent of employees surveyed believed their leaders were not good models of ethical leadership.[32] A number of headlines in the country's leading business periodicals and newspapers reporting unethical leadership practices support this survey finding. In early 2009, Bernie Madoff, the popular executive and founder of Bernard Madoff Investment Securities, sat in jail, arrested on charges of a massive securities fraud.[33] Madoff recruited friends, relatives, and others to invest in his company, all the while stealing their money through a massive Ponzi scheme, and failing to invest their money as he claimed. Ultimately, it was revealed that Madoff conned his investors for three decades and raked in over $50 billion in stolen money, making his crime one of the biggest Ponzi schemes on record.[34]

For most people, being ethical means being sensitive to others' needs, giving people choices rather than forcing them to behave in a certain way, keeping sensitive information private, not intentionally decreasing others' feelings of self-worth, and being honest in presenting information. Unethical communication does just the opposite.

Being honest is a key element of ethical communication. If you knowingly withhold key information, lie, or distort the truth, then you are not communicating in an ethical manner. Toyota Motor Corporation in 2010 faced record recalls of as many as 8 million defective vehicles that were deemed unsafe to drive because of a sticky gas pedal or possibly a faulty computer chip.[35] While the experts attempted to sort out what the actual safety issues were, tensions began to mount as Toyota remained quiet about "what they knew" and "how long they knew." Investigations into the issue revealed an "embarrassed" company that placed profit first and failed to communicate globally about safety questions they had for quite some time.[36] Although a public relations nightmare for Toyota, the U.S. government recently reported on the results from an investigation that found no electronic flaws to account for the reports of sudden and unintentional acceleration.[37] Leaders are confronted with a number of ethical challenges. It's important for you to be aware of these challenges and prepared to manage them, including challenges of deceit, responsibility, and consistency.[38]

Managing the Challenge of Deceit

Leaders usually have access to information that gives them power. Depending on how they decide to use the information, they may deceive people. If they decide to disclose the information, they must decide when to release it and to whom. If leaders decide to reveal the

Communication Ethics @ Work

Self-Assess Your Ethics

Evaluating your own ethical business practices is one way for you to become aware of your communication with yourself and others. Use the following self-assessment guide to identify your ethical strengths and weaknesses.[39] Answering "Yes" to any of the questions below can suggest some areas where you may be ethically weak.

- Have I conducted personal business on company time?
- Have I used or taken company resources for personal purposes?
- Have I called in sick when I really wasn't?
- Have I used a derogatory term when referring to another person?
- Have I told or passed along an ethnic joke or sexually oriented joke?
- Have I engaged in negative gossip or spread rumors about someone?
- Have I "bad mouthed" the company or management to coworkers?
- Have I pried into a coworker's conversations or private affairs?

- Have I passed along information that was shared with me in confidence?
- Have I knowingly ignored or violated an organizational rule or procedure?
- Have I failed to follow through on something I said I would do?
- Have I withheld information that others needed?
- Have I "fudged" on a time sheet, billing sheet, estimate, or report?
- Have I knowingly delivered a poor quality or defective good or service?
- Have I lied or manipulated the truth to make a sale?
- Have I accepted an inappropriate gift or gratuity?
- Have I taken credit for something that someone else did?
- Have I failed to admit to or correct a mistake I made?
- Have I knowingly let someone make an error and get into trouble?

information, they may run the risk of violating someone's trust. If they decide to keep the information to themselves, they may mislead others who may need the information. This type of misleading occurred at Toyota. The executive team had access to information that informed them that their vehicles may have been unsafe. Rather than sharing the information with others, they decided to keep the information to themselves so they could protect their image as a producer of safe, quality products.[40] Ethical leaders manage the challenge of deceit by avoiding the following behaviors:

- Lying, especially when the lies will lead to personal benefit.
- Using information solely for personal benefit.
- Withholding knowledge that may benefit others.
- Collecting information that violates others' privacy rights.
- Disclosing information to people who do not have a need for or right to the information.

Managing the Challenge of Responsibility

As a leader, you're not only responsible for your own ethical behavior; you're also responsible for the ethical behavior of your team members. How your followers behave ultimately reflects on you. Although you don't have direct control over how your team members behave, you do have indirect control, in that you set the ethical tone for how your team is to conduct business. For example, if your followers see you taking office supplies home for personal use, processing time cards inaccurately, or treating administrative assistants and custodians disrespectfully, then chances are they, too, will behave in a similar way. Ethical leaders manage the challenge of responsibility by:

- Modeling ethical conduct at all times.
- Acknowledging and trying to correct ethical problems.

- Taking responsibility for the consequences of their orders and actions.
- Taking reasonable steps to prevent the unethical treatment of others.
- Holding themselves to the same standards as their team members.

Managing the Challenge of Consistency

Leaders interact with a variety of different team members and in different situations, making it difficult to behave in a consistent manner. Not all team members have the same needs, and effective leaders are aware of these individual differences and try to meet the needs of each team member. The challenge of consistency occurs when team members perceive leaders treating team members differently. If a leader treats all followers consistently, then some team members' needs will go unmet. If the leader treats team members differently, then some team members may perceive the leader as having favorites. Ethical leaders manage the challenge of consistency by:

- Being proactive and informing team members that to lead in an ethical manner, it's important to treat team members as individuals with individual needs.
- Informing team members of the criteria they use for making decisions.
- Sharing with team members, when appropriate, how they went about making a decision.

Your awareness of these ethical challenges will influence the communication you use to manage them. Although working through such challenges is never easy, the five principles of communication will help you begin this process of leading in an ethical manner.

Wrap-Up

The first of five communication principles for leadership is *Be aware of your communication with yourself and others*. The process of becoming a more mindful communicator begins by becoming aware of social styles and why they're important.

- Identifying your social style remains important and is a combination of two primary dimensions: assertiveness and responsiveness. Assertiveness is the capacity to make requests, whereas responsiveness is the capacity to be sensitive to the communication of others.
- The four different social styles are expressive, amiable, driver, and analytical.
- It is also important to identify others' social styles to more effectively communicate with them.
- Style-flexing skills are strategies for adapting your social style to others' social styles to ensure productive communication.

Second, becoming a mindful communicator involves being aware of the leadership assumptions that ultimately influence your approach to motivating others. There are three approaches to motivation:

- The classical approach to motivation assumes there is one best way to perform a specific task and that people are often motivated by reward and punishment.
- The human relations approach to motivation assumes that people are motivated by their individual needs. The work environment and conditions impact a worker's motivation.
- The human resources approach to motivation assumes that workers want to be involved in determining how work should be accomplished.

Third, the chapter introduced the importance of organizational culture at work.

- Effective communicators are aware of how the communication symbols we use at work, such as written policies, stories, metaphors, ceremonies, and artifacts, create the organizational culture.

- In addition to creating the culture, these symbols also influence workplace communication. Effective leaders know that communication creates the culture and the culture influences the communication, and use this to their advantage.

    Leaders are confronted with a number of ethical challenges that must be managed well if the leader is to remain effective.

- The challenge of deceit focuses on how leaders should manage and use information. At times leaders must withhold important information, thereby deceiving a person. At other times, a leader must distribute information that may violate a person's privacy.

- The challenge of responsibility arises because leaders are responsible not only for their own behaviors, over which they have direct control, but also for the behaviors of others, which they control only indirectly.

- The challenge of consistency occurs when leaders are perceived as treating followers in an inconsistent manner. Although leaders strive for consistency, at times they must be inconsistent.

Reviewing Key Terms

Mindfulness *28*

Social style *28*

Assertiveness *29*

Responsiveness *30*

Amiable *30*

Analytical *30*

Driver *30*

Expressive *30*

Style flexing *33*

Classical approach to motivation *34*

Human relations approach to motivation *35*

Hygiene factors *35*

Motivation factors *35*

Human resources approach to motivation *36*

Organizational culture *38*

Ethics *42*

The Principle Points

Becoming an effective leader is an inside-out process. Leaders must first have a firm understanding of who they are as people before they can help develop and lead others.

Principle One: To become aware of your communication with yourself and others.

- Mindfulness is awareness of your own and others' thoughts, actions, and motivations. Being mindful is the process of actively paying attention not only to how you communicate and relate to your customers, employees, colleagues, or superiors but also to how they communicate with you.

- Awareness begins with leaders being able to identify their social style and then flexing their style to adapt to others' social styles. A social style is a pattern of communication behaviors that is visible to others, including amiable, expressive, driver, and analytical social styles.

- Becoming a mindful communicator and leader involves becoming aware of the beliefs you have about what motivates people to follow leaders. Three of these approaches include classical, human relations, and human resources.

- Leaders who have a keen sense of awareness are tuned into organizational culture, which is the learned pattern of beliefs, values, assumptions, rules, and norms that are shared by the people in an organization.

- Mindful leaders are aware that ethics play an important role in the leadership process. Ethics are the beliefs, values, and moral principles by which people determine what is right and wrong. Being sensitized to ethical communication and becoming aware of how to lead in an ethical manner will prevent leaders from being seduced into unethical leadership practices.

Applying Your Skills

1. Think of a time at work that you or someone you know was faced with an ethical challenge. What do you think you did right? What, if anything, do you wish you had done differently?

2. Compare your own results on Rating Scale 2.1 with those of a few classmates. Create a skit to demonstrate the styles represented in your group.

3. Describe in your journal an instance when you had to use style flexing to communicate effectively with someone at work.

4. Reflecting on your current job or a previous job, evaluate the organization in terms of the basic assumptions about leadership that guide the organization. Does your supervisor have a classical approach to leadership? Do you have a boss who consistently uses rewards and punishments? Or is the organization more aligned with the human resources approach? Give examples to support your ideas.

5. Discuss with another classmate one of the three ethical challenges leaders can face. Now, find a real-life example in current events of a leader struggling with an ethical challenge. What would you do if you were that leader? What could he or she have done better?

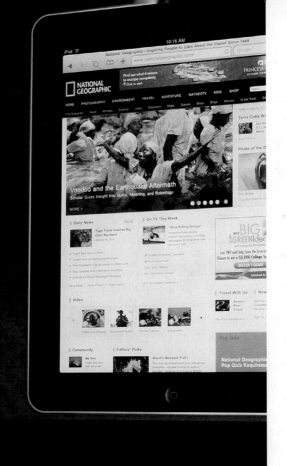

3

Using Verbal and Nonverbal Messages

chapter **outline**

After reading this chapter, you should be able to

- Explain the difference between the denotative and connotative meanings of a word.

- Differentiate the three aspects of communicating clear verbal messages: being concrete, being concise, and being relevant. Give an example of each.

- Implement the six strategies for supportive communication.

- Describe and implement the guidelines for effective use of text messages.

- List and describe the six functions of nonverbal communication.

- Explain and give examples of eight strategies for using nonverbal messages to enhance leadership.

- Differentiate between quid pro quo and hostile environment sexual harassment.

- Describe several ways to avoid or respond to sexual harassment in the workplace.

The late Steve Jobs, mastermind of Apple, understood the power of verbal and nonverbal messages. His command of nonverbal messages was obvious when he first introduced the iPad to the media on January 27, 2010. Rather than standing in front of the audience, Jobs sat comfortably on a sofa with the iPad in hand to demonstrate how this new technology allows people to flip casually through a magazine or book while relaxing on the sofa watching television. Jobs sitting on a sofa rather than an office chair also signaled to potential customers that this particular device was not necessarily intended for the office and work, but for home and pleasure.

Equally impressive was his command of verbal messages. According to communication consultant Carmine Gallo, Jobs's verbal messages were Twitter-friendly, chunked, and emotive. Jobs's iPad headlines were descriptive, tangible, and short, fitting well within a 140-character Twitter post. Jobs describes the iPad as "our most advanced technology in a magical and revolutionary device at an unbelievable price." The Twitter-appropriate headline was consistently used across all marketing channels including presentations, press releases, websites, and advertisements.

According to Gallo, Jobs's verbal messages were chunked in threes, which is consistent with cognitive neuroscientific findings that humans process and remember three chunks of information at a time. Jobs mentioned during his iPad presentation that Apple gets its revenue from three product lines: iPhones, iPods, and Macs; and that Apple has three competitors in the mobile devices category: Nokia, Samsung, and Sony.

Jobs's verbal messages also included emotional language rather than cold techno-jargon. For example, he mentioned in his iPad presentation that, "It's so much more intimate than a laptop and so much more capable than a SmartPhone," "It's the best browsing experience you've ever had," "It's a dream to type on," and "It's a screamer" (describing the A4, Apple-designed chip).

Taken together, Jobs's verbal and nonverbal messages complemented each other and created a casual and comfortable conversation that appeared to be between two people rather than a presentation to millions. His careful use of messages allowed his presentation to be high-tech but understandable. Through his conversational and emotive messages, Steve Jobs made the iPad out to be a product that the public must own. In fact, the public purchased between 5 and 7.5 million iPads during the 2010 holidays.[1]

leading **questions**

1. How much did Jobs's communication style affect his effectiveness as a leader? Were there other leadership attributes that you associate with Jobs? Explain.

2. What role did Jobs's use of nonverbal messages add to his effectiveness as a leader? Do you consider his casual style (sitting down) and informal dress (blue jeans) to have enhanced or detracted from his ability to lead?

3. Could other leaders adopt his communication style and be as effective? Why or why not?

4. Can you think of other corporate leaders (or just leaders) who use verbal and nonverbal messages effectively to influence others?

As a new leader, your first job will be to understand how to use and interpret messages that are appropriate for the workplace. To help enhance your leadership effectiveness, we're going to emphasize two more communication principles for leadership. Figure 3.1 illustrates where these principles fit in our model of communication principles and skills for leadership.

Principle Two: Effectively use and interpret verbal messages. **Verbal messages** are messages that use words to create meaning. Your ability to lead will depend on your ability to

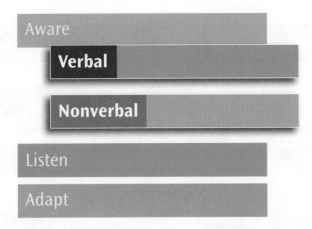

FIGURE 3.1 Communication Principles and Skills for Leadership

use and interpret verbal messages unique to your workplace. Using and interpreting verbal messages effectively will allow you to get the work done by making messages clear and supportive.

Principle Three: Effectively use and interpret nonverbal messages. **Nonverbal messages** are visual and audible symbols that do not rely on words or language to create meaning. Nonverbal messages are not only visual messages, such as hand gestures and posture, but also messages that we can hear. People sigh when they're bored; they use a vocal interrupter when they want to signal to others that they would like to add something to the conversation. Using and interpreting nonverbal messages effectively will allow you to get work done by focusing on the relational aspects of messages, those communicated by such means as physical appearance, posture and movement, facial expressions and eye contact, and touch.

> *"Don't use words too big for the subject. Don't say 'infinitely' when you mean 'very'; otherwise you'll have no word left when you want to talk about something really infinite."*
>
> — C. S. Lewis

Communicating Clear Verbal Messages

To communicate clear messages, it's important to understand how people interpret verbal messages, both denotatively and connotatively. When we interpret the **denotative meaning** of verbal messages, we interpret the words literally; we use the dictionary's definition. When we interpret the **connotative meaning** of verbal messages, we interpret the words based on our personal experiences. To illustrate the difference between denotative and connotative interpretations, let's take a look at the word *merger*. Some people interpret *merger* literally, to mean the joining together of two or more companies or organizations. However, people who have survived a corporate merger may interpret the word based on their personal experiences; to them the word stimulates feelings of fear, anxiety, and anger and has connotations of disruption and stress brought on by layoffs or unfamiliar new routines.

To make messages clear, it's important to consider how others will interpret your verbal messages. If people receiving your verbal messages have experience with the topic you're communicating about, chances are they will interpret your message on a connotative level. If the information you're conveying is unfamiliar to others, they are more likely to interpret the message on a denotative level.

Learning how to make your verbal messages concrete, concise, and relevant are three skills that will help you make verbal messages clear.

Use Concrete Messages

A word is **concrete** if you can experience what the word refers to (the referent) with one of your senses. If you can see it, touch it, smell it, taste it, or hear it, then it's concrete. If you

terms & definitions

Nonverbal messages visual and audible symbols that do not rely on words but create meaning for the receiver.

Denotative meaning the literal or dictionary definition of a word.

Connotative meaning the interpretation of a word based on personal experiences.

Concrete referring to something you can experience with your senses.

ABSTRACT				CONCRETE
Justice	Legal system		Attorney	Jonathan Butterfield, Attorney at Law
Money management		Financial plan		Budget
Human resource		Employee		Jane Smith, second-shift supervisor
Software		Operating system		MAC OS 10.4.11
Creature	Mammal		Dog	Mickey, a Border Collie
Employment		Blue-collar job		Second-shift production supervisor
Mobility	Vehicle		Compact car	2008 MINI Cooper S
Sweetness		Dessert		Crème brulée

FIGURE 3.2 **Abstract-Concrete Word Continuum**

cannot do these things with the referent, then the word is an abstract word. As illustrated in Figure 3.2, all words fall on a continuum from concrete to abstract.

For example, "interoffice communication" is abstract, and a "memo" is a concrete example of the process. "Professional development" is an abstract concept, whereas a "conflict-management training program" would be a concrete example of the concept. Using concrete words and phrases in the workplace helps avoid miscommunication. Being clear by using concrete words is especially important as workplaces become more diverse and international. Here are some additional ways of communicating concrete verbal messages at work.

USE SPECIFIC WORDS Specific words clarify meaning by narrowing down the discussion from a general category to a particular group within that category. For example, a district manager mentions in a meeting that she is concerned about employees' performance, when in reality she is only concerned about sales representatives' job performance. The "sales representative" employee group is a specific category within the larger employee group. The sales group may unfortunately miss the fact that the district manager's message is aimed at them and thus take it less seriously. By narrowing the topic, we make our verbal messages more specific and thus more concrete and clear, reducing miscommunication.

USE PRECISE WORDS Precise words are those that most accurately express meaning; they capture shades of difference. For example, when discussing a coworker's communication in a meeting, Armando mentioned that the coworker was too "aggressive." To some people, aggressive communication means communication that is hostile, demanding, attacks another person personally, or pushes a sale too hard. To others, an aggressive communicator is someone who is assertive and competitive. Because there are different types of aggressive communication, it is best to be as specific as possible. In this case, Armando might do better to describe the specific aggressive behaviors that were inappropriate. For example, Armando might point out that the person in question demanded that his coworkers work around his schedule, called his coworkers "a group of slackers," and threatened his potential clients by indicating that if they didn't purchase a particular product from him he would drop them from the preferred customer program.

USE JARGON CAREFULLY **Jargon** is language used by a particular group, profession, or culture and may not be understood or used by other people. Most professional workplaces are full of jargon. When we're new on the job, it usually takes us a while to learn the new language. Part of any new employee orientation program is to teach new trainees the language of the workplace. New employees at Walt Disney World, for example, attend the Disney University where they are introduced to a new vocabulary: the language of the theater. Rather than being an employee, you're a "cast member." Uniforms are referred to as "costumes" and customers are "guests." Use of jargon helps us fit in, makes our communication faster and easier, and makes us more likable to our coworkers.

Although jargon serves a useful purpose, it can be confusing to those who are not familiar with it. Who is receiving your verbal messages? Will they understand your jargon? Many working professionals quickly internalize new jargon and vocabulary; they forget that not long ago this jargon didn't make any sense. Just as jargon can create positive identity and affiliation among those who share it, it can also create negative identity and a lack of affiliation or a feeling of exclusion among those who are not familiar with the jargon.

Use Concise Messages

A concise verbal message is brief and one from which unnecessary words and phrases have been removed. For example, assume you're an employee listening to a human resource representative explain company policy regarding the use of the Internet while on the job. He says the following in his presentation: "Although it is our policy to provide Internet access to enable employees to conduct the online communications necessary to enact their job responsibilities, the Internet should not be used for personal communications or nonbusiness-related activities." You lose interest in the message because it's too wordy. Here's a concise message that conveys the same meaning: "Use the Internet only for company business." This message is targeted, concise, and efficient. It clearly articulates the company's policy on the Internet using as few words as possible. In fact, communication researchers have identified communication efficiency or conciseness as one of the criteria used to differentiate competent from incompetent communicators.[2] In the U.S. workplace, where "time is money" and productivity is highly valued, concise communicators are considered more competent than long-winded and verbose communicators.[3]

Following are some ways you can make your verbal messages more concise:

- *Use simple words and phrases.* Rather than talking about the Health Maintenance Organization, you discuss the health plan. Instead of talking about procurement processes, you refer to it as purchasing.

- *Reduce unnecessary contextual information.* Don't discuss detailed background information leading up to the point. Instead, get to the point.

- *Communicate solutions.* The workplace is about finding and implementing solutions to problems. Many professionals don't need to know all of the people and situations that contributed to a particular problem. They're not interested in learning about the problem. They are interested in solutions to problems.

Use Relevant Messages

Relevant messages are messages that satisfy others' personal needs and goals.[4] Much of your communication in the workplace will be instructional: Your goal will be to help others learn. Informing a coworker about a new procedure or training a group of new employees in a skill are examples of when you would want to use relevant messages. When you make messages relevant to others, you put yourself in the other person's shoes for a while and you answer the question "How does this information benefit me?" For example, effective teachers find ways of making course content immediately useful for students. Teachers' ability to use relevant messages in their teaching has been associated with a number of important instructional outcomes, such as student motivation and learning.[5]

Communication Skills FOR A **Digital Age**

The What, Why, and How of Microblogging

What Is Microblogging?

It's blogging using Twitter. Microblogging is a networking service that allows cell phone users and other Internet-connected devices to remain informed of activities within a particular group using 140 or fewer character message updates.[6] A few examples of microblogging include Jetblue (@JetBlue), which carefully used microblogging to pitch reduced airfares on select flights: "JetBlue has landed on eBay. We wanted to try something different. We're auctioning off some great packages on eBay http://jetblue.com/ebay/."[7] Another example is Popeyes Chicken (@PopeyesChicken), who reached out to their customer base during Hurricane Katrina: "Closed all the Popeyes in southern Louisiana so there is no need to stay. Please evacuate and BE SAFE! We'll be here when you return!"[8]

Microblogging provides a running commentary of what's going on in the organization. Text messages are uploaded to a microblogging service such as Twitter and then distributed to group members. All followers of the group are instantly notified of the microblog, enabling groups to keep tabs on one another's activities in real time.

Why Microblog?

Microblogging allows employees and customers to keep their finger on the pulse of what's going on without having to stop what they're doing unless a message is relevant. Compared to emails, microblogging messages tend to reach a wider range of people. When the message contains a question or a request for information, microblogging casts a bigger net, allowing organizational members to collect targeted information that enhances problem solving.[9]

Applying Your Skills.[10]

- *Share URL links and information with readers.* Inform others of your status, and engage others in decision making and problem solving

- *Re-tweet interesting information you've read to followers by using appropriate re-tweeting etiquette.* Preface the tweet with the "RT" designation. Re-tweeting extends the conversation. It's through re-tweeting that the most important and interesting bits of news ripple more broadly through the medium.[11]

- *Make sure tweets are relevant.* The key to effective institutional use of Twitter involves a disciplined approach of regular, relevant messages that will be of interest to the organization's clientele. It requires a commitment of resources to ensure a steady stream of interesting content over a sustained period of time.

- *Keep your online identity in line with your professional identity.* The 140-character limit imposed by Twitter should foster tight, concise statements that still reflect the voice of a professional.

Here are a few strategies for making your verbal messages more relevant to those receiving them, whether they are your superiors, subordinates, coworkers, or customers.

EXPLAIN THE USEFULNESS OF INFORMATION Instead of making the message about you and your needs, make the message about the other person's needs. For example, if your manager is reluctant to upgrade the software on your computer because of cost, use messages that inform your manager of how the upgraded software will ultimately help her reach her monthly performance goals.

USE OTHER-FOCUSED RATHER THAN SELF-FOCUSED MESSAGES Other-focused messages are receiver centered, whereas self-focused messages are source centered. Table 3.1 illustrates the two types of messages with excerpts from a sales presentation.[12] Although the content of the two types of messages in Table 3.1 is essentially the same, the messages are framed from two different perspectives. A potential customer will perceive the other-focused messages to be more relevant and may perceive a sales representative using the self-focused messages as self-absorbed and more interested in meeting his or her own personal needs than the needs of the customer.

USE FAMILIAR EXAMPLES If you're pitching a new product to a customer, make the new product relevant and familiar to the customer by comparing and contrasting the new product to an old product that the customer is currently using and is familiar with.

TABLE 3.1	Other-Focused Versus Self-Focused Messages
Self-Focused Messages	**Other-Focused Messages**
I'm Ricardo Gonzalez from Progresso Corporation. My presentation will cover the following four points: Progresso product line, our partnering criteria, our point-of-sale promotional plans, and what we need from you.	I'm Ricardo Gonzalez from Progresso Corporation. Let me make sure I understand your priorities for our time together. Based on our previous conversations, here's what I think you're after.
I'd like to cover the material I have in about 25 minutes and then open it up for questions.	You'd like to open up the Hispanic youth market, and you see an opportunity with Progresso's products to do that.
I'm very proud of the new Muzika2, which builds on the massive feature set of the Muzika product line. Although physical dimensions are somewhat larger, the Muzika2 includes Tortis and WAV playback support and a dedicated Optical Line-in i-Socket.	You've said that durable MP3 players are priced out of reach for most of your market. Our durable new Muzika2 has many features of the much more expensive MP3, but at half the cost. The only real sacrifice is that the Muzika2 is a fraction larger.

Communicating Supportive Verbal Messages

Like a state or a region of the country, every workplace has a climate. Some workplace environments are supportive, meaning that there is a climate of trust, caring, and acceptance. Other workplace environments are competitive, meaning that there is a climate of hostility and mistrust. Hostile climates develop when employees are disgruntled, which often happens when two companies merge and form one larger company. This was the case when Delta Airlines merged with Northwest Airlines in 2010. Although the combined airline was financially stronger and had a larger share of the airline passenger market, the two employee groups did not trust each other because of different corporate cultures, history of labor problems, and different ways of doing business.[13] What makes the difference in the climate of a workplace is the communication that is used in it.[14] Communication scholar Jack Gibb suggests the following verbal communication strategies for creating a supportive workplace environment.[15]

Use Descriptive "I" Language Rather Than Evaluative "You" Language

Most people don't like to be judged or evaluated. Criticizing and name-calling obviously can create relational problems at work, but so can attempts to diagnose others' problems or win their affection with insincere praise. In fact, any form of evaluation creates a climate of defensiveness. One way to avoid

Using "I" language when evaluating another's work contributes to a supportive workplace environment.

evaluating others is to eliminate the accusatory *you* from your language. Statements such as "Your work is always late" or "You're not a team player" attack a person's sense of self-worth and usually lead to a defensive reaction.

Instead, use the word *I* to describe the other person's behavior.[16] For example, suppose you are working with someone you perceive to have an attitude problem. Rather than saying, "You have an attitude problem," which will only provoke defensiveness, try describing what you see and hear the other person doing and saying. In other words, what does a "bad attitude" *look* and *sound* like? Try saying, "I see you rolling your eyes, sighing, looking away from me, and crossing your arms, which leads me to believe that you're unhappy with me." This type of message opens the door for conversation. "You" language is evaluative and judgmental; "I" language remains descriptive and detailed, which helps the other person see how his or her behavior is affecting you and your goals.

Solve Problems Rather Than Control Others

Most of us don't like others' attempts to control us. Someone who presumes to tell us what's good for us is likely to cause us to feel defensive and not supported. We suggest you communicate from a problem orientation rather than from a controlling orientation. A *problem orientation* is an approach that views a situation as a problem that can be solved together. Leaders who use this kind of approach make requests of others; in other words, they ask others for their help and support in solving a problem, hoping that they will "buy into" the solution. A *controlling orientation* is an approach that views a situation as a problem that one person solves by telling another person what to do. Leaders who use this kind of approach make demands on others. A problem orientation would sound like this: "We have a problem and I need your help solving it." A controlling orientation would sound like this: "There's a problem and I need you to do this to fix it." Again, the goal is to manage the situation without provoking defensiveness. Most people don't like being told what to do. Instead, people prefer being a part of the solution by being asked to help.

Be Genuine Rather Than Manipulative

To be genuine means that you seek to be yourself rather than someone you're not. It also means taking an honest interest in others and considering the uniqueness of each individual and situation. Try managing a difficult situation at work by being honest with the other person. For example, has your manager ever influenced you to work an extra shift by making you feel guilty? Have you ever been in a meeting where another person got his or her way by distracting the other group members from the real problem? Manipulation usually increases defensiveness and suspicion in others.[17] When they feel as though they've been manipulated, people usually say, "Why didn't he just come out and say what the problem was?" or "Why did she have to go behind our backs?" To be genuine is to be honest and upfront about problems and issues that affect the workplace.

Empathize Rather Than Detach from Others

The word **empathy** comes from the Greek word for "passion" and from a translation of the German word *Einfuhlung*, meaning "to feel with." To empathize with someone is to try to feel what he or she is feeling, rather than to simply think about or acknowledge the feelings of another person. Empathy occurs when we try putting ourselves into the other person's shoes or try seeing a problem as he or she sees it. Rather than remaining detached, try saying, "Help me to understand the problem from your perspective." When working through a difficult situation at work, some people say, "I don't care. I'm not going to deal with this." Although they may believe that this is the best way to manage the situation, what they don't know is that these messages of detachment only cause more anger, ill feelings, and distrust. Even if what another person is saying to you feels like a personal attack, try empathizing.

RECAP

Communicating Supportive Verbal Messages

Verbal Communication Strategies	Examples
Use descriptive "I" language rather than evaluative "You" language	Instead of telling a coworker, "You're not a team player," say something like "I didn't see you participating in the meeting today."
Solve problems rather than control others	Instead of telling an employee you supervise "Don't do that," say, "Maybe this will work better."
Be genuine rather than manipulative	Rather than making up an excuse about why you missed an important deadline (to get your manager to feel sorry for you), be honest with her about your mistake.
Empathize rather than detach from others	Don't ignore or quickly end a conversation with a member of your team if you know she needs someone to listen to her.
Be flexible rather than rigid	Rather than telling someone "I'm right; you are wrong," use more conditional language: "I may be wrong, but . . ."
Present yourself as equal rather than as superior	Ask an employee, "Can we get this done today?" rather than telling him, "I am the manager and I need you to do this now."

Be Flexible Rather Than Rigid

Flexible people qualify their language by using **conditional statements**, which qualify what is being said and leave room for interpretations. For example, a manager for a pharmaceutical sales company says, "*In my opinion*, one of the reasons sales are down is because the sales representative lacks communication skills." **Declarative statements** are expressed as truths and leave no room for interpretation. For example, a manager might say, "Sales are down because the sales representative lacks communication skills." Rigid people have a tendency to use declarative statements rather than conditional statements. Do you know anyone who always has the answer to every question and the solution to every problem? This type of "always right" attitude, which is perceived as rigid and unbending, usually increases defensiveness in workplace settings.

Present Yourself as Equal Rather Than as Superior

You can anger others by letting them know that you view yourself as better than they are. You may be educated and consider yourself intelligent. However, you don't need to announce it. In many ways, being a humble leader and presenting yourself as equal and similar rather than as superior and different will enhance your leadership effectiveness. Some people manage difficult situations at work by "pulling rank" with others; they might say, "I'm the leader and you're not," or "I have been here longer than you." We feel certain that you've already experienced these types of messages at school and work. Superior messages showcase differences rather than similarities. To enhance supportiveness, we encourage you to present yourself as an equal to others. For example, a message that reflects equality might be "Because we are colleagues and work together every day, it's important that we work out our differences."

Communicating with Text Messages

Texting has influenced how people use verbal messages to communicate in the workplace. In fact, many people consider texting to be a form of oral or spoken communication rather than a form of written communication.[18] According to linguistic researchers, "texters write it as though they are saying it."[19]

terms & definitions

Conditional statements
statements that qualify what is being said; they leave room for interpretation.

Declarative statements
statements expressed as truths that leave no room for interpretation.

Although text messaging is already quite popular as a means of social communication in the United States, texting has become increasingly necessary for U.S. businesses that want to compete globally.

CHARACTERISTICS OF TEXT MESSAGES Because texting is conducted using small and mobile communication devices (e.g., iPhones, BlackBerrys) with miniature keyboards, the technology has forced us to use verbal messages in new ways. Text messages share a number of common characteristics.[20]

- *Text messages convey relational rather than task information.* Rather than conveying information (e.g., "Where's the nearest Kinko's?"), texters usually use texting to convey relational information, including friendly greetings ("How are you?"), social arrangements ("You up for dinner tonight?"), and friendship maintenance ("Are you mad at me?").

- *Text messages are brief.* The average text message is 14 words per message, and these messages include, on average, three abbreviations. These abbreviations or shortcuts are becoming known in the popular culture as "textspeak." Although developed by teenagers, textspeak is being used by adults in their texts to their colleagues at work.[21] Most text messages don't include proper punctuation or capitalization of letters.[22]

- *Text messages are comprehensible.* Text messages are understandable and are equivalent to a note left on the filing cabinet, computer monitor, or next to the telephone. On average, text messages contain three abbreviations, which accounts for 20 percent of the content of text messages.[23]

GUIDELINES FOR USING TEXT MESSAGES[24] Although there are numerous guidelines for using text messages, here are a few that are geared toward the workplace:

- *Don't use text messaging to convey important information.* Put simply, don't discuss potential layoffs using a text message. Instead, have a face-to-face conversation. Text messaging is designed for casual information.

- *Don't text-message anything confidential, private, or potentially embarrassing.* You never know when someone might be looking over the recipient's shoulder—or, worse, when your message might be sent to the wrong person.

- *If you text-message someone who doesn't have your phone number, introduce yourself.* Start your message by stating who you are: "Hi—it's Tim from work. Call me when you get a sec."

Understanding Nonverbal Messages

It's your first day on the job and you're being introduced as the new leader of the team. You walk into a crowded room and notice that the only empty chair is at the front of the room. The person introducing you invites you to sit down in this chair. Although where people sit in a meeting may seem trivial, it's quite important. The positions of chairs in a room or around a conference table send nonverbal messages that communicate power and status. Understanding the significance and power of nonverbal messages will enhance your ability to lead effectively.

RECAP

Communicating Clear Verbal Messages

Goals	Tools	Definitions	Example
Be concrete	Use specific words	Specific words clarify meaning by narrowing down the discussion from a general category to a particular group within that category.	Rather than referring to all customers, refer to the specific group of customers (e.g., preferred customers, repeat customers)
	Use precise words	Precise words are those that most accurately express meaning; they capture shades of difference.	Rather than referring to your coworker as "lazy," point out that she consistently fails to help you with the quarterly report.
	Use jargon carefully	Jargon is language that is used by a particular group, profession, or culture and may not be understood or used by other people.	Instead of directing a new employee to the CCA building, tell her the name of the building (Corporate Communication and Advertising).
Be concise	Use simple words and phrases		Instead of saying, "We're going to work on the logistics," you simply say, "We're going to plan."
	Reduce unnecessary contextual information	State the point of a message and avoid detailed background information.	At a job interview, don't tell a potential employer unnecessary details about your recent termination.
	Communicate solutions		Report the committee's findings at the meeting; avoid discussing the problem-solving methods.
Be relevant	Explain the usefulness of information	Make a message about the other person's needs.	Explain to a supervisor the financial benefits of an upgraded computer system.
	Use other-focused rather than self-focused messages		Rather than saying, "Here's what I would like to talk about," ask "What would you like to know about?"
	Use examples familiar to your intended audience.		Rather than referring to a successful leader from the past, refer to a contemporary leader.

Researchers have found that people form impressions of strangers within as few as two seconds of meeting them by observing their nonverbal messages. What's interesting is that these instant impressions rarely change, even after the two people have become better acquainted.[25] If you are to interpret others' nonverbal messages accurately, it's important to understand what makes nonverbal communication unique, including its characteristics and functions.

Characteristics of Nonverbal Communication

A number of characteristics make nonverbal messages unique from verbal messages, including their ability to convey feelings, form relationships, express truth, and reveal a culture.

NONVERBAL MESSAGES CONVEY FEELINGS Social psychologist Albert Mehrabian concluded that as little as 7 percent of the emotional meaning in messages is communicated through verbal channels.[26] The most significant source of emotional communication is our face—according to Mehrabian's study, it carries as much as 55 percent of the emotional meaning in messages. Vocal cues such as volume, pitch, and intensity communicate another 38 percent of the meaning. In all, 93 percent of the emotional meaning in our messages is communicated through nonverbal channels. Although these percentages do not apply to every communication situation, the results of Mehrabian's study do illustrate the potential power of nonverbal messages in communicating emotion.[27] Researchers continue to find new ways to measure the impact of nonverbal messages in the communication of emotions.[28]

NONVERBAL MESSAGES FORM RELATIONSHIPS Nonverbal messages allow us to connect with others. Whereas verbal messages convey the content of a message (*what* is being said), nonverbal messages (*how* it is said) convey or establish the nature of the relationship. Nonverbal messages tend to convey meaning about the quality of the interaction that is taking place.[29] For example, upon leaving a job interview, the applicant hears the interviewer saying, "Thanks for coming to the interview. I will be giving you a call." The verbal message (*what* is said) sounds promising, and the nonverbal messages (*how* it was said) suggests that the interviewer is sincere and will probably be calling soon to extend the job offer: The interviewer makes direct eye contact and shakes the applicant's hand firmly and vigorously. If the interviewer had avoided eye contact and seemed awkward or rushed, the applicant would have been right to feel doubtful that the interviewer would call.

NONVERBAL MESSAGES EXPRESS TRUTH If you want to know how people really feel or what they think about a particular topic, pay attention to their nonverbal messages. Although people try to hide their true feelings, especially at work when others may be evaluating them, feelings have a tendency to "leak out" through nonverbal messages. Nonverbal leakage cues reveal how you really feel or think about a topic or a problem. For example, a man may say, "Her comment didn't bother me," but you know the comment did bother this person: You saw his face drop and his posture slump when his coworker made the comment. When someone's verbal and nonverbal messages don't match, we have a tendency to trust the nonverbal messages.

Why do we have a tendency to believe nonverbal more than verbal messages? Research suggests that people are not always consciously aware of their nonverbal messages. When you speak, you have a tendency to think about what you're going to say; even if it's just a brief statement, you encode your verbal message consciously. With nonverbal messages, there is very little, if any, conscious encoding. Nonverbal messages are more spontaneous and are conveyed by means outside of your conscious awareness. Your nonverbal messages "leak" from your body. You can slow down the leaking by becoming more aware of how you use nonverbal messages.[30]

NONVERBAL MESSAGES ARE CULTURE BOUND The nonverbal messages that work in one culture may not work in another culture. Every culture has its own rules and standards for what is appropriate nonverbal behavior. From a simple gesture to a design

Cross-cultural communication requires cultural sensitivity. The designers of the Shanghai World Financial Center learned this the hard way.

feature in a skyscraper, culture influences how messages are interpreted. For example, in the United States the thumbs-up sign usually conveys a positive meaning; however, in the Middle East the thumbs-up sign is an obscene gesture.[31] The Shanghai World Financial Center is a skyscraper that faced protest by the Chinese because of its design by an American architect. The original design included a small narrow opening at the peak in the form of a circular moon. The Chinese considered the design to be too similar to the rising sun depicted in the Japanese flag. A trapezoidal hole replaced the circle at the top of the tower, changing the controversial circular design.[32] This example illustrates what can happen when someone (in this case, the American company) with good intentions simply misunderstands what a symbol might represent to those from another culture.

Using and Interpreting Nonverbal Messages

Your ability to use and interpret nonverbal messages effectively at work depends on your ability to recognize various sources of nonverbal messages, including physical appearance, vocal qualities, gestures, eye contact, space, use of time, touch, and the environment.

Physical Appearance

Leaders in most organizations must project a professional image through their physical appearance. Enhancing your physical appearance, so that others in the workplace perceive you as a leader, is important.

PHYSICAL ATTRACTION Our attraction to others because of their appearance—their bone structure, weight, stylishness, and grooming—is referred to as **physical attraction**. Although many people don't want to believe that physically attractive people do better on the job than physically unattractive people, research suggests otherwise. For example, over a ten-year period, attractive MBA graduates earned more than unattractive MBA graduates.[33] (Individuals were deemed "attractive" based on a set of criteria established by the research, such as symmetrical facial features, among other characteristics.) Somewhat surprisingly, in the MBA study, good looks were more of a factor in men's salaries than in women's salaries.[34] In another study examining tipping behavior in restaurants, researchers concluded that female (and not male) servers earned more tips on average if they were physically attractive.[35]

Another important aspect of physical attraction, especially for men, is height. According to Henry Biller, a professor at the University of Rhode Island, "men of average or above-average height are seen as more mature, uninhibited, positive, secure, masculine, active, complete, successful, optimistic, dominant, capable, successful, and outgoing."[36] Other research studies concluded that graduating college seniors who were 6 feet 2 inches tall or taller enjoyed starting salaries $4,000 higher than seniors 5 feet 5 inches tall or under.[37] Although some people may be disappointed in these research findings, they allow us to become more aware of how physical appearance affects communication. The following section details some of the ways you can enhance your physical appearance and, in turn, others' perceptions of your leadership effectiveness.

CLOTHING Dressing for success has been the subject of many books, for good reason.[38] How we dress on the job not only conveys our personal sense of style, it also creates meaning in the minds of others.[39] In other words, people notice our clothing and they form impressions of us based on what we're wearing. This is one of the reasons some companies invest huge sums of money developing and designing company uniforms that communicate the appropriate image to customers.[40] It's important to dress not only in a manner appropriate for our workplace but in a manner that will lead other people to take us seriously and perceive us to be credible.

terms & definitions

Physical attraction the attraction we have toward others because of their appearance.

F MINUS: © Tony Carrillo / Dist. by United Feature Syndicate, Inc.

Most workplaces require employees to dress in a professional manner. Professional dress is associated with a number of important variables that benefit employees, such as perceptions of increased status, competence or knowledge, trustworthiness, and the ability to influence others.[41] Some organizations spell out professional dress. For example, flight attendants have to follow a rigid dress code that is detailed in a comprehensive employee handbook. There is different appropriate dress for walking through airports, boarding and deplaning passengers, and serving passengers while in flight.[42] Other organizations leave it up to the employees to figure out what professional dress entails.

Because our physical appearance in the workplace influences our ability to lead, it's important that you pay attention to this important source of nonverbal communication. Here are a few suggestions for how to communicate a professional physical appearance at work:

- *Monitor physical appearance standards.* Observe how a number of your coworkers dress in your office, unit, or division. What type of clothing are they wearing (suits or sport coats and slacks)? How are they wearing their clothing (shirts tucked in, hanging out)? What type of shoes are they wearing (open-toed or closed, wingtips, sneakers)? How much jewelry do they wear (earrings, nose studs)? What about their hairstyles (pulled back or down, facial hair)?

- *Match the formality of your manager's appearance.* Observe your manager: If you're uncertain of appearance standards, it's always a good thing to match your manager's appearance in terms of formality. Your manager ultimately sets the standards for appearance in your work unit. Is your boss's appearance formal, or is it more relaxed?

- *Dress for the occupation.* Another appearance suggestion is to dress for the job or the occupation. Most occupations have an established standard for dress and grooming. For example, most bankers dress in dark suits, construction foremen wear jeans and steel-toed boots, and health professionals who have contact with patients wear scrubs.

- *When in doubt, dress for the job you want.* Whenever you're in doubt about how you should dress and appear in the workplace, it's best to dress for the job you would like to have one day. In other words, appear more formal than informal. A more formal appearance gives the impression that you care about your work and your organization. Appearing too informal can give the opposite impression.

- *Appear neat and well groomed.* It is assumed that we will appear neat and well groomed when we go to work. Appearing neat means wearing clothing that is clean and pressed, shoes that are clean and polished, and appropriate artifacts (for example, a belt, a briefcase). Appearing well-groomed means being bathed, making sure your hair is styled, and having fresh breath and clean fingernails.

ARTIFACTS An **artifact** is a personal object we use to convey our identity; it's an accessory. Examples of artifacts include jewelry, eyeglasses, sunglasses, scarves, hairpieces, handbags, briefcases, and hats, to name a few. In many ways, we use artifacts to decorate the body. If used in moderation, artifacts signal to others our style and our unique sense of self.

terms & definitions

Artifact a personal object used to communicate some part of one's identity.

When researchers asked recruiters to determine the appropriateness of jewelry for men and women on the job, their findings were very stereotypical and sex typed. Recruiters found three items of jewelry acceptable for women: button earrings, chain chokers, and necklaces. And although necklaces, rings, and earrings were considered acceptable for women, they were less acceptable for men.[43]

Communication researchers John Seiter and Andrea Sandry found that job candidates with either a nose piercing or an ear piercing were perceived by interviewers as significantly less trustworthy, less sociable, and less knowledgeable than candidates not wearing any jewelry. Although a nose or an ear piercing did not significantly affect how attractive the interviewer perceived the candidate to be, a single body piercing lessened the perceived hirability of the candidate—candidates with a single body piercing were less likely to be hired.[44] Another researcher examining the effect of eyebrow piercing on employer perceptions of job candidates' hirability found a similar result, and found that neither the type of business nor the size of the organization made a difference in perceptions of hirability.[45]

Voice

How many times have you heard "It's not what you said, but how you said it that bothered me"? This common expression reveals the importance of **vocalics** (also referred to as *paralanguage*), which are the nonverbal aspects of our voice, including pitch (how high or low a speaker's voice is), rate (how fast the person speaks), and volume (how loudly the person speaks). Verbal messages help us to "say what we mean," whereas nonverbal messages, and especially vocalics, help us to "mean what we say."

Researchers have documented how our use of vocalic cues influences how others perceive us. In general, Americans who speak faster and louder than average are usually perceived as more powerful, knowledgeable, confident, trustworthy, and socially attractive by other Americans.[46] Of course, there are situations when speaking fast and loud would be entirely inappropriate. We are expected to adapt our vocalics based on the situation. For example, if you were to make a sales presentation to Japanese clients whose English comprehension was limited, it would be wise to speak more slowly and perhaps more quietly.

One study found that managers who were perceived by their employees as varying their vocalic cues were more well liked than those who did not vary the pitch, volume, and rate of their voices and were perceived as being more credible and influential than managers whose vocalic cues were more monotonous or flat.[47] People who alter their vocalic cues are perceived as expressive and sociable, two perceptions that serve leaders well.[48]

Gestures and Body Movement

The study of gestures and body movement is referred to as **kinesics**. In one of their most comprehensive contributions to nonverbal research, Paul Ekman and Wallace Friesen classified movement and gestures according to their functions. They identified three categories of gestures that are important for leaders: emblems, illustrators, and regulators.

EMBLEMS An **emblem** is a gesture that has a direct verbal translation and may substitute for a word or phrase. If you walk into your manager's office and he holds up an open palm without looking at you, you immediately know that your manager doesn't want to be interrupted. If you're giving a presentation and your supervisor holds up two fingers, you know you have two minutes to wrap up the presentation. Other common emblems that substitute for verbal messages include the time-out sign (a referee using two extended hands to form a T) and the quiet sign (placing an index finger up to the lips). Emblems are shortcuts that allow you to communicate with others, especially in situations when you cannot use verbal messages.

ILLUSTRATORS We frequently accompany a verbal message with an **illustrator** that illustrates (draws a picture) or complements the verbal message. Illustrators allow you to

terms & definitions

Vocalics the nonverbal aspects of the voice, including pitch, rate, and volume.

Kinesics the study of gestures, posture, and body movement.

Emblem a gesture that has a direct verbal translation and may substitute for a word or phrase.

Illustrator a gesture that illustrates or complements a verbal message.

An emblem is a gesture, such as a baseball umpire calling a player safe, that has a direct verbal translation and is immediately recognized by others.

clarify or intensify the meaning of the message. For example, when we are giving directions to another person, most of us use our hands to draw a picture in the air of where the other person should go. Not only does your use of illustrators help others decode and interpret your message, but illustrators also help you in encoding or developing a message.[49] Research has also suggested that our use of illustrators helps us to remember our messages. People who illustrated their verbal messages remembered 20 percent more of what they said than those who didn't illustrate, or use gestures, when communicating.[50]

REGULATORS A **regulator** is a nonverbal cue that helps control the interaction and flow of communication between people. Regulators help you manage turn-taking in a conversation. When someone tries to cut you off in a conversation, you hold up a hand or give the person a raised eyebrow, which signals "Wait, I'm not finished." When you're finished and you want the other person to speak, you give the other person a head nod, which signals his or her turn.

One type of regulator that is important in the development of quality relationships is a back channel cue. **Back channel cues** are nonverbal behaviors that signal to the other person that we are listening to them and we wish for them to continue talking. When listening to a friend, many of us will interject sounds such as "um," "uh-huh," and "hmm" to signal that we are listening and that we are interested in the conversation.[51]

Facial Expression and Eye Contact

Although there's a saying that some people "wear their emotions on their sleeves," they actually wear their emotions on their faces and in their eyes. In business and professional settings, it's important to monitor what your face and eyes reveal about who you are and how you're feeling.

Researchers have found that although our faces provide a great deal of information about emotions, we quickly learn to control our facial expressions.[52] In fact, some jobs require people to mask or hide their feelings.[53] These employees have learned to control the facial muscles that ultimately convey their feelings. Others try to mask their feelings and are less successful; their emotions leak from their faces and eyes.

In addition to conveying your emotions, your facial expressions and eye contact also influence how others perceive you. Researchers have concluded that people who smile more often are perceived to be more intelligent than those who smile less often.[54] Also, smiling behavior has been shown to enhance sales.[55] The research examining eye contact is equally powerful. Direct eye contact has been associated with a number of positive relational qualities that are valued and rewarded in the workplace. For example, researchers have concluded that direct eye contact enhances others' perceptions of your credibility, self-esteem, and emotional control or calmness, all perceptions that enhance leadership effectiveness.[56] Use of direct eye contact allows you to be more persuasive in getting others to comply with your wishes than someone who uses evasive or indirect glances.[57] Also, increased eye contact enhances your chances of being hired for a job and perceptions of your leadership potential.[58]

terms & definitions

Regulator a nonverbal cue that helps control the interaction and flow of communication between two people.

Back channel cues nonverbal cues that signal to the other person that we are listening and wish for them to continue talking.

Leaders on leadership

Communicate Verbally and Nonverbally with Clarity[59]

Jilly Stephens, executive director of City Harvest, based in New York City, learned that one of the most important tasks for either a leader or follower is to communicate with clarity. Whether you're the boss or not, using just the right words and being specific about what you need can make interacting with others much more effective. As Stephens explains,

It's important that you communicate clearly with people who are going to be reporting to you, that you be as open as possible about who you are, what they should know about you, what they should understand about you, and how you like to operate. Again, just be very clear about what you expect of the people who are going to be reporting to you. Meet with them regularly. Help keep them on track. Understand what it is they need to succeed. That's it.

Especially when you are in a leadership role it's important that those who report to you aren't trying to second guess what you need and want. Meeting with people often to clarify any misunderstandings is vital for effective workplace communication

It's important to not only monitor your words to make sure that your messages mean what you intend, but also consider what you are expressing nonverbally. Stephens noted,

I remember learning that very early on in my own career the importance of having to sit and think about what I needed to let people know about me. I even said to people that I've been told that I look angry a lot of the time, and I'm usually not. It's just my face, so just don't be put off by that.

What Stephens learned was that she had to be aware of how her nonverbal messages may be undermining her verbal messages. You may use the right words and think you're being clear, but the wrong nonverbal message can contradict your verbal message. As we've noted, the listener will believe your nonverbal message more than what you say. So be clear. Both in what you say as well as the way you say it.

Space

Have you ever had a conversation with someone who stood too close to you? You slowly edged backward to add some distance, and the other person took a step forward to maintain the close distance. Rather than focusing on the conversation and what the other person was saying, you were distracted and uncomfortable. This scenario, which many people have experienced, reflects the importance of **proximity**, or the space and distance we maintain from others in our communication with them.

In his study of *proxemics*, Edward T. Hall identified four spatial zones that we unconsciously define for ourselves.[60]

- *Intimate space.* Intimate space is the zone extending from 0 to 1½ feet from someone; it is reserved for only those with whom we are well acquainted, unless we're forced to stand close to another person, such as in a crowded elevator. Someone who wanted to intimidate another person might make a point to stand in that person's zone of intimate space.

- *Personal space.* Personal space is the zone that extends from 1½ to 4 feet from a person; it is our "comfort zone," where most of our conversations with family and friends occur.

- *Social space.* The zone of social space ranges from 4 to 12 feet from a person; it is reserved for most formal group interactions as well for as our professional relationships.

- *Public space.* Public space begins at 12 feet from us; it is the distance from the audience used by most speakers making public presentations.

It's important to respect others' personal space when communicating with them at work. Although you probably don't consciously recognize how you use space to communicate, chances are you do notice when others violate your personal space or when they penetrate your intimate space (also known as your *body-buffer* zone).[61] Research clearly suggests that when you invade another person's personal space, the other person notices that you're too close, and this usually causes the person to perceive you less favorably.[62]

terms & definitions

Proximity the physical space and distance that we maintain in our communication with others.

Culture also determines how we use space in our communication with others. For example, South Americans, Southern and Eastern Europeans, and Arabs communicate at closer distances than Asians, Northern Europeans, and North Americans, who require more conversational distance when communicating.[63] For these reasons, remaining respectful of others' use of space is important. Here are some behaviors to help you effectively interpret nonverbal proxemic cues in a diverse workplace environment:

- Increase distance. You will want to increase the distance between you and another person if you see the person stepping away from you, leaning back, crossing his or her arms, turning to the side, or failing to make direct eye contact.

- Decrease distance. You will want to decrease the distance between you and another person if you see the person stepping toward you, leaning forward, turning his or her body so that it directly faces yours, or making direct eye contact.

Time

Chronemics is the study of how people use and structure time. In U.S. workplaces, "time is money," and most working professionals take time seriously. Researchers have concluded that people pay attention to how coworkers use time on the job. In a study of administrative assistants, researchers found that people who arrived on time for appointments were perceived more positively than people who were late and even people who were early. On-time arrivers were perceived as being more knowledgeable, composed, and friendly than late or early arrivers.[64] Researchers have also found that leaving work before the boss does conveys the message that a person is not dedicated to work, and such people are often overlooked for promotions.[65]

At times, we are in control of our time. We sit down and plan our work; we develop a work schedule. At other times, time is in control of us—as when we have to drop everything to meet a deadline at work. Put simply, we use time and are used by time differently. Anthropologist Edward Hall studied how people use time.[66] For example, a manager who schedules a staff meeting for 1 P.M. and begins the staff meeting exactly at 1 P.M. is a manager who has a *displaced point pattern*. This type of person uses time in a precise manner. Other people have a *diffused point pattern* and use and structure time in an approximate manner. A manager who schedules a staff meeting for 1 o'clock and begins the staff meeting at 1:15 is someone who has a diffused point pattern. Working professionals quickly learn about their coworkers' patterns in use of time. This knowledge then guides them in how they work.

Touch

The study of how human touch communicates is referred to as **haptics**. Touch is the most misunderstood source of nonverbal behavior.[67] You can probably remember a situation when someone touched you and you walked away confused, wondering what the touch meant. There are a variety of reasons why people use and interpret touch differently. Some of these reasons are based in personalities.[68] Some people simply have a tendency to communicate using a lot of touching—it's a part of who they are, their personalities. They hug when saying hello or goodbye and they put their arm around others while communicating. Other people are more **touch avoidant**, which is the tendency generally to avoid touch in interpersonal interactions.[69] People with high touch avoidance have a tendency not to touch others when communicating and prefer not to be touched by others.

Culture also affects how touch is used to communicate with others. For example, certain cultures are **high-contact cultures**, which means that touching is quite commonplace.[70] In European and Middle Eastern cultures, men kiss each other on the cheek as a greeting. Other cultures are **low-contact cultures**, in which touching is uncommon. In some Asian cultures, touching as a way to show affection is rare and is considered inappropriate.[71]

Because touch is often misunderstood, we recommend that leaders limit their touching to what is referred to as *social/polite touch*. This type of touch is used to acknowledge the

terms & definitions

Chronemics the study of how people use and structure time.

Haptics the study of how we communicate through touch.

Touch avoidant the tendency to avoid touch in interpersonal interactions.

High-contact culture a culture in which touching is seen as commonplace and appropriate.

Low-contact culture a culture in which touching is uncommon.

presence of another person. An example would be a handshake when greeting someone.

Physical Environment

Your physical environment—the actual space that you work in—influences not only how others perceive you but also how you interact with others. In many organizations, physical environment is used to convey status. **Status** is an individual's importance and prestige. To communicate effectively and appropriately in professional settings, it's important to acknowledge status symbols. People in power assume you know that they have status. If you remain uncertain of who has status and power in your organizations, you can begin by observing offices.

In some large corporations, men and women with the most power usually occupy the largest offices with the most windows.[72] These offices often have floor-to-ceiling walls and a door. To gain access to the offices, you usually have to enter through an adjoining office, which is where the administrative assistant works and serves as a **gatekeeper**, a person who controls the flow of communication within an organization. The gatekeeper controls who gets in and who doesn't. In other words, the gatekeeper controls the level of privacy that the high-status person has earned. Those with the least amount of status usually occupy what has been referred to as a "cube." A **cube** is a small modular office unit that lacks floor-to-ceiling walls and a door. It includes no gatekeeper and offers minimal privacy. Cubes are usually spaced closely together to maximize office space. Some refer to these multiple modular office units as "cube farms."

Effective professional communication requires acknowledgment of an individual's power. Observing status symbols, such as this office, can help you determine who in an organization has power.

Managing Sexually Harassing Messages at Work

It is important to effectively use and interpret verbal and nonverbal messages at work, but it is equally important to know what verbal and nonverbal messages are inappropriate at work. As a leader, you need to be aware of (1) how verbal and nonverbal messages can be used to sexually harass others, and (2) how verbal and nonverbal messages can be interpreted as sexual harassment. According to Susan Webb, who runs a consulting firm that specializes in human relations issues and is editor of the *Webb Report*, a national newsletter on sexual harassment, **sexual harassment** is "deliberate and/or repeated sexual or sex-based behavior that is not welcome, not asked for, and not returned" (p. 12).[73] Sex-based behavior is expressed through both verbal and nonverbal messages in face-to-face communication. Sexting or sending nude photos via a cell phone is one example of mediated sex-based behavior.[74] To lead others more effectively, you need to know how sexual harassment is experienced and how to avoid sexual harassment.

Experiencing Sexual Harassment

To better understand how others experience sexual harassment, we examine three components of Webb's definition of sexual harassment.

The first step is to be able to recognize when the verbal and nonverbal messages and behaviors in question are sexual or sex-based in nature. This type of communication can be placed on a continuum from least to most severe. Examples of least severe include telling sexual jokes or making sexual innuendos, flirting, or asking someone out on a date. Examples of most severe include forced fondling, attempted or actual rape, and sexual assault.

The second step is observing that the verbal and nonverbal messages are deliberate and/or repeated. Some messages are so graphic that the first time they are conveyed, they are considered sexual harassment. Other messages are more subtle and can be considered sexual harassment only if they are repeated—for example, brushing up against someone in the break room. According to Webb, "the more severe the behavior is, the fewer times it needs to be repeated before reasonable people define it as harassment; the less severe it is, the more times it needs to be repeated" (p. 13).[75]

Third, sexual harassment is not welcome, not asked for, and not returned. Webb mentions that "the less severe the behavior is, the more responsibility the receiver has to speak up; the more severe it is, the less responsibility the receiver has to speak up" (p. 14).[76] In other words, if an employee is being harassed with sexual jokes or innuendoes or is in the room when others are viewing pornography on the Internet, then it's the employee's responsibility to inform the others of how the behavior is affecting him or her. If the behavior is severe, such as fondling or sexual assault, then the employee should immediately discuss the situation with a supervisor, whose responsibility it is to manage the situation.

Also, there are two major classifications of sexual harassment: quid pro quo harassment and hostile environment harassment. **Quid pro quo sexual harassment** is actual or threatened use of rewards or punishment to gain sexual compliance from a subordinate.[77] (*Quid pro quo* is a Latin phrase that roughly translates as "something for something else.") An example of quid pro quo sexual harassment in the workplace would be a manager threatening not to promote an employee unless the employee has sex with the manager. It's sex or no promotion—something for something else. **Hostile environment sexual harassment** is unwelcome conduct of a sexual nature that interferes with a person's ability to perform a job or gain an education and that creates a hostile, intimidating, or offensive working environment.[78] Examples of hostile environment sexual harassment in the workplace include constant use of lewd remarks and offensive language that demeans a person's sex.

Avoiding Sexual Harassment

Once you know what sexual harassment is, it's important to avoid it. Although most working professionals are aware of the more severe forms of sexual harassment, many are probably less aware of the more subtle forms of sexually harassing messages and behavior. Research suggests that men and women perceive sexual harassment differently. Kim Lane Scheppele, a political science and law professor at Princeton University, summarizes the male-female differences this way: "Men see the sex first and miss the coercion. Women see the coercion and miss the sex" (p. 26).[79] She points out that if sexual harassment were to occur in front of a mixed group, many of the women would call it sexual harassment and many of the men would probably call it a joke.

Debbie Dougherty, a communication researcher who studies sexual harassment, reported that

> Men perceive fewer behaviors as harassing than women . . . and men perceive most harassing behavior as normal. For the most part, men do not experience as many sexual overtures as harassment as do women . . . . When males do recognize that the behavior is harassing, they may feel complimented by the experience. (p. 445)[80]

The following sections present a few communication strategies for avoiding sexually harassing another person at work.

Communication Ethics @ Work

Apple Investors' Interests versus Steve Jobs' Health: Where Should the Lines Have Been Drawn?

On August 25, 2011, the late Steve Jobs resigned from his position as CEO of Apple. Although the message did not come as a surprise, his January 17, 2011 message that he was taking a medical leave of absence did surprise some investors and his communication even became an ethical issue. Jobs stated, "I will continue as CEO and be involved in major strategic decisions for the company . . . . I love Apple so much and hope to be back as soon as I can. In the meantime, my family and I would deeply appreciate respect for our privacy."[81]

Although the news didn't come as a surprise to many investors, there was a concern about what this would mean for the future of the company. Jobs had had health problems for years but had been notoriously quiet about the specific nature of the problem. In 2004, he was treated for a form of pancreatic cancer; in 2009, he underwent a liver transplant.[82] His weight fluctuations had become a fascination of the press, and his evasions about his weight and general well-being confused and angered Apple investors and leaders. Jerry York, a former member of Apple's board, was perhaps most vocal about his frustration. He reported that Jobs's lack of clarity "disgusted" him in an interview with the *Wall Street Journal* and said he considered quitting the board in protest.[83] Ultimately, the controversy surrounding Steve Jobs's disclosure came down to the cold value of his company. Most employees and investors knew Jobs was sick enough to take medical leave. But how sick? And from what? His verbal messages had been unclear. They lacked specificity and precision. Had he disclosed the diagnosis and prognosis, employees, investors, and customers would have been less anxious. Shareholders did not know whether he was leaving to undergo a procedure that might dramatically improve his health. They did not know whether he was seeking another unusual treatment. They had no idea whether he was on the verge of death. And they had no idea what would happen to Apple without Jobs at the helm.

However, Former U.S. Securities and Exchange Commission Chairman Arthur Levitt said the company had disclosed enough about Steve Jobs's health.[84] Levitt, who headed the SEC in the late 1990s, claimed the severity of Jobs's cancer was well established, and the board didn't need to share more details with the public. Although publicly traded corporations need to disclose events and changes that might "materially" affect the company, the SEC does not specifically require disclosures about CEO health. So while Apple's choice of disclosure was within legal limits, the ethical consideration concerned what was best for the company.

What do you think? Did Steve Jobs disclose enough about his health to keep the company moving forward? When considering the popularity of Apple's newest products (iMac, iPod, iPad, iPhone), is the company in danger of going under without Jobs? Did Apple and Steve Jobs have an obligation to be more straightforward with the public, or was this a matter of personal privacy?

AVOID SEXUAL MESSAGES AND BEHAVIORS Sexual jokes, inappropriate touching, and sexual teasing are to be avoided. We often assume that others are like us and that they share our attitudes, beliefs, values—and our sense of humor. In the diverse workplace, this assumption is inaccurate. What one person takes as joking, another may find offensive and degrading.

AVOID SEX-BASED MESSAGES Sex-based messages are not necessarily sexual in nature but are based on the person's sex. Here are a few examples:

"This is man's work. What are you doing here?"

"You should be home having more babies."

[To a stay-at-home dad] "Why aren't you out working like other guys? You need to bring home the bacon, not raise kids."

"You're here only because of the affirmative action program."

STOP COMMUNICATING HARASSING MESSAGES ONCE INFORMED Suppose that although you do not perceive your behavior as harassment, another person clearly does, and the individual takes responsibility and informs you of how he or she feels. To ignore this information is a clear violation of sexual harassment policy. Also, remember that jokes at first may not be bothersome, but over time, jokes cease to be funny and people become uncomfortable when they have to listen to them repeatedly.

MONITOR OTHERS' NONVERBAL MESSAGES AND BEHAVIORS Although people should be upfront and inform you when they find your messages sexually harassing, not everyone can be as assertive as they need to be in certain situations. Some may feel threatened; others may not want to be pegged as being "uptight" or "not a team player." Because of peer pressure, they may not express their discomfort. Some may even say "it doesn't bother me." But their nonverbal behavior reveals that they are bothered. (For example, their arms may be crossed, or they may be using an adaptor, such as tapping a foot.)

Wrap Up

Verbal and nonverbal messages are the tools of effective leadership. People in business and professional settings who use and interpret verbal and nonverbal messages effectively become leaders. Their leadership gives them the ability to influence others and to effect change in the workplace. Put simply, they make work happen.

Three sets of *verbal* communication skills will help you use and interpret verbal messages effectively.

- The first skill set focuses on making messages concrete, concise, and relevant.
- The second verbal communication skill set involves communicating supportive messages that enhance the communication climate.
- The third verbal communication skill set is aimed at communicating assertive messages—that is, making requests rather than demands.
- The use of text messages in workplace communication is effective when used appropriately, and not to convey important or personal information.

To use and interpret *nonverbal* messages effectively, it is important to understand the unique characteristics, functions, and sources of nonverbal messages.

- Nonverbal messages are unique in that they convey our feelings and emotions; they convey relational cues, which help us form relationships; they tend to be authentic and believable; and they are culture bound.
- Nonverbal messages function on a variety of levels, which means they serve a number of purposes. Nonverbal messages can be used to substitute, complement, repeat, regulate, accent, or contradict.
- The eight sources of nonverbal messages include physical appearance; vocalics; body movement, posture, and gestures; facial expressions and eye contact; use of space; use of time; touch; and physical environment.

It is essential to understand how verbal and nonverbal messages can be used in a destructive manner to sexually harass others in the workplace.

- The two types of sexual harassment in the workplace are quid pro quo and hostile environment sexual harassment.
- Communication strategies for avoiding sexually harassing messages include refraining from using sexual or sex-based messages and behaviors, communicating harassing messages once informed, and monitoring others' nonverbal messages and behaviors.

Reviewing Key Terms

Verbal messages *48*	Relevant messages *51*
Nonverbal messages *49*	Empathy *54*
Denotive meaning *49*	Conditional statements *55*
Connotative meaning *49*	Declarative statements *55*
Concrete *49*	Physical attraction *59*
Jargon *51*	Artifact *60*

The Principle Points

How you use verbal and nonverbal messages will influence your ability to lead others effectively. These two principles form the foundation for the study of communication and make the discipline of communication uniquely different from other academic fields of study such as psychology or sociology.

Principle Two: Effectively use and interpret verbal messages

- Verbal messages are messages that use words to create meaning for others. People interpret verbal messages in a couple of ways: denotatively and connotatively.
- Clear verbal messages are concrete, concise, and relevant.
- Supportive verbal messages are descriptive, uncontrolling, genuine, empathic, flexible, and equal.
- People interpret text messages as an oral or spoken form of communication rather than a written form of communication.
- Avoid use of sexual verbal messages such as sexual jokes and teasing and sex-based messages, such as "This is man's work. What are you doing here?"

Principle Three: Effectively use and interpret nonverbal messages

- Nonverbal messages are visual and audible symbols that do rely on words or language to create meaning.
- Nonverbal messages convey feelings, form relationships, express truth, and reflect culture.
- The following sources of nonverbal messages influence business and professional communication: physical appearance, voice, gestures and body movement, facial expression and eye contact, space, time, touch, and physical environment.
- Avoid nonverbal messages that are a form of sexual harassment, such as inappropriate touching.

Applying Your Skills

1. For each of the following terms, provide both a denotative and connotative definition.

Word	Connotative Meaning	Denotative Meaning
Justice		
Foreign		
Environment		
Leadership		
Home		
War		
Value		
Language		

2. In this chapter, you learned that the words you use can enhance or detract from the quality of your relationships. More specifically, using descriptive "I" language rather than evaluative "you" language is helpful to prevent a defensive reaction when addressing a conflict. Think of a specific conflict in your life and recreate the conversation you had at the time using "you" language. Then recreate the same conversation using descriptive "I" language.

3. Get together with some friends at a local mall or another public location. Watch the nonverbal behavior of those around you; observe the cultural norms. Take notes and compare yours with those of your friends, identifying any similarities and differences.

4. Start a nonverbal behavior journal, and take some time every week to reflect on the nonverbal communication you use during your daily routine. Jot down some behaviors you use and what they communicate.

   Now try an experiment: Choose some behaviors that you do regularly, and stop doing them for one day. For example, if you meet a friend at the same place for lunch every day, sit in a different seat or at a different table. Or, when you talk with your supervisor, make a point to shake his hand (if you don't normally do that) or avoid looking him in the eye. Do people notice the change in your behavior? How do they react? Are they confused? Defensive? Annoyed? What accounts for the reactions?

5. Think of a leader who has been very influential in your life. This can be someone you know personally or a more widely known leader. Now, list some of the verbal and nonverbal communication behaviors this leader uses. What are the messages that are effective? How does this person communicate his or her leadership using verbal and nonverbal messages?

4

Listening and Responding

chapter **outline**

After reading this chapter, you should be able to

- Discuss the importance of developing effective listening skills for the workplace.

- List and describe each of the five steps of the listening process: selecting, attending, understanding, remembering, and responding.

- Explain the Stop, Look, and Listen process for effective listening.

- Discuss the impact of learning style on the way we listen, both for details and the big picture.

- Describe strategies for effectively responding to others using verbal and nonverbal messages.

- List and describe the three steps for responding to others with empathy.

- Identify strategies for helping others effectively select, attend, understand, remember, and respond to your messages.

Leaders listen and listen well, according to Jim Collins, former Stanford University professor and author of the *New York Times* bestseller *Good to Great*. According to Collins, listening is emerging as one of the essential qualities that all effective leaders have in common. Norman Brinker was a leader who attributed much of his success to listening. Although you may not recognize his name, you know the Chili's restaurant chain he chaired from its inception in 1975 until his death in 2009. Norman Brinker prided himself and his restaurant chain on their ability to listen. He listened to store managers, his managers listened to employees, and employees listened to customers.

One way that Brinker listened to customers was by strolling through parking lots and asking them questions about their experience at Chili's.[1] He would ask customers what they liked and didn't like about the food, service, and restaurant. After learning about the value of listening to customers from spending time in parking lots, Brinker invested more heavily in more formalized methods of customer research, such as surveys and focus groups. From this feedback Brinker learned that the average age of a Chili's customer had increased, so they responded to their customer feedback by lowering the volume of the music, increasing the size of print on the Chili's menu, and reducing the size of food portions. At the same time, Brinker promoted Chili's as a friendly place for younger couples with children, providing fast and efficient service and low prices. "You have to stay in the energetic group of customers, but you try to tone it down enough so that you don't turn off the older group."[2]

According to Brinker, listening pays big dividends. Almost 80 percent of Chili's menu items come from suggestions made by store managers.[3] If you're a fan of Chili's fajitas, baby back ribs, or their infamous molten chocolate cake with vanilla ice cream, you have other customers to thank for these menu items. Because of their input and the Chili's leadership team's ability to listen, the menu reflects customers' tastes and preferences.[4] Chili's is now located in all fifty states and in thirty international locations including Khobar, Saudi Arabia, Lisbon, Portugal, and Makati City in the Philippines.

leading **questions**

1. When you make a suggestion at work, does your supervisor or team leader listen to you? What happens with your ideas? Do you see them being considered or are they immediately dismissed?

2. When you lead others, how well do you listen to your team members? How do you let others know that you're listening to them?

3. What strategies do you use to get others to listen to you? Would you consider these strategies to be effective?

> *"Most of the successful people I've known are the ones who do more listening than talking."*
>
> —**Bernard M. Baruch**

Listening is a communication leadership skill that most people struggle with on the job, primarily because people have not been taught how to listen.[5] Most of our communication training has focused on developing reading and writing competencies, and little if any attention has focused on developing listening and speaking competencies. This is unfortunate because research suggests that people who work in business and professional settings spend on average 32 percent of their communication time listening and 26 percent speaking, compared with 23 percent writing, and 19 percent reading.[6] Although it's certainly important to learn how to read and write, most of our communication time is spent listening to others—a skill in which we have the least amount of formal training and education.[7]

Business and professional organizations have noticed the listening skill deficiency and are beginning to voice their unhappiness. Corporations and various business organizations are putting pressure on colleges and universities to fix the problem.

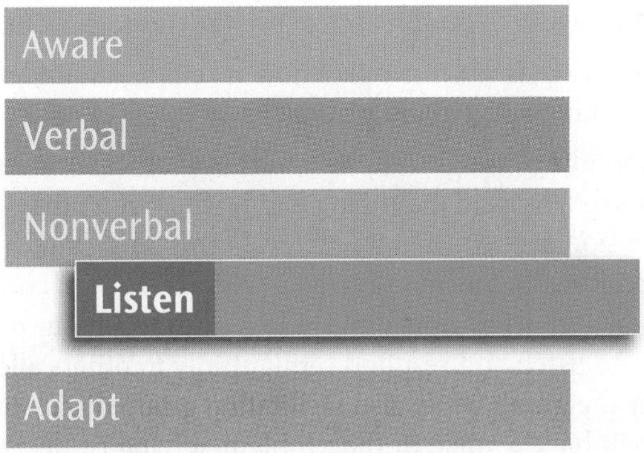

FIGURE 4.1 **Communication Principles and Skills for Leadership**

Here's what they're saying:

- The National Association of Colleges and Employers 2010 survey found the top skills employers wanted colleges and universities to focus on include listening, working in teams, and critical thinking skills.[8]

- Employers rate the potential of new employees based on their listening skills, which is revealed during the job interview by how well interviewees answer the question. Many questions are not answered because job applicants are not listening.[9]

- In Canada, Procter & Gamble's leaders engaging in active listening with their subordinates noted those workers produced better outcomes, were more satisfied in their jobs, and reported enhanced work relationships.[10]

- Information technology (IT) industry executives are placing increasing emphasis on listening as a missing yet vitally important skill in the new workforce, valuable for developing and enhancing relationships.[11]

- According to a report by the National Leadership Council for Liberal Education and America's Promise (LEAP), and the Association of American Colleges and Universities, 63 percent of employers say college graduates lack essential communication and listening skills to succeed in today's global economy.[12]

This chapter introduces you to our communication Principle Four: *Listen and respond thoughtfully to others*. Figure 4.1 illustrates where this principle fits into our communication principles for leadership model. Effective leaders do more than just listen to others; they also respond to what others are saying. Responding thoughtfully with a follow-up question or nodding our head lets others know that we're actively listening to them.

Some people confuse hearing with listening. Although listening requires hearing, not all hearing is listening. Have you ever heard someone speaking to you, but seconds later found yourself saying, "I'm sorry, what did you say?" You *heard* the person, but you were not *listening* to the person. **Hearing** is the physiological process of decoding sounds. We hear when the sound waves captured by our ears cause the eardrum to vibrate. The vibrating eardrum then causes the middle ear bones (the hammer, anvil, and stirrup) to vibrate. Eventually, the sound vibrations are translated into electrical impulses that signal the brain. In contrast, **listening** is the process of receiving, constructing meaning from, and responding to verbal and nonverbal messages.[13] When we listen, not only do we hear the messages, but we also decode, or assign meaning to them, and then we respond to the other person to let him or her know that the message was received. Listening is a process that involves five stages: selecting, attending, understanding, remembering, and responding.

1. To **select** a message is to focus on one sound as you sort through the numerous noises competing for your attention.

2. To **attend** to a message is to focus on a specific message. Just because you select a message doesn't mean you pay attention to it.

3. To **understand** a message is to assign meaning to (that is, to decode) the verbal and nonverbal messages that you're receiving.

terms & definitions

Hearing the physiological process of decoding sounds.

Listening the process of receiving, constructing meaning from, and responding to verbal and nonverbal messages.

Select to focus on one sound among all the sounds competing for attention.

Attend to focus on a specific message.

Understand to assign meaning to the verbal and nonverbal messages received.

4. To **remember** a message is to be able to retrieve the message from your memory.

5. To **respond** to a message is to let people know whether you understood their message and to validate or acknowledge them personally.

Listening and responding thoughtfully to others is a critical leadership communication skill because it helps us develop and maintain relationships with others in the three different workplace communication contexts that we review in this book: interpersonal, small group, and presentational speaking. In business and professional settings, good interpersonal relationships allow us to get the work done; they allow us to reach our goals. In small groups and teams, our ability to listen and respond thoughtfully to others allows us to provide vision and direction for the group while also facilitating group discussions and making sure that all group members have a voice in the problem-solving or decision-making process. Finally, when making presentations, our ability to listen and respond thoughtfully to others' questions before, during, and after the presentation allows us to continue clarifying our messages and persuading and influencing others.

This chapter is divided into three sections in which we discuss (1) listening effectively to others, (2) responding effectively to others, and (3) helping others listen effectively to you.

terms & definitions

Remember to recall information from memory.

Respond to let another person know whether you understood a message or to validate the other person.

Listening Effectively to Others

Although we spend a third of our communication time on the job listening, some say we don't use that time well. One day after hearing something, most people remember only about half of what was said. It gets worse. Two days later, our listening comprehension drops by another 50 percent. The result: Two days after hearing an informal discussion or a formal presentation, we remember only about 25 percent of what we heard.[14] What keeps you from listening well? Figure 4.2 includes a list of listening problems and solutions.

Listening Problem	Listening Solutions
I process information faster than the other person speaks. I get bored listening to others because I am way ahead of them.	• Take advantage of the extra time and mentally summarize what the speaker is saying. • Use nonverbal regulatory cues, such as head nods that let the speaker know that you understand and hand gestures that encourage the speaker to speak more quickly.
There's too much information. I cannot process all of it.	• Decide what you want to get from the speaker. Listen specifically for this information. • Ask the speaker for help in prioritizing information. • Record or take notes on the information.
I get nervous listening to new information.[15] I worry that I will get it wrong.	• Ask others to help clarify information. • Ask speaker for agendas, outlines, or copy of speaking notes. • Record or take notes on the information.
I have a habit of multi-tasking and end up missing important information.	• Recognize that researchers have concluded that the brain is not designed for multi-tasking.[16] • Commit to listening by paying attention to the speaker and message.
I'm a morning person. Seems like others want to talk to me late at night.	• If you're a morning person; and have an evening meeting, recognize that listening will he more challenging. • Let others know when it's not a good time for you to listen. If you're meeting deadlines, let others know.
I'm easily distracted by other sights, sounds, and smells.	• Change location—try to find a quiet place. • Let the speaker know if there is too much distraction.

FIGURE 4.2 Listening Problems and Solutions

Learning to listen effectively on the job involves developing a new set of skills. Although these skills appear simple, they're quite complex. To reduce the complexity, we encourage you to follow the Stop, Look, and Listen process for effective listening.

Stop: Turn Off Competing Messages

If you're serious about listening, then you need to be serious about turning off messages that compete for selection and attention, the first two stages in the listening process. It's not always easy to turn off competing messages in the workplace. A lot of literal and psychological noise distorts or interferes with the process of listening, such as cell phones ringing and vibrating or worries you may have about meeting a deadline. Many of these can become listening barriers, as we've seen.

Another barrier to effective listening is the desire to talk rather than to listen. An example would be a boss who says, "I want to listen to you" but ends up talking for an entire meeting. How can we listen when we're too busy talking? Listening occurs when we're silent. One team of researchers wanted to know the impact of a training program that developed listening skills, including the effects of being silent for twelve hours.[17] The researchers studied three groups of people. One group heard a lecture about how to be better listeners. A second group promised not to talk to anyone for twelve hours; rather than talking, they listened. A third group both heard the lecture on listening and were silent for twelve hours. Following the various activities, all groups took a listening comprehension test. The results: There were no differences among the three groups in listening test scores; all groups seemed to listen equally well. But those who were silent for twelve hours reported that they thought they were more attentive to others and more conscious of being good listeners. This research supports the saying that "You have been given two ears and one mouth so that you will listen more and talk less."

When you commit to listening, you must become other-oriented rather than self-centered. Listening is not about you. It's about the other person. Becoming other-oriented requires a process called **social decentering**, which is stepping away from your own thoughts and attempting to experience the feelings of another person.[18] Social decentering allows you to have empathy with another person, which was introduced in Chapter 3. To experience *empathy* is to feel what another person is feeling. In essence, you're asking yourself this question: "If I were the other person, how would I be feeling?" The process of social decentering requires mindfulness, or a conscious awareness, which is often difficult to achieve in a fast-paced and deadline-driven workplace. Social decentering occurs when you commit to turning off competing messages and to listening on both the content and the relational levels. Pay attention while listening to others. If your attention drifts, your self-awareness will help you redirect your attention back to the speaker.

Other strategies that may help you stop and turn off competing messages include the following:

- *Prepare yourself physically.* One way to prepare yourself physically to listen is to use the SOLER process.[19]

  S = Squarely face the person. Orient your body toward the person.

  O = Open the body position. Unfold arms and remove obstacles or barriers between you and the other person.

  L = Lean toward the person.

  E = Eye contact. Look directly at the person.

  R = Relax. Anxiety interferes with information processing. Try to be calm, and focus on the speaker or the interaction between people.

- *Prepare yourself by setting the scene for attentive listening.*[20] Avoid having serious conversations in locations that offer too many distractions. An overflowing desk, the instant messaging tone informing you of an ongoing conversation, or a ringing phone compete for your attention. As an alternative, use a conference room or go outside for a brief walk to talk and listen.

terms & definitions

Social decentering the process of stepping away from your own thoughts and attempting to experience the feelings of another person.

For many, information overload isn't limited to the workplace. A message meltdown is even more likely to occur when someone brings work home.

• *Prepare yourself by arriving early to meetings.*[21] A few extra minutes will give you the time you need to make a transition mentally and physically from one activity to the next. According to Richard Bierck, a communication consultant and writer for the *Harvard Management Communication Letter*, people need time to compose themselves by asking themselves the following questions: Am I ready to listen? What is the purpose for listening? What outcome do I want?

Look: Listen with Your Eyes

Is it easier for you to listen to someone when you can see the person? Have you ever been in a conversation with someone on the phone or while texting and felt that you had to meet with the person face to face instead? Do you get annoyed when you are attending a lecture and someone sits down in the seat immediately in front of you, blocking your view of the speaker? If you're like most people, you prefer to look at the person you're listening to. Research suggests that we listen more effectively when we can see the other person.[22] Specifically, there is a significant increase in our listening comprehension when we can see *and* hear, rather than only hearing the other person speak.[23]

Learning to listen with the eyes requires paying particular attention to others' nonverbal messages, which is *Principle Three: Effectively use and interpret nonverbal messages.* Although listening with the ears allows you to capture the content of another person's message, the eyes allow you to more accurately decode and interpret the relational aspects of the message.[24] Nonverbal communication researcher Albert Mehrabian has pointed out that verbal messages convey the *explicit* meanings (the content) of our communication, whereas nonverbal messages convey the *implicit* (relational) meanings. According to Mehrabian, implicit messages are nonverbal behaviors that express feelings and attitudes about the content conveyed by speech."[25] For example, we may not detect the urgency (implicit) in someone's request to complete a task until we actually see the person's face. Once we see the person's face we have a visual nonverbal message to couple with the verbal message, allowing us to decode and interpret the message more accurately.

How effective are you in reading other people's nonverbal messages? In the workplace, people don't always speak their minds for a variety of reasons. It's frustrating, but true. You'll be expected to hear what others are "really" saying, even when they don't say a word—you'll be expected to read between the lines. Although you may believe this to be a difficult process, Malcolm Gladwell, author of the best-seller *Blink: The Power of Thinking Without Thinking*, argues that humans have an uncanny ability to read people and to detect their attitudes and feelings automatically and instantaneously even without talking to them.[26] Gladwell refers to this ability as *rapid cognition*, which is our ability to know and understand something without being able to explain why or how we know it. If you have ever had a hunch about a person and later found out that this hunch was true or accurate, you've experienced rapid cognition.

There are a number of biological explanations for rapid cognition,[27] but we can improve our innate ability to listen with our eyes by improving our ability to interpret others' nonverbal behaviors. Mehrabian found that we synthesize and interpret nonverbal cues along three primary dimensions: pleasure (liking), arousal (interest), and dominance (status).[28]

• *Look for liking cues.* People who like what they're talking about and find the topic pleasurable will probably use some of the following observable behaviors: forward body lean, head nods, direct eye contact, smiling, open body orientation, and expressive gestures and voice.[29]

- *Look for interest cues.* People who have a genuine interest in and passion for what they're talking about will probably use some of the following observable behaviors: vibrant voice, dynamic gestures, excited facial expressions, and energetic body movements.[30]

- *Look for status cues.* People who consider themselves to be important (high status) will probably use some of the following observable behaviors when communicating with a person of lower status: relaxed body posture, less direct body orientation, a downward head tilt, and less smiling, head nodding, and facial animation.[31] People who perceive themselves to have less status than their communication partner will often display a tense body posture and a direct body orientation and are likely to break eye contact before the other person does.

When you attempt to interpret others' nonverbal communication, you must realize that there is a good deal of room for error. Humans are complex, and they don't always send clear messages. But the more you learn about nonverbal communication, especially the liking, interest, and status cues, the more likely you are to select, attend to, understand, remember, and respond to others effectively and appropriately.

Listen: Understand Both Major Ideas and Details

Here's a question to think about: Do you learn best when a teacher gives you the big picture first and then the details; or do you prefer to hear details first and then get the big picture? If you prefer the big picture first, you would have trouble listening to a customer who goes into detail about a complicated problem that she is having with a product that you sold her last week. In fact, after she finished speaking you might still be confused about the actual problem. You would need to ask the customer, "So what exactly is the problem?" If you prefer to hear details first, you would have trouble listening to a customer who explains in general terms a problem that she is having with the product. You would need to ask a number of detail-oriented questions to fully understand the problem. In many ways, learning and listening are very similar. Both processes require us to convert information into knowledge or to make sense out of what we're hearing from another person.

Communication Ethics @ Work

Do We Hold Leaders Accountable for Their Ineffective Listening?

As the workplace environment changes, and technology aids most of our communication at work, it becomes increasingly difficult to ensure we truly take the opportunity to listen to one another. When potential conflicts arise, effective listening skills become a vital component to solving our problems.

U.S. Department of Agriculture (USDA) employee Shirley Sherrod discovered the hard way how important listening can be. In July 2010, after an edited video of her surfaced where she made seemingly racist remarks, she was quickly terminated from her position. U.S. Secretary of Agriculture Tom Vilsack ordered the swift action so a potentially unpleasant and embarrassing story wouldn't gain traction in the media. The only problem was, it already had. However, within hours of her termination, the whole video was released, revealing a story that turned out to be quite the opposite of the original post. Eventually, government officials admitted that they had not seen the entire video prior to making the decision to terminate Ms. Sherrod. In fact, they had not even given her

the opportunity to speak with them personally or clarify the point of her seemingly controversial remarks. But when the story blew up after the entire video aired—exonerating Sherrod and leaving the Obama administration embarrassed by its hasty actions—the president soon apologized to Ms. Sherrod, expressing "regret" over the handling of the situation.[32]

How could this situation have been handled more effectively? To maintain the image of a department that won't tolerate discrimination by their employees, the USDA acted quickly to show their resolve. But in the end, their failure to listen to Ms. Sherrod resulted in an embarrassing attempt to backtrack and publicly apologize. Before the truth was known, however, many were praising the swift actions of Agriculture Secretary Vilsack. Is it ever appropriate to make hasty decisions to preserve an organization's image? Have you ever experienced a time when an employer failed to listen to your side of the story? How did that make you feel?

If you prefer getting the big picture first and then the small details, you're considered to have a **whole-part learning style.**[33] If you prefer learning the details first and then getting the big picture, you have what is considered a **part-whole learning style.**[34] Although we may have preferences for learning and listening, others don't always accommodate our particular preferences. To listen well, we have to be able to do three listening activities simultaneously: (1) listen for the major ideas in a message, (2) listen for the details in a message, and (3) link the details with the main ideas of the message.

LISTEN FOR MAJOR IDEAS IN THE MESSAGE Some of us get bogged down in the details and we miss the major idea of a message. In fact, studies suggest that poor listeners are more likely to focus on only facts and data, rather than the overall point of the message.[35] For example, you listen to a customer who is not happy with the service he has been receiving from your company. Rather than hearing the general idea that the customer is unhappy with the overall service, you're busy listening for the details of this customer's unhappiness: You want to pinpoint the cause of the unhappiness. Rather than listening on the relational level (recognizing that the customer is unhappy and wants you to acknowledge the unhappiness), you're listening on the content level (focusing on what's the problem and how to fix it). When this type of "micro listening" occurs, we unfortunately fail to hear the larger idea.

Asking "pre-questions" is a strategy that has been shown to enhance macro-level listening, or listening for the larger ideas in someone's message.[36] A pre-question is a question that one formulates mentally prior to listening to another person speak. Prior to listening to a manager, coworker, subordinate, or a customer, mentally formulate some questions that you want to find answers to while listening:

- How is this person feeling about the situation?
- What does this person want or need from me?
- Why does this person have this want or need?

Pre-questions serve to filter incoming information, preparing the brain to decode or process relevant information, which in this case are the "big ideas."[37] Research suggests that this type of listening strategy enhances the listening process.[38]

LISTEN FOR THE DETAILS IN THE MESSAGE Some of us listen for only the big ideas and we miss all the important details. This tendency can be a hindrance when you are trying to solve problems. How can you solve problems if you miss the important details? If you listen only on the relational level, you're going to miss important details you need to solve the problem. In many workplace situations, your job is to select, attend to, understand, and remember details. You can take notes or record the details in some other way and develop ways of jogging your memory. If details are not forthcoming, then you need to become more active in the listening process by probing and asking the other person the standard questions: Who? What? Where? When? How? and Why? Answers to these questions can provide you with the details you need.

LINK THE DETAILS WITH THE MAIN IDEAS Listening is a complex skill that requires us to be able to link information together. When we link information together, we organize it, making it understandable and useful; we convert information into knowledge. Our ability to link and organize information allows us to listen on both the content level (the details) and the relational level (the main ideas). We must be able to listen to and recognize a customer's dissatisfaction and frustration with our product or service while simultaneously listening for the Who? What? Where? When? How? and Why? Linking the customer's frustration with information about who is involved, what occurred, when it occurred, why it occurred, and how it occurred will allow us to address not only the customer's frustration (relational level) but also the customer's problem (content level).

terms & definitions

Whole-part learning style the style of a learner who prefers learning the big picture first, then the details.

Part-whole learning style the style of a learner who prefers learning details first, before the big picture.

One way to link information is to use **elaboration strategies,** which are mental processing strategies that give information new meaning by organizing the information. Elaboration strategies have been shown to enhance listening effectiveness.[39] Here are a few suggestions for linking details and main ideas:

- *Create interrelationships between the details and main ideas.* How are they related? Is there a direct relationship or is it an indirect relationship? Is there a cause-and-effect relationship? For example, Shelia is unhappy with how her team is performing. Try deciphering the cause-and-effect relationship while listening to Shelia. Is she unhappy with the team or is she frustrated with the current economic situation, the product line, or the lack of promotion and advertising? Or is it a combination? Ask questions to help clarify the relationships.

- *Create a mental map of the details and main ideas.* Now mentally draw arrows to show the various relationships. When asked to help others solve problems, picture the problem on a whiteboard. Using your imagination, put the problem in the middle of the whiteboard. To the left of the problem, mentally list the predictors or causes. To the right of the problem, mentally image the consequences or outcomes of the problem.

- *Connect the information (details and main ideas) to what you already know.* How is the information similar? How is it different? Think about how this problem or situation is similar or different from what you have experienced before. Rather than sharing your experiences, mentally check in and see how your experiences help you to understand the situation better. Because of your elaboration, you might be able to ask more informed questions to help the other person process the situation.

LISTEN ACTIVELY Another way to link details with main ideas is to listen actively, which is a distillation of the other recommendations we've offered thus far. Today's professional workplace requires active listeners who are engaged with both their minds and their hearts to capture both the content and the relational dimensions of others' messages.[40] Active listeners are engaged both physically and mentally in the listening process.[41] The following behaviors reflect an active listener:[42]

- Gives full attention to the other person.
- Focuses on what is being said.
- Asks questions for clarification.
- Withholds judgment until the full message is received.
- Has an alert and upright posture.
- Responds with forward body lean, head nods, and direct eye contact.

The best listeners are mentally alert, physically focused on the other person, and actively involved in seeking understanding. They stop what they're doing and consciously focus on the other person. They look for the nonverbal behaviors that convey the relational meanings in the message. And they listen actively by linking the details of the message to the main ideas.

terms & definitions

Elaboration strategies mental processing strategies that give information new meaning by organizing the information.

We mentioned that listening is very similar to learning. Just as you have a dominant style for learning, listening researchers argue that you have a dominant listening style.[43] To learn more about your listening style, take a few minutes to complete and score the Listening Styles Inventory in Rating Scale 4.1, developed by listening researchers Glenn Pearce, Iris Johnson, and Randolph Barker.[44]

RATING SCALE 4.1 Listening Styles Inventory

The following items relate to your listening style. Circle the number of the response that best reflects your behavior. Please be candid.

Items	Almost Always	Often	Sometimes	Seldom	Almost Never
1. I want to listen to what others have to say when they are talking.	5	4	3	2	1
2. I do not listen at my capacity when others are talking.	5	4	3	2	1
3. By listening, I can guess a speaker's intent or purpose without being told.	5	4	3	2	1
4. I have a purpose for listening when others are talking.	5	4	3	2	1
5. I keep control of my biases and attitudes when listening to others speak so that these factors won't affect my interpretation of the message.	5	4	3	2	1
6. I analyze my listening errors so as not to make them again.	5	4	3	2	1
7. I listen to the complete message before making judgments about what the speaker has said.	5	4	3	2	1
8. I cannot tell when a speaker's biases or attitudes are affecting his or her message.	5	4	3	2	1
9. I ask questions when I don't fully understand a speaker's message.	5	4	3	2	1
10. I am aware of whether a speaker's meaning for words and concepts is the same as mine.	5	4	3	2	1

Grand total = ____ + ____ + ____ + ____ + ____ +

Now consult the Interpretation Scale. Place an X on the part of the scale below that corresponds to your grand total score. Your listening style is described below.

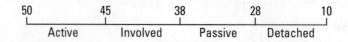

50   45   38   28   10

Active   Involved   Passive   Detached

The **active listener** gives full attention to listening when others are talking and focuses on what is being said. This person expends a lot of energy participating in the speaking-listening exchange, which is usually evidenced by an alert posture or stance and much direct eye contact.

The **involved listener** gives most of his or her attention to the speaker's words and intentions. This person reflects on the message to a degree and participates in the speaking-listening exchange. The involved listener practices some direct eye contact and may have an alert posture or stance, although this may be intermittent.

The **passive listener** receives information as though being talked to rather than participating as an equal partner in the speaking-listening exchange. Although the passive listener assumes that the responsibility for the success of the communication is the speaker's, he or she is usually attentive, although attention may be faked at times. The passive listener seldom expends any noticeable energy in receiving and interpreting messages.

The **detached listener** withdraws from the speaking-listening exchange and becomes the object of the speaker's message rather than its receiver. The detached listener is usually inattentive, uninterested, and may be restless, bored, or easily distracted. This person's noticeable lack of enthusiasm may be marked by slumped or very relaxed posture and avoidance of direct eye contact.

Note: The listening inventory gives you a general idea of your preferred listening style, based on how you view yourself. The scores indicating styles are approximations and should be regarded as such. Your listening style may change, depending on the given situation or your interests, intentions, or objectives.

RECAP

Skills for Listening Effectively to Others

Listening Skill	Listening Strategies	Examples
Stop: Turn Off Competing Messages	Prepare yourself physically.	Turn toward the person, look the person in the eye, and relax.
	Prepare yourself by setting the scene.	If necessary, move to another room away from distractions.
	Prepare yourself by getting to meetings early.	Arriving a few minutes early is best, but even being a few seconds early will help you to refocus on the new task.
Look: Listen with Your Eyes	Look for liking cues.	Look for forward body lean, head nods, direct eye contact, smiling, open body orientation, and expressive gestures and voice.
	Look for interest cues.	Observe for vibrant voice, dynamic gestures, excited facial expressions, and energetic body movements.
	Look for status cues.	Observe body posture, body orientation, head position, and amount of smiling, nodding, eye contact, and facial animation.
Listen: Understand Both Major Ideas and Details	Listen for the major ideas in the message.	Ask questions to get at the major point of the message, which may be the relational message.
	Listen for the details in the message.	Ask questions about the specific details in the message.
	Link the details with the main ideas.	Use elaboration strategies for organizing the information in order to fully understand the message.
	Listen actively.	Give the other person your full attention, focus, ask questions, paraphrase, and withhold judgment.

Communication Skills FOR A **Digital Age**

Listening to Your Social Media

In the digital age listening is no longer limited to audible messages, but also includes written messages. Today, companies engage in organizational listening, which means they carefully monitor how others are talking about them and their business practices using social media.[45]

Coca-Cola learned through their monitoring of social media that they were the target of international criticism for using limited sources of water for their Coke products in India that could have gone to thirsty villages.[46] Even though Coca-Cola's water practices were legal, the number of blog entries, Facebook posts, and tweets suggested that global resentment against the company was growing. Through careful listening, Coca-Cola quickly responded by saying that the company was going to invest $5 million toward water improvements to be "water-neutral" by 2020, which means that they will have systems in place to replace all the water they use. The response has been overwhelming with a number of stakeholders recognizing Coca-Cola for their corporate social responsibility.[47]

Organizational listening is a two-step process. First, you need to set up a listening station where you monitor the conversations that others are having about you and your organization. A couple of free tools can get you started:[48]

- Google alerts (http://www.google.com/alerts) inform you any time your organization shows up in online media, blogs, web pages, and news.

- Tweet beeps (http://tweetbeep.com/) is similar to Google Alerts, but for Twitter. Tweet beeps notifies you any time your organization is mentioned in a twitter conversation.

The second step is to learn to listen. Here are five types of information that you should focus on while monitoring social media:

- *Compliments*. They can be congratulations messages about a recent award. Or customers raving about the experience they just had with your product or with customer service.

- *Complaints*. Watch for posts complaining about your products or services, company, and staff. Catching

something early means getting a chance to respond and demonstrate your problem-solving abilities.

- *Expressed need*. People make known what they are doing and often ask the general public for advice when they are about to make a purchase. Both of these situations provide an opportunity for you to reach out with an offer of assistance or information related to your organization's products and services.

- *The competitor*. Listen to what your competitors are doing and the public's response to their products and services.

- *The crowd*. Topics will often pop up online that draw huge crowds, such as protesters against Walmart's carbon footprint.[49] Walmart immediately responded with a program to reduce greenhouse gas emissions in its truck fleet over five years by 20 million metric tons, an amount equal to that produced by 3.8 million cars.

- *The influencer*. Determine who the opinion leaders are. They gain their power from how frequently they post on a topic, the number of people who link to their posts, the number of people gathering to comment, and how engaged visitors to their posts become. You want these folks on your side.

- *The crisis*. Discussions happening in social media can serve as an early warning system. What concerns do people have that can be avoided?

Applying Your Skills.

Take a few minutes and listen to your social media. Try some of the following:

1. Sign up for Google Alerts or Tweet Beeps so you know when others are talking about you. What are they saying?

2. Visit some of your favorite organization's Facebook pages. Take inventory of what people are saying. Do the postings fit one of the categories just listed?

3. Based on what you're reading and hearing, how would you advise the leader of this organization to respond?

Responding Effectively to Others

The title of this chapter, "Listening and Responding," reflects the active listening process that we introduced in the preceding section. Active listeners not only stop, look, and listen, they also respond to the speaker. As you'll recall, listening is a process that includes *responding*. Thoughtfully responding to others serves several purposes. First, it tells a speaker how well we understand his or her message. Second, it lets a speaker know how the message affects us;

whether we agree or disagree with a message. Third, in many situations our response to a speaker validates the speaker; it lets the speaker know that we're "with" him or her. Ultimately, all of these responsive messages allow the speaker to adapt his or her communication more appropriately to ensure that listeners understand the messages.

In this section of the chapter, we review three sets of skills for responding to others while listening to them: responding with verbal messages, responding with nonverbal messages, and responding with empathic messages.

Responding with Verbal Messages

A number of verbal responses allow us to provide a speaker with important feedback. Here are a few of them:

- *Communicate messages that let the speaker know that you understand the message*; for example, "I understand. I see what you're saying."
- *Communicate messages that let the speaker know that you need clarification*; for example, "I'm confused. Can you give me another example?"
- *Communicate messages that let the speaker know that you're interested and need more information*; for example, "I find what you're saying fascinating. Do you mind going into more detail?"
- *Communicate messages that let the speaker know that you'd like him or her to continue speaking*; for example, "OK, then what happened?"
- *Communicate messages that let the speaker know that you'd like to say something*; for example, "May I add something to what you're saying?"

What all of these verbal responses have in common is that they all convey that we've been paying attention to what the speaker is saying. Again, it's important that speakers use these messages as feedback and adapt their communication appropriately.

Responding with Nonverbal Messages

In some business situations, such as at a formal board meeting, it may not be appropriate to respond to a speaker with verbal messages. In these situations, we can respond with nonverbal messages, which are as important as (if not more important than) verbal messages. Nonverbal responsive messages include visual (sight) and aural (sound) cues. We've already noted a few visual nonverbal responsive cues: forward body lean, head nods, taking notes, and making eye contact with the speaker. A few of the aural cues include back channel cues, which we discussed in Chapter 3, including vocal assurances that signal understanding and "vocal starters" or utterances that signal that the listener would like to add something to the conversation. To get an idea of how nonverbally responsive you are in conversations, complete the assessment measure in Rating Scale 4.2.

RATING SCALE 4.2   **Measure of Nonverbal Responsiveness**

How responsive are you when listening to others? Take a few minutes to complete this self-report measure of nonverbal responsiveness.[50] The items comprising this measure will also make you aware of various nonverbal responsive behaviors.

Rate each behavior in the list using the following scale: Never = 0, Rarely = 1, Occasionally = 2, Often = 3, Very Often = 4

When listening to others, how often do you:

_____ display facial expressions that reflect your positive attitude.

_____ show interest by taking notes on what the other person is saying.

_____ smile at the person who is talking to you.

_____ nod your head while the other person is talking to you.

_____ look at the other person who is talking to you.

_____ smile while you're asking the other person questions.

_____ sit up and lean forward while listening.

_____ gesture with your hands and arms while the other person is talking to you.

_____ use vocal inflections that convey your positive attitude toward the person talking.

_____ use vocal starters that suggest that you want to say something.

_____ respond quickly to the other person's questions or comments.

_____ use vocal variety in tone, pitch, rate, and volume to indicate that you're interested in what the other person is saying.

_____ use vocal assurances that let the other person know that you understand his or her message.

Scoring Instructions:

Sum your scores for the 13 items. Scores above 26 indicate high nonverbal responsiveness. Scores below 26 indicate low nonverbal responsiveness.

You might be asking yourself, "Does a smile, head nod, or forward body lean really make that much of a difference when listening to others?" It does! Not only does using nonverbally responsive behaviors enhance listening comprehension, but speakers who see others responding using these behaviors feel motivated, satisfied, and effective in their communication.[51] It's a win-win situation. How important is it to you that others be nonverbally responsive when they're listening to you? How do you feel when you're speaking to someone and you get a blank stare from them? Most people become distracted and begin to feel frustrated or insecure when this happens. Remember, nonverbal messages convey relational cues; when others don't respond to us nonverbally, we feel somewhat rejected and unsupported. We feel "unheard."

Responding with Empathic Messages

Empathy, as we noted earlier in this chapter and also in Chapter 3, is the process of feeling what another person is feeling. Empathizing is more than just acknowledging how another person feels; it is making an effort to feel what the other person is feeling. Responding with empathy is especially important when we want to support and encourage others. Although most people don't think of the workplace as a place where feelings are openly shared and people support and encourage each other by listening and responding with empathic messages, the role of emotions in the workplace is becoming more important.[52] For example, one study examined crying in the workplace and included seven hundred working Americans equally divided by sex and representing the full range of occupations and economic levels.[53] This

Listening and responding to others with empathy can accomplish many communication goals, including enhancing the quality of your workplace relationships.

study found that 48 percent of men and 41 percent of women reported that it's OK to cry and to express your emotions at work.

Empathy is a communication tool that can be used to accomplish a number of communication goals, such as building important workplace relationships, repairing workplace relationships, defusing workplace conflict, and even influencing clients and customers to purchase your products and services. Three strategies can enhance your ability to respond to others with empathic messages.

ASK APPROPRIATE QUESTIONS   As we listen for information and attempt to understand how another person is feeling, we may need to ask a number of questions. Most of our questions serve one of four purposes: (1) to obtain additional information ("Can you tell me more about the problem?"); (2) to check how the other person feels ("Are you frustrated because you didn't meet your deadline?"); (3) to ask for clarification ("What did you mean when you said we need to outsource?"); or (4) to verify that you have reached an accurate conclusion about the other person's intent or feeling ("So are you saying you'd rather work at home than at the office?").

PARAPHRASE MESSAGE CONTENT   After we have listened and asked appropriate questions, we need to check whether our interpretations are accurate by paraphrasing the content of a speaker's message. **Paraphrasing** is restating in our own words what we think the other person is saying. Paraphrasing is different from repeating what someone has said; that would be parroting, not paraphrasing. When we paraphrase content, we summarize the details and the main ideas. Here are some common scripts, or ways to begin paraphrasing:

"So here is what seems to have happened . . ."

"Let me see if I got this right. You're saying that . . ."

"Here's what I understand you to mean . . ."

"So the point you seem to be making is . . ."

"You seem to be saying . . ."

When a listener paraphrases the content and feelings of a speaker's message, the speaker is not only more likely to know that the message was understood but also more likely to trust and value the listener.

PARAPHRASE EMOTIONS   The most important goal of empathic responding is to make sure that we understand the speaker's feelings and let him or her know that we understand. How do we do this? Paraphrasing emotions is similar to paraphrasing content. For example:

"So you feel . . ."

"Emotionally, you're feeling . . ."

"I get a sense that you're feeling . . ."

"Is this how you're feeling: you're feeling . . ."

Paraphrasing emotions or content can be especially useful in the following workplace situations:

- Before you take an important action.
- Before you argue with or criticize your business partner or associate.
- When your business partner or associate has strong feelings.
- When your business partner or associate just wants to talk.
- When your business partner or associate is using jargon that you don't understand.
- When you encounter new ideas.[54]

terms & definitions

Paraphrasing restating in your own words what you think another person is saying.

Responding to Gender and Cultural Differences

How you respond to others at work also depends on gender and cultural differences, which we discuss more thoroughly in the next chapter. For now, think about how many times you have had problems understanding someone from a different culture or even a different subculture. What's interesting is that we don't have to travel far to have a cross-cultural experience. In fact, sociolinguist Deborah Tannen argues that men and women are socialized into two different cultural groupings that make it difficult for men and women to listen and respond to each other at work.[55] For example, during a break from a videoconference, a woman commented to her male colleague how wonderful it was for her to see, listen, and interact with her friends and colleagues from all over the world. The man agreed and then launched into a lengthy and detailed conversation about how the videoconferencing technology allows groups of people from all over the globe to see and hear each other at the same time. The woman became a bit irritated by his response, which focused on the technical detail, and ended the conversation.

As we can see in this case, people respond to each other based on their gender and cultural differences. The woman made her comment about seeing her friends from across the globe as a way of expressing her feelings for her international colleagues. She wanted her male colleague to listen and respond to her relational message. The male colleague took this opening as a chance to reveal his knowledge of videoconferencing technology and to teach his female colleague some of the things he knows. Although both colleagues had the good intention of listening and responding to a friendly conversation, they had differing expectations about the direction such a conversation should take. The male colleague may have believed that a "good response" was one with interesting, factual content; whereas the female colleague may have believed a "good response" to be one with personal content, which disclosed feelings.

What this implies for listening and responding is that when we hear someone speak, we are not only hearing the words they say. We are also activating our own expectations for how others should respond to our messages. If you understand how gender and culture influence how others listen and respond, you also better understand why others respond the way they do.

Listen Up[56]

When you talk you expect other people to listen to you. So does your boss. In fact, one of Sheila Lirio Marcelo's sources of frustration as a leader is people who don't listen to her. As the founder and chief executive officer of Care.com, she assumed that her followers would listen to her. But even as CEO, she found her employees not listening. When asked, "What are your pet peeves?" she said, "Having to repeat myself more than three times." Having one of her employees tune her out is only one of her concerns. Another concern she has is "people who jump to conclusions with one observation. I'm a big believer in getting a few data points of observable behavior before you give somebody the gift of feedback on something. And I typically will say: 'Look, I've observed this two or three times. Let's have a conversation about it.'"

Marcelo emphasizes listening by giving employees a new perspective. She does this by asking her employees to do another person's job for a while. "I give them a new seat at the table. And people don't have a choice where they sit; we rotate them. . . . You sit with somebody else from a different team so you get to know their job. What are they doing? What are they saying on the phone? How do they tick? It forces people to listen."

In this chapter we've emphasized what Marcelo and other leaders consider to be a weakness in new employees. Listening strategies that have been detailed include turning off competing messages, listening with your eyes, and linking both major ideas and details together. A number of responding strategies were also reviewed, including how to respond with empathic messages as well as responding by adapting to gender and cultural differences.

Whether you're listening to your boss, your colleagues, a client or a customer, make sure that you are listening at peak proficiency so that your listening behavior won't become a pet peeve of others—especially your boss's pet peeve.

leaders on leadership

Helping Others Listen Effectively to You

Have you ever thought about how others listen to you? Do you often have to repeat what you say to others because they quickly forget what you said to them? When others don't listen to you, who do you blame? Do you blame them for not listening? Or do you blame yourself for not making it easy for others to listen to you? If you're like most people, you probably tend to blame the other person for not listening to you. Have you ever thought that maybe you're the problem? Consider the following questions when diagnosing why others may not be listening to you as carefully as you would prefer:

- Do you bore others when you communicate with them? Do you leave a positive impression on others? Are you memorable?
- Do you convey information in a confusing manner?
- Do you communicate too much information to others?
- Do you give those listening to you an opportunity to ask questions, take notes?

In the following pages we focus on the five stages of the listening process—selecting, attending, understanding, remembering, and responding—and suggest ways you can help others listen to you in each stage.[57]

Helping Others Select Your Messages

Before someone can listen to your message, he or she must select it from other competing messages. How can you help other people select your messages? Here are a few suggestions:

MOVE CLOSER TO THE OTHER PERSON As we discussed in Chapter 3, proxemics is the study of space. We can help others select our messages by moving closer to them or by making ourselves available to them. Have you ever had a manager who claimed to have an open-door policy; but every time you dropped by her office, she gave you "that look" that clearly said "Don't interrupt"? If you want people to listen to you, you have to help them select your messages by physically moving closer to them or by communicating that it's OK to approach you, such as by making direct eye contact, using open body position, and gesturing (for example, waving someone into your office).

MAKE THE INFORMATION USEFUL People tend to select information that is immediately useful to them. You can enhance selection by increasing the utility or usefulness of your message. If you want people to listen to you, you have to give them a reason to listen. Show how the information will benefit them on the job: "Here's how what I'm about to say will benefit you."

ADAPT MESSAGES TO OTHERS' BELIEFS People have a tendency to select messages that are consistent with their attitudes, beliefs, and values. Give some consideration to how well your messages will fit your listeners' belief systems. If what you're about to say will go against their beliefs, find ways to make your messages more palatable or convincing. For example, if you're discussing sexual harassment with a group of guys who don't believe that sexual harassment occurs that often on the job, be prepared to share statistics with them.

Helping Others Attend to Your Messages

How can you help other people attend to your messages? They may have selected your message, but that doesn't mean they will necessarily pay attention to it. Try some of the following strategies for getting people to pay attention to your messages.

MAKE MESSAGES NOVEL People pay attention to messages that are unusual and unique. If we want others to pay attention to our messages, we need to make the messages stand out from all the others. Flight attendants who work for Southwest Airlines are known for making their routine and very boring safety demonstrations novel and humorous.[58] They make people want to listen to their safety instructions.

MAKE MESSAGES CONCRETE Use words in your messages that are vivid and clear; whenever possible, refer to things that listeners can see, smell, feel, taste, or touch. Avoid using words that are abstract. For example, Monica, a division leader for a large clothing retailer, is encouraging her store managers to be transformational leaders. She loses many of them because they don't understand what a transformational leader is. The leadership jargon is abstract to them. To make her message concrete so her store managers pay attention to her, Monica needs to explain that transformational leaders (1) develop clear sales goals, (2) invent new sales techniques, and (3) reward employees for reaching goals.

MAKE MESSAGES MODERATE IN LENGTH People pay attention to messages that are moderate in length. Staci, who is a wedding planner, tries to pitch her services to a prospective customer. But the bride-to-be loses interest in the sales pitch because it's too long. At an initial meeting, Staci doesn't need to go into detail about every possible service she can provide. Brief messages are equally problematic; a message that is too brief doesn't contain any relevant information and can be missed altogether. So what's moderate? It depends on the person who is receiving our message. Staci should use her prospective customer's nonverbal cues as a gauge. If the bride-to-be is engaged and asking questions, then Staci should continue. If the bride's attention is waning, then it's time to wrap up the sales pitch. Staci can also stop and ask a question to probe her customer's level of interest and engagement.

Helping Others Understand Your Messages

Assuming that others have selected and paid attention to your message, how can you help them understand, decode, or assign appropriate meanings to the message? Here are some possible strategies:

FIT MESSAGES INTO EXISTING SCHEMA A **schema** is a mental representation of knowledge. Think of a schema as a mental "box" or "filing cabinet" where you classify, categorize, and file concepts. For example, suppose you're training employees to use a new presentation software program. Chances are the employees have used PowerPoint—so they have a schema for presentation software, and that schema is PowerPoint. To enhance their understanding of your messages, show them how the new presentation software program is similar to and different from PowerPoint. Tapping into an existing schema helps others understand your message and makes listening easier.

DEVELOP A NEW SCHEMA Sometimes others don't understand us because they don't have an existing schema, or filing cabinet, for the new information. Using the preceding example, imagine that you were teaching employees how to use a new software presentation program, but they were unfamiliar with PowerPoint. Chances are they would be totally lost. To enhance their listening—and more importantly, their understanding—you would need to give them a new schema. You might begin by first telling the employees that developing a slide presentation is like being an artist who paints beautiful pictures. They begin with a blank slide, which is the canvas. Then, you could introduce the toolbox, which is like the painter's palette. Next, teach them how to create a background for all of the slides, which is like adding a first coat of paint. If people don't have a schema for understanding new information, it's important to develop one for them.

USE LISTENERS' FRAME OF REFERENCE Another way to enhance understanding and listening is to tap into the experiences of those who are listening. What is their frame of reference? In other words, rather than explaining something using your own experiences,

terms & definitions

Schema a mental representation of knowledge.

use the experiences of those who are listening. For example, if new employees don't understand the sick leave policy that you're trying to explain to them during orientation, ask them how the sick leave policy worked at their last company. Use their experiences with sick leave as a starting point, and then make the necessary adjustments in the conversation to ensure that the employees understand how your company's sick leave policy works.

Helping Others Remember Your Messages

How can you help other people remember your message? If you've been successful up to this point, your listeners have selected your message, are paying attention to your message, and understand your message. Now, how do you help them remember it? Here are a few suggestions:

Encourage your audience to respond to your message. Their responses will help you appropriately adapt information so that the audience can better understand and remember it.

USE REDUNDANCY For most of us, the more we hear something, the more important we think it is, and the more likely we are to remember the information. Making a message redundant is repeating the information or reiterating the information. **Repeating** is simply restating the information using the same words in the same order. **Reiterating** information is restating the information using different words. Saying, "Our number-one priority is your safety. Our number-one priority is your safety" is an example of repeating. Saying, "Our number-one priority is your safety. Your safety is immensely important to us" is an example of reiteration. Making messages redundant enhances others' ability to remember and recall information when needed.

USE MEMORY JOGGERS A **mnemonic device** is a short rhyme, phrase, story, joke, or other mental technique (such as a mental picture) for making information easier to memorize. A mnemonic is useful when trying to remember a list of terms or instructions. For example, if you're certified in cardiopulmonary resuscitation (CPR), you learned a mnemonic device for remembering how to save a person's life using ABC: A is for *airway*, B is for *breathing*, and C is for *circulation*. Memory joggers are shortcuts that enhance memory and recall of information.

USE THE PRINCIPLE OF PRIMACY AND RECENCY This principle states that people are more likely to remember information that is presented first (primacy) and/or last (recency) during a conversation or a presentation. Research suggests that messages in the middle of a conversation or a presentation are often forgotten. To enhance others' abilities to remember our messages, position the important messages toward the beginning and toward the end of our communication with them. Students preparing for the ministry are often instructed in how to prepare and deliver an effective sermon that people will remember: Begin by telling parishioners what you're going to tell them. Next, tell them. Finally, tell them what you just told them. This sage piece of advice recognizes the importance of the primacy and recency effect. If parishioners are going to remember any part of the sermon, they're most likely to remember what the minister said to begin the sermon and what he or she said to end it.

Helping Others Respond to Your Messages

How can you help other people respond to your messages? Whereas the selecting, attending, understanding, and remembering stages of the listening process are focused on the person who is listening and receiving the messages, responding aids the source of the messages—the person

terms & definitions

Repeating restating information using the same words in the same order.

Reiterating restating information using different words.

Mnemonic device a short rhyme, phrase, or other mental technique that makes information easier to memorize.

RECAP

Skills and Strategies for Helping Others Listen Effectively to You

Skills	Strategies	Examples
Helping Others Select Your Messages	Move closer to the person.	Move toward your listener to more effectively communicate the message.
	Make the information useful.	Show that the information is useful: "Here's something that you will find helpful . . ."
	Adapt messages to others' beliefs.	Share information in a way that makes it easier for others to pay attention: "I know you've been frustrated that work is piling up and it seems that nothing is being done to hire more staff. Here's where we stand on the staffing problem."
Helping Others Attend to Your Messages	Make messages novel.	Include humor in a monotonous message or tell a story from a different perspective.
	Make messages concrete.	Avoid jargon and abstract language. Rather than discussing the "interoffice communication problem," refer to the specific issue at hand: people aren't responding to their email.
	Make messages moderate in length.	Watch the nonverbal cues of the listener to gauge whether your message is too long; and if so, wrap things up.
Helping Others Under-stand Your Messages	Fit messages into existing schema.	When discussing a work situation with coworkers who are big sports fans, use a football analogy to help them understand.
	Develop a new schema.	When training coworkers to analyze workplace problems, have them consider the following questions about a particular situation: "What are the strengths? What are the weaknesses? What are the opportunities? What are the threats?"
	Use listeners' frame of reference.	When training new employees, refer to some of their experiences at their former employers to help them make sense of the policies and procedures at your organization.
Helping Others Remem-ber Your Messages	Use redundancy.	Repeating: "We care about the customer, we care about the customer."
		Reiterating: "We care about the customer. The customer is the reason we're in business."
	Use memory joggers.	During CPR training, the trainer encourages participants to remember the ABCs of CPR: A for Airway, B for Breathing, and C for Circulation.
		When trying to resolve a conflict, use the PUGSS model: P for Problem, U for Understanding, G for Goals, S for possible Solutions, and S for agreed-on Solution.
	Use the principle of primacy and recency.	Put the most important information at the beginning and end of the message.
Helping Others Respond to Your Messages	Encourage questions.	Let listeners know that it is OK to interrupt with questions, or set aside a time when they can ask questions.
	Encourage note taking.	Let the listeners know they can take notes while you talk. This can also help them to ask questions.
	Encourage nonverbal responsiveness.	Head nods, forward body lean, and other nonverbal respons-es allow listeners to develop a better understanding of the message.

who is talking. When receivers respond to a source, the source uses this information as feedback and adapts his or her messages accordingly. If messages are adapted appropriately, then the people receiving the messages will understand the information better and are more likely to remember the information. For example, if you're talking to a group of coworkers and they all look confused (raised eyebrows, wrinkled foreheads, sighs of frustration), it's important that you use this feedback and adapt your messages to clarify the confusion.

But sometimes people don't know how to respond, especially in more formal presentations. Because feedback cues are so important to a speaker, we encourage you to consider some of the following ideas:

ENCOURAGE QUESTIONS If the situation allows for this, encourage the receivers of your messages to interrupt you at any point with their questions. (If you would prefer not to be interrupted, assure listeners that you will answer their questions; and then have them hold their questions until a designated point in the conversation or presentation.) People need to be encouraged to ask questions. Many times, people don't ask questions out of fear that they will appear stupid. Give people permission to ask "stupid" questions.

ENCOURAGE NOTE TAKING Give people permission to take notes during your conversation or presentation. When people take notes, it lets the source know that the receivers consider the information important. In many ways note taking is validating to the speaker; it's a form of encouragement. Also, note taking encourages questions, which enables a speaker to know if he or she is making any sense to the audience.

ENCOURAGE NONVERBAL RESPONSIVENESS Because many listeners would prefer not to ask questions, encourage them to use nonverbal messages to convey *both* their understanding and their confusion. When people are engaged and understanding, they usually use direct eye contact, forward body lean, head nods, and vocal assurances that express their understanding. When people are disengaged and confused, they usually fail to make eye contact, lean back in their chairs, slouch, or sigh to express their frustration and lack of understanding. To a speaker, these nonverbal responsive messages are an invaluable source of information. If the nonverbal responses convey understanding, then we can continue our conversation or presentation. If the nonverbal responses convey confusion, then we need to slow down, repeat and reiterate, and answer listeners' questions to clarify the confusion.[59]

Research also suggests that when receivers of messages are engaged in the physical act of responding to and elaborating on messages (that is, asking questions, taking notes, responding nonverbally), they are more likely to have a better understanding of the information and be better able to recall and use it.[60] Put simply, the physical act of responding to messages enhances listening.

It's important to remember that when others don't listen to us, we might be part of the listening problem. Rather than blaming others for not listening to us, there is much that we can do to help others select, attend to, understand, remember, and respond to our messages.

Wrap-Up

Leading others begins by understanding others. To understand others, you must begin by first listening and responding to them. Developing your listening and responding skills is the fourth communication principle for leadership. Active listening is a five-step process of selecting, attending, understanding, remembering, and responding.

To develop effective listening skills, follow the 3-step process of Stop, Look, and Listen.

- Stop: Turn off competing messages and socially decenter.
- Look: Listen with your eyes.
- Listen: Listen for both the major ideas and the details.

Listening is a process that includes responding. Effectively responding to others involves using both verbal and nonverbal messages and communicating with empathy.

- Responding with verbal messages allows us to select messages that provide the speaker with important information about our understanding of the message, as well as offer feedback.

- Effective nonverbal responses include visual and vocal messages—such as eye contact, head nods, and vocal assurances—which indicate our attention and interest.

- Communicating with empathy involves asking appropriate questions, paraphrasing the content of the message, and paraphrasing the emotion.

  To help others effectively listen and respond to you, you can follow these guidelines:

- Move closer to the other person, make the information useful, and adapt your messages to the other's perspective to help others select your message.

- To help others attend to your messages; make them novel, concrete, and of appropriate length.

- To help others understand your message, use relevant information to help them develop or fit messages into a schema.

- Use redundancy, memory joggers, or the rule of primacy and recency to help others remember your message.

- To help listeners effectively respond to you, encourage verbal and nonverbal responsiveness, such as asking questions and taking notes.

Reviewing Key Terms

Hearing 73	Whole-part learning style 78
Listening 73	Part-whole learning style 78
Select 73	Elaboration strategies 79
Attend 73	Paraphrasing 85
Understand 73	Schema 88
Remember 74	Repeating 89
Respond 74	Reiterating 89
Social decentering 75	Mnemonic device 89

The Principle Points

This chapter opens with a quote from Bernard Baruch, who was a business leader and political adviser to both President Woodrow Wilson and Franklin D. Roosevelt. Baruch states, "Most of the successful people I've known are the ones who do more listening than talking." Although many leaders value listening, they don't always practice effective listening skills, which is the focus of this chapter.

Principle Four: Listen and respond thoughtfully to others.

- Hearing and listening are not the same. Hearing is the physiological process of decoding sounds. It occurs when the sound waves captured by our ear cause the eardrum to vibrate. Listening is the process of receiving, constructing meaning from, and responding to verbal and nonverbal messages. Although all listening involves hearing, not all hearing involves listening.

- Listening is a process that involves five stages: selecting, attending, understanding, remembering, and responding.

- Effectively listening includes turning off competing messages (Stop), listening with your eyes (Look), and understanding both major ideas and details (Listen).

- Effective listening includes responding to others' communication using verbal, nonverbal, and empathic responding behaviors.
- Helping others listen effectively to you includes helping others select, attend, understand, remember, and respond to your messages.

Applying Your Skills

1. Assess your receiver apprehension by completing the following assessment measure.[61] Respond to each item by indicating the extent to which it describes you using the following scale: 5 = Strongly agree, 4 = Agree, 3 = Sometimes, 2 = Disagree, 1 = Strongly Disagree

   _____ 1. When I am listening I feel nervous about missing information.

   _____ 2. I worry about being able to keep up with the material being presented in class.

   _____ 3. Sometimes I miss information in class because I am writing notes.

   _____ 4. I feel tense and anxious when I am listening to important information.

   _____ 5. I am concerned that I won't be able to remember information I've heard in lectures and discussions.

   _____ 6. Although I try to concentrate, my thoughts sometimes become confused when I'm listening.

   _____ 7. I worry that my listening skill is not very good.

   _____ 8. I regularly cannot remember things I have just been told.

   _____ 9. I feel anxious or nervous when I am listening in class.

   _____ 10. I prefer reading class material rather than listening to it, so I don't have to feel stressed about catching all the information the first time.

   Scores can range from 50 down to 10. The higher your score, the more likely you are to experience some anxiety when you listen to others; and the harder you may have to work at developing strategies to improve listening comprehension.

2. Think of a time when you felt your message was not understood by the receiver. In particular, have you experienced a situation at work when a supervisor or coworker didn't understand a concern you had? Discuss what you could have done differently, focusing on the strategies listed in this chapter for helping others understand you. How will you remember to use these strategies in your future communication?

3. Think back on a difficult conversation you have had. Then think about each of the five stages of listening in the conversation—at what point did you select, attend, understand, remember, and respond to the other person's message? Did you fail to adequately carry out any of the five stages? If so, try to identify any problems that may have prevented you from completing the stage.

4. Imagine you are training a group of new employees at a customer service firm. How would you teach them to listen actively? Could you explain the skill effectively?

5

Adapting to Differences

chapter **outline**

After reading this chapter, you should be able to

- Define willingness to communicate, communication apprehension, and argumentativeness; and describe the role each plays in our communication with others.

- Describe each of the cultural value dimensions, and identify how these might differ from your own.

- Identify communication strategies for adapting to cultural differences.

- Differentiate between sex and gender, and explain the role of gender conversational rituals in our communication.

- List and describe methods for adapting to gender differences in communication.

- Discuss strategies for adapting to generational differences at work.

Learning to adapt is a fundamental principle if you want to remain in business in the twenty-first century, according to Elise Mitchell, president and CEO of Mitchell Communications Group, which was recently named the 2011 *PRWeek* Small PR Agency of the Year. Her company's portfolio of clients includes a "who's who" of national brands, such as Walmart, Sam's Club, Tyson Foods, and J.B. Hunt.

Elise and her team need public relations professionals who have cultural competencies that will enable them to better serve their clients. Put simply, they need PR professionals who understand the nuances of a cultural group—including language, attitudes, beliefs, and values—and professionals who can help develop and adapt messages and interact with diverse groups of people in meaningful ways. For example, Mitchell Communications Group develops content for their clients' websites. When you develop content in both English and Spanish, you need a PR professional who is not only fluent in Spanish but also understands the Latino market to make sure the content is translated appropriately.

Because Elise wants her talent pool to be more diverse, she is developing innovative ways to enhance the ethnic makeup of her public relations team.[1] For example, Mitchell Communications Group launched a new talent initiative called "Big Break." This week-long mini-internship for high-performing college seniors from diverse ethnic backgrounds offers real-world work experience and a firsthand look at how her agency works. From a pool of more than a hundred applicants, they selected nine students from four universities, paying for the students' airfare, lodging, and meals, and preparing a daily schedule that included face time with agency leaders and an opportunity to develop and present a PR plan for two area nonprofits.

According to Elise, her goal is to cultivate and attract diverse talent to Mitchell Communications Group. And it's more than simply adding employees of different ethnic groups to her payroll. Diverse colleagues bring with them their cultural knowledge to the agency. They teach her and members of her team about the nuances and complexities of a cultural group. They help her group develop communication campaigns that appeal to the values and beliefs of diverse audiences while remaining respectful about the specific needs of these important markets.

leading **questions**

1. What cultural competencies do you possess and bring to the workplace? How comfortable are you in working and interacting with diverse groups of people?

2. How do you go about communicating with people who are different from you, whether it be because of their personality, culture, gender, or generational differences?

3. Can you recall a time when someone adapted a message to you to make sure you understood it? What did they do to adapt the message? Was it effective? How do you adapt your communication to others to make sure they understand you?

One characteristic of the workplace that is both a benefit and a challenge for leaders is that no two people are alike. We're different in terms of our personalities, cultural backgrounds, gender, and generational differences. Although this diversity adds a richness of ideas and perspectives to the business and professional setting, it also challenges leaders to adapt their communication. A communication style that works for one individual doesn't necessarily work for another. Effective leaders have the ability to assess how people are different and then adapt their communication to fit the unique needs of the individual.

"Adaptability is not imitation. It means power of resistance and assimilation."
—Mahatma Gandhi

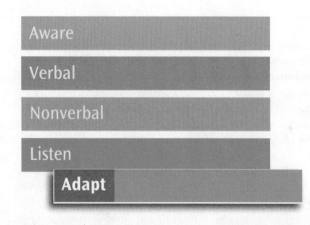

FIGURE 5.1 Communication Principles and Skills for Leadership

Principle Five: Appropriately adapt messages to others reminds us that a "one-size-fits-all" communication style doesn't work in the twenty-first-century workplace. Figure 5.1 presents our now-familiar model, which completes the discussion we started in Chapter 1. In the workplace, effective leaders are those who adapt messages to others rather than expecting others to adapt to the leader's messages.

The purpose of this chapter is to help you understand what makes people different from one another and to suggest ways you can adapt your messages to communicate more effectively with people on the job. The chapter is divided into four sections. The first section examines how personality influences communication at work. The second section focuses on how culture affects communication behavior on the job. The third section reviews how gender influences communication in the business and professional workplace. The final section identifies some of the unique qualities and characteristics of generation Y employees and how to adapt to them. Each section discusses the communication skills and strategies that will help you lead others by adapting to their personalities, cultural differences, genders, and generation.

Adapting to Personality Differences

The genetic code you inherited from your parents plays an instrumental role in the formation of your personality and your social style, discussed in Chapter 2. A **personality trait** is "any distinguishable, relatively enduring way in which one individual differs from another."[2] Some people are naturally nervous and anxious; others are more relaxed and easygoing. We get an idea of someone's personality by listening to the person and by watching him or her communicate. A **communication trait** is a label used to describe a person's communication behaviors.[3] When asked to describe others, you usually describe their personalities by describing their communication traits. For example, you might say, "He's very outgoing, talkative, funny, and animated" or, "She's very assertive and argumentative." In many ways, your communication is an expression of your personality.

Having an awareness of your own communication traits and the traits of others will give you additional insight into what motivates a person to communicate in a particular manner. This understanding will also enable you to more effectively adapt your communication to the other person. For example, if you're going to be communicating with someone you know is argumentative by nature, then it's important to approach the conversation with enough reasons and evidence to argue your case successfully.

Three traits that have been shown to influence how you communicate with others and how others communicate with you in the workplace include willingness to communicate, communication apprehension, and argumentativeness. The following sections provide a brief description of each of the traits, invite you to assess your communication traits by completing a series of self-report measures, and make recommendations for adapting your communication as a leader to accommodate these differences in communication traits.

terms & definitions

Personality trait any distinguishable, relatively enduring way in which one individual differs from another.

Communication trait a label used to describe a person's communication behaviors.

Willingness to Communicate

The most basic communication trait is **willingness to communicate (WTC)**, which is an individual's natural tendency to initiate communication with others.[4] Before reading any further, we recommend that you complete the WTC measure in Rating Scale 5.1 to become aware of your willingness to communicate with others.

RATING SCALE 5.1 Willingness to Communicate Measure

Below are twenty situations in which a person might choose to communicate or not to communicate.[5] Assume that you have *completely free choice*. Indicate to the left of each statement what percentage of the time you would choose to communicate in each situation: 0 = never, 100 = always.

_____ 1. Talk with a service station attendant

_____ 2. Talk with a physician

_____ 3. Present a talk to a group of strangers

_____ 4. Talk with an acquaintance while standing in line

_____ 5. Talk with a salesperson in a store

_____ 6. Talk in a large meeting of friends

_____ 7. Talk to a police officer

_____ 8. Talk in a small group of strangers

_____ 9. Talk with a friend while standing in line

_____ 10. Talk with a server in a restaurant

_____ 11. Talk in a large meeting of acquaintances

_____ 12. Talk with a stranger while standing in line

_____ 13. Talk with a secretary

_____ 14. Present a talk to a group of friends

_____ 15. Talk in a small group of acquaintances

_____ 16. Talk with a garbage collector

_____ 17. Talk in a large meeting of strangers

_____ 18. Talk with a spouse, partner, girlfriend, or boyfriend

_____ 19. Talk in a small group of friends

_____ 20. Present a talk to a group of acquaintances

Scoring Instructions: The WTC measure is designed to indicate how willing you are to communicate in a variety of contexts with different types of receivers. The higher your total WTC score, the more willing you are to communicate in general. Similarly, the higher your given subscore for a type of context or audience, the more willing you are to communicate in that context, or with that type of audience.

The WTC permits computation of one total score and seven subscores. The subscores relate to willingness to communicate in each of four common communication contexts and with three types of audiences.

Subscore	Scoring Formula
Group discussion	Add your scores for items 8, 15, and 19; then divide by 3.
Meetings	Add your scores for items 6, 11, and 17; then divide by 3.
Interpersonal conversations	Add your scores for items 4, 9, and 12; then divide by 3.
Public speaking	Add your scores for items 3, 14, and 20; then divide by 3.
Stranger	Add your scores for items 3, 8, 12, and 17; then divide by 4.
Acquaintance	Add your scores for items 4, 11, 15, and 20; then divide by 4.
Friend	Add your scores for items 6, 9, 14, and 19; then divide by 4.

terms & definitions

Willingness to communicate (WTC) an individual's natural tendency to initiate communication with others.

To compute your total WTC score, add the subscores for Stranger, Acquaintance, and Friend. Then divide by 3. *Norms for WTC Scores*

Group discussion	More than 89: High WTC;	Less than 57: Low WTC
Meetings	More than 80: High WTC;	Less than 39: Low WTC
Interpersonal Conversations	More than 94: High WTC;	Less than 64: Low WTC
Public Speaking	More than 78: High WTC;	Less than 33: Low WTC
Stranger	More than 63: High WTC;	Less than 18: Low WTC
Acquaintance	More than 92: High WTC;	Less than 57: Low WTC
Friend	More than 99: High WTC;	Less than 71: Low WTC
Total WTC	More than 82: High Overall WTC;	Less than 52: Low Overall WTC

High WTC individuals enjoy talking and look for opportunities to initiate communication with others. Low WTC individuals, in contrast, don't find communication as enjoyable and prefer to avoid communication with others. These individuals are usually labeled as shy because they don't readily engage in communication behavior. In the workplace, "high talkers" (high WTC people) tend to be the individuals who roam the hallways looking for people to engage in conversation. Low talkers (low WTC people), however, tend to leave their offices rarely, and when they do, it's for a specific purpose. If others engage them in conversation, they keep it short and return to their offices.

Because communication is valued in the United States and in the workplace, high talkers are usually rewarded for their willingness to communicate, and low talkers suffer some consequences for preferring not to communicate.[6] Research suggests that people who are willing to communicate are generally perceived more positively than those who are less willing to communicate.[7] "Low talkers" are perceived to have these characteristics:[8]

- Less likely to be hired
- Less likely to be promoted
- Less qualified to do their jobs
- Less motivated to do their jobs
- Less cooperative in the workplace

It's important to understand that this list of descriptions is based on people's *perceptions.* Low talkers and high talkers may be equally qualified, motivated, and cooperative on the job; however, working professionals tend to perceive low WTC individuals as less so compared to high WTC individuals.[9]

You can adapt to those with a low willingness to communicate so as to enhance workplace communication:

- *Refrain from forming premature judgments.* Sometimes we evaluate others simply based on their communication behaviors or lack of communication behaviors. Instead, we need to form perceptions based on the quality of people's work and other job performance factors that are important to the organization.
- *Do not take another person's quietness personally.* Some people are bothered or even offended when others don't communicate with them. You need to understand that someone's being quiet is a part of his or her personality; it's just the way the person is and it usually has nothing to do with you.

You can also adapt to and lead others who have high willingness to communicate:

- *Give them opportunities to communicate or place them in positions that are a fit for their communication trait.* Place high WTC individuals in positions where they represent the organization as spokespeople or representatives. For example, high WTC individuals are a natural fit for sales and marketing positions. Make their communication trait benefit the organization.
- *Monitor their communication behavior.* Too much communicating may prevent people from getting their work done or may prevent others from getting their work done.

Communication Apprehension

If you have ever experienced a bit of stage fright, then you've experienced **communication apprehension (CA)**, which is fear or anxiety associated with either ongoing or anticipated communication with another person or persons.[10] To become aware of your level of CA, complete the communication apprehension measure in Rating Scale 5.2.

RATING SCALE 5.2 **Personal Report of Communication Apprehension (PRCA-24)**

This instrument is composed of twenty-four statements concerning your feelings about communicating with other people.[11] Indicate in the space provided the degree to which each statement applies to you by marking whether you (1) strongly agree, (2) agree, (3) are undecided, (4) disagree, or (5) strongly disagree with each statement. There are no right or wrong answers. Many of the statements are intentionally similar. Work quickly and record your first impression.

_____ 1. I dislike participating in group discussions.

_____ 2. Generally, I am comfortable while participating in a group discussion.

_____ 3. I am tense and nervous while participating in group discussions.

_____ 4. I like to get involved in group discussions.

_____ 5. Engaging in a group discussion with new people makes me tense and nervous.

_____ 6. I am calm and relaxed while participating in group discussions.

_____ 7. Generally, I am nervous when I have to participate in a meeting.

_____ 8. Usually I am calm and relaxed while participating in meetings.

_____ 9. I am very calm and relaxed when I am called on to express an opinion at a meeting.

_____ 10. I am afraid to express myself at meetings.

_____ 11. Communicating at meetings usually makes me uncomfortable.

_____ 12. I am very relaxed when answering questions at a meeting.

_____ 13. While participating in a conversation with a new acquaintance, I feel very nervous.

_____ 14. I have no fear of speaking up in conversations.

_____ 15. Ordinarily I am very tense and nervous in conversations.

_____ 16. Ordinarily I am very calm and relaxed in conversations.

_____ 17. While conversing with a new acquaintance, I feel very relaxed.

_____ 18. I'm afraid to speak up in conversations.

_____ 19. I have no fear of giving a speech.

_____ 20. Certain parts of my body feel very tense and rigid while I am giving a speech.

_____ 21. I feel relaxed while giving a speech.

_____ 22. My thoughts become confused and jumbled when I am giving a speech.

_____ 23. I face the prospect of giving a speech with confidence.

_____ 24. While giving a speech I get so nervous I forget facts I really know.

Scoring Instructions: The PRCA permits computation of one total score and four subscores. The subscores are related to communication apprehension in each of four common communication contexts: group discussions, meetings, interpersonal conversations, and public speaking. To compute your scores, merely add or subtract the scores for each item as indicated below.

Subscore Desired	Scoring Formula
Group discussion	Add 18 to the total of your scores for items 2, 4, and 6; then subtract your scores for items 1, 3, and 5 from this total.

terms & definitions

Communication apprehension (CA) fear or anxiety associated with ongoing or anticipated communication with another person or persons.

Meetings	Add 18 to the total of your scores for items 8, 9, and 12; then subtract your scores for items 7, 10, and 11 from this total.
Interpersonal conversations	Add 18 to the total of your scores for items 14, 16, and 17; then subtract your scores for items 13, 15, and 18 from this total.
Public speaking	Add 18 to the total of your scores for items 19, 21, and 23; then subtract your scores for items 20, 22, and 24 from this total.

To obtain your total score on the PRCA, simply add your four subscores together. Your total score should range between 24 and 120. If your score is below 24, or above 120, you have made a mistake in computing it.

Scores on the four contexts (group discussion, meetings, interpersonal conversations, and public speaking) can range from a low of 6 to a high of 30. Any score above 18 indicates some degree of apprehension. If your score for the public speaking context is above 18, you are like the overwhelming majority of Americans.

Average scores on the PRCA-24 are as follows:

Total Score:	66
Group discussion	15
Meetings	16
Interpersonal conversations	14
Public speaking	19

People who score high in CA experience fear when communicating with others in a variety of contexts, including in meetings, in small groups, one on one, or when giving a speech. People low in CA rarely experience fear when communicating with others. One situation in which most people have a degree of fear and anxiety, even those low in CA, is when speaking in front of others in more formal situations, such as giving a business presentation.

Research suggests that one in five Americans experiences an abnormally high level of CA in all contexts.[12] For these individuals, CA is a disorder that prevents them from doing their best in the workplace. Highly apprehensive individuals have a tendency to behave in one of the following three ways.[13] First, they avoid communication. Rather than informally socializing with colleagues outside of work, for example, apprehensive individuals make excuses for not attending these social situations. Unfortunately, these informal situations are often opportunities for professionals to network with and influence each other. Second, when apprehensive individuals cannot actually avoid communication, they tend to withdraw from it. Rather than speaking up at a meeting and presenting their ideas, they tend to remain silent. Unfortunately, this reduces their ability to implement their ideas and influence others. Because of their communication withdrawal, individuals who are high in CA are often overlooked for promotions. Third, they experience communication disruptions. Apprehensive individuals have a tendency to communicate using improper articulation and pronunciation as well as too many vocal disfluencies or interrupters, such as "uhh," "ahh," "um," or "like." Because of these communication disruptions, apprehensive individuals tend not to be taken seriously.

You can adapt to and lead those who are low in CA by following these guidelines:

- *Place them in positions with high communication demands.* Many leadership positions require professionals who can make presentations and facilitate meetings with ease and comfort.

- *Monitor the quality and quantity of their communication.* Although nearly everyone experiences some degree of CA, it's important to monitor those who are low in this trait. These individuals are less guarded about their communication and may talk too much or say things they later wish they hadn't said. So a simple reminder of the possible consequences of phrasing statements carelessly or of not being discreet can help a person avoid "putting his foot in his mouth."

Here are a few recommendations for adapting to those high in CA so as to enhance workplace communication:

- *Monitor how you perceive quiet people.* Understand that a person's apprehensiveness is to a large extent outside his or her control. Check your perceptions of others by focusing on their work performance rather than their talk or lack of talk.

- *Refrain from putting highly apprehensive individuals in situations or positions requiring a high level of communication.* Goodness-of-fit is achieved when the communication demands of a position fit a person's personality and communication traits. For example, staffing a receptionist's position with a person high in CA would not be considered a good fit.

- *Provide alternative channels for communication.* For example, rather than requiring all staff members to make oral presentations at work, allow individuals options, such as communicating through memos, email, or voice mail.

- *Inform highly apprehensive individuals of options for interventions.* There are a number of instructional, treatment, and medical interventions for managing communication apprehension.[14] These are discussed in more detail in Chapter 12.

Argumentativeness

Argumentativeness is a communication trait of people who have a tendency to advocate strongly for their own position on an issue and criticize the positions of other people.[15] A person who is argumentative enjoys a good debate. To determine your own argumentativeness, complete the self-assessment instrument in Rating Scale 5.3. This will help you become more aware of this communication trait and how it may affect others' perceptions of you as well as how you perceive others.

RATING SCALE 5.3 Measure of Argumentativeness

This questionnaire contains statements about arguing controversial issues.[16] Indicate in the space provided the degree to which each statement applies to you by marking whether it is (1) almost never true, (2) rarely true, (3) occasionally true, (4) often true, or (5) almost always true. (Remember, consider each item in terms of *arguing or debating controversial issues;* the scale is not focusing on personal, emotional arguments.)

_____ 1. While in an argument, I worry that the person I am arguing with will form a negative impression of me.

_____ 2. Arguing over controversial issues improves my intelligence.

_____ 3. I enjoy avoiding arguments.

_____ 4. I am energetic and enthusiastic when I argue.

_____ 5. Once I finish an argument I promise myself that I will not get into another.

_____ 6. Arguing with a person creates more problems for me than it solves.

_____ 7. I have a pleasant, good feeling when I win a point in an argument.

_____ 8. When I finish arguing with someone I feel nervous and upset.

_____ 9. I enjoy a good argument over a controversial issue.

_____ 10. I get an unpleasant feeling when I realize I am about to get into an argument.

_____ 11. I enjoy defending my point of view on an issue.

_____ 12. I am happy when I keep an argument from happening.

_____ 13. I do not like to miss the opportunity to argue a controversial issue.

_____ 14. I prefer being with people who rarely disagree with me.

_____ 15. I consider an argument an exciting intellectual challenge.

_____ 16. I find myself unable to think of effective points during an argument.

terms & definitions

Argumentativeness a tendency to advocate strongly for one's own position on an issue and criticize the positions of other people.

_____ 17. I feel refreshed and satisfied after an argument on a controversial issue.

_____ 18. I have the ability to do well in an argument.

_____ 19. I try to avoid getting into arguments.

_____ 20. I feel excitement when I expect that a conversation I am in is leading to an argument.

Scoring Instructions: To compute your argumentativeness score, do the following:

Step 1: Add your scores on items 2, 4, 7, 9, 11, 13, 15, 17, 18, and 20.

Step 2: Add 60 to the sum you obtained in step 1.

Step 3: Add your scores for items 1, 3, 5, 6, 8, 10, 12, 14, 16, and 19.

Step 4: Subtract the total you obtained in step 3 from the total obtained in step 2.

If the number you obtain in step 4 is between 73 and 100, you tend to be high in argumentativeness. If the number is between 56 and 72, you tend to be moderately argumentative. If the number is between 20 and 55, you tend to be low in argumentativeness.

To determine your tendency to approach argumentative situations, add your scores on items 2, 4, 7, 9, 11, 13, 15, 17, 18, and 20.

To determine your tendency to avoid argumentative situations, add your scores on items 1, 3, 5, 6, 8, 10, 12, 14, 16, and 19.

Argumentativeness trait: subtract the total of the ten tendency-to-avoid items from the total of the ten tendency-to-approach items. Positive scores indicate a tendency to approach arguments. A higher positive score (between 20 and 40) indicates high argumentativeness. Negative scores reflect a tendency to avoid arguments. A higher negative score (between –20 and –40) reflects low argumentativeness.

Do you know people who like to argue? Although many people perceive arguing to be a destructive form of communication, if it's done well, it's quite constructive; and an ability to argue clearly is valued in business and professional settings.[17] People who are argumentative can think critically and argue for or against a particular proposal using reasons and evidence. Research clearly indicates that professionals who can argue well are also considered more effective in their jobs.[18] Specifically, highly argumentative individuals, when compared to less argumentative individuals, tend to be better at taking perspective or understanding another person's position on an issue. For example, when deciding how to operate the registration desk of a medical facility, a supervisor and her staff have different ideas. In a constructive argument, they each present their reason for operating the registration desk in a particular manner. Because the supervisor is high in argumentativeness, she values looking at an issue critically, from all perspectives, in order to make an informed decision. She is persuaded by the good reasoning staff members use, and she takes their perspective even though she had her own ideas of how the registration area should be arranged and organized. Individuals high in argumentativeness are naturally curious and thus tend to learn more about others, including their customers or their competitors' products and services. Another quality of people high in argumentativeness is that they tend to be better leaders and have followers who are more satisfied and committed to their jobs.[19] For example, when there is disagreement on a policy or procedure, argumentative leaders have a way of managing the emotions, while helping others critically examine the issues by focusing on the evidence or the facts rather than on what a few people might say.

Although there are a number of benefits to being argumentative, people who are low in argumentativeness tend to perceive highly argumentative individuals as verbally aggressive and overbearing at times. You can adapt to less argumentative individuals in the following ways to enhance workplace communication:

- *Be aware that individuals who are not argumentative tend to perceive highly argumentative individuals as being verbally aggressive.* If you get a defensive reaction from the other person when you begin to argue, know that they're probably interpreting your messages as an attack.

- *Use* **feed-forward messages**, *which are messages that inform others of how to process information.* For example, "What I am about to say is not intended to be verbally aggressive, but I would like to challenge your ideas."

terms & definitions

Feed-forward messages
messages that inform others of how to process information from you.

- *Use nonverbally immediate behaviors when arguing.* Monitor your tone of voice for warmth, keep an open body orientation, and lean forward rather than away from the other person (which can signal defensiveness). These nonverbal behaviors add warmth and communicate approachability rather than aggressiveness.

- *Use nonverbally responsive behaviors when listening to others argue.* Leaning forward, using direct eye contact, nodding your head, and using back channel cues are examples of nonverbally responsive behaviors. These nonverbal behaviors signal to others that you're actively listening to them and their arguments.

To adapt to highly argumentative individuals, try these guidelines:

- *Engage them in debates.* Make sure you have logical claims and evidence to support your claims. For example, when meeting with your supervisor to request more space for your retail business, make sure you go into the meeting prepared with sales figures that indicate how you are growing your business.

- *Play the devil's advocate.* A devil's advocate is someone who criticizes or opposes something purely to provoke a discussion or an argument. A devil's advocate is in many ways an ally whose goal is to help strengthen another's case by pointing out weaknesses. For example, if you own a restaurant and one highly argumentative waiter suggests that the restaurant is losing business because the menu doesn't include healthier food items, challenge his ideas rather than simply agreeing with him.

- *Learn how to argue.* Although argumentativeness is to some extent biologically based,[20] people can learn how to argue. It just may come more naturally for some than for others. Chapter 13 provides more detail on how to organize, develop, and present arguments.

The Power of Perspective[21]

You're undoubtedly familiar with the story of the three blind men who came across an elephant. The one who bumped into the elephant's trunk was certain that he'd found a snake. The unsighted man holding on to the elephant's tail thought he'd found a broom, and the man who embraced the elephant's leg was convinced he was clinging to a tree. A leader who relies only on her or his observations can easily miss seeing the whole picture. Effective leaders know the importance of looking at issues from diverse points of view to gain an accurate understanding of issues and problems.

Susan Docherty, who leads the U.S. sales, service, and marketing team at General Motors, wants to make sure she sees the elephant and not the snake, broom, or tree. She makes it a point to ensure that there are different types of people who offer her advice and opinions on a variety of issues.

> *I like building teams with people who come from very different backgrounds and have very different experiences. I don't just mean diverse teams, in terms of men and women or people of different color or origin. I like people who have worked in different places in the world than I have because they bring a lot more context to the discussion. That's something that I value a tremendous amount.*

> *I make sure that when I'm looking at people for my team, it's not just what's on their resume—their strengths or weaknesses or what they've accomplished—but it's the way they think. I can learn twice as much, twice as quickly, if I've got people who think differently than I do around the table.*

Whether you are in a leadership role or not, it's important to understand and value the perspective of others. Each of the blind men was undoubtedly convinced of the accuracy of their own conclusion as to what they had discovered when encountering the elephant. But if they would have shared their different perspectives, they would have reached a more informed conclusion. To make sure you know an elephant when you bump into one, seek diverse perspectives to make sure you're getting the whole picture.

Understanding the relationships between personality and communication traits reveals how and why individuals differ in their workplace communication. Understanding how and why people differ in their workplace communication will allow you to adapt your communication to them more effectively. Some of your communication behaviors are natural, meaning that they are influenced by your biology or the genes you inherited. However, you can learn to modify and adapt your communication in order to interact more effectively with others and become a leader in the workplace.

leaders on leadership

Adapting to Cultural Differences

Culture is a learned system of knowledge, behavior, attitudes, beliefs, values, and norms shared by a group of people.[22] Culture and communication, says anthropologist Edward T. Hall, are inseparable—you can't talk about one without discussing the other.[23] There is ample evidence to document the influence of culture on how you work and live.[24] According to researcher Geert Hofstede, your culture is like "mental software" that helps you understand the world.[25] Like the software and operating system in a computer, your culture provides a framework that shapes the messages you send and receive every day.

If you're like most people, you're unaware of your computer's software until a glitch occurs and your computer fails to work properly. Your cultural software is very similar. It remains invisible until there's a problem. Problems occur when you work with others whose "cultural software systems" are different from your own. For example, some cultures are less time sensitive than others. Rather than meeting an important deadline for a particular project or arriving early for a meeting, you might find people from some cultures not being worried about punctuality and deadlines. To them, deadlines and start times for meetings are fluid and can always be changed. Such problems occur with regularity in business and professional settings, particularly as the workplace becomes more diverse and as we interact more often with people from different or unfamiliar cultures.[26] For example, by 2050, whites will make up 46 percent of the population and blacks will make up 15 percent. Hispanics, who make up about 15 percent of the population today, will account for 30 percent in 2050. Asians, who make up about 5 percent of the population currently, are projected to increase to 9 percent by 2050.[27]

If there is a problem, one way to resolve it is to better understand the **cultural context** for the communication, which consists of the nonverbal cues that surround and give meaning to the messages. In this sense, *all* nonverbal cues are part of the cultural context. In some cultures, people give more weight to the surrounding nonverbal context than to the explicit verbal message when interpreting the overall meaning of a message. Other cultures place less emphasis on the nonverbal context and greater emphasis on what someone says.

For example, when you interview for a job, you may be scanning the face of your interviewer and looking for nonverbal clues about the impression you're making on the interviewer. These contextual cues give meaning to help you interpret the interviewer's message. Edward T. Hall helped us understand the importance of cultural context when he categorized cultures as either high context or low context.[28]

In **high-context cultures**, nonverbal cues are extremely important in interpreting messages. Communicators rely heavily on context—they gather subtle information from facial expression, vocal cues, and even silence in interpreting messages. People from Asian, Arab, and Southern European countries are more likely to draw on context to help them interpret messages.

People in **low-context cultures** rely more explicitly on language and on the meanings of words and use fewer contextual cues to send and interpret information. Individuals from low-context cultures, such as North Americans, Germans, and Scandinavians, may perceive people from high-context cultures as less attractive, knowledgeable, and trustworthy because they violate unspoken low-context cultural rules of conduct and communication. For example, people from high-context cultures may be perceived to be "beating around the bush" rather than getting to the point, and indirectness may sometimes be perceived as manipulation. Individuals from low-context cultures often are

To understand the cultural context of communication, it helps to attend to all nonverbal cues, including the attire of your communication partner.

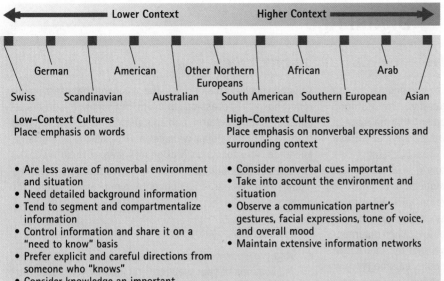

FIGURE 5.2 A Scale of High-Context and Low-Context Cultures

From James C. McCroskey, An Introduction to Rhetorical Communication: A Western Rhetorical Perspective, 9e. Published by Allyn and Bacon/Merrill Education, Boston, MA. Copyright © 2006 by Pearson Education. Reprinted by permission of the publisher.

less skilled in interpreting unspoken contextual messages.[29] Figure 5.2 summarizes differences in communication style between high-context and low-context cultures.

Cultural Values

By paying attention to what a culture values, you can learn important clues about how to adapt your communication so that you respond appropriately to others' communication, establish quality relationships, and avoid making embarrassing errors. Geert Hofstede has identified five dimensions of cultural values: individualism versus collectivism, distribution of power (either centralized or decentralized), avoidance of uncertainty versus tolerance for uncertainty, short-term versus long-term orientation, and masculine versus feminine cultural perspectives.[30]

INDIVIDUALISM VERSUS COLLECTIVISM People from **individualistic cultures**, like that of the United States, have learned to value their own interests more than those of the overall group. Individualistic cultures offer their members a great deal of freedom, based on the belief that freedom makes it possible for each person to achieve personal success. The U.S. workplace reflects the individualistic culture, with, for example, performance reviews that determine whether individuals are rewarded, based on whether they met their goals and objectives, and salary bonuses that reward individual effort.

People from **collectivistic cultures**, like that of Japan and other East Asian cultures, learn to value the interests of their group or community more than their individual interests. Collectivistic cultures offer their members a close-knit social network whose members have a primary loyalty toward one another and the group to which they belong. Collectivistic cultures value what people do together and reward group achievement. In collectivistic cultures, to receive individual recognition would be considered dishonorable because it elevates the individual above the group. One of this book's authors, who used to work in the airline industry, remembers a flight to Tokyo on which one of the employees of a Japanese company refused his first-class seat so as to not dishonor the other members of the group he was traveling with.

DECENTRALIZED VERSUS CENTRALIZED POWER Some cultures, referred to as **decentralized power cultures**, value a broad distribution of power. The power is in the

Communication Skills FOR A **Digital Age**

Making Organizational Websites Culturally Friendly

"I'm lovin' it." You may quickly recognize this popular slogan and jingle, used by McDonald's restaurants. The fast-food chain has been very successful in spreading this message of "love" for their people and products around the globe. Have you ever considered how they do that so successfully? One major consideration is their company's web presence. McDonald's executives and web designers have taken a careful and thoughtful approach to developing web presence that is relatable among various cultures.[31] They consider cultural values, such as high and low context, when determining color, content, layout, image choice, and the interactive nature of the site. In higher context cultures, images and content tend to focus on the value of a product to bring people together, and in low-context cultures they tend to market products as something that can directly benefit an individual. For example, in low-context Germany, the McDonald's site's main page contains an image of a young man, sitting on top of the hood of a car alone, enjoying the peace and quiet, and eating some McD's French fries. "I'm lovin' it" is plastered across the page, just above his face. In a high-context India, the website images focus on togetherness, such as one with a picture of a father and son, racing through a supermarket aisle. The boy sits in the cart, with a McDonald's Happy Meal in his hands, and looks up at his father, who leans down toward the boy as they both laugh. The "I'm lovin' it" text is on the side of the page, smaller in size. This page seems to highlight the relationship between the father and son as the idea they are both "lovin'."[32]

The explosion of the Internet in business in the last generation has led companies to examine their current web presence. Are businesses developing websites that are culturally friendly? A recent survey indicates that no, many companies are not ready for the global Internet marketplace. Almost two thirds of U.S. companies surveyed have not considered moderating their web presence for an intercultural audience.[33] When considering the new generation entering the workforce, and their reputation as a "wired" generation, organizations would be well-served to maintain a culturally friendly corporate website. What should a leader consider when developing a culturally-friendly web presence?

Researchers from New York University examined the cultural implications of several U.S. sites, and they related those to user-reported positive impressions and usability.[34] Specific cultural markers, font, language use, color choice, and image selection played a major role in the likelihood that users would report positive impressions of a site. Put simply, the organizations that took cultural considerations into account were more likely to have their website rated positively by a diverse audience. And following McDonald's lead, diverse websites can certainly enhance a product or organizations' image in a global marketplace, translating to more opportunities for growth.

Applying Your Skills[35]

- **Analyze your audience.** When considering the cultural implications of your website, first identify your target audience. You can make better judgments about the cultural implications of many items on your site if you first know which cultural categories to consider. McDonald's has done this successfully, and they use this information to adapt their web presence in various cultures accordingly.

- **Pay attention to content.** Consider the values and worldview of your audience. What is important to them? Make sure the content reflects information that would be relevant to the worldview of your potential audience. Using the high- and low-context cultural values, McDonald's selected content and images that fit best with the culture.

- **Focus on language.** Avoid colloquial language, jargon, and overusing symbolic language that doesn't directly translate. Also, if your site will have a language translator, consider how the verbal messages you use will translate into other languages. Keep in mind that some cultures value modesty, whereas others value taking pride in your accomplishments. All this should play in part in how you present yourself online.

- **Consider your color choices.** Colors have specific meanings in various cultures. For example, red can mean luck, death, blood, or life. Be aware of your audience and their interpretation of colors. Select colors that are aesthetically pleasing but also communicate the message you desire.

- **Use appropriate page design and technology.** Not everyone reads the same way, and that can translate into web design. In some countries, the people do not have the same level of broadband Internet access, which could impact the download speed. Keep this in mind when considering links, images, and other technologies such as animation and flash players.

people, or the many, not in any one single person or group. In the workplace, this cultural value is reflected in how decisions are made. For example, it's not unusual for a leader to conduct a meeting at which employees examine and discuss problems together, and then each employee has a vote on how the problem should be solved or what decision is going to be made. The power is in the individual votes or voices of the employees rather than in a single leader. Research suggests that people from Australia, Israel, Denmark, New Zealand, and Ireland typically prefer minimal power differences between members of the culture; they strive for more equal distribution of authority and control.[36]

Other cultures, referred to as **centralized power cultures**, value a more concentrated or narrow distribution of power. The power is in one person or a select few. The general assumption is that some people will have more power, control, and influence than others. Professionals from cultures that value centralized power are probably more comfortable with managerial styles in which clear lines of authority are followed. Rather than calling a meeting and asking employees to vote on how a problem should be solved or how a decision should be made, leaders are more likely to make the decision without consulting with group members and without group members objecting to the leader having most of the power.

ACCEPTANCE OF UNCERTAINTY VERSUS PREFERENCE FOR CERTAINTY The contemporary workplace is full of uncertainty and change.[37] **Uncertainty avoidance** is a measure of how accepting a culture is of a lack of predictability. Cultures low in uncertainty avoidance are those in which people tolerate uncertainty; they have learned to live with the fact that their ability to predict the future is limited. Many professionals from these cultures are more comfortable taking risks, and they tend to be more tolerant of others who engage in behavior that goes against what is considered normal. Verbal messages such as "It will work itself out" or "Let's go with the flow" are indicative of cultures in which uncertainty avoidance is low. People from Singapore, Hong Kong, Jamaica, Denmark, and the United States are more comfortable with uncertainty.[38]

Cultures high in uncertainty avoidance are those in which people don't like uncertainty; thus they learn ways to structure their lives to provide as much certainty and predictability as possible. Cultures in which people need certainty to feel secure are more likely to develop and enforce rigid rules for behavior and to establish elaborate codes of conduct. Verbal messages such as "Let's develop an action plan that includes the tasks that need to be completed, who is responsible for the task, and the deadlines" or "What does company policy say about that issue?" are indicative of cultures where uncertainty avoidance is high. People from Greece, Portugal, and Guatemala generally do not like uncertainty.[39]

SHORT-TERM VERSUS LONG-TERM ORIENTATION Given the pressure they are under to make money and turn an instant profit, it's difficult for some leaders and professionals from Western industrialized cultures to understand that not all of the world's organizations are interested in short-term results. Cultures that have a long-term orientation value long-term commitment, thriftiness, and perseverance. People in these cultures value delayed gratification and are willing to work hard knowing that the profits and rewards of their hard work may not materialize for a number of years. For example, companies who develop an expensive but high-quality product are willing to take an initial loss knowing that the product and loyal customer base will eventually lead to a profit. The massive Toyota recall of early 2010 was especially problematic for Toyota Motor Corporation of Japan. The Toyota recall was highly inconsistent with Japan's long-term orientation culture, and therefore the recall had a more damaging impact on Toyota's corporate image.[40] In addition to Japan, countries that tend to have a long-term orientation include South Korea, Taiwan, and China. In contrast, people in cultures that have a short-term orientation value fulfilling social obligations and protecting oneself from embarrassment. These cultures tend to be focused on short-term results, such as turning a profit by developing less expensive products. Countries that tend to have a more short-term orientation include Norway, Pakistan, Canada, East Africa, and the United States.[41]

MASCULINE VERSUS FEMININE VALUES Some cultures emphasize traditional male values, such as getting things done and being more assertive; other cultures place greater emphasis on traditional female values: building relationships and seeking peace and harmony with others. These values are not only about biological differences; they are general approaches to interacting with other individuals. People from **masculine cultures** tend to value more

terms & definitions

Centralized power cultures cultures that value a more concentrated or narrow distribution of power; power is held by one person or a select few.

Uncertainty avoidance a measure of how accepting a culture is of a lack of predictability.

Masculine cultures cultures in which people have a task orientation and tend to value achievement, heroism, material wealth, and more traditional roles for men and women.

Globalization requires workers to adapt to working with others despite different cultural orientations. This was exemplified by the crew members of Expedition 28, (including NASA astronauts, Russian cosmonauts, and a Japanese astronaut), who are shown here in the Service Module of the International Space Station

traditional roles for men and women. People (both men and women) from masculine cultures value achievement, heroism, material wealth, and making things happen. They tend to have more of a task orientation. People from Japan, Australia, Venezuela, Italy, Mexico, and Great Britain tend to have a cultural value that is more masculine than feminine.[42]

Men and women from **feminine cultures** tend to value caring for the less fortunate, being sensitive to others, and enhancing the overall quality of life.[43] They tend to have more of a social orientation and to focus more on collective concerns, such as cooperative problem solving and maintaining a friendly atmosphere. People from Sweden, the Netherlands, Denmark, Finland, Chile, and Thailand tend to have a cultural orientation that is more feminine than masculine.[44] A clear example of the impact of this cultural value was the cooperative spirit of the trapped Chilean miners who worked together to ensure their survival in August 2010. Through their own cooperative efforts in addition to their government's effort to work cooperatively with other countries and agencies, all thirty-three miners returned to the surface alive.[45]

Despite the distinctions just discussed, we caution you to avoid making sweeping generalizations about every person in any cultural group. Just as there are differences between and among cultures, there are differences *within* cultural groups. For example, for centuries, most countries had "masculine" cultures. Men and their conquests were featured in history books and men had more influence in all aspects of any society than women. But today's cultural anthropologists see some shift in these values. This is reflected in a very slowly growing number of women who serve in leadership roles in some of the world's major organizations and institutions.[46]

Strategies for Adapting

In their book *Globality: Competing with Everyone from Everywhere for Everything*, consultants Harold Sirkin, James Hemerling, and Arindam Bhattacharya examine how globalization is causing organizations to rethink how they do business.[47] The authors urge U.S. companies to "adapt, adopt, and synthesize ideas from everyone and everywhere" to compete in a global marketplace.[48] Put another way, our ability to survive in a global marketplace will depend on our abilities to cross cultures and to work with people who don't think, believe, or act as we do. The following strategies have been shown to help people interact more effectively in international and multicultural environments.

- *Be patient.* Keep in mind that working in an intercultural setting may be just as frustrating for the people you are trying to communicate with as it is for you. It is important to understand that being patient will communicate openness and tolerance.

- *Establish rules.* Because cultures place different values on things such as meeting deadlines and punctuality, some rules for business should be established. Rather than having the ground rules imposed from someone who is not directly involved in the exchange, try developing some rules by soliciting ideas and discussing these with team members.

- *Ask questions.* Do not be afraid to find out the answers to some confusing messages the old-fashioned way: by asking. A simple explanation may be all you require to move ahead with agreement. Often, such directness is what is missing from an intercultural exchange.

- *Respect others.* You cannot earn respect without first demonstrating it to others. This is the basis for all intercultural communication and will go a long way in enhancing your experience.

- *Write things down.* It has been shown that people who do not yet speak another language proficiently can generally better understand the written word. Writing things down is another way to ensure you have the most accurate communication possible.

- *Be aware of time.* Not everyone in the world thinks "time is money." Fostering an understanding about time and how it is viewed in another culture will help to build quality business relationships. Keep that in mind when making decisions about deadlines and meetings.

- *Exercise caution with humor.* Be very careful about using humor in an intercultural environment. What you may find funny could be quite offensive to another. In some cultures, such as in Russian culture, humorous banter is not appropriate in a business environment.

- *Double-check solutions.* In any business setting, double-checking is important to ensure that all parties are in agreement. This means repeating solutions, conclusions, meeting dates and times, and deadlines. Having everything in written form also helps with double-checking.

- *Be positive.* When faced with problems, steer clear of blame and conflict. Stay positive, analyze the problem, and work as a team to build strategies and solutions to ensure the problem never occurs again.

- *Engage in self-reflection.* A good intercultural communicator not only looks outward but also looks inward. Take time to reflect on your own communication and management style and see where you can improve as an individual.

Understanding the relationships between culture and communication traits allows us to better understand how people communicate and interact with each other. Next, we examine the relationships between gender and communication.

RECAP

Cultural Values

Cultural Values	Description
Individualism	Individualistic cultures value personal interests above group interests.
Collectivism	Collectivistic cultures value group or community interests above individual interests.
Decentralized Power Distribution	Decentralized cultures value putting power in the hands of the population, rather than one person or group.
Centralized Power Distribution	Centralized cultures value putting the power in the hands of one leader or a select few.
Tolerance of Uncertainty	Cultures that accept uncertainty tolerate "not knowing" and understand that their ability to predict the future is limited.
Need for Certainty	Cultures that value certainty learn ways to structure life to provide as much certainty and predictability as possible.
Short-Term Orientation	Short-term orientation cultures value change and are more interested in and focused on short-term results.
Long-Term Orientation	Long-term orientation cultures value long-term commitment and respect for tradition.
Masculine Values	Masculine cultures value a task orientation and being more assertive.
Feminine Values	Feminine cultures value caring for others and enhancing the overall quality of life.

Adapting to Gender Differences

Men and women communicate differently at work.[49] Becoming aware of these differences and adapting communication accordingly is just another way you can enhance your leadership effectiveness in the workplace. Although *sex* and *gender* are related, and although the terms often are used interchangeably, there are some distinctions that we would like to make. **Sex** refers to biological characteristics that are present from the time of birth. Different pairs of chromosomes—XX for females, XY for males—provide clear genetic coding for how the body will develop. We use the terms *male* and *female* to describe biological sex.

Gender refers to the cultural and psychological characteristics that are associated with our biological sex; gender is a cultural construction of what it means to be a man or women. The terms *masculine* and *feminine* are used most often when referring to gender. In many ways, your gender is an implicit rulebook that informs you of how you are to behave and communicate. Unlike sex, which is biological, gender is learned or developed through the nurturing process and through your interactions in your culture.

Although not all biological males (people of a particular sex) communicate in a masculine manner (that is, in a way considered typical or appropriate for their gender) nor all females in a feminine manner, your sex and gender are highly correlated. Research reveals that men in many cultures tend to approach communication by focusing on the content dimension of communication, whereas women tend to approach communication by focusing on the relational dimension.[50] As we first noted in Chapter 1, the **content dimension** of human communication focuses on *what* is said, or the verbal message. The **relational dimension** involves *how* the verbal message is said, based on tone of voice, facial expressions, and other nonverbal behaviors. The latter dimension often tells us how to interpret the former. Next we explore how gender affects communication at work by examining powerful and powerless language and conversational rituals.

terms & definitions

Sex biological characteristics present from birth that identify an individual as male or female.

Gender the cultural and psychological characteristics that are associated with biological sex.

Content dimension the communication dimension that focuses on what is said; the verbal message.

Relational dimension the communication dimension that focuses on how a message is said; the nonverbal message.

Powerful language language that is stereotypically masculine: direct, assertive, task-oriented, and focused more on the content of a message.

Powerless language language that is stereotypically feminine: indirect and focused more on the quality of a relationship than on the information being exchanged.

Powerful and Powerless Language

Linguist Robin Lakoff was one of the first researchers to identify a power difference between men and women's use of language. She described these different types as powerful and powerless language.[51] **Powerful language** is stereotypically masculine and is characterized by assertiveness. It tends to be task oriented—oriented toward getting things done—and it focuses more on the information being exchanged (the *what*) than on relational elements (the *how*) in the message. **Powerless language** is stereotypically feminine and is characterized by an emphasis on connecting with others and fostering harmonious relationships. Powerless language focuses more on the quality of the relationships between individuals than on the information being exchanged. More emphasis is placed on the nonverbal elements of communication (*how* something is communicated) than on content (*what* is communicated).[52]

Here are a few examples of powerful and powerless verbal messages and how men and women use them differently.[53]

- *Women use more hedges than men.* A *hedge* is a statement that limits the speaker's responsibility. It softens or weakens the

Gender differences in language use and conversational rituals affect communication in the workplace.

meaning of the idea. Examples of hedge words include *somewhat, perhaps, possible,* or *maybe.* For example:

Powerful Verbal Message: "They are entering our market. We need to develop a strategy that will prevent them from taking our customers."

Powerless Verbal Message: "It seems *possible* that they are entering our market. *Perhaps* we should develop a strategy that will prevent them from taking our customers."

- *Women use more tag questions than men.* A *tag question* is a combination of a sentence and a question, treated as a single unit. Sample messages include the following:

Powerful Verbal Message: "That's an interesting idea."

Powerless Verbal Message: "That's an interesting idea, isn't it?"

- *Women use more intensifiers than men.* An *intensifier* is a word that is evaluative and that conveys emotions. Examples of intensifiers include *extremely, tremendously,* and *incredibly.* For example:

Powerful Verbal Message: "I'm happy for you and proud of your accomplishment."

Powerless Verbal Message: "I'm incredibly happy for you and so proud of your *tremendous* accomplishment."

"Must you precede everything you say with 'This is your captain speaking'?"

The New Yorker Collection 2003 Leo Cullum from cartoonbank. com. All Rights Reserved.

Research has shown that people who use powerless messages are perceived as having a lower social status and as being less knowledgeable, trustworthy, and dynamic than people who use powerful messages.[54] In one workplace study, both male and female employees perceived female leaders as less effective if they communicated using powerless verbal messages.[55] In another study, researchers found that people who used powerful language were perceived as being more credible than those who used powerless language.[56]

Conversational Rituals

Linguist Deborah Tannen examines how men and women communicate differently on the job.[57] Tannen argues that men and women use different **conversational rituals**, which are routine scripts we have learned to use when talking and responding to others. According to Tannen, men learn to send and receive messages through a *status lens* (see Figure 5.3). A status lens is a perception process that leads men to focus on who has more prestige and power in the conversation. The language men use puts them in a "one-up" or "one-down" position in conversation and determines their status level. The stereotypical example of men one-upping each other with the size of fish they caught on their fishing trip illustrates how men use communication to assert status. According to Tannen, when men want to put someone down, they use direct statements, such as "Your fish is smaller than the one I caught."

Many women, according to Tannen, communicate using a *connection lens* (see Figure 5.3). A connection lens is a perception process that leads women to focus on who is closer or further away from them psychologically or emotionally. Many women use communication to bring others closer or to keep others at a distance. For example, a woman may fail to invite another woman to an after-work social function. According to Tannen, women punish others by pushing them away and keeping them at a distance.

The problem with conversational rituals is that they can sometimes misfire. Put simply, the message sent doesn't equal the message received. Tannen mentions that when someone

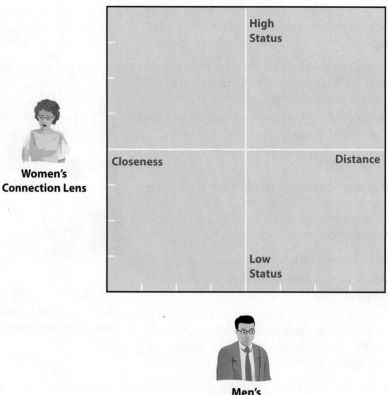

FIGURE 5.3 **Gender Lenses**

in the United States greets you, they often use the conversation-opening ritual, "Hi, how you're doing?" They expect the other person to interpret the question ritually rather than literally. They expect, "I'm fine. How are you?" If they get a complete health report, the ritual has misfired.

Here are a few of the conversational rituals that Tannen has identified in her research:[58]

RITUAL APOLOGY Women often say, "I'm sorry" and mean it not as an apology but as a *conversational smoother* or as a way of expressing concern. Like a drop of oil added to a squeaky hinge, a conversational smoother allows a person to communicate more smoothly and with less friction. For example, during a meeting Angelica states, "Oh, I'm sorry, I have one more item that I would like to add to the agenda." With this statement, Angelica is not actually apologizing but rather using ritual apology to appear less abrupt and possibly to express concern for other people's time. In terms of the female connection lens, Angelica uses ritual apology as a way to bring others closer. Ritual apology may misfire when men interpret the ritual as an actual apology. From the point of view of male status lens, Angelica may be undermining her authority by appearing less organized and therefore weak.

RITUAL OPPOSITION Men often play the role of devil's advocate in conversations with others, and this conversational ritual has been known to misfire when it is used with women. Consider the following conversation between Dean, who is editor of a men's fitness magazine, and Sarah, who is a writer for the magazine. Sarah pitches the following idea for a feature article:

Sarah: How about a story about men who are compulsive about fitness to the point that it's dangerous and unhealthy?

Dean: How does your idea fulfill the mission of the magazine, which is to promote health and fitness?

Sarah: Well, the article would conclude with a list of ways that men can be fit and healthy in a balanced manner.

Dean: But isn't compulsive fitness an issue that women face more than men?

A woman may interpret this conversation ritual as a challenge or a rejection of her idea, whereas a man might use the ritual to tease out ideas and explore them more critically. Based on this exchange, Sarah may decide the idea is not a good one and drop it. However, Dean may not be opposed to the idea but wants to probe Sarah's thinking and her angle for the feature article.

COMPLIMENTS Exchanging compliments is a conversational ritual, especially for women. According to Tannen, when a woman compliments another woman, she also expects to receive a compliment.[59] Exchanging compliments is a way to relate to and connect with another person. The ritual misfire can occur when men don't reciprocate compliments. Consider Dahlia and Tomas, who are colleagues. Following a meeting, Dahlia compliments Tomas on his presentation. Because Tomas doesn't reciprocate the compliment, Dahlia is forced to ask, "What did you think of my presentation?" Then, rather than following the ritual and complimenting Dahlia, Tomas provides a detailed critique of what he thought of her presentation. This is clearly a ritual misfire. At times, men interpret messages literally rather than ritually. Dahlia was not expecting a critique of her presentation. Instead, she expected her ritual compliment to be reciprocated with a compliment.

SMALL TALK RITUALS Men and women often use small talk to relate to others. Small talk is a type of social lubrication that allows conversations to run more smoothly. Men and women have different small talk rituals, which can be misinterpreted. As noted earlier, according to Tannen, many women use rapport talk and many men use report talk.[60] **Rapport talk** focuses on sharing information about relationships, whereas **report talk** focuses on sharing factual or statistical information. Both forms of small talk are used to relate and connect with others. However, men and women go about it quite differently in their conversation rituals. Women tend to interpret men's report talk as too impersonal and men tend to interpret women's report talk as too personal.[61]

Strategies for Adapting

Rather than communicating in a strictly masculine or a strictly feminine manner, research is beginning to suggest that flexibility is needed in the twenty-first-century workplace. The professional workplace will benefit if women adopt more masculine (powerful) ways of speaking and men adopt more feminine (powerless) ways of speaking. Tannen argues that both communication styles have benefits. Her claims have been supported by research indicating that employees who perceive their managers and supervisors using mixed or blended speech styles consider them to be more effective than supervisors who use the speech style associated with their sex (a man using powerful verbal messages, a woman using powerless verbal messages).[62] Being appropriate and effective in today's diverse workplace also requires understanding how men and women use conversational rituals. Here are a few recommendations to enhance your use and understanding of conversational rituals:

- *Be aware that men and women have different conversational rituals.* If you're male, understand that a woman's use of ritual apology is a way to express concern. If you're female, understand that a man's use of ritual opposition is a way to explore ideas.

- *Monitor others' nonverbal behaviors to confirm that they interpreted your ritual correctly.* Nonverbal expressions such as a raised eyebrow may signal misunderstanding.

- *If you're male and receive a compliment from a female, offer a compliment in return.* If a compliment is unwarranted, try sharing at least one positive comment about her job performance.

terms & definitions

Rapport talk talk focused on sharing information about relationships.

Report talk talk focused on sharing practical or statistical information.

- *If you're female and don't receive a compliment from a man in response to one you offer, understand that it's probably that he doesn't understand the conversational ritual.* Let him know how much you value and occasionally need compliments.

- *If you're male, try using ritual apology and rapport talk when communicating with a female.* A woman will likely appreciate it if you temporarily suspend ritual opposition and report talk rituals when communicating with her.

- *If you're female, try using ritual opposition and report talk when communicating with a male.* A man will likely appreciate it if you temporarily suspend ritual apology and rapport talk when communicating with him.

Adapting to Generational Differences

Human resource researchers and practitioners have learned over the years that it's critical to study generational differences at work and to use the research findings to help working professionals adapt to the generational differences.[63] Put another way, generational differences represent another form of intercultural communication; groups of employees born in one generation (cultural group) are communicating across another generation. Although it's important to understand that groups of people born in different generations share more similarities than differences, it's vital to be aware of, appreciate, and value the differences between the generations.

Understanding Generation Y

A new generation of employees are joining the business and professional workforce. They belong to what researchers refer to as generation Y, which includes those born between 1982 and 2000.[64] This generation is the "connected" generation, which reflects their tech savvy and need to remain connected and engaged. Members of generation Y seek work that is fulfilling and enables them to make a difference.[65] They are driven and desire growth and job success. One of the most common reasons younger workers leave their jobs is because they are not fully engaged. Leaders can keep them engaged by continually educating and training them and providing them with professional development opportunities.

One way to better understand how generation Y communicates is to compare and contrast it with other generations. Researchers have identified a number of small but important communication style differences across generational groups. A brief summary of these findings is depicted in Figure 5.4.

Strategies for Adapting

The International Association of Business Communicators conducted a survey of thirteen hundred of its members regarding generation Y and how to adapt to this new generation of employees.[66] Three key findings suggest 64 percent of those surveyed do not have a clear understanding of the communication preferences and perspectives of generation Y; 75 percent reported that current communication methods were ineffective with young professionals; 90 percent indicated that their own, or their client's, organization will be at risk if they fail to significantly adapt their communication methods and technology. Because of these concerns, researchers have identified a number of important ways that people can adapt messages to members of generation Y. Here are a few of the recommended strategies:[67]

- *Be direct and straightforward.* They need to know what is expected of them and be told what to do. Younger employees thrive under deadlines and like task-oriented projects.

- *Make them accountable by delegating tasks.* The accountability that comes from being given and then completing a project is extremely rewarding and is a good way to foster self-esteem and professional confidence.

Communication Characteristics	Veteran (Born before 1946)	Boomer (1946–1964)	X'er (1965–1981)	Y'er (1982–2000)
Style	Formal	Semiformal	Not so serious; irreverent	Eye-catching; fun
Content	Detail; prose-style writing	Chunk it down but give me everything	Get to the point—What do I need to know?	If and when I need it; I'll find it online
Context	Relevance to my security; historical perspective	Relevance to the bottom line and my rewards	Relevance to what matters to me	Relevance to now, today, and my role
Attitude	Accepting and trusting of authority and hierarchy	Accept the "rules" as created by the Veterans	Openly question authority; often branded as cynics and skeptics	Ok with authority that earns their respect
Strategies	Print; conventional mail; face-to-face dialogue or by phone, some online information and interaction	Print; conventional mail; face-to-face dialogue; online tools and resources	Online; some face-to-face meetings (if they're really needed); games; technological interaction	Online; wired; seamlessly connected through technology
Speed	Attainable within reasonable time frame	Available; handy	Immediate; when I need it	Five minutes ago
Frequency	In digestible amounts	As needed	Whenever	Constant

FIGURE 5.4 Adapting Communication for Generational Differences

"Adapting Communication for Generational Differences," by Leah A. Reynolds, Beth Campbell-Bush, and Ryan Geist, Deloitte Consulting, LLP, 2008. Reprinted by permission.

- *Keep conversation casual.* Conducting casual conversations at a coffee shop is a great way to engage Gen Y'ers and make them feel like part of the team.

- *Tell them why.* As much as the younger generation wants to be directed, they also want to know why they are being told to do what they are being told to do. They want to know why certain decisions were made and why particular rules were established. Gen Y'ers don't bow to authority just for authority's sake. They need to know who's making the rules, how they got into the rule-making position and the principles behind the rules being established.

- *Ask their opinion.* Open communication is critical. Leaders who ask for their ideas or opinions, and listen to their suggestions for how to improve the organization, will gain their respect.

- *Structure their work and meetings.* Agendas are very beneficial if meetings are to be productive. Providing agendas prior to meetings, and not just at the meetings start, will help them come prepared to produce and feel secure about their presence in the group.

Because of changing demographics, it's very likely that you may be leading others who are older than you and from the boomer generation.[68] Although you always want to be careful with broad generalizations, researchers who study the boomer generation consistently agree that members of this generation tend to competent, caring, and honest leaders.[69] Additionally, boomers are known for their strong work ethic and loyalty to organizations.[70] If you find yourself leading older employees, then you may want to consider the following adaptation strategies:

- *Communicate with older employees in a face-to-face manner or at least over the telephone rather than using email or text-messaging.* For example, when providing older employees with performance feedback, they expect a more formal, face-to-face meeting that is conducted in an office rather than through email.

- *Monitor use of slang and tech talk.* For example, words like *cool, you guys, like, dude, awesome, right on,* or *man* are commonplace in the vocabulary of younger employees. Other examples of slang that older employees may not understand include *drill down, friend me, avatar,* and *second life.*

- *Avoid stereotyping.* Not all older employees are inflexible, tired, or too old to change. The reality is that they can change if you involve them in the change and engage their experience to help you and your team move forward.

- *Take advantage of older employees' knowledge and experiences.* A number of organizations worry about knowledge vulnerability with the large number of baby boomers preparing to leave the workplace.[71] Losing your knowledge base can weaken some organizations and put a strain on leadership. More supervision is usually required and this becomes problematic as organizations are downsizing. Take advantage of the knowledge that the more mature worker brings to the organization or work team. Older employees, because of their age, have more life experience and the knowledge generated from these experiences can be invaluable to a new leader.

Wrap-Up

The fifth principle that is key to enhancing our communication at work is adapting to the growing diversity in the workplace. There are several ways we need to adapt our communication at work. Learning to communicate effectively across personality, culture, gender, and generational barriers makes us better leaders and more effective team members in the modern workplace.

- Willingness to communicate (WTC) is an individual's natural tendency to initiate communication with others. Adapting to those with low WTC means refraining from premature judgments and not taking a person's quietness personally. Adapting to those with high WTC means giving them opportunities to communicate.

- Communication apprehension (CA) is a fear or anxiety related to communicating with others. Adapting to those with low CA means getting them involved in people-oriented activities. Adapting to those with high CA means giving them responsibilities that involve less social interaction.

- Argumentativeness (ARG) is a person's tendency to advocate strongly for their own position on an issues and criticize the positions of other people. Adapting to those with low ARG means being aware that they may perceive argumentative behavior as verbally aggressive behavior and using feed forward messages. Adapting to those with high ARG means engaging them in debates and playing devil's advocate.

Growing cultural diversity in the workplace gives leaders an opportunity to tap into a variety of cultural knowledge and experiences. This also highlights the need for sensitivity to cultural differences in communication.

- Researchers have identified five dimensions of cultural values, including: high- and low-context cultures, individual and collectivistic cultures, high- and low-uncertainty avoidance, masculine and feminine cultures, and decentralized and centralized power cultures.

- Strategies for adapting to cultural differences include being patient, asking questions, writing things down and double-checking for clarification, remaining self-reflexive, or evaluating your own communication in these contexts.

Gender differences can also play a role in workplace communication. Becoming aware of these differences will benefit leaders working in a gender diverse society.

- One major difference in gender conversational style is use of language. A masculine style favors powerful, direct messages. A feminine style tends to contain more indirect, powerless messages.

- At work, we often converse ritualistically, rather than literally. These rituals, such as masculine ritual opposition and feminine ritual apology, are often interpreted literally, leading to communication problems.

- Adapting to gender differences in communication involves becoming aware of these differences, and monitoring your own communication to ensure you haven't incorrectly interpreted a message. In addition, it is beneficial to use more of the opposite gender's style in your own communication at work.

A final consideration for adapting our communication at work is generational differences. Although generations often have much more in common, the differences are important and leaders can learn to value the variety of experiences the different generations bring to work.

- Generation Y is the newest generation entering the job market. They are different from previous generations in their need for information, their style and preferences for communicating at work, and their ability to multitask.

- Adapting to these generational differences involves providing structure, communicating directly and authentically, and maintaining a casual tone.

Reviewing Key Terms

Personality trait *96*

Communication trait *96*

Willingness to communicate (WTC) *97*

Communication apprehension (CA) *99*

Argumentativeness *101*

Feed-forward messages *102*

Culture *104*

Cultural context *104*

High-context cultures *104*

Low-context cultures *104*

Individualistic cultures *105*

Collectivistic cultures *105*

Decentralized power cultures *105*

Centralized power cultures *107*

Uncertainty avoidance *107*

Masculine cultures *107*

Feminine cultures *108*

Sex *110*

Gender *110*

Content dimension *110*

Relational dimension *110*

Powerful language *110*

Powerless language *110*

Conversational rituals *111*

Rapport talk *113*

Report talk *113*

The Principle Points

Diversity adds a richness of ideas and perspectives to the contemporary workplace. This diversity can also become a challenge in that what works for one individual or group doesn't necessarily work for another person or group of people. Effective leaders have the ability to assess how people are different and then adapt their communication to fit the unique needs of the individual.

Principle Five: Appropriately adapt messages to others

- Adapting communication appropriately requires your understanding a person's personality and communication traits. Having an awareness of your own communication traits and the traits of others will give you additional insight into what motivates a person to communicate in a particular manner.

- Adapting communication appropriately requires your understanding how culture influences your communication. High-context and low-context cultures differ in terms of how nonverbal messages are used and interpreted. Cultural dimensions include individualism/collectivism, power distribution (decentralized/centralized), degree of avoidance of uncertainty, short-term/long-term orientation, and masculine/feminine perspective. Adapting to these cultural values has been shown to enhance workplace communication.

- Adapting communication appropriately requires your understanding how sex and gender have an impact on workplace communication. Specifically, men and women have been shown to differ in their communication in terms of how they use powerful/powerless language, conversational rituals, and nonverbal communication. Both men and women would do well to adapt their communication by using a combination of masculine and feminine communication styles.

- Adapting communication appropriately requires your understanding how generational differences influence how you communicate with others across generations. Veterans, Boomers, X'ers, and Y'ers have been shown to communicate differently on a number of different communication characteristics including style, content, strategies, speed, and frequency.

Applying Your Skills

1. As an exercise to help you understand gender-based communication, ask both men and women the following questions and pay particular attention to the major differences.

   - What is the basic reason for communicating?

   - Which of the following statements most accurately reflects your general attitude toward communication: (a) When asking for information or making requests of someone, it is best to get to the point; (b) It is better to take some time to talk and get to the background of a situation before getting to the bottom line of what you are trying to say.

   - What bothers you most when you talk to someone of the opposite sex?

   - Do you think men and women know how to really listen to each other? Why or why not? Compare your results to those of your classmates. Are there any general similarities?

2. Examine each of the following statements. Identify which use powerful and which use powerless language. Next rewrite the powerful messages in powerless language, and the powerless messages in powerful language.

   a. "I wonder, can I possibly get that report this afternoon?"

   b. "I need you to attend the meeting on Friday."

   c. "That was a fantastic seminar, wasn't it?"

   d. "Maybe we should consider dealing with this conflict another way."

   e. "I expect everyone to meet their deadlines this month."

3. Role-play with a member of the opposite sex a first conversation or conflict disagreement between dating partners. First, enact the conversation from the perspective of your own sex. Then, enact the conversation again but with the roles reversed. Note any differences that emerge in how the conversation plays out. Do you detect any stereotypical behaviors that emerge when you swap roles? Does this help you better understand the opposite sex and their communication patterns?

4. Take the personality measures from the beginning of this chapter (WTC, CA, ARG). Next, write down a brief description of your own communication style. How do these traits impact your communication at work? What can you do to adapt your communication to those around you?

5. Identify the cultural value illustrated in each of the following examples.

   a. Tomas arrives to work on time every day. He appreciates the structure and organization at his office job. He is a rule follower who feels he can be much more productive when there are clear guidelines for the task and written policies at work.

   b. Yesenia has trouble communicating with her supervisor at her new job. He is very direct, likes to give clear orders and has no problem telling her when he is unsatisfied with her work. This makes Yesenia uncomfortable because she is used to a more nuanced communication at work, where leaders are more likely to "beat around the bush" then to come right out and say they are not pleased.

   c. Mark has recently taken a new position with his employer that requires him to travel to other countries. As a leader, Mark is used to making decisions by consensus, requesting input and opinions from those he works with. He has found, however, that when he travels he often encounters employees who rarely give their own opinions and instead expect Mark, as the leader, to make all the decisions.

   d. Sarah has recently graduated from college. She is interested in pursuing a graduate degree in business at an elite university far from her home in Texas. She is encountering some problems, however, from her family. Although they want her to move on and further her career, she has pressure to remain close to home, and they encourage her to find a satisfying career that will keep her close to the family.

6

Relating to Others at Work

chapter **outline**

After reading this chapter, you should be able to

- Develop skills for effectively relating to those we work with—including upward, horizontal, and downward communication skills.

- Use effective outward communication skills when relating to customers, clients, and others outside the organization.

- Define relational conflict, and describe how to manage workplace conflict effectively.

- Differentiate between the five conflict styles: avoider, accommodator, competitor, collaborator, and compromiser.

- Discuss and apply strategies for effectively managing emotions at work.

- List and describe each step in the PUGSS Model of conflict management.

- Identify when bullying is taking place at work, and select an appropriate method for approaching the bully.

- Develop effective skills for negotiating a win-win solution in the workplace.

*F*rom *Worst to First* is the title of Gordon Bethune's book that chronicles how his leadership helped turn around Continental Airlines (now a part of United Airlines), guiding (or leading) the company from last to first in the industry in terms of on-time performance, missing luggage, and fewest number of customer complaints.[1] He attributes his success to the employees of Continental. Unlike other airline executives who failed to connect with employees, Bethune quickly reached out to various employee groups, developed strong trusting and committed relationships, provided his employees with the tools they needed to do their job, and then got out of the way.

According to Bethune, if you want to increase employee morale, you have to open up the communication. In an interview with the *New York Times*, he talked about his methods of communication:

> I did a weekly voice mail every week for 10 years, a three- to five-minute message. Every week I'd tell them what was going on. And we had a daily update with our stock price, our on-time performance, who did what to whom in our industry. So the employees always kind of knew what was going on. They had direct access to me, and direct access to the information. And we never lied. You don't lie to your own doctor. You don't lie to your own attorney, and you don't lie to your employees. And if you never lie, then when it hits the fan, and somebody says you're wrong—you can say, "No, I'm not," and they'll believe you.[2]

Bethune is known for his communication style of being approachable, authentic, caring, and responsive to employee needs and concerns.[3] Former employees recall how he would get to the airport an hour early before a flight to simply spend time with the employees.

"When you actually take the time to go over to somebody's office and personally thank them—whether their office is in a cockpit of an airplane, or in a break room—that's an actual manifestation of interest in them. You need to take the time to show the people around you who work for you that you're interested in them."[4]

Gordon Bethune's success in turning Continental Airlines around led to its recent merger with United Airlines to become the world's largest airline.[5]

leading **questions**

1. How well does your supervisor relate to others at work? What does your manager do to develop relationships with others? What advice could Gordon Bethune give to your boss?

2. How well do you relate to others at work? How would you describe the relationships you have with those above and below you? What have you learned from Gordon Bethune about relating to others?

3. How well do you think Gordon Bethune managed conflict at work? Do you think he was receptive to conflict or do you think he avoided conflict? Why?

A person's ability to lead depends on his or her ability to develop and maintain constructive relationships. A **relationship** is an ongoing connection made with another person through interpersonal communication. Have you ever worked for someone who took a genuine interest in you, listened to your needs, gave you work assignments that showcased your strengths, and recognized your efforts when you met performance goals? Chances are you have also worked for a supervisor who was only interested in getting the job done. Although this person may have said he or she was genuinely interested in you as a person, he

terms & definitions

Relationship an ongoing connection made with another person through interpersonal communication.

or she rarely listened to your needs, had a tendency to take credit for the work you and your team members completed, and assigned more work rather than taking time to recognize you for what you had just accomplished.

The first leader described is a **person-focused leader:** someone who understands the importance and value of getting to know people on a personal level. For this type of leader, the person takes priority over the work. When a leader gets to know an employee, the employee is more likely to be motivated to do the work and do it well. The second leader described is a **task-focused leader:** someone who believes that work takes priority over the person, who might be overheard saying, "Who's got time to get to know the employees on a personal level? There's too much work to get done in a short amount of time."

> *"Leadership is communicating people's worth and potential so clearly that they come to see it in themselves."*
> —Stephen R. Covey

The two leaders we've described reflect opposites ends of the task-person continuum of workplace relationships, but most leaders know that the workplace requires leaders who can balance both the tasks and the personal dimensions of the workplace. Figure 6.1 illustrates this relationship continuum.

At the left end of the continuum is the task dimension. At the right end of the continuum is the person dimension. Effective leaders develop workplace relationships that balance both of these extremes. Leaders know that if they are too task oriented, they forget about the person doing the work. If leaders are too person oriented, they forget about the work that needs to get completed. Effective leaders have learned how to manage both the task and the person dimensions of workplace relationships—that is, they operate in the middle zone of the continuum.[6]

The purpose of this chapter is to help you relate to others in a professional manner by helping you balance the task and person dimensions of workplace relationships. In Chapters 7 and 8, we continue our discussion of how to relate to others in a professional manner by examining the interview process. Relating to others requires using the five communication principles for leadership, discussed in Chapters 1 through 5 and illustrated in Figure 6.2.

terms & definitions

Person-focused leader a leader who values and makes a priority of getting to know people on a personal level.

Task-focused leader a leader who believes that work takes priority over personal relationships.

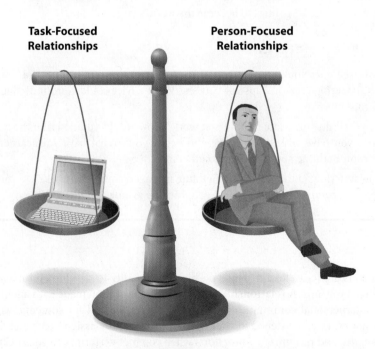

Task-Focused Relationships   **Person-Focused Relationships**

FIGURE 6.1 Workplace Relationship Continuum

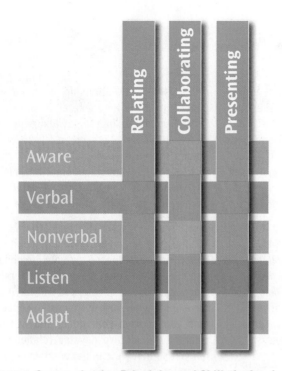

FIGURE 6.2 **Communication Principles and Skills for Leadership**

Understanding Relationships at Work

Effective leaders understand how the various types of workplace relationships differ and how to adapt communication accordingly to remain influential in these various types of relationships. This section reviews four different types of workplace relationships, including relationships with managers, coworkers, those you lead, and your customers.

Skills for Relating to Your Manager

One of the more important relationships that you have at work is the one you have with your manager or supervisor. The ability to relate to your manager is a major factor in determining your success at work.[7] Research suggests that your performance and job satisfaction improve as you communicate more effectively with your manager.[8] Because of the power difference between you and your manager, the relationship usually begins with a task focus. As your relationship develops, it usually becomes more balanced, focusing equally on task and the person. Unfortunately, some managers and employees lack the relational communication skills needed, and this limitation has a negative effect on employees' job performance and satisfaction. This communication skill deficiency prevents relational development and the relationship remains unbalanced—more task focused, less person focused.

To ensure that your relationship with your supervisor is balanced, it's important to develop skill in the use of **upward communication,** which is the communication that flows from employees to managers. Managers who are receptive to their employees' upward communication have employees who are more productive, motivated, satisfied with their work, and more likely to adopt change and to perceive their manager to be more open and approachable.[9]

"Managing up" is a communication concept that continues to receive attention in the academic literature and the popular press.[10] Managing up occurs when subordinates first identify their managers' goals, strengths and weaknesses, and preferred working style and

Develop a Diverse Relationship Network[11]

It's been said that *everything* happens because of the relationships we have with others. Stephen I. Sadove, chairman and chief executive of Saks, Inc., believes that our professional development depends not only on our ability to develop relationships with others but to help others develop important relationships. With new leaders, he stresses the importance of differentiating oneself from others. One way to do this is to develop relationships with others outside your chain of command. Sadove notes,

> I use opportunities to get involved and develop relationships with a diverse set of people, as opposed to the narrow group of people I was dealing with day-to-day, and that made a huge difference. It shaped my philosophy in terms of the importance of relationship-building. It really underlies my entire philosophy of how to run a business.

Sadove also brings social value to the organization; in other words, who and what he knows as a result of having a diverse network of relationships.

Equally important to Sadove is helping others develop relationships. Relationship building is particularly important in the luxury retail business, such as Saks. Customers are willing to pay luxury prices for services, which ultimately means a three-way relationship among the sales associate, client, and merchandise. Not only is the sales associate and client relationship important, but also the relationship that the sales associate develops between the client and the merchandise.

You may not yet have a philosophy of how to run a business, as Sadove does; but if your life philosophy is based upon developing quality interpersonal relationships with a diverse group of people, you will be well on your way to developing a network of friends and colleagues who can help you achieve your goals and with whom you can return the favor. We develop relationships with others not just so that we can get what we want out of life, but also so that we can enjoy the fellowship and friendship of others.

then adapt their communication to meet the needs of their managers. For example, if your manager has a tendency to conduct disorganized meetings, you may be able to manage up by asking if you can help plan meetings. If your manager agrees, you might recommend some strategies that would ensure a productive meeting, such as seeking input from others as to what should be discussed at the meeting and developing an outline or an agenda that will help your manager process the meeting.

Unfortunately, not all managers are receptive to upward communication. Here are five guidelines that have been shown to reduce manager resistance: Upward messages should be positive, timely, supportive of current policy, and sent directly to the person who can act on them; they should also have intuitive appeal (that is, they should make sense).[12] Although it is easier to communicate successes than failures, unfortunately, part of the relationship that you have with your manager is to communicate failures and negative information. Thad Green and Jay Knippen, management professors and consultants, have outlined eight communication procedures for communicating negative information or failures upward to a boss:[13]

1. Introduce the problem.
2. Provide background information.
3. Tell about the failure.
4. Discuss resolving the failure.
5. Acknowledge responsibility.
6. Note positive results of the failure.
7. Summarize key points.
8. Thank the manager.

According to Green and Knippen, these eight steps will help ensure that the negative communication flows upward and will help enrich the relationship that you have with your manager.

Skills for Relating to Your Coworkers

Developing quality relationships with your coworkers is important for several reasons.[14] First, you spend more time on the job with your coworkers than you do at home with your loved ones.[15] According to a Harris Interactive poll, the 9-to-5 workday is becoming a thing of the past. Americans are spending more time working than they did 30 years ago: In 1973, Americans spent 41 hours per week on the job; in 2008, they spent approximately 48 hours per week on the job, and the number of hours is expected to increase in the years ahead.[16] Although not a substitute for our families, quality workplace relationships make our working lives more meaningful. Another reason that quality relationships with coworkers are important is that your coworkers are instrumental in showing you the ins

Developing quality relationships with your coworkers is an important part of workplace satisfaction.

and outs of a new job—your coworkers teach you how to survive in the organization and provide you with information you need to do your job well. Finally, quality coworker relationships are positively related to job satisfaction, job productivity, job involvement, and negatively related to employee turnover.[17] In other words, having colleagues who are also your friends keeps you from quitting.

Because coworkers usually have equal power (meaning that they don't have any authority over each other), their relationships tend to be more person focused than task focused. This equality in power promotes **horizontal communication,** which is the communication that occurs between peers working at the same level within an organization.[18] One important aspect of the horizontal communication that occurs between coworkers is their use of the grapevine, or the informal network for workplace information. Coworkers use the grapevine to send and receive information about such news items as who got fired and hired, what is happening in the various units within an organization, and what job openings are available that would advance their careers.[19] Research suggests that information from the grapevine is valued almost as much as information from one's direct supervisor.[20] There are reasons why coworkers believe the information they get from the grapevine or other coworkers. Management researcher Keith Davis reported that between 75 and 95 percent of all grapevine information is correct.[21]

So what are employees talking about? It's not always about work. In fact, a group of researchers from the University of Wisconsin-Eau Claire reported that the Millennial generation, or those born between 1982 and 2000, talk a lot about what researchers refer to as "life-talk" or non–work life discussions. Researchers reported that Millennials are concerned about work/life balance, which is not becoming obsessed with work and continuing to have a life outside of work. In fact, Millennials are less likely to tie their personal identity to their work or professional identity. Research suggests that employees use "on-the-job" life talk conversations to develop closer relationships, to give and get advice, and for entertainment reasons.[22]

At times, "life talk" turns into workplace romances. According to a survey of a thousand employees, 47 percent of the employees reported having been involved in a workplace romance and an additional 19 percent would welcome the opportunity for an office romance.[23] Because Americans spend on average 48 hours per week on the job, it is not surprising that people find potential partners within their workplace.[24] **Office romances** are the romantic relationships that develop between workers who are employed by the same company.

Although workplace romances are common, they are often perceived as negative.[25] Some organizations even have formal policies regarding workplace dating because of the

terms & definitions

Horizontal communication communication between peers.

Office romances romances that develop between people who work for the same employer.

inherent challenges that such relationships may present to more people than just the dating couple.[26] This may be because individuals who are engaging in workplace romances are not always motivated by love. Some individuals date their bosses, peers, or subordinates to fill ego needs (e.g., excitement, adventure, sexual experience) or for job-related motives (e.g., advancement, money, job security).[27] Following are some of the primary issues associated with workplace dating:[28]

- *What is the rank of each person?* If a superior and a subordinate are dating one another, there could be concerns about each person's real motives (e.g., the superior is demonstrating power over the subordinate, the subordinate is using sex as a means to get a promotion).[29] Other workers could also feel jealous or suspect that the subordinate has an unfair advantage.[30]

- *Are individuals working in the same department?* When two workers in the same department date one another, this could make it awkward for the rest of the people in the department. For example, some coworkers may have problems with public displays of affection (e.g., a back rub) from their work associates.[31] Furthermore, it can be tricky to determine when coworkers consider the two people to be separate individuals and when they are considered a united couple.[32]

- *What happens if the relationship ends?* When office romances end, this may be problematic for more people than just the two employees who had been in the relationship.[33] Relationships with other coworkers may be affected. The organization may also have to invest additional resources if individuals are transferred or terminated or if there are legal issues associated with the breakup.[34]

Skills for Relating to Those You Lead

Many people who work in business and professional settings look forward to the opportunity to lead and manage others. Although some new professionals enter the workforce ready to manage, many do not possess the relational communication skills needed to lead others.[35] In fact, many fail to see management for what it is—a relational communication process. Successful managers understand that "work gets done through relationships." Managers who cultivate high-quality and trusting relationships with their employees have satisfied and committed employees who see to it that the manager and employees succeed together.[36] These employees comply with their managers' requests and directions and remain loyal to them.[37] Many of them go above and beyond the call of duty for their manager.

Because of the power difference that exists between managers and employees, the relationship usually begins with a task focus. Effective managers quickly learn that in order to cultivate nurturing and trusting relationships, they must learn to balance the relationship so that it is equally task focused and person focused.

As Figure 6.1 suggests, effective leaders manage from the middle of the workplace relationship continuum. These managers understand that by taking care of their employees (within reason), they will ensure that the employees take care of them. Managing from the middle of the continuum requires **downward communication,** or the communication that flows from managers to employees. (As noted earlier, managers must at the same time remain receptive to upward communication, or the communication that flows upward from their subordinates.)

An important part of how managers relate to those they supervise is how they delegate duties and

"There's no easy way I can tell you this, so I'm sending you to someone who can."

TABLE 6.1	DRGRAC Method of Delegating

Downward Communication for Delegation

Desired **R**esults	• Describe the task or project.
	• Define its purpose and note how it fits into the big picture.
	• Detail what the end result should look like.
	• Describe the intended outcomes.
Guidelines	• Describe guidelines for accomplishing the project.
	• Detail the rules for completing the project (e.g., it must be completed by a particular deadline, with a budget not to exceed a certain amount).
	• Discuss feasible deadlines for completing the project.
Resources	• Detail resources for completing the project (money, tools, materials, technology, special training).
	• Identify other personnel who will be involved, if any, and describe their roles.
Accountability	• Detail how the employee will be evaluated.
	• Establish agreed-on standards of performance and measures of success.
	• Describe individual responsibilities.
	• Establish metrics, or measures, for such things as quality (What level of quality is to be achieved? How will it be measured?), time (How will time be measured? Workdays only? Weekends?), and cost (What is over budget? Under budget? What's acceptable?).
	• Agree on a date to review progress.
Consequences	• Describe the rewards of accomplishing the project with the available resources.
	• Describe the consequences of not accomplishing the project with the available resources.

responsibilities. **Delegation** is a manager's assignment of a specific task or project to an employee.[38] Have you ever had a manager who told you to complete a project but didn't tell you how to do it, give you any additional help, or tell you when the project was due? When this happens, employees can feel "dumped on"; the manager is being too task focused and not person focused. To manage from the middle of the task-person continuum, managers must learn to delegate carefully by focusing not only on the task, but also on the person; and they must understand what the employee needs to complete the project. DRGRAC is an acronym that will help you delegate effectively to others.[39] Table 6.1 presents the DRGRAC method of delegation.

In many ways, DRGRAC is a quick summary of five types of downward messages. It covers job instructions, job rationale, policy and procedures, feedback, and motivation. The DRGRAC method of delegation and downward communication focuses equally on the task and the person. In each step, there is obvious attention to the task. Each step also protects the manager/employee relationship because each person in the relationship has a complete understanding of the desired results, guidelines, resources, accountability, and consequences. DRGRAC promotes a mature relationship based on mutual trust and respect.

Skills for Relating to Your Customers and Clients

Relating to your customers and clients is becoming increasingly important to your success in business and professional settings, especially because we live in a service economy.[40] A service economy is based on businesses' ability to anticipate the needs of customers and to

terms & definitions

Delegation a manager's assignment of a specific task or project to an employee.

Communication Ethics @ Work

Mixing Business with Pleasure

Best known for his snarky sense of humor and famous "Top Ten" lists, CBS funnyman *Late Show* host David Letterman made waves for an entirely different reason in the fall of 2009.[41] When word got out that he had an office romance with an intern on his staff, then another, then another, the story grew to scandalous proportions. Although release of this story was sensational (as it included stories from coworkers, graphic details, and the juicy little tidbit that Letterman was in a committed relationship at the time), it did highlight an ever-increasing issue for leaders in the workplace: office romance. Just how common is workplace romance? In a survey by Careerbuilder.com, 40 percent admitted to dating a coworker, with an additional 12 percent who hadn't but said they would.[42] Of the 40 percent who had dated a coworker, 42 percent said they had dated a boss or supervisor. Three of ten respondents also said they married someone they met at work. Leaders are now recognizing that workplace romances are inevitable.

Historically, workplace romance has been considered taboo. But now companies are recognizing that by permitting office romance, employees get what they consider an important benefit of working for the company: an opportunity to enhance their social life. However, an office romance almost certainly will have an effect on the interpersonal dynamics within a group.[43] In a related survey, 85 percent of respondents said that although common, workplace romances are a potential distraction for everyone at work. In addition, relationships between supervisor/subordinate, such as those Letterman engaged in, can have devastating consequences. There is the risk of retribution if the romance sours. Also, "third-party" employees can feel left out or begin to question the fairness of evaluations or rewards. In addition, these types of relationships have the potential to make the work environment so uncomfortable, that parties could file sexual harassment or hostile workplace complaints.

How does a leader navigate these legally and ethically murky waters? Do you believe the potential rewards for office romance outweigh the potential risks? As a leader, would you encourage or discourage these types of relationships? Would you participate in one?

develop and market products and services that meet these needs. For example, the late Steve Jobs, cofounder and CEO of Apple, identified a consumer need for portable and personalized tablet computers designed to deliver audiovisual media—including books, magazines, movies, music, and games—to users. Under his leadership, Apple developed and delivered the iPad to millions of people throughout the world.

Researchers are learning that task-focused relationships do not necessary result in satisfied or loyal customers.[44] With minor exceptions, customers who are treated in a depersonalized manner walk away feeling unsatisfied. To enhance the quality of the service provider–customer relationship, **outward communication,** which is the communication that occurs between a service provider and a customer, needs to be focused on meeting the needs of the customer. Wendy Zabava Ford has conducted a number of research studies examining customer-service communication.[45] Ford's research finds that personalized service, which occurs within a person-focused relationship, is "tailored service, or service that attempts to address the unique needs of the individual customer."[46] Examples of communication behaviors associated with personalized service include asking questions to identify customers' specific needs, offering options and advice to customers, and spontaneously sharing information on topics of interest to customers.

One service company that continues to set the standard for customer service is Disney. Much has been written about how Disney trains it employees or cast members to communicate and interact with customers (guests).[47] Whenever the word "Guest" is used in any of their internal or external communication, the "G" is capitalized as a symbolic way of showing how critically important the customer is to the Disney organization. To make sure guests received personalized customer service, Disney cast members practice the following "7 Guest Service Guidelines":[48]

1. Make eye contact and smile. Begin and end every interaction with a Guest with direct eye contact and a sincere smile.

2. Greet and welcome each and every Guest. Extend an appropriate greeting to every Guest you come into contact with. In some areas of the park, themed greetings are offered.

terms & definitions

Outward communication communication between a service provider and a customer.

3. Seek out Guest contact. Reach out to Guests who need assistance. Know all necessary information, from first aid and safety procedures to location of shops and restrooms.

4. Provide immediate service recovery. Resolve service problems from poorly prepared food to rooms that are not cleaned properly before check-in. Rapidly find the appropriate information or person when you don't have the solution.

5. Display appropriate nonverbal behavior at all times. Demonstrate appropriate posture, facial expression, and other aspects of professional appearance to create the best impression on Guests.

6. Preserve the "magical" Guest experience. Preserving the feeling of enchantment for the Guests is a core value at Disney and was first imagined by Walt Disney.

7. Thank each and every Guest. Show appreciation to each and every Guest. Complete each and every interaction with a thank-you and a smile.

In summary, when communicating with customers and clients, the research clearly suggests that building a relationship with the customer by using social courtesies and pleasantries and by providing personalized service—finding out the customer's needs and then meeting those needs—will ensure that customers are not only satisfied but prefer to give you their future business and to recommend your business to other potential customers and clients.

RECAP

Types of Workplace Communication

Relationship Type	Communication Direction	Definition
With Manager	Upward Communication	Communication that flows from subordinates to superiors.
With Coworkers	Horizontal Communication	Communication that occurs between those working at the same level in an organization. This tends to be more person-centered communication.
With Those You Lead	Downward Communication	Communication that flows from superiors to subordinates. This requires a conscious effort to communicate from both a task perspective and a relational perspective.
With Customers	Outward Communication	Communication that occurs between a product provider or a service provider and the customer. This needs to be focused on meeting the needs of the customer.

Managing Relational Conflict at Work

Relational conflict at work is inevitable. Conflict occurs when someone prevents you from reaching your goals. Workplace conflict is so common that you will experience it almost every day of your professional work life. You will experience conflict with your manager, with your colleagues and coworkers, with those you supervise and lead, and with your customers and clients. More specifically, **relational conflict** has been defined as an expressed struggle between at least two interdependent individuals, each of whom perceives incompatible goals, scarce rewards and resources, and interference from the other person in achieving his or her goals.[49]

Some workplace conflict is trivial, such as conflict arising from a person playing a radio too loud or an employee consistently arriving late to meetings. Other workplace conflicts are quite serious, such as conflict caused when a manager sexually harasses employees or a colleague bullies coworkers. In many ways, workplace conflict is like a disease. If it goes untreated, it becomes contagious and infects others. If the disease is properly diagnosed and treated, relationships can eventually heal.

terms & definitions

Relational conflict an expressed struggle between at least two interdependent individuals, each of whom perceives incompatible goals, scarce rewards and resources, and interference from the other person in achieving his or her goals.

Relational conflict is not uncommon in the workplace. The ability to manage such conflict is one of the most important skills a leader can have.

Understanding Conflict Styles

A useful tool for understanding different people's **conflict styles,** which is the way people are perceived to express and manage conflict, is the managerial grid developed by Ralph Kilmann and Kenneth Thomas, illustrated in Figure 6.3.[50] The horizontal axis (the bottom of the grid) reflects your concern for production, or tasks. This dimension focuses on getting the job done. If you have a high concern for task, your focus is on production or output; if you managed a coffeehouse, your concern would be on the total number of cups of coffee or coffee specialty drinks sold in a single day of operation. If you have a low concern for task, you are less concerned about output.

The vertical axis (the left of the grid) reflects your concern for people. This dimension focuses on the relationships you have with others including your boss, coworkers, subordinates, vendors, and customers. If you have a high concern for people, your focus is on meeting their needs rather than meeting your own needs. Again, if you managed a coffeehouse, your concern would be on ensuring that your employees were satisfied with their jobs by trying to meet their scheduling, social, and inclusion needs. You would also be concerned with whether your customers were satisfied with their coffee and the overall experience. If you have a low concern for people, you are less concerned about meeting others' needs and more interested in ensuring that your own needs are met. By rating

terms & definitions

Conflict styles the way people are perceived to express and manage conflict.

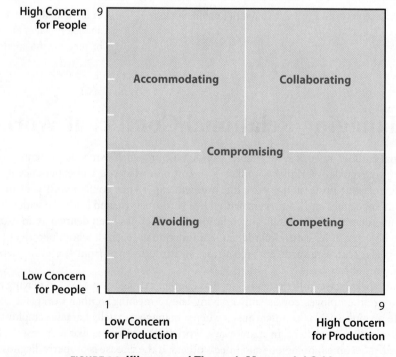

FIGURE 6.3 Kilmann and Thomas's Managerial Grid

your own or another person's concern for task and concern for people on a scale from 1 (low) to 9 (high), you can identify people's conflict styles, or the way they probably approach communicating conflict. Five conflict styles have been identified. Which style best describes how you communicate conflict? Becoming aware of your own conflict style will not only help you manage relational conflict more effectively, it will also help you adapt to others' conflict styles.

AVOIDER. An individual with a low concern for task and a low concern for people is an **avoider.** These individuals manage conflict by steering clear of it; if they do get involved in conflict, they quickly remove themselves from the situation. At other times, they deny that problems even exist. An avoider might manage conflict by stating the following:

- "This is not a problem for me. I don't have a conflict."
- "I need to run. See you later."
- "I'm going to go and let the two of you work this out."

ACCOMMODATOR. An individual with a low concern for task and a high concern for people is an **accommodator.** These individuals manage conflict by giving in and surrendering. They have a desire to please others and will often ensure that others' needs are met at the expense of their own needs and at the expense of the tasks or the jobs that need to get accomplished. An accommodator might manage conflict by stating the following:

- "Although this is not going to help us get the job done, I agree with you."
- "This is important to you, so let's do it your way."
- "To manage this conflict, I want what you want."

COMPETITOR. An individual with a high concern for task and a low concern for people is a **competitor.** These individuals manage conflict by being assertive and pushing their ideas or solutions to problems on others regardless of what others think, believe, or feel. A competitor might manage conflict by stating the following:

- "This is the way it's going to be; I don't care what you think."
- "To manage this conflict, there is only one solution."
- "I have experience with this issue and you don't. Let's fix it my way."

COLLABORATOR. An individual with a high concern for task and a high concern for people is a **collaborator.** These individuals manage conflict by working with others to solve problems and make decisions. They take into consideration others' opinions and feelings before making any final decisions. A collaborator might manage conflict by stating the following:

- "What do you think we should do to manage this conflict?"
- "Together, let's look at the various issues on the table."
- "This solution has been proposed. Can you support it?"

COMPROMISER. An individual with a moderate concern for task and a moderate concern for people is a **compromiser.** These individuals manage conflict by being able to give up part of what they want in exchange for the other person's giving up part of what he or she wants in a particular conflict situation. A compromiser may manage conflict by stating the following:

- "I'm willing to give this up if you're willing to give that up."
- "To manage this conflict, I'm willing to meet you halfway."
- "Let's both go back and revise what it is we need and want."

terms & definitions

Avoider someone who manages conflict by steering clear of it.

Accommodator someone who manages conflict by giving in rather than engaging in the conflict.

Competitor someone who manages conflict by being competitive and pushing ideas and solutions on others.

Collaborator someone who manages conflict by being willing to work with others to solve problems and make decisions.

Compromiser someone who manages conflict by giving up part of what he or she wants in exchange for the other person's giving up part of what of he or she wants.

TABLE 6.2	Adapting Conflict Style to Situation

Conflict Style	Situation
Use an Avoiding Style	• When an issue is trivial, or more important issues are pressing • When you perceive no chance of satisfying your own concerns • When potential disruption outweighs the benefits of resolution • When you need to let people cool down to regain perspective • When gathering information supersedes making an immediate decision • When others can resolve the conflict more effectively • When issues seem tangential or symptomatic of other issues
Use an Accommodating Style	• When you find you are wrong—to allow a better alternative to be presented, to learn, to show your reasonableness • When the issue is more important to others than it is to you—to satisfy others and maintain cooperation • When you need to build social credits for later issues • When you need to minimize the loss when you are outmatched • When harmony and stability are especially important • When you need to allow subordinates to develop by learning from mistakes
Use a Competing Style	• When quick, decisive action is vital • When the conflict is over important issues with unpopular consequences (such as cost cutting, enforcing unpopular rules, discipline) • When the conflict is over issues vital to company welfare and you know you're right • When working with people who take advantage of noncompetitive behavior
Use a Collaborating Style	• When both sets of concerns are too important to be compromised so you need to find an integrative solution • When your objective is to learn • When you need to merge insights from people with different perspectives • When you need to gain commitment by incorporating concerns into a consensus • When you need to address emotional issues that have interfered with a relationship
Use a Compromising Style	• When goals are important but not worth the effort or potential disruption of more assertive modes • When opponents with equal power are committed to mutually exclusive goals • When you need to achieve temporary settlement on complex issues • When you are under time pressure to arrive at expedient solutions • When you need a backup when collaboration or competition is unsuccessful

Although compromising is a realistic conflict management style in today's workplace, you don't always get what you want when you compromise—you've given up something in order to get something. Collaboration, in contrast, is probably the most preferred conflict style because rather than giving up something, you and the other person work together until you find a creative alternative solution that allows you both to get what you want.

Regardless of your conflict style, there are times when you need to adapt your style because of the situation. Table 6.2 provides some guidelines on when you might want to adapt your conflict style to fit the situation.[51]

Understanding the nature of relational conflict on the job is the first step in learning how to manage conflict at work. The elements of our definition will guide you in diagnosing the conflict and identifying the causes of the conflict. Also, knowing how relational conflict is communicated (through competing, collaborating, compromising, avoiding, or accommodating) allows you to be prepared to manage conflict, which is the focus of the next section of this chapter.

Skills for Managing Emotions

One problem that most people have when trying to manage conflict is controlling their emotions. Most conflicts provoke emotional responses: anger, hurt feelings, frustration, fear, or defensiveness. Of all the emotions that people can feel on the job, frustration and anger are the most commonly experienced emotions.[52] According to Anne Kreamer, who studies and reports on workplace emotions, the main cause of the frustration and anger is coworkers who are not doing their share of the work.[53] So what do you do with your emotions at work? Should you check them at the office door or should you recognize and process them? Kreamer argues that "it's high time we get rational about emotions in the workplace."[54]

Emotions play an instrumental role in how you solve problems. Again, research data does not support the old assumption that emotions only get in the way of rational thinking. Cognitive neuroscientists Mary Helen Immordino-Yang and Antonio Damasio argue that emotions and thinking should not be separated.[55] *Emotional thought* is the term they use to describe how people solve problems.[56] The emotional and thinking systems in the brain work together in a synthetic manner to solve important problems. For example, if you've ever been caught not doing your share of the work on an important project, you probably felt embarrassed and ashamed. These emotions have a "stickiness" that remain in your memory and prevent you from repeating the same mistake.

Although some people want to express their anger and frustration to show the other person their level of anger and frustration and to release bottled-up emotions, these emotional outbursts usually ignite the other person's emotions and result in emotional contagion. Like conflict in general, emotions are like a virus that spreads very quickly from one person to another.[57] We have a tendency to mimic each other's behaviors. If you approach a conflict situation in a hostile or defensive manner, the other person, maybe even without knowing it, starts mimicking your behaviors and begins feeling hostile and defensive too.[58] If you're going to be successful at managing a conflict, you must become aware of the contagion effect and try to prevent it from occurring. Although you do not have control over the other person's emotions, you can affect his or her emotions indirectly by managing your own emotions during a conflict conversation. Here are a few suggestions for how you might prevent the contagion effect.

SELECT A MUTUALLY ACCEPTABLE TIME AND PLACE TO DISCUSS THE CONFLICT. Let the other person know that you would like to discuss something important and find out when the other person might be available. Make sure this time works for you and your schedule too. If you or the other person is tired, there's a risk of becoming locked in an emotion-charged confrontation. It's best to have a conflict conversation when you're both well-rested. Also, make sure you have some privacy for your conversation.

MONITOR THE EMOTIONAL TEMPERATURE. Let the other person know that you expect the conversation to be respectful and that if the conversation becomes too emotional, you will call a "time-out" or postpone the conversation until the emotions have subsided. For example, you might say, "I know we both feel strongly about the decision not to promote Leslie to unit manager, but I hope we can calmly discuss other alternatives for her career development." Verbal messages like this acknowledge feelings but also reinforce expectations for being polite to one another.

BE NONVERBALLY RESPONSIVE TO OTHERS. Emotions are conveyed primarily through nonverbal messages. And remember that we don't have as much control over our nonverbal messages as we do our verbal messages; emotions have a tendency to "leak" out of us in our nonverbal behavior. Many times these leaked cues convey negative emotions. Although it is natural to have a closed body orientation (to cross arms and pull back) during conflict conversations, try remaining nonverbally responsive to the other person. Make appropriate eye contact. Ensure an open body position by facing the person, uncrossing arms and legs, leaning forward, and using appropriate head nods. Nonverbally responsive messages have a tendency to defuse or neutralize negative emotions.

AVOID PERSONAL ATTACKS, NAME-CALLING, PROFANITY, AND GUNNY-SACKING. Because conflict situations are usually emotionally charged, it is easy to resort to what conflict researchers refer to as "below-the-belt" fighting.[59] This type of conflict is expressed by attacking the individual and making the conflict personal. Profanity, which is usually not acceptable in the workplace, or a personal attack is usually reciprocated by the other person. This cycle of negative emotional expression needs to be broken if there is to be any hope of managing the conflict constructively. Another way to manage emotions is to avoid engaging in gunny-sacking, or kitchen-sink fighting.[60] Gunny-sacking occurs when a person begins discussing a single conflict situation and then continues to unload or dump on the other person all of the things that have been bothering him or her. Essentially, it's emptying the "gunny-sack" of grievances. This type of conflict management is perceived as unfair by most people and increases negative emotions. To avoid gunny-sacking, limit the scope of your conflict conversation to a single issue rather than multiple issues.

Skills for Managing Conflict Conversations

Imagine you're having a problem with your coworker Michael. Rather than talking behind his back, you discuss the problem with Michael directly. But while you're talking, something happens almost without your knowing it: Michael "spins" the conversation so that the problem seems to be about you and not him. It happens quite often, and it can be frustrating. If we're not careful, people can hijack conflict conversations. When this happens, we walk away from the conflict conversation asking ourselves, "How did that happen? Why did I let him do that?" In reality, the problem is not just the other person's and it's not just yours. Because you and the other person are interdependent, the problem belongs to both of you.

To keep your conflict conversation on track and work toward a solution acceptable to both individuals, consider structuring your conversation using what we refer to as the PUGSS model of conflict management. Each letter of the PUGSS acronym represents a different part of the conversation:[61]

- P = Describe the *Problem*
- U = Achieve *Understanding*
- G = Identify *Goals*
- S = Brainstorm *Solutions*
- S = Select the best *Solution*

The advantage to using the PUGSS model is that it keeps conflict conversations focused, and it helps people prepare their conflict messages. Here's how the process works.

DESCRIBE THE PROBLEM.   What is the other person saying or doing that is bothering you? Using "I" language, describe the problematic behavior. "This is what I see you doing. This is what I hear you saying. This is how I'm feeling."

ACHIEVE UNDERSTANDING.   Make sure the other person understands the problem. Simply ask, "Do you know why this is a problem?" You might want to ask the person to paraphrase what she or he hears you saying to confirm understanding. If the person doesn't understand, which is common, then continue to describe the problem but in a different way. It is important not to continue to the next step in the conversation until you're confident that the other person understands the problem.

Also, make sure the person doesn't hijack or deflect the conversation and make the problem about you. For example, if you're discussing with an employee the fact that the person is frequently late, the employee may change the subject and mention that you need to be less rigid and more understanding. If this occurs, tell the person that you'd be happy to follow up at another time to hear his or her thoughts about your being rigid and not understanding. Then redirect the conversation back to the employee's tardiness problem. In other words, keep the conversation focused on the employee's behaviors, not on yours. That's a different conversation that should be conducted at another time.

IDENTIFY GOALS.   Next, let the other person know what you want and need. Find out what the other person wants and needs. Once you have identified individual goals, identify the goals you have in common. Build on your common goals. For example, if you're working with an employee who is constantly late to work, you might mention that the goal you have in common is for this person to remain employed. You might say, "I know you want to keep your job, and I want you to keep your job too. Our goal is the same. Now let's work together to reach this goal." People are usually surprised to find out that they have a number of common or similar goals.

BRAINSTORM SOLUTIONS.   Now that the problem and goals have been identified, it's time to find a solution. Ask, "What can we do to fix the problem? How can we ensure that both of our goals are met?" Withhold all evaluation and generate as many creative solutions as possible.

SELECT THE BEST SOLUTION.   Finally, select the best solution. Evaluate each of the brainstormed solutions and compare each to the goals you've identified. If a solution doesn't meet the goals of both people, then it's not the *best* solution. Continue evaluating each solution until you come up with one that meets all the goals identified earlier.

Figure 6.4 reflects how PUGSS might unfold in a real relational conflict in the workplace. This particular conflict, which actually occurred, involves two employees who work in the same office. One of the employees, Marisa, brings her infant daughter to work because she has been unable to arrange child care. The other employee, Rick, is distracted by the child's crying and often ends up doing Marisa's work.

For most people, working through conflict is troublesome and difficult because there's so much uncertainty. We have no idea how the conflict conversation is going to go. This uncertainty produces a lot of anxiety. One of the advantages of using PUGSS to structure your conflict conversations is that it makes managing and resolving conflict like working through a script. To reduce the uncertainty and anxiety, we encourage you to plan your conflict conversations and structure them using the PUGSS model.

There is simply no way to escape relational conflict at work. To manage conflict when it occurs, first ensure that the workplace climate is conducive to managing conflict. Workplace environments that are supportive, trusting, caring, and accepting ensure that relational conflict is managed well. Second, manage your emotions carefully by managing

Describing the *Problem*

Rick: Do you have a second? I have a problem and I know that you can help me fix it.

Marisa: Sure, come in. What's the problem? How can I help?

Rick: Something has been bothering me.

Marisa: What is it?

Rick: I haven't been able to get much work done lately. I begin a project that requires concentration and then I hear your child crying. The other day she cried from 9:00 a.m. until 11:00. I was feeling very frustrated.

Marisa: Yes, she was not having a good day. I'm so sorry.

Rick: I have also had other employees assign me work that is usually given to you. Yesterday, the Director of Marketing asked me to stuff all of these envelopes and I don't even report to her. I feel like I'm getting dumped on because others don't want to burden you with additional work. I'm feeling a bit abused by this situation, and I'm frustrated and anxious.

Achieving *Understanding*

Rick: Do you understand why this is a problem for me?

Marisa: I think so. Here's what I hear you saying: My child bothers you and others are dumping my work on you because they perceive me as having too much to do, with my child and everything else.

Rick: Your child is not the distraction, but her crying is.

Marisa: I also didn't know that others perceived me as ineffective.

Rick: I don't think anybody thinks you're ineffective at all—I just think they perceive you as having your hands full with your workload and your child.

Marisa: I understand. Again, I apologize for this and I'm glad you brought this problem to my attention. Let's fix it.

Rick: What do you suggest we do to fix the problem?

Identifying *Goals*

Marisa: What do you need to get your job done?

Rick: I need a quiet work environment. I also need others to know that you're available so they stop giving me your work. I don't feel our work is equally distributed. What do you need?

Marisa: I need to be able to care for my daughter and work at the same time. Being a single working mother is challenging.

Rick: Well, yes—I can't even imagine how hard it must be.

Marisa: Well, we both need our jobs and we like working here. . . .

Rick: Also, we're good friends and I don't think we want this to damage our friendship.

Marisa: I agree completely. What do you see as being a workable solution?

Brainstorming *Solutions*

Rick: How about having your parents care for her while you're working?

Marisa: I could see if I could change offices so we wouldn't bother you.

Rick: How about seeing if the company might help you finance daycare?

Marisa: How about you change your work schedule and work nights? Is that a possibility?

Rick: Could you get a babysitter with whom you could exchange babysitting services? For example, you sit with the other person's child on the weekends and this person could sit with your child during the week.

FIGURE 6.4 **The PUGSS Approach to Conflict**

Selecting the Best *Solution*

Marisa: Why don't I see if I could change my office so that my daughter and I will be out of your way?

Rick: I think that would meet my need for a quiet workplace; however, I still believe people will perceive you as having your hands full and they will come to me. Is it possible for your parents to care for your child during the day?

Marisa: Well, unfortunately my parents aren't capable of caring for my daughter. They're not comfortable around babies. My mother pops Valium every time we step foot in the house and my dad leaves once my daughter begins to cry.

Rick: What about exchanging babysitting services with a neighbor?

Marisa: That idea might work. . . . My neighbor is a firefighter and he works two 24-hour shifts during the weekend. I could watch his kids all weekend, and I believe he would be willing to watch my daughter during the workday.

Rick: That would meet both of my needs and yours. Do you agree?

Marisa: I do agree. All I want is good childcare for my daughter and to keep my job.

FIGURE 6.4 (*continued*)

conflict at the appropriate time and place, explaining your expectations for how you will treat each other during the conflict conversation, being nonverbally responsive, and avoiding personal attacks, name-calling, profanity, and gunny-sacking. Third, plan and structure your conflict conversations to ensure that you reach a solution you both can agree on.

Skills for Managing Bullies

Although we're used to hearing about bullies on playgrounds and in high school hallways, we're not used to hearing about them in business and professional contexts. Unfortunately, bullying in the workplace is becoming more and more of a problem at work. Communication researcher Pamela Lutgen-Sandvik and her colleagues report that 1 in 3 of all workers in the United States have been bullied sometime during their work history.[62] According to Lutgen-Sandvik, **workplace bullying** is an extreme, negative, and persistent form of emotional workplace abuse achieved primarily through verbal and nonverbal communication.[63] Four characteristics differentiate workplace bullying from other forms of employee abuse: (1) bullying communication behaviors are extreme and intense, (2) the behaviors persist over long periods and result in negative effects, (3) targets or those bullied believe these communication acts are intentional, and (4) targets feel they cannot defend themselves in the situation.[64] Examples of bullying may include some of the following behaviors:

When someone criticizes you when there is no reason to justify the criticism

When someone falsely blames you

When someone treats you differently than the rest of your work group

When someone swears at you

When someone intentionally excludes you from important activities

When someone shouts at you or humiliates you

When someone makes you the target of practical joke

When someone excessively monitors you

A leader is held responsible for managing these difficult and often challenging situations. There are a number of strategies for managing bullies in the workplace. Figure 6.5 examines two best practices: talking to the bully and writing a letter to the bully.

terms & definitions

Workplace bullying an extreme, negative, and persistent form of emotional workplace abuse achieved primarily through verbal and nonverbal communication.

Talk to the bully

Appropriate when . . .	There are times when the working relationship is constructive. The problems are recent.
Not appropriate when . . .	There have been threats or threatening behavior.
Before the meeting, do the following:	Identify the bullying behaviors. Write down the behaviors in a journal; be specific including time and frequency of events.
At the meeting, do the following:	Use the PUGGS model from above. Clearly describe the behaviors to the bully. Say that these behaviors are unacceptable. Describe the appropriate behaviors. Seek agreement.
Benefits	Issues can be resolved quickly. Relationships can be improved.

Write a letter to the bully

Appropriate when . . .	Talking to the person has not brought about the expected results. A meeting is not possible due to time or location.
Not appropriate when . . .	The person is unprepared to talk about the difficulties directly.
Before writing the letter, do the following:	Identify the behaviors that you want the person to change. Identify alternative, appropriate behaviors.
While writing the letter, do the following:	Clearly describe the negative behaviors. Explain why the behaviors are inappropriate. Describe the appropriate behaviors. Ask the person to acknowledge receipt of the letter.
Avoid the following:	Do not make the letter too long. Avoid making it personal. Address the behaviors. Rather than saying. "You were disrespectful," say, "Your behaviors were . . ."

FIGURE 6.5 Two Approaches to Managing Bullies in the Workplace

Communication Skills FOR A **Digital Age**

The Do's and Don'ts of Using Facebook for Work[65]

Many of today's entrepreneurs are using their Facebook for work and for pleasure. Because of their careful use of social media, these ambitious leaders are blurring the lines between their private and public lives in a seamless manner. One example of this is Ms. Randy Yezak, an animal science major from Texas A & M University, who uses her Facebook to sell necklaces, bracelets, earrings, rings, and other accessories under the name "Southern Jewlz," in addition to managing her personal relationships. Her two-year-old business has 8,000 fans on Facebook and her online sales have doubled in a six-month period.[66]

Applying Your Skills[67]

- *Don't have two profiles—one for personal and one for professional.* If Facebook learns that you have two profiles, they may shut down your account. The lines between personal and professional are blurring. You should be transparent and confident enough to let them blur. Of course there are some photos that you may not want your workplace colleagues to view. Facebook has excellent privacy settings that can be customized so your professional connections are limited in what they can view. Become familiar with these privacy settings.

- *Do create a Facebook page for your business.* Profiles are meant for people, whereas pages are meant for business.

Because pages were meant for businesses, they have different features that make them more valuable for a business. For example, business pages don't need to "accept" friend requests; they can get "liked" by anyone. Also, business pages come with viewer information so you know if you're reaching your customers and market on Facebook.

- *Don't turn off wall posts for your business page.* The point of Facebook is to interact with your customers. Turning off wall posts or comments screams to your customers, "We don't want to hear from you." Be prepared for what customers might post, and be ready to respond in a timely and authentic manner. Every time a user interacts with your page, that interaction gets in front of that user's network, spreading your reach far beyond your existing customer base. Use this unique opportunity carefully.

- *Do update your business page on a regular basis.* If you ignore it, your customers are going to ignore it as well. Your Facebook page should be an interactive platform where you and your customers interact regularly. If you update your business page with interesting content, your users are more likely to engage with your page, and their interactions get shown to their networks, expanding your reach exponentially. This virality is what makes Facebook such an incredibly powerful tool for businesses.

Negotiating Solutions at Work

Another important tool essential to effective leadership is negotiation, which is a particular type of conflict management. **Negotiation** has been defined as an exchange of proposals and counterproposals as a means of reaching a satisfactory settlement to a conflict.[68] Whereas all negotiation is a form of conflict management, not all conflict management is negotiation. For example, if you supervise an employee who comes to work under the influence of alcohol, you have a conflict that needs to be managed. There is no negotiation. The employee violated one of the workplace rules that usually results in immediate termination. In contrast, negotiation occurs when there is room for bargaining or for give-and-take. You give some and the employee gives some until you reach a solution that suits both of you. In short, you exchange proposals and counterproposals until you can agree. During negotiation, your proposals change and evolve. It's rare to leave the negotiation process with your first proposal untouched.

You will use negotiation strategies during the interview process when a company offers you a job. You have an idea of what the position and your skills are worth; however, the company also has an idea of a starting salary for you. That's when you begin the negotiation process. For example, you will take the job for $35,000. The company offers $27,000 and an extra week of vacation. After a strategic conversation, you and the company's representative agree on an annual salary of $31,000 without the extra week of vacation. This illustrates the exchange of proposals and counterproposals. Another example would be when you're

terms & definitions

Negotiation an exchange of proposals and counterproposals as a means of reaching a satisfactory settlement to a conflict.

trying to arrange your work schedule. You have certain scheduling needs, and your manager has certain scheduling needs. Ideally, negotiation occurs when you and your manager exchange proposals for your schedule and revise the proposals until you reach a satisfactory settlement. Negotiation can allow you to create a better fit between the requirements of the organization and your needs, abilities, and preferences.[69] Negotiation allows you to tailor a particular job so that it fits you.

In the next section, we examine six negotiation strategies and communication skills for negotiating win-win solutions. Coupling the negotiating strategies with the negotiation communication skills will allow you to be effective in your leadership position by continually enhancing your relationships with your manager, coworkers, those you lead, and your clients and customers.

Negotiating Strategies

A **negotiating strategy** is the overall approach you take when you exchange proposals and counterproposals with another person when negotiating a settlement to a conflict. Stephen Covey, an expert in leadership studies, suggests that your negotiating strategy is influenced by your paradigm.[70] A **paradigm** is a worldview; it's a way of thinking or a set of attitudes that guide your communication and behavior. Six paradigms that may guide people in negotiation include win-win, win-lose, lose-win, lose-lose, win, and win-win or no deal.[71] Which paradigm influences how you approach the negotiating process? Becoming aware of your paradigm and how it influences your negotiating strategies will enhance your ability to negotiate solutions more effectively in the workplace.

WIN-WIN. This negotiating strategy seeks mutual benefit; it uses a cooperative rather than a competitive approach to finding a solution. People with a win-win paradigm are empathic listeners; they try see and understand the problem from the other person's perspective. Win-win negotiators also are appropriately assertive, which means that they make their needs and their feelings known without attacking the other person; they make requests. For example, "For both of us to be successful, I need you to increase your share of the market by the end of next month. In return, I'm willing to give you additional resources to help you make that happen." This message conveys a win-win strategy in that both individuals are getting their needs met.

WIN-LOSE. This negotiating strategy is unfortunately quite common among people in business and professional settings. In fact, in many businesses, this is standard operating procedure. This approach uses competition rather than cooperation in negotiating solutions to problems. People acting on the basis of a win-lose paradigm are more concerned with the self than with the other person and his or her needs. Win-lose negotiators are verbally aggressive—they are more likely to attack the other person's character or make demands to get their way. It is important to understand the difference between verbally aggressive people and assertive people. "I'm going to work the Monday through Friday schedule; you're not going to get your selfish way this time" is an example of verbal aggression. In contrast, "I would like to request a Monday through Friday work schedule so that I may take care of my aging parents on the weekend" is an example of being appropriately assertive.

LOSE-WIN. This negotiating strategy is one typically used by someone who is submissive, which means that the person yields or gives in to the needs of the other person while ignoring his or her own needs and burying his or her own feelings. A person who negotiates on the basis of a lose-win paradigm is a people pleaser but often ends up being dissatisfied.

LOSE-LOSE. This strategy might be best expressed as "If I'm going down, you're going down with me." The lose-lose approach is a destructive attitude rather than a negotiating strategy. This approach is never recommended. Although it may not be your own approach to negotiating a solution, it may well be the other person's, and oftentimes you'll be unable to influence the person's attitude. People who use a lose-lose strategy usually don't have a lot of consideration for the other person and don't have the courage or the assertiveness needed to pursue other alternatives or solutions. People with a lose-lose paradigm envy and criticize others while also putting themselves down. For example, you might hear a team leader say to another team leader, "Your team always meets its goals because they cut corners. My team couldn't meet its goals even if we cut corners. If you're not willing to do the extra work, then we aren't either."

An effective leader successfully uses negotiating skills to strengthen workplace relationships and resolve conflicts.

WIN. This negotiating strategy might be expressed as "As long as I win, I don't care if you win or lose." People who approach negotiation with this overall strategy or paradigm only think about what *they* want. They forget that effective negotiation involves at least two people. Although they don't actively seek to make others lose, they do whatever it takes to win.

WIN-WIN OR NO DEAL. This negotiating strategy might best be expressed as "If we both can't be winners, then let's not play this game." Some leadership experts consider win-win or no deal the highest form of negotiation because it requires that negotiators equally respect their own needs and the needs of others. With a "win-win or no deal" strategy, both parties agree that the only acceptable solution is going to be a win-win. If that kind of solution cannot occur, then both parties agree to disagree and terminate all negotiations until a later time.

For example, suppose you want to negotiate a printing job with FedEx Office. You need color brochures to market your new business and you want them to do the job because of their quality and reputation. You have a limited budget. FedEx Office wants your business because they know you will be a loyal and longtime customer. Unfortunately, their price for printing color brochures is too expensive for your operating budget. Because you both want to work together but cannot come to an agreement on the printing price, you simply say, "Let's wait on this. Let's give it some time and see if we can come up with another agreement." After a few days, you return to FedEx Office and propose something different. This time you ask if FedEx Office will agree to increase the number of brochures they print for you at the price they already quoted if you change the brochure from a five-color brochure to a two-color brochure. You get more brochures printed, and they get your business and reduce their printing costs (because color ink is significantly more expensive than paper). The situation is a win-win.

Skills for Negotiating Win-Win Solutions

In the preceding section we introduced the PUGSS model, which is a general model for managing conflict. The following skills will supplement the steps of the PUGSS model when you use it during the exchange of proposals and counterproposals that constitutes negotiation.[72]

SEPARATE THE PEOPLE FROM THE PROBLEM. In many negotiation situations, people have a difficult time separating the issues from the individuals involved. As the negotiator, try separating the people from the problem. When discussing the problem, don't associate

RECAP

Negotiating Strategies

Strategy	Description
Win-Win	This strategy uses a cooperative approach to finding a solution and seeks mutual benefit.
Win-Lose	This strategy uses a competitive approach to finding a solution; each negotiator is most concerned with his or her own needs.
Lose-Win	A negotiator using this strategy submits to the other person and ignores his or her own needs.
Lose-Lose	This strategy uses an "If I go down, you are going down with me" approach.
Win	This strategy occurs when negotiators are only concerned about getting their own needs met and winning.
Win-Win or No Deal	This strategy takes into account everyone's needs. The negotiator is not happy until everyone wins.

a name with it. For example, some people take it personally if they perceive that they are getting assigned too much work. Rather than saying, "Jesse believes that the workload in the department is not equally divided and that he is doing too much of the work," try saying, "*It has come to my attention* that the workload in the department may not be equally divided." Your goal is to depersonalize the issues that need to be negotiated. (In fact, if you're the leader, it might be beneficial for you to take responsibility for the problem. You might say, "I know I've divided up the department workload unfairly lately.")

FOCUS ON INTERESTS, NOT POSITIONS. When you negotiate solutions to problems, you usually focus on positions rather than on interests. A **position** is what each person wants to see in the negotiated outcome. An **interest** is a desire, need, concern, or fear. In many situations, interests remain invisible; all you see are people's positions. But the invisible interests are in many ways much more important than people's positions. According to professional negotiators Roger Fisher and William Ury, "Interests motivate people; they are the silent movers behind the hubbub of positions. Your position is something you decided upon. Your interests are what caused you to so decide."[73]

When negotiating, look below the surface at what is motivating a particular person's positions. The motivation is the interest. Rather than meeting the other person's position, see if you can meet the other person's interest. For example, Jesse wants to renegotiate his job description because he feels he is doing too much of the work in his department. His position is to ensure that the workload is equally distributed. His *interest* is to be recognized, appreciated, and possibly compensated for the extra work that he is doing. To enhance the negotiation process, spend time listening to those involved in the negotiating process. Try to understand their motivations—their interests—and to meet these important interests.

INVENT PROPOSALS THAT ARE MUTUALLY BENEFICIAL. Generate as many options or proposals as possible that will benefit *all* individuals in the negotiating process. If you're going to exchange proposals, you need a number of them. The more proposals you have, the more likely you are to find one that benefits all parties to the negotiation. Also, when inventing proposals, consider the other side's perspective. Would they consider a given option plausible or possible? Would they find it attractive? If not, then eliminate the option from your list of possible proposals. One of the proposals that you might offer to Jesse would be to redistribute the workload, which addresses his position. Other proposals that you might exchange focus on his underlying interest—his concern that he is not being recognized,

terms & definitions

Position in a conflict, what each person wants to see in a negotiated outcome.

Interest a desire, need, concern, or fear that motivates one to take a particular position.

appreciated, or valued for the extra work that he does. You could write a letter for Jesse's personnel file, commending him for going "above and beyond the call of duty," offer him a financial bonus for the extra work he does, give him "comp time" or a day off with pay, or promote him. Remember, inventing proposals that address the other person's *interest* is sometimes more important than meeting the person's *position*.

USE OBJECTIVE CRITERIA TO EVALUATE PROPOSALS. When exchanging proposals and counterproposals, it's important to have criteria, or acceptable standards, that both sides can use to evaluate the proposals. It's important to know what makes a proposal acceptable or unacceptable. If you don't know what you're looking for, you won't recognize it when you see it. When judges make a ruling, they use laws as their criteria. When teachers evaluate student work, they use the standards outlined in the assignment as their criteria. These criteria allow judges and teachers to make decisions that are consistent and understandable to others. Before entering into negotiation, it's best to identify a set of criteria that both sides will consider fair and reasonable. How do you do this? In the workplace some standards for fair and reasonable criteria have already been established. Consider the following:

- *Precedent:* What formal judgments have already been made pertaining to this workplace issue?
- *Tradition:* What's been done in the past in the workplace?
- *Professional Standards:* What do professional organizations advocate as acceptable workplace practices and procedures?
- *Rules of Conduct:* What policies does the company enforce with all employees, regardless of rank, position, or title?
- *Employment Law:* What state and federal standards must a company follow in order to be working within the law?
- *Industry Standards:* What do our competitors do? What guidelines do they follow?

When negotiating Jesse's grievance that the workload in the department is not equally distributed, you could use a number of the criteria just listed to evaluate the various proposals that both sides are exchanging. For example, you might use tradition, or what's been done in the past, as your criterion for evaluating proposals. To apply this criterion, you could consult Jesse's job description. A **job description** is a written description of the responsibilities and requirements that have been traditionally associated with a specific job. In other words, it describes how the job has been conducted in the past. After reviewing this document, you would both know whether Jesse is doing the work outlined in his job description or work that falls outside his job description. The job description provides you with standards that might enable you to reach a win-win solution.

terms & definitions

Job description a written description of the responsibilities and requirements of a specific job.

Negotiating Skills for Win-Win Solutions

Skill	Description
Separate the people from the problem.	When discussing a problem, don't associate it with a name. If you are the leader, take responsibility for the problem yourself.
Focus on interests, not positions.	Rather than focus on people's desired solutions, focus on their needs and ultimate goals.
Invent proposals that are mutually beneficial.	Consider the other's perspective when developing proposals, and generate as many as possible, withholding evaluation.
Use objective criteria to evaluate proposals.	Use mutually agreed-on criteria for evaluating proposals.

To summarize: The process of negotiating win-win solutions is similar to managing relational conflict; however, negotiation *always* involves the exchange of proposals and counterproposals. Some relational conflict situations may not require the exchange of proposals; the problem in question may not be subject to negotiation. To negotiate effectively, it's important to understand the paradigm (the overall negotiating strategy) that you're using and the paradigm that the other person is using to negotiate a solution. There are six negotiation paradigms, or overall strategies: win-win, win-lose, lose-win, lose-lose, win, and win-win or no deal. Finally, negotiating win-win solutions requires separating people from the problem, focusing on interests rather than positions, inventing proposals that are mutually beneficial, and using objective criteria to evaluate the proposals.

▌ Wrap-Up

Continental Airlines' Gorden Bethune's approach to management—placing enormous value on the employees—helped lead the company to a successful merger, and first place in the industry. Effective leaders know the importance of relationships at work. As professionals, we engage in several types of relationships. We are employees, leaders, coworkers, and customer service providers. Relating to each of these groups involves important communication skills.

- Effective upward communication is important for relating to your manager at work.

- Relationships with peers are an important part of job satisfaction. However, be cautious with workplace romances.

- Leaders who engage in effective downward communication balance person and task focus. Effective delegation skills are vital.

- Developing effective customer relations skills has a positive impact on an organization's outward communication.

Workplace conflict is common, but it doesn't have to be destructive. Effective management of conflict is important for relational communication at work.

- Researchers have examined conflict style in terms of concern for people and concern for task. There are five conflict styles: avoider, accommodator, competitor, collaborator, and compromiser.

- Develop awareness and skills for managing emotions during conflict.

- The PUGSS model of conflict management provides an effective tool for managing the conflict conversation in a way that treats the conflict as a problem and allows each party a chance to be heard.

- Bullying in the workplace remains a problem, and a leader shouldn't ignore a bullying situation. The three potential approaches for managing a bully are talking with the bully, talking with the bully and the victim together, or writing a letter to the bully.

Negotiating for effective solutions provides benefit for both participants. These skills enhance your value in an organization.

- A negotiating strategy is the overall way we approach this type of interaction. There are six negotiation strategies: win-win, win-lose, lose-win, lose-lose, win, and win-win or no deal.

- Negotiation for a win-win solution benefits both individuals, and it involves objectivity and a willingness to actively pursue both your own and the other person's goals and needs.

Reviewing Key Terms

Relationship *121*	Upward communication *123*
Person-focused leader *122*	Horizontal communication *125*
Task-focused leader *122*	Office romances *125*

The Principle Points

Principle One: Be aware of your communication with yourself and others.

- Be aware of how others perceive you in terms of interpersonal attraction, similarity, and status.
- Be aware of the types of communication you use in your various workplace relationships with supervisors, subordinates, coworkers, and customers.
- Be aware of your own and others' conflict styles when relating in the workplace.

Principle Two: Effectively use and interpret verbal messages.

- To delegate effectively, use verbal messages that follow the DRGRAC method: stating desired results, establishing guidelines, providing resources, clarifying accountability, and describing consequences.
- In a conflict conversation, use descriptive "I" language to communicate the problematic behavior clearly.
- When negotiating using a win-win strategy, use objective criteria to evaluate solutions.

Principle Three: Effectively use and interpret nonverbal messages.

- In a conflict conversation, manage emotions before working to resolve the conflict.
- To enhance others' perception of your relational closeness, use nonverbal immediacy behaviors.
- To reduce the chances of the other person's becoming defensive during a conflict conversation, use nonverbal responsive behaviors: forward body lean, eye contact, head nods, open body position, and uncrossed arms.

Principle Four: Listen and respond thoughtfully to others.

- Listening involves stopping competing messages, looking for nonverbal behaviors that enhance the meaning, and listening for the big ideas rather than getting bogged down in the details.
- In a conflict conversation, listen carefully to all needs before attempting to reach a solution.
- When negotiating solutions, use strategies designed to incorporate all perspectives, such as using objective criteria and inventing proposals that are mutually beneficial.

Principle Five: Appropriately adapt messages to others.

- Use appropriate communication in the various workplace relationships: upward, downward, horizontal, and outward communication.
- Become aware of others' perceptions of you, and adapt your messages accordingly.
- When using outward communication with your customers, remember to orient it toward their needs.

Applying Your Skills

1. Review the different types of conflict styles discussed in the chapter and decide what type of conflict style you often use. What makes you think so? What kinds of strategies can you use to be more effective in your conflict conversations? Share your thoughts with a classmate.

2. When facing a conflict in the workplace, we often begin the conversation by accusing another person. This commonly is done using evaluative "you" language. The first step of the PUGSS model tells us to describe the problem, rather than evaluate. Rephrase each of the following statements from "you" (evaluative) to "I" (descriptive) statements:

   a. "You're irresponsible! Why can't you figure out how to get to work on time?"

   b. "You really need to deal with your attitude problem. I'm tired of it."

   c. "You're sexist. Women feel uncomfortable working with you."

   d. "You're lazy. I work five times harder than you!"

3. Take a minute and write down everything that comes to mind when you consider the word *negotiation*. Now, examine the list. Referring to the paradigms discussed in the chapter, what does this say about your own perspective when approaching conflict? Based on what you wrote, what is your paradigm?

4. Develop your own negotiation strategy for a potential workplace issue. This can be either a current issue in your own workplace or a created issue. Write down how you would communicate each step of the process for negotiating a win-win solution, including the following: separate the people from the problem; focus on interests, not positions; develop mutually beneficial solutions; and use objective criteria to evaluate proposals.

7

Interviewing Principles and Skills

chapter outline

After reading this chapter, you should be able to

- Define an interview and differentiate interviews from ordinary conversation.

- List and describe the steps for preparing an interview.

- Describe the difference between structured and unstructured interviews, and explain the steps in structuring an interview.

- List and define each of the different types of interview questions, and describe the various sequences interviewers can use.

- Discuss the interviewer's and interviewee's roles during the opening, body, and closing portions of an interview.

- Explain what it means to be a responsible interviewer.

- Explain what it means to be a responsible interviewee.

CNN Journalist and news anchor Anderson Cooper has become known for his unique style of journalism that emerged during hurricane Katrina in 2005 in New Orleans. His ability to interview the people of New Orleans during and after Katrina allowed him to tell stories that ranged from the horrifying to the heroic. During a guest lecture to Columbia University's Journalism School, he talked to students about what it means to be a reporter.[1] According to Cooper, your job as an interviewer is to ask questions that will allow people to tell their stories. Once they begin telling their stories, you guide them, and then get out of the way so the camera can capture the interview.

During his interactive discussion with journalism students, Cooper stressed the importance of authenticity. During the Katrina crisis he was sometimes criticized for telling the story through his lens rather than through the eyes of the people of New Orleans. He noted that when you're on the scene before the relief workers, and people want to use your phone to call a loved one to let them know that they're still alive or to get on your boat because they're tired of swimming, the interviews and the story changes. According to Cooper, these were not staged events. The news was unfolding before our eyes; and through the interviews and stories he told, people at home literally watched others survive or perish.

Some media professionals have described Anderson's interviewing style as emotional, which is unusual because most reporters are trained to hide or mask their emotions.[2] Anderson responds to this description by saying, "Yeah, I would prefer not to be emotional and I would prefer not to get upset, but it's hard not to when you're surrounded by brave people who are suffering and in need. The best thing I can do is just be myself and not pretend to be this hard-bitten reporter."[3] According to reporter Jonathan Van Meter, Anderson removed the filter while covering the Katrina disaster in New Orleans. "But it wasn't just his raw emotion that set him apart; there are plenty of hotheads on television, and tearing up became more and more common as the tragedy continued to unfold. It was his honest humanity; he comes off as genuine because he is. He connected to those in the hurricane's path, and to the people watching at home."[4]

leading **questions**

1. How can you become more authentic during the interview process? Do different types of interviews allow you to be more authentic than others?

2. How do you see your emotions enhancing an interview? How can your emotions get in the way and become a distraction?

3. How would you describe your style of interviewing? Does your style change when you're the interviewer versus the interviewee? If so, how?

terms & definitions

Interview a form of oral interaction structured to achieve a goal; it often includes just two people (but can include more) who take turns speaking and listening.

Through the interview process, you're able to obtain information as well as inform and influence others in important ways. Consider the following everyday workplace examples of interviewing:

- Lisa, a department store manager, conducts an appraisal interview with Brian, a wardrobe consultant, about his job performance during the fourth quarter.

- Alexi conducts an information-gathering interview with Sophie, who is a project leader for a prominent software company. Alexi wants to find out more about Sophie's job duties and the skills needed in this profession.

- Nick, a journalist, interviews a church official about an allegation of child abuse between a pastor and a child of one of the parishioners.

- Monique is being interviewed by Celeste, her personal trainer at the gym, to identify her personal fitness goals.

"Interviewing is like ballroom dancing; to keep from stepping on each other's toes, you must lead and follow at the same time without the other person knowing."

—Anonymous

An **interview** is a form of oral interaction structured to achieve a goal; it often includes just two people (interviewer and interviewee) but can include more than two people, who take turns speaking and listening. Interviewing is an interpersonal process of asking and answering questions. An effective interview meets three criteria:

- It's *structured*. The interview is a planned conversation that includes an introduction, a body, and a conclusion.

- It's *goal oriented*. The planned conversation has a purpose. The goal of Nick's interview with the mayor was to obtain information. The goal of Lisa's interview with Brian was to review his job performance.

- It's *role directed*. The interview includes two roles: the interviewer and the interviewee. Usually, the primary role of the interviewer is to lead and facilitate the conversation by asking questions. The primary role of the interviewee is to answer questions. In most informal conversations, the talk time of two individuals is equal. In an interview, the talk time is unequal, with the interviewee usually talking 70 percent of the time and the interviewer talking only 30 percent of the time.[5]

In your professional life you will have an opportunity to be both an interviewer and the interviewee. When looking for a job, you will be the interviewee. When trying to get information for a news story to be published in a local magazine, you will be the interviewer. Many of the principles and skills we discuss in this chapter apply to both the interviewer and the interviewee. There are times, however, when a particular set of skills will be required for a particular role; those unique skills will be highlighted.

There are several different types of interviews. For example, an *information-gathering interview* is a focused, structured conversation whose goal is to seek out important information from another person. The goal of the structured conversation in a *job interview* is to assess the qualifications and skills of a person for employment. An *appraisal interview* is a conversation in which a supervisor or employer shares information with an employee about his or her job performance. If your goal is to sell a product or service, then you want to conduct a **persuasive interview,** which is a structured conversation intended to influence a person's attitudes, beliefs, or behaviors. For example, if you're selling wireless telephone services, you would want to ask the potential customer a series of questions to identify his or her needs and then demonstrate how your wireless phone services meet these needs. These various types of interviews are discussed more thoroughly in Chapter 8.

Regardless of the type of interview, the five communication principles for leadership, which are illustrated in Figure 7.1, are important to the interview relationship. Through

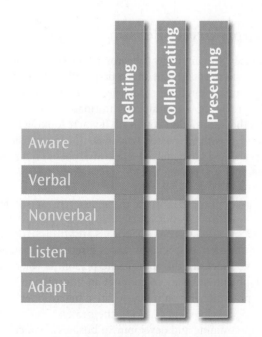

FIGURE 7.1 **Communication Principles for Leadership**

your use of these five principles, you will be able to interview others effectively as well as be interviewed by others.

Preparing the Interview

Unlike an ordinary conversation between two people, an interview is a planned conversation that needs to be prepared, which is the first stage of interviewing. Preparing an interview involves three skills: identifying the interview goal, identifying the appropriate person, and arranging the interview.

Identify the Interview Goal

Whether you're the interviewer or the interviewee, the interview has a goal. In fact, it has primary and secondary goals. The primary goals are obvious. If you're conducting an information-gathering interview, your goal is to obtain information. If you're interviewing for a job, your goal is to get the job. Although the primary goal is important and unique to the type of interview, the more important goals are the secondary goals, which fall into two types—task goals and relational goals—and are the same regardless of the interview type and whether you're the interviewer or interviewee. **Task goals** include asking and answering questions in a clear, concise, and thoughtful manner to acquire and convey appropriate information. **Relational goals** include using interpersonal skills so as to be perceived as interpersonally attractive and believable. Achieving the secondary task and relational goals allows you to reach your primary goal.

For example, if you're going for an employment interview, your primary goal is to get the job. Your secondary goal is to answer all of the interviewer's questions in a clear and concise manner that reveals how your educational background, job skills, and employment experiences meet the needs of the organization. Another task goal is to ask thoughtful questions of the interviewer that reveal your knowledge of the organization and your understanding of the organization's needs. Your relational goal is to demonstrate your interpersonal skills, such as your ability to listen carefully, self-disclose appropriately, and resolve conflict constructively while also appearing open and approachable.

Identify the Appropriate Person

Much time is wasted when you interview the wrong person or when the wrong person interviews you. It's important to spend time in the preparation stage of the interview process identifying the appropriate person for the interview. Who will allow you to reach your interview goal? If you're preparing to conduct an information-gathering interview, then you need to know who has the information you need. If you're looking for a job, then you need to make sure you interview with the person who makes hiring decisions. If you're conducting a persuasive interview and trying to sell a potential client on a new product, you need to make sure you interview the person in an organization who is approved to make such decisions.

Here are a few suggestions for identifying the appropriate person for an interview:

CONSULT PROFESSIONAL ORGANIZATIONS AND MEMBERSHIP DIRECTORIES. Most organizations have a professional association and a directory of names and contact information that can help you identify the appropriate person. If you're interested in careers in training and development and want to conduct an information interview with a training and development practitioner, you might locate a practitioner through the American Society of Training and Development (ASTD), the professional association for men and women who work in the training and development business. You could consult the ASTD membership directory at http://www.astd.org/ASTD.

USE ORGANIZATIONAL WEBSITES. The Internet makes it much easier to locate appropriate individuals. If you're a sales rep for a pharmaceutical company and you need to identify a specific physician at a local hospital with whom to conduct a persuasive interview, you can use the Internet to find the hospital, the appropriate physician, and additional biographical information about the physician that will help you conduct a more effective persuasive interview.

USE PERSONAL CONTACTS, ACQUAINTANCES, AND NETWORKS. Most people undervalue their personal networks—they don't think of them when they want to locate the appropriate person for an interview. It's important that you use both your primary and secondary networks. Your primary network is made up of your family and friends. Your secondary network includes your friends' friends. Your family members and your friends can connect you to their own personal and professional networks. This type of networking increases your chances of identifying the appropriate person for an interview.

USE YOUR INSTRUCTORS. Another great way to locate the appropriate person is to ask your instructors. College and university instructors and professors are experts in their fields and have a number of important personal and professional contacts. Your instructors may be able to refer you to the appropriate person.

CALL THE ORGANIZATION DIRECTLY. You can always contact the organization or office where you believe the appropriate person works and ask the receptionist for his or her assistance: "Can you put me in touch with the person who would be able to. . . ."

Arrange the Interview

If you're the interviewer, you need to arrange the interview, which includes arranging the time, location, and setting.

SCHEDULE TIME. Before beginning the interview, have an idea of how much time will be needed to reach the interview goal and then let the person you will be interviewing know how much time will be needed. It's important to structure and conduct the interview so as to honor this time commitment. It's also important to ensure that the interview time fits into the rhythm of the interviewee's workday. For example, if you're conducting an information-gathering interview with a restaurant manager to assess the manager's needs, it's probably best to schedule the interview after the breakfast rush or during the midafternoon lull to avoid the lunch and dinner rush.

IDENTIFY LOCATION. Finding the appropriate location is another aspect of arranging an interview. Because effective interviewing requires an intense period of listening, it's important to find a location with as few distractions as possible. If you are conducting a performance appraisal interview or a health interview, you will want a location that ensures privacy because such interviews can include conversations about sensitive and private information. If interviewees don't feel that their conversations are private, they may not divulge important and necessary information, thus preventing interviewers from reaching their goals.

ARRANGE PHYSICAL SETTING. How the furniture is arranged for an interview communicates how the interview is going to take place. When interviewers sit behind their desks, they communicate power, status, and formality. When interviewers sit face to face with interviewees at a small table, they communicate equality, accessibility, and informality. The physical arrangement influences the tone of the interview. Some airport lounges have lavish conference rooms that may at first glance seem quite appropriate for interviews. But closer inspection reveals that these ornate and formal rooms are cold and impersonal. The long and wide conference table puts a physical barrier between interviewer and interviewee. To remedy this physical barrier, the interviewer and interviewee may decide to sit side by

Communication Skills FOR A **Digital Age**

Ready for My Close-Up!

If you are planning on venturing into the job market soon, be prepared for the possibility that you will have to make a good first impression—in front of a webcam. Companies looking to cut expenses are streamlining their budgets, and that often means a big cut in funds for travel. So recruiters are moving to new technologies to facilitate face-to-face interactions from a distance. Software programs such as Skype, iChat, and other video instant messaging programs allow for an extra layer of nonverbal messages that phone interviews can miss. When online retailer Zappos.com wanted to cut expenses, they noticed how much the firm spent on travel.[6] They were already using Skype for internal communication, but in late 2010, recruiters started using the video chat program for interviews. Previously, the firm would have had to finance travel and hotel expenses for the top 20 candidates. Now Zappos .com saves thousands of dollars by screening the group through Skype and only flying in the top two or three.

Although using Skype or similar software can be beneficial for streamlining the interviewing process, it is important to pay attention to the specific nature of an interview using a webcam, combining effective use of technology with communication principles. Following are some strategies for effective webcam interviews:[7]

Applying Your Skills:

If you're an interviewer:

- *Watch for informality.* The relatively informal nature of the video chat can carry over into interviews, and interviewers often don't communicate with the same level of decorum as they would in a face-to-face setting. Treat this interaction with the same level of formality and professionalism as you would an interview in person.

- *Ensure you know the technology.* The first step to implementing video-chat interviews successfully is to install and practice with the technology. Know how to troubleshoot problems, and become comfortable with the software and setting.

- *Consider time zones.* When scheduling interviews, be aware of time zone differences. Because Skype interviews can save companies money on travel, it is common for these interviews to take place between faraway locations. It may be noon where you are, but your interviewee had to roll out of bed at 4 A.M. to talk with you. Keep that in mind.

- *Consider recording.* You may want to record Skype interviews for further review. Skype provides the recruiter with the option of reviewing an interview again to further vet a candidate or compare a few top candidates. It's always important to ask the candidate for permission if you're recording the interview.

If you are an interviewee:

- *Use technology thoughtfully.* Be aware of how to work the video-chat program. Practice with the webcam; make sure the microphone works. Don't wait until the interview is scheduled to discover there is something wrong with the technology.

- *Maintain typical interview protocol.* Although you do not have to show up to the interview in person, typical interview protocol still applies. Presenting a professional appearance and with any prepared notes/resume in hand provides a good start for an interview.

- *Pay attention to aesthetics.* Both the interviewer and interviewee need to consider the setup of the shot. Bright lights or windows behind the speaker make them look black or shadowed. Positioning the webcam too close or too low could provide an uncomfortable view. Show your head and shoulders in the shot, sit slightly off to one side, and light your face from the front.

- *Use eye contact.* We have a tendency to want to look down at the person on the computer screen when answering questions; however, for the person watching, that view often reveals the top of the head. However, webcams do provide us the opportunity to simulate eye contact. Looking directly into the camera while answering questions will allow you to make "eye contact" with the interviewer, because it will appear you are looking straight at them.

side. However, this physical arrangement makes it difficult to see each other. Setting up the room ahead of time while keeping in mind how the physical arrangement will influence the interview is an important aspect of arranging an interview.

Structuring the Interview

The second stage of interviewing is structuring the interview, which is the responsibility of the interviewer, not the interviewee. Before you begin structuring the interview, it's important to understand the differences between structured and unstructured interviews and how the interview goal determines the amount of structure. Once you determine the amount of structure you need, you begin structuring the interview by identifying interview topics and writing and sequencing interview questions.

Understand Structured Versus Unstructured Interviews

Construction workers use scaffolding when they are working on the outside of a building. Scaffolding is a framework made up of poles and platforms that supports the workers and allows them to do their jobs. Interview structure is the framework, or scaffolding, that supports the interviewer and the interviewee. As illustrated in Figure 7.2, interview structure falls on a continuum from structured to unstructured. **Structured interviews** are scripted and include a set of standard questions that are asked of every person who is interviewed. **Unstructured interviews** are unscripted conversations that are unique to the individual being interviewed; they do not include a standard set of questions. Unstructured interviews allow an interviewer to probe and follow up on an interviewee's response to a question ("Tell me more about that experience," "Can you elaborate more on that issue?"), whereas structured interviews usually don't allow for this type of detour. Most interviews, however, are moderately structured and fall somewhere between the two polar opposites of this continuum. **Moderately structured interviews** include elements of both structured and unstructured interviews. Interviews with this type of structure include some scripted questions and the flexibility to deviate from the script if necessary.

There are advantages and disadvantages to both structured and unstructured interviews. Structured interviews ensure that all interviewees are treated consistently. They usually take less time and are easier for the interviewer to control; they require less skill. Another advantage to a structured interview is that because all interviewees are asked the same questions, it is easier to compare interviewee answers. The largest disadvantage of a structured interview is that interviewers have no flexibility to follow up or probe interviewees' comments that may reveal important information.

Although unstructured interviews are usually more difficult to control and take more time to complete, they often reveal valuable information that allows interviewers to reach their goals. For example, Kimberly is interested in managing her family's landscaping business and wants to find out what it's like to work with and manage family members. She conducts an information-gathering interview with Brad, who manages his family's restaurant. Rather than going into the interview with a structured set of questions, Kimberly simply asks, "What's it like to work in a family business?" Kimberly can then follow up with additional questions to explore Brad's responses in detail.

Conducting an unstructured interview requires more skill on the part of the interviewer. Interviewers must listen carefully to the interviewee's answers and then follow up with probing questions that they hope will get the interviewee to reveal important information. This type of listening and probing can be time consuming. Despite this disadvantage, the unstructured interview allows interviewers to take detours that often lead to important information that may never have been uncovered in a structured interview.

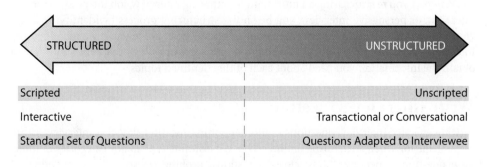

STRUCTURED	UNSTRUCTURED
Scripted	Unscripted
Interactive	Transactional or Conversational
Standard Set of Questions	Questions Adapted to Interviewee

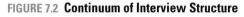

FIGURE 7.2 Continuum of Interview Structure

terms & definitions

Structured interview a scripted interview that uses a set of standard questions that are asked of every person who is interviewed.

Unstructured interview an unscripted interview that is unique to the individual being questioned; it does not include a standard set of questions.

Moderately structured interview an interview that includes some scripted questions but allows the interviewer the flexibility to deviate from the script.

Interviewers must understand the structure of the interview they're conducting and identify topics and questions appropriate for that structure.

Identify Interview Topics

When structuring an interview, interviewers need to identify the interview topics. An **interview topic** is a standard theme explored with a particular category of questions that are asked during the interview. Each type of interview has a standard set of topics; for each topic, there is a set of questions. For example, when news reporters and journalists conduct information-gathering interviews, they usually structure their interview questions around the five "W" questions: Who, What, Where, When, and Why. For example, with the "Who" interview topic, an interviewer might ask, Who was involved? Who are they? Who do they belong to? Who do they want to influence?

When conducting a job interview with a job applicant, an interviewer usually develops and arranges questions by employment-related topics: education, job skills, prior work experience, career path and goals. For each of these interview topics there is a set of specific questions that relate to the topic. For example, when focusing on the topic of education, the interviewer might ask interviewees questions about where they went to school, their degree programs, and their major fields of study. Interviewees, too, have a set of questions to ask the interviewer that are structured and arranged to cover such interview topics as job requirements, manager expectations, advancement opportunities, and salary and benefits. Such questions help interviewees reach their own interview goal: to appear competent, articulate, and ambitious. For example, an interviewee who asks an interviewer about the opportunities that new employees have for advancement within the organization reveals his or her level of motivation and ambition.

When managers conduct appraisal interviews, they usually structure and arrange questions by the following interview topics: employee's self-appraisal, performance gaps, causes of performance gaps, ways to reduce performance gaps. The manager may begin by asking a set of questions that tap into the topic of employee's self-appraisal, such as "Tell me how you think you're doing in your new position," and "Do you consider yourself to be reaching your performance goals?" Answers to these questions allow the manager to gauge the questions to ask when exploring the other interview topics. If an employee says that she's reaching her performance goals in her new position, the interviewer might use this response to explore a new line of questioning focusing on teamwork. For example, the interviewer might ask, "What role did the team play in helping you reach your performance goals?"

Whether you're structuring an information-gathering interview, job interview, appraisal interview, or persuasive interview, you begin the structuring process by identifying interview topics that will allow you to reach your interview goal. Once you have identified the interview topics, it's time to begin writing the interview questions that will allow you to obtain the information you need about each of the identified topics.

terms & definitions

Interview topic a standard theme that is explored with a particular category of questions that are asked during an interview.

Write Interview Questions

Writing effective interview questions is another communication skill that interviewers are responsible for when structuring an interview. We examine four major categories of interview questions: open questions, closed questions, probing questions, and hypothetical questions.

OPEN QUESTIONS. An **open question** is broad and unstructured and allows the respondent considerable freedom to determine the amount and kind of information she or he will provide. Most open questions are either questions of value, questions of process, or questions of policy. *Questions of value* ask respondents to discuss what they consider to be important. *Questions of process* ask respondents to talk about how they might do something. *Questions of policy* ask respondents to talk about what they might change or propose. For example, suppose you're conducting an information-gathering interview with the new president of the university for an article to appear in the school newspaper. Here are some open questions you might use in this type of interview:

- Question of value: What makes an *excellent* university?
- Question of process: *How* do you lead?
- Question of policy: What changes *should* be made to improve the university?

The italicized word in each of these questions is a clue to the question type. Questions of value usually include a word that gets at the worth of something (such as *excellent*). Answers to value questions usually reveal what a respondent considers to be important or the respondent's priorities. Questions of process usually begin with *How*, which encourages the respondent to discuss a series of actions. Answers to process questions usually reveal the steps a respondent would take to accomplish a particular goal. Questions of policy usually include the word *should*. Answers to policy questions can reveal the actions the respondent wants to take in the future or changes the respondent would like to make.

Here are some questions that tap into values, processes, and policies and that might be asked of an applicant in a job interview:

- Question of value: *What* are you looking for in a company?
- Question of process: *How* do you resolve conflict with coworkers?
- Question of policy: What *should* employers do to motivate employees?

Because open questions encourage an interviewee to share information almost without restriction, they are useful in determining opinions, values, and perspectives. Open questions are most appropriate in less structured interviews when time is not limited.

CLOSED QUESTIONS. A **closed question** is one that limits the range of possible responses and requires a simple, direct, and brief answer. Consider a personal trainer at a gym who is talking to someone who is considering purchasing a gym membership. The trainer conducts an informal persuasive interview to help the potential customer identify his needs and goals and to convince him that the gym can meet those goals. The trainer might ask a number of closed questions:

- What is your weight?
- How many complete meals do you eat daily?
- How many times per week do you exercise?

All of these questions can be answered with direct and brief responses. Some closed questions allow you to select from a range of responses:

How would you classify your physical condition?

    a. Very good

    b. Good

    c. Average

    d. Poor

    e. Very poor

Closed questions enable an interviewer to gather specific information because they restrict interviewees' freedom to express personal views or elaborate on responses. They also allow an interviewer to ask a greater number of questions in a limited amount of time. Closed questions are most appropriate in structured interviews.

terms & definitions

Open question an interview question that is broad and unstructured and allows the respondent considerable freedom to determine the amount and kind of information she or he will provide.

Closed question an interview question that limits the range of possible responses and requires a simple, direct, and brief answer.

PROBING QUESTIONS. A **probing question** is one that encourages the interviewee to clarify or elaborate on partial or superficial responses and that usually guides the discussion in a particular direction. The use of probing questions is one way to tell an experienced interviewer from a novice. The novice interviewer sticks to scripted questions and doesn't deviate from the script regardless of the interviewee's response to a question. The experienced interviewer, however, carefully listens for ways to deviate from the scripted questions to get additional relevant and precise information from an interviewee. The following paragraphs describe four of the more popular types of probes and ways to use them.[8]

A *nudging probe* encourages the respondent to continue responding to a question; it nudges the person. Interviewers use the nudging probe when they feel an interviewee's response is incomplete. The nudging probe is usually a single word or a very short phrase, such as:

- Go ahead . . .
- Please continue.
- And then . . . ?
- So . . . ?

A *clearinghouse probe* is used when interviewers want to make sure they have exhausted the questioning on a particular topic. Because interviewers sometimes don't ask important questions, clearinghouse probes encourage interviewees to volunteer information that may provide a more complete answer to an asked or unasked question. Following are examples of clearinghouse probes:

- Is there anything else that you would like to add about this issue?
- Is there anything that we have not covered that you consider important?
- What question have I not asked that you want to answer?

An *informational probe* is used when an interviewer wants the interviewee to elaborate on a response to clarify a point. For example:

- To clarify, can you tell me more about that concern?
- What do you mean when you say . . . ?
- How did you respond to that situation?

A *reflective probe* is used when an interviewer wants to ensure that he or she understands the interviewee's response to a question or a series of questions. Reflective probes are a way to resolve uncertainty. Here are a few examples:

- Are you saying that . . . ?
- This is what I hear you saying . . .
- You think, then, that in this situation you would . . .
- Am I correct in assuming that you believe that . . . ?

terms & definitions

Probing question an interview question that encourages the interviewee to clarify or elaborate on partial or superficial responses and that usually directs the discussion in a particular direction.

Hypothetical question a question that asks for an interviewee's reaction to an imaginary emotion-arousing or value-laden situation to gauge the person's likely response in a real situation.

HYPOTHETICAL QUESTIONS. A **hypothetical question** is one that asks for an interviewee's reaction to an imaginary emotion-arousing or value-laden situation to gauge the person's likely reaction in a real situation. For example, Gerri is a member of the human resources team at a large publishing company. She is interviewing people to assess the workplace environment. During her information-gathering interview with Chance, an employee in the information technology department, she asks the following questions:

- Would you want your son or daughter to work for this company? Why or why not?
- If you were the president of this company, what five changes would you make immediately and why?

Hypothetical questions are also used during job interviews to find out how potential new employees might respond to unique circumstances. For example:

- You believe one of your coworkers is stealing from the company, but you're not certain. What would you do?

RECAP

Writing Interview Questions

Question Type	Definition	Sample Questions
Open	A question that is broad and unstructured and allows the respondent considerable freedom to determine the amount and kind of information she or he will provide.	• What are you looking for in a company? • How do you lead others? • How should managers motivate employees?
Closed	A question that limits the range of possible responses and requires a simple, direct, and brief answer.	• Are you willing to relocate? • How many times have you missed work? • How many meals do you eat daily?
Probing	A question that encourages the interviewee to clarify or elaborate on partial or superficial responses and that usually directs the discussion in a particular direction.	• Tell me more about your concern. • What do you mean when you say . . . ? • And then what happened?
Hypothetical	A question that asks for an interviewee's reaction to an imaginary emotion-arousing or value-laden situation to gauge the person's likely reactions in a real situation.	• You believe that one of your coworkers is stealing from the company, but you're not certain. What would you do? • If you were to become the manager of this unit, what five changes would you make and why?

- Your coworkers continue to look at pornography on the Internet after you've told them that this makes you uncomfortable. If you discuss the problem with your manager, you know that your coworkers will make things uncomfortable for you. How would you handle this situation?

Sequence Interview Questions

Open, closed, probing, and hypothetical questions may be used in any combination, as long as their sequence is thoughtfully planned. An **interview schedule** is a guide that lists all of the questions and follow-up probes to be used in an interview so that the interviewer can sequence interview questions. An interview schedule serves as the interviewer's script. Depending on the goals of the interview, interview questions may be arranged into one of three basic sequences: funnel, inverted funnel, or tunnel.

FUNNEL SEQUENCE. A questioning sequence that begins with broad, open questions and proceeds toward more closed questions is a **funnel sequence**. Using a funnel sequence allows an interviewee to express views and feelings without restrictions, at least early in the interview. For example, Seth, a senior in college, is conducting an information-gathering interview with a corporate event planner because he thinks he would like to pursue event planning as a career. Seth structures his interview using the funnel sequence of questions shown in Figure 7.3, on the next page.

Seth's first question is an open-ended one about the rewards of the profession. He becomes a bit more specific in his second question by asking about the two different types of event planning. With his third question, he narrows the focus further by asking about only corporate events. His fourth question asks about specific steps the event planner took to get his job in corporate event planning. Finally, Seth's fifth and final question is a closed question that requires a yes-or-no response. With the funnel sequence, the interview begins with open questions and the increasingly closed questions serve as probes.

terms & definitions

Interview schedule a guide that lists all of the questions and follow-up probes to be used in an interview so that the interviewer can sequence questions.

Funnel sequence a questioning sequence that begins with broad, open questions and proceeds toward more closed questions.

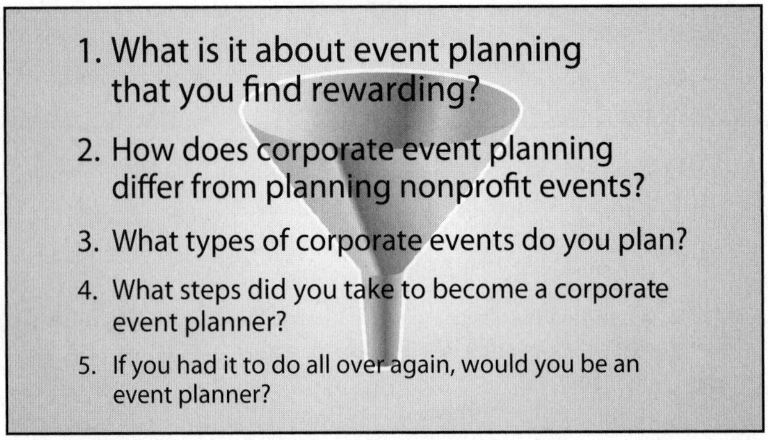

1. What is it about event planning that you find rewarding?

2. How does corporate event planning differ from planning nonprofit events?

3. What types of corporate events do you plan?

4. What steps did you take to become a corporate event planner?

5. If you had it to do all over again, would you be an event planner?

FIGURE 7.3 **Funnel Sequence**

INVERTED FUNNEL SEQUENCE. A questioning sequence that begins with closed questions and proceeds to more open questions is an **inverted funnel sequence.** Using the inverted funnel sequence encourages the interviewee to answer questions quickly. It's an easy way to begin an interview because the questions require only brief responses or descriptions. For example, Jamie manages a temp agency and is responsible for interviewing people to find out their job skills and work-related experiences so that she can place them in jobs that fit their skills and experiences. Figure 7.4 illustrates how Jamie structures her interview questions using the inverted funnel sequence.

Jamie's first two questions are closed questions that require only brief responses. Jamie's third, fourth, and fifth questions are more open-ended questions that require greater elaboration. These open-ended questions are intended to get interviewees to reveal not only their attitudes and values, but also how they might handle a particular situation at work. With the inverted-funnel sequence, the interview begins with closed questions and the open-ended questions serve as probes.

TUNNEL SEQUENCE. A questioning sequence that uses a combination of open and closed questions to gather a large amount of information in a short amount of time is a **tunnel sequence.** With this type of questioning sequence, no probing or follow-up questions are asked. The interviewer is interested in breadth rather than depth of responses. Rather than using an information probe ("Tell me more about that") or a hypothetical question to get at more detailed information (more depth), the interviewer simply moves to the next open

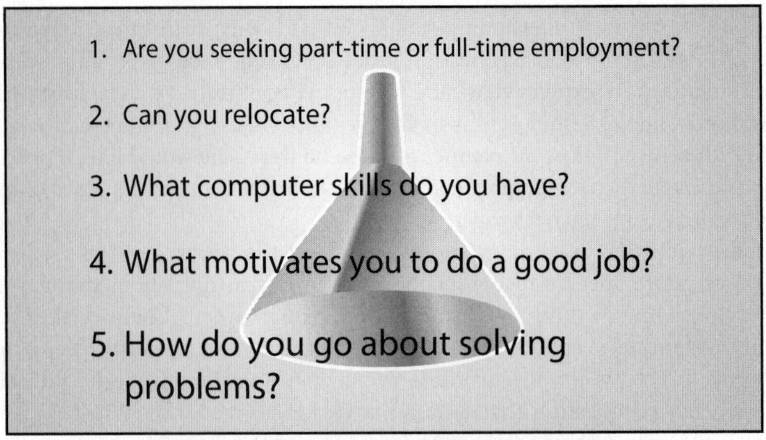

terms & definitions

Inverted funnel sequence a questioning sequence that begins with closed questions and proceeds to more open questions.

Tunnel sequence a questioning sequence that uses a combination of open and closed questions to gather a large amount of information in a short amount of time.

1. Are you seeking part-time or full-time employment?

2. Can you relocate?

3. What computer skills do you have?

4. What motivates you to do a good job?

5. How do you go about solving problems?

FIGURE 7.4 **Inverted Funnel Sequence**

or closed question to capture more breadth (more topics) during an interview. Again, the reason for using the tunnel sequence is that it allows an interviewer to gather a lot of general information in a limited amount of time. For example, Kole is a wardrobe consultant at an upscale department store. His goal is to persuade Leticia to let him pull together a wardrobe for her. He interviews Leticia to get a better idea of her wardrobe needs by asking a series of questions such as:

1. What type of outfits are you expected to wear at work?
2. What do you typically wear when you entertain friends at your home?
3. How do you dress when you go to the Ballet or theater?
4. What do you wear when working out at the gym?

All of Kole's questions focus on a different aspect of Leticia's lifestyle and her wardrobe needs. The questions are a way to "tunnel through" her lifestyle; they allow Kole to assess Leticia's needs quickly so that he can pull together a wardrobe that Leticia will purchase. Kole's interview goal is to capture the breadth of Leticia's fashion needs rather than to learn about them in depth. Again, with the tunnel sequence, the interview consists of a series of open and closed questions that capture as much breadth (the greatest number of topics) as possible. The interview doesn't include probing questions, which usually capture depth or details.

Conducting the Interview

Conducting the interview is the third stage. Although an interview differs from an ordinary conversation in being planned and structured, in one way an interview *is* similar to a conversation with a friend. Most conversations have three parts. First, you greet someone to open the conversation. Second, you conduct the conversation, which communication scholars refer to as "processing the body" of the conversation. Third, you bring the conversation to a

leaders on leadership

Look Them in the Eye. Always Tell the Truth.[9]

Bobbi Brown has interviewed hundreds of people during her successful business career as founder of Bobbi Brown Cosmetics. Her advice when participating in an interview is simple: Have eye contact and be truthful. She also recommends that when considering a specific organization for a job or career move, you optimistically start with realistic positions where you can enter the company and then look for opportunities to move up.

When you're talking to someone, look him or her in the eye. Always tell the truth. And you have to start at the bottom. I don't care who you are and what you do, you have to start at the bottom. If there's a job as a receptionist at a company you would love to work at and there's nothing else, get that job. And don't just sit there.

A lot of people have moved up in this company. Be open and be a sponge. I've always been a sponge. You're around really cool, creative

people, you see what they're doing, how they're dressing, what they're reading, what their tastes are. I mean that's what makes someone better at what they do—they're just open to what's going on.

Whether you've had a career for several years or will soon be entering the job market, her suggestions about being open and receptive to what you see around you is good advice, not only when trying to observe the organizational culture, but also when participating in an interview. Use your skill in observing nonverbal cues (principle three in our five principles for leadership) to help you enhance your leadership and communication skills. You will be more aware (principle one) of the possible common bonds with coworkers as well as how others are/have advanced or been promoted. And you will be better able to adapt (principle five) to others, both in the interview setting and in the organization as a whole.

close. Interviews have these same three parts. Although it is the interviewer's responsibility to structure and conduct the interview, it's important that interviewees become aware of how interviews are conducted so they know what to expect in the opening segment, the body, and the closing segment of the interview conversation.

Open the Interview

The opening of any interview is crucial because it sets the stage for the interview. The opening creates a climate that influences how the interview will unfold. Although most openings include both task and relational messages, they're more focused on relational messages. **Task messages** focus on the content of the interview and might include information about how the interview will be structured and how long the interview will take. **Relational messages** focus on building rapport and establishing a relationship; they're more personal. Asking the other person how she or he is doing, commenting on the weather, or discussing plans for the weekend are examples of relational messages.

Opening the interview includes three skills: making a positive first impression, establishing rapport, and clarifying the goals of the interview.

MAKE A POSITIVE FIRST IMPRESSION. First impressions are important, especially in interview situations; interviewers have been shown to treat interviewees more positively during an interview if their first impression of the interviewee is favorable.[10] In addition to being on time and being appropriately dressed for the interview, another way to make a positive first impression is to make direct eye contact and use a firm handshake. One study found that perceptions of conscientiousness or a person who is perceived to be intelligent, dependable, and goal-driven are created when interviewers see interviewees using direct eye contact.[11] Research on handshaking etiquette and business protocol strongly suggests that a handshake has a meaningful impact on people's first impressions of others and how they evaluate them.[12] Specifically, a firm handshake is associated with positive personality and communication traits, whereas a limp handshake is associated with negative personality and communication traits. A firm handshake is characterized by completeness of grip (palm to palm), moderate strength (not too weak, not too strong), a moderate amount of energy, and moderate length (not too brief, not too long), and is accompanied by direct eye contact.[13]

ESTABLISH RAPPORT. Developing a connection or an emotional bond makes the interview process more comfortable and enjoyable for both the interviewee and the interviewer. One way to establish rapport is to initiate conversations about current events, sports, film, or local items of interest. Linguist and communication researcher Deborah Tannen refers to these polite conversational starters as rapport talk. According to Tannen, rapport talk "greases the wheels" of a conversation and enhances liking for each other.[14] Both interviewer and interviewee can establish rapport by listening actively to the other, using nonverbal responsive behaviors, and by asking appropriate follow-up questions. Although establishing rapport, it is also important that the interviewee never uses profane language, even if the interviewer is using this type of language.[15] Sometimes as rapport is established and two people become more comfortable with each other, they have a tendency to begin talking like the other person. It's important to avoid this natural rapport-building strategy during an interview.

Interviewers treat interviewees more positively if they are on time and appropriately dressed for the interview. An interviewee's firm handshake, accompanied by direct eye contact, also contributes to a strong first impression.

terms & definitions

Task messages messages that focus on the content of an interview.

Relational messages messages that build rapport and are aimed at establishing relationships.

CLARIFY INTERVIEW GOALS. Finally, it's important to open the interview by clarifying the goals of the interview. To do this, the interviewer needs to state the purpose of the interview explicitly; for example, "The purpose of our interview today is to collect information about your job skills and work experiences." It's also important for the interviewer to clarify for the interviewee how the interview will be structured. An interviewer might say, "I'll begin with a set of questions about your job skills. Then I would like to discuss your accomplishments in your current position. To wrap up the interview, I would like to answer your questions." Finally, it's considerate for the interviewer to inform the interviewee of how long the interview will take.

To summarize, interview openings are usually more focused on relational messages than on task messages. Your goal when opening an interview is to make a positive first impression, establish rapport with the other person, and, if you're the interviewer, to clarify the goals of the interview.

Process the Interview

Once the interviewer has made efforts to put the interviewee at ease during the opening of the interview, the interviewer begins processing the body of the interview. This part of the interview tends to focus more on task-related messages than on relational messages. The body of the interview is where the interviewer and the interviewee ask each other questions. As noted earlier in the chapter, interviewing experts suggest that participation in most interviews (with the exception of persuasive interviews) ought to be distributed in roughly a 70:30 ratio, with the interviewee doing most of the talking. We first discuss the interviewer's role in processing the body of the interview and then the interviewee's role.

INTERVIEWER'S ROLE. The interviewer is responsible for processing the body of the interview by accomplishing several communication tasks. The interviewer begins by asking the prepared questions (open, closed, probing, hypothetical) from the interview schedule while following the questioning sequence (funnel, inverted funnel, tunnel).

Because the primary goal of an interview is to obtain information from the interviewee, it's important for the interviewer to listen actively to the interviewee. Listening actively means paying attention not only to what interviewees say but also to how they say it. Inexperienced interviewers sometimes become so distracted by keeping track of how much time they have or by thinking ahead to the next question that they fail to listen to interviewees' responses to questions.

The interviewer is also responsible for keeping the interview focused by controlling the breadth and depth of the questioning. If the goal is to obtain a lot of information on a variety of topics in a limited amount of time, then the interviewer is going for breadth (range of topics) and not depth (details of a single topic). If the goal is to probe one particular idea, event, or episode, then the interviewer will focus on depth by probing the interviewee's responses to questions.

It's important to keep a record of the interview. An interviewer does this either by recording the interview or by taking notes during the interview, or both. If you're going to record the interview, you must get the interviewee's permission before you begin. Note-taking must be done carefully. If you spend too much time taking notes, you may miss important information and the interviewee may perceive you as disrespectful.

Another important task for the interviewer is to answer the interviewee's questions. Anticipate what these questions might be and be prepared to answer them clearly and concisely. Finally, it's important for the interviewer to keep the interview on schedule. Being conscious of the interviewee's time is an effective way of communicating respect for the person.

INTERVIEWEE'S ROLE. The interviewee is responsible for processing the body of the interview by accomplishing three important tasks. The first is to listen actively, which is one way to impress an interviewer. One of the authors of this book used to conduct a number of interviews each year when he worked for a large corporation. He was surprised to learn how ineffective interviewees were at listening: They would answer questions that he hadn't asked! Carefully listen to the question and before responding, make sure you understand by paraphrasing the question: "This is what I hear you asking . . . Is that correct?" This ensures that you're not answering questions that were not asked. It also demonstrates a communication skill that many working professionals value.

Interviewees also need to provide thoughtful and clear responses. Many people are not comfortable with silence, and this discomfort creates a natural tendency to fill the silent void by responding immediately to an interviewer's question rather than taking a few moments to reflect on the question. When you begin responding too quickly, your responses may not be as thoughtful or as clear as you'd like. Thoughtful interview questions require thoughtful responses. Become comfortable with a few seconds of silence and mentally compose your response to an interview question so that your responses are meaningful.

Communication researcher Mary Mino found that interviewers evaluate not only *what* interviewees say but also *how* they say it. Interviewers perceived interviewees to be sincere and intelligent if their responses were thoughtful (the *what*). Also, interviewers perceived interviewees as outgoing, assertive, enthusiastic, emotionally stable, and creative if their responses were delivered clearly (the *how*). Clear responses are those in which the interviewee uses appropriate articulation (no mumbling or slurring), speaks at an appropriate speed (not too fast or slow), and uses appropriate pauses and phrasing.[16] Pauses signal the end of one idea and the beginning of a new idea; clarity is achieved when you use pauses to punctuate your thoughts, just as you use periods and commas when you write.

Finally, although in most interviewing situations it's the interviewer who asks the questions, it's also important for interviewees to ask appropriate questions. At some point most interviewers will ask the interviewee, "Do you have any questions for me?" Appropriate questions are those that reflect positively on the interviewee. For example, Audrey is interviewing for a job as a sales manager for an upscale hotel chain. During her interview she mentions that she is aware that the chain has received numerous prestigious awards for "service excellence" from travel magazines and that the company will be adding hotels on the West Coast. Audrey asks, "What makes your hotels different from other hotels?" and "Are there advancement opportunities on the West Coast for interested employees?" These questions show the interviewer that Audrey has prepared herself for the job interview by researching the company's background. Questions that demonstrate preparedness reflect positively on job candidates.[17]

Appropriate questions are those that help the interviewee reach his or her interview goal. For example, Jade manages a customer service call center for a large computer manufacturer. Throughout the year, she has reduced the amount of sick leave her employees have taken. Unfortunately, during her performance appraisal interview, Tony, her supervisor, does not ask her about sick time. Because he did not ask her about this important issue, Jade asks, "Tony, according to the vice president of human resources, the company has been paying out too much money in sick time and this hurts the company's productivity and bottom line. Is reducing the number of sick days taken by employees still a priority?" Tony answers, "Yes. How are your sick leave numbers?" Jade then answers the question with a report detailing how she has reduced sick leave. This allows her to bring to her supervisor's attention an important achievement and to demonstrate her responsible approach to her job.

Close the Interview

Like opening the interview, closing the interview tends to focus more on relational rather than task-related messages. Closing the interview requires four tasks: review and summarize the interview, encourage continued friendly relations, discuss the next step, and exchange thank yous.

SUMMARIZE THE INTERVIEW. A primary function of the conclusion of an interview is to summarize the interview. Both the interviewer and the interviewee should be aware of and agree on what happened during the interview. To ensure understanding and agreement, the interviewer needs to summarize the highlights of the discussion and ask for any clarification. Comments such as "Here is what I believe we accomplished today during our interview. . . . Do you agree?" or "Let me take a few minutes to summarize our interview. . . . What clarifications are needed?" help the interviewer and the interviewee review the highlights of the interview.

ENCOURAGE FRIENDLY RELATIONS. Another function of the conclusion is to encourage friendly relations. The rapport established during the opening of the interview needs to be threaded throughout the interview all the way through the conclusion. Because not all interviews are positive experiences for interviewees (as when a manager conducts a performance appraisal with an employee who is not performing up to expectations), it's important to maintain the relationship. Comments such as "I'm glad we had a chance to talk about this problem" or "Thank you for sharing and listening" enable both parties to feel that they have had a positive and productive interview.

"Your resume states that you've worked with 2 presidents, won the Nobel Prize and climbed Mt. Everest. That's all fine and dandy, but how are you at telemarketing?"

DISCUSS THE NEXT STEP. Have you ever left an interview wondering, "Now what?" All interviews, regardless of the type, need to be closed by discussing the next step. For example, if you're conducting an information-gathering interview to find out what

RECAP

Conducting the Interview

Interview Steps	Communication Skills
Open the Interview	Make a positive impression
	Establish rapport
	Clarify interview goals
Process the Interview	Interviewer's role
	• Ask questions
	• Listen actively
	• Control breadth and depth of questioning
	• Take notes
	• Answer interviewee questions
	• Monitor time
	Interviewee's role
	• Listen actively
	• Provide thoughtful and clear responses
	• Ask appropriate questions
Close the Interview	Summarize the interview
	Encourage friendly relations
	Discuss the next step
	Exchange thank yous

someone likes and dislikes about his or her chosen profession because you're interested in a similar career, the next step may be to ask the person to email you names of other individuals you may want to interview. If you're conducting an appraisal interview with an employee who is not performing his or her job well, then the next step is to inform the employee of the behaviors that need to be changed or modified and schedule a follow-up meeting. The next step after a job interview is to inform the applicant when decisions will be made and how applicants will be notified.

EXCHANGE THANK YOUS. The final task in closing an interview is to exchange thank yous. Interviewing requires another person's time, and in the business and professional setting, time is a limited resource. Linda Kaplan Thaler and Robin Koval, authors of *The Power of Nice,* argue that being nice (remembering names, saying thank you) is an undervalued habit.[18] Thaler and Koval attribute the success of their New York ad agency to their being civil to their clients. Although saying thank you is quite easy and is a matter of courtesy and common sense, it is not done enough, according to these authors.

Although closing an interview requires some task-related messages, the bulk of the messages have a relational focus. Without appropriate closure, interview participants leave the interview with questions and uncertainty. To ensure that this doesn't occur, interview participants need to review and summarize the interview, encourage continued friendly relations, discuss the next step, and exchange thank yous.

Interviewing Responsibilities

Our fourth and final interviewing stage is understanding the responsibilities of both the interviewer and interviewee. Because interviewing is a structured oral interaction in which important information is exchanged and decisions are made based on this information, it's important that you communicate in an ethical manner. Whether you're the interviewer or the interviewee, you have a responsibility to ensure that the interview is conducted ethically.

As we noted in Chapter 2, ethics are the beliefs, values, and moral principles by which we determine what is right and wrong. One way to better understand ethical communication is to examine unethical communication. Unethical communication manipulates listeners, restricts listeners' choices, and contains false information. In the interview context, both interviewers and interviewees have been known to engage in unethical communication. In fact, one study conducted by Ward Howell International, Inc., an executive headhunting firm, found that more than one in four executives reported that in the previous year, their organizations had hired employees whose job qualifications, educational credentials, or salary histories had been misrepresented during the interview process.[19]

Although some types of interviews are subject to specific ethical guidelines unique to those types of interviews (see Chapter 8), all interviewers and interviewees, regardless of interview type, should adhere to the following basic ethical principles:

- Don't manipulate the other person.
- Don't restrict the other person's choices or answers to questions.
- Don't convey false or misleading information to the other person.

The following section discusses communication strategies that both interviewers and interviewees can use to ensure that interviews are ethical.

Interviewer Responsibilities

There are several things an interviewer needs to do to interview another person in an ethical manner.

STATE YOUR PURPOSE IN ADVANCE. One way to avoid manipulating the interviewee is to state clearly and in advance what you, as the interviewer, need and want from the interviewee. For example, have you ever answered your door to find someone who wants to interview you about the last time you cleaned your carpets? If you're not careful, this person will end up in your living room cleaning your carpets with a new line of steam cleaners that you can purchase for "a low monthly fee." If you're like most people, you resent this type of persuasive interview and you feel manipulated. A more ethical approach would be for the salesperson to first state his name, the company he represents, and the purpose for his visit.

Both the interviewer and interviewee have a responsibility to communicate and conduct the interview in an ethical manner.

ALLOW THE INTERVIEWEE TO MAKE UNCOERCED RESPONSES. Because there is a power differential in many interview situations—the person conducting the interview has more power than the person being interviewed—it is important for the interviewer to avoid coercing or influencing the interviewee to answer a question he or she would prefer not to answer or to respond in a manner that would be against his or her will. For example, during a performance appraisal interview, your interviewer puts you in an awkward position by asking you about another employee's work performance. A more ethical approach would be to ask whether other employees' job performance affects your job performance. This question is more general and doesn't box you into a corner. According to communication researchers Steven Ralston and William Kirkwood, ethical interviewing occurs when interviewers equalize the power by allowing interviewees the freedom to respond without the threat of negative consequences.[20]

ASK UNBIASED QUESTIONS. Another way to make sure your communication is ethical during an interview is to avoid using biased questions, or **leading questions**, which suggest (implicitly, and sometimes even explicitly) the expected or desired answer. An interviewer using a leading question leads the interviewee toward a particular answer by making "it easier or more tempting for the respondent to give one answer than another."[21] For example, during an employment interview, an interviewer might ask, "I'm assuming that you're willing to relocate; is that correct?" A more ethical way to ask this important question would be "If this job were to require you to move to a new city, how willing would you be to relocate, on a scale from 1 (completely unwilling to relocate) to 10 (eager to relocate)?" This question doesn't make an assumption about moving or force the interviewee into answering yes or no but instead allows the interviewee to choose from a range of responses. Put simply, this type of unbiased question gives the interviewee the opportunity to make a free, uncoerced response.

AVOID UNLAWFUL QUESTIONS. A number of questions are illegal to ask during interviews, especially job interviews. The following interview questions are considered unlawful, and interviewers should not be asking interviewees these questions:[22]

- How old are you?
- What religion do you practice?

terms & definitions

Leading question a question that suggests either explicitly or implicitly the answer expected.

- Are you married? Divorced?
- Do you have a family? Do you intend to have a family?
- What is your race?
- What is your sexual orientation?
- What is your national origin/ethnicity/ancestry?
- Are you a citizen of the United States? (Although this information is important for an interviewer to know when seeking an employee to work in the United States, the question cannot be asked in this manner. Instead, the interviewer needs to ask, "Are you legally authorized to work in the United States?")
- Are you disabled or handicapped? (Again, because the answer to this question is important for some job descriptions, interviewers need to get the answer by asking a lawful question: "Are you able to perform the essential functions of this job without accommodation?")
- Have you been arrested? (Unless the interviewee is applying for a security-sensitive position, this question is unlawful.)
- Have your wages ever been withheld for legal reasons?

CONVEY HONEST, ACCURATE INFORMATION. To make sure that interviewees can make decisions in their best interests, it's important to be honest about the information you present during the interview and to avoid intentionally withholding information from the interviewee. For example, during a job interview, a candidate asks when the position is going to be filled. Knowing that the new job has not been approved by the vice president of human resources, the interviewer says, "We hope to extend an offer soon." This statement is misleading because the interviewer is intentionally withholding important information. It is the interviewer's responsibility to explain to the interviewee that she cannot give an exact date when the position will be filled because the job has not yet been approved.

Another important aspect of conveying honest information is keeping promises. If an interviewer says he plans to notify all job candidates on Friday about the status of their interviews, then he must do so—it's an ethical responsibility. At times, interviewers get caught up in the excitement of the interview conversation and make promises they know they cannot keep. For example, a job candidate mentions during an interview that the pay doesn't meet her salary expectations. Because the interviewer wants to hire the candidate, she promises her that the starting salary will be increased prior to her start date. This is an unethical interviewing practice because the interviewer knows that she cannot keep her promise but uses it to manipulate the job candidate into "signing on the dotted line."

RESPECT CONFIDENTIALITY. The ethical principle of **confidentiality** requires interviewers to keep information disclosed during an interview private. If an interviewee asks an interviewer to keep something said during the interview confidential, it is unethical for the interviewer to share that information with others. For example, during a job interview, the job candidate mentions that he is interested in transferring to a new position within the company because of poor management in his current department. It would be unethical for the interviewer, who happens to be friends with one of the managers in this interviewee's department, to share this information with the manager. During interview situations, "What's said in the office stays in the office."

terms & definitions

Confidentiality the ethical principle that requires interviewers to keep information disclosed during an interview private.

Interviewee Responsibilities

Someone who is being interviewed also has a responsibility to communicate in an ethical manner.

Communication Ethics @ Work

Is Honesty the Best Policy?

Ellen O'Hara, a book editor from New York, may be learning the hard way about lying on your resume.[23] When she told her new employer about her previous salary, she decided to bump up the number by $5,000, hoping to be hired in at the higher rate. It worked. However, when she decided to post to a blog about the idea, she was quickly chastised for her unethical behavior. The criticism was so loud that the blog had to pull down her post and apologize. The blog's founder, Amanda Steinberg, wrote on her site, "We've heard from a number of HR executives in the DailyWorth community that even slight salary history inflations are illegal and could jeopardize your job application, and to that extent, we will be retracting this post completely."[24]

Ms. O'Hara hasn't lost her job over the issue, but it has sparked an intense debate over compensation and unethical job search behavior. So what do you think? Current trends in employment show more workers available than jobs. Job hunting skills are essential in the sometimes vicious postgrad job search. However, employers are placing more and more scrutiny on their prospective new hires, and you need to stand out from the crowd.

During the job hunt, you must remain ethical. Behaviors that may help you land a job, if unethical, in the end may cost you that same job. Following are guidelines for remaining ethical during the job search:

- *Avoid misrepresenting yourself.* Don't lie on a resume, cover letter, or in an interview. Don't put inaccurate or embellished information about your education, experience, or training, or even salary. These things could cost you big time.

- *Don't accept on-site interviews if you are not serious.* Unless you are seriously considering a particular opportunity, don't accept an offer of an on-site interview. It can be quite clear if you are not serious about an employer, and they will likely not appreciate financing your trip if you don't intend to take their job.

- *Don't cancel an on-site interview.* Unless you have decided to accept another job offer, avoid cancelling on-site interviews, which makes you look irresponsible. Word could get around in a business.

- *Thoughtfully accept an offer.* Don't accept an offer if you are not certain you can commit. And don't back out of an offer, once you have accepted. It is best to contact any other employers you have been considering once you decide to accept an offer.

ANSWER QUESTIONS HONESTLY. It's the interviewee's responsibility to answer all of the interviewer's questions honestly. By giving honest answers to questions, we adhere to two of the three basic ethical principles: We avoid manipulating the interviewer, and we don't limit the interviewer's options and choices. For example, to say during a job interview that you can begin work immediately when you know you can't is dishonest. If the interviewer needs to fill the position immediately and he extends an offer that you know you cannot accept, you have both manipulated the interviewer into giving you a job and limited the interviewer's choices. Had he continued to interview additional job candidates, he might have found a qualified person who could begin the job immediately.

Answering questions honestly also means not misrepresenting the facts about prior positions you've held or your history when being interviewed. For example, a twenty-one-year-old college student who sold advertisements for the school newspaper for four semesters cannot honestly claim to have five years of full-time sales and marketing experience. Similarly, you can't say you have international work experience when the only experience you have is one month studying Spanish in a Mexican border town to fulfill your foreign language requirement for graduation. It is unethical to claim to have a skill needed for a particular position when you don't have the skill. Instead, you can say you will do what is necessary to acquire the skill as soon as possible.

Although, as noted earlier, businesses have been known to hire people whose job qualifications, educational credentials, or salary histories had been misrepresented during the interview process, research also suggests that both interviewers and work colleagues are able to detect when job applicants are not telling the truth or when they've misrepresented their credentials. One of the ways we detect deception is when verbal and nonverbal messages don't match. For example, while an interviewee is telling the interviewer how confident she is because of her extensive background experience, her nonverbal behavior is communicating a lack of confidence. She is fidgeting in her chair, her voice is soft, and it takes her a while to formulate answers to questions that should be easy to answer for a person with her background experience. Research also indicates that, once a person is hired, his or her colleagues can detect whether the person was dishonest during the interview process.[25]

KEEP YOUR WORD.   Don't make promises that you cannot keep. Interviewers are expected to keep their word, and the interviewee has the same responsibility. If you say that you can begin work in two weeks, you will be expected to begin the new job in exactly two weeks. Sometimes we make promises we know we cannot keep out of fear of the other person's response. Such empty promises will eventually backfire in business and professional contexts, where an individual's credibility is vital to his or her success in the organization.

RESPECT CONFIDENTIALITY.   Because some of the information that is exchanged in an interview can be personal or sensitive, it's important to keep the information to oneself and not to share it with others, particularly if the interviewer specifically asks you to keep the information confidential. For example, if you learn through an informational interview that an employee is about to be fired, you should not share this sensitive information with anyone. Violating this type of trust with an interviewer will ultimately backfire on the interviewee. Although the business and professional world appears very large, professionals are highly networked through professional organizations and technology—so their world is actually quite small. If you fail to respect confidentiality, or engage in any other unethical interviewing behavior for that matter, the word travels quickly, eliminating the likelihood of your reaching your interview goal.

Interviewers and interviewees are responsible to each other during an interview. A number of communication skills ensure that interviewers and interviewees conduct the interview in an ethical manner.

Wrap-Up

Interviews are a common and necessary mode of communication at work. Developing skills in this area is vitally important for many different workplace contexts, not to mention they will make you stand out as a job candidate. Preparing for an interview is the first step in the process.

- Effectively preparing for an interview starts with identifying the interview goals.
- After identifying your goals, next is selecting the appropriate person to interview.
- Arrange the interview, considering time, location, and setting.

Structuring the interview ahead of time is important for you to reach your interview goals successfully. Structuring the interview involves paying attention to specific details, such as what questions should I ask, and in what order?

- Consider the level of structure most appropriate for your interview goals. A highly structured interview provides a script of questions, whereas a moderately structured interview allows for the interviewer to ask probing questions.
- Identify the topics you need to cover to reach your interview goals.
- Identify the types of questions you want to ask, such as open, closed, probing, and hypothetical questions.
- Select an appropriate sequence for the questions, using a funnel, inverted funnel, or tunnel approach.

Conducting an interview is similar to a planned speech or presentation. Interviews include an opening, body, and closing.

- The interview opening has three main functions: to make a positive first impression, establish rapport, and clarify interview goals.

- The body of the interview is where the interviewer and interviewee ask questions. The interviewee should expect to talk approximately 70 percent of the time while the interviewer typically does about 30 percent of the talking.

- Close the interview by summarizing, encouraging friendly relations, and discussing the next step where appropriate. Finally, end with an exchange of thank yous.

Considering the frequency we use interviewing at work, we must make ethical decisions when working through the interview process. Both the interviewer and the interviewee are responsible for ensuring the interview is ethical.

- A responsible interviewer is straightforward with the interview's purpose and does not coerce answers or ask biased questions. In addition, the interviewer should avoid unlawful questions and be honest with the interviewee.

- A responsible interviewee must be honest and clear while answering questions and respect the confidentiality of the information shared during the interview.

Reviewing Key Terms

The Principle Points

Principle One: Be aware of your communication with yourself and others.

- When planning an interview, be aware of your interview goals.
- Understand how to prepare for and structure your interview.
- Be aware of the importance of being a responsible interviewer or interviewee.

Principle Two: Effectively use and interpret verbal messages.

- It is an interviewer's responsibility to foster clear communication by choosing appropriate, high-quality questions to ask the interviewee.
- For an interview to be successful, the interviewee must think through and clearly answer the questions.

Principle Three: Effectively use and interpret nonverbal messages.

- An interview provides relational as well as content information. This information is often transmitted nonverbally.
- It is important for an interviewee to keep in mind that nonverbal behaviors of punctuality, appearance, handshake, and eye contact communicate information.

Principle Four: Listen and respond thoughtfully to others.

- Interviewers must make an effort to listen actively to an interviewee's responses and to use both verbal and nonverbal responsive messages.
- For interviewees, listening carefully so as to respond in a clear and thoughtful way will ensure the communication of accurate information.

- To recognize the most appropriate opportunities for probing questions, an interviewer must be actively involved in the listening process at all times, even while taking notes.

Principle Five: Appropriately adapt messages to others.

- When developing interview questions, the interviewer's goal is to elicit a natural response from the interviewee. This requires adapting questions by wording and sequencing them appropriately.

- Although it is important to be prepared, interviews are dynamic conversations and interviewers need to be able to adapt to get the most from an interviewee.

- An interviewee may also need to adapt to effectively communicate the information he or she intends to communicate.

Applying Your Skills

1. Reflect back on your first job interview. In light of what this chapter had to say about the interviewee's roles, list three things you did incorrectly in that interview, and explain why. Then write down what you would do differently.

2. Think of someone you admire and would like to interview to gain information about the person's career path. Write a list of six questions to ask this person, keeping in mind the types of questions discussed in the chapter. Also, pay attention to sequencing. Be prepared to provide justification for the questions and the sequence.

3. Watch an information-gathering interview on a television program, such as *AC 360, 60 Minutes,* or *20/20*. Identify the different types of interview questions used in the interview. Also, discuss the question sequencing. Analyze how effectively the interviewer and the interviewee performed their particular roles.

4. Work together with a classmate to practice a performance appraisal interview. Assume the employee's performance has been lacking. Write out several questions and role-play the interview, remembering to listen and respond appropriately. Then switch roles.

5. Reflect on the ethical responsibilities mentioned in the chapter. Using a real-world example from your own experience, discuss interviewer and interviewee responsibilities in the specific situation.

6. Imagine you are a public relations coordinator for a major pharmaceutical company and you need to interview the supervisor of one division about a new program aimed at helping the company "go green." How would you prepare for the interview?

Interview Types

chapter **outline**

After reading this chapter, you should be able to

- Differentiate among the three types of interviews: information-gathering, job, and appraisal interviews.
- Identify and apply the strategies for preparing an information-gathering interview.
- Conduct an information-gathering interview with an opening, body, and closing.
- Describe the guidelines for following up an information-gathering interview.
- Define a job interview, and explain how to prepare for such an interview.
- Conduct a job interview, including opening, processing, and closing the interview effectively.
- Discuss ways to effectively follow up a job interview.
- List strategies for preparing for an appraisal interview.
- Describe how to effectively conduct and follow up an appraisal interview.

How to hire a good hotel desk clerk is a question that Chip Conley has finally figured out.[1] Chip is the CEO of Joie de Vivre Hospitality, which is California's largest boutique hotel company that he founded in 1987. While interviewing potential hotel employees, Chip asks candidates a number of questions to find out what motivates them to get up in the morning and go to work. He ultimately wants to know what the candidate considers to be "meaningful work." According to Chip's experiences, a paycheck doesn't motivate; meaningful work does.[2]

While interviewing others, Chip tries to find out what interviewees consider to be meaningful work. For example, when Joie de Vivre staff interview job candidates who want to work as a host at the front desk of one of their hotels, they ask the candidates to talk about a time in the last month when they did something for someone else that made the other person happy and made them happy, too.

Chip states, "It's obvious why we would ask that question, right? If making other people feel good makes you feel good, you're going to like working as a front-desk clerk. You'll greet every guest who approaches the desk with a smile, and genuinely look forward to helping them in any way you can. If you don't much like helping people, you'll see the job as eight hours of drudgery and the guests will notice."[3]

For the hotel, that's the difference between repeat business and a disappointed guest. For the front-desk clerk, it's the difference between a calling and a job. "A calling energizes you," Chip says. "A job depletes you."

Chip Conley is surprised by how casually companies interview and hire people. He invests considerable time on hiring the right people and creating a workplace where they can grow and thrive.

leading **questions**

1. If you were asked by an interviewer to describe the kind of work that would make you happy, what would you say?

2. Can you tell the difference between an employee who is doing a job versus one who is doing what he or she was called to do? What do you see him or her doing that makes the difference? Describe the communication behaviors.

3. As an interviewer, what is the best way to ask questions that will get an interviewee to tell you about what motivates him or her?

4. Why do you think some companies approach the interviewing and hiring process in a casual manner?

Leaders, like Chip Conley, participate in the interview process on a regular basis. Whether they're interviewers or interviewees, they apply the communication skills discussed in Chapter 7: preparing, structuring, and conducting the interview; listening and responding during the interview; and being responsible and ethical throughout the interview. As a professional, you will use these skills in three primary types of interviews: information-gathering interviews, job interviews, and appraisal interviews.

You take part in an information-gathering interview when you need information from others or when others need information from you. For example, if you're the editor of a company newsletter, you probably conduct information-gathering interviews with employees so you have information to include in the newsletter. You will take part in a job interview when you're looking for a job for yourself or when it's your responsibility to hire other people. An appraisal interview occurs when your manager reviews your work performance with you at the end of the year or when you conduct a performance review with one of the employees you lead.

"Be yourself; everyone else is taken."
— Oscar Wilde

Although interviews differ depending on whether you're the interviewer or the interviewee, it's important to remember that all interviews are relationships. Whether you're collecting information, trying to get a job, or informing employees about their work performance, an interview is a conversation in which people relate to each other by asking and answering questions to achieve a specific goal. To ensure that these interview conversations go well, you need to understand how to prepare, conduct, and follow up on information-gathering, job, and performance appraisal interviews.

Information-Gathering Interviews

An **information-gathering interview** is a focused, structured conversation whose goal is to seek out information from another person. Of all the three interview types, it is the most common and is one that leaders use daily.

Preparing an Information-Gathering Interview

IDENTIFY THE INTERVIEW GOAL. To prepare an information-gathering interview, the interviewer needs to first be aware of his or her goal for the interview. What type of information do you need? Here are some possible goals of information-gathering interviews:

- *To investigate an issue or an event.* Newspaper and television reporters are responsible for reporting the news, which includes finding and locating information. Reporters identify appropriate individuals and then ask them questions such as Who? What? Where? When? How? and Why? to uncover a news story.

- *To conduct research to identify patterns and trends.* Some businesses have research units that are responsible for conducting market research. These professionals make phone calls and survey customers to identify their needs and levels of satisfaction with products and services.

- *To diagnose and to solve problems and develop interventions.* For example, nurses and doctors interview patients to diagnose health problems and devise appropriate treatment. Personal trainers, who work in fitness centers, interview new members to identify physical fitness needs and goals in order to recommend appropriate cardiovascular, muscle toning, and resistance workout routines. Financial advisors interview clients to diagnose investing problems and help the clients develop new investing habits.

- *To learn why employees are leaving an organization.* In an **exit interview,** an employer gathers information from an employee about his or her work experiences. Because turnover can be expensive, leaders are interested in understanding why good employees leave an organization. They use this information to enhance the workplace environment and prevent additional turnover.

One interview goal of many students who are taking a class in business and professional communication is to gather information on the different types of careers and jobs that are available to them after graduation. This type of information-gathering interview is referred to as a **career-search information interview.** Research suggests that 25 percent of the people who get hired at any organization are known to the employer before a job opening actually exists, and half of all jobs are filled by the time they are advertised.[4] Conducting a career-search information interview is a way for those in an organization to get to know you even when a job is not available. When a position does become available, these people may consider you for

Newspaper and television reporters conduct information-gathering interviews to uncover and report on a news story.

the position even before they begin the search process. In the following sections we discuss this particular type of information-gathering interview.

IDENTIFY THE PERSON TO INTERVIEW.   Once you have a clear interview goal, it's time to identify the appropriate person to interview. You want to interview a working professional who holds a position that you find interesting and that you might like to have one day. According to sociologist Mark Granovetter, most people believe that their job contacts will be close friends and relatives, or their "strong ties"—when the reality is just the opposite. According to Granovetter, job contacts usually come from our friends' and relatives' network of friends (or, our "weak ties").[5] After surveying over 280 residents in a Boston suburb who had taken a new job within the past year, Granovetter learned that only 17 percent of the people surveyed had found their jobs through close friends and relatives. The majority learned about their new positions from people who were only distant associates—old college friends, former colleagues, friends of friends—or weak ties.[6]

The best way to identify a person for a career-search information interview is to use both your strong ties and your weak ties. Ask around. Use your network. Let others know what you're doing and why you're doing it. Let them know what you need. For example, one of the authors of this book decided during his senior year in college that he wanted to become a buyer for Macy's. Not knowing anyone in the Macy's organization, he started asking his family members for assistance. One of his uncles heard he wanted to talk with a Macy's employee. As it turned out, this uncle worked for a man at the Pepsi-Cola Corporation whose best friend's wife was a buyer for Macy's. Through this network of weak ties, your author identified the appropriate person for the interview. The interview went well and resulted in an offer from Macy's of a job as an assistant buyer.

SCHEDULE THE INTERVIEW.   Next, you need to schedule the interview. Some sources suggest writing a letter to arrange the information-gathering interview.[7] Others suggest emailing the identified person to make the necessary arrangements. However, according to some career consultants, because postal mail may get lost and email is too easy to dismiss, the phone is the preferred way to arrange a career-search information interview.

Arranging a career-search information interview tends to be quite easy because most people like talking about themselves and their work. Many professionals are flattered to be asked for an interview and enjoy helping others get started in a career.

Communication Ethics @ Work

Three Cups of Tea: Fact or Fiction?

Through a series of information-gathering interviews and life experiences, Greg Mortenson was able to author his *New York Times* bestseller *Three Cups of Tea*. This book details how Mortenson, who attempted and failed to climb the second highest mountain on earth, drifted into an impoverished Pakistani village whose inhabitants took care of and comforted him after his failed expedition. To repay the villagers for their kindness, Mortenson returned to the village and built fifty-five schools throughout Pakistan, many of which were for young girls.

Although Mortenson's work has supported the development of a number of schools for young girls in Pakistan, an investigative report by *60 Minutes* found that large portions of Mortensen's story had been fabricated and exaggerated for emotional impact and personal financial gain.[8] Through his books and public speeches, Mortensen was able to persuade people to donate money to his Central Asia Institute, which is a nonprofit organization that has as its mission "to empower communities of Central Asia through literacy and education, especially for girls, promote peace through education, and convey the importance of these activities globally."[9]

Although Mortenson's schools have empowered a number of young girls in Central Asia, he misused or misrepresented the information he collected. To make his "true story" more compelling, Mortenson added a number of fictional elements to the story.

Is it ever appropriate to misrepresent information you have collected to tell a more compelling story that has the potential to yield positive results, such as raising money for a nonprofit organization? If you have read Mortenson's *Three Cups of Tea*, how do you feel about his embellishing the information he collected? When, if ever, would it be appropriate to exaggerate or fabricate information?

Conducting an Information-Gathering Interview

OPEN THE INTERVIEW. As the interviewer, you open the interview by ensuring that you make a positive first impression, establish rapport, and clarify your interview goals, as discussed in detail in Chapter 7. It is important to arrive early to locate the appropriate parking lot and office and to dress appropriately. Although a career-search information interview is not a job interview, it is recommended that you dress as though it were and in a manner that reflects the culture of the organization. To do this, you might want to check with your friends and professional acquaintances who might have insight into the dress standards of the organization. You could also check for photos on a company website to get an insight into appropriate dress.

After a warm greeting, a firm handshake, and an expression of appreciation for the person's taking the time to meet, you need to state your goal or your purpose for the interview: "I am interested in learning more about the work that you do, since I believe it may be something that I would like to do after graduating from college." To remain mindful and respectful of the interviewee's time, it is recommended that you confirm the amount of time the interviewee has for the conversation and let him or her know how you're going to record answers to your questions. For example, if you decide to make an audio recording of the conversation, you need to obtain permission. If you're going to take notes, then you may want to let the person know that you may pause in your questioning from time to time to do that.

PROCESS THE INTERVIEW. To process the body of the interview, you ask questions, listen to answers, and respond appropriately. Table 8.1 lists some open-ended questions that would be appropriate for your interview schedule—which, as discussed in Chapter 7, is a guide that lists all of the interview questions in a single document and is helpful for sequencing the questions.

Now it's time to begin the interview dance—the give-and-take of the interview conversation. Remember the 70:30 ratio rule, which suggests that, ideally, the interviewee should talk about 70 percent of the time and the interviewer about 30 percent of the time. Following each question, it's important to listen carefully and show that you're listening by making as

TABLE 8.1	Questions for a Career-Search Information Interview

The following questions have been shown to be helpful for gathering information when interviewing people about jobs and careers that you find interesting.

- How did you get into this line of work? Into this particular job?
- What do you like most about your job? What do you like least?
- If you had to do it all over again, would you choose this line of work?
- Can you walk me through your typical workday?
- What has surprised you about your current position?
- Describe the ideal person for this career or job.
- What questions could I expect to be asked if I were interviewing for this position?
- What should I look for in a company when interviewing for this type of position?
- What trends do you anticipate occurring in this line of work over the next ten years, and how are you going to prepare to meet these changing trends?
- How do you recommend I begin preparing myself to adapt to these changing trends?
- In what ways were you prepared for your job? In what ways were you not prepared for your job?
- What college or university courses do you wish you had taken to prepare you for this position? Do you wish you had concentrated on a different major?
- What professional organizations do you recommend I join to begin building my professional network?
- Who else should I talk to about this type of career, position, or job? Could you provide me with additional names or contacts?

much eye contact as possible and by using nonverbal responsive behaviors. Another way to enhance listening effectiveness and note-taking accuracy, and to support the interviewee, is to paraphrase what you hear the interviewee saying. Depending on the amount of time you have and whether you're reaching your interview goals, you can continue to ask questions, using the various probes discussed in Chapter 7 to gain additional insight. Or, you can ask the interviewee if there are questions you have not asked that should be asked.

CLOSE THE INTERVIEW. To close a career-search information interview, it's important to summarize the interview, get the name of another contact if possible, and express your thanks and appreciation to the interviewee. Summarizing the interview may mean restating some of the main ideas or themes that you learned during the interview. Because of the importance of personal and professional networks in getting a job, ideally you'll want to leave the interview with a lead or the name of a contact for another interview. Finally, close the interview by expressing your thanks and appreciation to the interviewee for taking his or her time to meet with you.

Following Up an Information-Gathering Interview

EXPRESS THANKS. One of the goals when following up on an interview is to leave a positive impression and to thank the interviewee for his or her time. Immediately following the interview, send a note of thanks to the interviewee. The note can be short and simple: *"I wanted to thank you for talking with me yesterday about your job and career path. I very much appreciated your taking time out of your busy schedule to do this. Again, thank you. Best wishes,"* followed by your signature. Make sure you spell the person's name correctly in the note. To ensure that you know the correct spelling and address, take the person's business card.[10] It would also be a good idea to send an email or a note to thank the individual who referred you to your interviewee. This type of personal expression leaves a good impression on many people and reflects a maturity and thoughtfulness that is appreciated.

PROCESS YOUR NOTES. Another follow-up activity is to take time to process the interview notes. Review the questions and the interviewee's responses and summarize the key findings. Take a few minutes to write additional notes. What questions remain? What concerns did the interview uncover? What did the interviewee say that clarified your thinking?

leaders ON leadership

Do What You Love: Love What You Do[11]

Are you one of those people who have not yet settled on your specific vocational calling? The word "vocation" comes from the Latin word *vocare*, which means voice or "to call." Rather than thinking of your vocation as a job that you seek, think of it as "a calling" (a voice or *vocare*) that you hear that calls you to your life's work. But perhaps you've not yet decided on your specific vocation—perhaps you've not heard your personal call as to what you'll do when you complete your education. Maybe you've had advice from countless well-intentioned friends and family members, but you are still uncertain as to what job you'll pursue.

Steve Hannah, chief executive officer of the satirical newspaper *The Onion*, suggests that your vocational calling should ultimately be something that you have a passion for—something you love to do. Here's Hannah's vocational advice:

Find what you really love to do and then go after it—relentlessly. And don't fret about the money. Because what you love to do is quite likely what you're good at. And what you're good at will likely bring you financial reward eventually.

I've seen too many people who have plotted a career, and often what's at the heart of all that plotting is nothing other than a stack of dollar bills. You need to be happy in order to be good, and you need to be good in order to succeed. And when you succeed, there's a good chance you'll get paid.

As you read this chapter, we echo the advice of Steve Hannah. As you listen for your vocational call and make decisions about which company to interview with, consider this counsel: Do what you love and love what you do.

TAKE THE NEXT STEP. Finally, make sure to follow through on the next step. Make an appointment with your next interviewee, develop additional questions based on your prior interview experiences, and begin the process all over again. The purpose of conducting multiple career-search information interviews is not only to learn more about the career field that you find interesting, but also to develop your professional network.

Job Interviews

The goal of the structured conversation in a **job interview** is for the interviewer to assess the interviewee's qualifications and skills for employment. During the information interview, you played the role of the interviewer. In the job interview, you will be the interviewee.

Preparing a Job Interview

To prepare the job interview, you need to (1) identify your interview goal, (2) develop your resume, (3) identify and research the appropriate organization, position, and contact person, (4) write a cover letter, and (5) arrange the interview.

IDENTIFY THE INTERVIEW GOAL. As the interviewee, you need to clarify your interview goal. You do this by conducting a self-assessment and becoming aware of your skills. You begin by asking yourself what you know and what you can do that an employer would consider desirable. Your task is to identify skills that are marketable. According to one survey of employers, more than 90 percent of the people they interviewed could not adequately describe the skills they possessed.[12] To help you identify your skills, we describe three types: adaptive skills, transferable skills, and job-related skills.

Self-management skills, referred to as **adaptive skills,** are the skills that allow you to be social and to function every day; they allow you to adjust to a variety of situations. Some of these adaptive skills are based in your personality and include such social qualities as being approachable, warm, good-natured, humble, loyal, committed, and flexible. Other adaptive skills are functional and allow you to get things done, including being able to manage time and meet deadlines; being organized, punctual, and motivated; following instructions, taking initiative, and being resourceful. Although many of us take these social and functional skills for granted, a number of people have few or underdeveloped adaptive skills.

Skills that are useful in a variety of jobs and positions are referred to as **transferable skills.** You can begin by identifying the skills that you're learning in this business and professional communication class, including interviewing, conflict management, meeting management, group problem solving, and sales presentation skills. Other important communication-related transferable skills include leading, negotiating, instructing, establishing and maintaining relationships, and counseling. The ability to think critically, to analyze data, and to use technology are other highly valued transferable skills in today's organizations.

Many positions require **job-related skills** that are specific to that particular occupation. For example, to be an accountant, you need to understand standard accounting practices, (such as double-entry bookkeeping) and the various categories of accounting (such as financial, management, and tax accounting). To be considered for a position as an airline pilot, you need to be able to fly an airplane and to have logged a certain number of flight hours. Most jobs or professional positions have a **job description,** which is a document outlining the specific skills required for that particular position. The following resources will help you learn more about the various types of jobs and career fields that are available:

- *Occupational Outlook Handbook* and the *Dictionary of Occupational Titles,* which are more than likely located in your library
- The U.S. Department of Labor's *Occupational Information Network* (O*NET) at www.onetcenter.org

terms & definitions

Job interview a structured interview in which an interviewer assesses an interviewee's qualifications and skills for employment.

Adaptive skills self-management skills that allow you to adjust to a variety of social situations.

Transferable skills skills that are useful in a variety of jobs and positions.

Job-related skills skills that are specific to a particular occupation.

Job description a document outlining the specific skills required for and basic duties of a particular position.

RECAP

Assessing Your Skills

Adaptive Skills	Skills that allow you to interact socially and adapt to changing situations	Managing time, taking initiative, being resourceful, loyal, flexible, humble, and committed
Transferable Skills	Skills that are useful in a variety of jobs or positions	Team building, leading, negotiating, managing meetings, giving sales presentations
Job-Related Skills	Skills that are specific to a particular task or occupation	For example, an accountant needs to understand economics; a restaurant manager needs to have business skills; a pharmacy rep needs to have knowledge of trends in the pharmaceutical industry

- *JIST* is a publisher devoted to career information. The website at www.jist.com contains helpful information on job descriptions, self-assessment tools, sample resumes, and interview tips.

Before applying and interviewing for a position, you need to conduct an inventory of your job-related skills. Because many college students have limited professional work experience, it's important to identify job-related skills you have developed while a student. For example, many students interested in careers in public relations have taken courses focusing on public relations; students interested in journalism may have worked as staff members for the college newspaper. From experiences such as these, you can begin to identify job-related skills that you're developing that fit the job description. Although you may not be as proficient at the skills as you would prefer, such extracurricular activities are an excellent beginning.

It can be frustrating to read job descriptions that require applicants to have professional work experience or skills that come only after working in the profession for a number of years. It may help to know that although job-related skills are important, a study conducted jointly by the U.S. Department of Labor and the American Association of Counseling and Development, titled *Workplace Basics—The Skills Employers Want*, indicates that adaptive and transferable skills appear to be more important than job-related skills.[13]

The ultimate interview goal is to identify a job that is a good fit with your personality type, skills, and abilities. You begin this process by carefully assessing your adaptive, transferable, and job-related skill sets.

DEVELOP A RESUME. A **resume** is a concise, well-organized written description of your background, training, and qualifications for a job. How long should your resume be? Many employers don't expect a resume to be longer than two pages; some will look only at a one-page resume. (Resumes of experienced career professionals may be longer than two pages,

terms & definitions

Resume a concise, well-organized written description of your background, training, and qualifications for a job.

Jacqueline Vasquez
109 East 4th Avenue
Edinburg, TX 78539
(956) 282-1052
jlvasquez@yahoo.com

Professional Objective:
Seeking a position in human resources as a training specialist.

Education:
Bachelor of Arts degree
Major: Communication Studies; Minor: Business
The University of Texas–Pan American
Graduation date: May 20XX

Professional Experience:
20XX–Present: Intern, Convergys, McAllen, TX
Assisted in creating a leadership training program. Wrote copy for flyers and display ads. Made cold calls to prospective clients.

20XX–August, 20XX: Intern, Target, Edinburg, TX.
Developed sales training seminar. Coordinated initial plan for writing advertising copy for Crest, Inc.'s ad campaign.

20XX–20XX: Supervisor, S&B Associates, Mission, TX.
Supervised three employees and edited training materials.

20XX–20XX: Advertising sales representative and reporter, *The Pan American*, Edinburg, TX. Sold ads for the university paper and worked as student life reporter.

Other Experiences:
20XX–20XX: Summer jobs and part-time work

Skills:
Team Leadership, Photography, Computer Proficiency, Research and Analysis, Public Speaking, Customer Service

Accomplishments and Honors:
Paid for the majority of my college education while maintaining a 3.5 GPA
Presidential Scholarship
Vice-President of the University of Texas–Pan American's Communication Studies Club
Coordinator of *Panorama*, the student yearbook

Professional Organizations:
American Society for Training and Development
Communication Studies Club
National Communication Association

Interests:
Photography, tennis, softball, theatre

References:
Available on request.

FIGURE 8.1 **Sample Resume**

however.) Although your resume is important in helping you land a job, its key function is to help you get an interview—it's how you perform in the interview that determines whether you get the job. Employers rarely hire someone based only on a resume. Most employers spend less than a minute—and some only a few seconds—looking at each resume. Therefore, your resume should be clear and easy to read and should focus on the essential information an employer seeks.

Most employers will be looking for standard information on your resume. Study the sample resume in Figure 8.1, on the preceding page.[14] These essential pieces of information should be included on your resume:

- *Personal information*: Employers will look for your name, address, phone numbers, email address, and web page address (if you have one). Provide phone numbers where you can be reached during both the day and the evening.

- *Career objective*: Many employers will want to see your career objective. Make it brief, clear, and focused. You may need to customize your career objective for the different positions you seek.

- *Education*: Include your major, your degree, your graduation date, and the institution you attended.

- *Experience*: Describe your relevant work experience, listing your most recent job first. Include the names of employers, dates when you worked, and a very brief description of your duties.

- *Honors and accomplishments*: List any awards, honors, offices held, or other leadership responsibilities.

- *Optional information*: If you have volunteer experience, have traveled, or have computer skills or other pertinent experience, be sure to include this information if it is relevant to your objective and the job.

- *References*: **References** are people who can speak positively about your skills and abilities to an employer. At the bottom of your resume, indicate that your references are available on request. Some job postings may request applicants to provide a list of references' names, phone numbers, and email addresses. If so, you can attach a separate page to your resume.

IDENTIFY AND RESEARCH APPROPRIATE ORGANIZATION, POSITION, AND CONTACT PERSON. Once you have your resume in hand, you identify and research the organization, position, and person you will contact to arrange an interview. Some experts suggest that students may want to begin the process of identifying the appropriate position first and the organization second. Others suggest identifying the organization first and the position second. For example, if Seth is interested in a managerial position, he may want to identify as many entry-level management positions as possible and begin the research process. He doesn't care about the type of organization or industry that is offering the job, as long as it's an entry-level management position. He might end up interviewing to be a manager of a waste management company, a local coffee shop, or the accounts receivable department of a large hospital.

Seth could also conduct his job search by first identifying the type of organization or industry that he would like to be associated with, and then focusing on finding the right position within the industry. Many students tend to be more certain of the types of organizations they would like to be associated with and less certain of the types of positions that might be available. For example, some students may want to work in the entertainment industry (film, music, restaurants, nightclubs); some may want to work in the health-care field (hospitals, clinics, labs, surgical units, hospice care); others may want to work in the transportation industry (airlines, cruise ships, trains, mass transit). Let's assume that Seth is interested in airline marketing and sales, but there are no positions available. It may be wise for Seth to get his foot in the door of the industry by interviewing for a position as a ticket agent and then searching for jobs within the industry using trade publications, internal job postings, and professional networks.

According to Richard Nelson Bolles, author of *What Color Is Your Parachute?*, a popular job-hunting book, students tend to underestimate the power of their personal networks (friends, family, acquaintances) when researching and locating a job. The three worst ways to look for a job, according to Bolles—which also happen to be the ways most often used by college students—are

1. Using the Internet.

2. Mailing out resumes to employers at random.

3. Answering advertisements in professional or trade journals.

terms & definitions

References people who can speak positively about your skills and abilities to an employer.

The three best ways to look for a job, according to Bolles—and the least often used by college students—are

1. Asking for job leads from family members, friends, people in the community, and staff at career centers—in other words, using personal networks.

2. Knocking on the door of any employer, factory, or office that interests you, whether the firm currently has a vacancy or not.

3. Using the Yellow Pages to identify subjects or fields of interest to you in the town or city where you want to work, and then calling up the employers listed, to ask if they are hiring for the type of position you can do.[15]

WRITE A COVER LETTER.   Once you have inventoried your skills, developed a resume, and identified the organization and position you want to interview for and the person who will conduct the interview, you need to write a cover letter. A **cover letter** accompanies a resume and is a sales pitch that argues why you're the best candidate for the position. Cover letters need to be targeted to a particular job and person. You want your cover letter to result in a job interview, so it needs to be written persuasively and to argue that your educational training, work experience, and career interests are a fit for the position. Figure 8.2 is one example of a cover letter. For additional samples, visit www.jobweb.com/Resources/Library/Samples.

As Figure 8.2 illustrates, a cover letter should include the following parts:

- *Introduction*. In the introduction, you need to let the reader know what position you're applying for and how you learned of the opening. If you're responding to an advertisement, refer to the job title and the publication in which you found the ad. If you're applying for a position that someone referred you to, indicate the name of the person who referred you.

- *Body*. In the body of the letter, you need to sell yourself: You need to make a convincing argument that you have the skills and knowledge the position requires and that you're a good fit for the position and the organization. Provide enough details to let your reader know that you're familiar with the organization and the skills and knowledge needed in this particular position.

- *Action step*. In this part of the letter, you want to let your reader know the next step you will take—usually, this is a request for an interview. Let your reader know when you will call and your intentions when you call.

- *Conclusion*. End the letter by expressing your appreciation for the reader's time and consideration of your resume.

SCHEDULE THE INTERVIEW.   Finally, it's time to schedule the interview, which means communicating with the identified person and asking for an interview. According to career consultant Michael Farr, most jobs are filled before they are advertised, so if you have a choice, don't wait until the job is advertised to ask for an interview.[16] In fact, one study reports that up to 32 percent of all open positions are filled by internal transfers or promotions.[17] According to Farr,

> The best time to search for a job is before anyone else knows about it. Most jobs are filled by someone the employer meets before a job is formally open. So the key is to meet people who can hire you before a job is available. Instead of saying, "Do you have any jobs open?" say "I realize you may not have any openings now, but I would still like to talk to you about the possibility of future openings."[18]

Some career consultants suggest that arranging an interview by phone is preferred to using email because email is easily ignored. Phone calls get the contact person's attention and provide a more interactive experience, and saying no to a potential interviewee is harder on the phone. It is also recommended that you develop a phone script prior to

terms & definitions

Cover letter a document that accompanies a resume; a sales pitch that argues why you are the best candidate for a position.

1234 West Avenue
McAllen, TX 78541
April 10, 20XX

Ms. Maria Pulido
Director of Human Resources
University Hospital
1201 West University Drive
McAllen, Texas 78541-4646

Dear Ms. Pulido:

I am applying for the Communication Specialist position that was advertised through the University of Texas–Pan American Career Services Office. I consider this position to be a fit with my educational training, work experience, and career interests.

First, my educational training has prepared me to manage communication to internal and external audiences, two aspects of the position mentioned in the advertisement. I have completed a number of courses related to the position you advertised, including interpersonal communication, organizational communication, health communication, and writing for the media. These courses focused not only on developing messages targeted to specific audiences, but also on developing relationships with members of internal and external audiences.

Second, I have work experience in corporate communication that will allow me to immediately make a contribution to University Hospital. As a communication intern for Memorial Hospital, I was responsible for conducting survey research to assess employees' needs regarding internal communication and then developing communication products and services to meet those needs.

Third, this position is a fit in terms of my career interest, which is to become a communication professional in the health field. I enjoy the hospital environment and working with health professionals. University Hospital has an excellent reputation and I would like to become a part of the team responsible for this reputation.

Please consider my request for a personal interview to discuss further my educational training, work experience, and career interests. I will call next week to see whether a meeting can be arranged. Should you wish to reach me, please feel free to contact me at 956-566-0899 or pthomas@utpa.edu.

Thank you for your consideration.

Sincerely,

Patrick Thomas

Patrick Thomas

FIGURE 8.2 Sample Cover Letter

placing a phone call to ask for an interview. This script should take no more than 30 seconds to communicate. Here are a few pointers for developing your script:[19]

1. *Introduce yourself.* "Hello, my name is _____."

2. *State your interest in a position.* "I am interested in a position as. . . ." Do not ask, "Do you have any jobs?" This question is easily answered with a "No." If you're interested in a hotel management position, then you need to state, "I'm interested in a management position within the hospitality industry."

3. *Describe your strengths and skills.* Describe your transferable and job-related skills. "I have well-developed communication skills, including speaking clearly, listening actively, and solving customer service problems in a constructive manner. I also have experience using hotel reservation software."

4. *Mention your adaptive traits*: "I am a committed and loyal employee who is dependable, mature, and resourceful. I learn quickly and require minimal direction."

5. *Ask for the interview.* "When can I come in for an interview to discuss employment opportunities with your organization?" This appropriate and assertive question makes it more challenging for a potential employer to reject your request.

Conducting a Job Interview

OPEN THE INTERVIEW. In many ways, a job interview is like a first date. Although the interviewee and the interviewer are vaguely familiar with each other, assuming that both have done their homework, there is still much uncertainty. This uncertainty usually causes you to feel nervous and apprehensive because you don't know the outcome of the interview. Will the interviewer like me? Will the

To open a job interview, it is important for the interviewee to make a positive first impression, including dressing appropriately and greeting the interviewer in a pleasant, positive manner.

interviewer consider me qualified for the position? Will I get a second interview? Will I get the job? Interestingly, many interviewers also find the process of interviewing nerve-racking. Research suggests that many interviewers have limited experience in interviewing others. Because of this inexperience, they too experience anxiety and fear.[20] The purpose of the interview is to reduce this uncertainty; to determine if there is a good fit between the position and the organization and the interviewee's skills, experiences, and values. Both the interviewee and the interviewer must agree on whether there is a good fit.

To open the job interview, it's important for the interviewee to make a positive first impression. We usually know within the first few minutes of meeting someone how a first date is going to go, and an interview is no different. This ability is the "blink" concept that Malcom Gladwell wrote about in his bestseller *Blink*. Gladwell describes how and why people have the ability to make important decisions in seconds. According to Gladwell, our instantaneous judgments are for the most part accurate and can be trusted.[21]

The following paragraphs review some tools you can use to make a positive first impression. Research suggests that interviewees who manage their first impressions by engaging in appropriate waiting-room behavior, dressing appropriately, using technology strategically, and making a professional introduction are perceived as socially skilled and desirable by interviewers.[22]

Making a good first impression usually begins even before you meet your interviewer, the moment you step foot into the office or waiting area. Never underestimate the power and influence of an administrative assistant or other support staff. Because administrative assistants will be working alongside you if you're hired, some interviewers value their input and their impressions, such as how you treated them while waiting for the interview. Did you greet them in a pleasant manner? Did you establish rapport with them? Did you arrive early, just in time, or late for the job interview? Did you leave the waiting area as you found it when you arrived? Did you wish the person a pleasant day when you left? Although all of these behaviors may appear insignificant and unimportant, they're in fact quite revealing. Many executives have termed these "offstage" types of behaviors "the Waiter Rule." How people treat waiters (or others who wait on, serve, or support people) is usually how they treat people in general.[23] Take advantage of your waiting room time and begin making a positive first impression by developing relationships with those who work in administrative support positions.

How you dress for the job interview influences how others perceive you. For example, several studies have found that interviewers judged job candidates' credibility and attractiveness on the basis of their interview dress rather than on their interviewing skills.[24]

Video resumes and e-portfolios can capture an applicant's personality and showcase his or her presentation skills and abilities.

Although job applicants want to dress appropriately for their interview, many applicants don't know what is meant by the word *appropriate*. Some job applicants believe that what might be considered appropriate for one job and interviewer may not be appropriate for the next. Although there is some truth to this, there are standards or principles for appropriate interview dress that cross all types of jobs and industries.[25]

- Wear clean, pressed clothes that appropriately cover the body (no exposed midriffs); wear polished shoes (no flip-flops, sandals, or open-toed flat shoes).

- Be well groomed: clean and styled hair, clean and appropriate-length fingernails, fresh breath, no strong cologne or perfume.

- Wear moderate amounts of jewelry. Do not overdecorate the body. Remove hats, sunglasses, cell phone earpiece devices, MP3 player earphones, and chewing gum before the interview.

- Cover or hide tattoos, and remove any jewelry in a nontraditional location, such as nose, tongue, or multiple ear piercings.[26]

In addition to the preceding principles of appropriate interview dress, there are some standards of appropriate dress specific to women and men. For women, the standard interview outfit is classic: a navy blue skirt suit worn with a single strand of pearls, and matching dress shoes with a heel of moderate height. Interviewers seem to agree that a candidate can't go wrong with a well-tailored suit in a neutral color (black, navy, or gray). Minimal makeup can also help candidates look and feel their best in an interview.

For men, a suit in a dark, neutral color, a white or blue dress shirt, and a tie in a conservative pattern are considered appropriate for most formal job interviews. It is recommended that men wear natural fabrics, like wool or cotton, and black polished shoes with heels that are not worn down. Socks must match the color of the pants and not the color of the shoes and should not sag around the ankles.

Another way to ensure a positive first impression is to monitor how you represent yourself using technology. What would an interviewer learn about you if he or she were to Google your name? What would an interviewer learn about you by viewing your Facebook or MySpace page or searching on YouTube? Also remember that an interviewer may not have access to Facebook, but his or her family members might. This was the case with administrators with the San Antonio school district who were in the process of hiring new teachers for their schools. The children of the administrators were better able to do cyber background checks on future teachers than the administrators, who were limited to traditional ways of conducting background checks. What the administrators found (through their children) were teacher applicants whose interview personas were inconsistent with how they presented themselves online.[27]

Some companies are beginning to request video resumes in addition to the traditional paper resume.[28] For many employers, "showing" (video resumes) is becoming more important than "telling" (paper resumes). According to one human resource professional, video captures personality and helps an employer determine whether the individual would be a good fit for the organization.[29] Here are a few pointers on how to prepare a video resume to ensure a positive first impression.[30]

- *Keep it brief*. Managers have limited time. You don't want the interviewer or hiring manager to turn you off before you have showed them who you are and what you can do for them.

- *Dress appropriately*. Your video resume is going to be the first impression. You need to dress like you're going to a job interview.

- *Adapt to the audience.* Adapt your video to the position, organization, and industry. The video you prepare for a position at a bank should not be the same video you prepare for a position at an art gallery.

- *Show your personality.* This is your chance to go beyond your paper resume. Allow the future employer to see your personality and your communication style and to see why you're a good fit for their organization.

One final way to make a positive first impression is to be professional when introducing yourself: Offer a warm greeting, direct eye contact, and a firm handshake, and express your appreciation for the interview. Remember that in some situations, the interviewer may be as nervous as you are. This is an opportunity for you to make the interviewer more comfortable. One of the ways you can do this is by commenting on something in the interviewer's office: "I notice the picture of the sailboat. Do you sail?" This type of informal conversation has been shown to reduce the nervous energy that both interviewer and interviewee may be experiencing.[31]

PROCESS THE INTERVIEW. Be prepared to answer standard job interview questions. Numerous interview guides agree that the following are some of the most popular interview questions:[32]

- What can you tell me about yourself?

- Why are you interested in this position (or organization)?

- What are your major strengths and weaknesses?

- What are your plans for the future?

- What will your former employers (or references) say about you?

- Why did you leave your prior job?

To answer these questions, it's important to remember the five communication principles discussed in Chapters 2 through 6. First, be aware of the needs of the employer and how your skill sets meet these needs. Second, answer questions clearly, and ensure that your response directly answers the question. Use a confident voice when answering questions. A confident voice includes minimal pauses and a quick rate of speaking and can be easily heard.[33] Third, be aware of the interviewer's nonverbal messages. What is the interviewer telling you without telling you? Fourth, listen carefully to the questions; if necessary, paraphrase the questions to clarify understanding. Fifth, adapt your communication. Continuously find ways to demonstrate how you can help the organization meet its needs and goals. We'll discuss a few strategies that may help you appropriately adapt your message:[34]

- *Tell a story.* Discuss your accomplishments by discussing a specific situation you were involved in, the people involved, the challenge, how you overcame the challenge, and the outcome. Use enough detail so that the interviewer can visualize your accomplishment.

- *Provide quantity.* When discussing your accomplishments, quantify them—state the number of customers served, the dollar amounts you're responsible for, or the number of new accounts you generated.

- *Emphasize results.* Provide data regarding positive results, for example, "I increased sales by 5 percent each year I was with the organization." Use numbers to quantify your results.

- *Link your results to the organization's needs.* Make sure the interviewer can connect your accomplishment to the needs of the organization, for example, "With my experiences and accomplishments, I feel confident that I can meet the needs you have expressed during this interview, specifically, the need to increase sales."

There comes a time during most job interviews when the interviewer asks if you have any questions. This is your cue to take the lead in the interview dance. The questions you ask during the job interview can be revealing, so you want to make sure you're asking questions that reflect positively on you. Here are a few things you want to *avoid* asking or saying because they will reflect negatively on you:

- "What exactly does this company do?" This question suggests that you have not done your homework and are unfamiliar with the mission of the organization.

- "How much will I be paid?" This question is premature and usually should be reserved until a job offer has been extended. Also, it sounds presumptuous, as though you're assuming you will get the job.

- "I don't have any questions." This statement makes you appear passive and uninterested rather than actively curious and interested.

You want to ask questions that reveal you have done your homework. For example, suppose you're interviewing for an entry-level marketing position with AT&T. The following questions reflect your curiosity and showcase your research on and background knowledge of AT&T:

- "According to *The Wall Street Journal*, Verizon, Quest, and Sprint Nextel are AT&T's chief competitors. How has this competition changed how you do business over the years?"

- "I have been reading about David Dorman's [president of AT&T] management style. Does his style reflect the style of the other managers at AT&T?"

- "What problems do you anticipate AT&T encountering in the years ahead, and what skills will employees need to solve these problems?"

Here are five additional questions that job-hunting experts recommend asking. Listening carefully to how these questions are answered should give you a fairly accurate picture of what's going on behind the interview:[35]

1. "What priorities will need to be addressed immediately in this position?" Many times, the job description, which details the duties of the position, does not jibe with how the interviewer describes the duties of the job. It is important to have the duties and responsibilities clarified before accepting a position.

2. "How long was the previous person here?" If there is a "revolving door" with this particular position, meaning that the organization cannot keep anyone in the position, this reflects a problem with the position itself and/or the supervisory staff.

3. "Tell me about your management style. How do you bring out the best in your employees?" The answer to these questions reveals how the manager works with his or her employees. Is the manager a hands-on or hands-off manager?

4. "What types of people tend to excel here? Does the organization have a formal or an informal feel? Is the organization more traditional or is it more progressive?" Answers to these questions let you know about the work culture and if you're a fit with the culture.

5. "How long have you been here? Why do you stay?" The answer to these questions will give an indication of the health of the department or company. If there is constant turnover, then there are probably going to be a lot of inconsistencies in the work of the department and the department will feel splintered and fractured.

CLOSE THE INTERVIEW. To close a job interview properly, you need to do the following: (1) express thanks and appreciation for the interviewer's time, (2) ask for the job, and (3) and ask "next step" questions. A few task and relational messages may help you close a job interview.

The following relational messages reflect competent communication behaviors because they're other focused and illustrate your awareness of the interviewer's limited time and energies.

- "I would like to thank you for your time. I realize interviewing takes a lot of time and I appreciate the time you have given me."

- "I know you must be incredibly busy and I appreciate the time you have given me."

Although many interviewees find it awkward and difficult to ask for the job they just interviewed for, doing so is incredibly important and reinforces in the interviewer's mind your commitment to a particular position.

- "I hope I have made it clear why I feel my skills and experiences meet your needs. I would like to be given a chance to join your organization. Can you offer me the job?"
- "I would like to be given the opportunity to help you meet your needs and the needs of this organization. Could I have this job?"
- "I would like the opportunity to serve this organization in this position. Is that possible?"

To plan the next step of a job search, you need answers to the following questions before leaving the job interview:

- "Do you want me to come back for another interview, perhaps with some other members of the staff?"
- "When may I expect to hear from you?"

Following Up on a Job Interview

Following up on a job interview is very similar to following up on an information-gathering interview. You need to complete two tasks: express thanks and follow through on any additional requests made by the interviewer.

EXPRESS THANKS.   We noted in Chapter 4 that people have a tendency to remember and be influenced by information received at the beginning and end of a social interaction.[36] This effect is referred to as the principle of primacy and recency. There is a strong possibility that your interviewer will remember the first and last moments of his or her encounter with you. Because of this effect—and because it is common courtesy to do so—it is important to send a thank-you note to the interviewer immediately following the interview. Below are a few pointers for preparing and sending thank-you notes:[37]

- *Decide whether email or regular mail makes more sense.* Depending on the timing and formality, an email message may be more appropriate. For example, if the employer is going to fill the position immediately, you may want to forward an email to save time. If the organizational culture is more formal, a handwritten note may be more appropriate. Referring to Chapter 2 will guide you in what to look for to appropriately assess the formality of the organizational culture.
- *Use quality paper and envelopes.* Stationery stores have quality thank-you notes and cards in a variety of styles.
- *Handwritten or computer printed is acceptable.* If your handwriting is legible, then handwrite the note. If not, then a word-processed note is acceptable.
- *Use a formal salutation.* It's preferable to write "Dear Ms. Saavedra" rather than "Dear Marisa."
- *Keep the note friendly.* Remember that the purpose of the thank-you note is to thank someone for doing something for you. Although it's best to avoid making a hard sales pitch in a thank-you note, you can provide a subtle reminder of your skills, qualifications, and accomplishments.
- *Sign the note.* Sign your first and last names and make sure that both are legible.
- *Send the note immediately.* Prepare and mail your note within the first 24 hours following an interview.
- *Avoid text messaging.* "Thx for the IView! I Wud ♥ 2 Work 4 U!!" is too casual and highly inappropriate for a thank-you note. A recent article in the *Wall Street Journal* notes that corporate recruiters and hiring managers are turning away otherwise qualified job candidates because of their lack of judgment when it comes to using technology to communicate and the informality of their communication.[38]

March 8, 20XX

Dear Ms. Saavedra,

Thank you for giving me the opportunity to interview for the spa manager position at SPA360. After our interview, I am more convinced that I am a good fit for this position and your organization.

Although my experience managing a restaurant may at first appear to be unrelated to your position, I consider my management experience and skills to be highly transferable to your spa. I have a proven track record in managing a business that consistently provides superior service while also yielding a considerable profit at the end of each business cycle. I feel confident in my ability to manage your spa in a similar manner.

Per your request, I have enclosed a list of professional references, including their names and contact information. These individuals look forward to hearing from you soon.

Again, thank you for taking the time to meet with me. I enjoyed our visit and learning more about you and your organization.

Best wishes,

Rick Gonzalez
(956) 287-3421

FIGURE 8.3 Sample Thank-You

Figure 8.3 shows a sample thank-you note that would be appropriate following a job interview.

FOLLOW THROUGH. In many job interviews, the interviewer asks you for additional information, or you may have offered to provide additional information following the interview. If you said you would forward a list of professional references as soon as possible, then this is what you must do. Interviewers notice whether or not interviewees follow through. In fact, one of your authors worked with a manager who purposely made a number of tedious requests during job interviews to see if job candidates followed instructions carefully. The positions the manager was trying to fill required professionals who were detailed oriented, and this is how this particular manager assessed the job candidates' attention to detail.

terms & definitions

Appraisal interview an interview in which a supervisor shares information with an employee about his or her job performance; also known as a *performance review.*

Supportive feedback communication feedback whose goal is to encourage desirable behavior.

The most effective appraisal interviews are problem-solving conversations that use both top-down and bottom-up communication.

Appraisal Interviews

An **appraisal interview,** also known as a *performance review,* is an interview in which a leader or employer shares information with an employee about his or her job performance. The appraisal interview serves as a feedback loop between the leader and the employee, in which two types of feedback are usually discussed: supportive and corrective. **Supportive feedback** encourages

Communication Skills FOR A **Digital Age**

Getting LinkedIn to a Job

LinkedIn is a social networking site for professionals. Unlike Facebook, LinkedIn users are not looking to post something on your Wall or date you. Instead, LinkedIn users want to do business with you. They're looking for new business opportunities. Some LinkedIn users are looking for new jobs. Others are recruiters looking to hire new employees. As of April 2011, LinkedIn had more than 11 million recent college graduates around the world as members of their LinkedIn network.[39] If you don't already have a LinkedIn account, visit www.linkedin.com.

Applying your skills:

Here are ten tips for how you can use LinkedIn to enhance your jobsearch.[40]

- *Edit your profile.* Make sure your LinkedIn profile is complete and current. It's how you get found on LinkedIn. Give your profile the same amount of care and attention you give your resume. Provide prospective employers with detailed information on your skills and experience. If you're currently unemployed, list your current position as "open to opportunities."

- *Get the word out.* Tell your network that you're looking for a new position. The more people who know you're looking, the more likely you'll find a job.

- *Include a professional photo.* Make sure your photo reflects you as a professional and is no larger than 80 × 80 pixels. In this photo, wear what you would wear to a job interview.

- *Develop a professional summary.* The "Professional Summary" section of your profile is a good way to highlight your experience. Select an Industry because recruiters often use that field to conduct their own searches.

- *Identify keywords and skills carefully.* Include the keywords and skills from your resume in your profile. This will

make it easier for your profile to be found in search results conducted by others.

- *Select appropriate contact settings.* Your contact settings let your connections (and hiring managers and recruiters) know your availability. Options include some of the following: career opportunities, consulting offers, new ventures, job inquiries, and reference requests.

- *Find out the secret job requirements.* Job listings rarely spell out entirely or exactly what a hiring manager is seeking. Find a connection at the company who can get the inside scoop on the skills that are needed for the job. You can do this by searching for the company name; the results will show you who in your network connects you to the company. If you don't have an inside connection, look at profiles of the people who work at the company to get an idea of their backgrounds and important skills.

- *Showcase website links.* The "Links" section of your profile is a good way to provide even more information to potential employers and to your contacts. If you have blog or a personal website that is business related, include those in the Links section of your profile.

- *Build your network.* Connect with other members and build your network. You can find connections you've worked with, done business with, went to school with, or are otherwise affiliated with. The more connections you have, the more opportunities you have, but don't randomly connect with people you don't know.

- *Get recommendations.* To a potential employer, a LinkedIn recommendation is an opportunity to read a reference in advance. Having strong references can only help you when it comes to getting selected for an interview or for a job. The best way to get recommendations is to give them, so take some time to write recommendations for your contacts, and they will most likely reciprocate.

---

desirable behavior. **Corrective feedback** attempts to alter negative or inappropriate behavior. Leaders are wise to use both supportive and corrective feedback to achieve maximum benefit in a performance review.[41]

In most organizations, employees receive an appraisal interview from their supervisors, who detail where the employees are exceeding performance standards, where they are meeting standards, and where they are failing to meet standards. In traditional organizations, appraisal interviews usually include top-down communication with the supervisor sharing information with the employee; the structure of this type of interview is formal, and the interview occurs once a year. According to Norman Maier, an expert on appraisal interviews, this type of appraisal interview is referred to as the "tell and sell" method.[42] The supervisor's role is to tell and then to sell, or persuade the employee, that his or her observations are correct. Research reveals that the formal top-down approach to evaluating employee performance usually leads to disgruntled employees and fails to correct inappropriate behaviors.[43]

terms & definitions

Corrective feedback communication feedback whose goal is to alter negative or inappropriate behavior.

In less traditional organizations, appraisal interviews usually include two-way communication—top-down and bottom-up—with the supervisor and the employee sharing information with each other. The structure of this type of appraisal interview is less formal; some organizations refer to these as *coaching sessions*.[44] It is not uncommon for a manager and an employee to have a number of coaching sessions throughout the year. According to Dayton Fandray, this type of an appraisal interview is a problem-solving conversation with the supervisor serving as a coach or counselor.[45] Many of these appraisal interviews include an employee's self-appraisal of his or her performance. Rather than the manager informing the employee of appropriate and inappropriate behavior, the employee takes the lead and informs the manager of his or her performance. This approach to appraisal interviews has been shown to produce a number of positive outcomes for both employees and organizations.[46]

Many college graduates find themselves in entry-level leadership positions in which one of their duties is to conduct appraisal interviews with their team members. To assist you in developing this important interview skill, we next discuss preparing the interview, conducting the interview, and closing the interview.

Preparing an Appraisal Interview

To prepare the appraisal interview, you need to identify the interview goal, analyze the individual's performance, and arrange the interview.

IDENTIFY THE INTERVIEW GOAL. The primary goals of most appraisal interviews are for the interviewer (1) to acknowledge and reinforce employee behaviors that meet or exceed performance expectations by using supportive feedback, and (2) to identify and discuss employee behavior that fails to meet performance expectations using corrective feedback. Your secondary goals are for employees to feel supported and valued and to understand how their workplace behaviors affect others within the work unit or organization.

ANALYZE THE INDIVIDUAL'S PERFORMANCE. You begin preparing the appraisal interview by analyzing the individual's job performance. Most business and professional positions have goals or standards that employees are expected to meet. For example, one of the authors used to work for an international airline as a service manager. His annual performance review was based on how well he met the following performance standards:

- A 10 percent decrease in customer complaints
- A 20 percent reduction in employees' use of sick time
- A 5 percent increase in on-time departures
- A 15 percent reduction in employee injuries on the job

These four performance standards guided the annual appraisal interview that his manager conducted with him.

When preparing for the appraisal interview, an interviewer must be able to answer the following three questions prior to meeting with the employee:

1. Which performance expectations does the employee exceed?
2. Which performance expectations does the employee meet?
3. Which performance expectations does the employee fail to meet?

If the employee is failing to meet performance expectations, then the interviewer must also conduct what is referred to as a **gaps analysis,** which is an analysis of the identified gap between a performance standard and the employee's actual performance.[47] For example, if the airline service manager was only able to increase on-time departures by 1 percent for the year, then there would be a gap of four percentage points between the performance expectation and actual performance. To conduct a gaps analysis, an interviewer must be able to answer the following three questions:

1. Where is the employee's performance now?
2. Where does the employee's performance need to be?
3. What is causing the gap?

terms & definitions

Gaps analysis an analysis conducted by a supervisor of an identified gap between a performance standard and an employee's actual performance.

One of the main reasons appraisal interviews are conducted is to provide employees with corrective feedback to help them reach their performance goals. As an interviewer, you must be prepared to discuss what is causing any gap between the performance standard and an employee's actual performance and help the employee identify ways to close the gap. Ferdinand Fournies, a leading training consultant, conducted an important study in which he asked 25,000 supervisors and managers the following question: "Why don't employees do what they are supposed to do?" Here are the top thirteen reasons:[48]

1. They don't know what they are supposed to do.
2. They don't know how to do it.
3. They don't know why they should do it.
4. There are obstacles beyond their control.
5. They don't think it will work.
6. They think their way is better.
7. They are not motivated.
8. They are personally incapable of doing it (personal limits).
9. There is not enough time for them to do it.
10. They are working on wrong priority items.
11. They think they *are* doing it (no feedback).
12. They have poor managers.
13. They have personal problems.

When providing corrective feedback to your employees, you can use Fournies's research to guide how you provide corrective feedback. The reasons Fournies identified may assist you in helping the employee close the performance gap.

SCHEDULE THE INTERVIEW. Appraisal interviews need to be scheduled when both the interviewer and the interviewee have ample time to have a private conversation about the interviewee's job performance. Timing can be important and must be considered when arranging the appraisal interview. For example, if the interview is going to include considerable corrective feedback, is it best to conduct the interview at the beginning, the middle, or the end of the workday? If you conduct the interview at the beginning of the workday, the employee is probably rested; however, the interview may affect the employee's job performance for the rest of the day following the interview. If you conduct the interview at the end of the workday, you don't have to worry about affecting the employee's job performance because he or she will be going home following the interview. However, the employee is likely to be tired and may not be as receptive to corrective feedback as he or she might be when feeling rested. We suggest that you be mindful of the employee and provide him or her with some scheduling options so that together you can select the time that works best.

Conducting an Appraisal Interview

Like information-gathering and job interviews, an appraisal interview includes three activities: opening, processing, and closing.

OPEN THE INTERVIEW. An appraisal interview is a more sensitive conversation than an information-gathering or a job interview because it includes a discussion of job performance. Thus it's important to open the interview appropriately by establishing a supportive tone. Opening the appraisal interview involves three tasks: expressing thanks, stating your purpose, and describing the process.

First, thank the employee for his or her time. Although the appraisal interview is usually not optional (meaning that employees are usually required to participate), you can show your appreciation for the employee's time. This type of courtesy indicates that you are mindful of others, which may help set the tone for the appraisal interview.

After thanking the employee, you need to state the purpose for the appraisal interview. It's also important to set the appropriate tone in this step. The following examples not only state the purpose but also set the appropriate tone:

- "The purpose of an appraisal interview is to help us develop employees. We want employees to be successful, and this interview allows us to have a conversation about what's helping you to become successful and what's getting in the way of your becoming successful."

- "The main purpose for the appraisal interview is to give us an opportunity to discuss each other's performance. I would like to share some of my impressions with you and I also want to listen to some of your impressions."

Finally, you need to inform the employee about how the interview will be structured. Again, research suggests that productive and constructive appraisal interviews tend to be less formal and structured and to feel more like a give-and-take conversation in which interviewer and interviewee spend equal amounts of time talking and listening to each other.[49] Most appraisal interviews begin with a review of supportive feedback followed by a review of corrective feedback: "I would like this to be a conversation. I will begin by sharing with you some of my observations about where I see you excelling on the job. Following these observations, I would like to hear your assessment of areas where you excel. Then I'll provide you with some feedback about areas of your job performance that need more development. Following this, I'd like to have your impressions of my feedback: Where do you agree? Where do you disagree?"

PROCESS THE INTERVIEW. Processing the interview includes providing supportive and corrective feedback as well as being receptive to receiving supportive and corrective feedback. During this process you will use the principles and skills we have been discussing throughout this text, including having an awareness of your communication, using verbal and nonverbal messages, listening, and adapting appropriately.

The following strategies may help convey supportive feedback to another person in an appraisal interview:[50]

- *Make it timely*. Timeliness refers to how quickly you provide feedback to someone following the performance of appropriate behaviors. Have you ever received feedback too late? If so, you probably didn't even remember what you did to deserve the supportive feedback. It's best to provide supportive feedback immediately following the behaviors you find appropriate and desirable.

- *Make it specific*. Specificity refers to the level of detail contained in the feedback messages. Feedback messages that are more specific and detailed are preferable. For example, rather than saying, "You're doing a great job working with our customers," say, "During the past twelve months, you have grown your customer base by 50 percent and increased your sales by 62 percent over the prior year. This is exceptional performance."

- *Make it frequent*. Frequency refers to the number of times feedback is given. Unfortunately, people working in business and professional settings don't receive supportive feedback as often as is warranted.[51] To maximize the effectiveness of supportive feedback, it needs to be communicated frequently—not just once a year during the appraisal interview.

- *Be sensitive*. With all types of feedback (both supportive and corrective), it's important to be aware of the other person's feelings and to adapt the feedback accordingly. Sensitive feedback demonstrates a concern for the recipient's feelings.[52]

Although most people enjoy receiving supportive feedback, some people don't like the attention—it makes them nervous. One of your authors clearly remembers hearing in an appraisal interview that he did not accept praise well from others and that this behavior needed to be changed! When conveying feedback—whether supportive or corrective—prefacing your statements with a comment such as "I know you might be uncomfortable listening to what I have to say; however, it's important that you receive this type of feedback" is one way of showing your concern for the other person's feelings. When you receive supportive feedback, simply say, "Thank you. I appreciate receiving this recognition." If you're being recognized for a project in which others were involved, accept the supportive feedback, but also acknowledge and thank the others who helped you along the way.

One of the more challenging duties of a professional who is responsible for leading others is to provide them with corrective feedback. Research suggests that employees are more receptive to corrective feedback if they have a quality relationship with their supervisor and if they perceive their supervisor as successful, knowledgeable, and caring or understanding of others.[53] Many of these relational characteristics and the communication skills that have been shown to enhance these characteristics were discussed in Chapter 6. Put simply, a quality relationship between supervisor and employee will undoubtedly enhance how constructive the employee perceives corrective feedback to be.

Like supportive feedback, corrective feedback should be communicated in a specific, timely, and sensitive manner. Again, research suggests that rather than using a top-down, "tell and sell" approach, it's best to use a "problem-solution" approach, in which you engage the person in a conversation about his or her job performance.[54] Ferdinand Fournies refers to the appraisal interview as a coaching session in which the supervisor serves as a facilitator of a conversation. The following communication behaviors have been shown to enhance the effectiveness of the appraisal interview:[55]

1. *Describe the problematic behaviors.* Using "I" language, describe what you see the employee doing (nonverbal messages) or hear him or her saying (verbal messages) that remains a problem. For example, "I *see* you coming to meetings late and I *hear* you blocking all of the proposed ideas without offering any of your own ideas."

2. *Get agreement that a problem exists.* Ask, "Do you agree that this is a problem?"
   - If the employee agrees, ask the person to paraphrase. For example, "I'm glad you agree. In your own words, what do you hear me saying the problem is?"
   - If the employee does not agree, then adapt your communication accordingly. For example, "Let me try describing the problem from a different perspective."

3. *Mutually discuss alternative solutions.* It's best to get the person involved in generating possible solutions to the problem.
   - "What are some possible solutions or ways to remedy the problem?"
   - "What could you begin doing that would solve the problem?"

   According to Fournies, people are more likely to adopt solutions they generate than solutions that are imposed on them.

4. *Mutually agree on action to be taken to solve the problem.* To do this, the leader and the employee must carefully listen to each other and agree on which solution will be adopted to change the problematic behavior. To confirm your understanding, it's important to paraphrase. For example, "This is the solution that I hear you agreeing to in order to solve the problem. . . . Is that correct?"

5. *Be nonverbally responsive.* Many people, when receiving corrective feedback, have a tendency to become nonverbally *unresponsive.* They may take a step back, cross their arms, look away, and sigh. We usually interpret these verbal and nonverbal messages as defensiveness. Interestingly, defensiveness and the nonverbal behaviors that signal defensiveness are contagious. People have a tendency to "catch" each other's emotions.[56] When one person acts defensive, the other person has a natural tendency to mimic the person's nonverbal behavior (i.e., take a step back, cross arms, look away, and sigh) without being aware of it, and eventually this person becomes defensive.[57] To break this natural cycle of defensiveness, it is important to be aware that it happens. Interviewers are encouraged to remain nonverbally responsive even when their natural instinct is to become defensive.

Although communicating corrective feedback is difficult for an interviewer, equally if not more challenging is receiving corrective feedback as an interviewee. You may find the following guidelines useful when listening to corrective feedback; these are known as the four As: acknowledge, ask, align, and add.[58] First, *acknowledge* the feedback. Rather than jumping the gun and immediately explaining your behavior, making excuses for your behavior, or informing the interviewer that his or her observations are inaccurate, listen carefully. Acknowledge the corrective feedback both nonverbally and verbally, by paraphrasing what you heard. For example, "This is what I hear you saying. . . . Is that correct?"

Second, *ask* for additional information to help you better understand the problem. Your questions will also convey to the interviewer that you're interested in the corrective feedback, whether you agree with it or not. Also, the more the interviewer feels that you have fully listened to and understand the corrective feedback, the more likely the interviewer is to be receptive to your response.

Third, *align* with something the interviewer has said; in other words, find agreement. For example, "I agree with your observation that I am consistently late to meetings. I can see why this is a problem and why you might be frustrated with me." Following this agreement, offer an apology and detail how the behavior will be changed.

Fourth, *add* your point of view if you don't agree with the corrective feedback. You do this by first asking permission. For example, "Is this a good time for me to share my observations with you?" or "May I tell you my perspective?"

CLOSE THE INTERVIEW. To close an appraisal interview, you need to accomplish two tasks. First, you need to express your thanks for the interviewee's taking the time to discuss his or her job performance with you. Second, you need to inform the interviewee of how you plan to follow up the appraisal interview. Most interviews will result in an action plan or a detailed set of steps for addressing performance gaps. You want to be able to assess how well the plan works. Thus you might tell the employee, "Before you leave, I would like to recommend that we follow up this appraisal interview. I would like to meet in two months to review your progress."

Following Up an Appraisal Interview

Unfortunately, supervisors sometimes neglect to follow up on appraisal interviews because of time constraints or other tasks that take priority.[59] However, it's essential that you, as the interviewer, follow up your appraisal interview with additional feedback if you're serious about helping another individual change his or her behavior.[60] You do this by acknowledging changed behavior and by readdressing unchanged behavior.

ACKNOWLEDGE CHANGED BEHAVIOR. Acknowledging changed behavior communicates to the interviewee that you're serious about wanting the interviewee to change. It also communicates you care about the interviewee and his or her behavior. Finally, acknowledging changed behavior serves as reinforcement for continued behavioral change.[61] You acknowledge changed behavior by communicating supportive feedback that is timely, specific, frequent, and communicated in a sensitive manner.[62]

READDRESS UNCHANGED BEHAVIOR. If the interviewee has not changed the behavior discussed during an appraisal interview, then it's important to continue the dialogue. Keep in mind Fournies's research, which examined the reasons employees don't do what they're supposed to. Examining and probing some of these reasons with the interviewee may give you additional insight into why the interviewee has not changed his or her behavior.

RECAP

Providing Supportive and Corrective Feedback

Feedback Type	Strategy	Example
Supportive Feedback	Make it timely	Praise an employee who effectively leads a meeting as soon as the meeting is over.
	Make it specific	Tell an employee that he has the department's highest percentage of policy additions this month, rather than simply referring to him as a "top seller."
	Make it frequent	Share with an employee whenever you notice effective behavior throughout the quarter, rather than waiting for her quarterly review.
	Be sensitive	Understand that all messages, even supportive feedback, may need to be adapted to the listener.
Corrective Feedback	Describe the problematic behaviors	Say, "I see you using company time to shop online," rather than, "You never do your job."
	Get agreement that a problem exists	Ask the employee to confirm that she has been doing what you describe.
	Mutually discuss alternative solutions	Ask the employee if he has some ideas for solutions to the problem.
	Mutually agree on action to be taken to solve the problem	You have not come to a conclusion until both people agree on the solution. Ask the employee if she thinks a suggested action will solve the problem.
	Be nonverbally responsive	Make eye contact, listen respectfully to the employee's views, be careful not to mimic any defensive behaviors used by the employee, which could cause you to become defensive.

Wrap-Up

Interviews are one of the more common forms of structured workplace communication. As we discussed at the beginning of the chapter, Chip Conley knows about the value of the interview and places a high priority on developing effective employment interviews. This helps ensure that he is staffing his businesses with the best people. It is necessary for both potential interviewers and interviewees to learn effective communication skills for a range of interview types. The three main types of interviews discussed in this chapter are information-gathering, job, and appraisal interviews.

- Information-gathering interviews include any interview intended to get specific ideas, details, or information from others. This is the most commonly used interview.

- Preparing for an information-gathering interview involves first identifying the goal of the interview, then selecting the appropriate person, and finally, scheduling the interview.

- When conducting an information-gathering interview, properly open the interview by establishing rapport and clarifying the goals, then ask and answer questions honestly and clearly; and finally close the interview and include any important follow-up information.
- Follow-up an information-gathering interview by expressing thanks, processing your notes, and taking the next step where necessary.

Job interviews are intended to assess the interviewee's level of skill and qualifications for employment.

- To prepare as an interviewee for a job interview, first do a self-assessment and identify your interview goal. Then develop a resume and research the best organizations, divisions, and contact people for your industry. Use the Internet for a job search.
- For the job interview; make a good first impression, maintain a professional appearance and demeanor, establish rapport, answer questions clearly and honestly, and close the interview with a thank you. Be prepared with questions for your interviewer.
- Follow up a job interview with an expression of thanks, and follow through on any other actions that need to be taken.

Performance appraisal interviews, also called performance reviews, are a final interview type commonly used in the workplace. These interviews usually involve a leader or manager sharing information with the employee and providing feedback about his or her job performance.

- Preparing for an appraisal interview involves first identifying the goals of the interview, then analyzing the employee's performance against the goals or standards of the organization, and finally scheduling the interview.
- When conducting a performance appraisal interview; open, process, and close the interview using sensitivity, remaining verbally and nonverbally responsive. Use feedback strategies to help ensure mutual understanding.
- Follow up an appraisal interview by exchanging thank yous and also acknowledging any appropriate changes in behavior. If those changes have not taken place, then follow up by readdressing the unchanged behavior.

Reviewing Key Terms

The Principle Points

Principle One: Be aware of your communication with yourself and others.

- In any interview, it is important to be aware of the interview goals before beginning the process.
- In a job interview, the interviewee needs to be aware of the impression he or she is creating with the other person.
- When conducting a career-search interview, be aware that it can be a precursor to an employment interview.

Principle Two: Effectively use and interpret verbal messages.

- In all interviews, note-taking is a good way to ensure the most accurate record of the other's responses.
- In an appraisal interview, use supportive feedback messages to support the interviewee.
- When evaluating another's performance in an appraisal interview, use descriptive "I" language to get at a problem.

Principle Three: Effectively use and interpret nonverbal messages.

- In any interview, it is good to use nonverbally responsive messages such as forward body lean and eye contact.
- A firm handshake, direct eye contact, and a confident voice are all nonverbal behaviors that make a positive impression on an interviewer.
- When receiving corrective feedback, remain nonverbally responsive and avoid becoming defensive.

Principle Four: Listen and respond thoughtfully to others.

- In any interview, to enhance listening effectiveness and to support the interviewee, use verbally responsive behaviors such as paraphrasing.
- As an interviewer, asking follow-up questions or probing questions is a good way to demonstrate that you are listening.
- As an interviewee, when listening to corrective feedback, use the four As: acknowledge, ask, align, and add.

Principle Five: Appropriately adapt messages to others.

- In an appraisal interview, in order for corrective feedback to be well received it needs to be timely, specific, and sensitive.
- All interviews are structured conversations, but you should be able to adapt each interview to the individual interviewee.
- All messages in an interview should be other-oriented rather than self-focused; keep in mind what is relevant to the other party in the interview.

Applying Your Skills

1. Get together with a classmate and role-play a career-search interview. As the interviewee, take notes during the interview. Then take a few moments to take notes on your notes. Reflect on the note-taking process: Was it effective? Was your information thorough and accurate? Switch roles and do the exercise again. Present what you learned to the class.

2. For each description on the following list, identify the interview type. Next, write down a goal for each interview.

   a. Maria is talking with Marco, an apartment complex manager, about her leasing options, move-in date, deposits, and parking availability before she makes a decision about where to rent an apartment.

   b. Frank asks Marisol questions about information off her resume, such as her past work history and leadership experience.

   c. Alex has just joined a new gym. Sandra, a personal trainer, is asking about Alex's eating, exercise, and sleep habits.

   d. Cameron wants his team manager, Albert, to know he is impressed with the last five months' labor costs and decrease in scheduling conflicts. He sits down with Albert to discuss a pay raise.

3. Refer to the list of career-search interview questions in Table 8.1. Which questions would you remove from the list? Based on your particular career aspirations, which

questions would you add? Keep a record of these for future reference when doing career-search interviews.

4. For the following scenarios, describe what messages you might use to provide supportive or corrective feedback.

    a. Carlos joined the team at PemCall, a local customer service calling center, about two weeks after Jenna came on board. Both went through a portion of their training together and competed to be the top of their class. However, since that time Carlos is always considered first in promotions and special assignments, and he has moved up to team leader very quickly. Since taking over Jenna's team, he has noticed her performance slipping. She also calls into work sick more often and has taken less initiative during special promotions. He is concerned about her numbers, but at the same time Carlos feels sensitive to the fact that Jenna may feel overlooked or taken advantage of. How can he provide Jenna with feedback in a performance interview? What messages could he use that could communicate corrective feedback in a sensitive way?

    b. After her recent performance evaluation wasn't as positive as she had hoped, Rosalinda's performance has met or exceeded company standards for several weeks now. John, her supervisor, has noticed that she implemented all of the changes he suggested and really took to heart the constructive criticism he provided. How can John communicate positive, supportive feedback in a way that makes Rosalinda feel valued and appreciated?

5. With a classmate, invent a hypothetical organization that is currently hiring. Write out an exhaustive list of potential interview questions for a certain position. Then take turns role-playing the interview from each perspective. When you take on the role of interviewer, select questions randomly from the list, so the interviewee will need to prepare in advance as he or she would for a real job interview.

9

Collaborating in Teams

chapter **outline**

After reading this chapter, you should be able to

- Identify similarities and differences between a group and a team.

- List and describe the eight characteristics of effective teams.

- Describe and appropriately perform task and social roles in teams.

- Describe team communication networks.

- Develop team ground rules and a team mission statement.

- Appropriately manage team status and power differences and enhance team cohesiveness.

- Define and discuss the descriptive, functional, and prescriptive approaches to teamwork.

o you or your family own any Tupperware? Chances are the answer is *yes*. Tupperware, invented in the 1940s, consists of the ubiquitous plastic bowls and other kitchen storage containers that keep food fresh because of its unique way of "burping" air out of the container. A Tupperware party, a sales meeting usually in someone's home, is held every 2. 5 seconds resulting in annual sales of over $1.2 billion.[1] But the pervasive influence of Tupperware in American kitchens during the past half century almost didn't happen. The inventor of Tupperware, Earl Silas Tupper, was a genius in creating new products, but he didn't know how to sell them. Then Tupper met Brownie Wise, an energetic person with a gift for sales. Their meeting and working together is a testament to how people with different skills and talents can create something that neither one could do on their own. Wise was a marketing genius; Tupper was a brilliant inventor. Through Wise's sales ideas (home Tupperware parties), Tupperware became a household word and the Tupperware business flourished. Without Wise, Tupperware would probably be a forgotten product. But because of their collaboration, great things happened.[2] Working together and with teams of salespeople, Tupperware became a household word.

leading **questions**

1. Brownie Wise and Earl Tupper each had different talents: Wise was the salesperson and Tupper the inventor. When have you been part of a group or team that included people with different talents and backgrounds that accomplished more than was possible if the individual group members had worked alone?

2. When you have worked with people who were different from you, what strategies have you used to bridge the differences? What would you like to learn that would help you collaborate with people who have different skills, talents, and backgrounds than you?

In business and professional settings, most of the truly powerful transformations happen through collaboration. One person's idea connected to another person's vision has resulted in such innovations as eBay, Google, Infosys, Apple, amazon.com, and Dell computers. One person with one idea may be the seed that starts a company, but it's because two heads (or many heads) are often better than one that companies grow. Although one person may be appointed the team "leader," each person in a team can exhibit leadership skills to make a team successful. Not only *can* each team member exhibit leadership—he or she *should* do so. Leadership (influencing through communication) is a responsibility of all team members. In this chapter we discuss how to develop leadership skills when collaborating with others.

> *"Never doubt that a small group of concerned citizens can change the world. Indeed, it's the only thing that ever has."*
> —**Margaret Mead**

Some people enjoy working with others in groups and teams. Yet, despite the advantages of teamwork, others hate working in groups, attending meetings, or participating in *any* type of team collaboration. One researcher has even coined the term **grouphate** to label the loathing many people have for collaborating with others in groups and teams.[3] But whether you love them or would rather leave them, there is clear evidence that in contemporary organizations you *will* work in small groups and teams. Estimates suggest that lower-level to mid-level managers will spend at least one third of their time in groups and as much as two thirds of their day working in teams, attending meetings, or preparing for collaboration.[4] And the higher you climb in any organization, the more likely you are to spend *more* rather than less time working in small groups. Today's technology makes it easier for you to collaborate in teams even when you're not meeting face-to-face, regardless of whether you're collaborating with someone across the hall or across the globe. Your work will

terms & definitions

Grouphate the loathing many people have for collaborating with others in groups and teams.

undoubtedly revolve around what your kindergarten teacher evaluated you on: "getting along with others" in group and team meetings.

Research suggests you will most likely be working in or leading a team or team-based organization at some point in your career.[5] A **team-based organization** is one that has more of a flat structure than tall, hierarchical structure (one with many layers and levels of supervisors). One research study found that at the turn of the millennium, over 70 percent of corporations were team based and the number was continuing to grow.[6] Another study found that corporations spend over $200 million annually training people to work together in teams.[7] Given increased globalization and management's increased emphasis on collaboration, it's likely the number of team-based organizations will continue to grow.

There is a reason that collaboration and teamwork continue to be the way work is accomplished in the business world today. Teamwork gets positive results. Side by Side Consulting, an internationally recognized teamwork consulting group, documented dramatic increases in work productivity after providing teamwork training.

- At Advanced Micro Devices one team of microchip developers improved its productivity 20 percent, and another team cut defects on microchip wafers by 30 percent.

- At Asea Brown Boveri one manufacturing team doubled shipments from $1 million per month to $2 million while cutting engineering design time from 26 weeks to 14 weeks.

- At Texas Instruments a computer chip assembly team decreased its cycle time 42 percent.

- E-Systems Monteck increased team productivity and saved the division over 41,000 labor hours in just over two and a half years.[8]

Teamwork works, whether making microchips or potato chips. At the heart of effective teamwork is improved coordination that occurs through improved communication.

Because you'll spend considerable time collaborating with others, this chapter offers insights into how groups and teams work that can help you be successful in team-based organizations. In the next chapter we'll offer specific strategies for improving team meetings. The five communication principles for leadership that we introduced in Chapter 1 can serve you well as you interact with others at work.

Elements of Teamwork

Why do we spend so much of our work days collaborating with others? The simple fact is that two heads are indeed better than one (most of the time). We work collaboratively because research suggests that when we collaborate we usually end up with a better outcome.[9] Here's why:[10]

- Teams have more information available to them than individuals do.

- Teams stimulate creativity.

- Teamwork increases the likelihood that we'll remember what we discuss because we're actively involved in the process.

- Team members are usually more satisfied with a decision if they are involved in the discussion.

- Team members learn about themselves through feedback they receive from their fellow team members.

But if all of these advantages occur when we collaborate, why do we sometimes become frustrated when working collaboratively? The answer: Because there are also disadvantages to collaborating with others:

- One individual may dominate the discussion.

- Team members may pressure others to conform.

- Team members may rely too much on just a few people.[11]

- Teamwork takes more time than working individually.[12]

Differences Between Groups and Teams

Is there a difference between a *group* and a *team*? The two terms are often used interchangeably. By exploring this question, and building on the distinction introduced in Chapter 1, you can better understand what groups and teams do and develop strategies for improving group and team performance.

WHAT'S A GROUP? Or, more precisely, what is small group communication? **Small group communication** *consists of communication among a small group of people who share a common purpose, who feel a sense of belonging to the group, and who exert influence on each other.*[13] Let's look at this definition more closely.

A group consists of a small number of people. How many people does it take to be a group? At least three people; two people are a dyad, not a group. Yet if a group becomes too large, it typically operates as a collection of subgroups rather than a single body. When more than a dozen or so people meet together, it is difficult for all members to participate; usually, when the group gets too big for everyone to talk, it is likely that a few people will monopolize the discussion.

A group has a common purpose. To be a group, people need to be united by a common goal. They must all seek the same thing. A collection of people waiting for a bus may all want to go to Dallas, but they probably haven't organized their efforts so they are going to meet once there.

Group members feel a sense of belonging. To be a group, the members must realize that they are part of the group. For example, the commuters waiting for the bus don't think of themselves as part of a group. Group members develop a sense of identify with their group. They know when they are in the group or not in the group.

Group members exert influence on others in the group. By being in a group, your presence and participation influences other people in the group. Group members are interdependent; what one group member says or does affects other group members. Your comments and even your silence help shape what the group does next. Each member of a group potentially has some influence on others. Even silence, facial expressions, and eye contact (or lack of it) affects what the group does. It is this element of being a group that explains why each person in a group or team is, to some extent, a leader. Inherent in being in a group is the idea that each person in the group influences others—sometimes by speaking, other times by listening.

terms & definitions

Small group communication the transactive process of creating meaning among from three to fifteen people who share a common purpose, feel a sense of belonging to the group, and exert influence on each other.

WHAT'S A TEAM? Most of us have participated on a sports team at various times. Whether it was soccer, baseball, football, or water polo, the goal of a sports team is usually to win the game or competition. In business and professional settings, a work team has some of the same characteristics as a sports team.[14] Instead of winning the game, the goal may be to get the contract, decide where to build a new shopping mall, or reach a fund-raising target. *A* **team** *is a coordinated group of people organized to work together to achieve a specific common goal.*[15]

Given the increased importance teams have in the workforce today, it's important to know precisely how groups and teams are different from each other. Although both groups and teams are made up of a small number of people, who work to achieve a goal, teams are often more structured or deliberately organized to achieve the goal. For example, the Gomez real estate office holds a group meeting each month just to receive updates about what properties have sold and which are still for sale; they operate more as a group than a team. But at the Suarez Real Estate office, the office members

As evident in this group, the group members share a common purpose, feel a sense of belonging, and exert influence on each other through verbal and nonverbal messages.

work as an integrated team. One office worker handles new sales listings; another person manages the database and provides information to other members of the sales team; yet another team member only works in advertising and sales promotions. Workers have specifically assigned roles. When the team meets they discuss how to coordinate their work.

Every team is a group, but not every group is as highly organized or coordinated to meet the definition of a team. Because of the prevalence of teams and the fact that the word *team* rather than *group* is used in corporate and organizational settings, we primarily use the term *team* to describe a collection of people who work together to achieve a specific goal.

Several specific distinctions are made between groups and teams. Being aware of these differences can help you assess the nature and function of the collaboration process.

Teams develop clearly defined responsibilities for team members. On a sports team, most team members have specifically assigned duties such as shortstop, pitcher, quarterback, or fullback. On a work team, team members' duties and roles are usually explicitly spelled out. Team members may perform more than one function or role, but they nonetheless have well-defined duties,[16] such as the person who will research the new building site, the person who will take notes (or the "minutes"), or the colleague who will network with people outside the team.

Teams have clearly defined rules for team operation. Team members develop explicit rules for how the work should be done.[17] Just as there are written rules in a game of Monopoly, teams usually develop explicit rules that describe how the team will function. For example, a team may establish a rule that if someone is going to be absent, he or she should tell another team member. Team members know what the rules are and know how those rules affect the team.

Teams develop clear goals. Whereas groups have a common goal, it may be less specific or structured.[18] Team goals are usually stated in ways that the goal can be measured, such as to win the game, sell more cornflakes than the competition, or get to the North Pole before anyone else.

Teams develop a way of coordinating their efforts. Team members spend time discussing how to accomplish the goals of the team. Their work is coordinated to avoid duplication of effort. Watching a skilled sports team at work is like watching a choreographed dance. Team members have developed a system of working together rather than at cross purposes. When

terms & definitions

Team a coordinated group of people organized to work together to achieve a specific, common goal.

Communication Ethics @ Work

Should You Go Along to Get Along?

Although team members are encouraged to collaborate and to unite with other team members to achieve the mission, what if you disagree with the goal of the team or the actions of a team member? When is it appropriate to voice your concern? What if doing so means diverting the team from its stated objective?

A team of financial analysts was working on developing budget proposals for the new fiscal year. They had to cut the budget in some way. When reviewing the analysts' proposals, Alison noted that the entire training and development budget had been cut. She felt strongly this would be a major mistake. Cutting the training and development department budget would eliminate the department. The company would either have no training, which would decrease productivity, or would have to outsource the training, which would cost the company

more money, not less. Yet if the training and development department were cut from the budget, the result would be considerable savings for the company, and the financial team would immediately achieve its goal. Alison checked with other team members; they all agreed the training and development budget should be cut.

What should Alison do? Go along with the rest of the team, or try to argue for restoring the budget cuts? A prolonged argument with her team members could disrupt team morale and Alison could lose credibility among her team members. When you're the only person on a team who has reached a particular conclusion, do you give in to preserve team morale? Or do you stand your ground, even if doing so runs the risk of alienating you from team members?

teams are permitted the freedom to manage themselves, team members have reported greater satisfaction than when team members are told what to do by someone outside their team.[19]

Although we have differentiated between groups and teams, don't get the idea they are completely different entities. Both groups and teams are made up of a small number of people who are striving to achieve a goal. Think of groups and teams as existing on a continuum; some deliberations will be more like a group, whereas others will be closer to our description of a team—a more coordinated and structured process with clear rules and explicit goals. Because every team is a small group, whenever we refer to a team we are also suggesting it's a group as well.

Characteristics of Effective Teams

Several researchers have been interested in studying how to make teams function better.[20] One study found that team members need compatible work schedules, adequate resources to obtain the information needed to do the work, leadership skills, and help from their

RECAP

Comparing Groups and Teams

	Groups	Teams
Roles and Responsibilities	Individual responsibilities may not always be explicitly defined.	Team member roles and responsibilities are clearly stated and explicitly discussed.
Rules	Rules are often not formal or written down; rules evolve depending on the group's needs.	Rules and operating procedures are clearly identified to help the team work efficiently and effectively.
Goals	Group goals may be discussed in general terms.	Clearly spelled-out goals are the focus of the team's efforts.
Methods	Group members may or may not decide to divide the work among group members.	Team members develop clear methods of collaborating and coordinating their efforts to achieve the team goal.

organization to get the job done.[21] Another study concluded that it's not how smart team members are, but how well they communicate that improves teamwork.[22] Using studies of several real-world teams (such as teams at NASA and McDonald's, and sports teams), researchers Carl Larson and Frank LaFasto identified eight characteristics of an effective team. The more of these attributes a team has, the more likely it is to be effective.[23]

A CLEAR, ELEVATING GOAL. Having a well-defined goal is the single most important attribute of an effective team.[24] This goal should be perceived by the team as *elevating* and *important*—it should excite team members and motivate them to make sacrifices for the good of the team. An elevating goal is also one that could not be accomplished by an individual. Sports teams use the elevating goal of winning the game or the championship. Teams in business and professional

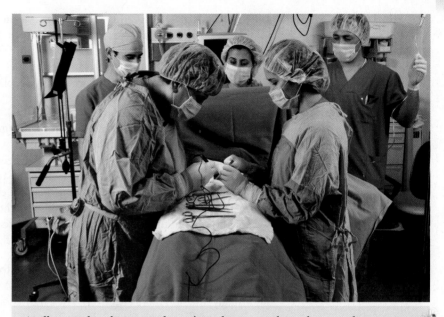

As illustrated in this surgical team's work, teamwork involves coordination among a group of people organized to work together to achieve a specific common goal.

settings also need an exciting goal that all team members believe is important,[25] such as selling more running shoes than the competition or landing the biggest contract in company history.

A RESULTS-DRIVEN STRUCTURE. **Team structure** is the way in which a team is organized to process information and achieve the goal.[26] A results-driven structure is one in which team members are looking for the *verb*—the action step; all activities of the team are focused on achieving the team goal. A structure that is not results driven is one that tolerates ineffective meetings, busywork, and "administrivia." It is useful, therefore, for teams to develop a clear sense of the roles and responsibilities of each team member.

COMPETENT TEAM MEMBERS. Team members need to know not only what their assignments are but also how to perform their jobs.[27] Team members need to be trained (to have the proper skills) and be educated (to have the information they need) so they know what to do and when to do it. Without adequate training in both teamwork skills and job skills, the team will likely flounder.[28] One research study found that the most effective team members have experience and problem-solving skill; are open, supportive, and action-oriented; have a positive personal style; and are optimistic about team success.[29]

UNIFIED COMMITMENT. It's vital for all team members to be "on the same page"—to have a common perception of how they are working together to achieve a goal. Josh and Amanda, for example, were on the same human resource development team. Although they shared the same goal—enhancing their company's success—they were not unified in their approach to achieving that goal. Josh's approach was to increase salaries for workers, whereas Amanda's was to try to hold down costs and limit pay increases to an absolute minimum. In successful teams, members need to be united in their commitment, dedication, and approaches to achieving the goal. When differences exist, team members should work collaboratively to clarify the overall goal and then identify differences. After the issues are identified, team members should address them using skilled approaches to managing conflict.

A COLLABORATIVE CLIMATE. Effective teams foster a positive, supportive group climate and encourage development of the skills and principles needed to achieve their goals.[30] Team members should affirm one another, support one another, and listen to one another as they perform their work.

STANDARDS OF EXCELLENCE. A team is more likely to achieve its goal if it establishes high standards. Goals that cause the team to stretch a bit can serve to galvanize team members into action. Unobtainable or unrealistic goals, however, can result in team frustration. If the entire team is involved in setting goals, the team is more likely to feel a sense of ownership of the standards it has established.

EXTERNAL SUPPORT AND RECOGNITION. Teams in any organization do not operate in isolation. They need outside support to acquire the information and materials needed to do the job.[31] Team members also need to be recognized and rewarded for their efforts by others outside the team. Positive, reinforcing feedback enhances team performance and feelings of team importance. There's evidence that receiving less support from others discourages some team members from giving their full effort; negative feedback causes more group members not to give their full effort. Most coaches acknowledge the "home field advantage" that flows from the enthusiastic support and accolades of team followers. Corporate teams, too, need external support and recognition to help them function at maximum effectiveness.

PRINCIPLED LEADERSHIP. Teams need effective leaders. However, a team does not require an authoritarian leader to dictate who should do what. On the contrary, teams usually function more effectively when they adopt shared approaches to leadership.

As profiled in Chapter 2, Indra Nooyi, CEO of PepsiCo, exemplifies the qualities of a principled leader. Her philosophy: "Don't ever think you've arrived, and remember that what you don't know is much more than what you do."[32] With this principle in mind, she encourages others, as well as herself, to learn, change, and grow.

In most effective teams, leadership responsibilities are spread throughout the team. An effective team leader not only collaborates with team members but also has a network of support outside the team. An effective team leader keeps the team informed about how events and factors external to the team may affect the team's work.[33]

One of the top-selling management books, *The Five Dysfunctions of a Team,* nominated five things team members should *not* do if the team wants to be effective:

1. Don't trust other team members

2. Fear conflict

3. Don't be committed to the team

4. Avoid accountability

5. Don't focus on achieving results[34]

If you've been in a dysfunctional team, these five characteristics may be familiar to you. If you want to have a dysfunctional team, be a dysfunctional team member. Or, if you want to be part of a highly functional team, flip those dysfunctions around to perform these positive functions:

- Trust others

- Embrace conflict

- Be committed to the team

- Be accountable for your team assignment

- Focus on results

It's one thing to know what effective team members should do to be effective, but more important than only *knowing* what to do is actually putting these prescriptions into practice. The research is clear: It helps if team members receive training in how to be a good team member. Teamwork training enhances teamwork.[35]

Working in Virtual Teams

Apparently email isn't fast enough for many people, especially young people. A recent survey found that teenagers were more likely to send a text message, connect via an instant message, or make a quick phone call than to send email to share a tidbit of news or just to chat. The least likely means of connecting with a friend was to visit in person.[36] And it's not

leaders on leadership

Clear Communication = Effective Collaboration

Simple, clear communication promotes simple, clear collaboration. That's the advice of Susan Docherty, who leads the U. S. sales, service, and marketing team at General Motors. Especially in the context of a group or team, with multiple points of view being expressed or people jockeying for position (or trying to get out of doing more work), it's important to be clear and to the point. When asked for advice about how to make collaboration effective, Docherty said,

> Whether you have a really small team or a really big team, communication needs to be at the forefront. It needs to be simple. It needs to be consistent. And even when you're tired of what the message is, you need to do it again and again and again. Because everybody listens at different levels, and everybody comes to the table with a different perspective and a different experience. And the same words mean different things to different people.
>
> On some very key things, people need to internalize it, and they need to own it. And when they do, you'll know that you're effective as a leader, because you hear them saying it.[37]

As Docherty suggests, one way you know your ideas are getting across to others is when you hear your friends or colleagues restating some of your ideas and suggestions. So listen to others to assess whether your ideas have been heard and understood. Whether you're part of a work team at General Motors or collaborating with others for a class project, what's the best way to make sure your ideas are accurately interpreted by others? Remember Susan Docherty's advice: Make messages clear and simple—then repeat as necessary.

just teenagers; increasingly when groups and teams need to collaborate in business and professional settings, especially if team members are not physically close to one another, they connect using technology rather than meeting face-to-face.

A **virtual team** is a team that interacts via a channel other than face-to-face communication. Email, video conferences, and a vast array of technological tools make it possible for us to be psychologically close to someone even if that person lives and works on the other side of the world. Because of the increased costs of travel, many businesses and professional organizations are doing more collaborative work using virtual teams.[38] And even if we work in the same building with our colleagues, we may nonetheless connect electronically rather than interacting face-to-face. Yet collaborating in virtual teams seems to have a tipping point. One study found that when virtual teams interacted via electronic channels more than 90 percent of the time, teams were *less* successful in achieving team outcomes.[39]

Your personal computer, your cell phone, and other technological tools give you the ability to collaborate with other people who are not all in the same place at the same time. To give you an idea of how rapidly worldwide Internet use is increasing, note these statistics: In 2005, over 950 million people used the Internet; that number had grown to over 2 billion people in 2011—and the numbers continue to grow exponentially.[40]

How is electronically-mediated, virtual teamwork different from live, face-to-face conversation? There are four key differences:[41]

- *Anonymity*: If you are interacting by text message or email only, you may not always know precisely with whom you are communicating when you receive a message.

- *Physical appearance*: There is typically less emphasis on a person's physical appearance and nonverbal communication online.

- *Distance*: Although we certainly can and do send email messages to people who live and work in the same building, there is typically greater physical distance between people who are communicating online.

- *Time:* You have greater control over the timing and pacing of the messages you send and receive. You can decide, for example, when to retrieve a text or email messages or when to respond to a message you receive. Your interaction with others can be **asynchronous**— which means your messages are out of sync with the time in which you send them; there often is a time delay between when you send and receive a message. Or they can be **synchronous**—the messages are received the moment they are sent.

terms & definitions

Virtual team a team that interacts via a channel other than face-to-face communication but rather uses email, video conferences, or other technological tools.

Asynchronous communication in which there is a time delay between when a message is sent and when it is received.

Synchronous communication which is received and responded to in real time.

Video conferencing allows virtual teams to collaborate, even when team members are in different parts of the country or the world.

Different types of technology make virtual communication possible. Let's take a closer look at these various technologies.

TELEPHONE CONFERENCES. The telephone conference call—one of the first uses of technology to support group and team meetings—involves a group of people agreeing to "meet" at a certain time by phone. To hold a conference call you need a special telephone service, available from most telephone companies, so that several people in different locations can be connected at the same time. Contemporary cell phones also have features that make conference calling easy.

EMAIL AND TEXT COLLABORATION. We don't need to tell you that email and text messaging are two of the most prevalent methods used to send and receive messages in organizations—or anywhere. If you're typical, you regularly send and receive email and/or text messages about both personal and work-related topics. In 2009 one report indicated that people in the United States sent a total of over 4 billion text messages per day.[42] The research on *group* use of email, however, is still in its early stages[43] and is somewhat contradictory.

- One research study suggests that electronic correspondence minimizes status differences that may be present if people meet face-to-face.[44]

- Another study found that language style has a significant impact on the impression created by email.[45] In general, someone who uses a more assertive language style (such as saying, "I want you to do this.") is perceived as more powerful, credible, and even physically attractive than someone whose language style is weak or timid. ("It might be nice if you consider doing this sometime.")

- Yet another research team found that groups that communicate by email while solving a problem are more likely to do a better job of analyzing the problem than groups that interact face-to-face.

- Being able to read and reread detailed information may help group members focus better on details and message content.

On the negative side:

- Although email and text messaging can be effective for discussing routine business, some messages (such as those intended to manage conflict) are best presented in person.[46]

- There is some evidence that groups that make decisions by email are *less* likely to reach agreement.[47]

- Once a message is sent, you can't take it back. Although it's possible to retract or apologize for something you've sent, as the Russian proverb puts it, "Once a word goes out of your mouth, you can never swallow it again."

- With text-only messages, there is some loss of emotional information communicated by facial expression, vocal inflection, gestures, and body posture that may lead to misunderstanding.[48]

Although emotional information may be less prevalent, we nonetheless try to express emotions when we send messages. We're sure you've noticed that some people use emoticons—keyboard symbols that are typed in certain combinations to express emotions—or

just put their feelings into words: "I have a big grin on my face as I read what you sent me." (Some people believe that all capital letters in an email message is another way to add emotional richness. But you should be careful using all capital letters: IT'S LIKE SHOUTING AT SOMEONE.) Emotions can be expressed when using email; it just may take more time for relationships to develop and emotions to be expressed.[49]

VIDEO CONFERENCES. The video conference—a relatively media-rich use of technology—takes place between two or more individuals who are linked by the Internet or by closed-circuit TV. Free and easy-to-use software programs such as Skype have dramatically increased the use of video conference meetings. Video conferences have the obvious advantage of permitting groups to interact over long distances when it may be very expensive to have all members travel to one destination. And video conferences have an advantage over a conference phone call because participants can see the nonverbal behavior (facial expressions, eye contact, and posture) that allows the transmission of relational messages. When participating in video conferences consider these research conclusions and tips:

- A video conference is more likely to be successful if team members have met *before* the video conference.[50]

- Video conferences are more productive when an agenda is sent to all video conference participants *before* the video meeting (a good practice in any meeting situation).

- Video conferences work best when what is to be discussed follows a more linear, logical, structured format rather than free-wheeling, unstructured conversation.[51]

- Team members seem to be better prepared for video conferences than face-to-face meetings, perhaps because in some organizations they are a novelty and people spend more time preparing for something that is new and unusual.

ELECTRONIC MEETING SYSTEMS. Electronic meeting systems (EMS) consist of both computer hardware and software programs that help group members do their work when they are not meeting face-to-face.[52] Sometimes this technology is called Group Decision Support Systems (GDSS) or Group Support Systems (GSS). One popular commercial software is called Go To Meetings. Whatever the name and abbreviation, EMS, GDSS, and GSS and other systems like them are all based on similar principles. EMS permits you to send simultaneous messages, including PowerPoint slides, to an entire team, including before or after meeting.

Wikis are another specific type of web-based collaborative site that permit collaborators to jointly edit and revise information on the site. Popular Wiki sites include Wikipedia (an encyclopedia) or WikiHow ("how-to" manuals).

WEB PAGE COLLABORATION. Group and team members can collaborate in the same electronic space using a common web page that functions as an electronic bulletin board. Members can go to the web page for information and may be permitted to add, edit, or delete information. Each member has access to what others have gathered and shared. If you have a Facebook web page, you are well aware of the power and uses of a web page to connect with others, share and receive information, and enhance the quality of existing relationships.

terms & definitions

Wiki a web-based site that permits collaboration and access to edit and revise information.

Research on the impact of technology on team problem solving is continuing. The following strategies and observations may offer some guidance to you and your team as you participate in virtual groups and teams.

- Electronically mediated communication seems to work best for more structured, linear tasks, such as reacting to a report or defining a problem.

- The application of computer and e-technology does not inherently result in better solutions and decisions. Technology may allow greater access to accurate information, help structure the process, and keep a group focused on facts, but problems are solved and decisions are made by people.

- The increased speed of information transfer allows less time for reflection. Thus, technology sometimes allows us to make mistakes faster.

- In computer-mediated meetings, ideas can be captured and recorded with speed and accuracy.

- Ultimately, it's not technology that makes teams better; it's the ability of team members to think critically, communicate effectively, and relate positively to others.[53]

Communication Skills FOR A Digital Age

Best Practices for Collaborating Electronically

When the Xerox Corporation wanted to redesign its global advertising campaign, executives knew they would need input from their offices located around the world. It would be too costly to fly all advertising staffers together for a one-hour initial brainstorming meeting, so they decided to hold a conference call and then follow up with a video conference. Increasingly companies large and small are collaborating via virtual groups and teams rather than holding a face-to-face meeting. Collaborating via the Internet, conference phone calls, or Skype video can save costs in terms of travel time; and e-collaboration makes it possible to connect with coworkers instantly.[54] But what you may want to know is how collaborating virtually differs from face-to-face collaboration. Specifically, what are dos and don'ts when collaborating virtually?

Two researchers recommend these six best practices that can enhance virtual team success:[55]

- *Get started early*. It takes longer to develop relationships when participating in virtual teams.

- *Communicate frequently*. The messages need not be lengthy, but more frequent exchange of messages lets other group members know you're still involved and connected.

- *Multitask elements of the team project*. Teams can work on more than one task at a time by dividing and conquering the work. So it's OK to make assignments and have different team members working on different parts of the project all at the same time.

- *Overtly acknowledge that you have read another person's message*.

- *Be clear about what you are thinking and doing*. People can see you or easily guess what you're thinking because they can't see you. So spell out what you think and feel.

- *Set deadlines and stick to them*. Team members should have clear, specific due dates and report whether or not they are meeting those deadlines.

Applying Your Skills

When you are in a leadership role and are encouraging others to collaborate virtually, there are several things you can do to support a virtual group. Here's what seems to help virtual teams function best:

- Provide teams with adequate resources, such as the right people, enough time to do the work, and enough money to buy what they need to get the job done.

- Make sure teams have the right technology. For mere exchange of information, a conference phone call may be best. But for more detailed, emotion-filled conversations, media-rich video conferencing is needed.

- Recognize team members for their work and reward them fairly. Two of the biggest conflict triggers are (1) perceptions of lack of fairness—someone is rewarded or punished in accurately, and (2) lack of equity—a team member has received an disproportionate share of resources or pay.

- Provide the proper training for team members to use whatever technology the team is using.

- Give team members appropriate training in communication skills, technical skills, customer service skills, and information about how to collaborate from remote locations.

Understanding Team Dynamics

At his first day of work at Samsung, Shuntaro was assigned to a team that was developing new solar energy panels. He noticed that other team members were an average of ten minutes late to the two staff meetings held that day. Although Alex was the supervisor, the other team members treated him no differently than anyone else; in fact, they sometimes ridiculed Alex behind his back. The most influential member of the team was Hailey, who although quiet and soft-spoken, seemed to wield the most power because of her knowledge and experience. What Shuntaro was observing were team dynamics—the various factors that determine what it feels like to belong to a team.

Team Roles

How you communicate with others in a team is a function of your role. Your **role** is the consistent way you communicate with others on a team. Your role is based on your expectations of yourself and the expectations others have of you. There is also evidence that your personality and the personality characteristics of other team members have major influences on team role development.[56] All five of our communication principles for leadership have an impact on the development of your role in a team. How aware you are of your behavior and the behavior of others has a major impact on your verbal and nonverbal messages. Your role develops as you listen and respond and as other team members listen and respond to you, and as you adapt to the communication behavior of other team members.

Your role is worked out as you balance your own expectations of yourself and the expectations others have of you. If no leader has been assigned to a team you're part of, do you often take charge, or are you more comfortable blending in and taking directions from others? Are you the one who makes sure the team gets the work done instead of just having a good time? Maybe you're the team member who seems especially gifted in managing conflict and disagreement. Or, perhaps you have no typical pattern—your role depends on the group and who else is in the group. In business and corporate settings, your specific role may be prescribed by your job title or position. If you are the boss, you may be expected to be the procedural leader and conduct meetings, set the meeting agenda, or assign people to do certain jobs. But even if your position in the organization prescribes your role, there are still some roles that are shaped by the specific situation and job at hand. The roles people assume in teams can be classified into three types.

TASK ROLES. **Task roles** are those behaviors that help the group achieve its goal and accomplish its work: gathering and sharing research with the group, taking minutes of meetings, and writing ideas on a chalk board are examples of task role behavior.

SOCIAL ROLES. **Social roles** focus on behavior that manages relationships and affects the group climate; these roles help resolve conflict and enhance the flow of communication. Soothing hurt feelings and helping the group celebrate its accomplishments are examples of social role behavior.

INDIVIDUAL ROLES. **Individual roles** are those that focus attention on the individual rather than the group. These are roles that do *not* help the group; they emphasize individual accomplishments and issues rather than those of the entire group. Dominating group discussions to talk about personal issues or concerns, telling jokes that get the group off track, and constantly complaining are examples of individual roles.

Over sixty years ago, group communication scholars Kenneth Benne and Paul Sheats identified a list of group roles that remains a classic way of identifying the group and individual roles that group and team members typically assume.[57] Table 9.1 presents a summary of these roles. As you look at the list of roles in Table 9.1, you may think to yourself, "Yes that's what I usually do in meetings. That's the role I usually take." And you can probably see roles that other team members usually take on. Most of us typically enact several roles when we collaborate with others. Effective team members adapt their behavior to what is happening or needed in the group.

terms & definitions

Role the consistent way someone communicates with others in a team, based on the person's own expectations and what others on the team expect of the person.

Task roles behaviors that help a group achieve its goal and accomplish its work.

Social roles behaviors that manage relationships and affect group climate; these roles help resolve conflict and enhance the flow of communication.

Individual roles behaviors that focus attention on an individual rather than the group.

TABLE 9.1	A Classification of Group Roles	
Task Roles	**Description**	**Example**
Initiator/contributor	Offers new ideas or approaches to the group; suggests ways of getting the job done.	"How about developing an agenda to help us organize our work?"
Information seeker	Asks for additional clarification, facts, or other information that helps the group with the issues at hand.	"Can anyone tell me how many times we have had to cancel our fall conference because of bad weather?"
Opinion seeker	Asks group members to share opinions or express a personal point of view.	"So, what do you all think of the new uniform that all of the service workers have been asked to wear?"
Information giver	Provides facts, examples, statistics, or other evidence that relates to the task confronting the group.	"Within the past year, the Vice President for Information Technology has told us to use two different information management systems."
Opinion giver	Offers opinions or beliefs about what the group is discussing.	"I think the new information technology policy will decrease our productivity."
Elaborator	Provides comments or examples to extend or add to the comments of others.	"Jessica, that's a good point. The same thing happened to me when I worked for our main competitor two years ago."
Coordinator	Clarifies and notes relationships among the ideas and suggestions that have been offered by others.	"Travis, your ideas sound a lot like Sondra's suggestion. Sondra, why don't you elaborate on your idea and we'll see if Travis agrees or disagrees with you."
Orienter	Summarizes what has occurred and seeks to keep the group focused on the task at hand.	"I think we're getting a bit off track here. Let's go back to the issue on the agenda."
Evaluator/critic	Assesses the evidence and conclusions that the group is considering.	"How recent are those statistics? I think there are newer figures for us to consider."
Energizer	Spurs the group to action by making comments to motivate the group to work harder.	"Come on, team. We can do it if we just keep at it! Don't stop now."
Procedural technician	Helps the group accomplish its goal by handling tasks such as distributing reports, writing ideas on a chalk board, or performing other tasks that help the group.	"I'll write your ideas on the board. After the meeting, I'll copy them and summarize them in an email to each of you."
Recorder	Makes a written record of the group's progress by writing down specific comments, facts, or the minutes of meetings.	"I'll take notes of today's meeting."

Social Roles	**Description**	**Example**
Encourager	Offers praise and support and confirms the value of other people and the ideas they contribute.	"You're doing a great job. Thanks for working overtime on this project."
Harmonizer	Manages conflict and mediates disputes between group members.	"Grover, you and Nicole seem to be agreeing more than you are disagreeing. Both of you want the same goal. Let's brainstorm some strategies that can help you both get what you want."
Compromiser	Resolves conflicts by trying to find an acceptable solution. Seeks new alternatives.	"Muriel, you want us to meet at 7:00 PM, and Samantha, you'd like us to start at 8:00. What if we started at 7:30? Would that work?"
Gatekeeper	Encourages people who talk too much to contribute less and invites those who are less talkative to participate.	"Blair, we've not heard what you think. What do you suggest we do?"

TABLE 9.1	(*continued*)	
Follower	Goes along with the suggestions and ideas of other group members.	"I can support that option. You have summarized the issue about the same way I see it."
Emotion expresser	Verbalizes how the group may be feeling about a specific issue or suggestion.	"We seem to be frustrated that we are not making more progress."
Group observer	Summarizes the group's progress or lack of progress.	"We are making great progress on all of the issues except how much salary we should offer the new person we've just hired."
Tension reliever	Monitors stress within the group and offers suggestions for breaks, using humor or other appropriate strategies.	"Hey, what we need is a good laugh. Here's a joke I saw on the Internet today."
Individual Roles	**Description**	**Example**
Aggressor	Deflates or disconfirms the status of other group members or tries to take credit for the work of others.	"Lee, your idea is awful. We all know that what I suggested two meetings ago is clearly the best option."
Blocker	Is negative, stubborn, and disagreeable without an apparent reason.	"I just don't like it. I don't have to tell you why; I just don't like it."
Recognition seeker	Seeks the spotlight by dwelling on his or her personal accomplishments; seeks the praise of others.	"I offered that suggestion two meetings ago I'm the one who usually makes things happen for this team."
Self-confessor	Uses the group as a forum to disclose personal feelings and problems unrelated to the group's task.	"I'm not happy at home, so that's why I seem a bit off at this meeting. My kids are driving me crazy."
Joker	Wants to crack jokes, tell stories, and have fun instead of focusing on the task or what the group needs.	"Hey, let's just go have coffee. Then I'll tell you the gossip about Harvey in accounting. What a nutcase!"
Dominator	Tries to take control of the group, talks too much, and uses flattery or aggression to push his or her ideas on the group.	"Now here's what we're going to do: Martin, you will take notes today; Alice, you go get us some coffee; and Luke, I want you to just sit there in case I need you to run back to my office to get the Simpson file."
Special-interest pleader	Seeks to get the group to support a pet project or personal agenda.	"My boss would like it if we would support the new downtown renovation project. I'll stand a good shot at a promotion if I can get you on board."
Help seeker	Seeks to evoke a sympathetic response from others. Often expresses insecurity stemming from feelings of low self-worth.	" I'm not very good with people. I just feel like I don't relate well to others or have many friends."

What are the best or worst roles to assume? We recommend that you avoid assuming *any* individual role; by definition, these roles focus attention on an individual rather than the group. Groups need people to take on a balance of task and social roles, not draw attention to themselves.

What is the proper balance between task roles and social roles? Some experts recommend a 60:40 balance between task and social roles.[58] What is clear is that groups seem to operate most effectively when it's not all work and no play. Conversely, an out-of-balance group that focuses on just having a good time is not going to achieve its task goals. In general, more of the group's interactions should be about getting the work done than about having fun or managing the social climate—but don't forget to make sure that there are good working relationships among group members.[59]

Team Norms

When George Lucas, president of Lucasfilm, and Micheline Chau, chief operating officer of Lucasfilm, wanted to merge two separate units of the company into one unit, they decided it would be best to create new work norms by moving the teams together into one building rather than keeping them in their separate locations. They wanted the new teams to develop new collaborative norms for work productivity and procedures. **Norms** are standards that determine what is appropriate and inappropriate behavior in a group. Common team norms help develop team coordination and cooperation. Norms reflect what's normal behavior in the group; they influence how group members are supposed to behave—such as the type of language that is acceptable or the casualness of the clothes they wear. Norms can evolve into more formal rules, which are more explicit prescriptions that spell out how group members should interact.[60] Lucas and Chau believed the development of new common norms would help the new Lucas film team develop a better sense of team identity.

How can you discover what the norms of any group are? Watch the group. Listen and observe any repeated verbal or nonverbal behavior patterns. Note, for example, consistencies in the way people talk or dress. To help you spot norms in your groups, consider the following questions:

- What are group members' attitudes toward time (do meetings start and stop on time)?
- How do group members dress?
- Is it acceptable to use informal slang terms or to use obscenity?
- What kind of humor is acceptable?
- How does the group treat the leader?

Noting when someone breaks a norm can also help you spot a norm. If a member waltzes into a meeting twenty minutes late and several folks grimace and point to their watches, that's a sure sign that a norm has been violated. The severity of the punishment corresponds to the significance of the norm.[61] Mild punishment is usually unspoken—silent glances or a frowning stare. More serious punishment can be a negative comment about the behavior in front of other group members or even expulsion from the group. You don't have to worry about whether your group will have norms or not; norms happen. You should, however, monitor the group norms to ensure that your behavior doesn't distract from the work of the group or to note whether an unproductive group norm has developed that the group should talk about.

Cliques may create rivalries or inhibit the flow of communication among team members. Fostering inclusiveness and open communication can help prevent conflict in a group.

Team Networks

Do you have your own Facebook page? Chances are you do. If you are a member of one of the popular social networking sites, you have some idea of the power and significance of social networks. People have a need to connect to others. And just as on Facebook, in groups and teams, **communication interaction patterns** emerge based on who talks to whom and how often. Some groups have an equal distribution of interaction among members; others develop distinct patterns of interaction between two or more people.[62] Whether we're communicating via the Internet or in person, it's normal to develop preferences for talking to certain people but not others. Group communication scholars have studied and classified the various patterns that emerge when people talk to one another in groups. Who you talk with in a group is a function of the communication networks and interaction patterns that emerge.

In most teams, people speak to certain individual people rather than to the team as a whole. We tend to speak to people who have more power and status. In addition, we talk to people we like more than to people we don't like. There will also be more communication directed toward someone on the team who holds an opinion different from the rest of the group. This person is called a **group deviate**. (Some members may call this person a pain in the neck.) Group members may spend considerable talk time trying to change a group deviate's opinion.

ALL CHANNEL. A group in which everyone talks to everyone else is called an all-channel network. As illustrated in Figure 9.1, all channels are open and used. There is considerable interaction and there are no cliques or subgroups that emerge. A **clique** is a smaller group of people within a larger group who form a common bond among themselves. Perhaps you have special friends on your team whom you seek out and who seek you out when you attend meetings. During meetings you probably sit together, share private jokes and stories, and may talk about other members. Although there is nothing wrong with having special friends and colleagues at work, cliques can become detrimental to a team if they foster rivalries within the team or if they inhibit the flow of communication with others. Teams should avoid cliques that can develop divisive power plays that foster conflict. You don't want cliques ratcheting up the emotional tension as the team seeks to deliberate rationally. The first step to avoiding cliques is to be aware that one exists. Then make a conscious effort to be less exclusive and more integrated into the conversation of the entire group.

CHAIN NETWORK. In a team with a chain network, people send messages through one person at a time rather than to all group members. Many business and professional organizations have a hierarchical chain communication pattern. For example, the president of the company sends a message to the vice president, who, in turn, talks to the director; the director talks to a manager, who eventually gives the message to the other employees. As you might suspect, passing a message through many different ears and minds often results in misunderstanding by the time the message reaches the last person in the chain.

WHEEL NETWORK. The wheel network pattern occurs when one person in the team or organization *receives* more messages from other members; this pivotal communicator also is the prime *source* of information to other team or organization members. Perhaps in your group of friends there is one person who seems to know everything that's going on. The wheel pattern emerges when there is a strong leader or when the group members do individual tasks and need someone to keep them informed about what others are doing.

What's the best interaction pattern? It depends. There may be times when the structured nature of the chain or wheel pattern may be called for. For example, during the huddle before a football play, when time is short, usually the quarterback does most of the talking while others listen (wheel network). But most teams function best if there is an all-channel pattern of communication, especially when the group is not too large and is trying to generate new, creative ideas.

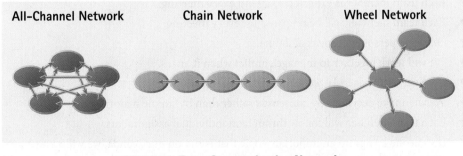

FIGURE 9.1 Team Communication Networks

As you participate in or lead team meetings, be aware of the general pattern of communication. Are all members participating? Do some people whisper their ideas only to a few and not share with the rest of the group? Is a group deviate monopolizing the conversation or blocking progress? By being observant of interaction patterns, you can help the team enhance cohesiveness and develop appropriate roles to get the work done.

Improving Team Dynamics

Now that you can describe team roles, norms, and networks, you may wonder if there are specific ways to improve team dynamics. One way to clarify roles is to establish clear ground rules about how the team should best operate. Making sure the team has a clear mission statement contributes to good dynamics: Effective teams have a clear, elevating goal. Managing differences in status and power can also help reduce tension. And implementing strategies to enhance team cohesiveness can help teams work together more effectively.

How to Develop Team Ground Rules

Team ground rules are explicit, agreed-on prescriptions for acceptable and appropriate behavior. An effective team takes the time to develop clear rules that will help to organize routine tasks and procedures. Although team norms typically develop without anyone explicitly spelling out what the norm should be, a team may decide to develop more explicit rules to help get the work accomplished. For example, although it may be a norm that meetings usually start on time, a team could decide to establish a ground rule that all meetings will *always* begin on time. There's evidence that teams are more effective if they develop explicit rules that help the team operate efficiently.[63] Rules help keep order so that meaningful work can be accomplished. Rules also state what the team or organization values. Honesty, fairness, adherence to schedules, and personal safety are typical values embedded in team ground rules.

How does a team develop ground rules? Soon after the formation of a team, the team leader may facilitate a discussion to establish the ground rules. If a team has no designated leader, any team member can say, "To help us get organized and accomplish our task, let's develop some ground rules." Teams clearly operate better if team members develop their own ground rules rather than having them imposed from "on high." Following are some questions that can help a group develop clear and appropriate ground rules:

- How should we record the results of our meetings?
- Who should set meeting agendas?
- How long should our meetings last?
- Should we have a regular meeting time and place?
- What should a member do if he or she can't attend a meeting?
- Should we make our decisions by majority vote or seek a consensus on every decision?

These questions might result in the following team ground rules:

- Every meeting will begin on time.
- Each team member is expected to attend every meeting.
- Each team member will be prepared for every meeting.
- Only one person will speak at a time.
- We will work together to manage conflict when it arises.
- If we get off the agenda, we will return to the agenda.
- We will make decisions by consensus rather than by simple majority vote.
- Each team member will follow through on individual assignments.
- If someone brings up an important topic that is not on our agenda, we will write it on a sticky note, place it in the "parking lot," and return to it later rather than get off our agenda.

How to Develop a Team Mission Statement

A **team mission statement** is a concise description of a team's goals or desired outcomes. A clearly worded mission statement helps a team know not only whether it's on task or off task but also when it has completed the task.

A good team mission statement should pass the SMARTS test—it should be Specific, Measurable, Attainable, Relevant, Time-bound, and should Stretch the team.[64]

- *Specific*: It should clearly describe what the team should accomplish.
- *Measurable*: The team must be able to assess whether the mission was achieved.
- *Attainable*: The mission statement should be realistic given the time and resources of the teams.
- *Relevant*: The mission should be appropriate to what the team has been assigned to do.
- *Time-bound*: Teams should set a deadline or time frame for achieving the mission.
- *Stretch*: The goal should be a bit of a challenge so as to stretch the team.

Here are examples of team mission statements that pass the SMARTS test:

- Our team will make 10 percent more widgets by the end of the month.
- Our team will sell more life insurance policies than any other sales team in our sales area.
- Our team will attract two new businesses to our community, which will result in an increased tax base by the end of the year.

How to Manage Team Status Differences

Status refers to an individual's importance and prestige. Your status in a group influences whom you talk to, who talks to you, and even what you talk about. Although some people underestimate their perceived status and influence in a group, research suggests that you are probably quite aware of your own status level when communicating with others.[65] Your perceived importance affects both your verbal and your nonverbal messages. Typically, a person with high status

- Talks more than those of lower status.
- Directs comments to other high-status group members.
- Has more influence on the decisions the group makes.
- Is listened to by group members.
- Makes more comments to the entire group.[66]

Being aware of status differences can help you predict who talks to whom. If you can discern status differences, you'll also be better able to predict the type of messages communicated.

Status influences group communication, but just because a person has high status does not mean that his or her ideas are good ones. Don't let status differences influence your perceptions of the value of the ideas contributed. Some groups get into trouble because they automatically defer to the person with more status without reviewing the validity of the ideas presented. Similarly, don't dismiss ideas out of hand because the person who suggested them doesn't have high status or prestige. Focus on the quality of the message, not just on the messenger.

How to Manage Team Power Differences

Power is the ability to influence others' behavior. You have power if you can get others to do what you want. Although status (prestige and importance) and power (ability to influence) sometimes go hand in hand, a group member could have status and still not be able to influence how others behave. You could, for example, be the designated team leader but not be perceived as having much influence on the team because your ideas aren't valued or you may have no resources to back up what you say and do. Because leadership is the process of influencing others through communication, it's important to understand the sources of power and those factors that enhance someone's ability to influence others.[67] Ultimately who does and doesn't have power in a group influences how people relate to one another.

A power struggle often creates ripples of conflict and contention through a group. And on the surface a conflict may seem to revolve around a simple disagreement, such as when a report is due, but underlying the disagreement may be a power struggle. The real issue may be who gets to decide when the report is due.

Power struggles also frequently focus attention on individual group members. People with less power tend to participate less in group discussion, unless they're trying to gain power. A group in which power is not balanced could have problems; the "power people" might dominate the discussion. When one or more members dominate the discussion, the group loses the contributions and insights of others. Research supports the conclusion that teams with equal power distribution usually have better quality outcomes.[68]

One classic discussion of how individuals become powerful identified five power bases: legitimate, referent, expert, reward, and coercive power. These power bases explain why certain people have power and why others don't.[69]

LEGITIMATE POWER. You have **legitimate power** if someone elected or appointed you to a position of power. Your power source comes from holding a position of responsibility. The president of your university or college has the legitimate power to establish and implement school policy. Senators from your state, the chief executive officer of a company, or the manager of a department store are other examples of people who have legitimate power. A group or team member who has been designated team leader or elected chair or president of the group is given legitimate power to influence how the group operates.

REFERENT POWER. You have **referent power** if people like you. Put simply, people we like have more power over us than people we do not like. If you are working on a committee with your best friend, your friend exerts power over you in that you may give more credence to what your friend recommends. Just the opposite occurs if you are working with someone you don't like; you will be more likely to ignore that person's advice.

EXPERT POWER. Knowledge is power. People who have **expert power** are perceived as informed or knowledgeable and have more influence than people who are perceived as uninformed.

REWARD POWER. People who can grant favors, money, promotions, or other rewards have **reward power**. Someone who can take away a punishment or other unpleasant experience (rescinding a restrictive dress code or establishing a more flexible work schedule, for example) also has reward power. People who have greater power to reward typically are sent more positive, supportive messages than people who don't have the ability to reward others. But reward power is effective only if a person being rewarded finds the reward (or the removal of a punishment) satisfying or useful. What is rewarding to one person may not be rewarding to another person.

COERCIVE POWER. You have **coercive power** if you can punish others; coercive power is the flip side of reward power. If someone can cut your salary, lower your grade, demote you, or force you to do unpleasant jobs, that person has coercive power. The power results from the perception that the person with the power will actually use the power. If someone has the authority to punish, but if group members don't perceive that the person will use this power, then he or she doesn't really have power.

Even though we have categorized power into five different types, don't get the idea that group members have just one type. In reality, every group or team member typically has more than one source of power. For example, a group member who is the elected leader (legitimate power) may be able to offer rewards (reward power) or punishment (coercive power).

terms & definitions

Legitimate power power that stems from being elected or appointed to a specific position or office.

Referent power power that stems from being liked.

Expert power power derived from having knowledge and expertise.

Reward power power arising from the ability to grant favors, money, or other rewards.

Coercive power power stemming from the ability to punish others.

RECAP

Types of Power	
Legitimate power	Power that arises from being elected, appointed, or ordained to lead or make decisions for a group or a team.
Referent power	Power that arises from being well-liked.
Expert power	Power that arises from having information and being knowledgeable about issues or ideas.
Reward power	Power that arises from having the ability to bestow gifts, money, recognition, or other rewards valued by group members.
Coercive power	Power that arises from having the ability to punish others.

One of the first things to be aware of when managing power differences is the power basis. Say you're having a power struggle with your boss over when a project should be completed. Because your boss has legitimate power to fire you (coercive power) or give you a raise (reward power), it would be politically prudent to note the power resources your boss has and that you don't possess. In addition to being aware of people's power bases and the conflict resolution strategies discussed in Chapter 6, it is useful to keep in mind the other communication principles that we've discussed throughout the book. Your verbal and nonverbal messages can either create more tension or help to manage the tension that a power struggle produces. And the sensitivity established through listening and responding will help you appropriately adapt your messages to help manage power issues that arise in teams.

How to Enhance Team Cohesiveness

Perhaps you've read about the Three Musketeers or have seen a movie about them; if so, you know that their motto was "one for all and all for one." They were a cohesive group; they liked being with each other. Group **cohesiveness** is the degree of attraction that members of a group feel toward one another and the group. In a highly cohesive group, the members feel a high degree of loyalty to one another; the goal of the team is also the goal of the individuals.[70] Members of cohesive groups listen to one another, care about what each other think, and feel a sense of collective belonging to the team.

Teams become cohesive because of a variety of forces that attract people to the group and to each other. Similarity of goals, feelings of genuine liking, and similarity of background and culture are variables that influence group cohesion. Cohesiveness also is more likely to develop when team members' emotional needs are satisfied by participating in the group.[71] In the case of the Three Musketeers, the desire to do good deeds and assist those in need provided the clear, elevating goal that gave them satisfaction. Think of a team you belong to in which there is a high degree of *esprit de corps* and cohesiveness. You will also probably find that you both like the group members and support the overall goals and objectives that the group is trying to accomplish.

What enhances team cohesiveness? Table 9.2 summarizes some strategies that enhance team cohesiveness. Cohesiveness is more likely to occur if group members have the opportunity to talk freely with one another about the group goal and if this interaction increases affection and liking for one another. Teams that have greater control over how they conduct their work are also likely to be more cohesive.[72] Teams that aren't cohesive typically don't have a clear, shared goal, and the team members don't like one another and haven't spent much time focusing on relationship development roles. An uncohesive team is also likely to include people who perform individual roles rather than team task or relationship development roles.[73]

terms & definitions

Cohesiveness the degree of attraction that members of a group feel toward one another and the group.

TABLE 9.2	Suggestions for Enhancing Team Cohesiveness[74]

Cohesive Teams	Uncohesive Teams
Talk about the group in terms of "we" rather than "I."	Tend to emphasize the individual contributions of group members.
Reinforce good attendance at group meetings.	Make less effort to encourage group members to attend every meeting.
Establish and maintain group traditions.	Make less effort to develop group traditions.
Set clear short-term and long-term goals.	Avoid setting goals or establishing deadlines.
Encourage everyone in the group to participate in the group task.	Allow only the most talkative or high-status members to participate in the group task.
Celebrate when the group accomplishes either a short-term or a long-term goal.	Discourage group celebration; group meetings are all work and little or no fun.
Stress teamwork and collaboration.	Stress individual accomplishment.

Can a team be too cohesive? Yes: If team members are focused only on developing a positive, cohesive relationship to the exclusion of getting their work done, group productivity can suffer. If the team becomes focused primarily on enjoying one another's company, they will produce *less* work. Strive for team cohesiveness, but balance cohesiveness with a focus on accomplishing the team's task.

Approaches to Enhancing Teamwork

What's the best approach to analyzing teams so as to understand how they work and to make them more effective? Some team experts suggest that it's best to develop a detailed knowledge of team processes and understand how a team moves through various phases of development. So you would approach a team by getting close enough to *describe* what occurs in the team. Others suggest the best approach is to assess whether a team is using certain communication *functions*. The *functional approach* suggests that effective team members are those who meet certain task requirements in the way they communicate with other team members. Yet a third approach emphasizes using specific skills and techniques to help a team work better. This approach *prescribes* precise strategies that effective teams should employ, such as how to develop an effective meeting agenda, how to reach agreement, or steps to follow in solving a problem. A key element of being an effective team leader is understanding which approach may be best in developing the team's potential.

The Descriptive Approach: Describing Team Development

When you describe an object or experience, you look for ways to categorize or classify it. A **descriptive approach** to team development seeks to identify the typical ways teams behave when they attempt to solve a problem. It is based on the assumption that all groups experience a natural or normal process of development. Researchers have attempted to describe the way group members talk and behave to see if they can discern predictable patterns.

Some researchers have found that groups go through certain phases or sequences of talk when they meet to solve a problem.[75] Researchers don't agree on the exact nature of these phases, or even on the number of phases; some researchers have found three phases, most have found four. One of the most descriptive four-phase models was developed by group communication researcher Aubrey Fisher.[76] His four phases of group talk are (1) orientation, (2) conflict, (3) emergence, and (4) reinforcement.

terms & definitions

Descriptive approach an approach to team development that seeks to identify the typical ways teams behave in solving problems.

ORIENTATION. As you might suspect, when people first get together in a group, they must become oriented to what they are doing. This happens in both face-to-face and virtual groups. During the **orientation phase**, group members become oriented to at least two things: (1) who's in the group and (2) what they will be doing. When you join a group for the first time, you have high uncertainty about how the group will be organized, who's in charge, and exactly how things will work. Research on the orientation phase suggests that your early communication is directed at orienting yourself toward others as well as to the group's task.[77] During the orientation phase people often experience **primary tension**, which results from the uncertainty and discomfort they feel when the group meets for the first time.[78] Some group members who don't like uncertainty and are eager to start sorting things out may suggest an agenda: "Hello, my name is Steve. Let's each introduce ourselves." Other group members are quite content to simply sit quietly in the background and let others take the lead. As people begin to become acquainted and group members start talking about the group's purpose, typical groups experience the second phase: conflict.

CONFLICT. People are different. That unprofound observation has profound implications for human communication, and nowhere is it more evident than in a group discussion after the group gets down to business. The **conflict phase** typically, but not always, follows the orientation phase. During the orientation phase, group members form opinions about what the group should be doing and who should be doing it. As they become more comfortable in and oriented to the group, they start asserting these opinions.

The conflict phase is necessary for both solving problems and maintaining group relationships. The conflict phase occurs when people are honest about sharing their opinions. If there is no conflict, it usually means people aren't being honest about how they really feel. When ideas aren't challenged and tested, the group usually makes stupid decisions. Also, honest yet tactful expression of personal disagreement is more likely to foster genuine relationships rather than phony ones. You can take some comfort in knowing that conflict is an expected part of group deliberations.

EMERGENCE. You know your group is in the **emergence phase** when decisions begin to be made and the group begins to solidify a common point of view. Though conflict is still a part of phase three, what sets the emergence phase apart from the conflict phase is the way in which group members manage the conflict. Norms, roles, ground rules, and leadership patterns that have been established in the group now help the group get work accomplished. In the emergence phase, a group settles on norms and moves toward consensus or agreement.

REINFORCEMENT. Group members become more unified in the fourth phase, the **reinforcement phase**. During the orientation, conflict, and emergence phases, group members struggle through getting acquainted, developing cohesiveness, competing for status and prominence, and puzzling over issues and action the group could take. The group eventually emerges from those struggles and develops a new sense of direction; this results in a more positive feeling about the group. The group more clearly develops a sense of "we." In fact, one of the ways you can identify the reinforcement phase is when group members use more collective pronouns (*we, us, our*) than personal pronouns (*I, me, my*) to talk about the group.

THE PROCESS NATURE OF TEAMS. Although we have identified four distinct phases that teams can experience, all teams do not neatly process through these phases exactly the same way at every meeting. The descriptive approach to team problem solving has identified these phases and can help provide a general overview of how many groups operate, but more recent research suggests some teams don't go through these phases at all.[79] Teams may spiral through phases, get stuck on one or more phases or bounce between two phases, or quickly gloss over a phase.

Teams may spiral through phases. For example, a team trying to design a new health-care policy may spiral through several phases during the same meeting. They could go through several rounds of getting oriented on a specific issue, having conflict, experience a decision emergence, reinforce their decision, and then get oriented on a different issue or

terms & definitions

Orientation phase the first phase of group interaction, in which members become adjusted to one another and to the group's task.

Primary tension the tension that results from the uncertainty and discomfort people experience when they meet in a group for the first time.

Conflict phase the second phase of group interaction, in which group members experience some disagreement about social issues and group tasks.

Emergence phase the third phase of group interaction, in which conflict or disagreement is managed and decisions are made.

Reinforcement phase the fourth phase of group interaction, in which group members express positive feelings toward each other and toward the group.

problem. Even if you have difficulty identifying these phases or their precise order in your group, you will probably see some elements of these four types of talk during the history of your group meetings.

Teams may get stuck on one or more phases. Have you ever participated in a group that could never quite figure out what it was supposed to do? If so, your group may have gotten stuck on the orientation phase and not have overcome the initial uncertainty of who does what when or determined what its goal was. The group started bewildered and stayed there. Some groups get stuck in the conflict phase, or perhaps they bounce between orientation and conflict, trying to figure out what to do and then disagreeing about what to do. Eventually something will emerge (phase three) from the group even if it is not a wise decision or quality solution. Or, the group may decide to disband and never meet again because the team members are so dysfunctional. Something emerged—the group members quit—but that's not the reason the group was formed. Reinforcement is likely to occur because we like to make sense out of what happens to us. Even if the group disbands we are likely to celebrate its demise or reinforce the decision to disband. Some groups get stuck in reinforcement; they simply want to have a good time, but little gets accomplished.

Teams may gloss over one or more phases. Many groups, especially those that emphasize efficiency and productivity, may spend very little time on the reinforcement aspects of group celebration. Wise group leaders and participants make sure that victories are celebrated and both group and individual efforts are recognized. The cohesiveness and positive feelings that result from such celebrations will be helpful as the group prepares for its next task. It becomes oriented all over again, experiences conflict, has something emerge as a course of action, and reinforces the action. Again, these phases may not occur as orderly and predictably as it appears, but most groups do experience some elements of these phrases.

The Functional Approach: Understanding Team Functions

The **functional approach** to team development suggests that for a team to be effective, certain communication functions must occur. Researchers have spent several years trying to identify what functions help teams improve communication and effectiveness.[80] Researchers have identified these essential communication functions by studying both effective and ineffective groups. Effective group members did things differently than the ineffective group members. Identifying what these behaviors are led to the labeling of key behaviors or functions that, when present, are more likely to produce better results.

An important skill of an effective group member is to be a vigilant thinker.[81] **Vigilant thinkers** pay attention to the *process* of how work is done in teams rather than focusing only on techniques used to achieve a goal. A vigilant thinker also assesses, evaluates, and tests ideas. One research team identified four essential questions that vigilant-thinking group members should consider:

1. Does something in the present situation need to be changed?

2. What goal does the group want to achieve?

3. What choices does the group have that will help achieve the goal?

4. What are the positive and negative implications of the choices?[82]

Even though these questions are usually discussed in the order listed, some groups don't follow this sequence.[83] What is clear, however, is that if one or more of these critical questions is *not* discussed, the group is less effective. These questions lead to the achievement of the critical functions that groups need to consider. The following five functions seem critical to effective group performance.

GOAL FUNCTION. As we've discussed, it is important for a group or team to have a clear goal and to develop a team mission statement. Thus taking time to talk about the team goal is an essential team function. Articulating a clear and elevating goal is one of the earliest functions that team members should enact. It is important therefore, for group members to ask and answer the question, "What's our clear, elevating goal?" The goal is developed by the group's asking itself, "Do we need to change something that is happening now?" Most group goals boil down to something that you want either more of or less of. If there is no need for a change, then there is nothing that the group wants more or less of.[84]

ANALYSIS FUNCTION. Another critical function of team communication is to analyze the data, information, or evidence that can help the group achieve the group goal.[85] To analyze something is to break it into parts and critically evaluate its causes, symptoms, and history. An effective team does at least these three things:

1. Identifies the data, information, or evidence the group currently has.

2. Identifies the additional data, information, or evidence the group needs in order to make a decision.

Effective groups, such as this team at NASA, have a clear goal; and they analyze situations, generate ideas, and evaluate those ideas to help achieve that goal. In the process, group members listen to what others have to say.

3. Draws accurate conclusions from the data, information, and evidence that it has.

As is true of other team communication functions, when group members don't do these things, or do them poorly, the group is more likely to make inappropriate decisions. For example, the team that coordinates the space shuttle landing has to decide whether the weather will permit the shuttle to land either in Florida or in California. If the team doesn't interpret the weather data accurately, then a poor decision may be reached. Having too little evidence—or no evidence at all—is one of the reasons groups sometimes don't analyze their present situations correctly. Even if group members do have plenty of evidence, they may not have tested the evidence to see if it is true, accurate, or relevant.

IDEA-GENERATION FUNCTION. Another hallmark of an effectively functioning team is that team members generate many ideas and potential solutions after analyzing a situation. Effective teams don't just settle on one or two ideas and then move on; they list multiple approaches. The most effectively functioning teams have members who make high-quality statements. Researchers define high-quality statements as precise rather than unfocused and abstract. High-quality statements don't ramble, and they are consistent with evidence, relevant to the topic under discussion, and positively reinforce what other group members are saying.[86] We provide specific tips and strategies for generating ideas and enhancing team creativity in the next chapter.

Sometimes teams get stuck and ideas just don't flow. Rather than continuing to hammer away at the problem, the group may want to take a break from it for a while. Perhaps you've had a great idea come to you when you were taking a walk, or driving home. Taking a break can give your subconscious mind a chance to thrash through some of the issues and perhaps generate a breakthrough solution.[87] The principle of awareness operates here: Team members need to become aware of the group's ability to generate high-quality ideas. Leaders have a special responsibility to be mindful of the team process and help steer the team back to productive territory.

EVALUATION FUNCTION. Another characteristic of high-performing teams is that team members know a good idea when they see it. They are able to evaluate evidence, opinions, assumptions, and solutions and separate the good from the bad. Low-performing teams are less discriminating. A team that is eager to make a decision to get their job over with usually comes up with poor-quality decisions.

An effectively functioning team examines the pros and the cons of an idea, issue, or opinion. When the team is zeroing in on a particular course of action, an effective team member says "Let's consider the positive and negative consequences of this decision." Some teams literally make a written list of the pros and the cons on a chalk board, whiteboard, or flip chart. Teams that do this are more likely to come up with a better decision than teams that don't systematically evaluate the pros and cons of a potential solution or decision.[88]

PERSONAL SENSITIVITY FUNCTION.   Most of the group functions we've described so far focus on getting the work done effectively and efficiently. But team success is about more than just focusing on the task. Effectively functioning team members also are sensitive to the needs of others. They listen to what each group member has to say—even those who may hold a minority opinion. One of the benefits of working collaboratively comes from hearing a variety of ideas. If opinions of others are quickly squelched because they are not what most other team members think or believe, the team loses the power of many different points of view. Effective team members are aware of how the comments they make might be perceived by other group members. Finally, effectively functioning group members use appropriate verbal and nonverbal communication and appropriately adapt their communication to others.

Effective team members balance the concern for the task with concern for the feelings of others. As we noted when discussing cohesiveness, being too task-oriented is not beneficial to the functioning of a team.

The Prescriptive Approach: Identifying Team Strategies

The descriptive approach to teams suggests that there is a natural order or sequence to how groups and teams operate, although each group is unique and a group doesn't always follow a pattern. The functional approach to teams is based on the assumption that effective teams perform certain functions or communication behaviors that ineffective teams don't perform. A **prescriptive approach** to teams is based on the assumption that team members need to use specific steps and techniques to stay on task and remain productive while still being sensitive to other team members. Just as a prescription from your doctor is a specific medicine that is intended to treat a particular ailment, a prescriptive approach *prescribes* things to do to enhance the communication health of the team. In the next chapter we offer a wealth of suggestions, strategies, and techniques to help improve the process of collaborating with others.

Wrap-Up

If you work in business or a profession you are likely to work in a group or a team.

- Definition of a group: three to fifteen people who share a common purpose, who feel a sense of belonging to the group, and who exert influence on each other.

- Definition of a team: A coordinated group of people organized to work together to achieve a specific common goal. A team differs from a group in that it is more structured and involves greater coordination of roles and procedures.

- Effective teams have (1) a clear, elevating goal, (2) a results-driven structure, (3) competent team members, (4) unified commitment, (5) a collaborative climate, (6) standards of excellence, (7) external support and recognition, and (8) principled leadership.

- Virtual teams differ from face-to-face teams: There is greater anonymity, you're often not able to see the other person, there is typically a physical distance between you and others, and you have greater control over the timing of the messages you send and receive; your approach to managing conflict may be different and you may find a need to meet face-to-face to resolve differences.

- These key factors influence team dynamics:
- roles (task, social, and individual roles)
- norms (standards that determine what is appropriate and inappropriate behavior)
- communication networks within a team
- There are three approaches to teamwork: descriptive, functional, and prescriptive.

Reviewing Key Terms

Grouphate *200*

Team-based organization *201*

Small group communication *202*

Team *203*

Team structure *205*

Virtual team *207*

Asynchronous *207*

Synchronous *207*

Wiki *209*

Role *211*

Task roles *211*

Social roles *211*

Individual roles *211*

Norms *214*

Communication interaction patterns *214*

Group deviate *215*

Clique *215*

Team ground rules *216*

Team mission statement *217*

Status *217*

Power *217*

Legitimate power *218*

Referent power *218*

Expert power *218*

Reward power *218*

Coercive power *218*

Cohesiveness *219*

Descriptive approach *220*

Orientation phase *221*

Primary tension *221*

Conflict phase *221*

Emergence phase *221*

Reinforcement phase *221*

Functional approach *222*

Vigilant thinkers *222*

Prescriptive approach *224*

The Principle Points

Principle One: Be aware of your communication with yourself and others.

- Be knowledgeable of the differences between groups and teams.
- Be aware of the role you and others typically assume in teams as well as team norms and rules.
- Be aware of the descriptive phases of orientation, conflict, emergence, and reinforcement that many teams go through during their deliberations.

Principle Two: Effectively use and interpret verbal messages.

- Clarify team goals; clear elevating goals are one of the key determinants of an effective team.
- Provide supportive, positive comments to help encourage team members.
- Talk about your team in terms of "we" rather than "I" to enhance team cohesiveness.

Principle Three: Effectively use and interpret nonverbal messages

- Accurately observe nonverbal cues to help you understand team norms.
- Provide positive, reinforcing nonverbal behaviors such as eye contact, forward lean, and appropriately positive facial cues to enhance team climate and cohesiveness.

Principle Four: Listen and respond thoughtfully to others.

- Listen attentively to others to establish a positive, supportive climate.
- Use active listening skills to clarify misunderstandings and help manage primary tension in groups.

Principle Five: Appropriately adapt messages to others.

- Adapt to determine if the team needs to perform certain communication functions as identified in the functional approach to team development.
- Effective team members appropriately adapt to cultural differences within the team.

Applying Your Skills

1. Make a list of the groups and teams of which you are a member. Using the definitions of small group communication and a team from the discussion of the differences between a group and a team on pages 202–204, place your groups and teams on a continuum with those entities that are more like a group at the top of your list and those gatherings that are more like a team at the bottom of your list. Explain why your groups are groups and your teams are teams according to the distinctions made in the chapter. How many of the characteristics of effective teams and effective team members are illustrated by the teams of which you are a member?

2. Identify the many ways you have communicated using media and technology during the past week. Identify how the presence of anonymity, physical appearance, distance, and time (as discussed on page 207) have had an effect on your virtual communication.

3. Of the roles listed on pages 211–213, which role or roles do you typically assume in groups, teams, and meetings? Identify two task and two social roles you usually do not assume. Why don't you assume these roles?

4. Identify a team that you are currently participating in or a team with which you have worked in the past. Identify norms, rules, and any explicit ground rules that were developed for the team. Even if the team did not have an explicit mission statement, as you reflect on the team goals and objectives, develop a team mission statement for the team presented in this chapter.

10

Enhancing Team Meetings

chapter **outline**

After reading this chapter, you should be able to

- Decide whether you should or should not hold a meeting.

- Develop clear meeting goals, which may include sharing information, discussing information, and taking action.

- Describe and implement strategies for developing an effective meeting agenda.

- Identify and practice the steps of team problem solving.

- Use strategies that enhance team creativity and result in the generation of ideas and solutions to problems.

- Describe and implement strategies for facilitating team meetings avoiding groupthink, and fostering team consensus.

Most of us wouldn't do what Donald Fisher did to solve a simple problem. When he tried to exchange a pair of Levi's at a jeans store in San Francisco because they were an inch too short, he was told, "No, we don't make exchanges." So he decided the world needed a store that sold jeans in various sizes that could be returned if they didn't fit. Donald and his wife Doris opened their first store in 1969. Because the late 1960s was the era dubbed "the generation gap," he called this first store simply *Gap*. Within a year there were six Gap stores. By the mid 1970s there were more than 100 stores. But after ending up on the losing end of price wars, in the late 1970s and early 1980s, Gap experienced a major dip in profits and looked like it was headed for bankruptcy. Then in 1983 Donald hired Mickey Drexler, who had recently revitalized Ann Taylor, another clothing store that almost lost its shirt but, thanks to Mickey's help, became highly successful.

The real turnaround for Gap came when Mickey came to executive meetings with a single simple strategy. Soon after the meeting started he distributed plaques to all meeting participants, embossed with one word: "Simplify." He used the technique not at just one meeting, but in many meetings. When purchasing executives wanted to branch out selling other brands, Mickey evoked his "simplify" meeting mantra. When designing a new look for the retail stores, once again "simplify" was the goal. "Simplify" was not only a meeting-management strategy but became the leadership strategy that made Gap flourish. They not only simplified the number of brands the store carried, but also made the shopping experience simple and easy. After encouraging customers to try on clothes, sales clerks swiftly refolded, restacked, and replenished the stock to keep the stores tidy and contemporary looking and simple for customers to find their size. Despite a roller-coaster retail economic reality, Gap has used its simplicity approach to keep it lean and viable. They have spun off several new sister stores with the same philosophy—keep it simple. The company started as a solution to a problem of meeting a simple customer need. By focusing on simplicity as a company mission statement that percolated through each meeting, Gap has flourished. Including Old Navy and Banana Republic, the Gap organization has over four thousand retail stores worldwide.[1]

leading **questions**

1. Think of a recent meeting you participated in that seemed to go on much too long. How could Mickey Drexler's mantra of "simplify" have improved your unnecessarily long meeting?

2. How does the mantra "simplify" apply to being an effective leader? Think of a leader you know, from your own experiences or from politics, business, or other professions, who has a clear, simple elevating goal that keeps the group moving forward. Or identify a leader who doesn't but should be more focused on a clear goal. What could the leader do to enhance his or her effectiveness?

"None of us is as smart as all of us."
—Ken Blanchard

For better or worse, the context leaders use to make decisions, solve problems, and unleash the power of collaboration is a meeting. Yet, in spite of their prominence in business and professional settings, meetings don't enjoy a good reputation. Perhaps humorist Dave Barry had heard the phrase "death by meeting" when he compared business meetings with funerals. He noted that at both meetings and funerals, "You have a gathering of people who are wearing uncomfortable clothing and would rather be somewhere else. The major difference is that most funerals have a definite purpose. Also, nothing is ever really buried in a meeting."[2] It's not just Dave Barry who doesn't like meetings. Most people who spend a considerable amount of time in meetings would probably agree with the following sentiments:

- A committee meeting is a collection of the unfit chosen from the unwilling by the incompetent to do the unnecessary.

- A meeting should include at least three people: But one should be sick and another should be absent.

- On judgment day the Lord will divide those entering his kingdom by telling those on his right hand to enter the kingdom and those on his left hand to break into small groups.

Why does meeting participation inspire such negative reactions? Often it's because meeting participants have not mastered the communication and leadership principles we've introduced in this book. In this chapter we apply communication and leadership principles to meetings in the hope that the multiple meetings you will lead and attend are lively rather than deadly dull.

Meeting Essentials: A Balance of Structure and Interaction

A **meeting** is a structured conversation among a small group of people who interact to accomplish a specific task. Because meetings are the ever-present format for collaborating in most contemporary organizations, you have undoubtedly been to many meetings.[3] And you'll attend more. As we noted in Chapter 9, you simply can't escape meetings. Research suggests that most managers spend about a quarter of their time in meetings. Top-level leaders spend even more time, about two thirds of their time in meetings or preparing for meetings.[4] The simple fact is this: The broader your leadership responsibilities, the more time you'll spend in meetings.

Meetings need a balance of structure to stay focused and interaction to enhance collaboration.

How can you ensure that meetings you attend and lead are productive? Note two key elements in the definition of a meeting: (1) a *structured* conversation and (2) people who *interact* to accomplish a specific task. Being able to ensure both meeting structure and interaction is vital for the success of any meeting.

Providing Meeting Structure

Meeting **structure** consists of the agenda and other techniques that help a group or team stay focused on the task at hand. A meeting without structure is like a ship without a rudder. Rudderless it would aimlessly chug through the ocean without a clear direction. The lack of structure—a lack of clear meeting goals and a fine-tuned meeting agenda—results in an unfocused, off-task meeting. What are the most irritating elements of business meetings? Most of them are about the lack of proper meeting structure. Note the following list of the top-ten "meeting sins" people report about meetings.[5]

1. Getting off the subject
2. No goals or agenda
3. Too lengthy
4. Poor or inadequate preparation

terms & definitions

Meeting a structured conversation among a small group of people who interact to accomplish a specific task.

Structure the way discussion is organized; using an agenda and other techniques that help a group stay focused on the task at hand.

5. Inconclusive

6. Disorganized

7. Ineffective leadership and lack of control

8. Irrelevance of information discussed

9. Time wasted during meetings

10. Starting late

Each of these problems are symptoms of a meeting without proper structure to keep conversation productive and focused. Meetings get off the subject because there's no structure, no goals or agenda to bring discussion back on track. Meetings go on too long, are disorganized and waste time because there is a lack of structure to keep them focused.

Given this list of meeting problems you'll not be surprised to learn that research has found that meetings with no planned structure or agenda have many more procedural problems than structured meetings. Groups that are "naturally occurring," in which conversations rattle on without leadership, direction, or an agenda, are much more likely to evidence these problems:

1. Meetings are overly long.

2. Members focus on a solution rather than analyzing the issues.

3. People inappropriately jump at the first solution mentioned.

4. Team members hop from one idea to the next without focusing on the big picture.

5. The team is more likely to be controlled by one person.

6. Conflict is more likely to be unmanaged.[6]

The bottom-line conclusion to this research: People who meet in groups and teams need structure to keep them on track, because meeting members have relatively short attention spans. Several researchers have documented a profound observation: *Meetings without leadership and structure are likely to shift topics about once a minute unless there are specific goals and an agenda to keep them focused.*[7]

Can a meeting have too much structure? Yes. A meeting run by a heavy-handed leader who dominates the discussion and allows no or a minimum of discussion does not capitalize on the benefits of why meetings are held—to benefit from the conversations and ideas of others. Meetings need something to balance the structure: interaction.

Encouraging Meeting Interaction

Interaction is the give-and-take talk and conversation that occurs when people collaborate. It is vital for the exchange of ideas. For a meeting to be productive, the group or team should be small enough so that each participant can participate in the conversation.[8] Without interaction the meeting would be more like a speech in which one person talks and the others simply listen. An effective meeting has rich high-quality interaction that is focused on helping the group manage the task or maintain relationships. Group researcher Robert Bales found that most task-oriented groups spend a little over 60 percent of their time talking about the task and almost 40 percent of their time talking about social, relational, or maintenance matters.[9]

Can a meeting have too much interaction? Yes. A meeting in which there is too much off-task talk, no one listens to one another, and people don't connect what they say to what someone else has said is an overly interactive meeting gone amuck. As suggested in Figure 10.1, the key is to find the right balance between structure and interaction. Too much interaction, and meeting members experience the chaos of unbridled, unfocused talk; it's hard to stay on task. Too much structure, and one person dominates; the team loses the freedom to listen and respond with sensitivity to what others are saying.

In this chapter we help you prepare for meetings, structure problem-solving and creative meetings, facilitate meeting interaction, and lead meetings to create a balance of structure and interaction.

terms & definitions

Interaction the give-and-take conversation that occurs when people collaborate.

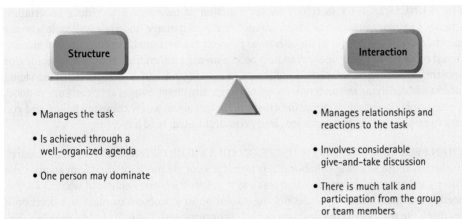

Structure
- Manages the task
- Is achieved through a well-organized agenda
- One person may dominate

Interaction
- Manages relationships and reactions to the task
- Involves considerable give-and-take discussion
- There is much talk and participation from the group or team members

FIGURE 10.1 **Groups Need a Balance of Structure and Interaction**

Preparing for Meetings

Effective meetings don't just happen. The best way to have a good meeting is to prepare. It's like the old carpenter's adage: "Measure twice, saw once." Investing time in preparing for work before actually beginning the work will pay dividends, especially if you're in charge of leading the meeting. The first key task in preparing for meetings is deciding whether you even need to hold a meeting. If a meeting is needed, you'll need to determine what the meeting goals are and how to structure precisely what you'll talk about to achieve the meeting goals. And perhaps the most important task in preparing the meeting is to develop the meeting agenda.

Determining Whether to Have a Meeting

To meet, or not to meet? That is the first question. In your role as a leader, one of your jobs is to determine whether a meeting is needed. The cardinal rule of meetings is this: *Meet only when you have a reason to meet*. This principle may seen like common sense but it is often not common practice. If you want to be a hero in your organization, regardless of whether you work in a small three-person office or for a large Fortune 500 corporation, don't hold a meeting if you don't need to have one.

You can accomplish quite a bit of work without meeting face-to-face. For example, if you just need to share information and need no commentary or interaction, sending a memo or email message may suffice. One leader we know periodically sends out what he calls a "meeting in a memo" that summarizes key announcements, reports, or reminders. You may want to ponder whether a meeting is premature: If people aren't prepared for the meeting, aren't well-informed, or are embroiled in tension and conflict, holding a meeting will only make things worse. So rather than calling a meeting, you may need to share written information, delegate some tasks to one individual, talk to people individually to manage interpersonal conflict, or invite people to read existing policies and procedures before calling a meeting. But when do you really need to hold a meeting? Read on.

WHEN COLLABORATION IS NEEDED Perhaps you've heard it said that many hands make light work. When a task is too big for one person and you need a team effort to gather information, evaluate information, make a decision, or solve a problem, you probably need to call a meeting to sort through the myriad of options and choices. As we've noted, groups and teams have more information available to them and can be more creative than a single individual. A meeting brings the team members together to share information and to coordinate their efforts.

WHEN UNCERTAINTY IS HIGH   A key function of meetings is to reduce uncertainty. Actually, a primary function of *all* communication is to manage uncertainty. People who are uncertain don't know what to do or how to proceed. As we noted, sending an information-packed memo is certainly one way to help people manage uncertainty about an issue, idea, or problem. But during an interactive, collaborative meeting you can do a better job of managing uncertainty, clarifying misunderstandings, and ensuring that messages are clearly understood. When people need clear, accurate information, such as about a new company policy, and you want to ensure that the messages are clearly communicated, hold a meeting.

WHEN PEOPLE MAY RESIST A DECISION OR A PROPOSED SOLUTION   One research conclusion about working collaboratively is that people are more satisfied with an outcome if they participate in the process that leads to it, rather than just being told what to do.[10] A meeting is a good method for developing a solution to a problem or making a decision if you think the solution to the problem could be controversial. But don't hold a meeting simply to manipulate a group. Giving people the illusion of control without the power to shape the outcome will likely create resentment, mistrust, and dissatisfaction. Do hold a meeting when you seek honest input and participation.

WHEN THERE IS NO INDIVIDUAL OR SINGLE SOURCE THAT HAS THE ANSWER YOU SEEK   If you want to know what the company budget is for next year, you can simply email the chief financial officer to get the information; you don't need to hold a meeting. Of, if you want to know demographic data, changes in customer buying patterns, or other work-related information that an individual expert could readily tell you, go ask the expert rather than holding a meeting. Meetings are best used to process and evaluate information. There may be times when you need a lot of information from different sources; in that situation, a team meeting can help coordinate the efforts to get the information. But if all you need is a single piece of information from a single source, call or email someone, or check a website—a meeting is not necessary.

WHEN THE TASK OR PROJECT IS COMPLEX   Simple tasks can often be delegated to one person. But if you have a multistage complex project to complete, a meeting (or several meetings) may be needed to coordinate the process. Or if you need to address multiple questions, issues, or problems or make multiple decisions, using meetings to tap into the collaborative power of more than one person will probably ensure a high-quality outcome. Of course, it's the complexity of a decision or a problem, such as trying to figure out why sales are slumping and then fixing the problem, that makes managing meetings a challenge. In Chapter 9 we noted that team members typically assume different task and maintenance roles during collaboration. With a complex task or project, it is useful to establish clear roles and responsibilities, develop a clear mission statement, and establish ground rules to ensure efficient and effective collaboration.

Once you're convinced that a meeting is the best way to accomplish a task, you'll need to determine the precise outcome you want to achieve.

Determining the Meeting Goal

Every meeting should have a goal. (If you don't have a goal, don't hold a meeting!) Regardless of the task or project, most meetings are intended to achieve one or more of the following three outcomes: (1) sharing information, (2) discussing information, and (3) taking action. The first step in preparing for a meeting, especially if you're leading the meeting, is to determine its goal or goals.[11]

SHARING INFORMATION   An information-sharing meeting is like a briefing or a series of short speeches. Many weekly staff meetings are primarily gatherings during which someone shares information with others. Although these information-giving sessions are called meetings, a gathering really isn't a meeting in the true sense of the word if only one person presents information. Yes, a collection of people are present and do indeed meet; but if there's virtually no interaction and the "meeting" is so heavily structured that one person does all or most of the talking, you're really attending a presentation or briefing, not a meeting. If the person doing most of the talking is giving her spiel with PowerPoint slides, that's a good indication that the speaker views her primary purpose as imparting information rather than soliciting feedback. If the only task during such a meeting is to share information, you may not really need a meeting at all—perhaps a "meeting in a memo" or email will suffice.

There certainly are times when you want to share information in person to emphasize its importance or to get a reaction from others—such as when you need to explain a change in policy, procedures, or sales goals. If you want reactions to what you present, make sure to budget time for discussion and reactions. Sometimes you may need to give information during the early part of the meeting and then move into discussion before taking action. However, if the goal is to explain a new policy and you want or expect minimal discussion, then you're presenting a briefing, rather than holding a meeting.

Briefings have an important function in business and professional settings; sometimes, particularly in businesses with global divisions, the purpose can be simply to see other team members once a week to get an update on projects and assess team member needs. However, a briefing does differ from a collaborative meeting. There is value in the ritual of seeing other people on the team and enhancing relationships. But if people think they are going to attend a meeting and it's really a speech or a briefing, the participants may end up feeling frustrated rather than enlightened.

DISCUSSING INFORMATION An information-discussing meeting is one in which there is considerable interaction and give-and-take, such as nurses reviewing a medical case, real estate agents providing feedback about a new electronic multiple listing website, or student teachers discussing policies. The goal is to gather and assess reactions to information, policies, or procedures. It's important not to let a discussion meeting become a series of long-winded speeches. You want to encourage interaction. Also, at a discussion meeting it is easy for conversations to get off the topic. The meeting leader or meeting participants should be particularly careful to keep the goals of the discussion in mind so that the comments remain relevant. If gathering information is a key meeting goal, it's important to develop strategies to ensure that meeting participants can freely share information, particularly new ideas or statistics. There is a tendency for group members to only share information that all group members already know. It's important when the goal is to discuss information to encourage all group members to participate in the conversation and share ideas, data, opinions, and information.[12] There are structured conversation techniques that can ensure that all members feel free to participate; we'll discuss those strategies later in the chapter.

TAKING ACTION A meeting to take action often involves making a decision, solving a problem, or implementing a decision or solution. For example, deciding who to hire for a job vacancy or figuring out how to save money on travel expenses involves taking action. Prior to taking action, a team must gather information, analyze the information, and discuss it. A meeting can have a single agenda item of making a decision; but if so, team members have likely had prior conversations and have shared information and options, and come to the meeting with the background needed to make the decision.

We've Got to Stop Meeting Like This

The best meetings do more than simply shovel piles of information at people. They provide an opportunity for discussion, on-task conversation, and on-point dialogue. If a meeting is where people merely give speeches, then it's not a meeting—it's a speech. Susan Docherty, whom we noted in the last chapter served as the leader of the United States sales, service, and marketing team at General Motors, abhors "speechy" meetings, especially meetings that overly rely on mind-numbing PowerPoint presentations. She notes,

I actively despise how people use PowerPoint as a crutch. I think PowerPoint can be a way to cover up sloppy thinking, which makes it hard to differentiate between good ideas and bad ideas. I would much rather have somebody type something longhand, send it in ahead of the meeting and then assume everybody's read it, and then you start talking, and let them defend it.

The question from the beginning of the meeting to the end of the meeting is, "Have we added value: yes or no?" And I would say that if the meeting is mostly the presentation of a deck of PowerPoint slides, you conveyed information, but you didn't actually add value.[13]

Make sure your meetings aren't merely occasions for people to give speeches. If you're the meeting leader, develop an agenda that includes an opportunity for discussion. If you're a meeting participant, gently and politely ask for a memo that summarizes key information, a policy summary, or data analysis *before* the meeting. There may be times when information needs to be shared with other members during the meeting; but if that's the primary function of the meeting, consider writing a memo, sending an email, sharing a podcast, or distributing a video.

Many, if not most, meetings have multiple goals. Those attending a meeting may first hear information presented, then discuss the information, and finally take some action to accomplish the meeting goal. If you are the meeting leader, before beginning to draft your agenda, you need to know the meeting goal; you want to identify what you would like to have happen as a result of the meeting. A typical goal might be, "At the end of this meeting we will have decided who to hire for the new advertising job," or "At the end of the meeting we will have discussed and evaluated the sales figures for the last three months." Without a specific goal, it's likely you'll accomplish little.

Developing the Meeting Agenda

Once you have identified goals and assessed what you need to talk about, it's time to develop an agenda—to arrange the items in the most effective way to achieve your goals. An **agenda** is the written list of issues, questions, or topics that serves as the primary tool to help you structure the order in which you talk about each topic. If you are leading a meeting, it's your responsibility to develop the meeting agenda. The agenda is your key tool to give your meeting structure. Here are the key steps to developing a meeting agenda:

1. IDENTIFY MEETING ISSUES AND QUESTIONS   Your first task in developing your agenda is to consider all of the topics, issues, and questions you need to discuss to achieve your meeting goals. As you start to identify the various agenda items, you don't need to worry about what order to place them (you'll make those decisions later). First, just identify the agenda items. Once you have a first draft of your agenda items, you arrange the topics and issues in a logical structure.

We recommend that rather than using a single word as an agenda item, or even using a short phrase, *make each agenda item a question to be answered.* Instead of simply writing "hiring policy" on the agenda, write, "What changes should we make in our hiring policy?" By using a question you invite interaction. You and other meeting participants also know precisely why you are having the discussion—to answer a specific question. Using a question as an agenda item, as shown in Figure 10.2, also helps meeting participants be better prepared for the meeting. They will have a clearer idea about what will be discussed. You'll also know when you have finished a particular agenda item. You're finished when you've answered the question.

Agenda a written list of issues, questions, information, or topics to be discussed or tasks to be completed in a meeting.

Meeting Place: The Centennial Building, Abernathy Conference Room

Meeting Time: Tuesday, September 19, at 3:30 PM

Meeting Goals: At the end of the meeting, meeting participants should be able to
1. Identify positive and negative reactions to the finance report.
2. Describe how the new employment policy will influence hiring practices.
3. Identify strategies to increase sales.

I. DISCUSSION ITEMS
  A. Are there any other agenda items we need to discuss today?
  B. What are positive and negative reactions to the finance report distributed
     before the meeting?
  C. How will the new employment policy influence hiring practices?

II. ACTION ITEMS
  What can be done to improve our sales figures during the next sales period?

III. INFORMATION ITEMS
  Announcements

FIGURE 10.2 **Sample Agenda**

2. GROUP ISSUES AND QUESTIONS ACCORDING TO MEETING GOALS Organize the agenda around your meeting goals. Use subheadings of information items, discussion items, and action items to signal to team members the goal of the discussion. If your meeting goal is to discuss the pros and cons of the new strategic plan, then your agenda would likely include such straightforward questions as, "What are the benefits of the new strategic plan?" and "What are the disadvantages of the new strategic plan?"

3. ESTIMATE HOW MUCH TIME TO BUDGET FOR EACH QUESTION OR ISSUE Before making final decisions about which items you will discuss, estimate how long you think the team will need to discuss each item. How much time you budget for a discussion will help you decide where to place the item on the agenda.

4. STRATEGICALLY SEQUENCE AGENDA ITEMS There is an art to determining the order in which you introduce agenda items. Your goal in developing the agenda sequence is to maximize the efficient use of meeting time while also balancing structure and interaction.

Some meeting management experts suggest putting your most important item first because usually what is introduced first takes the most time. When you have lots of money in your bank account you probably don't monitor every penny you spend; but when you're down to only a few dollars in your account, you're aware of everything you spend. This same analogy holds in meetings. It's time rather than money that is the "currency" of meetings. When you are at the beginning of your meeting you have a "full bank account" of time, so team members may be more likely to talk without monitoring how long they talk. So rather than beginning a meeting with routine information items that are likely to spark digressions from the agenda, it may be best to make your first agenda item something of vital importance to the group that clearly relates to one or more of your meeting goals.

Consider these additional meeting agenda sequencing tips and suggestions:

- Start your meeting by actively involving members in finalizing the agenda; ask them for reactions to how you have structured the discussion. Ask participants if they have other items to include on the agenda in an effort to avoid digressions and surprise agenda additions later.

- Consider making your first agenda item a question or issue that will immediately involve all meeting members in active discussion. By placing a high-priority item early in the meeting, you take advantage of having people talk about an issue when they are fresher.

- Consider placing the most challenging issues for discussion in the middle of the meeting, thus giving the group a chance to get oriented at the beginning and ease out of the discussion at the end.

- If you have an issue that you know is contentious and will generate conflict, place it after an agenda item on which you think the team will reach agreement. Use the positive energy of the issue of agreement to help when there are issues that may divide the team.

- You may want to first string together several small issues so you can dispense with them before getting into the meat of the meeting. Quickly zipping through several agenda items can give the team energy.

- Consider placing routine reports at the end of the meeting; if you run out of time you can distribute the information in a memo or by email.

Always distribute an agenda to meeting participants *before* the meeting. Without an agenda or some knowledge of what will be discussed at the meeting, participants won't know how to prepare. In addition to asking for feedback about the meeting agenda before you begin the meeting, periodically ask meeting participants if the agenda is serving its purpose. Ask, "Are we still discussing useful information?" or "Is our agenda helping us achieve our meeting goals?"

In addition to distributing copies of the agenda before the meeting and having copies of the agenda to distribute when you meet, it's sometimes useful to display the meeting agenda using a flipchart, a PowerPoint slide, or some other visual means. Having a common image to look at can help keep a group focused on its goal.

Having adequate structure is important not only for meetings that take place in person, but also for virtual groups that meet via teleconference or the Internet. Research suggests that a virtual team will make better decisions during a meeting if it has appropriate instructions for framing the decision as well as enough time to process the information. Table 10.1 summarizes potential meeting agenda problems and how to manage those problems.

Leading Team Meetings

Leaders often are the ones who determine whether to have a meeting. They help set the meeting goal and shape the agenda. Although the leader is a key influence in making these

TABLE 10.1	Meeting Agenda Pitfalls and Strategies for Managing Them
Potential Pitfall	**Suggested Strategy**
Participants tend to spend too much time on early agenda items.	Make the first agenda item something worthy of discussion rather than beginning with a trivial report or announcement.
Participants find a way to talk even if you don't want them to talk.	Invite input and discussion early in the meeting rather than having participants trying to interrupt.
Participants aren't prepared for the meeting; they have not read what they were supposed to read.	Clarify the team's ground rules about being prepared for meetings. Consider taking a few minutes to have participants read information or have them prepare by writing ideas or suggestions using this silent-brainstorming technique.
Participants won't stick to the agenda.	Remind the group what the meeting goals are, or, with input from the group, change agenda items.
A meeting is scheduled late in the day or participants are tired.	Begin with an agenda item that involves all meeting participants rather than having participants sitting silently at the beginning of the meeting.
The agenda includes a controversial item that will create conflict and disagreement.	Put one or more noncontroversial items on the agenda ahead of the conflict-producing item. Addressing easier agenda items first will establish a feeling of accomplishment and agreement before the group tackles the more controversial item.

decisions, the wise leader collaborates with other team members and works side by side with others.[14] In most situations, an effective meeting leader facilitates rather than dictates how the group will conduct the meeting. One study found that groups generated more and better ideas when team leaders simply listened and waited for team members to contribute ideas before stating their own ideas than they did when the leader spoke first.[15] Different groups accept (or tolerate) different levels of directions from their designated leaders. One simple rule of thumb is this: *A group will generally allow a leader who emerges naturally from the group or who leads a one-time-only ad hoc group to be more directive.*

Beyond giving direction, and taking a leadership role in goal setting and developing the agenda, certain tasks are generally expected of meeting leaders. In general, meeting leaders are expected to do the following:[16]

- Call the group together, which may involve finding out when participants can meet.
- Call the meeting to order.
- Review the agenda. Ask if there are additional agenda items to discuss.
- If it is a formal meeting, determine if there is a quorum—the minimum number of people who must be present to conduct business.
- Keep the meeting moving; go on to the next agenda item when a point has been thoroughly covered.
- Use a flipchart, chalkboard, or dry-erase board to summarize meeting progress; the written notes of a meeting become the "group mind" and help keep the group on track.
- If the meeting is a formal one, decide when to take a vote. Make sure the issues are clear before a vote is taken.
- Prepare a committee report (or delegate someone to prepare a report) after one or many meetings. Groups need a record of their progress. Many groups designate someone to be secretary and prepare the minutes or summary of what occurred at the meeting.

One of the time-tested strategies for leading a large group is **parliamentary procedure**—a comprehensive set of rules that prescribe how to take action on specific issues that come before the group, such as crafting a new energy-saving policy, or making budget decisions; it provides an orderly way for large groups of twenty or more people to conduct business, although it is less useful for small groups. With smaller groups, parliamentary procedure can be overkill. Research suggests that for small, informal discussions, the formal rules of making motions and amending motions can get in the way of having people just talk and listen to each other.[17] But for larger groups, parliamentary procedure provides the needed structure to help

RECAP

How to Prepare for a Meeting

Determine Whether You Need a Meeting: Determine Meeting Goals

- Sharing Information: The team needs to know something it does not know now.
- Discussing Information: The team needs to express ideas and understand information.
- Taking Action: The team needs to do something or make a recommendation.

Develop the Meeting Agenda

- Identify items that need to be discussed to achieve the meeting goal(s).
- Organize the agenda items to achieve the goal(s). Consider:
  - Making the first agenda item a chance for participants to offer input about the meeting agenda.
  - Placing the highest priority agenda item first on the agenda.
  - Placing an item on which the group is likely to reach consensus first on the agenda to build a positive team climate.
  - Placing routine information items last on the agenda.

them stay focused on the business at hand. For a summary of *Robert's Rules of Order*, the standard source for parliamentary procedures, see www.robertsrules.com.

After you have decided that a meeting is needed, developed your goal(s), and prepared your agenda, you need to develop strategies to accomplish the tasks you've outlined. Whether your meeting goals include solving problems or developing creative approaches to issues, decisions, or problems, you'll need to develop strategies to structure the discussion to achieve those outcomes.

Planning Problem-Solving Meetings

Do you have any problems in your life? *Almost every problem can be phrased in terms of something you want more of or less of.*[18] Perhaps what you want more of is time, money, sales, information, or how to cut costs without sacrificing quality. How to decrease errors, customer complaints, or absenteeism are examples of what you may want less of. Although it may be easy to identify the problems in your life or workplace, it's more challenging to figure out how to solve them. Because of the power of collaboration, groups and teams are often called on to solve challenging problems in business and professional settings. Understanding the nature of the problem-solving process and how to implement the steps of problem solving can help you and your team figure out how to get more or less of what you want.

The Nature of Problem Solving

Problem solving is the process of overcoming obstacles to achieve a specific goal. For groups and teams, a problem consists of three elements: (1) an undesirable existing situation, (2) a goal the team wants to accomplish, and (3) one or more obstacles that prevent a team from achieving its goal.[19]

The problem-solving process begins with assessing the present situation. What's wrong with what we currently are experiencing? What are the most common barriers that keep teams from achieving the goal? Communication researchers Benjamin Broome and Luann Fulbright spent over six years asking business and professional people who participated in group and team discussions what barriers keep their team from operating at full capacity. What they found can be summarized as either lack of a clear goal or lack of opportunity for meaningful interaction. Not having a clear goal or agenda was the most likely barrier to effective problem solving (lack of clear structure). For example, a sales team who gets together to discuss how to enhance Internet sales will make better progress if they seek to answer specific questions and follow a well-crafted agenda rather than just visiting about how things are going. Other problems include poor communication, lack of cultural sensitivity to others, time pressures, and generally not being supportive of others.[20]

The prescriptive approach to teamwork focuses on giving teams specific structures, agendas, or using structured techniques to help them do their work. One researcher suggests that problems can be classified on a continuum of structured or unstructured.[21] An unstructured problem is one in which there is high uncertainty about how to solve the problem; there is little information and the team is confused. The team needs information to help orient its members. For example, how to best merge two well-functioning departments in an advertising firm is an unstructured problem; there is no one right answer, uncertainty is high, and many possible strategies could accomplish the outcome.

A more structured problem might be: What is the best way to purchase and install new energy-saving light bulbs in our manufacturing plant? This problem is more straightforward; doing a simple cost-benefit analysis is a more structured process than trying to predict how well two departments can merge.

One researcher has identified over seventy methods or sequences of prescriptive steps and techniques that can be used to solve problems.[22] Several researchers have sought to identify the sequence that works best. However, they found that *no one single prescriptive method works best. But having some structured sequence of steps or questions works better than having no structure.* The following problem-solving steps and strategies can help you structure a problem-solving meeting.

The Steps of Problem Solving

The problem-solving steps that we present here were developed to help individual people structure problem solving, but they have by groups and teams. These steps were originally developed by educator and philosopher John Dewey in his 1910 book *How We Think*.[23] In essence, his steps follow the scientific method of defining and analyzing a problem, identifying solutions, picking a solution, and putting the solution into practice—a method scientists still use. Dewey's approach, which he called *reflective thinking*, is not a one-size-fits-all prescription. However, it is one useful way of structuring the problem-solving process to manage uncertainty and to ensure that the key functions identified in Chapter 9 (identify the goal, analyze the issues, generate ideas, evaluate ideas, and be sensitive to interpersonal dynamics) are included in your team discussion.

STEP 1: IDENTIFY AND DEFINE THE PROBLEM As we pointed out in Chapter 9, teams work best when they have identified a clear, elevating goal that focuses their problem-solving effort. And, as we've also noted, the goal is often to have more of something (money, time, work quality) or less of something (errors, conflict, wasted time). To reach a clear specification of the problem, consider asking the following questions:

- What is the specific problem that concerns us?
- What do we want more of, or less of?
- What terms, concepts, or ideas do we need to define to understand the problem?
- Who is harmed by the problem?
- When do the harmful effects of the problem occur?

Most team experts agree that an effective way to give your problem-solving task appropriate structure is to phrase your problem in the form of a policy question. A policy question is phrased so the answer is some action (policy) intended to eliminate, reduce, or manage the problem. Policy questions begin with the words, "What should be done about . . ." or "What could be done to improve . . . ." For example:

- What should be done to lower the cost of tuition at our university?
- What could be done to decrease property taxes in our state?
- What should be done to make health care more affordable for all U.S. citizens?

One specific technique for identifying a problem is the Journalists' Six Questions technique.[24] Most news reporters are taught to include the answers to six questions when writing

This team has already analyzed the situation, identified its goals, and generated several alternative ideas. Team members are now evaluating each alternative before selecting the best one.

Communication Ethics @ Work

Truth in Agenda Setting

Your colleague Chad, who is chairing the next meeting of the Personnel Committee, has distributed the meeting agenda before the meeting, just as he should, to help people prepare for the meeting. When he emailed the meeting agenda to all the committee members, Chad asked whether anyone had any other agenda items for the meeting. Missing from the agenda is an item about increasing employee benefits, which you are in favor of; you know that Chad opposes this move. You're certain that if you ask to have the item placed on the agenda, Chad will not do so. Is it ethical for you to wait until the meeting begins to have your agenda item added to the discussion, or should you tell Chad before the meeting begins that you'd like to have your item about employee benefits added to the meeting agenda? What is the most ethical way to proceed?

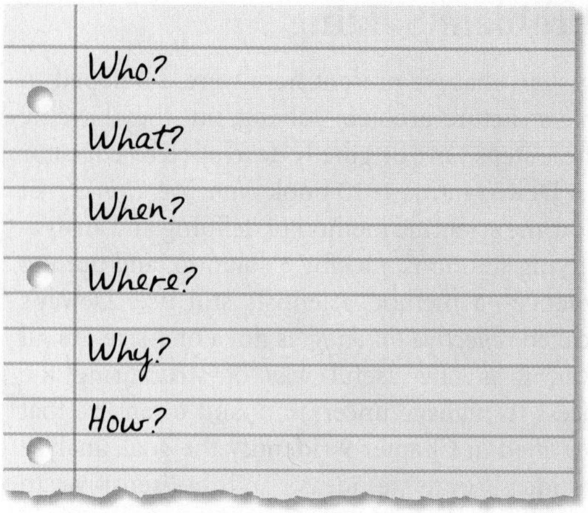

FIGURE 10.3 **Journalists' Six Questions**

a news report: Who? What? When? Where? Why? and How? Posing these six questions can help your team identify and then further define and limit the problem, as well as help you move to the next step in the process—analyzing the problem. You could make a chart, like the one in Figure 10.3, that includes these sample questions and invite group members to answer each question individually, then pool their responses.

STEP 2: ANALYZE THE PROBLEM   Many teams want to "cut to the chase" quickly and start spinning out solutions before taking the time to thoroughly analyze the problem. But research clearly suggests that analyzing the problem well is an important prerequisite to finding an effective solution. To analyze something is to break it down into smaller pieces; to analyze a problem is to consider its causes, effects, symptoms, history, and other information that will inform the team about how to best solve the problem. Here are some essential questions that can help your team analyze problems:

- How long has the problem existed?
- How widespread is the problem?
- What are the causes of the problem?
- What are the effects of the problem?
- What are the symptoms of the problem?
- What methods already exist for managing the problem?
- What are the limitations of existing methods?
- What obstacles keep the team from achieving the goal?

In addition to considering these questions, when analyzing a problem team members should develop criteria—standards and goals—for an acceptable solution. Identifying clear criteria can help you spot a good solution when you see one. Here are some sample criteria for solutions:

- The solution should be inexpensive or within our budget.
- The solution should be implemented by a certain date.
- The solution should be agreed on by all team members.
- The solution should be agreed on by all persons affected by our recommendations.

STEP 3: GENERATE POSSIBLE SOLUTIONS You've now identified a specific problem, analyzed it (causes, history, and so on), and are ready to identify possible ways to solve the problem. The classic technique for identifying possible solutions is called *brainstorming*. An advertising executive developed it more than half a century ago to encourage a team to be creative. You've probably already used this technique. With brainstorming, team members are encouraged to suggest many options or ideas without evaluating them first. We discuss this technique in more detail later in the chapter.

Pros	Cons

FIGURE 10.4 T-Chart

STEP 4: SELECT THE BEST SOLUTION Once they have completed step 3 and generated different options to solve the problem, the team takes the list of ideas generated and determines which ones best meet the criteria identified in the initial analysis of the problem (step 2). They also determine which solutions best achieve the team's clear, elevating goal.

It is usually easier for teams to expand alternatives (brainstorm) than it is to narrow alternatives. Teams can use one of the following three methods to whittle down a long list of alternatives to a manageable number for more serious debate:

- *Ranking:* Tell team members to rank their top five choices from 1 to 5.
- *Rating:* Ask team members to rate each solution on a scale from 1 to 5. The solutions rated best get the most serious discussion.
- *Voting:* Team members simply vote for the alternatives they like.

What seems to work best is for team members to first discuss the criteria and remind themselves of their analysis of the problem before taking a vote or even before rating or ranking. The following questions can help focus the discussion on analysis before selecting a solution:

- Which of the solutions deals best with the obstacles identified?
- Does the suggestion solve the problem in both the short term and the long term?
- Does the solution meet our criteria?
- Do we have the resources to implement the solution?

Once you've narrowed your list of solutions to a handful or a couple of options, it's time to systematically evaluate the pros and the cons of each potential solution. An easy way to structure this discussion is to use a T-chart like the one shown in Figure 10.4. Simply write down the possible solution at the top of the chart (displayed on a flipchart, chalkboard, or whiteboard) and then list both the pros and the cons. This technique will help you look at the positive and negative consequences of an action. For example, suppose one option for a company that needs to cut costs is to move the corporate headquarters to a new location. Team members studying this issue could list on a T-chart the advantages and disadvantages of moving. The team leader could compile a master list of all pros and cons and then use the list to spark discussion on whether the corporate headquarters should be relocated.

STEP 5: TEST AND IMPLEMENT THE SOLUTION Once you have identified your solution(s), your team needs to consider the question "Will it work?" You may want to do a pilot test or ask a small group of people what they think of your idea before you "go public" with it. Bouncing your proposed solution off an expert and checking to see if the solution was successful for others who may have adopted it can help you test the solution's likely effectiveness.

If the team not only has to identify a solution but also put it into action, it will need structure to make sure that the job gets done and that everybody has a role and assumes specific responsibilities. Perhaps you know the people in the following story:

This story is about four people: Everybody, Somebody, Anybody, and Nobody. There was an important job to be done and Everybody was asked to do it. Everybody was sure Somebody would do it. Anybody could have done it but Nobody did it. Somebody got angry about that because it was Everybody's job. Everybody thought Anybody could do it but Nobody realized that Everybody wouldn't do it. It ended up that Everybody blamed Somebody when actually Nobody asked Anybody.

Making sure you have clearly identified who does what can keep everybody from blaming somebody and ensure that the solution is implemented.

RECAP

Problem-Solving Steps and Techniques

Steps	Techniques
1. Identify and define the problem.	• Phrase the problem as a policy question. • Use the Journalists' Six Questions (Who? What? When? Where? Why? How?) to help define the issues.
2. Analyze the problem.	• Develop clear criteria that clarify the issues and can help in evaluating solutions.
3. Generate possible solutions.	• Use brainstorming.
4. Select the best solution.	• Narrow alternatives using ranking, rating, or voting. • Evaluate the pros and cons of each solution.
5. Test and implement the solution.	• Develop a clear action plan. • Make a written list of who should do what.

Developing Creative Solutions

Ingvar Kamprad, the founder of IKEA furniture stores, had a creative idea: He would sell quality furniture disassembled in flat containers at a price lower than any of his competitors. IKEA started in a shed used for storing milk churns and is now an international corporation worth over $17 billion. IKEA (an acronym—the first two letters stand for Ingvar Kamprad; the E is for Elmtaryd, the Swedish farm where Kamprad was born, and A is for Agunnaryd, the name of the village in which the farm was located) is successful because Ingvar Kamprad, working with a team of colleagues, was able to implement his creative idea.[25]

Creativity may seem like a mystical process, but it can be developed. Group and team members often want to know "What techniques will enhance our creativity?" Beyond understanding general principles of creativity and promoting conditions to enhance creativity, what are specific methods, approaches, or techniques that can boost creativity? As we noted earlier, sometimes groups and teams need the structure of a technique to stimulate a creative breakthrough.[26] Such techniques include brainstorming, the nominal-group technique, the Delphi technique, and electronic brainstorming. There is evidence that sometimes creative groups make intuitive decisions—decisions that just feel "right" based on hunches and team members' gut feelings. And sometimes creative teams simply stumble on a discovery while looking for something else. For example, Spence Silver was a researcher at 3M trying to develop a new glue for adhesive tape when he discovered a "low-tack" adhesive. His colleague Art Fry was irritated when the little bookmarks he used to keep his place in a hymnbook kept falling out of his book. Fry had a creative idea: He thought that if he used Silver's "low-tack" adhesive on little pads of paper, he would have sticky bookmarks that wouldn't fall out. Eureka! Post-it Notes were born.[27]

Gut feelings and chance discoveries aside, in the long run, teams are more creative if they take the time to thoughtfully consider a number of alternatives when trying to solve a problem, make a decision, or invent a new process or product.[28] In this section we identify strategies and techniques to help develop creativity in groups.

Brainstorming

Imagine that your employer assigns you to a task force whose goal is to increase the productivity of your small manufacturing company. Phrased as a policy question, the problem is, "What can be done to increase efficiency and productivity for our company?" Your group is supposed to come up with ideas to help solve the problem. Assume that your boss has clearly identified the problem and has provided your group with several documents analyzing the problem in some detail. Your group may decide that reflective thinking, which focuses on identifying and analyzing problems, is not the best process to follow—you need innovative ideas and creative, original solutions. Perhaps your group could benefit from brainstorming.[29]

Brainstorming has been used by businesses, committees, and government agencies to improve the quality of group decision making. Although it can be used in several phases of many group discussions, it may be most useful if a group needs original ideas or has trouble coming up with any ideas at all. Research suggests that a trained facilitator can improve the execution of group brainstorming.[30]

And it's not only verbal interaction that enhances creativity and collaboration during brainstorming; nonverbal communication also can contribute to effective brainstorming. One study found that group members who build off and are in sync with one another's gestures are more likely to develop more collaborative and creative ideas than group members who aren't nonverbally in sync with one another. It is speculated that being nonverbally in sync with other team members enhances the overall creative climate.[31]

How do you structure a traditional brainstorming session? Here are the guidelines:

1. *Identify the problem that needs solving.* Be sure that all group members can identify and clearly define the problem.

2. *Set a clear time limit.*

3. *Ask group members temporarily to put aside all judgments and evaluations.* The key to brainstorming is ruling out all criticism and evaluation. Alex Osborn, the advertising executive who originally conceived of brainstorming, had these suggestions:[32]

   - Acquire a "try anything" attitude.
   - Avoid criticism, which can stifle creativity.
   - Remember that all ideas are thought-starters.
   - Today's criticism may kill future ideas.

4. *Have group or team members think of as many possible solutions to the problem as they can and share the ideas with the group.* Consider the following suggestions:

   - The wilder the ideas, the better.
   - It is easier to tame ideas down than to think ideas up.
   - Think out loud and mention unusual ideas.
   - Someone's wild idea may trigger a good solution from another person in the group.

5. *Make sure that the group understands that "piggybacking" off someone else's idea is useful.* Combine ideas; add to previous ideas. Adopt the philosophy that once an idea is presented to the group, no one owns it. It belongs to the group and anyone can modify it.

6. *Have someone record all the ideas mentioned.* Ideas could be recorded on a flipchart, chalkboard, or an overhead projector so that each group member can see them. You could also record your discussions.

7. *Evaluate ideas when the time allotted for brainstorming has elapsed.* Consider these suggestions:

   - Approach each idea positively and give it a fair trial.
   - Try to make ideas workable.

- Encourage feedback about the success of a session.
- Remember that if only a few of the ideas generated by a group are useful, the session has been successful.

Silent Brainstorming: Nominal-Group Technique

The **nominal-group technique** is a procedure that uses some of the principles and methods of brainstorming but has members write their ideas individually before sharing them with the group.[33] The nominal-group technique gets its name from the notion that because members work on problems individually rather than during sustained group interaction, the group is a *nominal* group (it is a group in name only). Nominal-group technique uses "silent brainstorming" to overcome some of the disadvantages researchers have discovered with exclusively using oral brainstorming. For example, during traditional brainstorming groups, team members shout out their ideas. When a fast-food restaurant team was meeting to figure out how to jump-start sales and Cale blurted out, "Let's just give away our hamburgers," several people laughed. Cale interpreted the laughter as criticism and he was less likely to suggest other ideas because he thought group members would ridicule his ideas. During brainstorming it's important to come up with lots of ideas, even odd or unusual ones. But if someone laughs at a suggestion, nods in appreciation, says "That's cool," or comments "That's stupid," the idea has been evaluated. *The key to making brainstorming work is to separate the generation of ideas from the evaluation of ideas.* In oral brainstorming it's hard not to evaluate ideas—but evaluation can stifle the sharing of ideas. Criticism and evaluation diminish creativity.[34] Even if group members do not verbalize their evaluation, their nonverbal expressions often convey positive or negative reaction to ideas. Another problem is that some people are apprehensive or nervous about speaking up in a group, and using traditional oral brainstorming makes it less likely that the communication-apprehensive members will participate. In addition, researchers have found that sometimes with traditional brainstorming, the creative talents of some members seem to be restricted just by the very presence of others.[35] Silent brainstorming overcomes these problems by encouraging even apprehensive team members to participate by first writing their ideas. Once they have a written "script," they are more comfortable sharing their ideas. Researchers have also found that people work more diligently if they have an individual assignment than if they have a group assignment.[36] Team members using the nominal-group technique are also more likely to remember the ideas suggested.[37]

Research suggests that group and team members may generate more ideas if members first work alone and then regroup. However, although the nominal-group technique can result in more ideas being generated, they may not always be better ideas. It still takes creative, intelligent team members to develop high-quality ideas. No single technique automatically makes ideas better, but team members who are trained to use nominal-group technique do develop more creative ideas than untrained members.

After writing their own ideas individually, group members can come together to modify, elaborate on, and evaluate ideas. The generation of ideas (writing them down) has been separated from the evaluation of ideas. Silent brainstorming can be done even before a group meets for the first time; you could describe a problem and ask group members to brainstorm individually before assembling. Email makes this approach easier. Communication researchers Henri Barki and Alain Pinsonneault found that electronic brainstorming worked just as well as face-to-face brainstorming in generating ideas.[38] The following steps summarize how to use the nominal-group technique.

1. All group members should be able to define and analyze the problem under consideration.
2. Working individually, group members write down possible solutions to the problem.
3. Group members report the solutions they have identified to the entire group, one at a time. Each idea should be noted on a flipchart, chalkboard, or whiteboard for all group members to see.
4. Group members discuss the ideas gathered, not to advocate for one idea over another but rather to make sure that all the ideas are clear.

terms & definitions

Nominal-group technique a brainstorming method in which members work individually on ideas, rank suggested solutions, and then report their findings in a group discussion.

5. After discussing all proposed solutions, each group member ranks the solutions. If the list of solutions is long, group members can rank the five solutions they like best. The results are tabulated.

6. The entire group discusses the results of the rankings. If the first round of ranking is inconclusive or if the group is not comfortable with the results, the options can be ranked again after additional discussion. Research suggests that using this organized method of gathering and evaluating information results in better solutions than attacking a problem in a disorganized fashion.[39] One researcher has found that the nominal-group technique works better than other prescriptive approaches such as reflective thinking.[40]

Both traditional brainstorming and the nominal-group technique can be used at any phase of the problem-solving process.

Absentee Brainstorming: Delphi Technique

Whereas the nominal-group technique invites participants to contribute ideas by first writing them down and then sharing them with the group, the Delphi technique takes this idea one step further. This method, named after the ancient oracle at Delphi, has been called "absentee brainstorming" because individuals share ideas in writing or via email and do not meet face-to-face. One person coordinates the information and shares it with the rest of the group. This approach is especially useful when conflict within a group inhibits effective group interaction, or when time and distance constraints make it difficult for group members to meet.[41] Here is a step-by-step description of the Delphi technique:

1. The group leader selects a problem, issue, policy, or decision that needs to be reviewed. For example, the leader may pose this question: "Should we support the development of a new convention center to be located near the environmentally sensitive river that runs through our community?"

2. The leader corresponds with group members in writing, informing them of the task and inviting their suggestions and input; often a specific questionnaire is developed. Group members are asked individually to brainstorm suggestions or reactions to the issue confronting the group.

3. The respondents complete the questionnaire or generate a list of their brainstormed responses and send it to the leader.

4. The leader then summarizes all the responses from the group and shares the summary with all group members, asking for additional ideas, suggestions, and reactions. Team members are asked to rate or rank the ideas and return their comments to the leader.

The leader continues the process of summarizing the group feedback and asking for more input until general consensus emerges. Several rounds of soliciting ideas and evaluating them may be needed to achieve consensus. For example, when Software.com, a multinational company, wanted to develop a new computer game, they involved teams from their London, Tokyo, Austin, and San Francisco offices using the Delphi technique. The coordinator of the brainstorming session, using the Delphi technique, simply described the goal to the teams and asked them to generate ideas. The coordinator collected the ideas and then shared them with all groups for evaluation.

This method often produces many good ideas. All participants are treated equally because no one is aware of who submitted which idea. It is, however, a time-consuming process. And because there is no face-to-face interaction, some ideas worthy of elaboration and exploration may get lost in the shuffle. Using the Delphi technique in combination with face-to-face meetings can help eliminate some disadvantages of the procedure.

Electronic Brainstorming

Electronic brainstorming is a technique whereby team members generate ideas and enter them in their computers; the individual lists are then displayed to the entire group. This high-tech method resembles the nominal-group technique in that group members write

One of the benefits of electronic brainstorming is that team members—those in the office and those working elsewhere—can look at lists of ideas together and then build on those ideas.

ideas before sharing them with the group. It also is similar to the Delphi technique, but improves on it because team members can see ideas in written form; with other ideas in view group members can piggyback off the ideas of others. Electronic brainstorming can be performed by group members who are all in the same room or by members at their own home or office computers.

Research suggests that groups using electronic brainstorming generate more ideas than traditional face-to-face brainstorming groups.[42] One research team found that when some members of a group meet face-to-face, and are supported with ideas from group members who are not physically present but who are using electronic means to share information, more ideas are generated and these are of higher quality than if all members meet face-to-face.[43] Some electronic meeting software programs permit team members to submit ideas and suggestions without other team members knowing who made them. Members feel less fear or anxiety about being criticized for unconventional ideas because no one knows who suggested them.[44] Thus, when group members move to the phase of evaluating ideas, they are not sure whether they are evaluating an idea coming from a boss, a group leader, or a new intern. All ideas are considered on their own merit.

One obvious disadvantage of electronic brainstorming is the need for all group members to have access to a computer network and appropriate software. But recent evidence strongly supports the value of this variation of the brainstorming method, in which computers add structure to the process.

Managing Meeting Interaction

Without interaction—the give-and-take of dialogue and the contributions that participants make during meetings—meetings become monologues. But with too much interaction, meetings can become disorganized, with rambling, redundant, or digressive discussions that waste time and are inconclusive. Meeting leaders and participants can help ensure a balance of structure and interaction by using facilitation skills, such as gatekeeping, reminding the group of meeting goals, helping the group to be sensitive to the passage of time during discussion, and using strategies that structure group interaction.

Facilitating Discussion

The essential task of a meeting facilitator is to manage the interaction to achieve the goals of the group. A meeting facilitator may be someone other than the leader, boss, or the supervisor of the team. A facilitator's job is to help manage the flow of conversation and keep the group on track. Research suggests that one of the key duties of a meeting facilitator is to ask questions that help the group uncover information, ideas, and strategies for making decisions and solving problems. Specifically, facilitators should:[45]

- Ask questions that help the group identify information it needs at the beginning of team deliberations.
- Get as many people in the team as possible to participate in the conversation.

RECAP

Comparing Creative Techniques

	Advantages	Disadvantages
Brainstorming	• Easy to use • No special materials needed • Group members can piggyback off each other's ideas	• High potential for group members to evaluate ideas as they are being generated • Takes more time than more highly structured methods, such as the nominal-group technique or the Delphi technique • Quiet group members less likely to participate
Nominal-group technique	• Group members can build on ideas of others • Provides a written record of ideas suggested • Controls more talkative, dominating group members by limiting participation	• A good leader is required to organize the process • Less time is allotted for free flow of ideas • Difficult to implement with a large group
Delphi technique	• Group does not have to meet in person • Provides a written record of ideas suggested • Helps group members prepare for upcoming meeting	• No synergy created by hearing the ideas of others • Minimizes opportunities for elaborating on ideas • Group members may be suspicious that someone has manipulated the results
Electronic brainstorming	• Very efficient • Anonymity increases number of ideas generated	• Need computers and software and training to use them • It takes time to describe procedures of electronic brainstorming to team members

- Make sure team members understand the comments and suggestions offered by other team members.
- Solicit high-quality, on-task, relevant contributions from team members.

Communication researchers Fred Niederman and Roger Volkema, in studying the effects of meeting facilitators on group productivity, found that the most experienced facilitators helped orient the group toward the goal, helped members adapt to what was happening in the group, and involved the group in developing the agenda for the meeting.[46]

BE A GATEKEEPER   Meetings should not consist of a monologue from the meeting leader or be dominated by just a few participants. A gatekeeper encourages less talkative members to participate and tries to limit lengthy contributions by other group members. A meeting facilitator needs to be a skilled listener who is sensitive to both individual members' needs and the overarching team goals and knows when to step in. Gatekeepers make comments such as, "Alice, we haven't heard your ideas yet. Won't you share your thoughts with us?" Or, "Mike, thanks for sharing, but I'd like to hear what others have to say." Polite, tactful invitations to talk or limit talk usually work. If worse comes to worst, a facilitator may need to speak to an unruly talker privately to let him or her know that a more balanced discussion is preferable.

FOCUS ON THE GOAL Team members need to understand the group's goals. Once they do, the group's agenda for each meeting should provide a road map for moving toward those goals. A leader often has to keep the group on course, and one of the most effective tools for doing so is summarizing. Periodically, use metadiscussional skills (discussion about discussion, which we will consider shortly) and review your understanding of the group's progress with brief comments such as, "Okay. Dennis agrees with John that we need to determine how much our project will cost. Are we ready for the next issue?" Such summaries help a group take stock of what it has done and what it has yet to accomplish.

MONITOR TIME Another job of a meeting leader is to keep track of how much time has been spent on the planned agenda items and how much time remains. Think of your agenda as a map, helping you plan where you want to go. Think of the clock as your gas gauge, telling you the amount of fuel you have to get where you want to go. In a meeting, just as on any car trip, you need to know where you are going and how much fuel you need to get you to your destination. If you are running out of fuel (time), you will either need to fill up the tank (budget more time) or recognize that you will not get where you want to go. Begin each meeting by asking how long members can meet. If you face two or three crucial agenda items, and a third of your group has to leave in an hour, you will want to make certain to schedule important items early in the meeting.

STRUCTURE INTERACTION To ensure that all members participate in the discussion, you may need to use some of the problem-solving tools and techniques mentioned earlier in the chapter, such as the Journalists' Six Questions, or the various brainstorming techniques for generating creative options. For example, if your meeting goal is to identify new ideas for reducing customer complaints, consider using brainstorming or the nominal-group technique as a way to generate ideas. A key task of the meeting facilitator is to orchestrate meaningful interaction during the meeting so that all participants have the opportunity to give input. Structured methods of inviting involvement are effective in garnering contributions from all group members.

RECAP

Strategies for Effective Meetings

How to Give a Meeting Structure

Prepare an effective agenda by

- Determining your meeting goals
- Identifying what needs to be discussed to achieve the goals
- Organizing the agenda to achieve the goals

How to Ensure Managed Interaction

Keep discussion on track by

- Using effective gatekeeping skills
- Using metadiscussion to help the group focus on the goals
- Reminding the group of elapsed time and time remaining for deliberation
- Using strategies to manage interaction (for example, nominal-group technique or silent brainstorming)

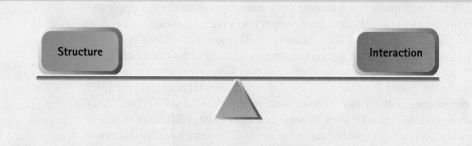

Avoiding Groupthink

Be cautious if all team members agree too quickly. Your team may be experiencing groupthink instead of consensus. **Groupthink** is a faulty sense of agreement that occurs when team members seemingly agree, but they primarily just want to avoid conflict. On the surface it seems as if team members have reached consensus—but it's an illusion of agreement, or an ineffective consensus.

Too little disagreement often reduces the quality of team decisions. If a team does not seriously examine the pros and cons of an idea, it's likely that the quality of its decision will suffer.[47] Effective groups do experience conflict, and then they seek productive ways to manage the conflict. When conflict occurs in a group, the entire group may experience a feeling of dissonance or discomfort. Some group members may

The tragedy of the Challenger explosion might have been avoided had group members been willing to challenge the decision to launch in cold weather.

want to manage the dissonance by quickly agreeing. But members of a well-functioning group realize conflict is part of the process of collaborating in groups and teams.[48]

There are several causes of groupthink. Sometimes it occurs because team members are not particularly interested in the topic. Or the team may just be tired and want to get on with other work. If a team has a highly revered leader, someone that all team members respect, the team is more likely to agree with the leader rather than testing and challenging the leader's ideas. Groupthink also occurs when team members feel they can do no wrong; they feel invincible. Rather than taking time to test and evaluate ideas, the team may quickly decide and assume that the decision is a good one. Groupthink is also likely to occur when (1) the team feels apathetic about its task, (2) team members don't expect to be successful, (3) one team member has very high credibility, so team members tend to believe what he or she says, (4) one team member is very persuasive, or (5) team members don't usually challenge ideas; it's expected that team members will agree with one another.[49] Be on the lookout for these symptoms in your groups and teams.

Failure to test ideas and the resulting groupthink can have serious consequences: Wrong, dangerous, or stupid decisions can be the result. On January 28, 1986, schoolchildren all over the United States were watching the televised launch of the first teacher into space on the space shuttle *Challenger*. Their excitement soon turned to horror when, only moments after liftoff, the space shuttle exploded, killing all astronauts on board. A technical flaw in the design of the shuttle was traced to a problem with O-rings, which provide a seal between components of the shuttle. But the root cause of the accident was groupthink. A review of meeting minutes and memos revealed that at least some people at NASA knew that the O-rings would not work in cold weather. It was below freezing the morning of *Challenger*'s launch. It is now evident that groupthink occurred: Despite the weather, no one spoke up to challenge the decision to launch. Tragedy was the result.[50]

To overcome groupthink, consider the following strategies:[51]

1. *Encourage team members to be independent, critical thinkers.* Reward people for being honest and stating their true feelings. Establish a climate of acceptance of others' ideas.

2. *Don't agree with someone just because he or she has high status; examine the ideas of others carefully, regardless of their position.* Consider the merit of the idea, not the rank or title of the person making the suggestion. Of course, you have to be tactful when disagreeing with individuals who may have more power and status than you do.

terms & definitions

Groupthink a faulty sense of agreement that occurs when team members seemingly agree, but they primarily want to avoid conflict.

3. *Consider asking someone from outside the group to evaluate the group's decisions and decision-making process.* Or, take a few moments to evaluate the group's decision-making skill at the end of the meeting.

4. *Assign someone to be a devil's advocate—to purposely look for disadvantages of a proposed idea.* This strategy is especially useful if no one disagrees with an idea. There is evidence that teams that have team members who are skilled in arguing for and against ideas and evidence make better quality decisions.[52]

5. *Ask team members to break into smaller teams or pairs to consider both the pros and the cons of a proposed solution.* Sometimes team members may feel more comfortable expressing their disagreement in a smaller group than in a larger group or team.

Reaching Consensus

Consensus occurs when all group members support and are committed to a decision. To manage conflict and disagreement to reach consensus takes time and skill, but to reap the benefits of group and team deliberations, it's useful, if time permits, to strive for team consensus on key issues and decisions.[53] Conflict, whether in face-to-face or virtual teams, can be helpful in ensuring that groups don't experience groupthink, but too much unmanaged conflict can lower team member satisfaction and overall team performance.[54] So it's important for teams to invest energy in seeking consensus and managing conflict.

Table 10.2 compares the behavior of effective and ineffective members in a group that is attempting to achieve consensus. Three strategies can help teams reach consensus. First, because teams often bounce from topic to topic, it's important to keep the team oriented toward the goal. When you see the team starting to stray from its task, whether you are the official team facilitator or not, remind the team what the goal is. It also helps to write ideas and facts on a flipchart or chalkboard to keep the team focused.

terms & definitions

Consensus group agreement that occurs when all group members support and are committed to a collective decision.

TABLE 10.2	Suggestions for Reaching Group and Team Consensus
Effective Group Members	**Ineffective Group Members**
Keep the group oriented toward its goal: • Remind the group what the goal is. • Write facts and key ideas on a flipchart or chalkboard. • Talk about the discussion process; ask questions that keep the group focused on the agenda.	• Go off on tangents and do not stay focused on the agenda. • Fail to summarize or rely on oral summaries to keep group members focused on the goal. • Do little to help clarify group discussion.
Listen to the ideas of others: • Clarify misunderstandings. • Emphasize areas of agreement. • Maintain eye contact when listening to someone and remain focused on the speaker without interrupting.	• Do not clarify misunderstandings or check to see whether others understand their messages. • Ignore areas of agreement. • Avoid eye contact with a speaker, do not focus attention on the speaker, interrupt the speaker.
Promote honest dialogue and discussion: • Seek out differences of opinion. • Do not change their minds simply to avoid conflict. • Try to involve everyone in the discussion.	• Do not seek other opinions from group members. • Quickly agree with other group members to avoid conflict. • Permit one person or just a few people to talk too much and dominate the conversation.

Source: Adapted from Steven A. Beebe and John T. Masterson, *Communicating in Small Groups: Principles and Practices*, 10th ed. (Boston: Allyn and Bacon, 2012).

Communication Skills FOR A **Digital Age**

How to Plan a Virtual Meeting

In the twenty-first century it's increasingly likely you'll be involved in meetings without meeting face-to-face. Virtual meetings are rapidly replacing face-to-face interactions. For example, companies providing videoconferencing services generated $6.7 billion in 2007; that figure jumped to almost $12 billion in 2010, and the trend continues to escalate.[55] Even large conferences are being replaced by virtual gatherings. In 2009 Cisco held a global sales conference for more than 19,000 people; sales staff from 89 countries, in 600 conference rooms, spanning 24 time zones participated in the event.[56]

Why are virtual meetings so popular? It saves money. With a virtual meeting participants don't have to travel (no airline or hotel costs). It also saves time. It's not only costly to travel but it takes time to gather people together in one location. Another benefit: Virtual meetings are a way of "going green" and saving the planet. T-mobile calculated that the over 40,000 virtual meetings that the company held between 2004 and 2007 saved 7,000 tons of carbon dioxide (because of reduced air travel) as well as more than 200,000 hours of people's time.[57] Businesses and other organizations are increasingly turning to virtual meetings to save money, time, and the planet. With the increase in virtual meetings you may be called on to organize or facilitate a virtual meeting.

Applying Your Skills

Leslie Wolf, a virtual meeting consultant, recommends the following strategies to ensure a productive virtual meeting.[58]

Before the meeting
- *Always distribute an agenda prior to the meeting.* A good practice for any meeting but especially important in a virtual meeting.
- *Ask someone to assist you as a backup facilitator.* Review the agenda with one or more people *prior to* the meeting to help you keep the meeting productive and positive.

- *Test the technology.* Don't wait until just before the meeting begins to see if the technology works.

At the beginning of the meeting
- *Get to your meeting room early.* In case some virtual meeting members are connected early, you will be there to help them get oriented.
- *Greet each person when they "arrive."* As each person connects to the meeting, welcome them by name and make sure team members know each other.

During the meeting
- *Start on time.* Establish a ground rule that meetings begin on schedule.
- *Don't multitask.* Also make it a ground rule that during the meeting, members aren't checking email, tapping text messages, or taking phone calls.
- *Facilitate interaction.* Listen to make sure one or more people aren't dominating and that others are not participating. Be a gatekeeper just as you would in a face-to-face meeting.
- *Know when to end the meeting.* When the work has been accomplished or conversation lags because the major task is complete, end the meeting. Don't worry about ending the meeting too early. People like it when meetings take *less* rather than more time.

After the meeting
- *Distribute meeting notes.* Ask participants to correct errors or add anything that is missing.
- *Post the notes.* Send each person the link where the meeting summary is posted.
- *Follow up.* Make sure that meeting assignments are completed on time.

A key strategy to keep a team focused on its goal is to use metadiscussion. **Metadiscussion** literally means "discussion about discussion"—it is comments about the discussion *process* rather than the topic under consideration. A metadiscussional comment helps the group stop and reflect on what it's doing or become aware of how it's operating. The fundamental communication principle of being aware that we've emphasized throughout the book is especially important when several people are talking (sometimes at the same time), and people are thinking about what they are saying rather than really listening to what others are saying.[59] A metadiscussional statement might be, "I'm not following this conversation. What is our goal?" or "Can someone summarize what we've accomplished so far?" Periodically using metadiscussional statements can help keep the team on track and focused. For example, saying, "Peggy, I'm not sure I understand how your observation relates to our meeting goal" can help gently guide a team member back to the topic at hand.

terms & definitions

Metadiscussion discussion about discussion; comments that describe the discussion process rather than the topic under consideration.

Obviously, we're not suggesting that you attack others personally. Don't just blurt out "You're off task" or "Oh, let's not talk about that anymore." Metadiscussional phrases need to be tactful and respectful. Use "I" messages rather than "you" messages to bring the team back on track. Rather than saying, "You're not following the agenda" or "Your point doesn't make any sense," you can express these same ideas, but with less of a negative edge, by saying, "I'm not sure where we are on the agenda" or "I'm not sure I understand how your point relates to the issue we are discussing." Being able to use metadiscussion is an exceptionally powerful skill, and you can offer metadiscussional statements even if you are not the appointed leader.

A second general strategy for promoting consensus is to listen carefully to the ideas of others. Work to clarify misunderstandings. When you do agree with something that is said, say so. Maintain eye contact with the speaker and give him or her your full attention. The active listening technique, whereby you sometimes paraphrase key ideas to ensure that you understand what someone is saying, is another useful tool to help a team get unstuck when consensus seems elusive. When listening to others, try to find areas of agreement rather than just trying to convince someone that his or her idea is wrong and yours is right. Consensus is more likely to blossom when the team can find some areas of agreement rather than just hammering away at the most contentious issues. Team members who help promote a positive climate, express agreement, are open to new ideas, and look for ways to support other team members enhance the likelihood that consensus will occur.[60]

A third general strategy is to promote honest dialogue and discussion. True consensus is more likely to occur if many ideas are shared and team members don't just give in or change their minds to avoid conflict. Those tactics are likely to result in groupthink. Some teams may be tempted to take a quick vote to settle issues. Although voting can be a useful way of seeing where team members stand on an issue, be wary of taking a vote too quickly before the team has had an opportunity to discuss it. Consensus is most likely to be genuine if the team has explored several alternatives, despite the time it takes to have these discussions.

Wrap-Up

When leading meetings, your primary task is to consider how you can provide a balance between needed structure to keep a meeting on track and meeting interaction—the give-and-take talk that occurs during a meeting.

To manage meeting structure:

- Develop a well-organized meeting agenda, giving consideration to placement of high-priority items and information items.

To facilitate interaction during a meeting:

- Be a gatekeeper by encouraging quieter members to participate and more talkative members to balance their talk with listening.
- Focus on the goal.
- Be aware of the time left for conversation.
- Structure interaction (such as using silent brainstorming or nominal-group technique).

One of the most traditional ways of structuring a problem-solving discussion is to use the standard problem-solving agenda, which consists of:

- Identifying and defining the problem.
- Analyzing the problem.
- Generating possible solutions.
- Selecting the best solution.
- Testing and implementing the solution.

Teams are often called on to develop creative solutions when making decisions or solving problems.

- Brainstorming is one of the most used techniques to structure creative conversation in meetings.

- Other forms of "silent" or "absentee" brainstorming including nominal-group technique and Delphi Technique to avoid some of the pitfalls of oral brainstorming.

To minimize groupthink (a false sense of agreement), we suggested:

- Encourage independent, critical thought: Don't agree just to agree; ask someone from outside the group to make sure there is appropriate discussion.
- Assign someone to be a devil's advocate to challenge ideas.
- Break into smaller teams (even in two-people dyads) to evaluate the pros and cons of ideas proposed.

There are three strategies to help a team reach consensus:

- Orient the group toward its goal.
- Listen to the ideas of others, especially minority viewpoints.
- Promote honest dialogue and discussion.

Reviewing Key Terms

Meeting *229*

Structure *229*

Interaction *230*

Agenda *234*

Parliamentary procedure *237*

Problem solving *238*

Nominal-group technique *244*

Groupthink *249*

Consensus *250*

Metadiscussion *251*

The Principle Points

Principle One: Be aware of your communication with yourself and others.

- Be aware of your team's need for structure to keep meetings on track and moving forward when people get off task and off topic.
- Be aware of team members' need for interaction when one or more members are talking too much or members are talking too little.

Principle Two: Effectively use and interpret verbal messages.

- Assess the solutions by systematically evaluating the pros and the cons.
- Develop an agenda to give a meeting appropriate structure.
- Use the metadiscussion skill to keep a meeting focused on the agenda.

Principle Three: Effectively use and interpret nonverbal messages.

- Use appropriate nonverbal messages to establish and maintain a positive team climate.
- During brainstorming sessions, avoid evaluating others using nonverbal cues, such as frowning or shaking your head.
- Monitor the eye contact of team members to assess leadership, power, status, and norms.

Principle Four: Listen and thoughtfully respond to others.

- Listen to other team members to express your sensitivity to other team members' ideas and opinions.
- Listen and respond to assess whether the team needs more structure or more interaction to help the team achieve its goals.

Principle Five: Appropriately adapt messages to others.

- Adapt your messages to give team meetings an appropriate balance of structure and interaction.
- Adapt your messages to help keep the team focused on the team's agenda during meetings.

Applying Your Skills

1. Think of a past group or team meeting that you attended. What was the balance of structure and interaction based upon the discussion of structure and interaction on pages 229–230. If your meeting was out of balance (either too much structure or too much interaction), what specific strategies could have been used to make the discussion more balanced?

2. Develop a meeting agenda for an upcoming meeting. Develop a meeting goal or goals, and identify the sequence of agenda items. After you have written your agenda, write a brief explanation of why you structured your agenda as you did. Use the discussion on pages 234–236 as a basis for your rationale.

3. Attend a public meeting, such as your local school board, city council, or campus council. Using the principles and skills discussed in this chapter, evaluate the meeting using the five principles of leadership discussed in this book. Were group members self-aware and aware of comments and actions of others? How effectively did group members use verbal messages to make their points and organize their ideas? Did nonverbal messages provide supportive and positive reinforcement of others' comments? How effectively did group members listen and respond to messages? What evidence did you find that group members appropriately adapted their message to others during the course of their conversations?

11

Developing Your Professional Presentation

chapter **outline**

Confidently Communicating to Others 257

Consider Your Audience 260

Select and Narrow Your Topic 267

Support Your Presentation 271

Organize Your Presentation 280

After reading this chapter, you should be able to

- Implement several strategies to help manage communication apprehension.

- Identify several strategies for analyzing an audience before, during, and after a presentation.

- Select and narrow a presentation topic.

- Determine the specific purpose, central idea, and main ideas for a presentation.

- Identify strategies for choosing interesting and relevant supporting material.

- Describe how to organize and outline a message that includes an attention-catching introduction and an effective summary.

ierre Omidyar and Jeff Skoll had a major presentation to make. They were giving a talk asking executives from Benchmark Capital to invest millions of dollars in their new idea. It was originally called AuctionWeb. They also considered using a variety of different ways to present their information and organize their talk. They also thought about which method of delivery—a formal style or a more informal, relaxed approach—would be most effective. They decided that because they were speaking to an audience that might initially be skeptical and might not jump at the chance to invest in their idea, they needed to present facts, strong statistical evidence, and clear arguments as to why an Internet auction might be the next big marketing innovation. After presenting all of the facts and figures of their investment deal in a logical, clear outline, while also using their best presentation skills, they were delighted to get the go-ahead from Benchmark Capital executives to invest in their little company. Because of their skill in presenting the idea, as well as the idea itself, that investment it is not so little today. Within ten years of starting the company, they made nearly $10 billion. You know it as eBay.[1]

leading **questions**

1. If you were Pierre Omidyar and Jeff Skoll and were pitching eBay to a group of investors, how would you have described the concept to your listeners?

2. What are the key skills of presenting information to an audience? What strategies do you think would be most effective in establishing your credibility with listeners?

3. Why are presentation skills so valuable in business and professional settings?

Not all of your presentations will have as much at stake as the investment pitch make by Omidyar and Skoll. Yet regardless of your precise professional or business role, you will be expected to give presentations to others. Although the Internet makes it possible to share volumes of information with others, a presentation—whether live and in person, presented on streaming video, "narrowcast" via Skype, or captured on YouTube—speaking to others remains an integral part of business and professional communication. Some of your talks will be presented to only one person, but many talks will be presented to a larger audience—whether live or delivered via satellite. During some presentations you'll likely be seated around a conference table, perhaps to promote a new product that you hope your customers will buy. If you aspire to a major leadership role in an organization, it's possible that you may find yourself speaking to a large audience who are anxiously waiting for you to tell them whether they are still employed. As management consultant Tony Jeary has noted, *"Life is a series of presentations."*[2]

To lead is to speak. Of course you can lead, or influence others, while listening—but effective leaders are also effective speakers. Delivering public presentations is an essential part of being a leader in contemporary business and professional settings. Although it's true that you could simply hand your listeners a written report that provides the information you want to share, the written word alone does not have the same impact as a live presentation. This chapter is about the inevitable public presentations that will punctuate your professional life.

As with the other communication skill sets we've discussed in this book (relating and collaborating), when presenting a message to an audience you will draw on all five of the fundamental communication principles we've presented throughout our application of communication principles and skills.

> *"Everything that can be said can be said clearly."*
>
> —Ludwig Wittgenstein

• Principle One—be aware of self and others—is important when speaking publicly. Mindlessly blathering about your topic in front of an audience can be embarrassing, or worse—it could lead to the loss of your job if you say the wrong thing.

Effective leaders are mindful of their own communication behaviors as well as the behaviors of those they lead.

- Principle Two—effectively using and interpreting verbal messages—is definitely applicable to public presentations. A speech is called a speech because spoken words express the ideas of the presenter.

- Principle Three—effectively using and interpreting nonverbal messages—emphasizes the role of delivery when presenting a speech. Effective leaders use eye contact, gestures, and even their appearance to establish their credibility and develop a relationship with the audience.

- Principle Four—listening and responding thoughtfully to others—is important because it's through listening and observing that you learn how to thoughtfully respond to your audience. Leaders who are effective listeners are also better speakers.

- Principle Five—appropriately adapting your message to your audience—is essential. One definition of public speaking describes it as "adjusting ideas to people and people to ideas."[3] Skilled leaders appropriately and ethically adapt what they say and how they say it to their audience.

Confidently Communicating to Others

Some people believe if they don't talk about "it," then "it" will go away. The "it" we're talking about is the anxiety and apprehension many people feel when they give a presentation. If you get nervous when you speak in public, you are not alone, many—if not most—people are nervous about giving presentations. Comedian George Jessel once noted, "The mind is a wonderful thing. It starts working the minute you're born and never stops . . . until you get up to speak in public." In a frequently cited survey seeking to identify people's fears, public speaking ranked as the top anxiety-producing experience most people face.[4] Forty-one percent of all people responding said public speaking was their greatest fear; fear of death ranked only sixth! Other research suggests that more than 80 percent of people feel nervous when they give a presentation.[5] And about 20 percent of all college-age students are highly apprehensive about speaking with others.[6] Because there may be much at stake when you speak in business and professional contexts (such as getting the sale, getting the contract signed, or negotiating a major deal), the anxiety of giving a public presentation may seem overwhelming. Although you may find some comfort in knowing that you are not alone in experiencing public speaking anxiety, you may still welcome some tips and strategies to help you manage your nervousness. One of the biggest comforts can simply be having more information about *why* you experience nervousness and anxiety.

Understanding Your Apprehension

You are not alone if you get nervous when you speak publicly. Virtually every speaker gets nervous to some degree. Many well-known polished presenters admit they get nervous. Speakers and TV personalities such as Katie Couric, Conan O'Brien, Jay Leno, and Oprah Winfrey admit to getting nervous before a speech.[7] In the last century both President John Kennedy and British Prime Minister Winston Churchill were hailed as outstanding orators. Both got very nervous before speaking.

WHY DO WE BECOME NERVOUS?   Believe it or not, your anxiety stems from your brain trying to help your body adapt to a stressful situation. Sometimes, however, your body offers more "help" than you need.

Your view of the speaking assignment, your perception of your speaking skill, and your self-esteem interact to create anxiety.[8] You want to do a good job, but you're not sure you can or will. Presented with this conflict, your body responds by increasing your oxygen supply through increased breathing, pumping more adrenaline to give you energy, and causing more blood to rush through your veins. Your brain switches to its default fight-or-flight mode: You can either fight to respond to the challenge, or flee to avoid the trigger of the anxiety.

To put things technically: You are experiencing physiological changes because of your psychological state, which explains why you may have a quicker heartbeat, wobbly knees, trembling hands, a higher, quivering voice, and increased perspiration.[9] As a result of your physical discomfort, you may have less eye contact with your listeners, use more vocalized pauses ("Um," "Ah," "You know"), and speak more rapidly than normal. And although you view these physical responses as problems, your body is simply trying to help you with the task at hand—to speak effectively.

WHEN ARE YOU MOST LIKELY TO FEEL NERVOUS? You are most likely to feel apprehensive about giving a presentation just moments before you deliver it. Anxiety is also likely to surge when you learn you have a presentation to deliver, such as when your boss assigns you to talk about your team's project.[10] As you begin preparing your presentation your anxiety decreases somewhat; that's because you are taking positive action to respond to the speaking opportunity. The practical application of this research is that now you know when you need the most help managing your apprehension—right before you give your speech. It is also helpful to remember that your anxiety begins to decrease as you begin delivering your speech.

To help you mentally prepare for a presentation, consider the following thoughts: You are going to feel more nervous than you look. Realize that your audience cannot see what you feel. In fact, worrying about your speech and continuing to focus on your fear may actually increase your fear. Just realize that the audience can't see your fear unless you announce your fear.

Use your anxiety to help you. Being aware of the causes of the communication apprehension can help you rather then hurt you. Extra adrenaline, increased blood flow, increased endorphins to block pain, increased heart rate, and other physical changes triggered by anxiety actually enhance your energy level and help you function better than you might otherwise. Speakers who label their feelings of physiological arousal as "nervousness" are more likely to feel anxious and fearful, but the same physiological feelings are experienced as enthusiasm or excitement by speakers who don't label the increased arousal as fear. Don't let your initial fear convince you that you cannot speak effectively.

Tips for Building Your Confidence

Other than understanding what is causing your fear, are there specific things you can do to enhance your confidence? We're happy to report that the answer is "yes"! Here are some tips and strategies to decrease anxiety and increase your poise.[11]

DON'T PROCRASTINATE One research study reached this commonsense conclusion: Speakers who are more apprehensive about speaking put off working on their speeches.[12] There is a link between how far in advance you start preparing and the amount of anxiety you'll experience. The lack of thorough preparation often results in a poorer performance, thereby reinforcing the perception that making a presentation is difficult. Take charge by preparing for your talk early; give yourself every chance to be successful.

KNOW YOUR AUDIENCE Learn as much as you can about your listeners. The more you can anticipate their reactions to your presentation, the more comfortable you will be in delivering your message.[13] Consider their needs, goals, and hopes as you prepare your message. As you are rehearsing your speech, periodically imagine what your audience members may be doing or how they may respond to your presentation. In other words, be audience-centered, not speaker-centered. Don't keep telling yourself how nervous you are going to be; that's being speaker-centered.[14] An audience-centered speaker focuses on connecting to listeners.

RECREATE THE SPEECH ENVIRONMENT WHEN YOU REHEARSE When you practice your presentation, imagine you are actually delivering the speech to the audience you will be addressing.[15] Picture what the room looks like. Practice rising from your seat, walking to the front of the room, and beginning your speech. Stand up, and practice out loud; don't just think about what you are going to say. The more your brain and body experience actually presenting your speech, the less they will try to deal with the challenge by increasing adrenaline, heart rate, and breathing. A realistic rehearsal will increase your confidence when your moment to speak arrives.

VISUALIZE SUCCESS   Imagine not just giving your speech, but giving it effectively and comfortably. Studies have found that positive visualization can help you feel more confident and reduce anxiety.[16]

BREATHE   You can't not breathe—or else you'd be dead. Yet nervous speakers often tend to take short, shallow breaths. To help break this anxiety-induced breathing pattern, consider taking a few slow deep breaths before you speak. No one will be able to detect that you are taking deep breaths if you just slowly inhale and exhale before beginning your talk. While breathing deeply, relax your entire body. Deep breathing coupled with visualizing your success can help you relax.

CHANNEL YOUR NERVOUSNESS   Typical symptoms of anxiety are shaking hands and wobbly knees. Your muscles may move whether you've asked them to move or not. One way to release tension is to take a leisurely walk before you arrive wherever you will be speaking. Another technique is to grasp the edge of your chair (without calling attention to what you are doing) and gently squeeze the chair to release tension. Just squeeze and relax, squeeze and relax. You can also purposely tense and then release the muscles in your legs and arms while you're seated. You may also want to keep both feet on the floor and ever so gently wiggle your toes. These tactics will ensure that every body part will be wide awake and ready to go when it's your turn to speak.

GIVE YOURSELF A PEP TALK   Mentally tell yourself positive, encouraging messages rather than negative, fear-laced messages. There is research evidence to support this advice: Worry begets more worry and anxiety. There's also research to suggest that if you can *cognitively restructure* the defeating messages you tell yourself, you can decrease your anxiety.[17] Cognitive restructuring is the technical term for telling yourself positive messages instead of negative messages. So break the chain of negative thoughts by mentally telling yourself, "I've practiced this speech. I've got good notes. I'm prepared." Or, "I can do this! My listeners want me to succeed." If you find yourself drifting back into self-defeating negative self-talk, stop those thoughts and replace them with more positive, encouraging messages.

LOOK FOR FRIENDLY FACES WHEN YOU SPEAK   If you think your audience is not going to like you or agree with your message, you are more likely to feel nervous.[18] So look for friendly, positive support when you speak. Find the people who will nod affirmatively in agreement with your message.[19] Look for smiles, reciprocal eye contact, and other positive reinforcement. Although you may find some audiences that won't respond positively to you or your message, the overwhelming majority of listeners will be positive. Finding reinforcing feedback can help you feel more confident.

SEEK SPEAKING OPPORTUNITIES   The way you get better at anything is through practice. There is evidence that as you gain public speaking experience your anxiety will

© *2003 King Features Syndicate*

RECAP

Tips for Speaking with Confidence

Before You Speak

- Don't procrastinate—start early.
- Know your audience.
- Be well prepared.
- Rehearse by re-creating the environment in which you will speak.
- Visualize your success.
- Use breathing techniques to help you relax.
- Channel nervous energy.
- Give yourself a mental pep talk.

During Your Speech

- Focus on connecting to your audience rather than on your fear.
- Look for and respond to positive listener support.

After Your Speech

- Seek other speaking opportunities to boost your experience level and confidence.
- Focus on your success and accomplishments.

decrease.[20] So, rather than fleeing from speaking opportunities, look for ways to increase rather than decrease your public speaking experience, such as volunteering to present your teams' report at the sales meeting. At the end of each speech, resist the temptation to focus on your initial fear; instead, celebrate your accomplishment. Mentally replay your success in connecting to an audience.

BE PREPARED Here's a formula that applies to most speaking situations you are likely to experience: *The better prepared you are, the less anxiety you will experience.* Being prepared means you have researched your topic and practiced your speech several times before you deliver it. Being prepared also means being able to adapt your message to your audience on the spot.[21] If you thought you were giving a twenty-minute presentation, be prepared to cut your speaking time in half if you need to. Or, if you have more time to speak than you thought, consider adding a relevant example (but don't talk longer than you need to talk to make your point, even if you are given extra time). Being prepared also means you have developed a logically coherent outline rather than one that is disorganized and difficult to follow. Transitional phrases and summaries can help you present a well-structured, easy-to-understand message. By preparing, even overpreparing, you'll gain confidence and skill.

Consider Your Audience

When attempting to sell a product, a good businessperson knows that one of the keys to success is marketing—which is considering who will buy the product and having a detailed sense of the needs, interests, and goals of the people in that market. When giving a professional presentation, you'll need to practice good marketing skills by considering the specific market for your ideas—your audience. The audience "writes" the speech[22]—not literally, but certainly metaphorically. By suggesting that the audience "writes the speech," we mean the audience plays a central role in determining what you should say. If the audience is not foremost in your thoughts as you design and deliver your presentation, you are less likely to accomplish your purpose. Constantly think about connecting your message to your listeners; you'll be more likely to achieve your speaking goal.

As shown in Figure 11.1, at the heart of the professional speaking process is considering your audience. You'll notice that double-headed arrows connect the center of the model with every other element in the speaking process. Effective leaders ethically adapt or customize their message to their audiences. View the model as you would a clock. You'll find "Select and Narrow Topic" at 12 o'clock. The process proceeds clockwise in the direction of the arrows to "Deliver Speech." Focusing on the audience is ever-present—it is where you start and end the speaking process.

Why should the central focus of professional speaking be the audience? Because ultimately your listeners will determine whether you get the sale,

These audience members, who are clearly engaged in a presentation, appear to be listening to a speaker who considered their needs, interests, and goals when developing his or her presentation.

land the contract, convince a philanthropist to give your organization money, or achieve whatever your speaking goal is.

Being audience-centered involves making decisions about what you say and how you say it before you speak. It also means being aware of your audience's responses during the presentation so that you can make appropriate adjustments to your message or your style of delivery. Finally, effective speakers acknowledge that cultural, ethnic, and other traditions affect the way people process messages. In addition, each organization, whether a for-profit business or a nonprofit organization, has its own organizational culture. Audience-centered

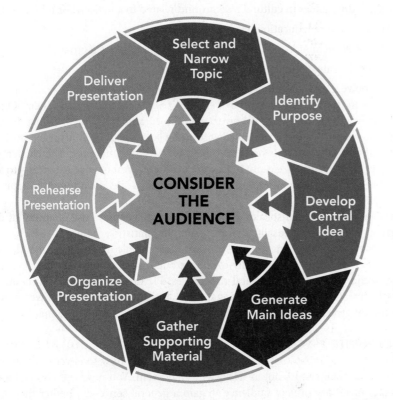

FIGURE 11.1 An Audience-Centered Model of the Presentational Speaking Process

professional speakers are inherently sensitive to the variety of ethnic and cultural backgrounds of contemporary audiences.

Analyzing Your Audience Before You Speak

As we've noted, before thinking about how to narrow your topic or proceeding with any other task in preparing for your presentation, you *consider your audience*. One way to do this is to gather information about them: **demographic information** such as age, gender, and cultural background, and **psychological information** such as likes, dislikes, and possible biases against you, your topic, or your speaking goal. You'll also want information about the speaking situation (including where you will speak and the overall environment in which you'll talk).

After you have gathered the information, you'll need to think about how the information you've gathered can help you. Reflecting on this information is a key task—something less experienced speakers fail to do. The information you gather about your audience won't help you if you don't take it into account at each step of developing your presentation.

CONSIDER DEMOGRAPHIC INFORMATION As every good salesperson knows, before trying to sell someone something, it's important to qualify the customer. To **qualify** customers is to learn as much as you can about them—their backgrounds, likes, dislikes, interests, needs, and goals. If you have the right information, you can determine if customers are interested in what you are selling. Whether you are qualifying a customer to make a sale, or presenting a short report to a corporate board, the more background information you have about your listeners, the better able you will be to adapt to them and ethically achieve your speaking goal. Among the key types of information to learn are demographic details, or statistics about such audience characteristics as age, gender, and ethnicity. Consider the following questions about your listeners:

- How old are your listeners?
- What is the ratio of men and women in the audience?
- Are there differences in cultural background related to a national or religious heritage?
- What is the typical education level of your audience?
- Are listeners members of religious, political, social, or service groups?
- What are the range of income and the occupations of your audience?

Once you've gathered demographic information about your listeners, you'll need to ponder how to use the information to help you adapt your message to them. One of the biggest challenges speakers face is how to adapt to an audience that is highly diverse. You may have to focus on a target audience within the larger audience. A **target audience** is a specific segment of your audience that you most want to influence. The challenge when focusing on a target audience is not to lose or alienate the rest of your listeners—to keep the entire audience in mind while simultaneously making a specific attempt to appeal to the target segment.

Another strategy when speaking to a diverse audience is to use a variety of different supporting materials—such as illustrations, examples, statistics, opinions—which we discuss in more detail later in the chapter. Tell stories. Most people like to hear a good, well-told, relevant story. With an exceptionally diverse group, consider relying on visual materials that transcend language and cultural differences. Pictures and images can communicate universal messages—especially emotional ones. Finally, with a highly diverse audience, seek common ground: Identify values that many people in the audience may hold.

CONSIDER THE PSYCHOLOGICAL PROFILE OF YOUR AUDIENCE Because you are probably not a trained psychologist, you may wonder how to develop a psychological profile of your listeners. It's not as tricky as it may seem. You need not conduct a detailed personality inventory of your audience to gain a general sense of whether they are interested, uninterested, favorable, or unfavorable toward you and your topic. But you can ask

terms & definitions

Demographic information statistics about audience characteristics such as age, gender, and cultural background.

Psychological information listener attributes such as attitudes, beliefs, and values.

Qualify to learn as much as possible about a customer or an audience, such as backgrounds, likes, dislikes, interests, needs, and goals.

Target audience a specific segment of your audience that you most want to influence.

someone who knows your audience well about their attitudes, beliefs, and values. Or you could speculate about their position on the issues you will discuss based on their demographic characteristics, as well as the nature of their jobs and their roles in the organization.

- What are their attitudes (likes and dislikes)? Overall, does your audience have a positive attitude toward you and what you are going to say? Or are they, like many audiences, simply neutral or apathetic toward your message?

- What are their beliefs (what they hold to be true or false)? Do they have a different sense of what the world is like compared to your view of the world?

- What are their values (concepts of good and bad, right and wrong)? Values are the hardest to change.

For example, if it's your job to announce there will be a 10 percent cut in employment in your department, your listeners will be both attentive and fearful that their jobs are on the line. Or, if it's your turn to present a mandatory routine reminder of safety tips for your work team, your listeners are likely to be somewhat apathetic because they've heard this message before. Knowing your audience's attitudes toward you or your topic is important—it determines how you organize your message, the types of examples and illustrations you use, and many other facets of your talk that we will discuss in this chapter and the chapters ahead.

CONSIDER THE SITUATION Situational audience analysis includes a consideration of the time and place of your presentation, the size of your audience, and the reason you are speaking. Although these elements are not technically characteristics of your audience, they can have an important effect on how your listeners react to what you say.

Key factors in the situation are the time at which you are expected to speak and the length of your presentation. If you're speaking to people who are not quite awake or are tired, you may have to throttle up your energy level when talking. Another key piece of information to know before any presentation is when your listeners expect you to conclude. A general rule of thumb is to *never exceed your time limit*—in fact, if possible, conclude just slightly before your listeners expect you to end. Most listeners don't complain if a talk is too short; but they will not appreciate you if you take too much of their time.

The size of your audience directly affects your speaking style. Usually, the larger the audience, the more likely they are to expect a more formal style. With an audience of ten or fewer, you can be more conversational; but in a professional or business setting, formality may be expected. If, as during many professional presentations, you and your listeners are so few that you are all sitting around a table, you'll probably be expected to stay seated for your presentation.

The location of your presentation will influence your overall style and speaking approach. As shown in Table 11.1 (on the next page), the seating arrangement can have an effect on the interaction patters during or following a presentation. A key variable that affects audience interaction is the amount of eye contact audience members have with the speaker and with one another. Eye contact encourages interaction.

Analyzing Your Audience as You Speak

Being audience-centered involves more than thinking and planning your message before you speak; it also is a process that occurs as you are speaking. An effective speaker looks for cues from the audience during the speech to help him or her adjust speaking content or delivery. such as shuffling papers, confused looks, or discreetly trying to check their cell phone messages. Delivering a presentation is a lot like playing in a jazz ensemble and responding to what the other musicians are playing. If you know what to look for, you can find cues from your listeners that will help you know how to connect with them. Here's where Principle Four is applicable to presentational speaking: A good speaker is listening with both ears and eyes to monitor the audience so that he or she can adapt by adding an example, repeating a key idea, or stopping to ask or questions if the listener seems confused.

During most presentations, your listeners will not be talking back to you. Unless your presentation is part of an interactive meeting in which there is lots of discussion, you'll talk

TABLE 11.1

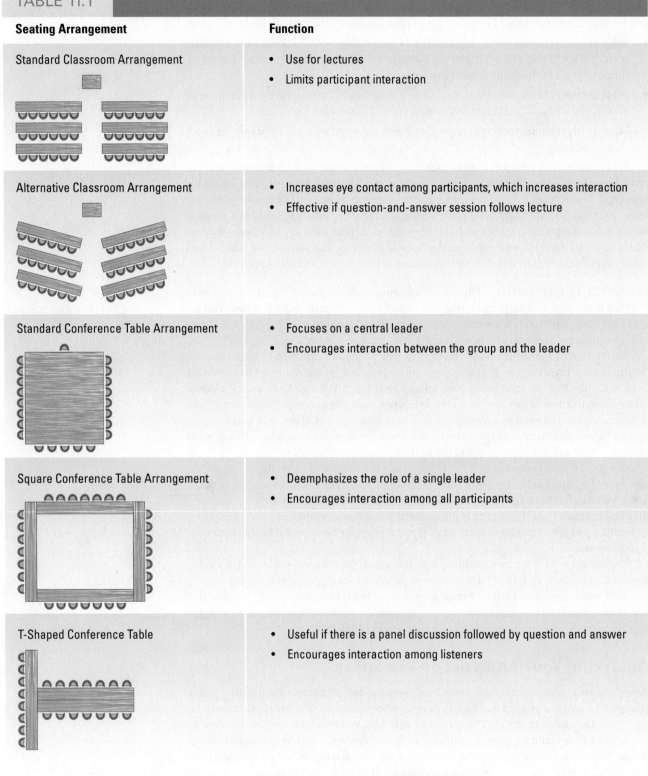

Seating Arrangement	Function
Standard Classroom Arrangement	• Use for lectures • Limits participant interaction
Alternative Classroom Arrangement	• Increases eye contact among participants, which increases interaction • Effective if question-and-answer session follows lecture
Standard Conference Table Arrangement	• Focuses on a central leader • Encourages interaction between the group and the leader
Square Conference Table Arrangement	• Deemphasizes the role of a single leader • Encourages interaction among all participants
T-Shaped Conference Table	• Useful if there is a panel discussion followed by question and answer • Encourages interaction among listeners

and others will listen. It's your audience's nonverbal cues that will tip you off to how successful you are and whether you need to modify your message or delivery. Nonverbal cues are the primary way people communicate likes and dislikes, feelings, and emotions; and if you know what to look for you'll be able to interpret your listeners' unspoken cues accurately.

Communication Skills (FOR A) **Digital Age**

Using Technology to Analyze Your Audience

We have stressed the importance of understanding your audience in any speaking situation. Sometimes it can be a challenge to gain information about an audience you have not yet met. Imagine you have been asked to give a talk to a company that you've never visited. Consider checking out the company's website to learn more about the audience to which you'll be speaking. Here are some strategies to help you gather information from the organization's website:

- Look for information you can use to customize your message. For example, look at the organization's mission, vision, or values statement for ways you can align your message with the organization's overall mission and goals.

- Use success stories or other examples or illustrations that can sometimes be found on an organization's website to illustrate a point or key idea you are making. Of course, you should acknowledge the source of anything you may use.

- Find information that describes job duties and responsibilities of the people to whom you will be speaking to help you adapt your message to their specific job responsibilities.

- Make a note of news that the organization may post on its website. Let your audience know you are aware of the stories and issues that are important to the organization.

Applying Your Skills

For an important presentation, you may want to gather information more formally to assess your listeners' opinions, attitudes, and beliefs. Consider these strategies:

- Develop a short or brief questionnaire and via email distribute it to your potential audience members asking for their responses.

- Selectively email a few people you know will be in your audience to ask for their opinions or attitudes about issues you will present.

- Consider inviting audience members to click on a website or a Facebook page that you've developed to gather audience-member demographics and assess their attitudes and opinions.

OBSERVE EYE CONTACT The best indicator that your listeners are with you is their eye contact. The more eye contact your listeners make, the more likely it is they are connecting to your message. If they are flipping through notes, looking out the window, looking at someone else, or sitting with eyes closed, it's a good bet you're not connecting with them.

OBSERVE FACIAL EXPRESSION Another key indicator of interest is audience members' facial expressions. Someone who is looking at you with a slight head tilt and a frozen, "in-a-stupor" expression is probably not mentally in the same room with you. An interested listener not only looks at you, but also responds to your messages with facial expressions. Smiling at appropriate times, laughing at your humor, nodding their heads in agreement, or even shaking their heads in disagreement means audience members are listening. A bored listener has an expression that doesn't change, no matter what you are saying.

OBSERVE MOVEMENT A bored audience expresses its boredom with movement, especially finger tapping, toe jiggling, foot wagging, and other squirms and jitters. An attentive audience doesn't move much while you are speaking; but if you ask for a show of hands in response to a question, an attentive audience will respond. When you "have" an audience, they look at you and focus on your message. When you don't "have" them, their inattentiveness manifests itself with nervous, restless movement.

An inattentive, unengaged audience just sits there. An inert, motionless, nonresponsive audience is a bad sign. If you see bad signs, you'll need to modify your message content or your delivery. Effective speakers use and interpret others' nonverbal messages.

LISTEN FOR VERBAL RESPONSIVENESS During smaller, informal presentations your listeners may respond verbally to questions you ask or ideas you express. Even in a large group, audience members may respond verbally; they may mouth "yes" or "no" to a question you ask or respond aloud to something you've said. If your listeners express disagreement with an idea, you now have information you can use to adapt to them. The effective speaker not only watches the audience, but also listens for any audible information that may indicate that the audience is in agreement or opposition.

More important than just observing your listeners is *responding* to them. If audience members are responsive to you and in agreement with your ideas, you have the luxury of presenting the message you planned. But if you see indicators of disagreement or inattentiveness, you'll be wise to adapt and adjust either your message, your delivery, or both. It takes experience to both "read" an audience and then respond appropriately to listeners.

There are several classic audience reactions to be mindful of. If your listeners appear bored they may decrease their eye contact with you, have more finger fidgets and toe wiggles, and be generally unresponsive. When audience members aren't understanding what you are saying they may slightly tilt their heads to one side, furrow their brow, and display a quizzical facial expression. If they disagree with you, they may sit politely and try not to let their opposition show, but look for sideways head movements, frowns, or smirks while making a whispered comment to someone else. Table 11.2 presents a summary of ways to adapt to your listeners (Principle Five) if you see these things happening while you speak.[23]

One strategy to use to help you respond to your audience on the spot is to *overprepare* your message. By this we mean you may need to have stories, examples, statistics, or facts

---

TABLE 11.2   How to Respond to Audience Nonverbal Messages

If Your Listeners Appear Bored

- Tell an appropriate story.
- Use a personal example.
- Remind your listeners why your message is of interest to them.
- Eliminate a planned discussion of abstract facts, statistics, and details.
- Consider using appropriate humor.
- Make a direct reference to the audience; consider using members' names or mentioning something about them.
- Encourage the customers to participate by asking them for an example.
- Ask a rhetorical question.
- Speak a bit faster with more intensity and energy.
- Pause for dramatic effect.

If Your Listeners Don't Seem to Understand You

- Ask someone in the audience to summarize a key point you are making.
- Repeat your main points.
- Restate your information using a different example, if you have one. Effective speakers have backup examples and illustrations they could use if they need to add depth or clarity to their ideas.
- Use a presentation aid (such as a whiteboard, chalkboard, or flip chart) to focus listener attention.
- Clarify the overall organization of your message, noting what point you are on now and what point you will make next.

If Your Listeners Appear to Be Disagreeing with You

- Identify those parts of your message in which you and your listeners do agree.
- Provide additional data and evidence, if you have it, to support your key point.
- Rely less on anecdotes and emotional support and more on facts to document your case.
- Write key facts on a whiteboard, chalkboard, or flip chart.
- If you don't have the answers, tell your listeners you will get back in touch with them with more information.

you could add to your message once you actually see your audience and observe how they are responding. You may not use all the information you've prepared. You may, for example, have a handout that spells out detailed costs of the project you're proposing; you'll distribute the handout only if you find your listeners have questions about your project's expenses. Yes, it takes additional time to overprepare. But an investment in extensive preparation can be worth it. As we've noted, effective leaders adapt and respond to others.

Analyzing Your Audience After You Speak

You may think that after you give your talk there is nothing left to be done. But post-presentation analysis can help you prepare your next presentation. The effective leader is interested in results. So gauging the outcomes of your presentation can help you achieve your goals. Following are ways of assessing how effectively your listeners received your presentation.

NONVERBAL RESPONSES Did your audience applaud? Gauging the level and intensity of applause you received is a simple way to determine if your audience liked what you had to say. Smiles, head nods, and eye contact are also cues to observe when you conclude. Although the nonverbal response can give you a general sense of how well your message was appreciated, you may not be able to determine which parts of your talk were the best or if there were things you said that were less well-received.

VERBAL RESPONSES You may need to listen to audience members' comments and ask them for feedback to gather more specific information about your message. If a listener says, "Nice job," or "Good talk," follow up by asking what part of the speech was the most helpful or what part she agreed with the most. Asking, "Is there anything you disagreed with?" may also help you glean useful feedback.

SURVEY RESPONSES If you presented a more formal presentation to a large audience, you may want to survey your audience after you speak. A short written survey that can be distributed to company employees right after your talk, a telephone survey, or an Internet survey can help you gather precise information about your message.

BEHAVIORAL RESPONSES The ultimate test of whether your message was effective is whether your listeners do what you wanted them to do following your presentation. If you were selling a product or service, did they purchase it? Did they sign the petition or vote as you wanted them to vote? If you presented training, can they now perform the skill you taught them? Or, if you were delivering an informative briefing or report, can they remember and use the information you shared? Your listeners' subsequent actions are the best indicators of your success.

Select and Narrow Your Topic

When speaking professionally you typically don't have to rack your brain trying to think of a presentation topic. Unlike a high school or college public speaking class in which your instructor asks you to give an informative or persuasive speech on a topic of your choice, your professional presentation topic is typically a "no-brainer," in that you are speaking for a specific reason—such as selling a product or service, trying to enhance the image or reputation of your organization, seeking donations, or reporting on a project.

On those occasions when you do have the latitude to select your topic, such as being invited to say a few words at a conference, the best presentation topics are those that are of interest to both you and your audience. Your topic should also have a link to your job, background, or expertise so you can establish your credibility. **Credibility** is a listener's perception of you as competent, trustworthy, and dynamic. We discuss how to develop your credibility in more detail in Chapter 13. What is less obvious, however, is how you narrow your topic and adapt your specific purpose to fine-tune the outcome you wish to achieve.

terms & definitions

Credibility a listener's perception of a speaker as competent, trustworthy, and dynamic.

Although the topic of your presentation may be evident, you will need to narrow and customize it to fit your time limits and to adapt to your listeners. For example, if you've been working for three weeks with a team of people studying ways to trim the budget and you only have five minutes to give your report, you'll have to be selective. To narrow your topic, you'll need to consider three things: your audience, the occasion, and yourself.

Given what we've already said about the centrality of the audience, it shouldn't be surprising that your topic should be one your listeners are interested in. The occasion will also dictate the type of presentation you make. Whether you are giving a sales talk, briefing stockholders, presenting a short report, or addressing the media, the specific purpose helps you decide how to approach your topic. The third element is you: your own interests and skills, your role in the organization you represent, and whether you are presenting information or persuading others all help you tailor your topic.

Determine Your Purpose

Your presentation topic and your presentation purpose are two different things. Your *topic* is what you are talking about; your *purpose* is the goal you seek to accomplish.

DETERMINE YOUR GENERAL PURPOSE In business and professional contexts, that goal will likely be to inform (as when sharing information at a briefing, seminar, or lecture) or to persuade (as when trying to convince your listeners to buy something or support the organizations mission statement). (Some presentations have a third goal: to entertain. This might be your goal if you were delivering a speech that your audience expected to be funny, such as an after-dinner speech. And you could certainly use entertaining humor when informing or persuading.) So with your topic settled, you'll need to decide what your overarching purpose is—to inform, persuade, or to entertain others.

Many presentations may have more than one purpose. You may first need to inform listeners about a product or service before you persuade them to purchase it. Although you may have multiple purposes, it's a good idea to think about and be aware of the ultimate purpose or purposes of your presentation.

DETERMINE YOUR SPECIFIC PURPOSE After making sure you understand your general purpose, you will need to develop your specific purpose. A **specific purpose** is a concise statement that indicates precisely what you want your listeners to be able to do, remember, or feel when you finish your speech; your specific purpose statement indicates the *audience response* you seek. Once again, we emphasize the importance of focusing on the audience as you develop your specific purpose. If you don't know what your precise purpose is, chances are your audience won't know either. Here are some examples of specific purpose statements:

- At the end of my presentation, the audience should be able to identify the three reasons our stock price increased during the last quarter.

- At the end of my presentation, the audience should be able to restate the two new security measures our company has instituted to enhance employee safety.

- At the end of my presentation, the audience should increase their order for one or more of the products our company makes.

Note that each of the examples just cited all begin with the same words: "At the end of my presentation, the audience should be able to . . . ." The next word should be a verb that describes an observable, measurable action that the audience should be able to complete when you finish your presentation. If your general purpose is to inform, then you will use verbs such as *list*, *explain*, *describe*, or *write*. If your general purpose is to persuade, then you'll use such verbs as *purchase*, *order*, *act*, or *write*. Don't use words such as *know*, *understand*, or *appreciate* because you cannot measure what an audience knows, understands, or appreciates unless your listeners perform a specific behavior such as explaining, describing, or listing.

A specific-purpose sentence states what you want the *audience* to be able to do, not what you, the speaker, will do. A sentence such as, "I want to describe the history of our company" is not a specific-purpose statement because it is not audience-centered; it's a speaker-centered

terms & definitions

Specific purpose a concise statement of precisely what you want your listeners to be able to do, remember, or feel when you finish your speech. Your specific purpose statement indicates the *audience response* you seek.

statement. It's not effective because it is not focused on the primary reason for speaking—the audience. If you phrase your specific-purpose sentence as, "At the end of my presentation, the audience should be able to describe the four transforming events in our company's history," then the focus of the presentation shifts to the listeners rather than the speaker.

Your specific-purpose sentence usually isn't something that you explicitly state to your audience. It's a technique that you use to help you achieve your speaking goal. Yes, typically you will preview for your listeners what you will be talking about, but you don't necessarily say, "At the end of my speech you should be able to list and describe the four new organizational goals of our company." You may simply tell them, "Today I'll visit with you about four new directions our company will take."

Use your specific-purpose sentence to guide you in accomplishing your speaking goal. Some speakers write their specific purpose sentence on a note card or a sticky note so that they can refer to it as they prepare their message. The shorter the speech, the more important it is to have a clear sense of direction because a short talk needs to be tightly focused; you don't have extra time to be off topic. If you have a clear specific purpose, you can make sure that as you are gathering information, examples, and ideas for your talk, your research is helping you achieve your specific purpose. If what you are gathering is not related to your specific purpose, don't include it in your talk.

Develop Your Central Idea

Imagine you hop on an elevator at the first floor of your office building and are traveling to the twentieth floor. Traveling with you is a client to whom you'd like to sell your company's services. What would you say during the short ride to communicate your key ideas? Whether you have one minute or one hour to pitch your ideas to listeners, you need to distill your message into a short, specific statement. The essence of your message is your **central idea** (sometimes called a *thesis sentence*): a one-sentence summary of your presentation. The difference between a central idea and a purpose statement is that the central idea focuses on the content of your presentation, whereas the purpose statement focuses on audience behavior.

The central idea should be a complete sentence—not a phrase, a sentence fragment, or a question. The language in the central idea sentence should be clear and direct. The central-idea sentence should also contain just one major idea. Here's a good example of a central-idea sentence: "The Acme Computer Store is the best computer store because of our low prices, high quality, and excellent customer service." This sentence summarizes the key content of the presentation. It has one idea that is supported by several reasons. Here's another example: "New federal laws require every company to increase security at manufacturing plants." It's an effective statement because it's short, clear, and contains only one idea.

A less effective central idea might be "Federal laws and business." The statement is not a complete sentence and it doesn't provide a sense of the key content of the message; it's a description of a topic, not a central idea sentence. A statement such as, "In my opinion, our West Coast factory is overstaffed and we spend too much money on staff development" is also not well-phrased because it contains two different ideas (overstaffing of the factory and expensive staff development). The phrase "in my opinion" is not needed; you don't need to include qualifiers such as "I think," or "from my point of view" in a central-idea sentence. Just state your key conclusion or essential idea in a clear, direct, well-worded sentence.

Finally, your central-idea sentence should be audience-centered. The content of your speech, as summarized in your central idea sentence, should be tailored to your listeners. If the key idea of the message doesn't relate to your audience, your presentation will not connect with them effectively. For example, speaking to plant workers about four ways to increase security at manufacturing plants is appropriately audience-centered. But the same central idea is not appropriate for a talk to the plant's customers gathered for a new product demonstration. Your audience should be the prime factor that determines how you develop your central idea sentence.

terms & definitions

Central idea a one-sentence summary of your presentation; sometimes called a thesis sentence.

RECAP

Identify Your Purpose and Central Idea

Your General Purpose

- To inform: To define, describe, or explain a thing, person, place, idea, or process
- To persuade: To change or reinforce a listener's attitude (likes or dislikes), beliefs (sense of what is true or false), values (view of what is good or bad), or behavior
- To entertain: To amuse an audience

Your Specific Purpose

- A description of the specific behavior you want your audience members to be able to do by the end of your presentation: "At the end of my presentation, the audience should be able to . . ."
- Includes a verb, such as *list, describe, identify, purchase,* or *build*

Your Central Idea

A one-sentence summary of your presentation that

- Is a declarative sentence
- Is short, clear, and direct
- Contains only one idea
- Focuses on the audience's interests and needs

Generate Your Main Ideas

With your central idea sentence in hand, you are now ready to add depth and dimension to your presentation by identifying the key ideas you will talk about. Although we've suggested that your central idea sentence should contain a single idea, it will probably be an idea that you can subdivide and organize into smaller ideas that you will present to your audience one at a time. Most listeners like a clearly organized presentation rather than a hodgepodge of information. At times it's a challenge for speakers to figure out what the major points of their talk will be. But if a speaker hasn't taken the time to think about how to divide the information into manageable pieces, it will be more difficult for listeners to follow the speaker's train of thought. In fact, "train of thought" is an apt metaphor: Think about your speech as a train with separate cars being pulled by the engine; the major ideas are the cars. Each car is separate, but all are connected to make up the entire train. Your speech will have separate pieces as well; each piece is a main idea.

An effective strategy is to ask yourself three questions about your well-worded central-idea sentence to help you chunk your speech into manageable pieces.

- *Does the central idea have logical divisions?* These may be indicated by such phrases as "there three types of software I'll discuss" or "there are four different ways to perform the same computer function using this technology." If, for example, your central idea is, "There are three parts to completing your corporate insurance claim forms," your presentation can be organized into three parts. At this point in developing your presentation, you don't need to worry about the order of the points; just note there are separate pieces of the talk you will discuss.

- *Can you think of several reasons the central idea is true?* If you are trying to persuade someone to do something, you may identify several reasons why they should do what you are suggesting. Here's an example: "The San Marcos Advertising Agency is the best advertising agency for any company to use to advertise their product or service." The main ideas in the speech could consist of several reasons why this central idea is true. A speaker could cite these reasons:

- The San Marcos Advertising Agency gets results.
- The San Marcos Advertising Agency is affordable.
- The San Marcos Advertising Agency is creative.

Note that each of the reasons is a complete sentence that summarizes a key reason why the central-idea sentence is true. Once you have chiseled your talk into these smaller pieces, you are well on your way to begin organizing the overall structure of your message.

- *Can you support your central idea with a series of steps or a chronological progression?* If you are giving a talk telling someone how to perform a task, then you'll probably be able to organize your presentation into a series of steps by noting what should be done first, second, third, and so on, to perform the task. Your central-idea sentence would describe the steps in the process: "Requesting an office transfer is easy and simple." First, there is a form to be filled out by his or her boss. Second, the employee must submit a request to the corporate office. And finally, the employee must submit a request online". Training presentations, orientation programs, and teaching people how to perform a skill will most likely use a chronological pattern (organized by the sequence) of describing a series of steps needed to accomplish the task. Most training sessions involve teaching people how to do something that involves a step-by-step approach.

Virtually any central-idea sentence can be subdivided by finding out the answer to one of these questions. Your presentation can be subdivided by considering its logical divisions, the reasons the idea is valid, or the steps involved.

Support Your Presentation

When Jack Welch was the CEO of General Electric, he was awakened early one morning with the news there was an emergency at the General Electric jet engine plant in Ohio. He zipped to Ohio on his corporate jet, and two hours after hearing about the problem he found himself speaking to his beleaguered plant workers in Ohio. How did he begin his message to address the problem that had developed? Statistics about sales figures? Power-Point slides showing his solution? No. He began with a story about his grandmother. His grandmother had always told him to be prepared for the unexpected. Rather than using a barrage of data, Jack Welch knew the power of a well-told story to provide encouragement and motivation.[24] Stories are just one of the powerful ways you can support the key points you make in a presentation.

Supporting material includes illustrations, explanations, descriptions, definitions, analogies, statistics, and opinions—material that will clarify, amplify, and provide evidence to support your main ideas and your thesis. You could simply rattle off your main points and subpoints without supporting material, but it's likely your message would be unclear and unconvincing. It's your supporting material that helps clarify your ideas and makes your message memorable, interesting, and credible.

What's the secret to keeping your listeners interested in you and your message? Pace the flow of new ideas and information. Communication expert Frank E. X. Dance recommends a 30:70 ratio: 30 percent of your speaking time should be spent presenting new ideas and information, and 70 percent of your time should be spent supporting the ideas with vivid examples and interesting stories.[25] We'll first discuss sources of supporting material and then offer tips and strategies for using the material you find in your professional presentation.

What makes supporting material interesting? Consider these three tips:

- *Make it personal*: Tell stories based on your own experiences and, like Jack Welch, people you know. Where appropriate, describe events that have happened to you.

- *Make it concrete*: Provide vivid descriptions of things that are tangible so your audience can visualize what you are talking about. Make it real. Describe events and scenes so they come to life.

terms & definitions

Supporting material
illustrations, explanations, descriptions, definitions, analogies, statistics, and opinions that clarify, amplify, and provide evidence to support the main ideas and the thesis of a presentation.

The Internet is typically the first place to find supporting materials for a presentation; but other sources include periodicals, databases and news programming, as well as friends, colleagues and other people you know.

- *Appeal to the senses*: The more senses of touch, hearing, taste, and smell you trigger with words, the more interesting your presentation will be. Help your listeners mentally "hear" what it was like to experience the grating crunch of metal during a car crash, or describe the sweet smell of gardenias wafting through the greenhouse when you first made a fundraising pitch to a client during a visit to her home.

Sources of Supporting Material

How do you go about finding just the right supporting material for a presentation? By developing good research skills. President Woodrow Wilson once revealed, "I use not only all the brains I have, but all that I can borrow." It is not only important to have good ideas, it is also important to build on your existing knowledge by searching for good ideas. Three potential sources of supporting material are the Internet, the library, and people you know.

THE INTERNET Typically, the Internet is the first place you turn when faced with a research task. Rather than heading off to the library, in the comfort of your own office or home, you tap out a few key terms and quickly are deluged with information. You have probably accessed material on the web through a directory or search engine, such as Google, Yahoo!, Ask.com, or another popular site.

The websites and web pages you discover may include personal pages, books, periodicals, newspapers and wire services, reference material, and government documents. In addition, you may discover indexes and catalogs for accessing these various kinds of resources. You can even find sites designed to help you prepare and deliver your speeches.

First, explore the advanced, or **Boolean search**, capabilities of your directory or search engine. Most will offer directions on how to limit your search to sites that are most relevant to what you are looking for. Boolean searches let you enclose phrases in quotation marks or parentheses, so that a search yields only those sites on which all the words of the phrase appear together, rather than sites that contain any one of the words. You can also insert the word *or* between two parenthetical phrases, directing your search to include documents in which either phrase appears. Or you can insert the word *and* between parenthetical phrases to indicate that you wish to see results that contain both phrases. These relatively simple strategies can help you narrow a list of hits from, in some cases, millions to a more workable number.

THE LIBRARY Despite the explosion of Internet resources in recent years, the library remains a rich source of supporting material. Most libraries, from the largest research university library to the smallest village public library, house the following kinds of resources: books, periodicals, full-text databases, newspapers, reference resources, and government documents.

- *Books*. The word *library* is almost synonymous with the word *book*. In spite of the predictions of some that electronic resources will someday make books obsolete, for now books remain central to the holdings of most libraries. A library's central catalog of all its books is called the card catalog. Today large library card catalogs are not literal cards but electronic ones that are accessible online as shown in Figure 11.2.

- *Periodicals*. The term *periodicals* refers both to magazines, such as *Time*, *People*, and *Sports Illustrated*, and to professional journals, such as the *Quarterly Journal of Economics*. Both types of periodicals can be useful for professional speeches. Periodical indexes are the equivalent of card catalogs in helping you locate information you need. A number of such indexes cover many topics and most of the thousands of periodicals published. Most periodical indexes are available online, and many can be accessed either from the library or from remote locations.

terms & definitions

Boolean search an advanced web-searching technique that allows a user to narrow a key word search by specifying certain parameters.

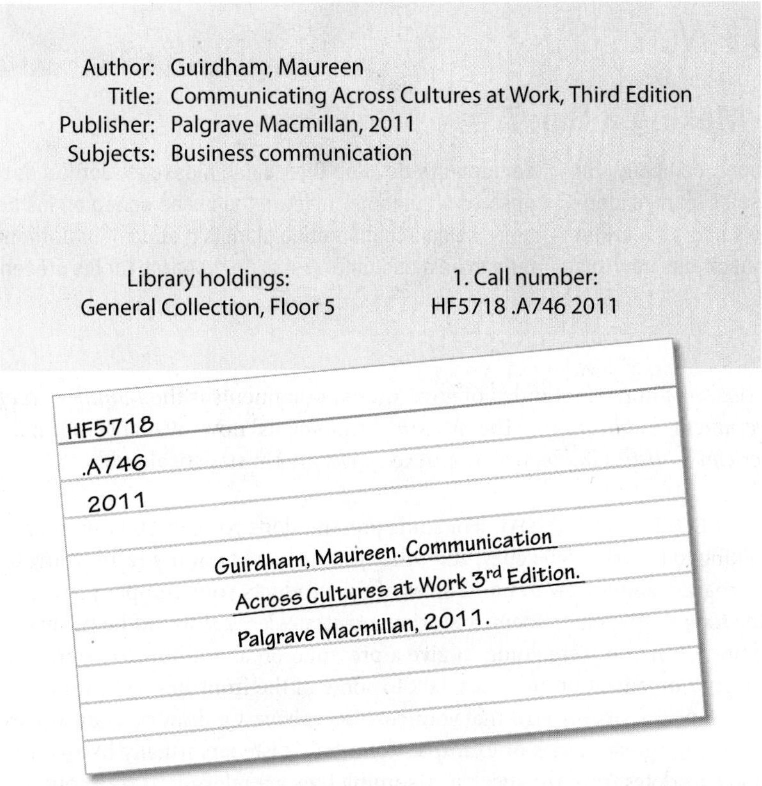

Author: Guirdham, Maureen
Title: Communicating Across Cultures at Work, Third Edition
Publisher: Palgrave Macmillan, 2011
Subjects: Business communication

Library holdings: 1. Call number:
General Collection, Floor 5   HF5718 .A746 2011

HF5718
.A746
2011

Guirdham, Maureen. *Communication
Across Cultures at Work 3rd Edition.*
Palgrave Macmillan, 2011.

FIGURE 11.2 Entry from an Electronic Card Catalog and Corresponding Bibliography Card

- *Full-Text Databases.* Although each library is different, many provide access to a wide array of full-text databases. Some of the frequently used periodical indexes and full-text databases include the following:

  - *Academic Search Complete* offers many full-text articles on a wide variety of subjects.

  - *Lexis/Nexis* is an extensive full-text subscription database of periodicals, newspapers, and government documents that focus on business, industry, and law.

  - *ABI/Inform Global* includes full-text articles in business and trade periodicals from 1971 to the present.

  - *JSTOR* is a multisubject full-text database of journal articles.

- *Newspapers.* You can find information that is only hours old by reading the latest edition of a daily newspaper or, more likely, finding news stories form an online version of the newspaper. Newspapers and their online versions typically offer the most detailed coverage available of current events and breaking news. As with books and periodicals, you need an index to help you find newspaper articles of potential value to the topic you are researching. Newspaper indexes are published for a number of medium to large newspapers. In addition, several electronic indexes, including the *National Newspaper Index* and *NewsBank*, index multiple newspapers.

- *Reference Resources.* A library's reference resources include encyclopedias, dictionaries, directories, atlases, almanacs, yearbooks, books of quotations, and biographical dictionaries. Virtually all of these resources are now available online.

- *Government Documents.* The federal government publishes information on almost every conceivable subject, as well as keeping records of most official federal proceedings. Once a dauntingly complex collection of pamphlets, special reports, and texts of speeches and debates, **government documents** today are much more readily accessible through the World Wide Web.

terms & definitions

Government documents published federal information on almost every subject, including records of official federal proceedings, pamphlets, special reports, and texts of speeches and debates.

Communication Ethics @ Work

Is All Fair in Love, War, and Making a Sale?

Jordan is a sales manager for a major phone company. He was assigned to give a presentation to his sales team to identify a new strategy to compete with a new smart phone that his chief competitor had developed. To check out how his competitors develop their sales message, Jordan decides to pose as a customer to learn the inside scoop on his competition's sales and marketing plan. Is it ethical for Jordan to pretend to be a customer just to do research for his presentation?

The most important index of government documents is the *Monthly Catalog of U.S. Government Publications*. The *Monthly Catalog* is now available online, as is the *American Statistics Index*, which indexes government statistical publications.

YOU AND PEOPLE YOU KNOW   For some presentations you can find rich sources of material by talking to friends, colleagues, and other people you know. If you are going to present a training program about how to boost sales of the products your company makes, you could talk to the top salespeople to identify stories and strategies that would help you develop useful sales tips. Or if you were going to give a presentation about how to improve the quality of service your organization provides, talk to some of the front-line receptionists to identify common complaints or concerns that your customers have. Or draw on your own experiences when looking for great stories or examples for a talk. Listeners usually like to hear personal stories and anecdotes from the speaker, assuming they are relevant to your topic.

The point is that you don't necessarily need to click on the Internet or run to the library for every piece of supporting material for every topic on which you speak. Don't overlook your own expertise and experience or those of the people you know. As an audience-centered speaker, realize, too, that personal knowledge or experience has the added advantage of heightening your credibility in the minds of your listeners. They will respect your authority if they realize you have firsthand knowledge of the topic on which you are speaking.

Types of Supporting Material

If you have discovered material on the Internet, examined a variety of library resources, and explored your own knowledge and the insights of people you know, you will probably have a wealth of potential supporting material. Now you need to decide what to use in your speech. Keeping in mind your audience's knowledge, interests, and expectations will help you to determine where an illustration might stir their emotions, where an explanation might help them to understand a point, and where statistics might convince them of the significance of a problem.

ILLUSTRATIONS   An **illustration** is a story or anecdote about an idea, issue, or problem a speaker is discussing. It can be as short as a sentence or two, or as long as several well-developed paragraphs. Sometimes speakers will offer a series of brief illustrations. Other speakers may present longer and more detailed illustrations. Here's an example of a short illustration used by business executive Tami Longaberger when speaking about her friend and former editor of *The Washington Post* Kay Graham and about the importance of leadership:

> A great leader reflects integrity in the hardest times, as well as when times are good. Let me go back to Kay Graham at *The Washington Post*. Not a day went by when Kay Graham wasn't challenged by some major government or business official to change a story or do something that was outside the ethics or integrity of the paper. She never compromised. Her editors and reporters took great heart from this and redoubled their efforts. That's one of the reasons *The Washington Post* continues to stand for a level of quality and integrity that is now known around the world.[26]

terms & definitions

Illustration a story or anecdote about an idea, issue, or problem a speaker is discussing.

Sometimes, instead of a real example, a speaker will use a **hypothetical illustration**, a description of something that has not actually occurred but that could happen. If you decide to use a hypothetical illustration, it is important to make clear to your audience that the scene you describe never really occurred. Using such phrases as "Imagine what you would do . . ." or "What would you do if the following experience happened to you?" are typical ways of signaling that your illustration is hypothetical. A speaker effectively gained and maintained his listeners' attention with this hypothetical illustration:

> Imagine you've just received a call from your boss informing you that she has to reduce the number of employees in your organization by the end of the day. She's asked you to report to her office in one hour to document your worth to the company. What evidence would you offer? Do you know how to prove your worth to your organization on a moment's notice?

Business leader Soloman Trujillo speaking to an audience about technology, used the following hypothetical example about Paul Revere:

> Imagine if Paul Revere, at the beginning of the American War of Independence, had at his disposal the technology we have today. His horse would certainly not be as footsore. Revere could record himself on his 3G phone, addressing the approaching British troops and then send a broadcast email of that recording to all of his contacts. They might receive those messages on their own mobile handsets or their BlackBerrys—at work or at home. If the recipients were sleeping, the receiving device would be smart enough to alert its owner to the importance of the message by using a sensor network, which turned on the lights in the house and stirred up its inhabitants to respond to the call to arms.[27]

Whether you choose to use brief or extended illustrations, actual or hypothetical ones, remember this principle: *Everybody likes to hear a story.* A well-told and relevant story almost always ensures audience interest. In addition, the following suggestions should help you use illustrations effectively in your speeches.

- Be sure that your illustrations are directly relevant to the idea or point they are supposed to support.
- Choose illustrations that are typical, not exceptions.
- Make your illustrations vivid and specific.
- Use illustrations with which your listeners can identify.
- Remember that the most effective illustrations are often personal ones.

Should you tell jokes to illustrate your talks? One well-known professional speech writer suggests using anecdotes rather than jokes to make your point. The speechwriter notes the difference this way:

> What's the difference between a joke and an anecdote? It is the difference between fiction and fact. An anecdote is supposed to be true—even if many are apocryphal (an anecdote doesn't have to be authentic to be told). The subject of an anecdote is famous or at least real, and what that subject did has to be believable. As professional speech writer James Humes suggests, a story about "Jesus on the golf course" . . . fails to meet the test.[28]

Nonetheless, a joke can be a good attention-getter and can relax your audience and win their goodwill. But be sure you can tell the joke well and that it will have the effect you intend. If you're no Leno, Seinfeld, Degeneres, or Letterman, it may be best to stick with material that you know will achieve your intended result.

DESCRIPTIONS AND EXPLANATIONS Probably the most commonly used forms of supporting material are **descriptions** and **explanations**. To describe or explain is to provide detailed images that allow an audience to see, hear, smell, touch, or taste whatever you are describing. Descriptions can make people, places, and events come alive for an audience, as does this description of being a drug addict, from a speech presented by Nora Volkow, director of the National Institute on Drug Abuse, to a group of business people:

> I want to share with you what it is to be an addicted person from the perspective of the individual suffering from it. This happens to be an individual who sent me an email and I chose this particular email because it does highlight some of the characteristics of addiction: "I am a Dutch thirty-year-old male, very addicted to marijuana, alcohol, and crack cocaine. I have no social life and no job and feel more and more isolated. I have less and less hope to break free of this hell. My life is a mess and I did several attempts to break with my addictions in the past. Now, as I am so tired of trying, I find it very difficult to keep on fighting, even more so because of the depressed mood and feelings of dissatisfaction while being clean. I do not feel whole without the damn drugs anyway."[29]

Although descriptions and explanations are found in most speeches, they lack the inherent interest of illustrations. To keep audiences from yawning through your descriptions and explanations,

- Avoid too many descriptions and explanations.
- Keep your descriptions and explanations brief.
- Describe and explain in specific and concrete language.

DEFINITIONS Here's our definition of **definition**: a brief explanation that identifies and clarifies what something is through classification or description of how something operates. Speakers should offer definitions of all technical or little-known terms in their presentations. But only use them when you think your listeners won't understand the term. Note the two ways a word or concept can be defined: by classification or operational description.

Classification is the typical approach used in a standard dictionary definition of first placing a term in the general class, group, or family to which it belongs and then differentiating it from other members of its class. Besides simply turning to a dictionary for a word or phrase, you could define a term in your own words. William Harrison clearly defines the word *globalization* by classifying what it is:

> *Let's begin with a simple and easy-to-understand definition. As I am going to use the word, globalization relates to "the death of distance." It relates to intensified global connectedness and the whole raft of changes—economic, social, political, and cultural—that spring from that. As Tom Friedman declared in "The World is Flat," globalization has "accidentally made Beijing, Bangalore and Bethesda next-door neighbors." Inside this accidental, virtual neighborhood, we find that we—as Americans—no longer have a lock on many of the best jobs inside the United States. Candidates from other countries are now just a "mouse-click" away.*[30]

Operational definition, a second way of defining a word or concept, is explaining how the word or phrase being defined works or what it does. Here's an example of an operational definition—defining something based upon how something works or the general operation:

> *Here's what I mean by high-performing local economy: New housing starts increase 10 percent over the previous year, the Chamber of Commerce fields several calls a day from businesses that want to relocate to our community, and sales tax revenue is up by double digits for the past three years. Now that's what I call a high-performing economic base.*

terms & definitions

Definition a brief explanation that identifies and clarifies what something is by classifying it or describing how it works.

Classification defining something by placing it in a group or category based on its qualities or characteristics.

Operational definition an explanation of how an item being defined works or what it does.

To use definitions effectively, consider the following tips:

- Use definitions only when necessary because they can be less interesting and abstract.
- Be certain that your definitions are clear to your listeners.
- Be sure that your definition accurately reflects your use of the word or phrase throughout the presentation.

ANALOGIES **Analogies** are comparisons that demonstrate how unfamiliar ideas, things, and situations are similar to something the audience already understands. Speakers can use two types of analogies in their speeches. The first is a **literal analogy**, or a comparison of two similar things—for example, comparing the available memory in a flash drive to a CD's storage capacity.

One business leader who wanted to illustrate the value of the European Union to a group of chief financial officers used the following literal analogy:

> What if each state in the United States had its own currency, had different requirements and rules for weights and measurements, and had no unified constitution that provided basic rights for its citizens? That would not encourage economic prosperity, would it? So perhaps you can understand why the countries in the European Union want to band together to develop common political and economic principles: It's good for business. It's important to collaborate to succeed economically.

A literal analogy can help clarify an idea or persuade listeners to support the speaker's point.

A **figurative analogy** is one that compares two unlike things or events that nevertheless share some feature. Figurative analogies, although less useful to prove a point, can be especially useful when clarifying an idea. Comparing the memory capacity of a computer to a person's mental capacity to remember something would be a figurative analogy. Eric opened his speech on the National Flood Insurance Program with this figurative analogy comparing gambling on horse races to gambling with nature:

> If someone were to lose thousands of dollars gambling on horse races, would you want your tax dollars to bail them out? . . . Currently in the United States there are millions of people gambling, not on horse races, but on Mother Nature, by living on flood plains or coasts. When these people lose, they lose big: beach houses, farm houses, and apartment houses go out to sea, down the river, or simply soak up catastrophic damages.[31]

Two suggestions can help you use analogies more effectively in your speeches:

- Be certain that the two things you compare in a literal analogy are very similar so that listeners can immediately see the connection.
- Make the similarity between the two objects in a figurative analogy apparent to the audience by providing specific detail and explanation.

STATISTICS **Statistics** are simply numerical data that summarize several examples. Numbers can represent hundreds or thousands of illustrations and can thus help a speaker express the significance or magnitude of a situation. Statistics can also help a speaker express the relationship of a part to the whole. Note communication expert Richard Weaver's clever use of statistics from his speech titled "Sticky Ideas":

Visual aids, such as the chart this man is using for his presentation, can be very effective when presenting statistics to an audience.

terms & definitions

Analogy a comparison between an unfamiliar idea, thing, or situation and something the audience already understands.

Literal analogy a comparison between two similar things.

Figurative analogy a comparison between two essentially unlike things or events that nevertheless share some feature.

Statistics numerical data that summarize several examples.

Trying to get listeners to understand what the word *billion* means is a good example of making statistics meaningful. Politicians use the word *billion* in a casual manner, and there is no doubt it is a difficult number to comprehend. Did you realize that a billion seconds ago it was 1959? A billion minutes ago, Jesus was alive; a billion hours ago, our ancestors were living in the Stone Age; a billion days ago, no one walked on the earth on two feet; a billion dollars ago was only 8 hours and 20 minutes, at the rate our government is spending it—and that does not include spending for the war.[32]

Skilled speakers learn how to use statistics to their advantage. For example, they try to make huge numbers more readily understandable and more dramatic to their audiences. Rather than saying, "There are 525,600 people this year who turned 65," the speaker more memorably said, "Every seven seconds another American turns 65."[33]

In addition to simplifying and dramatizing your information, statistics can be effective if you utilize the following two suggestions:

- Round off large numbers.
- Use visual aids such as bar, line, or pie graphs to present your statistics.

Cite the sources of your statistics. To integrate an **oral citation** into your speech, simply tell your listeners the source of your information. For example, when describing the number of Facebook users, you might say, "According to the Facebook website, published in October 2011 on the Facebook Pressroom Online Version, there are more than 800 million active Facebook users worldwide."[34] Note that this citation includes three things:

- The title of the report
- The date when it appeared
- The organization responsible for the website.

The address itself need not be given in the oral citation, although the speaker should have that information available if someone wants to confirm the information.

OPINIONS The opinions of others can add authority, drama, and style to a speech. A speaker can use three types of opinions: expert testimony, lay testimony, and literary quotations. **Expert testimony**, the opinion of a recognized authority on a topic, is perhaps the most frequent type of opinion employed by speakers. If you yourself lack authority on your topic, cite someone who can offer such expertise. For example, to convince company employees that the winter months are the most common time of year to contract the flu, a speaker noted "Influenza virus is more likely to be transmitted during winter on the way to the subway than in a warm room, according to Dr. Peter Palese, a flu researcher who is professor and chairman of the microbiology department at Mount Sinai Medical College in New York City."[35]

Lay testimony is an opinion or a description offered by a nonexpert who has firsthand experience. Like illustrations, lay testimony can stir an audience's emotions. And, although neither as authoritative nor as unbiased as expert testimony, lay testimony is often more memorable.

Literary quotations—opinions or descriptions by writers—can be used to illustrate or clarify a point. The best literary quotations make a point in an interesting, memorable, or humorous way. One speaker quoted humor columnist Dave Barry to make a point about different types of newspapers:

"The more boring a newspaper is," Barry explained, "the more it is respected." The most respected newspaper in the United States, Barry pointed out, is *The New York Times*, which has thousands of reporters constantly producing enormous front-page stories on bauxite. On the other hand, Barry said, "the least respected newspaper in America, *The New York Post*, would write about bauxite only if celebrities were arrested snorting it at an exclusive New York nightclub."[36]

terms & definitions

Oral citation an oral statement of the source of information used in a speech.

Expert testimony an opinion offered by someone who is an authority on the subject under discussion.

Lay testimony an opinion or a description offered by a nonexpert who has firsthand experience.

Literary quotations opinions or descriptions by writers used to illustrate or clarify a point.

RECAP

Supporting Your Speech

Type of Supporting Material	Guidelines for Use
Illustrations	• Make them directly relevant to the idea you are discussing or point you are making. • Choose illustrations that are typical, not exceptions. • Make them vivid and specific. • Use illustrations with which your listeners can identify. • Remember that the most effective illustrations are often personal ones.
Descriptions and Explanations	• Avoid too many descriptions and explanations. • Keep descriptions and explanations brief. • Describe and explain in specific and concrete language.
Definitions	• Use definitions only when necessary. • Be certain that definitions are clear to listeners. • Be sure that a definition is accurate.
Analogies	• When using a literal analogy, be certain that the two things you compare are very similar. • When using a figurative analogy, make the similarity between the two objects apparent to the audience.
Statistics	• Round off large numbers. • Use visual aids to show comparisons and trends. • Cite your sources.
Opinions	• Be certain that any authority you cite is actually an expert. • Identify your sources. • Cite unbiased authorities. • Cite representative opinions, or identify dissenting viewpoints as such. • Quote or paraphrase accurately and in context. • Use literary quotations sparingly.

Whether you use expert testimony, lay testimony, or literary quotations, consider the following suggestions for using opinions effectively in your speeches:

- Be certain that any authority you cite is actually an expert on the subject you are discussing.
- Identify your sources with an oral citation.
- Cite unbiased authorities.
- Cite opinions that are representative of prevailing opinion. If you cite a dissenting viewpoint, identify it as such.
- Quote or paraphrase your sources accurately and within the context in which the remarks were originally made.
- Use literary quotations sparingly.

As you select your illustrations, descriptions, explanations, definitions, analogies, statistics, and opinions, be guided not only by the suggestions we've provided for each type of supporting material, but also by the five fundamental communication principles. The best supporting material reflects self-awareness, taking advantage of your own knowledge and experience. Effective verbal supporting material is appropriately worded, concrete, and vivid enough that your audience can visualize what you are talking about. Effective visual supporting material enhances, rather than detracts from, your verbal message. Sensitivity to your audience will help you choose the supporting material that is most appropriately adapted to them.

Organize Your Presentation

Developing a presentation is like building a house. Just as a construction contractor develops the frame for a house early in the building process, a speaker develops the frames for a presentation by completing the first four stages of the speech-preparation process—selecting and narrowing a topic, identifying a general and a specific purpose, determining a central idea, and generating main ideas. Framing completed, the contractor assembles all the materials needed for the house: windows, doors, cabinets, hardware, and flooring; the speaker finds and adds supporting materials to the speech "frame." Once the house is framed out and the building materials are ready, the contractor must organize the work of the electricians, plumbers, carpenters, and carpet layers. Similarly, the speaker must organize ideas and supporting material.

Organizing Your Main Ideas

An organized message is easier for your listeners to remember *and* easier for you to remember. Note the following two columns of words. Don't you find the words in column B easier to remember than the ones in column A?[37]

Column A	Column B
be	to
question	be
to	or
that	not
not	to
the	be
be	that
is	is
to	the
or	question

Giving careful thought to how you structure your message, whether you use a pattern that is already familiar to your audience or one that you create to help your listeners make better sense of your message, is the mark of an effective communicator.

We'll first discuss strategies for organizing the main ideas of a speech and then focus on organizing supporting material and developing signposts and transitions. Next, we will identify how to effectively introduce and conclude your presentation and, finally, how to outline your ideas and supporting material.

ORGANIZE IDEAS CHRONOLOGICALLY **Chronological organization** is organization by sequential order, according to when each step or event occurred or should occur. If you are explaining a process, you will want to organize your explanation of the steps of that process from first to last. If you are providing an historical overview of an event, movement, or policy, you might begin with the end result and trace its history backward in time.

Examples of presentation topics that might lend themselves to chronological organization include a training presentation on how to perform a skill or task or a description of the development of an idea or process. Here's an outline of a speech that follows a chronological organizational pattern.

Central Idea: There are three steps to developing a business meeting agenda.

I. Determine whether the goal of the meeting is to give information, to get information, or to take some action.

II. Identify the agenda items that need to be discussed to achieve the meeting goal or goals.

III. Organize the agenda items.

ORGANIZE IDEAS TOPICALLY. If your main ideas are natural divisions of your central idea, you will likely want to use **topical organization**. Topical organization may be simply an arbitrary arrangement of main ideas that are fairly equal in importance. For example, if you are giving a briefing in which you describe the athletic apparel your company makes, you could use a topical organization plan to group the three primary types of products your organization manufactures—running shoes, clothes, and hats. The order in which you discuss the products may not really matter.

Like a contractor who builds the framework for a house, a speaker constructs the framework of his or her presentation by completing the first four stages of the speech-preparation process.

A topical organization plan for a talk designed to recruit salespeople to join the organization would look like this:

Central Idea: People who join our company have several education options for their children.

I. Parents can send their children to the local, nationally recognized public school.

II. Parents can send their children to one of two private schools.

III. Parents can apply for low-interest loans from our company to cover college tuition.

In this example, the order of the ideas may not be important. At other times, topical organization is less arbitrary; you may decide to arrange your major points in a specific order.

ORGANIZE IDEAS BY IMPORTANCE What comes first or last is often viewed as more important than what comes in the middle. That's because first and last impressions are more likely to make an impact than what happens in-between. So when organizing a message, you can use the principles of primacy or recency to augment the importance of your ideas based on how you sequence the ideas.

The principle of **primacy** suggests that what comes first will gain extra prominence. If you think your audience may tune you out early, perhaps because they disagree with you, present your most convincing idea first. Or, to adapt to audience members who may be skeptical of some of your ideas, discuss first those points on which you all agree. Building good will early in the message can pay off once you present your specific action steps or recommendations.

The principle of **recency** suggests that audiences remember best what they hear last. So if you want your audience to remember a specific point or to emphasize its importance or significance, put it last.

ORGANIZE IDEAS BY THEIR COMPLEXITY Another type of topical organization is organization according to **complexity**, moving from simple ideas and processes to more complex ones. Many skills you have learned in life have been taught by order of complexity. In first grade, you learned to read easy words first, then moved on to more difficult ones. In

leaders on leadership

Get to the Point

Guy Kawasaki, cofounder of Alltop, a news aggregation site, and managing director of Garage Technology Ventures, doesn't like long, boring presentations. Who does? After all, in business, time is money. Belaboring a point that could be made concisely can do more harm than good in business and professional contexts. When asked what he thought the most important point college instructors should teach their students, Kawasaki said,

> They should teach students how to communicate in five-sentence e-mails and with 10-slide PowerPoint presentations. If they just taught every student that, American business would be much better off.[38]

In making the case for efficient communication, Kawasaki noted that life moves at a fast pace, so whether you're composing an email message or making a presentation, make your point and move on.

[N]o one wants to read "War and Peace" e-mails. Who has the time? Ditto with 60 PowerPoint slides for a one-hour meeting.

What you learn in school is the opposite of what happens in the real world. In school, you're always worried about minimums. You have to reach 20 pages or you have to have so many slides or whatever. Then you get out in the real world and you think, "I have to have a minimum of 20 pages and 50 slides."[39]

What's the takeaway message from this recommendation? As with every other aspect of developing a message, consider the needs and expectations of your audience. Making the switch in writing style from longer academic messages to shorter, to-the-point presentations can not only help you make your point, but you'll win "points" for making your message clear and succinct. You, Guy Kawasaki, and most people you meet don't like unnecessarily long messages. Get to the point.

---

third grade, you learned single-digit multiplication tables before moving on to more complex double- and triple-digit multiplication problems. In junior high school, you learned to use the library's card catalog before you undertook a multistage research project. And in high school, you learned to drive by practicing simple maneuvers in the parking lot before cruising on the highway.

ORGANIZE IDEAS SPATIALLY. "Go down the hill two blocks and turn left by the florist. Then go three blocks to the next stoplight and turn right. The place you're looking for is about a block farther, on your right." When you offer someone directions, you organize your ideas spatially. **Spatial organization** is arrangement according to location, position, or direction. Speeches that rely on description are good candidates for spatial organization; for example, a speech about the layout of a manufacturing plant or a new shopping center would lend itself to spatial organization. For example:

Central Idea: Our corporate headquarters includes buildings that have three major functions.

I. At the western edge of the campus is the employee recreation and sports complex.

II. In the central part of the campus are the buildings that house the financial operations.

III. At the eastern edge of the campus are the top executive offices.

ORGANIZE IDEAS TO SHOW CAUSE AND EFFECT **Cause-and-effect organization** actually refers to two related patterns: identifying a situation and then discussing the resulting effects (cause–effect), and presenting a situation and then exploring its causes (effect–cause).

A speaker who discusses the consequences of tax increases and their impact on the local economy will probably use a cause–effect pattern, establishing first that the tax rate is a major burden on local business and then providing evidence that the high taxes are causing business owners to close their doors. A speaker who does the opposite, documenting the loss of businesses in a downtown area and then providing statistics on recent tax increases instituted by the local county commissioners, is using an effect–cause organizational pattern. A cause–effect pattern emphasizes effects; an effect–cause pattern emphasizes causes.

terms & definitions

Spatial organization organization based on location, position, or direction.

Cause-and-effect organization identifying a situation and then discussing its effects (cause–effect) or presenting a situation and then exploring its causes (effect–cause).

Here's how one speaker organized a presentation using a cause–effect organizational pattern:

Central Idea: Higher taxes will force many businesses in our community to close.

I. (Cause) Our school board and city council have raised our tax rate for the past five years.

II. (Effect) The hardware store has closed because it can no longer afford the business tax levied by the school board and city council.

III. (Effect) One of our two grocery stores has closed because it can no longer afford the business tax.

ORGANIZE IDEAS BY PROBLEM AND SOLUTION If, instead of exploring causes or consequences of a problem or issue, you want either to explore how best to solve the problem or to advocate a particular solution, you will probably choose **problem-and-solution organization**. When addressing the dip in your company's stock price, you could first identify the problems associated with the downturn in the stock and then suggest strategies that could boost the stock price. Or, when delivering a motivational speech to new employees, you could first describe the implications of poor customer service—loss of company revenue and the potential loss of employment for workers. You could then offer specific solutions so that the problem of poor customer service doesn't occur.

Here's an outline of a speech organized using a problem-and-solution organizational framework:

Central Idea: Because of higher mortgage rates, the U.S. economy has experienced a significant downturn.

I. (Problem) When the mortgage rates in adjustable rate mortgages increase, many people can no longer afford to pay the mortgage and end up losing their homes.

II. (Solution) The federal government should implement a new guaranteed home mortgage plan to help homeowners avoid foreclosures.

As you make final decisions about organizing your presentation, keep the following general strategies in mind:

- *Organize the body of your presentation before you prepare your introduction or conclusion.* You won't know how to introduce your ideas or summarize your message until you've made decisions about the major points you are presenting.

- *Most business and professional presentation will have from three to five major ideas.* Audiences are more likely to remember fewer key points than a lengthy list of abstract ideas. If your have more than five major ideas, make sure you have ample time to develop each idea with clear and interesting supporting material.

- *Make sure each major point in your speech presents only one idea.* Don't confuse your listeners by having multiple ideas jumbled into one point. The major points are the big ideas of your speech. Keep them separate.

terms & definitions

Problem-and-solution organization organization that describes a problem and then offers one or more solutions to it.

RECAP

Organizing Your Main Ideas

Pattern	Description
Chronological	Organization by time or sequence
Topical	Organization of natural divisions of an idea according to recency, primacy, or complexity or in an arbitrary arrangement
Spatial	Organization according to location, position, or direction
Cause and effect	Organization by discussing a situation and its causes or a situation and its effects
Problem and solution	Organization by discussing a problem and then various solutions

ADAPT ORGANIZATION TO CULTURAL EXPECTATIONS OF YOUR AUDIENCE

What's the shortest distance between two points? Why, a straight line, of course. In organizing a message, it may seem that the most logical strategy is to develop a structure that moves from one idea to the next in a logical, "straight" way. But not every culture organizes ideas using that logic. In fact, each culture teaches its members unique patterns of thought and organization that are considered appropriate for various occasions and audiences.

In general, U.S. speakers tend to be more linear and direct than do Semitic, Asian, Romance, or Russian speakers.[40] U.S. listeners prefer direct cause-and-effect examples. For example, a U.S. speaker might say, "There are two reasons you should move your company to our city. First, we have a university located in our town so you'll have a steady supply of educated employees. And second, the nearby international airport means you can easily travel from our city to anywhere in the world." In contrast, Semitic speakers support their main points by pursuing tangents that might seem "off topic" to many U.S. listeners. When speaking to someone from a Semitic culture, instead of ticking off points one and two, you could offer several anecdotes about others who have enjoyed having corporate headquarters in your city. Or, a short story about how college-educated workers help companies flourish may implicitly make the point that your city is advantageous because of its ample supply of well-educated workers. Asians may only allude to a main point through a circuitous route of illustrations and parables. Instead of using well-documented points when speaking to Asian listeners, you could tell a story about how those who are in the best location flourish and those in the wrong place are subject to disaster. And speakers from Romance and Russian cultures tend to begin with a basic principle and then move to facts and illustrations that are only gradually related to a main point and that to a North American listener may seem less relevant. Yet listeners from Romance and Russian cultures may find the illustrations more compelling than too quickly getting to the "bottom line" with explicit facts and statistics. A more gentle, circuitous route to get to the point may be best. Figure 11.3 illustrates these culturally diverse patterns of organization.[41]

Of course, these are very broad generalizations. As an effective speaker who seeks to adapt to your audience, you should investigate the organizational strategies best suited to your particular audience. In addition, when you are listening to a speech, recognizing the existence of cultural differences can help you appreciate and understand the organization of a speaker from a culture other than your own.

ORGANIZING YOUR PRESENTATION FOR THE EAR You now have a fairly complete, logically organized plan for your speech. But if you tried to deliver the speech at this point, your audience would probably become confused. What are your main ideas? How is one main idea related to the next? What supporting material develops which main idea? To adapt your logically organized message to your audience, you need to provide organizational cues for their ears. You do this by adding **signposts**—previews, verbal or nonverbal

terms & definitions

Signpost a verbal or nonverbal signal that a speaker is moving from one idea to another.

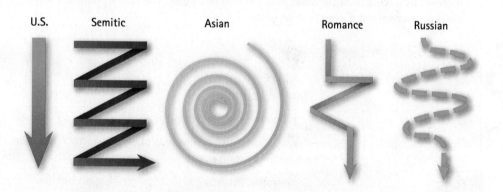

U.S.   Semitic   Asian   Romance   Russian

FIGURE 11.3 Cultural preferences of message organization

Source: D. A. Lieberman, *Public Speaking in the Multicultural Environment,* Second Edition (Boston: Allyn and Bacon, 1997), 23.

transitions, and summaries that allow you to move smoothly from one idea to the next throughout the speech.

PREVIEWS A **preview** is a statement of what is to come in a speech—it "tells them what you're going to tell them." Previews help your audience members anticipate and remember the main ideas of your speech. They also help you move smoothly from the introduction to the body of your speech and from one main idea to the next.

The **initial preview** is a statement of the main ideas of a speech, usually presented in conjunction with, and sometimes as part of, the central idea of the speech. In addition to offering an initial preview, a speaker may also offer **internal previews** at various points throughout a speech. These previews introduce and outline ideas that will be developed as the speech progresses.

VERBAL TRANSITIONS Effectively using and understanding verbal messages includes using **verbal transitions**, words or phrases that show relationships between ideas in your speech. They include simple enumeration (*first, second, third*); repeated words or synonyms or pronouns that refer to earlier words or ideas (the word *they* at the beginning of this sentence refers to the phrase "verbal transitions" in the previous sentence); and words and phrases that show relationships between ideas (*in addition to, not only . . . but also, in other words, in summary, therefore, however*). As you begin to rehearse your speech, you might need to experiment with various verbal transitions to achieve coherence that seems natural and logical to you. If none of the verbal alternatives seems quite right, consider a nonverbal transition.

NONVERBAL TRANSITIONS **Nonverbal transitions** are behaviors used alone or in combination with verbal transitions help to show relationships among ideas in a speech. An effective nonverbal transition might be a facial expression, a pause, a change in vocal pitch or speaking rate, or movement. Most good speakers use a combination of verbal and nonverbal transitions to help them move from one idea to the next throughout their speeches.

SUMMARIES Like previews, summaries provide an additional opportunity for an audience to grasp a speaker's most important ideas. Most speakers use two types of summaries: internal summaries and a final summary.

Internal summaries, like internal previews, occur within and throughout a speech. You might want to use an internal summary after you have discussed two or three main ideas, to ensure that the audience keeps them firmly in mind as you move into another main idea. You can combine an internal summary with an internal preview.

You may also want to provide your audience with a restatement of your main ideas, in the form of a **final summary** in your conclusion. Just as your initial preview gave your audience their first exposure to your main ideas, your final summary will give them their last exposure to those ideas.

Introducing Your Presentation

At this point, you have well-developed ides and content for your presentation, and you have strategies for organizing that material. But you have not yet given much thought to how you are going to begin the speech. That's OK. Even though you will deliver your introduction first, you usually plan your introduction last. You first need to know what you're introducing, especially your central idea and main ideas. Although they make up a relatively small percentage of the total speech, your introduction and conclusion provide your audience with important first and final impressions of you and your speech.

Your **introduction** should convince your audience to listen to you. More specifically, it must perform five functions: get the audience's attention, introduce the topic, give the audience a reason to listen, establish your credibility, and preview your main ideas.

GET THE AUDIENCE'S ATTENTION If an introduction does not capture the audience's attention, the rest of the speech may be wasted on them. You have to wake up your listeners and make them want to hear more.

---

terms & definitions

Preview a statement of what is to come in a speech.

Initial preview the first statement of the main ideas of a presentation, usually presented in conjunction with or as part of the central idea.

Internal previews previews that introduce and outline ideas that will be developed as a speech progresses.

Verbal transitions words or phrases that show relationships between ideas in a speech.

Nonverbal transitions nonverbal behaviors (facial expressions, pauses, changes in vocal pitch or speaking rate, or movement) that are used either alone or in combination with verbal transitions to show relationships among ideas in a speech.

Internal summaries summaries that occur within and throughout a speech to help listeners keep ideas in mind as the speech progresses.

Final summary the final part of a speech, which restates a speaker's most important ideas.

Introduction the opening sentences of a speech, intended to get the audience's attention, introduce the topic, give the audience a reason to listen, establish the speaker's credibility, and preview the main ideas.

There are several potentially effective ways to gain an audience's attention. One commonly used and quite effective one is to open with an illustration. Other strategies include asking a rhetorical question, stating a startling fact or statistic, quoting an expert or a literary text, telling a humorous story, or referring to an historical or recent event. Note the following clever introduction that refers to the date of the speech.

> It is perhaps fitting that we are meeting on this particular day, because this is the 15th of March, the dreaded "Ides of March". . . and I am going to address a subject of growing concern and distress to many people—the subject of globalization. In the play *Julius Caesar,* the Ides of March are a "strange-disposèd time." Thunder and lightning fill the air, and people are amazed to see the owl, or "the bird of night," sitting in the marketplace at noon, "hooting and shrieking."[42]

Still other speakers might get their audience's attention by referring to a personal experience, referring to the occasion, or referring to something said by a preceding speaker. While these strategies will not work for every speech, at least one of them should be an option for any speech you deliver. And with a little practice, you may find yourself being able to choose from several good possibilities for a single speech.

INTRODUCE THE TOPIC Within the first few seconds of listening to you, your audience should have a pretty good idea of what your topic is. The best way to achieve this objective is to include a statement of your central idea in your introduction.

GIVE THE AUDIENCE A REASON TO LISTEN Not only do you have to get your audience's attention and introduce your topic, you have to motivate your listeners to continue to listen. Show the audience how your topic affects them directly. By the end of your introduction, your audience should be thinking, "This concerns *me!*"

ESTABLISH YOUR CREDIBILITY A credible speaker is one whom the audience judges to be competent, trustworthy, and dynamic. Be aware of your skills and talents and the experiences you have had that are related to your topic. You can increase your credibility by telling your audience about your expertise.

PREVIEW YOUR MAIN IDEAS As we discussed above, you should provide an initial preview of your main ideas at or near the end of your introduction, to allow your listeners to anticipate the main ideas of your speech.

Here's how Gupta Yash, dean of the Carey Business School at Johns Hopkins University, clearly introduced his four key ideas in a speech about the business implications of an aging population:

> I think there are four areas in which it will have enormous importance [on an aging population]. First: at the societal or sociological level. Second: in the economic and thus the political sphere. Third, in all matters related to health care, and in particular, how resources within this $2 trillion industry are allocated. And finally, number four, in the realm of education. In the next few minutes I'd like to consider what the demographic changes ahead mean in each of these four areas.[43]

Note how he effectively enumerated each of his key ideas. His listeners have a clear road map that lets them know where they are headed.

Concluding Your Presentation

Whereas your introduction creates a critically important first impression, your conclusion leaves an equally important final impression. Long after you finish speaking, your audience may mentally hear the echo of effective final words. An effective **conclusion** serves four

terms & definitions

Conclusion the closing sentences of a speech, intended to summarize the speech, to reemphasize the main idea in a memorable way, to motivate the audience to respond, and to provide closure.

functions: it summarizes your speech, reemphasizes the main idea in a memorable way, motivates the audience to respond, and provides closure.

SUMMARIZE THE SPEECH The conclusion offers a speaker a last chance to repeat his or her main ideas. Most speakers summarize their main ideas between the body of the speech and its conclusion or in the first part of the conclusion.

REEMPHASIZE THE CENTRAL IDEA IN A MEMORABLE WAY The conclusions of many famous speeches contain many of the lines we remember best:

> . . . government of the people, by the people, for the people, shall not perish from the earth. (Abraham Lincoln)[44]

> Old soldiers never die; they just fade away. (General Douglas MacArthur)[45]

> Free at last! Free at last! Thank God almighty, we are free at last! (Martin Luther King Jr.)[46]

Although business and professional presentations don't usually have such memorable or emotion-packed conclusions, consider how even the most routine briefing or report can be enhanced by a strong call to action or reiteration of the expense budget statistics or other points. Word your final thoughts so that your audience cannot help but remember them.

MOTIVATE THE AUDIENCE TO RESPOND Think back to your specific purpose. What do you want your audience to be able to do by the end of your speech? If your speech is informative, you may want your audience to think about your topic or to seek more information about it. If your speech is persuasive, you may want your audience to take some sort of action—to write a letter, make a phone call, or volunteer for a cause. Your conclusion is where you can motivate your audience to respond.

PROVIDE CLOSURE You may have experienced listening to a speech and not being certain when it was over. That speaker did not achieve the last purpose of an effective conclusion: providing **closure**, or cueing the audience that the speech is ending by making it "sound finished." One good way to provide closure is to refer to your introduction by finishing a story, answering a rhetorical question, or reminding your audience of the startling statistic you presented in your introduction.

You can also achieve closure by using verbal and nonverbal signposts. For example, you might use such transitions as "finally" and "in conclusion" as you move into your conclusion. You might pause before you begin the conclusion, slow your speaking rate as you

terms & definitions

Closure a sense of being complete or "sounding finished," provided in the conclusion of a speech by finishing a story, answering a rhetorical question, or reminding the audience of a statistic presented in the introduction.

RECAP

The Purposes of Introductions and Conclusions

Your speech introduction should	• Get your audience's attention • Introduce your topic • Give your audience a reason to listen • Establish your credibility • Preview your main ideas
Your speech conclusion should	• Summarize your speech • Reemphasize your central idea in a memorable way • Motivate your audience to respond • Provide closure

A preparation outline of your speech helps you rehearse the speech; a delivery outline provides notes that you can use as reminders as you deliver your speech.

deliver your final sentence, or signal by falling vocal inflection that you are making your final statement. Experiment with these strategies until you are certain that your speech "sounds finished."

Outlining Your Presentation

With your introduction and conclusion planned, you are almost ready to begin rehearsing your speech. By this point, you should have your preparation outline nearly complete. A **preparation outline** is a fairly detailed outline of your central idea, main ideas, and supporting material; it may also include the specific purpose, introduction, and conclusion of your speech. A second outline, which you will prepare shortly, is a **delivery outline**, a condensed, abbreviated outline that provides the notes you will use when you present your speech.

PREPARATION OUTLINE   Although few speeches are written out word-for-word (manuscript form), most speakers develop a fairly detailed preparation outline that helps them to ensure that their main ideas are clearly related to their central idea, and that their main ideas are logically and adequately supported. A speaker who creates a preparation outline is applying the first fundamental principle of communication: becoming aware of his or her communication. In addition to helping the speaker judge the unity and coherence of the speech, the preparation outline serves as an early rehearsal outline.

When outlining a speech, it is helpful to use **standard outline format**. Standard outline format lets you see at a glance the exact relationships among various main ideas, subpoints, and supporting material in your speech. Even if you haven't had much experience with formal outlines, the following guidelines can help you produce a correct outline.

Use standard numbering. Outlines are numbered by using Roman and Arabic numerals and uppercase and lowercase letters, followed by periods, as follows:

I.   First main idea

   A.   First subdivision of I

   B.   Second subdivision of I

      1.   First subdivision of B

      2.   Second subdivision of B

         a.   First subdivision of 2

         b.   Second subdivision of 2

II.   Second main idea

You will probably not need to subdivide beyond the level of lowercase letters in most speech outlines.

Use at least two subdivisions, if any, for each point. You cannot divide anything into fewer than two parts. On an outline, every I should have a II, every A should have a B, and so on. If you have only one subdivision, fold that information into the level above it.

Line up your outline correctly. Main ideas, indicated by Roman numerals, are written closest to the left margin. The *periods* following these Roman numerals line up, so that the first letters of the first words also line up:

  I.   First main idea

 II.   Second main idea

III.   Third main idea

Letters or numbers of subdivisions begin directly underneath the first letter of the first *word* of the point above:

I. First main idea

    A. First subdivision of I

    B. Second subdivision of I

If a main idea or subdivision takes up more than one line, the second line begins under the first letter of the first word of the preceding line:

I. First main idea

    A. A rather lengthy subdivision that runs more than one line

    B. Second subdivision

Within each level, make the headings grammatically parallel. Regardless of whether you write your preparation outline in complete sentences or in phrases, be consistent within each level. In other words, if I is a complete sentence, II should also be a complete sentence. If A is an infinitive phrase (one that begins with *to* plus a verb, such as "To guarantee greater security"), B should also be an infinitive phrase.

DELIVERY OUTLINE As you rehearse your speech, you will find yourself needing to look at your preparation outline less and less. You have both the structure and the content of your speech well in mind. At this point, you are ready to develop a shorter outline—your delivery outline.

Your delivery outline should provide all the notes you will need to present your speech as you have planned, without being so detailed that you will be tempted to read it rather than speak to your audience. Here are a few suggestions for preparing a delivery outline:

- *Use single words or short phrases whenever possible.*
- *Include your introduction and conclusion in abbreviated form.*
- *Use standard outline form.*

Although you may write the first version of your delivery outline on paper, eventually you may want to transfer it to note cards. They don't rustle the way paper does, and they are small enough to hold in one hand if there is no lectern. Three or four note cards will probably give you enough space for your delivery outline. Type or print neatly on one side only, making sure that the letters and words are large enough to read easily. Organize your note cards to reflect blocks of material, using one note card for your introduction, one or two for the body of your speech, and one for your conclusion. Number your note cards to prevent getting them out of order while you are speaking.

A final addition to your note cards as you rehearse your speech will be **delivery cues**, such as "Louder," "Pause," or "Walk two steps left." These will remind you to communicate the nonverbal messages you have planned. Write your delivery cues in a different color ink so that you don't confuse them with your verbal content.

terms & definitions

Delivery cues notes a speaker uses to remind himself or herself of nonverbal behaviors to use while making a presentation.

Sample **Speech** *by* *Douglas Starr*

Presented to the International Association of Business Communicators. [47]

Writing for the Web

The best news is that you don't need to learn a different writing style to write for the World Wide Web.

Writing news stories and news releases for the World Wide Web, writing online, is no different from writing for print, particularly writing for newspapers. It is amazing how many newspaper techniques are recommended for web writing.

Starr began his speech by simultaneously catching attention and summarizing his key idea.

(continued)

The speaker makes a personal, direct connection with his listener.

And the best part is that you already know all of those techniques. You learn them in journalism school, and you've been doing it all your professional lives—at least, you should have.

I am speaking about only the writing, not the audio, the video, the blinking buttons, and other gimmicks of websites. Moreover, researchers agree that web readers, like newspaper readers, are attracted by the headline and the text rather than by graphics or pictures.

The technique of writing for newspapers—as taught in schools of journalism throughout the country—is simple: Write tight, be clear and concise, write short sentences and short paragraphs, use words correctly, obey the rules of grammar and spelling, and get to the point quickly with the inverted pyramid lead: the Who, What, Where, When, How, and Why of the story.

The addition of the web to the time-honored tools of writing has no effect on those techniques of writing. They remain the same. The web does not require a different style of writing; it only provides a more broadly based medium for much wider dissemination of information.

In past centuries, some of the finest writing was done with a goose quill pen and a pot of ink. Over time, as technology advanced, the goose quill pen and pot of ink gave way to pens and pencils, to movable type and linotype machines, to typewriters, to computers, to desktop printing, and, finally, to the Internet and the World Wide Web. Along the way, a curious thing happened. With each change in technology, writers and scholars equated the tools with the techniques of writing, holding that if the tool changed, so must the writing change.

Nothing could be further from the truth. The tool of writing has little to do with the technique of writing. Writing is writing. It is a means of communicating information to a large number of readers. The challenge to the writer using the Internet remains the same as the challenge to the writer using the goose quill pen—to communicate, to hold onto and to inform the reader.

Here the speaker is effectively enhancing his credibility by citing research by other sources that his audience would find credible.

This conclusion is borne out by continuing research by writing research centers—the Pew Research Center, the Poynter Institute for Media Studies, Sun Microsystems—and by individual scholars, teachers, and professionals who publish in *Communication World*, *Public Relations Tactics*, *Poynter Report*, *Writer's Digest*, and *Quill Magazine*, and on various websites.

A survey of that research and those publications shows almost unanimous agreement on the techniques for writing on the web. They grew out of the demands of reporting from the field and have been taught in journalism schools almost from the beginning.

Today, in general, researchers and professionals agree that web readers, like newspaper readers, want to know quickly what the story is about, and most of them do not want the details of a full story. Therefore, the recommendation is that web stories follow the traditional inverted pyramid style of writing news—summary lead to get to the point quickly, short sentences, short paragraphs, and no more than one screen of copy. That's 250 words, or one sheet of paper, double-spaced.

Most public relations news releases are too long. Studies show that newspapers seldom use more than half of any news release, and most use only the first one or two paragraphs, preferring not to give away too much space to an outside writer.

One of the pioneer researchers in web writing, Jakob Nielsen, recommends that because readers read 25 percent slower on the web than in newspapers, writing for the web ought to be half as long as newspaper stories.

Starr makes his point by comparing the words in a typical news story with the number of words in the Bible creation story.

A researcher for the Poynter Institute for Media Studies in St. Petersburg, Florida, Roy Peter Clark, believes that any story can be told in 800 words. The Bible story of creation is told in 754 words.

Because large blocks of type tend to lose readers, the recommendation is that no paragraph be longer than five lines on screen and that paragraphs be separated with a blank line. All of that is nothing more than the electronic equivalent of newspaper white space.

There is no question about the writing; it must be accurate, clear, concise, vivid, and with strong verbs. Researchers recommend using a conversational style that avoids overuse of punctuation marks, all of which provides for a smooth flow of language and ease of understanding.

If you do need a lengthy story, the recommendation is that you rely upon the old newspaper technique of using subheads to break up the copy, to provide more white space, and to alert readers as to what is coming next. In addition, you should write in "chunks," that is, completing one topic before moving on to another. Chunk writing normally is restricted to under 100 words, further attesting to the value of tight writing.

The speaker does a good job of providing specific recommendations that his audience would find practical and useful.

But be careful. Web readers generally are newspaper readers, and they read the web the way they read newspapers. Most newspaper readers don't scroll; they read no more than the first four or five paragraphs and move on to another story.

On the web, those who do scroll read an average of six websites, though some read up to three times that many. These readers are seeking additional information because they are interested in that specific topic. Those additional websites are called "hypertext," meaning "beyond text" or "additional text," and they are nothing more than the electronic name for the newspaper "sidebars."

Here are specific suggestions for making website news releases readily understandable and interesting.

Starr continues to keep his audience's attention by providing a list of cogent ideas that will help them with their work as well as summarizing his key advice.

- Write in the conversational active voice: subject, verb, object. Tell, rather than write, your story.
- Avoid synonyms; repeating key words reinforces understandability.
- Obey the rules of grammar, punctuation, syntax, precise word use and spelling, subject-verb agreement, noun-pronoun agreement.
- Write objectively; no opinion words.
- Use strong verbs.
- No paragraph longer than five lines on screen.
- No line longer than five inches on screen.
- Paragraphs separated with a blank line.
- Write tight. No story longer than one screen, 250 words.
- For lengthy stories, use subheads and hypertext sidebars.
- Get to the point quickly with the summary lead—the Who, What, Where, When, How, and Why of the story—and the inverted pyramid.

Wrap-Up

Virtually everyone feels some apprehension about speaking in public. Here are some of the most powerful tips to help you manage your apprehension:

- Don't procrastinate
- Know your audience
- Be well-prepared
- Visualize your success
- Use breathing techniques to help you relax
- Look for and respond to positive listener support

There are several key steps to help you develop your ideas for a presentation:

1. Consider your audience. Thinking about your audience at every step of the process is one of the most important elements of developing and delivering a presentation.

2. Select and narrow your topic. In business and professional settings your topic grows organically from the reason you are speaking to an audience.

3. Determine the general and specific purpose for your presentation.

4. Develop your central idea for the presentation; this is a one-sentence summary of your major idea.

5. Generate your main ideas. Use your speech's central idea to help you generate your main ideas, which are usually logical divisions of the central idea, reasons the central idea is true, or a series of steps or a chronological sequence that develops the central idea.

6. Gather supporting material. The more personal, concrete, specific, and varied your supporting material the more likely it will be that you will gain and maintain the attention and interest of your listeners.

7. Organize your presentation. To make sure that your listeners remember your message, it is useful to tell your audience what you're going to tell them (in the introduction of your message), tell them you key ideas (in the body of your message) and then tell them what you told them (in your presentation's conclusion).

Reviewing Key Terms

The Principle Points

Principle One: Be aware of your communication with yourself and others.

- Be aware of your own interests and experiences when searching for a topic.
- Give yourself a mental pep talk before getting up to speak to boost your confidence.
- Remember that the most effective illustrations are often personal ones.

Principle Two: Effectively use and interpret verbal messages.

- Your central idea should reflect a single topic, be a complete declarative sentence, and use specific language.
- Be sure your illustrations are vivid, concrete, and directly relevant to the idea or the point they are supporting.
- Organize your presentation logically to by using verbal transitions to show relationships between ideas in your presentation.

Principle Three: Effectively use and interpret nonverbal messages.

- Remember that the physical symptoms of speaker anxiety are rarely visible to an audience.
- Use nonverbal transitions—pauses, facial expressions, altered vocal pitch or speaking rate, and movement—to indicate when you are moving from one idea to the next.

Principle Four: Listen and respond thoughtfully to others.

- Seek out information about your audience and how they are likely to respond to your message to increase your comfort with speaking in public.
- As you listen to presentations, consider the cultural differences in the organization of speakers from cultures other than your own.

Principle Five: Appropriately adapt messages to others.

- Revise your ideas or strategies at any point in the presentation-preparation process, as you seek out and learn more about your audience.
- Be sensitive to and adapt to the diversity of your audience.
- Keep in mind your audience's knowledge, interests, and expectations as you select supporting material for your presentation.
- Use illustrations with which your audience can identify. Consider making your audience members part of the scenario in a hypothetical illustration.

Applying Your Skills

1. Generate at least three main ideas from each of the following central ideas. Apply the questions suggested in this chapter: Does the central idea have *logical divisions*? Can you think of several *reasons* the central idea is true? Can you support the central idea with a series of *steps* or a *chronological sequence*?

   - Our company's new smart phone is the best camera on the market.
   - There are several things you need to do as a new employee to complete your benefits package.
   - There are several elements to designing and delivering an effective sales presentation.
   - Business ties between the United States and Iran have been strained over the last decade.
   - Sleep deprivation on the job is dangerous.
   - Three specific strategies can help you deal with unsolicited sales managers.
   - There are three reasons why our product underperformed and did not meet sales expectations.

2. Develop a general and a specific purpose sentence for the following speech topics:
   - The history of consumer credit cards in the United States
   - Encouraging business investment
   - Invest in U.S. savings bonds
   - Corporate mergers downsizing
   - Slowing sales of houses in the United States
   - The impact of globalization on the economy
   - The impact of technology of the workforce

3. Imagine that as you are presenting a sales talk to a group of business persons you begin to notice that your listeners seem to be losing interest in your presentation. Identify several possible strategies that could increase interest in your presentation.

4. Select a story from the newspaper or a weekly newsmagazine such as *Time* or *Newsweek*. Identify the different types of supporting material you find in the article. Evaluate the supporting material you identify as information that could be used in an oral presentation.

5. Select several statistics that you find in a news story. Identify strategies for adapting the statistics for a presentation, such as rounding off the statistics and developing a way to relate the numerical data to something an audience could visualize.

12

Delivering Professional Presentations

chapter outline

After reading this chapter, you should be able to

- List and describe four methods of delivery and provide tips for effectively using each one.

- Identify and describe characteristics of effective eye contact, posture, movement, gestures, facial expression, vocal delivery, and personal appearance.

- Identify strategies for adapting your speaking style to the media.

- List and describe strategies for responding to questions following your presentation.

- Identify the types of presentation aids a speaker might use, and provide suggestions for using each type effectively.

- Offer general guidelines for preparing effective presentation aids for a professional presentation.

- Identify tips and strategies for designing effective PowerPoint presentations.

S he was born in Kosciusko, Mississippi, on January 29, 1954, and raised on a pig farm. Although she lived with her parents, her paternal grandparents were her primary caregivers until she was 6. When her parents separated in 1960 she lived with her mother for several years, terrible years—she was repeatedly sexually abused by male family members and "friends." At age 13 she was almost locked up in a youth training center but instead sent to live with her father. Life continued to be a struggle. She had a baby at age 14, who died shortly after birth. Her first big break in life came at age 16 when she was named Miss Fire Prevention for Nashville, which led to a gig as a newsreader on a local radio station. It quickly became evident that she had the gift of speaking to others. After studying speech, theater, and English at Tennessee State University, she became coanchor of a TV news program. Others spotted her talent. She was hired as an anchorwoman at a Baltimore TV station's news program—but because she kept adlibbing during the news, the station dropped her after a few months. But they then moved her to a morning talk show called *People Are Talking*, where she truly found her voice. We'll bet you've heard her voice: The voice and face of Oprah Winfrey are among the most recognized in America. Despite an early life of obstacles and challenges, because of her communication skills and her abundant empathy, today Oprah (her first name is all she needs) is among the wealthiest people in the communication industry.[1]

Clearly Oprah has many talents, but chief among them is her skill in connecting to an audience. She knows how to deliver messages that hold and maintain interest. A leader's energy, charisma, and overall perception of leadership competence are communicated through his or her delivery of messages.

leading **questions**

1. You've undoubtedly seen Oprah communicate with an audience. What are the communication skills that she uses that make her one of the most admired communicators today?

2. Oprah is an influential leader as well as communicator and is often rated as one of the most influential people in America. What factors make her one of the most admired and influential leaders today? How would you describe her leadership style?

In this chapter we focus on the delivery skills that can help you create a favorable impression of you and your message, regardless of whether you're giving a formal speech to hundreds of people, sharing a few impromptu ideas in an informal meeting, or convincing your boss to give you a raise. Specifically, we focus on methods of delivery and the use of delivery cues such as eye contact, gestures, posture, movement, facial expression, vocal delivery, and your overall appearance. In addition, we'll discuss PowerPoint and other types of visual and technological tools to enhance your presentations.

As we begin this chapter, consider this age-old question: What's more important, the content or the delivery of your message? People have debated that question since ancient times. Some have concluded that when all is said and done, what is done (a speaker's delivery) is more important than what is said. There is considerable research to support the observation that delivery is the foremost factor in determining the overall impact of your message. One classic research study found that listeners believe the most important factors that make a speaker effective are direct eye contact, alertness, enthusiasm, a pleasant voice, and animated gestures.[2] Another researcher concluded that delivery was almost twice as important as content when students gave persuasive presentations.[3] Although there is clear support to tip the scales toward delivery over content, especially when a speaker is

> *"You can speak well if your tongue can deliver the message of your heart."*
> —**John Ford**

expressing emotion, most contemporary communication teachers suggest that *both* content and delivery are important. They are both vital because, as one executive communication coach has suggested, "In the real world—the world where you and I do business—content and delivery are always related. And woe be to the communicator who forgets this."[4]

So how do you achieve a delivery style that makes your message memorable and interesting? That's what you're about to find out.

Methods of Delivering Your Presentation

Whether you are selling insurance, summarizing quarterly profits, or just making a few brief remarks, you have a decision to make about your delivery. You first need to determine, from among the four common methods, the delivery method you'll use to communicate your ideas to others. The four methods of presentation delivery are as old as the hills but also as contemporary as today's news headlines. Whether you choose to read your speech, memorize it, make it up on the spot, or speak conversationally from an outline, the method of delivery you choose will have an impact on your listeners. And in keeping with our emphasis on adapting to your audience, focusing on your listeners' expectations and the specific speaking situation will help you determine which delivery method to select.

Reading: Manuscript Speaking

You could write your speech word-for-word and then read your speech. This method is called **manuscript speaking**. One advantage of manuscript speaking is that you don't have to worry if you forget what you're going to say. You simply write exactly what you're going to say and then read it. Manuscript speaking also has the advantage of letting you carefully craft each word so that you can prepare a speech that has power and pizzazz while also focusing on precise word choices. When possible, during times of crisis, statements to the press by government, business, or education leaders should be carefully crafted rather than tossed off casually. An inaccurate or misspoken message could have serious consequences. Yet, despite these advantages, manuscript speaking is *not* a preferred method, because listening to someone reading a speech is not inherently interesting.

In fact, it can be one of the *least* effective methods of maintaining audience interest. It takes considerable skill to make a manuscript speech sound interesting and lively. Another disadvantage: When reading a speech, you'll have minimal eye contact with your audience. Also, when you read a message your voice tends to fall into a singsong pattern that sounds like you're reading rather than talking naturally with your listeners. So consider manuscript speaking only when you need to make sure your message is clearly worded or when you need to be very careful about what you are presenting.

When you do use a manuscript speaking style, consider these tips from media consultant Roger Ailes, who has advised leaders including U.S. presidents and corporate CEOs:[5]

- Type your speech in short, easy-to-scan phrases on the upper two-thirds of the paper so you don't have to look too far down into your notes.

- Rehearse your speech so you can have maximum eye contact when reading your message.

- Use an index finger to follow along on each line of your message so when you do break for eye contact you'll be able to quickly find your place and seamlessly keep on reading without missing a beat.

- Don't read too quickly; try to speak as you typically do when not using a manuscript.

- Vary your vocal inflection to mirror the way you normally talk.

- Use appropriate gestures and movement to add interest and emphasis to your message.

The goal when delivering a manuscript speech is to sound like you are not reading a speech.

terms & definitions

Manuscript speaking reading a speech from a written text.

Recalling: Memorized Speaking

If you've ever been in a play and had to memorize lines, you already know both the advantages and the disadvantages of delivering a speech from memory. **Memorized speaking** has the advantage of allowing you to have constant eye contact with your audience while also saying precisely what you want to say. As with manuscript speaking, you can carefully develop your message and work on both word choice and the overall message.

A prime disadvantage of memorized speaking is that you might forget what you've rehearsed. Another disadvantage: Most memorized speeches sound like they are memorized—stiff, stilted, and overrehearsed. Also, you won't be able to adapt to your listeners if you've memorized every word.

Given those disadvantages, are there instances when it is appropriate to memorize your message? If you have a very short message to present, such as when accepting an award, introducing a speaker, or making an announcement, a memorized talk may be best. But even in those situations you may want to have notes available so you can use them if you need them. And if you do memorize your message, avoid rehearsing it using exactly the same vocal inflection each time you practice. Vary your voice to sound as natural and as conversational as possible. Memorize this: *Unless a speech is short, don't try to memorize it.*

Improvising: Impromptu Speaking

You've given more impromptu speeches in your life than any other type of speech. **Impromptu speaking** is delivering a speech without any advance preparation. You simply respond to a question, comment, or invitation to speak. Impromptu speaking is also called "thinking on your feet" or "speaking off the cuff." Whether in a meeting when someone turns to you for a short briefing on a topic or when you respond to something said during a conference call, you'll undoubtedly give many impromptu speeches. Leaders are expected to think on their feet and to speak fluently.

The key advantage of impromptu speaking is that you can speak conversationally (because you didn't prepare your message ahead of time) while maintaining direct eye contact with your listeners. You can also adapt your comments to your listeners, based on the remarks of a previous speaker or something that has just occurred. A skilled impromptu speaker can customize a message to hold an audience's interest and attention. The problem is that a speaker needs to be especially skilled and talented to be a good impromptu speaker. Another potential disadvantage is that an impromptu speech may lack a coherent organizational structure. You're also not able to carefully gather facts and other information for an impromptu speech; you can include only the supporting material that comes to mind when you're speaking.

Mark Twain said, "A good impromptu speech takes about three weeks to prepare." What Twain knew is that the best impromptu speakers are always thinking about what they might say if they were called on to say a few remarks. In business and professional settings, when you find yourself in a situation with an audience present and others are speaking (such as when your team is reporting its findings to stockholders), you would be wise to think about a few remarks you could present, even if you were not invited in advance to talk.

The following tips can help you present impromptu speeches that sound professional and polished.

IDENTIFY THE NUMBER OF POINTS YOU WISH TO MAKE Before you open your mouth to respond to another speaker or to ask to speak, think about how many major ideas you will mention. Maybe you'll just have one major idea; you'll probably not have more than three or four. Just as in any speech, as you develop a brief introduction to your comments, you could say, "I have two responses" or "There are three points I want to make." You'll impress listeners with your clarity of thought and give your message an immediate structure.

ORGANIZE BEFORE YOU SPEAK In addition to enumerating your major points, think about the order of your major ideas. For example, consider using the primacy-recency principle: Whatever you present first or last is most likely to be remembered. If you think your audience may be opposed to your message, start with your strongest idea. Or, you may want to build to a strong conclusion, saving your strongest point for last. Or, use a simple problem-solution, topical, or chronological pattern. With just a few seconds of reflection, you can develop a mental outline of your key points and place them in an order for maximum impact.

BE BRIEF Because it's an impromptu speech, most listeners won't expect (or want) your message to be lengthy. A typical impromptu speech lasts from one to three minutes, although depending on the issue, or your leadership role, and the specific audience you are addressing, an impromptu speech could be longer than three minutes.

SPEAK HONESTLY AND DRAW ON PERSONAL EXPERIENCE More than likely, you will support your key ideas with personal experience or stories, since you've not had time to conduct research. But be careful to self-censor your remarks to make sure you're not making a heat-of-the-moment response. Don't let your emotions lead you to say something you'll later regret. When you do provide impromptu personal examples and illustrations, we recommend using short—and we emphasize *short*—anecdotes or stories to make your point; long, rambling offerings will likely not be well-received.

ALWAYS KEEP YOUR AUDIENCE IN MIND As we've stressed throughout our discussion of professional speaking, be audience-centered. Always think about your audience's needs, interests, and background as you begin an impromptu message. A quick way to be audience-centered and adapt your message to your listeners is, for just a few moments, to *be* your audience: Imagine that you are different members of your audience, with their different roles and experiences. If you were them, what would you expect or want a speaker to say? Being audience-centered is always good advice when speaking on short notice.

Conversing: Extemporaneous Speaking

The delivery style advocated by most communication experts is extemporaneous delivery. **Extemporaneous speaking** is speaking from a written or memorized outline without having memorized the exact wording of what you are going to say. You have rehearsed your message so that you know the key ideas and how to organize them, but not to the degree that your speech sounds memorized. An extemporaneous delivery style gives your audience the impression that the speech is being created as you're presenting it. But you've worked hard to gather research, refine your ideas, organize your message, and even practice saying what you'll say. Extemporaneous speaking sounds conversational, fluid, and thoughtful. Yet, because you haven't memorized the exact wording of your talk, you really are creating your message in front of the audience. As one communication consultant noted, "Great presentations, masked as conversations, always get you closer to your audience. The closer you get, the better the chance you get what you want."[6]

To make an extemporaneous speech sound conversational yet evidence ample research and reflection, follow the steps of the audience-centered speaking process discussed in Chapters 11. With the content of your message in hand, you move to the rehearsal phase of preparation. As you rehearse your message, try rely less on your notes, but don't memorize your message word for word. In fact, if you find yourself starting to say exactly the same things during rehearsal, stop rehearsing. You don't want to sound like a computer-generated voice—you want to sound live and immediate. As you master the overall structure of your message, you'll rely less on your notes and focus more on adapting your ideas to your audience. The final draft of your speaking notes may be an abbreviated outline or a few key words, facts, quotations, statistics, or other bits of information you don't want to commit to memory.

terms & definitions

Extemporaneous speaking speaking from a written or memorized speech outline without having memorized the exact wording of the speech.

RECAP

Methods of Delivery

Delivery Method	Tips
Manuscript speaking Reading your speech	Write like you speak. Use shorter sentences. Use personal pronouns (*I*), contractions (*don't* instead of *do not*), and be more redundant than when you write.
Memorized speaking Giving a speech from memory with no notes	Use only for short messages. Budget time to rehearse your memorized message.
Impromptu speaking Delivering a speech without advance preparation	Enumerate your main points. Be audience-centered. Organize. Be brief. Be honest, but monitor what you are saying.
Extemporaneous Knowing the major ideas, which you have outlined, but not memorizing the exact words of a speech	Follow the steps for preparing a speech, including developing a full-content outline. Rehearse the speech until you know the overall structure of the message, but stop rehearsing when you start saying exactly the same words each time you rehearse.

Effective Delivery Strategies

"Should I look over their heads so I don't get nervous?"

"Should I stand or sit when delivering my presentation?"

"What do I do with my hands while speaking?"

"Should I vary the pitch, rate, and intensity of my voice?"

The answers to these common questions about delivering a speech (No; It depends; It depends; and Yes) have important implications for you the next time you deliver a speech. However, you may need more than one-word responses to gain worthwhile insights about how to best deliver a presentation. In this section we offer tips about eye contact, gestures, posture, facial expression, vocal cues, and your personal appearance to help you deliver a speech with power and credibility.

Look Up: Maximize Eye Contact

The most important tip to remember, if you do nothing else during a presentation, is to look at your listeners. As James Humes, famed speech writer for business leaders and several presidents, says, "There is only one rule you have to follow: *Never, never, never let words come out of your mouth when your eyes are looking down.*"[7] Known for being an excellent speaker, President Ronald Reagan used a specific technique to ensure maximum eye contact when delivering his presentations. He would look at his notes, make a mental "snapshot" of what he would say next, and then look up to deliver his lines.[8] For most Americans, having direct eye contact with audience members has been shown to increase speaker credibility and listener comprehension.[9] A study by one of your authors found that speakers with less than 50 percent eye contact are considered unfriendly, uninformed, inexperienced, and even dishonest by their listeners.[10] Don't look over listeners' heads (listeners know if you're not looking directly at them). Look at them and they will like you more and will be more likely to remember what you tell them.

Is there such a thing as too much eye contact? Probably not for most North American listeners. But you don't want to stare at just one person; that will likely make him or her uncomfortable. And be aware that not all people from all cultures prefer as much eye contact as North Americans do. Asians, for example, typically prefer less.

When it's your time to speak, walk to the lectern or the area where you've been asked to stand while speaking, pause briefly, and look at your audience before you say anything. Eye contact nonverbally sends the message "I am interested in you; tune me in; I have something I want to share with you." Have your opening sentence firmly in mind so you can deliver it without looking at your notes or away from your listeners.[11]

Keep these eye contact tips in mind as you speak:

- Establish eye contact with the entire audience, not just with those in the front row or only one or two people.

- Make eye contact with individuals, establishing person-to-person contact with them—not so long that it will make a listener feel uncomfortable, but long enough to establish the feeling that you are talking directly to that individual.

- *Don't* look over your listeners' heads.

Move Meaningfully: Use Appropriate Gestures, Movement, and Posture

When you write, you use punctuation, CAPITALIZATION, *italics*, and boldface to help your reader interpret your message and add emphasis to words. When you speak, gestures, movement, and your overall posture often serve those functions. You move to emphasize ideas, enumerate items, and describe objects.

GESTURES Some people (maybe you're one of them) gesture easily and appropriately during the course of everyday conversations, yet aren't sure what to do with their hands when they find themselves in front of an audience. If you don't know what to do with your hands, think about the message you want to express. As in ordinary conversation, your hands should simply help emphasize or reinforce your verbal message.

Here are some tips for using gestures when you speak in public:

- Focus on the message you want to communicate. Your gestures should naturally coincide with what you are saying.

- Be definite. If you want to gesture, go ahead and gesture. Avoid minor hand movements that may appear accidental to your audience.

- Vary your gestures. Don't use the same hand to gesture or one all-purpose gesture all of the time.

- Don't overdo your gestures. Listeners should focus on your message, not your gestures.

- Adapt your gestures to fit the situation. When speaking to a large audience in a formal setting, use bolder and larger gestures. For a smaller group, your gestures would likely be less dramatic.

- Adapt your gestures to the cultural expectations of your audience. Listeners from Asia, for example, typically prefer a quieter, less flamboyant use of gestures. British listeners seem to prefer a speaker to stay behind a lectern and use few gestures. Europeans often say they can spot an American speaker because Americans typically are more animated in the use of gestures, movement, and facial expression.

We've provided several do's and don'ts for using gestures, but the most important point about gestures is this: *Use gestures that work best for you.* Your gestures should fit your personality. It may be better to use no gestures—to just put your hands comfortably at your side—than to use distracting, awkward gestures or to try to mimic someone else's gestures.

MOVEMENT   Oprah Winfrey does it and so do many newscasters: They sometimes move around when they talk. When speaking in a business or professional situation, should you move when you speak? The best advice we can give you is to be aware of and adapt to the expectations of your listeners. If you're seated at a conference table and all of the other speakers have delivered their presentations while seated, then probably you should remain seated too, unless you purposely want to change the mood or momentum of the meeting. Consider these tips as you evaluate whether to add movement to your message:

- *Move—but don't distract listeners from your message.* You don't want your listeners to be thinking about your graceful movements; you want them to listen to your message. Movement should make sense—it should be neither artistic expression nor aimless meandering.

- *Move to reduce physical barriers.* Barriers such as a lectern, rows of chairs, or a projector may act as obstacles between you and your audience. If such physical barriers make you feel too far removed from your audience, move closer and reduce the physical separation.

- *Move to signal a new idea or tone.* Your movement can signal the beginning of a new idea or major point in your speech. As you move into a transition statement or change from a serious subject to a more lighthearted one, movement can be a good way to signal that your approach to the speaking situation is also changing.

POSTURE   Your posture is a strong nonverbal cue that communicates your credibility, power, and the overall intensity of your message. Research has found that a slumped-over, casual posture violates what listeners expect to see and can lower your credibility.[12] Whereas your face and voice play the major role in communicating a specific emotion, your posture communicates the intensity of that emotion. If you are happy, your smile and your laughter reflect your happiness; your upright posture and quick movements communicate the intensity of your joy. So make sure that your posture is consistent with your verbal message. Slouching lazily across a lectern does not communicate enthusiasm for or interest in your audience or topic. If you announce how happy you are to speak to an audience, yet your frozen posture expresses your discomfort, your listeners will believe your nonverbal message rather than your claim that you're pleased to be there.

Adapt your posture to your topic, your audience, and the formality or informality of the speaking occasion. For example, it may be perfectly appropriate, as well as comfortable and natural, to sit on the edge of a desk during a very informal presentation, such as a brief update on a project to a small team of colleagues. For a class presentation, however, most teachers frown on casually sitting on a desk and dangling your feet. In professional speaking sessions, always consider the expectations and culture of the audience members to guide you in the posture you adopt. An effective and audience-centered leader would tend to adopt a more formal posture to convey a professional approach.

Regardless of the specific situation, consider these suggestions to enhance your posture when speaking to others:

- *Plant your feet.* When standing, place your feet on the floor with one foot slightly in front of the other one; this will keep you from being tempted to sway from side to side. With one foot in front of the other one, you may move slightly forward and back, but this is less noticeable or distracting than swaying.

- *Stand tall.* To enhance your posture, pull your shoulders back a bit (as one posture expert suggests, "put your shoulders in your back pocket") and then imagine a string holding up the top of your head. Shoulders back, head up.

Like your gestures your posture should not call attention to itself. It should reflect your interest in and attention to your audience and your message.

Express Emotions: Use Appropriate Facial Expressions

Telling you to have a facial expression is like telling you to breathe; you can't help but have some kind of expression on your face. But the specific facial expression you display can be positive or negative, energetic or lethargic, expressive or neutral. Your audience sees your face before they hear what you are going to say. Thus, through your facial cues, you have an opportunity to set the emotional tone of your message before you utter a word.[13]

Throughout your presentation, your facial expression, like your body language and eye contact, should be appropriate to your message. Your face is the primary source of whatever specific emotion you communicate to your audience. The Roman orator Cicero said that you could help your listeners experience the emotion you wish them to experience by displaying the emotion yourself. If you want listeners to be joyful, you must express joy. To have them feel sorrow, communicate your sadness with your face. Not in a fake way—audience members can spot a phony—but with a facial expression that genuinely expresses how you feel. Present somber news with a serious expression. Tell a funny story with a smile.

Audience members attending a speech by Steve Jobs, the late CEO of Apple, would have been surprised to see him appear in a suit and tie. Remember to adapt your personal appearance to the norms of the situation so that you meet your audience's expectations.

Although humans are capable of producing thousands of different facial expressions, researchers have classified six primary emotions that are expressed on the face: happiness, anger, surprise, sadness, disgust, and fear.[14] But when we speak to others, our faces communicate a blend of expressions, rather than a single emotion. According to cross-cultural studies by social psychologist Paul Ekman, facial expressions conveying emotions are virtually universal; in most situations even a culturally diverse audience will be able to interpret your emotional expressions.[15]

Consider these suggestions to enhance your use of facial expressions when speaking to others:

- *Be aware of your facial expressions.* When you rehearse your speech, stand in front of a mirror or, better yet, videotape yourself. Note whether you are allowing your face to help communicate the emotional tone of your thoughts.

- *Ensure that your facial expression supports your verbal message.* As we've suggested throughout our discussion of delivery, your nonverbal message should be consistent with your verbal message.

- *Ask someone to watch you rehearse, or make a video paying special attention to your facial expressions.*

Look Good: Monitor Personal Appearance

What you wear tells people how you wish to be treated. For example, wearing jeans and a T-shirt to class says, "I just want to blend in with other students." Wearing a business suit to an upscale office says, "I want to be perceived as credible and competent like my colleagues." Your personal appearance affects how other people respond to you and your message. A key principle to keep in mind when monitoring personal appearance is to adapt to the norms of your situation. At the California corporate offices of Google, for example, casual clothing is the norm. Someone who wore a coat and tie or a dressy suit would not be perceived as part of the team. Whenever possible, monitor the audience's dress code before deciding what to wear or what not to wear.

The ultimate judge of your style choices is not a fashion editor from New York or Paris, but the people in your audience. Steve Jobs typically wore jeans and a black turtleneck sweater. Bill Gates often leaves his tie at home in favor of an open-collared shirt. Our point is that you should be wary of "one-size-fits-all" prescriptions for how to dress. Fashion styles change. What doesn't change is this: If you violate your listeners' expectations or the style or culture of the organization where you are making a presentation, you will be less successful in achieving your purpose.

Consider these general guidelines to help you adapt your personal appearance for maximum credibility:

- *If you're in doubt about the dress code, ask someone who is familiar with the audience and the occasion to help you decide whether to dress up or dress down.*

- *Dress slightly better than your audience members.* Your grooming and attention to appearance suggest that you care about your listeners and have given special thought to how you will be perceived by them.

- *Never wear clothing that would be potentially distracting—for example, a shirt or blouse that displays printing that advertises something unrelated to your topic.* You want your listeners to listen to you, not read you.

- *When in doubt, select clothing that is conservative.* You want your listener to focus on your message, not on your wardrobe.

Speak Clearly: Use Appropriate Vocal Delivery

Have you ever heard a radio announcer's voice and conjured up a mental image of what the person looks like, based only on the sound of his or her voice, only to see a photo and discover that your mental picture is completely inaccurate? Your voice is a powerful projector of personality, energy, and overall credibility. As a leader, you can influence others not only with the power of your ideas, but with the power of your vocal delivery. We don't mean you need to shout or try to sound like someone you're not—but thoughtfully monitoring your voice can help you enhance your leadership image.

A speaker has at least two important vocal obligations to an audience: Speak to be understood and speak to maintain interest. How do you achieve both of those goals? Monitoring your volume, pitch, rate, articulation, pronunciation, and dialect are the key elements in being both understood and interesting.[16]

VOLUME Your speaking *volume*—how loud or soft your voice is—is the most fundamental aspect of your voice. The volume of your speech is determined by the amount of air you project through your larynx, or voice box. More air results in a louder sound. Your diaphragm, a muscle in your upper abdomen, helps control sound volume by increasing air flow from your lungs through your voice box. Breathing from your diaphragm—that is, consciously expanding and contracting your abdomen as you breathe in and out—can increase the volume of sound as well as enhance the quality of your voice.

With many speakers the problem is not the volume of the voice, but a lack of intensity. You can enhance the intensity of your voice by increasing vocal energy using a combination of increased volume, varied pitch, and clear articulation of speech sounds.

ARTICULATION **Articulation** is the enunciation of speech sounds. You should articulate distinctly to ensure that your audience can clearly determine what words you are using.

Many errors in articulation result from bad habits, from emulating the sounds of others who use poor articulation, or from simple laziness. It takes more energy to articulate speech sounds clearly. Sometimes we are in a hurry to express our ideas, but more often we simply get into the habit of mumbling, slurring, or abbreviating—saying "dint" instead of "didn't" or "lemme" instead of "let me." Such vocal flaws may not keep your audience from understanding you, but poor enunciation does reflect on your credibility as a speaker.

How do you improve your articulation? First, identify words or phrases that you have a tendency to slur or cut short. Once you have identified these, practice saying the words correctly. Work to hear the difference between improper and proper articulation. Listen to the way newscasters or other media announcers articulate speech sounds. Consult a dictionary, which, in addition to defining words, provides guidelines for articulating the sound of words.

PRONUNCIATION Whereas articulation refers to the clarity of speech sounds, *pronunciation* is the degree to which words conform to standard English. Mispronouncing words can detract from your credibility. You may not be aware that you're mispronouncing a word unless someone tells you.

Some speakers reverse speech sounds, saying "aks" instead of "ask." Some allow an *r* sound to intrude into some words, saying "warsh" instead of "wash," or "Warshington" instead of "Washington." Another common pronunciation error is to leave out sounds in the middle of words, as in "ackchally" instead of "actually" or "Febuary" instead of "February." Some speakers accent syllables in nonstandard ways; they say "pólice" instead of "police" or "úmbrella" rather than "umbrella."

If English is not your native language, you may have to spend extra time working on your pronunciation and articulation. Try these strategies:

- Make an effort to prolong vowel sounds. Speeeeeak tooooo prooooolooooong eeeeach voooowel soooound yooooou maaaaake. Such exaggerations of speech sounds will help you become more aware of how to avoid clipping vowel sounds.[17]

- To reduce choppy-sounding pronunciation, blend the end of one word into the beginning of the next. Make your speech flow from one word to the next, instead of separating it into individual chunks of sound.

DIALECT A **dialect** is a consistent style of pronouncing words that is common to an ethnic group or a geographic region such as the South, New England, or the upper Midwest. In the southern part of the United States, people prolong some vowel sounds when they speak. And in the northern Midwest and Canada, the word *about* sometimes sounds a bit like "a boat."

Although a speaker's dialect may classify the person as being from a certain part of the country, it won't necessarily affect an audience's comprehension of information, unless the dialect is so pronounced that the listeners can't understand the speaker's words. Research does suggest, however, that listeners tend to prefer a dialect similar to their own.[18] If your word pronunciation is significantly distracting to your listeners, you might considering modifying your dialect (although radically altering a dialect is difficult and time consuming). However, you don't want to try to develop a fake dialect—unless you have the acting skill of Meryl Streep or Tom Hanks, people will be able to detect that your dialect is phony.

PITCH Vocal **pitch** is how high or low your voice sounds. When you sing, your pitch changes to produce a melody. When you speak, your pitch also has a natural variation. Not varying your vocal pitch is one of the worst things you can do while speaking; a monotone voice is boring.

Everyone has a habitual pitch. This is the range of the voice during normal conversation. Regardless of your habitual pitch, it's important to have a varied inflection when you speak. Vocal **inflection** is the variation in pitch as you pronounce words or sounds. Your inflection helps determine the meaning of your utterances. A disappointed "Ah" sounds different from a surprised "Ah!" or a quizzical "Ah?"

For English-speaking people, vocal inflection adds interest and helps communicate emotions and subtle nuances of meaning. In some languages, vocal inflection plays a significant role in determining the meanings of words. Thai, Vietnamese, and Mandarin Chinese languages use such inflections as monotone, low, falling, high, and rising inflections to vary the meaning of messages.[19] If you are a native speaker of a language in which pitch influences meaning, be aware that listeners do not expect these kinds of variations in many Western languages, although all languages rely on some variation in inflection to communicate emotions and nuances of meaning.

RATE Another way you express your interest and energy is by your speaking *rate*. Most speakers average between 125 and 180 words per minute. Research suggests that speaking more than 300 or less than 125 words per minute makes listening difficult.[20] At the upper end of that range you'd be speaking at a fairly fast clip. The ideal speaking rate depends on the topic, the occasion, your own natural style of speaking, and the preferences of your audience.

terms & definitions

Dialect a consistent style of pronunciation and articulation that is common to an ethnic group or a geographic region.

Pitch how high or low a speaker's voice is.

Inflection variation in vocal pitch.

Presence Is Powerful

There's more to communication than just presenting information—just ask Robert W. Selander, chief executive of MasterCard. To him, speaking well is about making an impact not only with the content of your message but with your *presence*. To have presence is to have charisma, energy—a certain electricity that keeps your listeners riveted on you and your message while you're speaking and helps them remember you after you sit down. How do you achieve presence? Is it merely a speaker's delivery and nonverbal message that makes a message pop? According to Selander, it's more than body language; it's also about the level of audience-centered message detail you present. Present too much information and you'll bore them; present too little and you'll confuse them. According to Selander,

I think you can be a good communicator and you still may not have presence. There may be someone who is very articulate on a subject and they know considerable levels of detail. When you get with a particular audience, it may not be appropriate to go into those levels of detail, or you may create doubt by even going into the subject matter. There's inside information in a company, for example. You never cross that bright line, but you can get varying degrees of proximity to that line, depending on your audience.[21]

Note his last four words: "depending on your audience." It's your audience that does or does not determine if you have presence. Sensing whether your listeners want details or merely the big picture can determine if you connect to them or not, whether you have a charismatic presence or make your listeners wish they weren't present. What else adds to presence? Selander adds this advice:

Some people are not very good communicators, but boy, when you get them into their subject matter they know exactly where to go and how far to go. Others are brilliant communicators, but because of the connection between their thoughts and the synapses firing and the words coming out, there isn't enough time and introspection. Therefore they will brilliantly communicate something that they shouldn't be talking about. Presence is knowing what to communicate, and how.[22]

To have presence is to read your audience to give them the information they need and want—not to smother them with details or make up for lack of substance with a overly-slick delivery style. You'll have presence if you know what to edit out of your message and what to keep. Bottom line: What is the key factor that determines what information stays in the message and what gets cut? Your audience.

Sometimes when speakers are nervous they speak rapidly. This is because their anxiety leads to an increase in adrenaline and thus extra energy; speaking rapidly is a manifestation of their anxiousness.

Effective speakers vary their speaking rate. You need not deliver your entire speech at the same pace. When you are excited or wish to communicate excitement and interest, speak faster. Slow your pace to emphasize an idea. As with any aspect of delivery, you don't want listeners to focus on your speaking rate—you want them to focus on your message. The pace of your delivery should make sense in terms of the ideas you are sharing with your listeners.

Your use of well-timed *pauses* can greatly enhance the overall impact of your message. Whether you are trying to tell a joke, a serious tale, or a dramatic story, your use of a pause can determine the effectiveness of your anecdote.

Although pauses can add impact and dramatic effect, many beginning speakers are uncomfortable with silent pauses and fill them with "Umm," "Er," "You know," and "Ah." Try to avoid making these unnecessary vocalizations.

Silence can be an effective tool in adding emphasis to a particular word or sentence. A well-timed pause coupled with eye contact can powerfully accent your idea. Silence is a way of saying to your listeners, "Think about this for a moment."

Speak Up: Tips for Using a Microphone

In many business and professional settings, especially with a large audience, you will be expected to use a microphone so that all your listeners can hear you clearly. There have been some classic blunders when speakers didn't know the microphone was on, including the

2009 gaffe when Vice President Biden dropped the f-bomb when congratulating President Obama on the passage of a major overhaul of health care. A good guideline: Any time you're near a microphone, assume that it's on.

You will likely encounter one of two kinds of microphones. A lavaliere microphone is the clip-on type often used by newspeople and interviewees. Worn on a collar or lapel, it requires no particular care other than not thumping it or accidentally knocking it off. In contrast, a stationary microphone is attached to a lectern, sits on a desk, or stands on the floor. Generally, the stationary mikes used today are multidirectional. You don't have to remain absolutely anchored to the floor in front of a stationary microphone while delivering your speech—it can pick up your voice even if you're a couple of feet away. Regardless of the type of microphone you use, here are a few tips for using it well.

- Microphones amplify sloppy habits of pronunciation and articulation. You'll need to speak clearly and crisply when using a mike. Be especially careful when articulating *b* and *p* sounds; they can be overamplified and produce slight popping sounds. Microphones can also intensify the sibilance of the *s* sound at the beginning or ending of words. You may have to articulate these sounds with slightly less intensity to avoid overamplifying them.

- If you must test a microphone, ask the audience whether they can hear you. Blowing on an active mike produces an irritating noise. Just say "microphone test" or "one, two, three" in your normal speaking voice.

- Don't tap or pound the microphone or shuffle anything nearby. If you are using note cards, quietly slide them aside as you progress through your speech. Full sheets of paper are more difficult to handle quietly; if you must use them, try to shuffle them as quietly as you can.

- When you are delivering your presentation, talk directly into the microphone at your normal volume. Some speakers lower their volume and become inaudible when they have a microphone in front of them.

- If you can, practice before you speak with the type of microphone you will use. If you have the opportunity, conduct the microphone test before your audience arrives. Practicing in the room where you will be speaking will help you adapt to echoes or other distortions so that these sounds don't surprise you during your presentation.

RECAP

Characteristics of Effective Nonverbal Delivery

- Gestures should be relaxed, definite, varied, and appropriate to your audience and the speaking situation.
- Movement should be purposeful.
- Posture should feel natural and be appropriate to your topic, your audience, and the occasion.
- Eye contact should be established before you say anything and sustained as much as possible throughout your presentation.
- Facial expression should be alert, friendly, and appropriate to your message.
- Vary your vocal volume, pitch, and rate; articulate your words and pronounce them correctly.

Adapting Your Presentation for the Media

Whether your message will be broadcast on national TV, transmitted using Skype on the Internet, or presented during a videoconference, it is increasingly likely that you will deliver a presentation that will be conveyed via video transmission. Should you use a different style of speaking when your message will be on TV? For the most part, you'll follow the same guidelines for delivery we've already discussed. Good eye contact, varied vocal inflection, and appropriate posture and gestures are expected, but consider these strategies if there is a video camera present.

CONSIDER TONING DOWN YOUR GESTURES. You don't need to use large sweeping gestures when speaking via the media. Dramatic gestures that are appropriate when addressing a large audience will likely appear too demonstrative on TV. Most newscasters use subtle head nods and facial expressions rather than gestures to emphasize their points. Use fewer gestures, and don't fidget with pens, your hair, or your clothing. Also, keep your hands away from your face. When you watch someone on TV or Skype, it's more like having an interpersonal conversation than hearing a formal oration. If your primary audience is the live audience in the room when you present your message, then that should be the key audience to whom you adapt your speaking style. But if the target audience is watching on monitors elsewhere, tone down the gestures a bit.

DRESS FOR TV SUCCESS Avoid large patterns, stripes, jangling or shiny jewelry, and overly frilly or complicated necklines, especially if you're being televised in high-definition TV.[23] Solid colors typically look best. The camera can add five to ten pounds to your appearance. You don't need to go on a crash diet, but do wear clothes that make you look and feel your best.

MONITOR YOUR FACIAL EXPRESSIONS Because TV amplifies your facial expressions, your listeners are seeing your expression up close rather than from a distance. Therefore, if you have a tendency to use exaggerated or dramatic facial expressions, realize that they will be seen from the camera's perspective rather than from the audience's perspective. Smile appropriately, but make sure you're not smiling at inappropriate times. If you are asked a serious question about company layoffs but you have a big grin on your face when the camera cuts to you, it will appear that you are insensitive to the question.

KEEP IT SHORT If you are speaking for the media, realize you will only be given a few seconds (or sound bites) of airtime. Short answers, short phrases, quotable lines are what editors are looking for.

CHOOSE YOUR WORDS WITH CARE AND STYLE The sound bites often broadcast are those phrases that are particularly memorable or attention catching. Repeating key words, speaking in parallel structures, and using alliteration and other stylistic devices enhance the likelihood that your message will be quoted or broadcast.

BECOME FAMILIAR WITH THE TECHNOLOGY BEFORE YOU SPEAK If you are being taped or broadcast from a studio, be sure to arrive in plenty of time so that you won't have to rush around making last-minute adjustments to your microphone.

Responding to Questions

Often the sale is made or lost, or your client decides whether you get the contract, during the Q & A (question and answer) portion of your presentation. During a Q & A period following a prepared presentation, your delivery methods change to impromptu speaking. In addition to the strategies for impromptu speaking that we offered earlier, here are additional tips to make a Q & A period effective.[24]

PREPARE How can you prepare for a question that hasn't been asked yet? Anticipate the kinds of questions listeners may have and prepare responses to those. How do you anticipate questions? You analyze your audience. Think of possible questions those particular listeners might ask you, and then rehearse your answers.

REPEAT OR REPHRASE THE QUESTION There are several reasons why it's a good idea to repeat questions. First, your restatement makes sure that everyone can hear the question. Second, paraphrasing ensures that *you* understand the question before you respond. Third, by paraphrasing, you can succinctly summarize long, rambling questions. And finally, by repeating the question, you give yourself more time to think about your answer.

ASK YOURSELF THE FIRST QUESTION One way to prime the audience to ask questions is to ask yourself a challenging question first. For example, you might say, "As we move into the question and answer portion of the presentation, several of you may be wondering . . . ." State the question and answer it. Doing this also gives you a comfortable way to make a transition between the presentation and the Q & A period. Asking yourself a tough question tells the audience that you're open for serious questions and that they'll have your attention.

STAY ON MESSAGE Sometimes listeners may ask questions unrelated to your talk. If so, you'll want to find a way to gently guide your questioner back to the message you have presented. Your answers, rather than the questions, are what are important. We're not suggesting that you dodge questions, but you can ensure that your key ideas remain the focus of the Q & A session. Some seasoned speakers suggest that you save a bit of your presentation to deliver during the Q & A session. It's called giving

During the Q & A portion of your presentation, your delivery methods change to impromptu speaking and may include gestures that add emphasis to your responses or help focus your listeners' attention.

a "double-barreled" talk.[25] You first deliver your presentation, and then, during the Q & A period, you give your second, much briefer talk.

LISTEN CAREFULLY AND NONJUDGMENTALLY Your listeners expect you to be polite and attentive. When you listen to questions, keep your eyes focused on the person asking the question and lean forward slightly to communicate your attentiveness. If you think a question is stupid, don't say so. Just listen and respond courteously. Audience members will judge for themselves whether a question was appropriate or not. Don't wince, grimace, or scowl at the questioner. You'll gain more credibility by keeping your cool than by losing your composure.

NEUTRALIZE HOSTILE QUESTIONS We're not suggesting that you should celebrate when you get a hostile or mean-spirited question, but such a question gives you opportunity to score points with your listeners. Why? Because you'll have your listeners' attention; use that attention to your advantage. Here are some tips to help you do that.

- *Restate the question.* If the question was a lengthy diatribe attacking you, focus on the essence of the issue. If the question is "Your ideas are just stupid! I'm angry that you have no idea how to proceed. The program has been a complete failure. Why are you still trying to make it work?" a paraphrase could be, "You're asking me why I'm still trying to make a program successful. From your perspective, the program has failed."

- *Acknowledge emotions.* For example, you could say, "I can certainly understand why you're angry. I share your anger and frustration. It's because of my frustration that I want to give my proposal more time to work."

- *Don't make the issue personal.* Even if the question has made you the villain, don't counterattack the questioner. Keep the conversation focused on issues, not personalities.

- *Get to the heart of the issue.* Respond directly to a hostile question. Consider restating the evidence you presented. Or provide a new example to support your position. A hostile listener is more likely to be persuaded with evidence and facts than by opinions or increased vocal volume.

- *When you don't know the answer, admit it.* It's better to admit you don't know an answer to a question than to try to fake it. Promise to find out more information and get back to the person later. And if you make such a promise, follow through on it.
- *Be brief.* Make your responses short and to the point.

USE ORGANIZATIONAL SIGNPOSTS   Listeners will be impressed if you can enumerate the number of points you'll make in response to a question. For example, you might say, "I have two responses to your question." When you get to your second point, say, "My second point is . . . ." Signposts will both help you stay organized and impress your listeners with your clarity.

SIGNAL WHEN THE Q & A PERIOD IS CONCLUDING   You might say to the audience, "I have time for two more questions." Let them know that the Q & A session will soon conclude. Even if you have someone helping you moderate the discussion, you should remain in control of concluding the presentation.

Presentation Aids

Because of the power of visual image, Jared Fogel has made Fred Deluca, cofounder of Subway sandwiches, rich. Photos of Jared when he weighed 425 pounds, before he shed 245 pounds eating Subway sandwiches, are startling when compared to the new, slimmer 180-pound Jared who appeared in Subway's TV ads. Subway's pitch that their sandwiches are a healthy alternative to other fast-food choices was successful—Subway is second in sales to McDonald's—because people could *see* for themselves that if you eat lower-fat sandwiches you can lose weight. So thanks in part to a trimmer Jared, Fred Deluca now makes an estimated $1 million a week.[26]

Seeing is indeed believing when it comes to communicating to others. It was Ernest Hemingway who said, "Don't tell me about it—show it to me." Because visual information can be so powerful, we now turn our attention to the visual (and sometimes auditory) support that audience members see (and hear) when you supplement your speech with presentation aids.

In many professional settings, you'll be expected to use some kind of presentation aid when you speak. A **presentation aid** is any object or image that reinforces your point visually so that your listeners can better understand it. Today's audiences often expect to see PowerPoint slides, those ubiquitous computer-generated lists of bulleted words, phrases, images, and even video; if you don't use professional-looking presentation aids, you'll lose credibility. In this section, we offer tips, pointers, and strategies to make sure you gain rather than lose credibility when using presentation aids.

Why Use Presentation Aids?

The short answer to the question "Why use presentation aids?" is "For many professional presentations, you're expected to." But there are several research-based reasons why presentation aids enhance professional presentations.[27]

ENHANCED UNDERSTANDING   People are more likely to comprehend what they can both see and hear. Because your audience has become accustomed to visual reinforcement by watching TV and images on the Internet, it is wise to consider how you can increase their understanding of your message by using presentation aids.[28]

ENHANCED MEMORY   It's well-known that you remember most what you understand best. Your listeners will not only have an improved understanding of your presentation, they will also better remember what you say as a result of visual reinforcement.

ENHANCED ORGANIZATION   Listing major ideas on a chart, a poster, or a PowerPoint slide can add clarity to your talk and help your audience understand your overall organizational strategy. Using verbal signposts ("I have three points. My first point is . . .") and clear transition statements is helpful, but visually displaying your major points ensures that your listeners understand your presentation's architecture. But use words sparingly; audiences respond more favorably to pictures and images than to complete sentences. Presentational speaking expert Granville Toogood even suggests getting rid of all text-heavy slides.[29] Consider using visual images such as a photo, chart, or picture as organizational markers of key ideas (or even very brief bullet points) instead of detailed verbal messages.

ENHANCED ATTENTION   Appropriate and well-chosen visual images not only can grab the attention of your listeners but also can maintain interest when words alone might not. Rather than just describe the new manufacturing plant, show a picture of it. The key to gaining and maintaining interest is not in just using presentation aids, but using them in interesting and novel ways. Using the same old PowerPoint slides or other presentation aids may not necessarily make your presentation pop with pizzazz.

ENHANCED SEQUENCING   If you're giving a how-to or training presentation, visually listing the steps or procedures in a process can help your audience understand a step-by-step process. Showing rather than just describing how to do something is more likely to teach your audience how to perform a task or function.[30]

Types of Presentation Aids

Almost anything tangible can be used as a presentation aid, including objects, models, photos, graphs, charts, videos, and audio recordings. Perhaps the most pervasive presentation aid in business and professional settings is PowerPoint slides. Because of the importance and ubiquity of PowerPoint, we'll give special emphasis to the dos and don'ts of PowerPoint in a later section. For now, let's consider the various types of presentation aids a speaker might use.

OBJECTS   Objects add interest because they are tangible. They can be touched, smelled, heard, or even tasted, as well as seen. Make sure any object you use is large enough to be seen clearly by your listeners. One powerful prop you can use is a copy of the daily newspaper if you are referring to a late-breaking news event—it adds immediacy, and you can connect the events of the day with your topic.

MODELS   If it is not possible to bring the object you would like to show your audience, consider showing them a model. Again, make sure the model is big enough for your listeners to see.

DRAWINGS   Today, unless they are artists, most speakers use computer-generated drawings. Yet there may be some situations in which a small freehand drawing on a flipchart or whiteboard may be more appropriate, such as when you want to show a very simple diagram.

PHOTOGRAPHS   A photo can show objects, places, and people that can't be illustrated with drawings or that an audience cannot view directly. To be sure that a printed photo will be effective as a presentation aid for a large audience, enlarge it or project it. A digital photo can be easily added to a PowerPoint presentation.

GRAPHS   A graph is a pictorial representation of statistical data in an easy-to-understand format. Most listeners find that graphs help make data more concrete. Graphs are particularly effective in showing overall trends and relationships among data. The four most common types of graphs are line graphs, bar graphs, pie graphs, and picture graphs. Presentation software programs such as PowerPoint let you quickly and easily create charts and graphs.

   Line graphs show relationships between two or more variables and they organize statistical data to show overall trends. A line graph can cover a greater span of time or numbers than a bar graph without looking cluttered or confusing. A simple line graph, as in Figures 12.1 and 12.2, communicates better than a cluttered one.

terms & definitions

Line graph a graph that shows trends over time and relationships among variables.

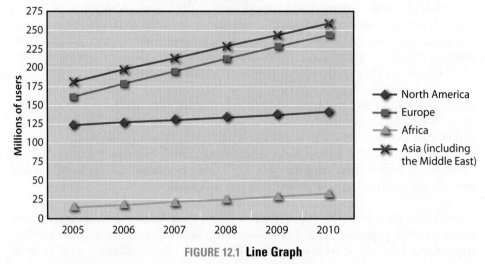

FIGURE 12.1 Line Graph

Source: http://www.ferris.com/research-library/industry-statistics/

A **bar graph** consists of flat areas—bars—of various lengths to represent data or information, as shown in Figure 12.3.

A **pie graph** shows the general distribution of data. Pie graphs are especially useful in helping your listeners quickly see how data are distributed in a given category, as in Figure 12.4.

Picture graphs look less formal and less intimidating than other kinds of graphs. One of the advantages of picture graphs is that they need few words or labels, which makes them easier for your audience to read.

Here's another tip: Consider using a simple graph to show positive news, such as an upward sloping line to communicate that sales are up or a simple downward line to indicate

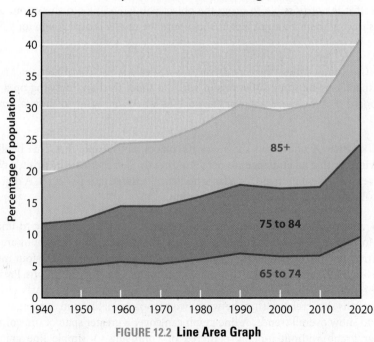

FIGURE 12.2 Line Area Graph

Source: S. Roberts, *Who We Are Now* (New York: Times Books, 2004), 50.

terms & definitions

Bar graph a graph that uses bars of different lengths to represent statistical data.

Pie graph a circular graph that shows the distribution of data as a proportion of a total.

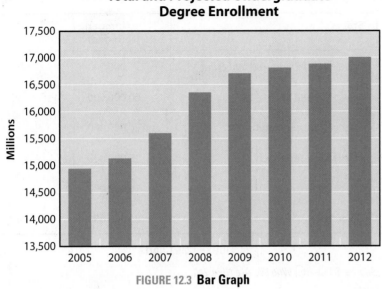

FIGURE 12.3 **Bar Graph**

Source: http://nces.ed.gov/programs/coe/2010/section1/table-hep-1.asp

that customer complaints are down. Use a more detailed (but still clear and easy-to-read) chart when you have a more complex point to make or the news is less than positive.[31]

CHARTS Charts summarize and present a great deal of information in a small amount of space. They are easy to use, reuse, and enlarge. They can also be displayed in a variety of ways. You can use a flipchart, a poster, or an overhead projector, which can project a giant image of your chart on a screen. Simple, professional-looking, large charts using a large font, such as 24-point type, are best. Figure 12.5 shows an example of a chart.

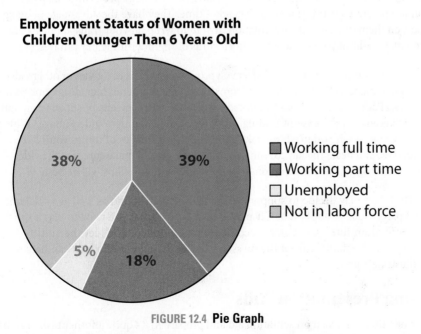

FIGURE 12.4 **Pie Graph**

Source: S. Roberts, *Who We Are Now*, 42.

Marital Status in the United States

Status	Number (rounded)	%
Population 15 years old and older	221,000,000	100.0
Never married	60,000,000	27
Married (not separated)	120,000,000	54
Married but separated	5,000,000	2
Widowed	15,000,000	7
Divorced	22,000,000	10

FIGURE 12.5 **Charts**

Source: S Roberts, *Who We Are Now,* 244.

FLIPCHARTS A flipchart consists of a large pad of paper resting on an easel. You can either prepare your visual aids on the paper before your presentation or draw on the paper while speaking. Flipcharts are easy to use; during your presentation, you need only flip the page to reveal or create your next visual. If you prepare your flipchart ahead of time, leave a blank page between your images so you can reveal your information when you are ready to refer to it. Lettering should be two or three inches tall. Flipcharts are best used when you have brief information to display or when you want to summarize comments from audience members during a presentation.

OVERHEAD TRANSPARENCIES Overhead projectors project images drawn or printed on clear sheets of plastic, called transparencies, onto a screen so a large group can see the images. As with other types of presentation aids, overhead transparencies have been replaced by PowerPoint slides. We mention them here because some speakers like to make overhead transparencies of their PowerPoint slides as a backup in case there are technical problems with the PowerPoint slides. As with PowerPoint slides, an overhead projector transparency permits you to prepare your transparencies ahead of time. They have the advantage of being able to mark on them during your presentation. If you do write on your transparencies during your presentation, limit yourself to a few short words or to underlining key phrases.

VIDEO DVDs (digital video disks) let you project short clips of movies or other video images for your audience. DVDs and images from digital video cameras, including cameras in mobile phones, iPods, and iPads, have replaced videotapes as the means of showing an audience a movie because of the ease of finding, freezing, and cueing up a video image. With a video camera, you can, if you need to, make your own video images of things you'd like your audience to see and hear. The key to using any video image is to make sure that the video selection doesn't take over your presentation. In most instances, short clips will be best.

AUDIO You may decide to support your message with sound as well as visual images. An MP3 player such as an iPod or CD player, may be just what you need to play a short excerpt of music or an interview you've recorded. As with video, don't let the audio sound track become the primary focus of the message. Used sparingly, audio aids can help set a mood or illustrate a point.

Using Presentation Aids

It's one thing to select a presentation aid and prepare it; it's quite another task to actually use your presentation aid in your talk. Just as there is an art to developing presentation aids, there is an art to using them. As you review the following list of suggestions, you may think that some of them are fairly obvious (like making sure that the presentation aid is big enough to be seen). However, even some of the most seasoned presenters violate these tips and techniques.

REHEARSE WITH YOUR PRESENTATION AID   The opening sentences of your sales presentation to the marketing team extolling the virtues of the new product should *not* be the first time you use your PowerPoint slides. Practice with your presentation aids until you feel at ease with them.

MAKE EYE CONTACT WITH YOUR AUDIENCE, NOT WITH YOUR PRESENTATION AID   Don't be tempted to talk to your presentation aid rather than to your audience. Your focus should remain on your audience. Of course, you will need to glance at your visual aid to make sure that it's the correct one and it isn't upside down. But do not keep looking at your PowerPoint slide, chart, or poster; keep making eye contact with your audience.

TALK ABOUT YOUR PRESENTATION AID, DON'T JUST SHOW IT   "Well, here are our production statistics for the second quarter," says Meredith. "Now let's move to the third quarter. And here are the fourth-quarter statistics." Don't do what Meredith just did—she simply projected information and data without explaining. Remember that a presentation is a talk, not just a slide show. Visual support performs the same function as verbal support. It helps you communicate an idea. Make sure that your audience knows what that idea is.

"I'll pause for a moment so you can let this information sink in."

DO NOT PASS OBJECTS AMONG MEMBERS OF YOUR AUDIENCE   It's usually not a good idea to pass a small object or handout around from listener to listener while you are speaking. Your listeners will stop being listeners and will focus on the object that is coming their way instead of on your message. It may be best to let people observe your object after your talk. Or, if the audience is only two or three rows deep, you can hold up the object and move in close to audience members to show it while you maintain focus and control.

USE HANDOUTS EFFECTIVELY   Audiences in many business and professional settings often expect to be looking at written material you've distributed while they are listening to your presentation. The problem is, however, that your listeners may focus on the written message instead of on your oral message. Consider these tips for using handouts:

- Only distribute handouts during the presentation if your listeners must refer to the material while you're talking about it. If your listeners don't need to have the handout material while you speak, tell them you will distribute a summary of the key ideas at the end of your talk.

- If you see that your listeners are giving the written material more attention than they are giving you, tell them where in the handout you want them to focus. For example, you could say, "I see that many of you are interested in the third page of the report. I'll discuss those points in just a few moments. Let's look at the information on page one."

- After distributing your handouts, ask audience members to keep the material face down until you're ready to talk about it; this will help listeners focus on you rather than on your handout.

- Number the pages of your handout material so you can easily and quickly direct audience members to specific pages. You may even add numbers to paragraphs to help point your listeners to specific passages.

Be sure to rehearse with your presentation aid and to time its display to control your audience's attention. A skilled presenter knows when to show a presentation aid and when to put it away.

- By projecting the handout on an overhead projector or a PowerPoint slide, you can nonverbally let your audience members know which page of the material they should be looking at.

TIME THE USE OF VISUALS TO CONTROL YOUR LISTENERS' ATTENTION A skilled presenter knows when to show a supporting visual and when to put it away. It's typically not a wise idea to begin your speech with splashy, eye-popping graphs or charts while you are presenting your opening remarks. Your visuals would just compete with your verbal message. Time the display of your visuals to coincide with your discussion of the information contained in them.

- Remove your visual aids when you move to your next point.

- Have your PowerPoint image already cued up and ready to display.

- If necessary, ask a colleague beforehand to help you change slides or transparencies; if you do ask someone to assist you, it's best to have a short rehearsal so that the presentation is professional and polished.

No matter what medium you plan to use, you should give your audience enough time to absorb what you place in front of their eyes and to listen carefully to your verbal message before asking them to shift their attention to another image.

Designing Presentation Aids

Whether you are using PowerPoint slides, a whiteboard, or a flipchart, there are some basic principles to keep in mind when designing visual images for a speech. Although we'll offer several specific suggestions for developing PowerPoint slides later in the chapter, the following suggestions are basic principles of "visual rhetoric" that can help you develop appealing as well as effective visual messages.[32]

MAKE THEM EASY TO SEE The most violated principle of visual aids is also the most basic: Make visual images and words large enough to be seen easily by everyone in your audience. If you don't do anything else, do this: Make messages big.

MAKE THEM SIMPLE Simple and brief are usually better than cluttered and lengthy. Limit text to essential words or phrases. If you have a considerable amount of information, use two or three simple charts or slides rather than putting all of your information on one visual. Keep the emphasis on your speech rather than on your visual message. Simple drawings and easy-to-grasp images or pictures have more power than images that take the viewer a long time to decipher.

"For God's sake, Edwards. Put the laser pointer away."

ALIGNMENT The alignment you choose for your text and images also affects the open space on the visual aid and directs the reader's eye. Alignment can be flush left, flush right, or centered. Centered alignment is often effective for titles, but centered body text can be difficult to read. A flush left or right alignment makes the text look crisp and allows the eye to move easily from point to point.

DEVELOP A CONSISTENT VISUAL THEME Choose one basic design and color scheme and use it throughout your presentation. Repeating words, symbols, styles, or fonts throughout the presentation conveys a sense of unity. Yes, repetition can be boring, so you may want to vary your visuals a little, but keep in mind that a consistent graphic theme will help your audience process and remember complex information.

COMMUNICATE NUMERICAL DATA VISUALLY Numbers and statistical summaries are abstract. Listeners like concrete, visual information. A well-developed graph can often convey the information that you wish to present without requiring your audience to absorb and interpret complex numerical data. If your listeners need or want more detailed data, consider sharing it with them in a handout that you distribute after your talk. If you absolutely must present complex data during your talk, walk the audience through the information rather than just pointing to a number-laden sheet of paper or briefly displaying a complex graph.

CHOOSE A FONT WITH CARE A font is a typeface of a particular style and design. Font size is measured in points; a point is 1/72 of an inch. The larger the point size, the larger the letters.

A single font (typeface) includes a collection of uppercase and lowercase letters, as well as numbers, symbols, and punctuation that have a consistent structure and form. Each font has a name, and many have variations in size, weight, and spacing. Fonts are divided into four types: serif, sans serif, script, and decorative, as shown in Figure 12.6.

1. **Serif fonts** (like those in the text you are reading) have lines (serifs) at the tops and bottoms of the letters. Serif fonts are easier to read for longer passages, because the serifs guide the eye from one letter to the next.

2. **Sans serif fonts** do not have extra lines, and all the lines in the letters are of uniform thickness.

3. **Script fonts** imitate handwriting, but are precise and uniform. They can be fancy and complicated as well as hard to read, so be cautious about using them.

4. **Decorative fonts** are designed to convey a feeling or tone. The letters in a decorative font may even be stylized drawings (for example, flowers) in the shape of letters. Use these fonts sparingly for emphasis.

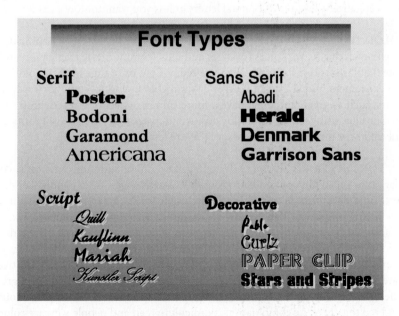

FIGURE 12.6 Typefaces Grouped by Font Type

Communication Skills FOR A **Digital Age**

Beyond PowerPoint: Power Tools to Make Your Point

A wide array of technological tools can enhance your ability to present your message to others. In addition to PowerPoint, a technology that according to researchers may be losing some of its novelty because it's often overused (or used inappropriately), consider using some of the newest technology to amp up the power of your message.

- MP3 players or iPods, the ubiquitous music storage and playback technology, can easily be connected to speakers to provide audio information to enhance your message. You not only can supplement your message with music, but recording and downloading prerecording interviews can easily be used to supplement your speech.

- iPads and other tablet computers can play video, audio, and YouTube and other Internet-based information to easily add visual and audio support to your message. Using Wi-Fi or cellular phone technology, although small in size, can connect you to websites from around the globe.

- Video projectors are now the size of a pack of playing cards. With contemporary technology you no longer need to lug around even medium-size projectors that just a few years ago were bigger than a breadbox. Small, compact projectors let you easily use video support even in a meeting of two or three people.

- Many professional presentation venues now have capabilities to receive instant feedback from audience members. Whether it's a handheld electronic clicker that listeners use to push buttons to respond to options given to the audience, permanent mounted buttons on desks or seat arm rests, there are new ways to find out precisely how your listeners are responding to you and your message. Some presenters are inviting listeners to use their Twitter or Facebook account to tweet or send messages to the speaker to assess immediate reactions to a message.

Regardless of the style of font you use, your visuals must be big enough to be seen by people in the back row of your audience. Consider using 44-point type for titles, 32-point type for subtitles or for text if there is no subtitle, and 28-point type for the text if there is also a subtitle.

DON'T USE ALL CAPITAL LETTERS It's harder to read a message in all capital letters than one that doesn't use all capital letters.[33] Because our eyes are used to seeing contrasting shapes, when we read we recognize not only the individual letters but also the shapes of the words. A word in all capital letters is less familiar to us; we have more practice reading words that aren't capitalized. So don't use capital letters unless you want to slow a reader down.

USE COLOR TO CREATE A MOOD AND MAINTAIN ATTENTION Graphic designers have long known that warm colors (oranges and reds) communicate excitement and interest. (Note that fast-food restaurants often use red, yellow, or orange in their color schemes to create excitement and stimulate hunger.) Warm colors tend to come forward, whereas cool colors, such as green and blue, have a more calming effect and recede into the background. Consider using warm colors for positive messages (for example, "Profits are up") and cool colors for more negative messages ("We're losing money").

DESIGN FOR CONTRAST If you're designing PowerPoint slides or overheads, consider using dark type on a light colored background. Research suggests that audiences don't like white text on a dark background.[34] Black, dark blue, or dark red type stands out crisply from a white, light gray, or light yellow background. Two different colors of text on one background color are usually sufficient. To unify your presentation, consider using the same color for all of your backgrounds and then varying the complementary colors you use for the text. The use of purple, for example, against a blue background is not effective; both colors are dark, so the purple letters don't stand out. Yellow against a blue background is more effective because the colors are contrasting yet harmonious. Be cautions about using green and red together; the combination is difficult to read and people who are color-blind will not be able to distinguish between these two colors.

USE BLACK AND WHITE EFFECTIVELY If your budget or equipment limits you to using only black and white, you can still use contrast to create attractive graphics. By choosing contrasting typefaces, spacing text widely or more compactly, using larger or smaller text, and using both bold and lightface text, you can create differences in textual emphasis.

USE A STORYBOARD TO PLAN YOUR MESSAGE A *storyboard* is a technique for planning how words and pictures will be used in a presentation. Each page of a storyboard is a sheet of paper or a flipchart page that discusses a single point in the presentation. The point is described in sentences, phrases, or key words and then illustrated with rough sketches to help you visualize how the words and images will work together in your presentation. Experienced speakers sometimes use storyboards as a substitute for a detailed formal outline when they are preparing a presentation.

To use this method, first, as when planning any message, think about your audience. Then, with your audience in mind, make a list of the main points you'd like to cover, knowing that each one will become a page on your storyboard.

Once you have decided on your main points, you can begin creating your storyboards. Divide a piece of paper down the middle and label it "Storyboard." In the left column, write the main idea followed by notes about supporting points. In the right column, sketch the visuals you plan to include. Don't worry if you are not a skilled artist. These sketches are simply placeholders for the finished visual aid that you will prepare later on a computer.

When you draft your sketches, be conservative about the number of visuals you plan to use. Select key supporting points to be illustrated with a few memorable words or images.

When you finish your storyboards, convert them into a more formal presentation outline. Prepare your PowerPoint slides or whatever other form of visual you plan to use. Then practice with your outline and visuals to ensure that your visuals are large enough, that they communicate your key points, and that you talk about them as you show them.

Using PowerPoint

According to Microsoft, in the early twenty-first century, over 30 million PowerPoint presentations occurred every business day.[35] That number has undoubtedly increased. Yet, according to surveys of the people attending those presentations, there are a lot of bad PowerPoint presentations. What are the biggest problems with PowerPoint presentations? According to a survey of business professionals, these are the top five PowerPoint problems:

1. The speaker read the slides to us.
2. The text was too small.
3. There were full sentences instead of bullet points.
4. Poor use of color: Slides were hard to read.
5. There was annoying flying text or graphics (sometimes with annoying sound).[36]

The advantage of PowerPoint is that it is relatively easy to use, and it adds a professional look to a presentation. But it also has the potential to create problems if used improperly. PowerPoint images can distract from your verbal messages; listeners may be tempted to focus on the visual message and not hear your verbal message. Many listeners may feel they're watching a competing TV program being projected behind the speaker while they are trying to hear the message. If overused, PowerPoint can turn a live speaking event into a canned media presentation that may lack immediacy. Used effectively and appropriately, however, PowerPoint slides can add to rather than detract from your presentation.[37]

KEEP SIGHTS AND SOUNDS SIMPLE In most aspects of communication, simple is better. The purpose of a presentation aid is to support rather than to compete with your message. Resist the temptation to add sound effects. Cute sounds often lose their novelty after the first slide or two and can become irritating. *You* should be the soundtrack, not your computer.

"I need someone well versed in the art of torture—do you know PowerPoint?"

APPROPRIATELY TIME THE DISPLAY OF YOUR POWERPOINT SLIDES It's best to introduce a slide verbally before you show it. By talking about your slide first you let your audience know you are the master of the material rather than needing the slide as a prompt to speak. As one expert noted, "You don't want your audience thinking that if the electricity goes down, you would suddenly be at a loss for words."[38] What we're suggesting is that you *tell and show*, rather than *showing and telling*.[39]

REPEAT VISUAL ELEMENTS TO CREATE UNITY Use a common visual element, such as a bullet or a symbol, at the beginning of each word or phrase on a list. Use common color schemes and spacing to give your visuals coherence. Also, avoid mixing fonts in the same presentation. You get a professional, polished look if you use a similar visual style for each of your images.

USE CLIP ART AND OTHER IMAGES Clip art consists of images that are in print form or stored in a computer file. You can easily incorporate these images into your visuals, as shown in Figure 12.7, even if you did not excel in art class. But try to avoid using the cartoonish clip art that comes with the PowerPoint program; most people have seen those same stick figures or graphics that come prepackaged with the software. Many clip art graphics are available on the Internet for sale for a nominal fee. Or customize your PowerPoint slides by taking your own photos or use the software program Photoshop.

ALLOW PLENTY OF TIME TO PREPARE YOUR PRESENTATION AIDS Consider developing your PowerPoint slides as you are developing your message. Using the storyboarding method we discussed earlier can help you integrate your visual message with your verbal message. Waiting until the last minute to develop your visuals can result in a sloppy, amateurish presentation that will detract from your credibility.

USE WORDS SPARINGLY Research suggests that the best use of PowerPoint is to present pictures, images, and other non-text information.[40] Don't clutter a slide with lots of text;

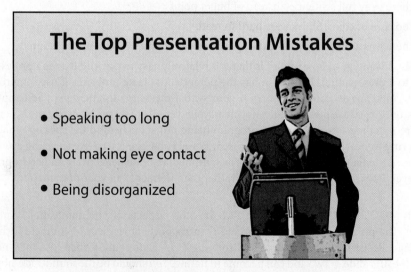

FIGURE 12.7 Clip Art Can be Used to Illustrate Visuals

let your speech communicate your message and use PowerPoint to support your points. Using too many words on your slides tempts listeners to become readers instead of listeners. A presentation is powerful because it's live and happening now. Used poorly, PowerPoint slides can make listeners assume the catatonic pose of watching TV rather than participating in a live presentation. Using words sparingly on your PowerPoint slides keeps the cognitive and linguistic focus on you rather than on prepared words and text.

Preparing a Presentation with PowerPoint

PowerPoint is ubiquitous—it's everywhere. Although you can easily learn to use this software program with the built-in tutorial that comes with the software, here are a few tips.[41]

CREATE CONSISTENCY PowerPoint is designed to give your presentations a consistent appearance. In addition to choosing from the menu of design templates, you can use the program's Slide Master, Title Master, and Color Schemes features to control the look of your slides.

The Slide Master controls the format and placement of the titles and text you type on slides; the Title Master controls the format and placement of the title slide and any other slide you designate as a title slide. Masters also hold background items such as graphics that you want to appear on every slide.

Color Schemes are sets of eight balanced colors designed to be used as the main colors of a slide presentation—for text, background, fill, accents, and so on. Each different element on a slide is automatically given a color in the scheme. You can pick a color scheme for an individual slide or for an entire presentation. If you create unique slides—for example, slides with backgrounds that differ from the master or fill colors that aren't part of the master color scheme—these slides retain their uniqueness even when you change the master. If you change your mind later, you can always restore slides you altered to the master format.

ADD TEXT The easiest way to add text to a slide is to type directly into any placeholder on the slide. When you want to add text outside a placeholder or shape, you can use the Text Box tool on the Drawing toolbar. But as we've noted, use text sparingly. Too many words may cause your listeners to tune you out and turn them into readers rather than listeners. It's a better idea to put more details in your handouts than to display all of the details in your PowerPoint slides.

INSERT PICTURES PowerPoint comes with its own set of pictures in the Clip Gallery, a wide variety of clip art that makes it easy for you to dress up your presentations with professionally designed images.

Select a picture by clicking Insert Clip Art and then clicking on Clip Art or Pictures. The Clip Gallery includes a handy Find feature to help you locate just the right images for your presentation. You can also insert pictures and scanned photographs from other programs and locations.

INSERT CHARTS AND GRAPHS PowerPoint includes subprograms you can use to add charts, scanned pictures, and equations to your presentations. Organization Chart, Graph, Photo Editor, and Equation Editor all create embedded objects that you can insert into a presentation. When you embed data in a PowerPoint document, you can edit it in your document without having to return to the source files. When you create or modify a chart, a scanned picture, or an equation in your presentation, PowerPoint subprogram toolbars replace the PowerPoint menus and toolbars.

PRINT A PRESENTATION You can print your entire presentation—the slides, outline, speaker's notes, and audience handouts—in either color or black and white. To print your presentation, open the file and choose whether you want to print slides, handouts, note pages, or an outline. Then identify the slides to be printed and the number of copies you want. When you print handouts, you can print one, two, three, or six slides on a page; or you can use the Microsoft Word Send To command (under the File menu) and then use Word to print other layout variations.

RECAP

Tips for Preparing and Using Presentation Aids

Preparing Presentation Aids

- Keep drawings simple and large.
- Be sure photographs are large enough to be seen easily.
- Limit the amount of information you put on a single chart or PowerPoint slide.
- Keep graphs simple and uncluttered.
- Use only brief excerpts and clips from DVDs or video- or audiotapes.
- Be sure that any models you use are large enough to be seen easily.

Using Presentation Aids

- Rehearse with your presentation aids.
- Rehearse with people who will assist you with presentation aids.
- Have any needed equipment set up and ready to go before you speak.
- Maintain eye contact with your audience, not with your presentation aids.
- Explain your presentation aids.
- Time the display of your presentation aids to coincide with your discussion of them.
- Do not pass objects, pictures, or other small items among your audience.
- Use handouts effectively.

You can create notes pages while you're creating your presentation and then use these pages as speaker notes when you give a slide show. You can also print handouts of your slides for the audience.

USE SPECIAL EFFECTS SPARINGLY   Transitions and animations, when used in moderation, can add interest to your presentation, help highlight important points, and control the flow of information. PowerPoint comes with music, sounds, and videos you can play during your slide shows. You can also animate text, graphics, sounds, movies, and other objects. You can insert a sound or video clip where you want it to play during a slide. But use these special effects the way you would add hot chili powder to chili—sparingly. Too much "spice" distracts from the main meat of your message.

Wrap-Up

The four types of delivery are manuscript, memorized, impromptu, and extemporaneous speaking. In most business and professional settings, extemporaneous speaking—using an outline and speaking conversationally—is best.

Regardless of the specific delivery method used, these several principles will serve you well when speaking to North American listeners:

- Look up: Maximize your eye contact with your listeners and don't look over their heads or bury your eyes in your notes.

- Move meaningfully: Use appropriate gestures, movement, and posture to reinforce key ideas in your presentation.

- Express emotions: The key source of expressing your emotion to your listeners will be via your facial expressions and your voice.

- Look good: If you're not sure about the dress code, ask others who know the audience expectations what you should wear.

- Speak clearly: Use appropriate volume, inflection, and intensity.
- Speak up: Use a microphone appropriately when needed.

Pay special attention to your use of visual as well as auditory aids when delivering a presentation.

- Presentation aids include objects, models, people, drawings, photographs, maps, charts, graphs, video images, and audio.
- The most ubiquitous method of displaying images (as well as sound) in professional settings is through the use of PowerPoint.

Guidelines for using any type of presentation aid include:

- Select the right presentation for the audience, occasion, and room.
- Make the presentation aid simple, clear, and big.
- As you prepare to use any presentation aid rehearse with it and look at your audience, not at your presentation aid, both during rehearsal and during your presentation.

Reviewing Key Terms

Manuscript speaking *297*

Memorized speaking *298*

Impromptu speaking *298*

Extemporaneous speaking *299*

Articulation *304*

Dialect *305*

Pitch *305*

Inflection *305*

Presentation aid *310*

Line graph *311*

Bar graph *312*

Pie graph *312*

Serif font *317*

Sans serif font *317*

Script font *317*

Decorative font *317*

The Principle Points

Principle One: Be aware of your communication with yourself and others.

- If your subject is sensitive or your information is classified, be cautious and noncommittal in any impromptu remarks you might be asked to make.
- Pay attention to your nonverbal delivery when you rehearse your presentation.

Principle Two: Effectively use and interpret verbal messages.

- Give a manuscript or memorized speech when exact wording is critical.
- Phrase your ideas so that they will be clear, accurate, and memorable.
- Do not memorize an extemporaneous presentation word-for-word; vary the ways in which you express ideas and information.

Principle Three: Effectively use and interpret nonverbal messages.

- When you deliver a manuscript speech, try to memorize an entire sentence at a time so you can maintain eye contact throughout the sentence.
- Move during your presentation to signal the beginning of a new idea or major point, or to signal a transition from a serious idea to a humorous one or vice versa.
- To heighten your credibility and to increase listener learning, use eye contact to let your audience know you are interested in them and ready to talk to them.
- Vary the volume and rate of your voice to emphasize ideas and sustain the audience's interest.

Principle Four: Listen and respond thoughtfully to others.

- Use eye contact to help you determine how your audience members are responding to you.
- Listen to what audience members tell you before and after your presentation to give you insights about how to best deliver you message.

- If possible, rehearse your presentation for someone and seek feedback about both your content and delivery.

Principle Five: Appropriately adapt messages to others.

- Although audiences today generally expect speakers to use everyday language and a conversational delivery style, you will need to adapt your delivery to audiences of different sizes and from different cultures.

- Adapt your gestures to your audience. Use bolder, more sweeping, and more dramatic gestures with large audiences. Tone down gestures if you are speaking to a culturally diverse audience who might prefer a more subdued style.

- Adapt to your audience's expectations for your appearance.

Applying Your Skills

1. Attend or watch on television or YouTube a political campaign speech or a speech broadcast on C-SPAN by a business or professional leader. Pay particular attention to the leader's delivery. Critique his or her use of gestures, movement, posture, eye contact, facial expression, vocal delivery, and appearance. What advice would you give this speaker based on the principles of effective delivery presented in this chapter?

2. Imagine you are a speech consultant to the chief executive officer of a large paper company. Your boss is about to begin working on her annual "State of the Company" address, which she gives to an audience of about 500 employees, stockholders, and community members. This year, she wants to enliven her presentation of sales statistics, stock prices, and the state of the physical plant with some presentation aids. Make a list of suggestions for the types of visual aids she might employ, and offer suggestions for using each one effectively.

3. Improving Your Speech Delivery

   Make a video of your speech as you rehearse it. Before presenting your speech to your audience, use the following evaluation form to evaluate your delivery.

Delivery Style

- Did I use an extemporaneous delivery style?
- Did I use appropriate notes, but not read or memorize my speech?

Eye Contact

- Did I establish eye contact with my audience before I began my speech?
- Did I maintain eye contact during my speech?

Physical Delivery

- Did I use gestures in a natural way?
- Did I have an appropriate posture?

Facial Expression

- Did I have an appropriate facial expression?
- Did I vary my facial expression?

Vocal Delivery

- Did I speak loud enough to be heard clearly?
- Did I speak with vocal variety?

4. Imagine a colleague of yours will be delivering a ten-minute report from the national office to twenty branch offices via web camera. The colleagues who will listen to your message will be seated in conference rooms around the country and your image will be projected on large screens. Based on the principles and strategies provided in this chapter, what suggestions would you give your colleague who will be making the Webcam presentation?

Achieving Your Presentation Goals: Informing, Persuading, and Relating

chapter outline

After reading this chapter, you should be able to

- Describe and use effective strategies to present a briefing, a report, and a public relations presentation.

- List and illustrate the nine steps in designing and delivering a training presentation.

- Identify and describe four strategies to motivate and persuade listeners.

- Define and provide an example of inductive reasoning, deductive reasoning, reasoning by analogy, and reasoning by cause and effect.

- List and explain eight logical reasoning fallacies.

- Explain three ways to use emotional appeals ethically and appropriately in a persuasive presentation.

- Describe and illustrate four ways to organize a persuasive message.

- Design and deliver an effective sales presentation.

- Describe and give examples of special occasion speaking situations, including introducing others, presenting and receiving an award, and giving a toast.

Mrs. P. F. E. Albee first started selling perfume door to door in 1886. Entrepreneur David McConnell, intrigued by the idea of selling cosmetics in homes rather than in a store, established the California Perfume Company. In just twenty years McConnell had 10,000 women selling more that 110 products door-to-door. The company changed its name to Avon in 1928. Although the company flourished in the mid-twentieth century, by 1990 Avon was in big trouble. With more women in the daytime labor force, the "Ding dong, Avon calling" slogan was not a message for success because selling door-to-door was much more challenging.

When Andrea Jung joined Avon in 1993 as a consultant, she knew the company could do better. She joined the marketing department in 1994 and, because of her communication talents and sales instincts, became CEO in 1999.[1] Andrea reengineered the company from top to bottom by rejuvenating the brand and establishing a trendy Flagship store and spa on Fifth Avenue. She also reached out to untapped markets throughout the world. Rather than being perceived as an oldtime line of cosmetics that people bought only in their home, Avon is now recognized as being available in stylish boutiques, online, and at other cosmetic stores around the globe. She also enhanced the sales force by upgrading the use of online sales tools. You can still purchase Avon from individual salespersons, but you have many more options to buy Avon products. Since Andrea took over the company's leadership, the stock price has risen 165 percent. Avon was a $4 billion-a-year company when she became CEO; in 2010 it had grown to a $10 billion company.[2] To remind her of the importance of leadership and being number one, she has a pillow in her New York office that reads, "If you are not the lead dog, the view never changes."

Andrea not only knows how to sell cosmetics. She also knows how to sell "trendy" ideas that change the culture of a company. She is an excellent communicator. As we have emphasized throughout this book, leadership and communication are linked—two sides of the same coin. Andrea was able to reinvent Avon by articulately expressing her vision to her executive colleagues. She also knows something about how to both present and persuade. Her application of the five principles for leadership was the prime factor in her success. She became aware of what needed to be done, communicated well both verbally and nonverbally, listened, and appropriately adapted her message to transform a company. When persuading others it's especially vital that you adapt or customize your message to the listener.

leading **questions**

1. Andrea Jung is a good salesperson. She first had to sell her new colleagues on the idea that Avon needed a makeover before company salespersons could sell more Avon products. What are the characteristics of a good salesperson?

2. Women have made dramatic gains in serving as corporate CEOs and in other top leadership roles, yet there are challenges that women continue to face in achieving top leadership positions. What factors contribute to these challenges? What needs to change for more women to serve in top leadership roles?

terms & definitions

Inform to share information with others to enhance their knowledge or understanding of the information, concepts, or ideas presented.

"Make sure you have finished speaking before your audience has finished listening."

—**Dorothy Sarnoff**

To **inform** is to share information with others to enhance their knowledge or understanding of the information, concepts, or ideas presented. When you inform someone, you assume the role of a teacher by defining, illustrating, clarifying, or elaborating on a topic. In a professional context, briefs, reports, lectures, and training presentations are typical formats for informing others. Speaking to inform others can be a challenging task. The information you communicate to someone else is rarely, if ever, understood exactly as you intend it: Simply presenting information does not mean that communication has occurred. Communication happens when listeners make sense of the information they receive.

To **persuade** someone is to change or reinforce the person's attitudes (likes and dislikes), beliefs (what is perceived to be true or false), values (what is considered good or bad), or behavior. A sales presentation is a type of persuasive presentation you'll commonly encounter in a professional setting. When you interview for a job, you're doing more than simply presenting information about yourself; you're presenting a sales pitch on why the organization should hire you. Informative and persuasive speaking are related processes. A key difference is that in a persuasive presentation, you want the listener to do more than merely remember what you say; you want to change or reinforce what the listener likes, believes, values, or does. Persuasive speakers *intentionally* try to change or reinforce listeners' feelings, ideas, or behavior.

In addition to informing and persuading, there are special occasions on which you will be called on to say a few remarks. These special occasions can be informative, such as when you introduce someone before he or she speaks; but more often they will be ceremonial, such as when you are presenting or receiving an award, giving a toast, or giving a short speech of thanks or congratulations. Throughout the discussion of informative, persuasive, and special occasion speaking, keep in mind the five communication principles for leadership.

Informing Others

Think of the best teacher you ever had. He or she was probably a great lecturer with a special talent for making information clear, interesting, and memorable. As a leader, you no doubt will be called on in your professional life to present information to others. Leaders explain and help keep others informed. Skilled leaders are also expected to be skilled educators. What do effective leader/educators do to communicate information to others? They simplify so listeners understand the message, pace the information to avoid information overload, directly address the needs and problems of their listeners, and reinforce their messages nonverbally or visually.

USE SIMPLE IDEAS Mark Twain told a story about a Missouri farmer who ran for the state legislature five times but lost each election. He didn't lose because he didn't practice his campaign speeches; he gave his speeches to his cows each morning. The problem was, according to Twain, that he used "high-falutin'" words when he should have used shorter terms. He described his audience as "my enlightened constituents" and suggested he was trying to "obtain a mandate" for his "legislative mission." During one of his morning oration rehearsals, one of his cows knocked out his front teeth. He could then only use one-syllable words. The result: He won every election in his career from that day on.[3]

When you inform others, your job is to get your ideas across to your audience, *not* to see how much information you can cram in. The simpler your ideas and phrases, the greater the chance that your audience will remember them. We don't mean you should talk down to your audience. Listeners can sense a speaker's superior know-it-all attitude, and they won't like it. Simplify your message, but don't be condescending.

PACE INFORMATION FLOW Organize your talk so that you present an even stream of information, rather than bunch up a number of significant details around one point. If you present too much new information too quickly, you may overwhelm your audience, and your listeners' ability to understand may falter.

USE ADULT LEARNING STRATEGIES If your audience consists of adult listeners, you will need to ensure that you deliver your message in the way that adults learn best. **Adult learners** prefer the following:[4]

- To be given information they can use immediately
- To be actively involved in the learning process

terms & definitions

Persuade to change or reinforce a person's attitudes, beliefs, values, or behavior.

Adult learners people who prefer to be given information they can use immediately, to be actively involved in the learning process, to connect their life experiences with the new information they learn, to know how the new information is relevant to their busy lives, to know how the information will solve a problem, and to receive information that is relevant to their needs.

- To connect their life experiences with the new information they learn
- To know how the new information is relevant to their busy lives
- To know how the information will solve a problem
- To receive information that is relevant to their needs

Most people who work in business have in-baskets on their desks to hold work that must be done. Similarly, each of us has a kind of "mental in-basket," an agenda of what we want or need from a presentation. Remember the characteristics of adult learners and the importance of adapting your message to others. You will hold your audience's interest, and also have more success in informing them, if you tailor your information to address what is in your audience's literal or metaphorical "in-basket."

REINFORCE IDEAS NONVERBALLY   You can also signal the importance of a point with nonverbal emphasis. Gestures serve the purpose of accenting or emphasizing key phrases, as italics do in written communication. A well-placed pause can emphasize or reinforce a point. Pausing just before or just after making an important point will focus attention on your thought. Raising or lowering your voice can also reinforce a key idea. Movement can help emphasize major ideas. Moving from behind the lectern to tell a personal anecdote can signal that something special and more intimate is about to be said. Finally, in business and professional settings you will likely present briefings, reports, public relations sales presentations, and training sessions. Photos, images, charts, and other visual information may be just what your listeners need to better understand your key ideas.

Presenting Briefings

A **briefing** (or a *brief*), as you might guess from the name, is a short talk that provides information to an audience. A briefing can focus on what has happened in the past, what is currently happening on a given project or topic, or what may happen in the future. The military, public safety organizations (police departments, security departments), medical organizations, and other organizations that need clear, short summaries of information almost exclusively rely on briefings to ensure the exchange of information.

Because briefings are short (from five to fifteen minutes), they typically don't have an extended or formal introduction. You should still be mindful of catching your listeners' attention, but not with a lengthy story or illustration. Just get to your points after a very short overview. Listeners expect a brief to be quick. Whereas in a more formal fifteen-minute presentation the introductory remarks and overview could take one-and-a-half minutes, for a briefing the introductory remarks may take thirty seconds or less. Beginning with a short question or stating the purpose of your briefing is typically expected.

Because several briefs are often presented one after another, the first brief may provide a longer introduction to introduce the briefings that will follow. For example, if you're giving a briefing about the income and loss statement for the past quarter and you're part of a four-person team, each of whom is sharing information, provide a short overview of your message, present your key ideas, summarize them, link to what the next person will say, and sit down.

The organizational pattern for briefings is usually topical or chronological. It's still appropriate to use transition phases and signposts ("I have three points to make. First, . . ."), but the transitional phrases are shorter and less pronounced than in a more extended informative presentation.

Some briefings can be quite formal, and listeners may expect a no-nonsense delivery style with little use of humor and lots of information. In some organizational cultures, however, a briefing is expected to be informal and casual. It's important to be aware of your audience as you make decisions on how to customize your briefing content.

Presenting Reports

A **report** is a summary of what has been accomplished in the past or an update on a project. In contrast to a briefing, a report is often a longer, more detailed summary of a past,

terms & definitions

Briefing a short talk that provides information to an audience.

Report a summary of what has been accomplished in the past or an update on a project.

present, or future event. For example, a briefing might include a short update on a new development at a manufacturing plant; a more lengthy report may summarize the history of the plant, what it produces, why the plant is being upgraded, and what is expected to happen to plant operations in the future. A briefing could provide a summary of reactions to the new employee training program; a report on the same topic could include information about the rationale for the new training, a summary of the training content, and a review of methods of assessing the training. Briefs are brief; reports are longer. Some organizations, however, use the terms *report* and *briefing* interchangeably. You may be asked to report on how to increase sales in the next quarter or to present the findings of a market survey your division has conducted in the past several months. Whatever the specific objective of the report, the general purpose is to communicate information or policy; some reports include a persuasive appeal to try some new course of action. Consider the following when preparing a report:

- *Adapt to your audience.* When you are presenting your report, keep in mind that your audience is there to hear you address a particular need or problem. Begin by briefly acknowledging that situation.

- *Present conclusions, then explain how you reached those conclusions.* If you are reporting on a particular project or study, first discuss what your research group decided to do to explore the problem. Then explain how you gathered the information.

- *End a report with solutions or identify what happens next.* Your listeners often want to know what the bottom line is. The most important part of some reports is this outline of new courses of action or changes in present policy. When your report proposes changes, tell your audience what's in it for them—what benefits will accrue to them directly as a result of the new proposal. One business consultant suggests this report technique:

> Tune your audience into radio station WIIFM—What's In It For Me. Tell your listeners where the benefits are for them, and they'll listen to everything you have to say.[5]

In addition to listening to a report, audience members usually expect to receive a hard copy or email version of the report, or at least a summary of the report's key conclusions.

Presenting Public Relations Presentations

In a **public relations presentation**, the speaker is specifically providing information to promote a positive public image for the person or organization the speaker is representing. People who work for professional associations, blood banks, utility companies, government agencies, universities, religious organizations, or charitable institutions, as well as those employed by commercial enterprises, are often called on to speak to an audience about what their organization does or about a special project the organization has taken on. Public relations (PR) speeches are designed to inform the public and improve relations with them—either to present general impressions of the organization, or, because a particular program or situation has raised some questions or concerns, to emphasize the positive features of the organization. So although the purpose of many public relations presentations is to present information, there is often a persuasive edge to public relations messages. The speaker may be trying to enhance or maintain a positive, polished public image.

Here are some suggestions for developing PR presentations:

- Often a PR speech should simply describe the virtues and positive aspects of the policy or program the speaker is promoting. Note how the company, organization, or policy has significant benefits for the listener.

- If a specific problem or issue has prompted the speech, the speaker should identify the concerns. Then he or she should go on to explain how the company or organization can meet the need, solve the problem, or why there really is no problem.

- PR speeches should anticipate criticism and objections, especially if the primary purpose of the speech is to change opinions or address a controversial issue. The speaker should acknowledge the listeners' points of view and then counter potential problems or objections. Explain how the company or organization has carefully worked through potential pitfalls and drawbacks and demonstrate how what may look like a problem can easily be addressed.

Presenting Training Sessions

Many organizations have extensive training departments whose function is to orient new employees to the organization and teach specific job skills, including communication skills. Business and professional organizations invest billions of dollars each year in training employees.[6] **Training** is a special type of informative speaking through which the trainer seeks to develop specific skills in listeners to help them perform a specific job or task more effectively.[7] The goal of a training session is for listeners to be able not just to recall information but to perform specific tasks. Since the goal of training is to implement behavior change, training presentations also seek to motivate listeners to perform the skill or task being taught.

Training is similar to any presentation, in that it's essential to focus on the needs, interests, and backgrounds of listeners. More specifically, what do trainers do, and how does training differ from other types of presentations? Figure 13.1 presents a needs-centered model of training that closely resembles the audience-centered model of communication that we introduced in Chapter 11. The model in Figure 13.1 is called a *needs-centered model* because the primary purpose of any training program is to respond to the learning needs of the trainee. Training that does not address a trainee's needs or specific job functions is not effective training.

What are the differences between training and traditional classroom education? In a nutshell, training focuses more on behavioral learning, whereas education emphasizes the cognitive domain. Table 13.1 summarizes the key differences between training and education.[8]

FIGURE 13.1 A Needs-Centered Training Model

TABLE 13.1	**Comparing Training and Education**
Training	**Education**
Emphasizes doing.	Emphasizes knowing.
Emphasizes achieving a certain level of skill. The goal is for each person to perform the skill correctly.	Emphasizes achieving, often in comparison to what others know. Learning may be assessed by grading "on the curve," in which people are compared with one another.
Is more of a closed system in that there are specific right and wrong ways of performing a skill.	Is more of an open system in that there are often many ways to achieve the goal; creativity and critical thinking are encouraged.
Emphasizes analyzing how to perform specific skills following a prescribed step-by-step approach.	Is less focused on learning a linear sequence of behaviors but on acquiring information.

Drawing on adult learning theory, a trainer should view himself or herself less as a lecturer and more as a facilitator. Adult learners bring their own experiences to the training session; they want to focus on real problems that are in their literal or metaphorical "in-baskets" or on their "to-do" lists. A trainer follows the steps in Figure 13.1 in order to draw on those experiences and equip trainees to address problems.

ANALYZE ORGANIZATIONAL AND TRAINEE NEEDS At the center of the model in Figure 13.1—and the first and crucial ongoing step in any training—is the process of identifying the needs of the organization and those of the specific trainees who will attend the training session. How do you know what trainees need? One way to assess their needs is to ask them what those needs are, using surveys, questionnaires, or interviews. The process of identifying trainee needs is quite similar to analyzing your audience when delivering a presentation. *Every other aspect of designing and delivering a training presentation depends on the needs of the trainees.* In addition to analyzing the needs of individuals, it's also important to consider the needs of the organization.

ANALYZE THE TRAINING TASK Viewing the model in Figure 13.1 as a clock, begin at the top and work your way around clockwise to explore the steps of designing and delivering a training presentation. After you've figured out what trainees need (for example, skill in listening or conflict management), an early critical step in designing a training program is to thoroughly analyze the specific task you want the trainees to perform. You conduct a task analysis. A **task analysis** is a detailed, step-by-step description of precisely what a trainee should do and know in order to perform a particular skill. As the trainer, if you are going to teach someone how to prepare and deliver a sales presentation, you first need to know what the steps in that process are before you teach them to others. You perform a task analysis to create a comprehensive outline of what you would be teaching others if you had unlimited time. You may only have three or four hours to teach a skill, so you may have to focus only on the most critical steps. A task analysis lets you discover what the essential elements of a task are. (Our needs-centered training model is itself a simplified task analysis of how to train someone. Each piece of the model represents an essential step in the process.)

DEVELOP TRAINING OBJECTIVES After you have figured out the steps in teaching a particular skill, it's important to develop objectives or learning outcomes that you want your trainees to achieve. It's important to specify the precise behavior you want trainees to perform at the end of the training. What do training objectives look like? We begin each chapter in this book with a list of learning objectives. Reviewing those objectives will give you an idea of the format and style for training objectives. Training objectives are also similar to the specific purpose statement for a presentation, discussed in Chapter 11. Training objectives specify what you want trainees to be able to do following the training presentation.

terms & definitions

Task analysis a detailed, step-by-step description of precisely what a trainee should do and know in order to perform a particular skill.

A trainer's job is to facilitate rather than to lecture. Demonstrating a skill and then having trainees practice performing it is much more effective than merely describing the skill.

ORGANIZE TRAINING CONTENT Once you have your precise training objectives in hand, you can begin drafting the information that trainees need to know and describing in more detail the behaviors that they will be expected to perform. The most typical organizational patterns for training content include (1) chronological (a step-by-step sequence of what someone does first, second, and so on), (2) by complexity (from simplest or easiest to learn to more complex or more detailed information), and (3) topical (identifying the natural divisions in a topic).

DETERMINE TRAINING METHODS To train someone, you don't just talk to them. Adult learners are not interested in hearing a three- or four-hour lecture; that's not good training. So you'll need to develop effective methods of presenting information to your trainees. You may decide that, rather than presenting a lecture, it would be better to have trainees participate in role-playing situations, discuss a case study, or brainstorm solutions to a problem that you pose. A typical training session may involve a mix of methods, including the following:

- *Tell.* At times it may be important to lecture—but lecture should not be the prime focus of a training presentation. Trainees need to see how to perform a skill and practice their new behavior.
- *Show.* Provide models, videos, or demonstrations of how to perform a skill.
- *Invite.* Ask trainees to practice performing the new skill you are teaching.
- *Encourage.* Provide positive reinforcement when trainees perform the skill the proper way.
- *Correct.* Provide feedback that lets a trainee know when he or she is not performing a skill properly.

SELECT TRAINING RESOURCES Perhaps you've discovered an excellent video that masterfully illustrates the skill you want to teach in the training session. Or, maybe you've decided to use a small-group method and you want trainees to respond to discussion questions. Whether it's a video, a list of discussion questions, PowerPoint presentation slides, or some other type of resource, you'll need to decide what materials you'll need to prepare for the training presentation.

COMPLETE TRAINING PLANS After you've developed your objectives and settled on the content of the training, the methods you will use to present your message, and the resources you need, it is important to develop a comprehensive written plan that describes how you will present your session: a training plan (sometimes called a *lesson plan* in educational settings). There are many different formats. Some training plans are simply detailed outlines of the training content and methods. Other plans offer a complete narrative transcript of the training lesson. Most training plans include a description of the objectives, methods, training content, and training resources needed, along with an estimate of how much time each part of the training will take.

DELIVER TRAINING After developing a well-crafted plan, you are now ready to bring the training presentation to life. You deliver your training not only by presenting lectures, videos, and activities, but also by asking good questions to facilitate class discussion. An effective training presentation should be much more interactive than a speech, although the elements of effective speech delivery (such as eye contact, good posture, effective gestures, and varied vocal inflection) are essential when training others.

ASSESS THE TRAINING PROCESS When the training session is over, a trainer's job is not complete. Effective trainers evaluate how their training was received (Did trainees like it?) and even more importantly, whether trainees learned what they needed to. The ultimate test of a training session is whether trainees can use the new skills on the job. Did the training make a difference?

Each piece of the needs-centered model of training in Figure 13.1 reflects an essential element in what a trainer does. Trainers first and foremost focus on the needs of learners and then carefully develop a training program that meets those needs. Training others well involves more than just talking to them. Effective training develops a specific skill by having trainees practice and receive feedback to master the skills being taught.

Persuading Others

Go to any bookstore and peruse the shelves of books on management and leadership and you'll find books about how to influence others. The best-selling business management book of all time is Dale Carnegie's classic *How to Win Friends and Influence People*. At the heart of influencing others is being able to persuade them. We've noted that to lead is to influence, so being able to persuade others is a vital leadership skill. As we're noted, persuasion is the process of changing or reinforcing attitudes, beliefs, values, or behavior. Think of any great leader, in business or politics, past or present, and undoubtedly you'll be thinking of someone who possessed effective persuasion skills. Not all leaders use the same persuasive methods. Martin Luther King, Jr., and Mahatma Gandhi led through promoting nonviolent means of achieving their goals. In leading the United States out of the Depression and through World War II, Franklin Roosevelt used his skill as a communicator as well as his behind-the-scenes power and influence to achieve his goals. Lee Iacocca (former CEO of Chrysler Corporation), Jack Welch (former CEO of General Electric), and the late Sam Walton (founder of Walmart) are examples of business leaders who could inspire and motivate others.

To develop strong leadership and persuasive skills, you need first to understand principles of persuasion and then learn specific strategies for persuading others.

Principles of Persuasion

How does persuasion work? What makes you reach for your phone so you can call and order a gadget you've just seen advertised on TV? What motivates people to do things that they wouldn't do unless they are persuaded to do so? Let's look at four possible explanations.

PEOPLE RESPOND TO RESOLVE DISSONANCE When you are confronted with information that is inconsistent with your current thinking or feelings, you experience a kind of psychological discomfort called **cognitive dissonance**. You can be persuaded by being convinced that you have a problem and then pointed in a direction that will solve your problem. For example, if you have ever driven an automobile after consuming a drink or two, then seen a public service announcement from Mothers Against Drunk Driving documenting how even two drinks can contribute to serious traffic accidents, you've likely experienced

terms & definitions

Cognitive dissonance psychological discomfort experienced when a person is presented with information that is inconsistent with his or her current thinking or feelings.

Communication Ethics @ Work

Is Manufacturing Dissonance Ethical?

Advertisers on TV, the Internet, and billboards frequently use the principle of cognitive dissonance to entice you to buy their product. They try to make you feel inferior, unglamorous, or unpopular if you don't use their product. Is it ethical to "manufacture" problems or dissonance to get you to buy something or do something? Is it appropriate to make listeners feel harm will come to them by trying to convince them they have problems of which they may not be aware? Research documents that fear appeals are effective in motivating people to take action. But is it *ethical* to create fear and panic by arousing listener's emotions by threatening them?

cognitive dissonance. The incompatibility of your behavior and your knowledge is likely to make you feel uncomfortable. And your discomfort may prompt you to change your thoughts, likes or dislikes, feelings, or behavior so that you can restore your comfort level or sense of balance—in this case, by not driving after drinking.

Skilled persuasive speakers know that creating dissonance and then offering their listeners a way to restore balance is an effective persuasive strategy.

PEOPLE RESPOND TO MEET NEEDS Besides creating cognitive dissonance, effective persuaders attempt to identify your needs and then convince you that they can meet your needs. For example, executives of a manufacturing company who observe people moving out of your town in search of jobs elsewhere might be able to persuade the town council to provide tax incentives to build a new plant in the area, reasoning that the town's need for jobs will make council members receptive to the request. The manufacturing company's executives can see the town's need for jobs and can craft a message explaining how the company will meet the need. As a speaker, the better you understand what your listeners need, the better you can adapt to them and the greater the chances that you can persuade them to change an attitude, belief, or value or get them to take some action.

Abraham Maslow developed the classic theory that outlines basic human needs.[9] If you've taken a psychology course, you have undoubtedly encountered this theory, which has important applications to persuasion. Maslow suggests that all human behavior is motivated by a **hierarchy of needs**.

- *Physiological needs*: Basic physiological needs (such as the need for food, water, and air) have to be satisfied before we attend to any other concern.

- *Safety needs*: We need to feel safe and to be able to protect those we love.

- *Social needs*: Comfortable and secure, we attend next to social needs, including the need to be loved and to belong to a group.

- *Self-esteem needs*: The next level of needs is for self-esteem, or thinking well of ourselves.

- *Self-actualization needs*: Finally, if the first four levels of need have been satisfied, we attend to the need for self-actualization, or achieving our highest potential.

Although research does not completely support the notion that humans have a fixed hierarchy of needs (as Maslow originally thought), the theory does serve as a useful way of classifying basic human needs. Figure 13.2 illustrates Maslow's five levels of needs, with the most basic at the bottom.

terms & definitions

Hierarchy of needs Abraham Maslow's classic theory that humans have five levels of needs and that lower-level needs must be met before people can be concerned about higher-level needs.

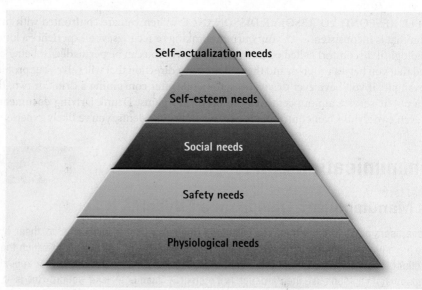

FIGURE 13.2 Maslow's Hierarchy of Needs

Source: Maslow, Abraham (1954). *Motivation and Personality*. New York: HarperCollins.

As a persuasive public speaker, understanding and applying the hierarchy of needs helps you to adapt to your audience. One practical application is to do everything in your power to ensure that your audience's physiological needs are met. For example, if your listeners are sweating and fanning themselves, they are unlikely to be very interested in listening to your sales presentation. If you can turn on air conditioning or fans, you will have a greater chance of successfully making a sale.

Another way in which you can apply the need hierarchy is to appeal to an audience's higher-order needs. The U.S. Army once used the recruiting slogan "Be all that you can be" to tap into the need for self-actualization, or achievement of one's highest potential.

PEOPLE RESPOND TO FEAR MESSAGES One of the oldest ways to convince people to change their minds or their behavior is by scaring them into compliance. Fear works. The appeal to fear often takes the form of an "if-then" statement: *If* you don't do X, *then* awful things will happen to you. "If you don't buy this insurance policy, then your loved ones may not be able to pay the mortgage and they may be homeless." "If you don't wear a seatbelt, then you are more likely to die in an automobile accident." "If you don't support the development of a new hospital in our community, lives could be lost if we have to travel to the next county for medical attention." A variety of research studies support the following principles regarding the use of fear as a motivator.[10]

- A strong threat to a family member or someone whom members of the audience care about will often be more successful than a fear appeal directed at the audience members themselves.

- The more respected the speaker, the greater the likelihood that the appeal to fear will work.

- Fear appeals are more successful if you convince your audience that the threat is real and will affect them unless they take action.

Strong gestures can be helpful in conveying your message, but you must also understand the principles of persuasion and learn specific strategies for persuading others.

PEOPLE RESPOND TO POSITIVE MESSAGES A TV commercial for a "big box" department store pledges, "For every dollar you spend in our store, we will return 5 percent to the public schools in your community; your students will have new computers to help them learn." A candidate for chair of the board of directors asserts, "If you support me for board chair, I can assure you our stock price and sales will increase." We've all encountered these kinds of positive appeals. Politicians, salespeople, and most successful business and professional persuaders know that one way to change or reinforce your attitudes, beliefs, values, or behavior is to use a positive motivational appeal. Positive motivational appeals are verbal messages promising that good things will happen if the speaker's advice is followed. The key to using positive motivational appeals is to know what your listeners value. Most people value a comfortable, prosperous life; stimulating, exciting activity; a sense of accomplishment; world peace; and overall happiness and contentment. In a persuasive speech, you can motivate your listeners to respond to your message by describing what positive things will happen to them if they follow your advice.

Strategies for Persuading

Greek philosopher and scholar Aristotle said that rhetoric is the process of discovering the available means of persuasion.[11] What are those available means? Aristotle singled out three primary strategies: (1) emphasize the credibility or ethical character of a speaker, which he called **ethos**; (2) use logical arguments, or **logos**; and (3) use emotional appeals, or **pathos**, to move an audience. The following strategies for developing your credibility as

terms & definitions

Ethos the credibility or ethical character of a speaker.

Logos the use of logical arguments.

Pathos the use of emotional appeals to move an audience.

a speaker—using logic, evidence, and emotion to persuade and motivate listeners—are based on Aristotle's three strategies and bolstered by contemporary research. We'll also revisit some of our strategies of message organization and discuss how to adapt ideas to people and people to ideas.

EFFECTIVELY ESTABLISH YOUR CREDIBILITY If you were going to buy a new computer, to whom would you turn for advice? Perhaps you would consult your brother, the computer geek, or your roommate, the computer science major. Or you might seek advice from *Consumer Reports*, the monthly publication of studies of various consumer products. In other words, you would turn to a source you consider knowledgeable, competent, and trustworthy—a source you think is credible.

As introduced in Chapter 11, **Credibility** is a listener's perception of a speaker's competence, trustworthiness, and dynamism. It is not something a speaker inherently possesses or lacks; rather, it is based on the listeners' mindset regarding the speaker. Your listeners, not you, determine whether you have credibility. Regardless of your professional goal as a communicator, you must be perceived as a credible communicator. The more credibility you have, the more likely that your listeners will believe you, trust you, and like you. It's important to be perceived as credible when presenting any message, but especially critical when trying to persuade someone.

The credibility of a speaker, such as well-known soccer star David Beckham—here launching "Four Codes of Football" for Adidas—increases the chances that listeners will be persuaded or motivated to do or buy something or to change a behavior.

How do you establish your credibility? It's a centuries-old question. Aristotle thought public speakers should be ethical, possess good character, display common sense, and be concerned for the well-being of their audience. Quintilian, a Roman teacher of public speaking, advised that a speaker should be "a good person speaking well." Modern research has generally supported these ancient speculations about the elements that enhance a speaker's credibility.

Credibility is not a single factor but consists of multiple elements. Your goal is to be perceived as highly credible on each element of credibility when you speak. Ideally you should be perceived as competent, trustworthy, and dynamic.

- **Competence** is the perception that a person is skilled, knowledgeable, and informed about the subject he or she is discussing. You will be more persuasive if you can convince your listeners you know something about your topic. How? You can use verbal messages effectively by talking about relevant personal experience with the topic. If you have lived in a high-rise condominium you'll have more credibility as a high-rise condo salesperson than someone who has only lived in a ranch-style house. You can also cite evidence to support your ideas. Even if you have not lived in a high-rise condo yourself, you can be prepared with information about the advantages of apartment living such as convenience and efficiency.

- **Trustworthiness** is a second element of credibility. While delivering a speech, you need to convey honesty and sincerity to your audience. You can't do this simply by saying, "Trust me." You have to earn trust. You can do so by demonstrating you are interested in and experienced with your topic. Again, speaking from personal experience makes you seem a more trustworthy speaker. Conversely, having something to gain by persuading your audience may make you suspect in their eyes. That's why salespersons and politicians often lack credibility. If you do what they say, they will clearly benefit from their sales commissions or political influence.

- **Dynamism**, or energy, is the third element of credibility. Dynamism is often projected through delivery. Applying the communication principle of effectively using and understanding nonverbal messages, a speaker who maintains eye contact, has enthusiastic vocal inflection, and moves and gestures purposefully is likely to be seen as dynamic. **Charisma** is a form of dynamism. A charismatic speaker possesses charm, talent, magnetism, and other qualities that make the person attractive and energetic. Former General Electric CEO Jack Welch, well-known talk show host Oprah Winfrey, and motivational speaker Anthony Robbins are considered to be charismatic speakers by many people.

A speaker has opportunities throughout a speech to enhance his or her credibility. The first such opportunity is called **initial credibility**. This is the impression of your credibility your listeners have even *before* you begin speaking. They grant you initial credibility based on such factors as your appearance and your credentials. Dressing appropriately and having a brief summary of your qualifications and accomplishments ready for the person who will introduce you are two strategies for enhancing your initial credibility.

The second credibility-building opportunity, **derived credibility**, is the perception your audience forms as you present your speech. If you adapt your message appropriately to your audience, you will enhance your derived credibility. Specific strategies include establishing common ground with your audience (emphasizing what you have in common with your listeners), supporting your arguments with evidence, and presenting a well-organized speech. Using effective eye contact, posture, and vocal delivery also enhances your derived credibility.

The last phase of credibility, called **terminal credibility**, is the perception of your credibility your listeners have when you finish your speech. A thoughtfully prepared and well-delivered conclusion can enhance your terminal credibility, as can maintaining eye contact throughout and even after your closing sentence. Also, apply the communication principle of listening and responding thoughtfully to others. Be prepared to answer questions after your speech, regardless of whether there is a planned question-and-answer period.

EFFECTIVELY AND ETHICALLY USE EVIDENCE AND REASONING Besides knowing how to motivate listeners, an effective persuader knows how to structure a persuasive message for maximum effect. In addition to being considered a credible speaker, you will gain influence with your audience if you can effectively use logically structured arguments supported with evidence. The goal is to provide logical proof for your arguments. **Proof** consists of both evidence and the conclusions you draw from it; **evidence** is the illustrations, definitions, statistics, and opinions that are your supporting material. **Reasoning** is the process of drawing conclusions from your evidence. There are three major ways to draw logical conclusions: inductively, deductively, and causally.

Reasoning that arrives at a general conclusion from specific instances or examples is known as **inductive reasoning**. You reason inductively when you claim that a conclusion is probably true because of specific evidence. For example, if you were giving a sales pitch to convince your customer that Hondas are reliable cars, you might use inductive reasoning to make your point. You have a 2002 Honda Civic that has 140,000 miles on it and has required little repair other than routine maintenance. Your brother has a Honda Accord and has driven it twice as long as any other car he has ever owned. Your friend just returned from a 3,000-mile road trip in her Honda Odyssey minivan, which performed beautifully. Based on these specific examples, you ask your listener to agree with your general conclusion: Hondas are reliable cars.

Reasoning by analogy is a special type of inductive reasoning. As you recall from Chapter 11, an analogy demonstrates how an unfamiliar idea, thing, or situation is similar to something the audience already understands. Analogy is not only a type of supporting material; it can also be used to reason inductively. For example, you might reason, "Even though we're a small business, we should start a retirement plan for our company. If we don't we could lose our top employees. Our top competitor started a new 401(K) retirement plan for her employees and she's had much less employee turnover." The key to reasoning by analogy is to make sure that the two things you are comparing (your company and your competitor's company) are similar so that your argument is a sound one.

terms & definitions

Dynamism an aspect of a speaker's credibility that reflects whether the speaker is perceived as energetic.

Charisma a form of dynamism; a charismatic speaker possesses charm, talent, magnetism, and other qualities that make the person attractive.

Initial credibility the impression of a speaker's credibility that listeners have before a speech begins.

Derived credibility the perception of a speaker's credibility that the audience forms as he or she presents a speech.

Terminal credibility the perception of a speaker's credibility listeners have at the conclusion of a speech.

Proof evidence and the conclusions you draw from it.

Evidence the illustrations, definitions, statistics, and opinions presented as supporting material in persuasive speaking.

Reasoning the process of drawing conclusions from evidence.

Inductive reasoning reasoning that arrives at a general conclusion from specific instances or examples.

Reasoning by analogy a special kind of inductive reasoning that draws a comparison between two ideas, things, or situations that share some essential common feature.

Reasoning from a general statement or principle to reach a specific conclusion is called **deductive reasoning**. Deductive reasoning can be structured as a **syllogism**, a three-part argument that has a major premise, a minor premise, and a conclusion. In attempting to convince the marketing department at a car dealership to advertise on television, you might offer this syllogism:

MAJOR PREMISE: All of the top-selling automobile dealers in our county advertise on television.

MINOR PREMISE: Your automobile dealership is in this county.

CONCLUSION: Your automobile dealership should advertise on television.

Contemporary logicians note that when you reason deductively, your conclusion is certain rather than probable. The certainty of the conclusion rests primarily on the validity of the major premise and secondarily on the truth of the minor premise. If you can prove that all top-selling auto dealers advertise on TV, and if it is true that those that advertise sell more cars, then your conclusion will be sound.

You use **causal reasoning** when you relate two or more events in such a way as to conclude that one or more of the events caused the others. For example, you might argue that public inoculation programs during the twentieth century eradicated smallpox.

As we noted when we discussed cause and effect as a persuasive organizational strategy, there are two ways to structure a causal argument. One is by reasoning from cause to effect, or predicting a result from a known fact. You know that you have had an inch of rain over the last few days, so you predict that the aquifer level will rise. The inch of rain is the cause; the rising aquifer is the effect. The other way to structure an argument is by reasoning from a known effect to the cause. National Transportation Safety Board accident investigators reason from effect to cause when they reconstruct airplane wreckage to find clues to the cause of an air disaster.

Trying to establish a causal link where none exists is one type of **logical fallacy**. Unfortunately, not all people who try to persuade you will use sound evidence and reasoning. Some will try to develop arguments in ways that are irrelevant or inappropriate. To be a better informed listener, as well as a more ethical persuasive speaker, you should be aware of the common logical fallacies described in Table 13.2.

EFFECTIVELY ADAPT YOUR REASONING TO THE CULTURAL EXPECTATIONS OF YOUR LISTENERS Effective strategies for developing your persuasive purpose depend on the background and cultural expectations of your listeners. Most of the logical, rational methods

terms & definitions

Deductive reasoning reasoning from a general statement or principle to reach a specific conclusion.

Syllogism a three-part argument that has a major premise, a minor premise, and a conclusion.

Causal reasoning reasoning that relates two or more events in such a way as to conclude that one or more of the events caused the others.

Logical fallacy false reasoning that occurs when someone attempts to persuade without adequate evidence or with arguments that are irrelevant or inappropriate.

RECAP

Inductive, Deductive, and Causal Reasoning

Type of Reasoning	Reasoning begins with …	Reasoning ends with …	Conclusion is …	Example
Inductive	specific examples	a general conclusion	probable	Dell and IBM computers are all reliable. Therefore, PCs are reliable.
Deductive	a general statement	a specific conclusion	certain	All financial officers at this company have advanced degrees. Tom Bryson is the chief financial officer at this company. Therefore, Tom Bryson has an advanced degree.
Causal	something known	a speculation about causes or effects of what is known	likely	The number of people with undergraduate degrees has risen steadily since 1960. This increasing number has caused a glut in the job market for people with degrees.

of reasoning we've presented evolved from Greek and Roman traditions of developing arguments. Rhetoricians from the United States typically use a straightforward factual-inductive method of supporting ideas and reaching conclusions. First, they identify facts and link them together to support a specific proposition or conclusion. North Americans also like debates involving a direct clash of ideas and opinions. Our low-context culture encourages people to be more forthright in dealing with issues and disagreement than do high-context cultures.

Not all cultures assume a direct, linear, methodical approach to supporting ideas and proving a point.[12] People from high-context cultures, for example, may expect that participants in a debate will establish a personal relationship before debating issues. People from some cultures, such as those of Eastern Europe, use a deductive pattern of reasoning rather than an inductive pattern. They begin with a general premise and then link it to a specific situation when they attempt to persuade listeners.

TABLE 13.2   Reasoning Fallacies

Fallacy	Example	Explanation
Causal Fallacy An inappropriate or inaccurate cause-and-effect connection between two things or events.	If we annex the new subdivision into our city, then we are likely to have more days of sunshine.	There is no logical or causal connection between the annexation of a subdivision and the days of sunshine.
Bandwagon Fallacy The argument that because everyone believes something or does something, the belief or behavior must be valid, accurate, or effective.	Everybody knows this product is defective.	Saying "everybody knows" is a fallacious attempt to suggest that because everyone agrees, others should "jump on the bandwagon" and also agree.
Either-Or Fallacy The oversimplification of an issue into a choice between only two outcomes or possibilities.	Because of the overcrowding at our schools, either we pass the school bond to build new schools or we'll have to bus our students to another school district.	There are more than two options for solving the problem. For example, less expensive portable classrooms can be purchased without a bond election.
Hasty Generalization Reaching a conclusion from too little evidence or nonexistent evidence.	Because I didn't receive the correct change when I made my purchase at Mega-Low Mart, this is evidence that Mega-Low Mart is trying to cheat their customers.	One example does not provide enough evidence to reach a sweeping general conclusion that Mega-Low Mart is trying to cheat customers. It could simply have been an isolated error.
Personal Attack Attacking the personal characteristics of someone connected with an idea, rather than addressing the idea itself.	Janice's idea that we decrease property taxes is a crazy idea because Janice never had a good idea in her life.	The idea may be a sound one. Simply attacking the person without critiquing the idea proposed does not address the proposal itself.
Red Herring Using irrelevant facts or arguments to distract the listener from the issue under discussion.	When a member of Congress is attacked for inappropriately using funds, the representative responds by talking about the sexual indiscretion of a colleague.	The representative is not directly addressing the issue but merely trying to distract from the issue at hand.
Appeal to Misplaced Authority Using someone without the appropriate credentials or expertise to endorse an idea or product.	Because superstar Bart McCoy likes this breakfast cereal, you will like it too.	Simply because a well-known athlete endorses a breakfast cereal does not prove the cereal is good, healthy, or tasty.

People in Middle Eastern cultures usually do not use standard inductive or deductive structures. They are more likely to use narrative methods to persuade an audience. They tell stories that evoke feelings and emotions, allowing their listeners to draw their own conclusions by inductive association.

Although we've emphasized the kind of inductive reasoning that will be persuasive to most North Americans, you may need to use alternative strategies if your audience is from another cultural tradition. If you are uncertain about which approach will be most effective, consider using a variety of methods and strategies to make your point. Use facts supported by analysis, but also make sure you provide illustrative stories and examples. Also, try to observe and talk with other speakers who have experience addressing your target audience.

USE EMOTION EFFECTIVELY AND ETHICALLY TO PERSUADE People often make decisions based not on logic, but on emotion. Advertisers know this. Think of the soft-drink commercials you see on television. There is little rational reason that people should spend any part of their food budget on soft drinks; they are "empty calories." So soft-drink advertisers turn instead to emotional appeals, striving to connect their product with feelings of pleasure. Smiling people, upbeat music, and good times are usually part of the formula for selling soda pop.

One way to make an emotional appeal is with emotion-arousing verbal messages. Words with positive connotations (such as *mother, flag,* and *freedom*) and those with negative connotations (such as *slavery, the Holocaust,* and *terrorism*) trigger emotional responses in listeners. Patriotic slogans, such as "Remember 9/11" and "Give me liberty, or give me death," are examples of phrases that have successfully aroused emotions in their listeners. McDonald's "I'm lovin' it" and Nike's "Just do it" are short phrases that appeal to positive feelings and the satisfaction of accomplishment.

Another way to appeal to emotions is through concrete illustrations and descriptions. Although illustrations and descriptions are themselves types of evidence or supporting material, their impact is often emotional. When trying to convince her listeners to purchase high-quality child safety seats, a speaker used this example to evoke an emotional response in support of her goal:

> Michelle Hutchinson carefully placed her three-year-old daughter into her child safety seat. She was certain that Dana was secure. Within minutes Michelle was involved in a minor accident and the seat belt that was never designed to hold a child safety seat allowed the seat to lunge forward, crushing the three-year-old's skull on the dash. Dana died three days later.[13]

Effective use of nonverbal messages can also appeal to an audience's emotions. Visual aids can provide emotion-arousing images. A photograph of a dirty, ragged child alone in a big city can evoke sadness and pain. A video clip of an airplane crash can arouse fear and horror. A picture of a smiling baby makes most of us smile, too. As a speaker, you can use visual aids to evoke both positive and negative emotions.

When you use emotional appeals, you do have an obligation to be ethical and forthright. Making false claims, misusing evidence or images, or relying exclusively on emotion without any evidence or reasoning violates standards of ethical public speaking.

ORGANIZE YOUR PERSUASIVE MESSAGE EFFECTIVELY Most persuasive speeches are organized according to one of four strategies: problem and solution, cause and effect, refutation, and the motivated sequence—a special variation of the problem-solution format that lends itself well to sales presentations.

Even though we discussed **problem-and-solution organization** in Chapter 11, we mention it again here as the most basic organizational pattern for a persuasive speech. The problem-and-solution strategy works best when a problem can be clearly documented and a solution or solutions proposed to deal with the problem. When describing the problem, your goal is to create dissonance or to identify an unmet need.

When you use problem-and-solution organization, apply the principle of appropriately adapting messages to others. If you are speaking to an apathetic audience or one that

terms & definitions

Problem-and-solution organization a strategy for organizing a persuasive speech that works best when a clearly evident problem can be documented and a solution or solutions proposed to deal with the problem.

is not even aware that a problem exists, you can emphasize the problem portion of the speech. Your fellow members of the Chamber of Commerce, for example, who don't see how a new shopping mall in a nearby community will affect retail sales in the downtown area, may need to be jolted from apathy: You can point out that the presence of malls has resulted in drastically declining retail sales in other communities. If your audience is already aware of the problem, you can emphasize your proposed solution or solutions (perhaps to try to stop the mall from being built or to aggressively promote your community as the best destination for shopping). In either case, your challenge will be to provide ample evidence that your perception of the problem is accurate and reasonable. For example, you would need to find statistics that document how a mall can lower sales. You'll also need to convince your listeners that the solution or solutions you advocate are the most appropriate ones to solve the problem. Again, evidence in the form of statistics or examples are needed. As another example, note the problem-solution structure in the example below. The president of a Chamber of Commerce is trying to convince the local school board to address the public perception that the school district is inferior compared to nearby school districts. The community is not attracting new businesses because of perceptions of academic mediocrity. The Chamber of Commerce president analyzes the problem and proposes a solution:

I. PROBLEM: Students in public schools in our community are not learning as well as students in other nearby communities.

   A. Our student test scores are down.

   B. Our teachers are paid less than teachers in nearby school districts.

   C. Parents are not volunteering in our schools.

II. SOLUTION: We should slightly increase property taxes to increase revenues to finance improvements in our schools.

   A. We could hire additional teachers to help improve test scores.

   B. We could increase compensation for our best teachers.

   C. We could hire a volunteer coordinator to increase parent volunteers in our school.

Like the problem-and-solution strategy, the **cause-and-effect organization** pattern was introduced in Chapter 11. We noted that a speaker could either identify a situation and then discuss the resulting effects (cause-effect) or present a situation and then explore its causes (effect-cause).

Regardless of which variation you choose, you should once again apply the principle of being aware of your communication with yourself and others. Specifically, you must analyze the problem and determine the critical causal link and then convince your listeners that the link is valid. An effect may have more than one cause. For example, sales at your company are 10 percent behind sales figures at this time last year. As sales manager, you are responsible for analyzing the issues and presenting your analysis to the company CEO. Here's a way you could organize your message:

I. CAUSE: The design of our product line is out of date.

   A. We have not hired any new engineers in the past five years.

   B. Our engineers are using outdated computer equipment.

   C. Our engineers are relying on outdated software to design our product.

II. EFFECT: Our sales are down.

   A. Our customers find our competitor's product more up-to-date.

   B. Our customers are replacing the products they have purchased from us with products from our competitor.

   C. Our customers have indicated that they do not intend to purchase our product in the future.

When using a cause-and-effect organizational strategy, it's not enough just to assert your causes and probable effects. You need to provide evidence to provide the link between the causes and effects.

terms & definitions

Cause-and-effect organization a strategy for identifying a situation and then discussing the resulting effects (cause-effect), or presenting a situation and then exploring its causes (effect-cause).

A variation on cause and effect is organizing a presentation from effect to cause. For example:

I. EFFECT: Holiday sales are sluggish. People aren't buying as many gifts as they did in previous years.

II. CAUSE: The recession has decreased customers' purchasing power.

A third way to organize your efforts to persuade an audience is especially useful when you are facing an unreceptive audience—one that does not agree with your point of view or your specific proposition. **Refutation** is an organizational strategy by which you identify objections to your proposition and then refute those objections with arguments and evidence. It is better to present both sides of an issue rather than just your own position if you are certain that your audience is skeptical of your position.

You will be most likely to organize a persuasive speech by refutation if you know your listeners' chief objections to your proposition. In fact, if you do not acknowledge such objections, the audience will probably think about them during your speech anyway. Credible facts and statistics will generally be more effective than emotional arguments in supporting your points of refutation.

Suppose you represent a large hotel chain that wants to build a new luxury hotel in a southwestern city. The hotel chain has purchased most of the property it needs to start construction, except for one prime piece of property owned by two sisters who have a tamale stand on their property. You have approached the sisters, but they don't want to sell. They have agreed to meet with you to hear your final offer, so you'll need to be especially effective in refuting their concerns. You understand that the price you're offering is not the reason they are balking at selling. Rather, they promised their mother, who passed away last year, that they would always maintain the family business on the same location where their mother started the business. Here's an outline for a presentation to the two sisters based on the refutation organizational strategy.

I. We would like to build a hotel on this property and we will honor your mother by naming our exclusive roof-top restaurant after her.

II. In addition to purchasing your property, we would like to purchase your mother's recipe for tamales and feature them in our new restaurant.

III. We would like to hire both of you as consultants to the hotel to work in the restaurant and be in charge of quality control of all food served in the hotel.

The presentation to the sisters consists of major points offered to directly refute their objections. When you use a refutation strategy, you address the specific concerns and offer solutions to the objections you know you will encounter.

Like refutation, the fourth organizational strategy is unique to persuasive speaking. The **motivated sequence**, devised by Alan Monroe, is a five-step organizational strategy for a persuasive presentation.[14] This simple yet effective strategy integrates the problem-and-solution organizational method with principles that have been confirmed by research and practical experience. The five steps involved are attention, need, satisfaction, visualization, and action.

1. **Attention.** Your first task, and the first stage in appropriately adapting your message to others, is to get your listeners' attention. Using a rhetorical question, illustration, startling fact or statistic, quotation, humorous story, or a reference to historical or recent events are ways of starting a speech to gain favorable attention. The attention step is, in essence, your application of one of these strategies.

    Business executive Raymond Kotcher used this attention-catching opener to begin a speech in which his goal was to encourage recent graduates with communication degrees to become involved in the global marketplace:

    Now, I have a request. I want you graduates to consider what I have to say to you this afternoon not as a commencement address. Rather, think of my remarks—and I'll keep them brief—as an email, written just to you. An email written to you, an emerging communicator. And as with most personal notes

terms & definitions

Refutation an organizational strategy by which you identify objections to your proposition and then refute those objections with arguments and evidence.

Motivated sequence a five-step plan for organizing a persuasive message: attention, need, satisfaction, visualization, and action.

Attention the first step of the motivated sequence involves capturing the audience's attention so that they will listen to the message.

that are written to mark milestones in our great and privileged society—setting off for college; yes, graduating from college; that first job; committing to that someone special; the first child—the email offers advice, encouragement, warnings about and hope for the future. Don't hit delete just yet![15]

2. **Need**. After getting your audience's attention, establish why your topic, problem, or issue should concern them. Tell your audience about the problem. Adapt your message to them by convincing them that the problem affects them directly. Argue that there is a need for change. During the need step (which corresponds with the problem step in a problem-and-solution speech), you should develop logical arguments backed by evidence. It's during the need step that you create dissonance or use a credible fear appeal to motivate listeners to respond to your solution.

In trying to convince his audience that the world is changing and that they ought to be contributing to the global conversation, Kotcher points out that in order to be contemporary, they need to be up-to-date on cyberworld applications:

A persuasive speaker, such as former US Treasury Secretary Henry Paulson, addressing Columbia Business School students, might use an organizational strategy such as the motivated sequence to craft an effective message.

> The audience of widely read blogs . . . rivals the size of the audiences of the online versions of major newspapers. Each day, 200 million Google searches are conducted, and half aren't in the English language. There are two billion cell phone subscribers in the world today. . . . And while I don't want to overburden this email with statistics, have you, like the estimated twenty million people around the world, played and worked in the cyberworlds created by Entropia or Second Life? Second Life is an online society where you can explore, or socialize, or buy goods and services or even build, rent, and sell real estate—using your credit card! Earlier this month, *Business Week* reported on this 3-D world, and estimates in the article put the size of this virtual economy at $1.5 BILLION—that's in real U. S. dollars—and growing.[16]

3. **Satisfaction**. After you explain and document a need or problem, you identify your plan (or solution) and explain how it will satisfy the need. You need not go into painstaking detail at this point in your talk. Present enough information so that your listeners have a general understanding of how the problem may be solved. You'll provide the specific action you want them to take later (in the action step). For now, identify in general terms what the solution to the problem is—satisfy the need you have identified. Here's the satisfaction step in Raymond Kotcher's message:

> Relish the idea of joining the conversation. Today's media are participatory—integrating people with people to build community. Gone are the days of command and control. And this new networked world requires a new generation of communication leaders and leadership. Apply what you've learned at [college] and in your life so far. Already, one in five college-age students has traveled abroad in the past three years. More than one in three of you speaks at least two languages. And your generation truly wants to help build this global community.[17]

4. **Visualization**. Now you need to give your audience a sense of what it would be like if your solution were adopted or, conversely, if it were not adopted. **Visualization**—using words to create an image in audience members' minds—applies the principle of

terms & definitions

Need the second step of the motivated sequence, establishing the rationale, problem, or need for a listener to make a change so that the listener will agree with the action requested by the speaker.

Satisfaction the third step of the motivated sequence, which includes telling the listener of a persuasive message how the proposed solution will meet or satisfy the need.

Visualization using words to create an image in audience members' minds.

effectively using verbal messages. With a **positive visualization** approach, you paint a rosy picture of how wonderful the future will be if your satisfaction step is implemented. With a **negative visualization** approach, you paint a bleak picture of how terrible the future will be if nothing is done; you use a fear appeal to motivate your listeners to do what you suggest to avoid further problems. In either case, you use **word pictures**—lively descriptions that appeal to listeners' senses (sight, taste, smell, sound, and touch). Or you might combine both approaches: The problem will be solved if your solution is adopted, but things will get increasingly worse if it is not.

Here's how Kotcher helped his listeners visualize how the world is changing and how some previous college graduates have capitalized on being globally aware and active:

> Justin Lane, for instance, a 1995 . . . graduate, is the New York bureau chief for the European Pressphoto Agency. He won the Pulitzer in 2002 for breaking news photography for his freelance contributions to *The New York Times'* coverage of the September 11 attacks. A year later, he traveled to Iraq to document cultural looting, the crisis facing Iraqi women, and the uncovering of mass graves. His photographs from Iraq garnered two gallery shows in New York and appearances in numerous newspapers, magazines, and books.
>
> Then there's Chris McKee, also class of 1995. . . . He made an award-winning documentary that has opened up the little-known world of Mongolian nomads to the rest of the world. And Tyler Hicks, class of 1992, named by *American Photo* magazine as one of the twenty-five most important photographers, in large part because of his compelling images from war-torn places like Kosovo, Iraq, and Afghanistan.
>
> And Michael Williams.... This Academy Award–winning producer is a pioneer in delivering some of the most original content to be seen in theaters and on television. He won an Oscar in 2004 for producing *The Fog of War*, a film that delivered a riveting look at former Defense Secretary Robert S. McNamara and his controversial role in the Vietnam War.[18]

The implication of these positive examples is that if you join the global technology revolution, you too will be successful.

5. **Action**. The action step is your speech's conclusion. You remind your audience of the problem (outlined in the need step), give them the solution (the satisfaction step), remind them of the great things that will happen if they follow your advice (positive visualization) or the bad things that will happen if they don't (negative visualization). Finally, you tell them what they need to do next (the action step).

To finish his presentation, Raymond Kotcher made this specific recommendation to his listeners:

> So, this email to you is just about finished. Yet I can't close without giving you some personal advice—about what I have gleaned in my career and life since those impossibly cold mornings walking to class at 640 Comm Ave. Here goes:
> ENGAGE YOUR CURIOSITY. Be indefatigable in ferreting out the answers to questions that will inform a world, assist a client, uncover an injustice, right a wrong.
> NEVER FORGET YOUR INTEGRITY AND CREDIBILITY.
> DEVELOP YOUR VOICE. You're a skilled communicator. Always strive to improve and develop your communication skills and apply them atop a deep understanding for all that has preceded you. Combine that with your personal experiences and what is important to you. And be willing to listen and to be taught, because learning NEVER ends.
> FOSTER YOUR CREATIVITY. Oh, how the world, especially the business world, seeks creative and innovative thinkers who can communicate their imaginative ideas.[19]

terms & definitions

Positive visualization a rosy word picture of how wonderful the future will be if your solution is implemented.

Negative visualization a bleak picture of how terrible the future will be if nothing is done; a fear appeal used to motivate listeners to adopt a particular solution to a problem.

Word picture lively descriptions that help listeners form a mental image by appealing to their senses (sight, taste, smell, sound, and touch).

You can adapt the motivated sequence to the needs of your topic and your audience. For example, if you are speaking to a knowledgeable, receptive audience, you do not need to spend a great deal of time on the need step. The audience already knows that the need is serious. They may, however, feel helpless to do anything about it. Therefore, you would want to emphasize the satisfaction and action steps.

However, if you are speaking to a neutral or apathetic audience, you will need to spend time getting their attention and proving that a problem exists, that it is significant, and that it affects them personally. You will emphasize the attention, need, and visualization steps. And if you are speaking to a hostile audience, you should spend considerable time on the need step. Convince your audience that the problem is significant and that they should be concerned about it. You would probably not propose a lengthy, detailed action. In the final

RECAP

Organizational Patterns for Persuasive Speeches

Organizational Pattern	Definition	Example
Problem and Solution	Organization by discussing a problem and then various possible solutions	I. Problem: The company's sales revenues dropped in the last quarter. II. Solution: The company should beef up advertising efforts to bolster sales.
Cause and Effect	Organization by discussing a situation and its causes, or a situation and its effects	I. Cause: Most HMOs refuse to pay for treatment they deem "experimental." II. Effect: Patients die who might have been saved by "experimental" treatment.
Refutation	Organization according to objections your listeners may have to your ideas and arguments	I. Although you may think that our new, higher-premium insurance policy will reduce your standard of living, its comprehensive coverage will save you money over time. II. Although you may think that the high cost of insurance may cost the organization more money and place your jobs in jeopardy, it will actually help us attract and retain higher quality workers.
Motivated Sequence	Alan H. Monroe's five-step plan for organizing a persuasive speech: attention, need, satisfaction, visualization, and action	I. Attention: "An apple a day keeps the doctor away." What has happened to the old adage? Why has it changed? II. Need: Pesticides are poisoning our fresh fruits and vegetables. III. Satisfaction: Those of you who purchase food for hotels and restaurants should purchase organic fruits and vegetables for your guests. IV. Visualization: Remember the apple poisoned by Snow White's wicked stepmother? You may be feeding such apples to your own guests if you don't buy organic fruits and vegetables. V. Action: Buy fruits and vegetables raised organically.

section of this chapter, we will offer additional strategies for persuading receptive, unreceptive, and neutral audiences.

Is there one best way to organize a persuasive speech? The answer is no. The organizational strategy you select must depend on your audience, your message, and your desired objective. What is important is to remember that your decision can have a major effect on your listeners' response to your message.

HOW TO ADAPT YOUR MESSAGE TO RECEPTIVE, NEUTRAL, AND UNRECEPTIVE LISTENERS Donald C. Bryant's definition of rhetoric emphasizes the principle of appropriately adapting a message to an audience: "Rhetoric," he said, "is the process of adjusting ideas to people and people to ideas."[20] And with this thought we've come full circle in the process of developing a persuasive message. As we have emphasized throughout our discussion of public speaking, analyzing your audience and adapting to them is at the heart of the speech-making process; it's one of the fundamental communication principles for leadership. In a persuasive speech, that adaptation begins with identifying your specific purpose and understanding whether you are trying to change or reinforce attitudes, beliefs, or values. It continues with your selection of an organizational strategy. For example, if your audience members are unreceptive toward your ideas, you might choose to organize your speech by refutation, addressing the audience's objections head-on. Both research studies and experienced speakers can offer other useful suggestions to help you adapt to your audience. Table 13.3 summarizes key strategies to use when adapting to receptive audiences (listeners who agree with your ideas and like you), neutral audiences (they are either uncertain or simply don't see how your ideas affect them), or unreceptive audiences (they have ideas that are in direct opposition to yours).

Presenting to Sell

Dietrich Mateschitz, a former toothpaste salesman, had an idea. He thought the world might just be ready to buy a fizzy energy drink, even though there didn't appear to be a market for such a product. When he was on a trip to Thailand as a marketing executive for Procter & Gamble, Mateschitz tasted a drink called Krating Daeng, which is Thai for "red water buffalo."

terms & definitions

Web 2.0 the second generation of presenting and gathering information on the Internet using "read-write" technology.

Wikis collaborative web-based sites that permit numerous people to share information with one another.

TABLE 13.3　How to Adjust Ideas to People and People to Ideas

Persuading the Receptive Audience	Persuading the Neutral Audience	Persuading the Unreceptive Audience
• Identify with your audience by stating how you are similar to them, stressing characteristics you have in common. • Emphasize common interests and describe areas of agreement. • Provide a clear objective; because they are receptive to you, tell your listeners what you want them to do. • Use emotional appeals appropriately. Using stories, illustrations, and other methods of ethically appealing to emotions can be effective with a receptive audience.	• Because your listeners are not engaged or may be uninterested in you or your topic, gain and maintain their attention using appropriate attention-catching methods such as rhetorical questions, quotations, startling statistics, and interesting examples. • Refer to beliefs, attitudes, and concerns that are important to the listener. • Identify the needs of the listener and address those needs. • Show how the topics affect people your listeners care about. • Be realistic about what you can accomplish given that your listeners are neutral or apathetic.	• Because your listeners are not in agreement with your goals and objectives, don't tell them you are going to try to convince them to change their minds and support your position. • Make sure you present your strongest arguments first. • Acknowledge opposing points of view and then use evidence and facts (rather than emotional appeals or opinion) to refute their ideas. • Don't expect a major shift in attitudes or behavior.

Communication Skills FOR A **Digital Age**

Communicating via the Web

As companies have gone global and embraced technology, there is an increasing need to be able to connect with others in far-flung locations. Workers have to share information quickly and efficiently. Given the likelihood that you'll be communicating with others from around the world, it's important to use a variety of web-based tools that permit you to share ideas with others via the Internet. As an alternative to face-to-face business presentations, here are a few of the technology-based methods of connecting with an audience.[21]

- **Web 2.0**. Web 2.0 is a general term that describes the second generation of presenting and gathering information on the Internet. Web 1.0, the first generation of Internet technology, was "read-focused": The primary function was to present messages that were only designed to be read by someone. Web. 2.0 is a "read-write" technology. In addition to sharing information, the receiver of the message can easily respond by writing back to the message sender. Facebook is an example of a read-write Web 2.0 technology that permits communicators to interact with one another with seamless ease, including sharing photos, videos, web links, and instant messaging capabilities.

- **Wikis**. Wikis are collaborative web-based sites that permit many people to share information with one another. The distinctive feature of wikis is the open-editing function that permits all users to develop a resource collaboratively. Well-known sites, such as Wikepedia (encyclopedia), Wiki Travel (travel guide), and WikiHow (how-to manuals), are places on the web where you can not only share information with others, but also contribute to the information presented. Of course, when retrieving information from a Wiki source, consider the source. Although evidence indicates that the self-policing of the content helps keep the information current and accurate, there is always the potential for misinformation to be posted on a wiki site.

- **Skype**. If you've used Skype you know how easy it is to hold a video conversation with someone who is miles or continents away from you. Using the free software at skype.com, users need a video camera and microphone (often built-in to most computers) to communicate with one another.

- **Podcasts**. A podcast is a radio broadcast that uses the technology of an iPod through iTunes to share a message with others. Originally podcasts were audio messages, but through **Vodcasts** it's now relatively easy to share video and audio messages. You don't need to travel to India, China, or even San Francisco; you can present your report to your superiors with a podcast or vodcast.

Contemporary technology is making it easier to share messages with others who are separated in space and time. But it is still human beings who craft and interpret messages. Malcolm Gladwell, in noting the importance of the human element in communicating with others, said this:

> [T]here is a class of social problems for which there is no technological solution. Look. Technology is going to solve the energy problem. I'm convinced of it. Technology is going to give me a computer in ten years time that will fly me to the moon. Technology is going to build a car that goes 100 miles to the gallon. *But technology does not and cannot change the underlying dynamics of "human" problems: it doesn't make it easier to love or motivate or dream or convince.*[22]

Gladwell's point: Regardless of the technology used to solve problems and share information, it's *people* that make communication possible, an important point to keep in mind in all your workplace interactions.

He thought it might have possibilities as a beverage that could be sold to people who needed an energy boost. After considerable marketing research and product development, Mateschitz debuted his product in 1987 in Europe. It sold well, and he launched it in the United States in 2001. Chances are you've sampled his creation—Red Bull.[23]

Dietrich Mateschitz figured out how to sell a product even before people had expressed a need for the product. Now that's a good salesman. What did Mateschitz know that could help you be a top-notch salesperson? We're about to tell you.

Between billboards, posters, TV, the Internet, and radio commercials, you experience hundreds of sales messages every day. Perhaps wherever you are reading this book there is a radio jingle or TV commercial in the background, a billboard attempting to get your attention to sell you something, or a poster on a wall enticing you to spend your spring break in Colorado. If your computer is connected to the Internet, there may be sales messages bouncing around on your computer screen. Sales and marketing experts spend billions of dollars crafting messages to get you to buy or use what they are selling.

To sell is to persuade someone to buy or use a product or service. You can also sell an idea, a proposal, or a policy rather than a tangible object. Since selling is persuading, the principles

terms & definitions

Skype video-conferencing software that enables face-to-face communication between people miles or continents apart.

Podcasts a radio broadcast that uses the technology of an iPod through iTunes to share messages with others.

Vodcasts an easy way to share video and audio messages to anyone around the world.

of and skills for persuasion that we've already discussed are the key strategies that you will use when selling someone something. To maximize your sales potential, we suggest that you first, analyze the sales situation, and second, plan your persuasive sales message using time-tested strategies that, to paraphrase Donald C. Bryant, help you adjust products and services to people and people to products and services.

Sales skills are important leadership skills. We've noted that to lead is to influence others through communication, and often leaders need to sell ideas and methods. So, as we discuss the principles and strategies of sales, keep in mind that leaders sell ideas—whether informally and one on one, in groups and teams, or when speaking to many people. Sales involves more than simply selling a product.

Developing Your Sales Message

We've discussed several strategies for organizing presentations. Some organizational strategies, such as topical or chronological organization, are best suited for informative messages. Most sales presentations are organized using the problem-and-solution pattern. The five-step motivated sequence (which, as we noted, is a form of the problem-and-solution approach) is a good overarching organizational strategy to consider for sales presentations. Catching attention, establishing need, satisfying the need by offering a solution, visualizing the benefits of the solution or describing how the need will not be met if the solution is not adopted, and identifying a specific action to take is a good formula for structuring a sales presentation. Communication consultant Granville Toogood reminds his sales clients that when making a sales pitch, you need to connect with the customer's needs. As Toogood puts it,[24]

- You're not selling soap. You're selling sex.
- You're not selling perfume. You're selling love.
- You're not selling cars. You're selling excitement.
- You're not selling jeans. You're selling adventure.

The suggestions for organizing a sales presentation we describe below are based on the motivated sequence.[25]

The five-step motivated sequence provides a good way to organize an effective sales presentation that will close the deal.

HOOK YOUR LISTENER A good salesperson does more than merely get a customer's attention; a good salesperson is able to "hook" the customer to gain and keep the person's focus. How do you do that? You must know your customer's interests, needs, and hopes and adapt your message to address them. And, in most cases, you have to grab your listeners quickly. To hook them, ask them an opening question that is based on what you suspect they may need ("Are you interested in a car that costs less yet looks expensive?") or addresses a fear they may have ("Would you like a car that will protect your family if you have an accident?"). Television, radio, and Internet sales pitches spend considerable time simply trying to hook you to get and keep your attention. Unless you hook your customers, they will undoubtedly get away.

IDENTIFY THE CUSTOMER'S KEY ISSUE After hooking the customer, you need to address what he or she needs or wants. Knowing your customer's interests, needs, desires, fears, and hopes is essential for making a sale. How do you find out what your customer likes and needs? Ask. After you ask, you have one more task: Listen. An effective sales message doesn't begin with the salesperson immediately extolling the virtues of the product. First, ask questions that qualify your customer. To **qualify** a customer is to identify whether the customer can afford the product or service you are selling and to learn how to best approach the customer. Does the customer have a family? If so, would he or she be motivated by appealing to concerns for their safety? Is the customer most interested in a low price? Knowing what the customer wants can help you customize your message to your customer.

It's also important to have a positive relationship with your customers. Joe Girard, the number-one car salesman in the United States for eleven years in a row, would send over 13,000 cards to his customers. He'd wish them everything from happy birthday to happy George Washington's Day. The message on the front of each card was simple. It said, "I like you." He sold twice as many cars as whoever came in second place. Customers identified with Joe; they liked him. And they came back to buy more cars from him.[26]

If you already suspect what the customer's needs are, then you can directly identify how what you are selling meets the needs, solves a problem, or addresses an issue that concerns the customer. Your knowledge of what your competitor has to offer and what the customer needs and your ability to briefly and quickly get to the heart of what the customer wants will increase your chances of making the sale.

To identify the customer's needs or issues, you may need to ask specific questions (unless the customer explicitly tells you what he or she wants). Here are some possible questions to ask to help identify a customer's need:

- What do you like best about what you are currently using?
- What would an ideal product look like?
- What do like least about what you are currently using?
- What is missing from what you're currently using?
- How many of these do you use each week?
- What are the key things you're looking for in a new . . . ?
- If you bought our product, when would you need it delivered?
- What could we do to get your business?

MAKE THE RECOMMENDATION After you have analyzed, or qualified, the customer, you'll want to note how your product or service addresses the issues you've identified. Although you don't need to ask for the sale quite yet, you need to describe what you're selling and link your product or service to the the customer's needs. Especially if you're selling several models or versions of the same product (such as a car, a computer, or an insurance benefit package), you'll need to direct the customer to a specific recommendation. If you have over a dozen different models, select one or two that you think are best aligned with your customer's needs. Having too many options can be overwhelming for both you and the customer. If you've understood what your customer's concerns are, you'll be in a good position to begin to steer your customer to a recommendation that is best for him or her.

When making your recommendation, explain and demonstrate how the product works. Provide a step-by-step overview of what the product does. If appropriate, let the customer try the product. Most grocery stores know that one way to sell cheese is to give away free samples. Letting your customer use the product to experience the benefits may be your most important sales tool.

STRESS BENEFITS, NOT FEATURES All customers are interested in the benefits of what you're selling to them. This next point is essential: *You must stress the benefits of what you're selling, not just list the features.* What's the difference between a feature and a benefit? A feature is simply a characteristic of whatever the product or service is. For example, if you say, "This computer screen is very bright," you're describing a feature of the product. A benefit is a good result or something that creates a positive response in a customer. Rather than simply noting that the computer screen is bright, you could describe a benefit of the bright screen: "This means that you won't experience eye strain or headaches, and you can get your work done more quickly." Describing a benefit is a customer-centered way of helping the customer visualize the positive things that will happen to him or her if he or she buys what you are selling. Table 13.4 provides additional examples of features and their corresponding benefits.

A skilled salesperson can quickly assess how to describe a product or service in terms of the benefits the customer will receive. Stressing benefits helps the customer have a positive

TABLE 13.4	Features and Benefits
Customer Features	**Customer Benefits**
This floor is a no-wax floor.	Because this is a no-wax floor, you will never again have to get down on your hands and knees to scrub another floor.
If you sponsor this concert, your company name and logo will be listed in the program.	Sponsoring this event promotes your company and lets everyone in the community know how much you care about supporting the arts. People will view your company in a positive light, which will increase your sales and maintain the goodwill of your customers.
This ergonomically designed chair will keep your back straight.	This ergonomically designed chair will eliminate backaches, increase your productivity, and give you more time to spend on more pleasurable tasks.

feeling about what he or she is buying. To help the customer experience the good things that will happen if he or she makes the purchase, it's not enough to just state a benefit—you'll need to provide evidence. Testimonials from satisfied customers, demonstrations, and evidence from unbiased sources such as *Consumer Reports* are helpful in documenting the truth of your claims. You have an ethical responsibility not to promise too much or make a claim you can't support. By realistically identifying the benefits, you'll increase your credibility and have the best type of customer—a repeat customer.

MAKE THE CLOSE Every good salesperson knows the most critical part of making a sale is the close. The close is when you ask for (and ideally get) the sale. Most closes involve summarizing how the product or service solves a problem or meets a need, cogently listing the benefits, and then asking for the sale.

Some closes use the "yes technique." A salesperson using the yes technique asks the customer a series of questions to which the answer is always yes. If, for example, the customer has already disclosed that he likes a particular model of car, the color of the car, and the features of the car, the salesperson asks a series of questions to which the answer is yes:

Salesperson: "So, Mr. Affolter, you like the Oxford model the best?"

Customer: "Yes."

Salesperson: "And you like the cobalt blue?"

Customer: "Yes."

Salesperson: "You also like the cruise control, satellite radio, and GPS system, right?"

Customer: "Yes, I do."

Salesperson: "So if I can get the Oxford model, in blue, with the features you like, and we can agree on a price, will you buy the car today?"

Customer: "OK, yes."

The yes technique is based on the principle that "It's better to get a message out of someone than to put one in him or her." Get the customer to state what he or she likes and to reach no other conclusion when asked to make the purchase than that the correct answer is yes.

RESPOND TO OBJECTIONS Textbooks have a way of presenting models or specific strategies that make it seem as though all you need to do is follow the suggested sequence of steps or specific prescriptions and you'll be successful. When attempting to sell something to someone, you'll soon discover that it's usually not quite that easy. In most sales situations, the customer is not likely to simply say yes or "I'll take it" after you've hooked the person, identified the issue, made the recommendation, stressed the benefits, and provided a closing. Customers will likely have questions, concerns, and objections to the claims you've made. How you respond to those will often determine whether you get the sale or not. Consider the following suggestions.

Some customers may not explicitly state what is bothering them. For example, they may not say, "I don't have enough money to buy what you're selling." So, you need to "listen between the lines" if the customer says something like "I'm not sure I'm prepared to buy this product now" or "Buying this product doesn't fit into my plans right now." If price appears to be the objection, suggesting a payment plan spread over a period of time, directing the customer to a less expensive option, or reconfiguring the product so it costs less may be what you need to do to respond to the unspoken issue of price. The more you can remove hidden agendas, the more likely you are to be able to address the specific concern. Open-ended questions such as, "What questions do you have about this product?" or "Is there something that I could do today that would help you make a commitment?" can help you find a customer's underlying objection. The closer you can get to a customer's real objection, the more likely it will be that you can address it and get the sale.

How do you determine a customer's real objections? You listen, observe, ask good questions, and listen some more. If you can find the true objection and then successfully address that objection, you've got the sale.

"If they don't like our proposal I'll show them the kittens. Everybody likes kittens."

© *The New Yorker Collection 2007 Peter C. Vey. From cartoonbank.com. All Rights Reserved.*

If a customer says no, or, "I'll need to think about this," or "I'm not sure I'm ready to decide today," do your best to listen and see if you can identify what it is that is keeping the customer from saying yes. Keep the conversation going. By asking follow-up questions, exploring objections, listening for clues, and observing nonverbal behavior, you may be able to successfully respond to a rejection. Once the customer has left or hung up the phone, it's less likely that the person will return (although some customers simply need more time to ponder the options). You're more likely to get the sale if the customer is physically present or if you are in contact with the customer. We don't encourage such high-pressure tactics as, "This is a one-time offer, only good in the next hour" or "You must decide today." It's also unethical to claim that the product is the last one left when there are more in the back room.

Ethics Is Everything

According to Barbara J. Krumsiek, chief executive and chair of the Calvert Group Ltd., an investment firm, ethics is everything when it comes to leadership. When asked what she thought the most essential lessons students should be learning in college, Krumsiek replied,

> Weave ethics and responsibility through every course. Every single course should have an ethical component. I think the notion that ethics is a code of conduct or a set of rules or a set of principles is one of the big culprits in the meltdown. Ethics is how you think about things when it's not written down.
>
> I tell Calvert people you make decisions every day, hundreds of them, that have ethical content.

> We couldn't possibly write codes of ethics to cover everything you do. So therefore, you're going to have to do the right thing. I'm counting on you to do the right thing.[27]

Although ethics will permeate all aspects of your work life, your ethical obligation is especially important if you're trying to persuade someone to do something or sell them something. You have an ethical responsibility to present information that is honest, accurate, relevant, and on point. As Krumsiek's comments suggest, ethics is an element in every communication action—it's implicit in every communication and leadership action you undertake, especially when you're sharing information or persuading others.

A customer may ask you something about what you're selling that you don't know. *If you don't know the answer to a question, say so, and find the answer quickly.* Promise to get back to the customer with the answer by a specific time or date. Be sure to keep your promise.

One maxim that has served salespeople well is "Underpromise and overdeliver." Don't promise more than you know your product or service can offer, and work to provide even more than the customer expects. Although customers generally do not like surprises, they are usually delighted when what they've purchased surprises them with more than what was promised.

One of the biggest sales mistakes new salespeople make is talking too much after they have made a sale. Once the customer has made the decision to buy a product or service, don't keep describing additional benefits.

Relating to Others: Making Special Presentations

Besides informing and persuading others, you may be called on simply to introduce a speaker, present an award, receive an award (because you're such a good leader and communicator), or make a toast. In these special presentation situations, the audience has certain expectations of what you may say. When introducing someone, for example, it's assumed you will extol the virtues and credentials of the person you're introducing. Toasts are expected to be brief yet interesting.

Introducing Others

The ultimate purpose of an introduction is to arouse interest in a speaker and his or her topic and establish the speaker's credibility. When you are asked to give a speech of introduction for a featured speaker or honored guest, your purposes are similar to those of a good opening to a speech: You need to get the attention of the audience, build the speaker's credibility, and introduce the speaker's general subject. You also need to make the speaker feel welcome while revealing some of the speaker's personal qualities so that the audience can feel they know the speaker more intimately. There are two cardinal rules for giving introductory speeches: Be brief and be accurate.

- Be brief. The audience has come to hear the main speaker or honor the guest, not to listen to you.

- Be accurate. Nothing so disturbs a speaker as having to begin by correcting the introducer. If you are going to introduce someone at a meeting or dinner, ask that person to supply you with biographical data beforehand. If someone else provides you with the speaker's background, make sure the information is accurate. Be certain that you know how to pronounce the speaker's name and any other names or terms you will need to use.

The following short speech of introduction adheres to the two criteria we have just suggested: It's brief and it's accurate.

> This evening, friends, we have the opportunity to hear one of the most innovative mayors in the history of our community. Mary Norris's experience running her own real estate business gave her an opportunity to pilot a new approach to attracting new businesses to our community, even before she was elected mayor in last year's landslide victory. The Good Government League recently recognized her as the most successful mayor in our state. Not only is she a skilled manager and spokesperson for our city, but she is also a warm and caring person. I am pleased to introduce my friend Mary Norris.

Finally, keep the needs of your audience in mind at all times. If the person you are introducing truly needs no introduction, do not give one! Just welcome the speaker and step aside.

Presenting an Award

Presenting an award is somewhat like introducing a speaker or guest: Remember that the audience did not come to hear you but to see and hear the winner of the award.

First, when presenting an award, refer to the occasion. Awards are often given to mark the anniversary of a special event, the completion of a long-range task, the accomplishments of a lifetime, or extraordinary achievements.

Next, talk about the history and significance of the award. This section of the speech may be fairly long if the audience knows little about the award; it will be brief if the audience is already familiar with the history and purpose of the award. Whatever the award, a discussion of its significance will add to its meaning for the person who receives it.

In the final section of an award presentation, name the person to whom the award is given. The longest part of this segment is the description of the achievements that elicited the award. That description should be given in glowing terms. Hyperbole is appropriate here. If the name of the person getting the award has already been made public, you may refer to the person by name throughout your description. If you are going to announce the individual's name for the first time, you will probably want to recite the achievements first and leave the person's name for last. Even though some members of the audience may recognize the recipient from your description, still save the drama of the actual announcement until the last moment.

Acceptance speeches have a reputation for being boring. If you keep your speech brief and behave graciously, your audience will agree that the right person received the award.

Accepting an Award

Anyone who receives an award or nomination usually responds with a brief acceptance speech. Acceptance speeches have received something of a bad reputation because of the lengthy, emotional, rambling, and generally boring speeches delivered annually on prime-time TV by the winners of the film industry's Oscars.

The same audience who may resent a lengthy oration will readily appreciate a brief, heartfelt expression of thanks. In fact, brief acceptance speeches can actually be quite insightful, even inspiring, and can leave the audience feeling no doubt that the right person won the award. Two months before he died in 1979, John Wayne accepted an honorary Oscar with these touching words:

> Thank you, ladies and gentlemen. Your applause is just about the only medicine a fella would ever need. I'm mighty pleased I can amble here tonight. Oscar and I have something in common. Oscar first came on the Hollywood scene in 1928. So did I. We're both a little weatherbeaten, but we're still here and plan to be around a whole lot longer.[28]

If you have the good fortune to receive an award, your acceptance speech may be impromptu, because you may not know that you have won until the award is presented. A fairly simple formula should help you compose a good acceptance speech on the spur of the moment.

First, thank the person making the presentation and the organization that he or she represents. It is also gracious to thank a few people who have contributed to your success—but resist thanking a long list of everyone you have ever known, down to the family dog.

Next, comment on the meaning or significance of the award to you. You may also wish to reflect on the larger significance of the award to the people and ideals it honors.

Finally, find some meaning in the award for your audience—people who respect your accomplishments and who may themselves aspire to similar achievements. In what has become one of the most often quoted acceptance speeches ever made, William Faulkner dedicated his 1950 Nobel Peace Prize for Literature to:

> the young men and women already dedicated to the same anguish and travail, among whom is already that one who will some day stand here where I am standing.[29]

Making a Toast

It's not uncommon in a business or professional setting to have an opportunity to propose a toast. It could be at a business lunch or dinner, or at the beginning or ending of an informal or social meeting with a client or customer. A **toast** is a brief salute to the occasion or is dedicated to a particular person, usually accompanied by a round of drinks and immediately followed by the raising or clinking together of glasses or goblets. The purpose of a toast is to enhance relationships, celebrate an accomplishment, or remember a past event. The custom is said to have taken its name from the old custom of tossing a bit of bread or a crouton into a beverage for flavoring.[30] "Drinking the toast" was somewhat like enjoying a dunked doughnut.

The modern toast is usually quite short, only a few sentences at most. Some toasts incorporate a quotation you might remember that seems appropriate to the occasion as, for example, one given at a business dinner by a client:

> I propose a toast. We are a long way from home this evening. But as we have worked together in our meetings today you and your staff have made us feel very welcome. It was Robert Frost who said, "Home is a place where when you go there they have to take you in." Thank you, colleagues, for taking us in this evening and making us feel so much at home.

If you are asked to make an impromptu toast, let your audience and the occasion dictate what you say. Sincerity is more important than wit. At a dinner one of your authors attended in Moscow a few years ago, all the guests were asked to stand at some point during the meal and offer a toast. Although this Russian custom took all of us by surprise, one of our friends gave a heartfelt and well-received toast that went something like this:

> We have spent the past week enjoying both the natural beauty and the many marvels of your country. We have visited the exquisite palaces of the czars and stood in amazement before some of the world's great art treasures. But we have also discovered that the most important resource of Russia is the warmth of her people. Here's to new and lasting friendships.

Our Russian hosts were most appreciative. The rest of us were impressed. Mary's toast was a resounding success because she spoke sincerely about her audience and the occasion.

terms & definitions

Toast a brief speech saluting a momentous occasion.

Wrap-Up

Principles of informing others, whether in a presentation, brief, or report, include these ideas:

- Use simple ideas.
- Pace the flow of the information.
- Relate new information to what listeners already know.
- Use adult learning strategies.
- Relate to listeners' interests.
- Build in redundancy.
- Reinforce ideas verbally and nonverbally.

These are the nine steps of the need-centered training model:

- Anchor all training processes in analyzing the organizational and trainee needs.
- Analyze the training task: Break the skill into sequential steps.
- Develop training objectives: Identify what you want to accomplish.
- Organize training content: Structure the training information and skills.
- Determine training methods: Decide how you will present the content.
- Select training resources: Identify the written and visual materials you need.
- Complete the training plan: Display all elements of the training lesson.
- Deliver the training: Bring the training to life.
- Assess the training: Determine if the trainees liked it, learned it, and can perform it.

Persuasion is the process of attempting to change or reinforce attitudes, beliefs, values, or behaviors. Several principles explain how persuasion works.

- Cognitive dissonance is a sense of mental disorganization or imbalance that arises when new information conflicts with previously organized thought patterns. People are persuaded to resolve the dissonance.
- Maslow's classic hierarchy of needs suggest that people are persuaded when the proposed persuasive goal helps to meet an unmet need.
- Both fear appeals and positive motivational appeals motivate listeners to respond to persuasive messages.

The steps of presenting an effective sales talk include:

- The hook: Getting customer attention and interest
- Identifying the issues: Identifying what's in it for the customer
- Making a recommendation
- Identifying the benefits including providing evidence for the benefits
- Making the close: Ask for the sale

There are special occasions in the workplace when you may be invited to say a few words, including introducing others, presenting and receiving and award, and giving a toast.

Reviewing Key Terms

Inform *326*

Persuade *327*

Adult learners *327*

Briefing *328*

Report *328*

Public relations presentation *329*

Training *330*

Task analysis *331*

Cognitive dissonance *333*

Hierarchy of needs *334*

Ethos *335*

Logos *335*

Pathos *335*

Credibility *336*

Competence *336*

Trustworthiness *336*

Dynamism *337*

Charisma *337*

Initial credibility *337*

Derived credibility *337*

Terminal credibility *337*

Proof *337*

Evidence *337*

Reasoning *337*

Inductive reasoning *337*

Reasoning by analogy *337*

Deductive reasoning *338*

Syllogism *338*

Causal reasoning *338*

Logical fallacy *338*

The Principle Points

Principle One: Be aware of your communication with yourself and others.

- Be consciously aware of using strategies that will make your informative messages clear, interesting, and memorable.

- Be prepared to make your credentials known to your listeners by having a brief summary of your qualifications and accomplishments ready for the person who will introduce you, to help enhance your initial credibility.

- To be a better informed consumer of persuasive messages, as well as a more ethical persuasive speaker, be aware of and avoid using common logical reasoning fallacies.

Principle Two: Effectively use and interpret verbal messages.

- To create negative visualization, describe in detail how bleak or terrible the future will be if your solution is not implemented.

- To create positive visualization, describe in detail how wonderful the future will be if your solution is implemented.

- To make yourself seem more competent to your audience, cite evidence to support your ideas.

- Use concrete illustrations and descriptions to appeal to an audience's emotions.

Principle Three: Effectively use and interpret nonverbal messages.

- Observe the nonverbal behavior of your audience to help you determine whether your message has been communicated clearly.

- Nonverbally reinforce ideas to make your message memorable.

- Use presentation aids to help evoke both positive and negative emotions as well as positive and negative visualizations.

Principle Four: Listen and respond thoughtfully to others.

- Before you deliver your presentations to an audience, talk and listen to audience members to help you customize your message for them.

- Be prepared to answer questions after your presentation, regardless of whether there is a planned question-and-answer period.

Principle Five: Appropriately adapt message to others.

- If you are speaking to an apathetic audience or one that is not even aware that a problem exists, emphasize the problem portion of your problem-and-solution presentations.

- If your audience is aware of the problem you are discussing, emphasize the solution or solutions in your problem-and-solution presentations.

- Be realistic about what you can accomplish with neutral and unreceptive audiences.

- Focus on areas of agreement with an unreceptive audience.
- If you audience is unreceptive, advance your strongest arguments first.

Applying Your Skills

1. Based on the suggestions provided on page 344, write a word picture—a vivid, colorful description that appeals to the senses—for one of the following scenes:
   - Your first day on a new job.
   - A difficult situation you faced at work
   - The implication of enduring no health insurance for all employees
   - Your work team receiving an award

2. Identify the logical fallacy in each of the following arguments:
   - We must raise taxes to finance the construction of new schools in our community. Otherwise, we will have to close the schools because our students won't be able to pass the state-required tests.
   - Everybody knows you can't find a decent job in our small town.
   - My dentist recommends we vote in favor of the proposition to reduce immigration so you should vote for it too.
   - The reason our children don't do well in math and science is because the stock market went down 300 points last week.
   - Sarah grew up in a state that spends less money on education than any state in the country; she could not possibly have any useful ideas about how to improve our children's test scores on standardized tests.

3. Select a product that you like and use. Based upon the steps of designing an effective sales presentation presented on pages 348–352, design a sales message imagining that you are selling the product to someone who is similar to you in age, interests, and experiences. Next, select a person who is considerably different from you, and redesign your sales presentation for him or her.

4. Prepare a short toast or no more than three or four sentences for one of the following occasions:
   - A business dinner with clients visiting from Russia.
   - A retirement party for one of your coworkers.
   - A party to celebrate your company reaching a sales goal.
   - A dinner hosted by a colleague of yours to celebrate that she and her spouse recently adopted a child.

14

Writing for Business

chapter **outline**

After reading this chapter, you should be able to

- Describe different methods for organizing a business document.
- Describe business writing style and explain what is meant by tone and unbiased messages.
- Describe ways to prepare clear written messages.
- List and discuss three strategies for appropriate use of technology in business writing.
- Identify and apply the strategies for effective use of email.
- Define business correspondence and give four examples of common business correspondence.
- Identify the elements of an interoffice memo.
- Differentiate between progress reports, activity reports, and formal reports.

The quote on this page from newspaper legend Joseph Pulitzer, the father of writing's famous Pulitzer Prize, sums up the essence of good and powerful writing in one thirty-four-word statement. It's one of the great writing quotes of all time and focuses on what have often been called the "ABC's of writing" (accuracy, brevity, and clarity). When Pulitzer took over the struggling *New York World* in 1883, the world was a vastly different place.[1] He most likely couldn't have envisioned today's digital media and our ever-increasing reliance on technology to assist us in our writing. However, the value of his statement, and the value of good clear writing, has never changed. In today's world of 140-character Twitter posts and text messages full of abbreviations, it remains extremely important to focus on developing effective writing skills. In our current economy, with more job seekers than positions available, honing writing skills may be the one thing that puts a prospective hire over the top.

leading **questions**

1. Why is Pulitzer's quote timeless? Why are writing skills vital to the twenty-first-century leader?

2. What about your own writing skills? Can you write a properly formatted business letter? An accurate and clear email message? Do you know the elements of an office memo?

3. Why are leaders concerned with the lack of writing skills in the new workforce? What does that mean in an increasingly competitive job market?

Leaders must know how to write in an effective manner. The lack of adequate writing skills among U.S. businesspeople is well-documented.[2] A study published in *Management Review* noted that poor writing skills among business leaders were putting companies at risk.[3] Executives have identified a lack of writing skills among job candidates interviewing for jobs. The study found that employers were beginning to place greater emphasis on writing and that job offers were going to those who can write. To address this concern, many employers have adopted policies requiring job candidates either to submit a brief written report as part of the screening process or to complete a writing exam as a part of the interview process.[4]

"Put it before them briefly so they will read it, clearly so they will appreciate it, picturesquely so they will remember it, and above all, accurately so they will be guided by its light."

— **Joseph Pulitzer**

This chapter introduces you to some of the more important skills for business writing and the preparation of business reports. The chapter focuses primarily on Principle Two, *Effectively use and interpret verbal messages*. We examine the general rules and styles used for business documents and stress the benefits of clear and effective writing. We examine the customary format of business reports and the tone, content, and purpose of their component parts. Samples of various business documents are provided to give you the opportunity to develop and sharpen your written communication skills.

Developing Business Writing Skills

Certain business writing skills apply to a number of different types of business documents. Writers must be able to organize and develop paragraphs. They must be able to write in a style that reflects appropriate tone and use vocabulary that is adapted to the organization.

They must be able to write clearly using appropriate terminology while being concise. Finally, writers must be sure to use correct spelling and grammar. All these skills require planning and preparation before the writing process begins.

Organizing and Developing Paragraphs

Maintaining a clear organizational pattern that flows naturally and is easy for the reader to understand will increase the effectiveness of your written communication. Making the document pleasing to look at and easy to read means "chunking" the information into visually distinct sections, using paragraphs.

ORGANIZE THE DOCUMENT   Appropriately organizing a document is the first step a business writer can take to make sure the reader understands the message. There are several methods for organizing a document, depending on the type of document, its content, and the audience. The following paragraphs discuss some options for organizing a business document:

Problem-solution development begins with a description of a problem and moves on to discuss possible solutions or a proposed solution to the problem. A variation on this method is the *cause-and-effect* style of development, which outlines a cause and its possible effects. For example, if you were writing a report on employee turnover, you would start by describing the problem of turnover and its magnitude, then move on to discuss some possible ways to retain employees and minimize turnover. You would then outline the proposed best solution and offer reasons for selecting this solution.

The *chronological* or *sequential* organizational pattern begins with the first in a series of events or steps and moves on to the second, third, and so on. This organization pattern allows you to report on events or steps in the order in which they occurred or will occur. Using sequential development is helpful when writing a training manual, for example. When training someone in how to perform a skill, the steps must be enacted in a particular order. A team leader overseeing fifteen service agents at a customer service call center may need to develop a short training program on how to process a call. The training manual would likely include a step-by-step description of each behavior involved in processing a call effectively and successfully.

Priority development focuses on the most urgent or important information first, then moves on to less important or urgent information. This style would work well when developing an agenda for a business meeting. An agenda lists the items to be discussed in the meeting in the order they will be discussed. If, for example, an increase in customer complaints were an important priority item to discuss in a meeting, then that would be listed first on the agenda.

General-to-specific development is a format that allows you to begin with the big picture and move on to specific details. When preparing a sales proposal, for example, you may want to start by discussing the overall goals and move on toward the specifics of the product or service you are offering. Another way to use this method is to go from specific to general. For example, a restaurant chain marketing agent might describe a recent drop in sales at one store location and move on to outline the larger, global effects of this decline on the entire organization.[5]

Although this list of organizational patterns is not exhaustive, it can give you an idea of the various methods used to organize information. While organizing your document, you need to be aware of the reader and to select a method that best fits with the subject matter. An effective way to determine a method that works well for your message is to first develop an outline, or a basic skeleton of the information you want to write about. You can review the format to ensure that it fits with your message and makes sense to the reader before you fully develop the document.

DEVELOP PARAGRAPHS   The paragraphs in your document are important tools that you can use to divide your information into logical sections. Paragraphs also provide visual breaks on the page, making the message easier to read. Three factors to consider when developing a paragraph are the topic sentence, length, and coherence.

The **topic sentence** of a paragraph is generally the first sentence, and it states the main idea. In other words, the topic sentence informs the reader about the content of the paragraph. The sentences that follow the topic sentence support the idea asserted in the topic sentence. For example, when writing in support of a proposed travel budget increase, you could start with the following sentence: "As a result of the rising cost of fuel, transportation costs have nearly tripled in the last quarter." The sentences following the topic sentence in the paragraph describe and offer evidence of the increased cost.

The second factor to consider in developing a paragraph is length, which again depends on your subject matter, reader, and the type of document. A memo, for instance, may have short paragraphs. In a letter or report, making the paragraphs too short could result in an underdeveloped message and information that is not clear to the reader. Paragraphs that are too long are not visually appealing and can be difficult to read if they fail to chunk information into manageable sections for the reader.

The third factor to consider when constructing paragraphs is coherence. **Coherence** refers to unity created by common underlying concepts, logical organization, and clear, natural development of the content.[6] Coherence can be created, for example, by writing in one tense or from one point of view. For example, suppose a manager writes the following in a memo: "The employee training sessions *are being conducted* on Wednesday afternoons. We *trained* six employees in these sessions." The switch from present tense in the first sentence to past tense in the second sentence undermines coherence and makes little sense. Transitions can be used within and between paragraphs to help the paragraphs flow smoothly. Also, to make the information easier to read, headers can be used when separating paragraphs or main ideas. Headers also help to break the page up into visually distinct and easy-to-read sections.

Using Appropriate Writing Style

When writing for business, consider both style and clarity. **Writing style** refers to the tone, language, voice, and overall viewpoint of the sentences. Compared to other forms of writing, business writing style is generally more precise, brief, and direct. Also, the style of business writing has evolved from a previously formal and elaborate style to one that is more personal, although this may vary depending on the organization. The business writer also needs to take into consideration the tone and bias of the language used.

USE APPROPRIATE TONE AND VOCABULARY Whatever the type of document they are preparing, writers should consider the tone of their message. **Tone** refers to the attitude of the writer toward both the reader and the subject matter. In many ways the tone of a written document has an effect similar to that of the tone of voice in face-to-face communication—the tone of a document (courteous, brusque, demanding, deferential, or friendly) complements the words used in the document. The following questions will help you to determine the appropriate tone for your message.

- Why am I writing this document?
- Who am I writing to and what do I want them to understand?
- What kind of tone will complement and reinforce my written message?

Fortunately, you can use the same tone for most business messages. Remember that the main goal is to adapt your message to your reader. Using difficult vocabulary or phrases that demonstrate a lack of confidence, such as "I think you will find our product to be useful and beneficial to your organization," may not effectively communicate to your reader that you are convinced of the benefits of your product. Follow these general guidelines when considering what kind of tone to use in your letters and how to present information in that tone:

- Be confident.
- Be courteous and sincere.
- Adapt to the reader by stressing benefits.
- Write at an appropriate level of difficulty.

terms & definitions

Topic sentence generally, the first sentence of a paragraph that states the main idea.

Coherence unity in writing created by common underlying concepts, logical organization, and clear, natural development of the content.

Writing style the tone, language, voice, and overall viewpoint of the sentences in a piece of writing.

Tone the attitude of the writer toward both the reader and the subject matter that is communicated in a written document.

USE UNBIASED LANGUAGE One of the ways you can make your business writing effective is to avoid biased messages. **Biased messages** include words and expressions that offend because they make inappropriate assumptions or repeat stereotypes about gender, ethnicity, physical or mental disability, age, or sexual orientation. Although some people dismiss the notion that they should use unbiased messages as mere "political correctness," in reality, it is what most parents have been teaching their children for years—to be considerate of others. Following are several ways to use unbiased verbal messages:

Avoid use of the generic *he*. Generic verbal messages include words that may apply to only one sex, race, or other group, as though that group represents everyone. For example, using the word *he* to include both men and women is no longer appropriate in the diverse professional workplace. Some people argue that the use of *he* automatically includes both men and women. But research does not confirm this widely held belief.[7] The use of *he* is exclusionary; it leaves women out.[8] Using *he/she* is awkward in many situations; it's best to use plural pronouns. Rather than writing "A manager is effective because *he* is a competent communicator," write "Managers are effective because *they* are competent communicators."

Contrary to popular belief, when writers use the generic *man* to refer to both men and women (as in the word *mailman*), women feel excluded.[9] In fact, research suggests that people usually visualize men when they hear that label. Additionally, when job titles end in "man," individuals in those positions are assumed to have stereotypically masculine personality traits. Rather than using the generic word *man*, try using the following to make your business writing style more effective and appropriate:

Instead of . . .	Use . . .
Chairman	Chair
Freshman	First-year student
Fireman	Firefighter
Salesman	Sales representative
Mailman	Mail carrier

Parallel verbal phrases use language and phrases that are symmetrical. Nonparallel verbal messages treat groups differently and therefore are perceived negatively, as biased. Here are a few examples to clarify the difference between parallel and nonparallel verbal messages:

Nonparallel Phrases	Parallel Phrases
Ladies and men	Ladies and gentlemen
Men and girls	Men and women
Boys and women	Boys and girls

terms & definitions

Biased messages messages that include words or expressions that offend because they make inappropriate assumptions or repeat stereotypes about gender, ethnicity, physical or mental disability, age, or sexual orientation.

Clarity the specificity of a message and how easily the reader can comprehend the information.

Writing with Clarity

Have you ever tried to read something, and you couldn't understand it? Maybe the words were all spelled correctly and easy to read, but the message was still unclear? **Clarity** refers to the specificity of a message and how easily the reader can comprehend the information. Many of the ideas discussed in this section were also discussed in Chapter 3, which examined how to use and interpret verbal messages. However, Chapter 3 discussed clarity as it pertains to oral, or spoken, messages. In this section, we discuss clarity as it relates to the written word.

When writing for business, as opposed to other forms of writing (such as creative writing), clarity of message and thought is very important. Ambiguous messages or unclear sentences can prevent your writing from communicating to the reader. A clear paragraph is coherent; it has a logical sequence and smooth transitions between the sentences.

Another consideration in achieving clarity is the choice of words. Abstract phrases, such as "use a bright color palette," will not communicate as much or as clearly as concrete phrases, such as "use bright oranges, yellows, and reds." The business writer should also be cautious about jargon. As defined in Chapter 3, **jargon** is language used by a particular group, profession, or culture that may not be understood or used by other people. Jargon is common in the workplace, and it tends to become overused.[10] If you've ever worked as a restaurant server, for example, you probably recognize the phrase "in the weeds," which you have used anytime you are so overwhelmed with customers that you feel like you can't catch up. But for those who haven't worked in the food industry, that statement holds little meaning. Phrases such as "Let's dialogue" (instead of "Let's discuss this") can become clichéd and can seem inappropriate to a reader outside of the organization. Jargon can be effective if readers are familiar with the terms. When writing for an outside audience, however, avoid jargon.

A final consideration when writing for clarity is to be concise. **Concise writing** avoids unnecessary words and phrases but does not sacrifice clarity or necessary detail. A report need not be brief to be concise, and making something shorter is not appropriate if clarity is sacrificed. Here are some suggestions for writing concisely.[11]

USE SUBORDINATION   Instead of writing "We received the sales report this afternoon. It was five pages. The report clearly illustrated a drop in sales marketwide," subordinate, using conjunctions to combine the ideas from these sentences to make one coherent, concise sentence: "This afternoon we received the five-page sales report, which clearly illustrates a marketwide drop in sales."

AVOID REDUNDANCY   Even if you are not repeating whole phrases and sentences, a report can still be redundant. Eliminate qualifying terms that are not necessary, such as "first and foremost" or "basic and fundamental."

DO NOT OVERUSE INTENSIFIERS   Sometimes intensifiers are relevant and help convey the importance of an idea. However, their overuse can become redundant and cause your writing to lose some of its clarity. It is not necessary to write "The report was perfectly clear and completely accurate." Instead, just say "The report was clear and accurate." Although intensifiers are sometimes appropriate, take caution to avoid overusing them because they lose their intensity.

AVOID TELEGRAPHIC LANGUAGE   One pitfall in attempting to write concisely is the tendency to oversimplify. **Telegraphic style** is a writing style that condenses a message by eliminating articles, pronouns, conjunctions, and transitions. Although telegraphic style may make a document brief, the document may not necessarily remain clear. Consider the following examples:

Telegraphic style: Per May 5 memo, meeting agenda attached. Supervisor wants report by Houston office. Meeting as soon as report received. August almost full, please advise to set date.

Clear message: As I mentioned in my May 5 memo, I have attached the next meeting agenda. The supervisor wants the report to be completed by the Houston office. As soon as we get the report, we can schedule a meeting. Our August calendar is almost full, so please suggest a date soon.

Using Correct Spelling and Grammar

Readers often view how you communicate in written messages as a measure of your effectiveness.[12] Paying close attention to spelling and grammar will help you develop credibility with your readers. A document that contains spelling or grammatical errors can be difficult to read and may fail to communicate the message completely. Mistakes generally reflect poorly on the writer and often on the organization as well.

terms & definitions

Jargon language used by a particular group, profession, or culture that may not be understood or used by other people.

Concise writing writing that avoids unnecessary words and phrases.

Telegraphic style a writing style that condenses the message by eliminating articles, pronouns, conjunctions, and transitions.

The spell-check tool on most word-processing programs is a good place to start when you want to identify spelling errors. Spell-checkers are not foolproof, however, and relying solely on a spell-check tool may not give effective results.[13] It is always a good idea to go over a hard copy of any document yourself and then pass it on to a friend or a colleague to proofread before delivering it to readers. Reread your notes to confirm the spelling of names and places; a proofreader often cannot catch such mistakes. For example, Mr. Schmitt; may not appreciate receiving a letter addressed to Mr. Schmidt; but because the latter is a more common spelling, it will likely not be identified as an error by a spell-check program or a proofreader. Examine the following sentences to see if you can identify the mistakes that a spell-checker would miss.[14]

- Of all the perspective employees we have interviewed, you have the most impressive resume and work experience. (*prospective*)

- A background in education training has proven to be a real compliment to my experience as a trainer. (*complement*)

- . . . identified potential roadblocks to ensure that project operations preceded smoothly. (*proceeded*)

- . . . organized and lead a fifteen-member customer service team who processed all the calls in the customer retention department. (*led*)

Communication Skills FOR A **Digital Age**

Growing up in a Digital World

According to a recent report in the *New York Times*,[15] the effects of growing up in an increasingly digital world can be seen in the new generation of young people, and they are not all good. Researchers have discovered students have less and less ability to focus on one activity, read longer prose, or even comprehend longer messages that require extended periods of attention. In fact, the constant stimulation from video games, phone calls, text messages, and social media updates (all often accessed from one or two mobile devices) has lessened their ability to concentrate at all. In addition, the interactive nature of these programs is often preferred to homework, studying, and reading books, none of which provide the reward of immediate feedback.

However, the same generation can often run laps around older generations in their ability to make full use of digital media and new technologies. New graduates may be experts at using new media, but has it harmed their ability to read and write accurate, clear material? With cell phone keyboards that encourage responses such as "ill text u after the mtg," future business professionals need to know when and how to "turn off" the shorthand. Effective development of basic writing skills is still necessary to present a positive, competent image.

Applying Your Skills

Take stock of your own social media use. Do you find yourself composing more and more shorthand abbreviated messages? Do you read these types of messages more every day? How has that affected your own ability to focus? When was the last time you read a book? (If you are reading this text, you are off to a good start.)

Here are some keys to developing writing skills in an age of informal communication:

- *Learn proper grammar.* We often rely on word-processing programs to "tell" us when there is a grammatical problem in our writing. And many writers have grown so accustomed to the "little green squiggly line" under their sentences that they ignore the grammatical problems altogether.

- *Take time to read longer prose.* Read textbooks, read long-form journalism, read the articles in a magazine, and read works of fiction. Just take the time to read. Our vocabulary increases when we read often, but it must be more than "omg."

- *Take care with your spelling.* Shorthand has become common and can be used effectively in the workplace. But Twitter users, for example, know how misspellings are commonplace because of the need to condense a message to a limited number of characters. Although appropriate for Twitter, remember the accurate spelling of words when crafting a more formal document.

- *Give your brain some downtime.* Take away or turn off the new media barrage. New imaging studies have found that periods of rest for the brain are vital to allowing it to make connections, process new information, commit that information to longer term memory, and even develop our sense of self.[16]

All the words in these four sentences are spelled correctly and would not be caught by a spell-checker. However, the indicated words are not appropriate for the context. Although helpful, a spell-check program is no replacement for editing and proofreading.

Equally important in business writing is proper usage of grammar. **Grammar** refers to the functions of words and the way they work together to form coherent language. Standard English grammatical rules apply in business writing, and being familiar with these rules will help in the writing process. Many word-processing programs have grammar check tools, but be aware that these programs may not correct all mistakes. Once again, proofreading a hard copy of your document for grammatical errors is always a good idea.

The skills discussed in this section apply to all forms of business writing. They help make your writing clear, precise, effective, logical, and accurate. The first skill is to clearly develop and organize your document, using structure and clear paragraphs. The second skill is to use the appropriate writing style for your document, audience, and subject. A third skill is to write clearly, using concise, effective messages to enhance communication. The fourth skill we discussed is to make sure your spelling and grammar are correct, which can develop your credibility with the reader and ensure you have effectively communicated your message. Use these skills when developing any business document.

terms & definitions

Grammar the study of the functions of words and the way they work together to form coherent language.

RECAP

Skills for Effective Business Writing

Skills	Strategies	Examples
Organize the document	Decide on an organizational structure or format.	A persuasive sales proposal might use a problem-solution format.
	Use paragraphs with topic sentences.	Start a new paragraph with a new topic sentence for new ideas, to highlight the main ideas and make the document easy to read.
	Develop an outline	Lay out your main ideas first to see how they fit together. Then support with subpoints where necessary.
Use appropriate style	Select appropriate tone and vocabulary	"Hi, how are you doing, Sarah?" works well for an informal greeting, whereas "Good afternoon, Dr. Strong," strikes a more formal tone.
	Avoid biased language.	Say *police officer* instead of *policeman*, or cop.
Write with clarity	Be concise.	The statement "Please come to the meeting which will be today at 5 o'clock in the afternoon." is too wordy. A more concise statement would be "Please come to the meeting at 5 P.M. today."
	Avoid jargon.	Don't use words or phrases that only certain people might understand, particularly when composing for an audience outside the organization.
Use correct spelling and grammar	Use more than word-processing programs' spell-check tools.	Have a friend, family member, or coworker assist by proofreading; read the document aloud; and double-check the spelling of proper nouns.

Using Technology and Email

As the workplace becomes increasingly media saturated, we cannot ignore the importance of remaining professional and effective in our use of technologically mediated communication. Business leaders report an increasing pressure from new graduates to develop or maintain a wired workplace, with easy Wi-Fi access that allows users to integrate their many digital devices seamlessly.[17] Although technology can expand efficiency, leaders must be cautious that mediated communication doesn't result in messages not being expressed clearly. Effective, appropriate use of technology and email can enhance a group's image both within and outside the organization.

Learning to Use Technology Thoughtfully

Although perfecting business writing skills is challenging, what might be more challenging for new leaders is learning when and how to use technology to communicate. Many times the question that confronts a leader is, "Should I communicate to others in writing or should I communicate in person?" Leaders need to be aware of when writing a document is more appropriate and when speaking in person is preferable. If a leader decides to communicate through writing, then which format is best? Is an email appropriate, or should a letter be sent? If a leader decides to communicate orally, is a voice-mail message appropriate, or should he or she schedule a face-to-face meeting? These questions are important, especially because *Business Week* writer Michael Mandel reported that 25 percent of 7,800 leaders who were surveyed reported that voice mail, email, and meetings were completely ineffective in the workplace; nearly 40 percent of the leaders spent a half to full day per week on communication activities that were ineffective.[18]

To use technology effectively when writing and speaking, it's important to understand what communication researchers refer to as **media richness**, or how closely a technology simulates face-to-face communication.[19] As we noted in Chapter 9, according to media richness theory, a method or channel of communication is rich if it offers the possibility of instant feedback; allows both verbal and nonverbal cues to be processed by senders and receivers; allows the use of natural, informal language rather than formal language; and customizes messages to individuals rather than communicating to a mass of people. Management and marketing researchers Robert Lengel and Richard Daft describe how the channel (face-to-face conversation, email, text message, or whatever it may be) influences how messages are received. Lengel and Daft assert that different media have different degrees of richness; some channels are rich, others are lean. For example, flyers or posters advertising a meeting are considered a lean medium because they convey messages using a single channel (the visual channel) and because readers of a poster have no interaction with the creator of the poster. In contrast, face-to-face meetings are considered a rich medium because they convey messages using multiple channels (sight, sound, smell, touch) and allow people to interact. Figure 14.1 illustrates the media richness continuum.[20]

As you can see from Figure 14.1, as the number of channels through which messages are conveyed increases, communication becomes more interactive and personal. As the number of channels decreases, communication becomes less interactive and more impersonal. The following section offers guidelines to help you become aware of media richness and how to apply this model in business and professional settings.

The completely wired and media-saturated workplace increasingly demands effective, professional use of technology, as well as the ability to express oneself clearly.

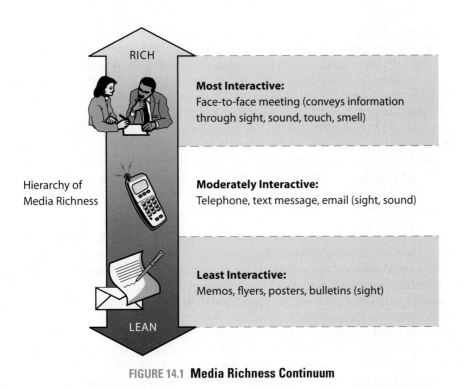

Hierarchy of Media Richness

RICH

Most Interactive:
Face-to-face meeting (conveys information through sight, sound, touch, smell)

Moderately Interactive:
Telephone, text message, email (sight, sound)

Least Interactive:
Memos, flyers, posters, bulletins (sight)

LEAN

FIGURE 14.1 Media Richness Continuum

CONSIDER THE QUALITIES OF THE MESSAGE Messages have certain qualities that will help you decide which channels or media are most appropriate to use to convey them. If your message is routine—meaning that it is simple, straightforward, contains no surprises, and is task related—then lean media such as flyers, letters, and memos are probably most appropriate. If your message is nonroutine—meaning that it is complex, confusing, contains a surprise, or is time sensitive—then rich media such as face-to-face meetings or video or web conferences are probably better.[21] When information is complex and confusing, you want to make sure you receive immediate feedback from your team members so you can clarify and correct any misunderstandings.[22] A rich medium allows such feedback.

CONSIDER THE EMOTIONAL IMPACT OF THE MESSAGE When a fabricated scandal resulted in the quick termination of U.S. Department of Agriculture (USDA) employee Shirley Sherrod in 2010, she was notified of her expected resignation through text message while she was driving to work.[23] The channel (text message) alone caused an uproar, showing a lack of respect for a longtime employee. As the USDA learned, sometimes text messages are not the most appropriate mode of communication. If you've ever been notified by a text message that you were fired, you know how important it is to match the communication channel to the emotional impact of the message. What hurt was not only the message, but also the way the message was delivered. Even less powerful messages can be destructive if communicated through text message alone, such as critical performance reviews. Although both sending and receiving emotionally sensitive information are difficult, the channel—

© 1999 Ted Goff

"Can't talk now. I'm in a seminar about improving communication with technology."

the way the message is transmitted—makes a big difference. For example, if you're laying someone off, the ideal way to do this is face-to-face (a rich medium) rather than with a text message (a lean medium). A face-to-face discussion allows you to effectively interpret and use nonverbal communication while explaining the layoff and to answer any questions. Taking the time to meet face-to-face conveys respect for the person being laid off.

Organizational communication researchers suggest that it may be more effective to use leaner media (e.g., email or text messages) in some emotionally charged situations, such as a conflict between coworkers. Researcher Phil Salem suggests that leaner media may be more effective in some conflict situations when individuals are more likely to say something out of anger that they may later regret.[24] According to Salem, leaner media don't allow for immediate feedback and interaction. This lack of feedback provides a "cooling-off" period that may be helpful in emotionally charged situations.

FOLLOW THE COMMUNICATION NORMS OF THE ORGANIZATION When deciding what channel is best to use to convey your message, it's always important to be aware of the communication norms of the workplace. As we noted in Chapter 9, **norms** are general standards that determine what is appropriate and inappropriate behavior in an organization. For example, in some offices you would violate a norm if you were to phone someone in the office next to you or even someone on the same floor; the norm is to phone only people who are not in your immediate location. In other organizations, the norm may be sending email rather than using the phone or talking to the person face to face. One study of over 150 senior executives at the nation's 1,000 largest companies found that only 13 percent of leaders used the telephone as their primary means of communication, which was down from 48 percent five years previously. Also, just 14 percent of the leaders reported relying on face-to-face meetings, compared with 24 percent five years before. Instead, email had become the most common channel for dialogue at work, according to 71 percent of the leaders surveyed.[25] This research data suggests that communication norms may be changing, moving away from rich communication media and toward more lean communication media. However, with the advent of smartphones and other new technologies, our continued use of lean media can be efficient timesavers. Regardless of the research data, it's important to carefully observe the communication norms in your office and work unit and follow the norms already established.

USE MULTIPLE CHANNELS Organizational communication researcher Keri Stephens recommends that leaders use multiple channels when communicating with employees and team members.[26] Stephens argues that employees are not tied to any one communication technology and that to be effective in your communication, it's important to communicate using a variety of channels. For example, if you're preparing to facilitate a meeting next week, you might do the following:

- Send out an email, voice mail, and a text message asking for team members' input on what they would like to discuss at the meeting.
- Send out a paper memo outlining the agenda for the meeting in addition to attaching the memo to an email message.
- Send a text message on the day of the meeting reminding team members of the meeting time and location.
- Communicate face-to-face at the meeting.

Stephens mentions that by using multiple channels to communicate with team members, you are more likely to reach more of your audience members than if you relied solely on a single technology.

Using Email

Email messaging now exceeds telephoning as the dominant form of business communication.[27] Many people claim that handling their emails can consume half of their day. One *Wall Street Journal* report predicted that employees would soon spend three to four hours a day on email.[28] With the increased use of email as an accepted form of business communication,

terms & definitions

Norms general standards within an organization that determine what is appropriate and inappropriate behavior.

some basic etiquette rules are being established to keep email usage both effective and professional. Here are some tips for composing professional email messages, either in the workplace or in an academic context:[29]

- *Be concise.* Keep messages brief and to the point. Correct writing doesn't have to be lengthy. Make your writing as concise as possible; it can be frustrating for a reader to have to wade through an email twice as long as needed.

- *Use proper letter case.* Letter case indicates whether words are written using capital (uppercase) letters or lowercase letters. Using all capital letters gives the impression you're shouting; using all lowercase letters gives the impression you're either whispering or lazy.

- *Use blind copy (BCC) and courtesy copy (CC) appropriately.* Use courtesy copy to keep others informed. Use blind copy only when you prefer to keep recipients from seeing who else received a copy of your email message. You would do this if your email involved issues of confidentiality or if the information in it might damage a relationship. For example, suppose you want to let your district manager know how you're handling an employee problem. You email the employee himself to notify him of your plan, and you send a blind copy of the email to the district manager. This way, the district manager knows the problem is being managed, but the employee doesn't know the district manager has been informed. If the problem employee was to know this, his relationship with the district manager might be compromised. Also use BCC when sending to a large distribution list, so recipients won't have to scroll through a long list of names to get to the message.

- *Use the subject line.* When sending a new email, always include the important and pertinent information in the subject line. The subject line can be anything relevant—an ID number, a claim number, a meeting date, a project name—or it can be a descriptive subject line that reveals to the reader the nature of your email. Sometimes to get an email out quickly, we ignore the subject line. This can be ineffective because it fails to let the recipient know the topic of your email. Also, a subject line assists in later filing or searching for your message.

- *Use correct grammar and punctuation.* The advent of smartphones and other text messaging devices has led to a decline in the formality of electronic communication. When sending email, use proper grammar and punctuation. Just because the channel is less formal does not mean the writing can be sloppy.

Communication Ethics @ Work

Social Media and the Blurring of Personal/Professional Boundaries

Smartphones, laptops, iPads, and other electronic devices all increase Internet access for many business professionals. If we bring these items to work, and use them to manage our online presence on social networks, we may be violating a workplace policy. Many companies discourage or even ban social media use at work, fearing that it can quickly become a distraction. In addition, more and more organizations are developing rules, guidelines, and policies regarding employee social media use, regardless of whether or not they are used in the workplace.[30]

For example, in 2009, the *Los Angeles Times* released their newly developed social media guidelines for employees.[31] They include a warning that although employees may try to keep their personal and professional identities separate online, they often merge together. Employees are warned not to post anything online that might embarrass the *LA Times* or appear to compromise workers' ability to do their job. In addition, employees' choices of who to "friend" in social media forums are being regulated by their employer, to help maintain an impression of objectivity. For example, "friending" someone on one side of the debate means "friending" someone on the other side, to appear impartial.

As a student, take stock of your own online presence. Do you use a social media site, such as Twitter, LinkedIn, Facebook, or MySpace? You might expect a level of privacy related to these accounts, so how would you respond to an employer's request to limit or regulate your online identity? Do you think these organizations have a right to manage their employees' social network sites? Does an employee's presence on social networks reflect an image of the employer as well?

RECAP

Skills for Effective Use of Technology and Email

Skill	Strategies	Examples
Use technology thoughtfully	Consider the qualities of the message.	A confusing or complex message is better communicated in a face-to-face manner. Routine messages such as meeting times or weekly sales numbers can benefit from a leaner medium.
	Consider the emotional impact of the message.	Emotionally charged messages-such as bad news about missed promotions, layoffs, or termination-should be handled in a face-to-face conversation.
	Follow the norms of the organization.	If most people in your office prefer a face-to-face conversation instead of a phone call or email, then walk over and talk with them, instead of relying on technology.
	Use multiple channels.	Send a memo, remind people in person, and post the meeting time on the office bulletin board.
Use email effectively	Be concise.	Use short, to-the-point statements in emails because they are typically read quickly.
	Use proper letter case and punctuation.	The statement "MR. GONZALEZ, WE MIGHT NEED TO SCHEDULE A MEETING FOR THIS AFTERNOON" appears to be yelling, whereas one that reads "mr. gonzalez we might need to schedule a meeting for this afternoon" looks sloppy.
	Use a subject line.	Include names and identification information if necessary, or at least identify the topic of your email.
	Use CC and BCC appropriately.	Large distribution lists may be better handled with BCC, so the reader doesn't have to scroll through a long list of recipients.
	Pay attention to grammar and spelling.	Reading over your email aloud before sending it often helps you catch mistakes.

- *Consider the appropriateness of your content.* Employees have been fired for using email inappropriately (e.g., forwarding items with sexual or off-color content) or for personal use. Never put in an email message anything you wouldn't put on a postcard. Remember that email can be forwarded, so unintended audiences may see what you've written.

- *Don't use email as an excuse for not communicating through more appropriate channels of communication.* Don't forget the value of face-to-face or voice-to-voice communication. Email communication isn't appropriate for sending confusing or emotional messages. Don't use email to avoid an uncomfortable situation or to cover up a mistake.

Writing Business Letters

Business letters are standard communication formats that are important and common in the workplace. As a leader, you will likely need to communicate with those outside of your organization—for example, with clients or those in other organizations. Being able to apply the skills discussed earlier to business letters is important and valuable.

Correspondence

Correspondence refers to business letters sent to customers, coworkers, superiors, and subordinates. Because business correspondence often is more personal than formal proposals and reports, it should generally be written in a conversational style. Suggestions for writing effective correspondence include the following.

DEVELOP GOODWILL **Goodwill** is a positive perception of the author on the part of the audience. A good way to build goodwill is to keep correspondence audience focused. Put simply, adapt to your reader. Rather than saying, "*We* need to see a receipt before *we* can process a return or exchange of the merchandise," say, "*You* may receive a full refund or exchange of the merchandise if *you* mail or fax a receipt." The two sentences say essentially the same thing, but the focus in the second sentence is on the needs of the customer. In this case you could build even more goodwill by sending an acknowledgment letter letting the person know the receipt arrived and thanking the person for being prompt.

INCLUDE STANDARD ELEMENTS OF CORRESPONDENCE Although the general appearance and format of correspondence may vary, following is a list of elements present in most business correspondence. Use this list as a guideline when deciding what to include in your business letter. Figure 14.2 illustrates a sample business letter.

- *Return address.* The return address contains the sender's address and the date the letter was written. If the letter appears on letterhead that includes an address, a date is enough for the return address.
- *Inside address.* Include the name and address of the recipient of the letter before a salutation.
- *Salutation.* A salutation should address the recipient of the letter directly and appropriately. A letter intended to be social and friendly can have a comma after the salutation; a more formal letter should include a colon. Avoid "Dear Sir" unless you are certain the recipient is male. The overused "To Whom It May Concern" is too impersonal. Take the time to determine exactly to whom the letter should be addressed.
- *Body.* The body contains the content of the letter. It should be written in paragraph form. Including a non–task-related message at the beginning of the letter can help to build rapport, for example, "Thank you for expressing interest in exploring the employment options offered at our institution." Then enter into the main message.
- *Closing.* The end of the letter should include a closing expression before your signature. This can be the common and effective "Sincerely," "Cordially," or something more personal such as "Best," or "Respectfully yours." The letter should include both a handwritten signature and a typed signature block. The block usually contains your name, as well as your title and the name of your organization (unless your letter appears on letterhead).

DELIVER BAD NEWS TACTFULLY Occasionally correspondence must contain bad news. This must be handled tactfully. A general rule for handling bad news is to deliver it gently and courteously. When presenting bad news through correspondence, consider:

- *Opening with a description of the context, to provide a buffer.* For example, you might begin a letter with "Thank you for applying for the position of service manager at TRH, Inc."

1532 1st Lane
Edinburg, Texas 78541
July 5, 20XX

Mr. Joseph Castillo
InnoTech Associates
817 Freddy Gonzalez Drive
Edinburg, TX 78539

Dear Mr. Castillo:

We appreciated the customer service training program you provided to our company last month. This letter is intended as a follow-up to that training and to thank you for your time and attention to detail.

The training was effective and productive. Our customer service agents have greatly increased morale and motivation when interacting with customers. We have seen great results from your training just in the last month.

We are considering a telephone etiquette course as a follow-up to the customer service training you provided. We were impressed with your demeanor, training style, and attention to detail, and would like InnoTech Associates to conduct the training program. If you are interested in providing us with a training program in customer service telephone etiquette, please contact me.

Once again, thank you for your interest in helping our employees work to improve their customer service skills. You have taught us some invaluable lessons and our company and workers are grateful.

Sincerely,

Sylvia Rodriguez

Sylvia Rodriguez
Training Department Supervisor
PemCo Inc., West Call Center
Phone: (956) 989-3347
Fax: (956) 989-3300
srodriguez@pemcowest.org

FIGURE 14.2 **Sample Business Letter**

- *Explaining the bad news rather than simply stating it.* For example, an explanation of a hiring decision might be, "Because of the extensive pool of applicants, we have chosen to place someone in the position with ten years of experience who will need minimum training to begin."

- *Closing with a goodwill message that reinforces a positive relationship with the recipient.* For example, you might close with a statement such as, "With your excellent academic record and ability to put others at ease, we have no doubt you will be successful in finding a position with another organization."

USE A STANDARD FORMAT When developing a business letter, you also need to consider the format. A common format for correspondence is the full-block, or standard letter style shown in Figure 14.2. Although organizations may have their own preferred correspondence format, this format is standard for any letter. Many word-processing programs contain templates for correspondence. If you are using letterhead paper, consider the bottom of the letterhead to be the top of the page when creating margins. Although the length of the letter may vary, it is a good idea to center the letter on the page. A short one- or two-sentence correspondence may be better sent by email. The main consideration with format is that once an organization has developed a standard for outside correspondence, you should be consistent in following the standard in all your correspondence.

Complaint Letters

There will be times when you are not satisfied with a product or service and believe some restitution is in order. A **complaint letter** expresses dissatisfaction with a product or service. A letter of complaint can be an effective method for resolving a dispute, if it is written with the appropriate tone and does not sound as though you are being accusatory or whining. You might even get more than you expected. Many businesses appreciate knowing when something is going wrong, and they will do what they can to create goodwill with a dissatisfied customer.

The following suggestions will help you write a letter of complaint that's likely to be read and acted on.[32]

- *Complain only when appropriate.* Sending numerous frivolous letters of complaint will get you nowhere. Send your letters only for genuine problems and only after initial communication with company representatives has failed. In other words, if the widget you bought didn't work as expected, ask the salesperson or the customer service department to correct the problem before you fire off a letter of complaint to the head office.

- *Address the letter to the correct person.* You need to reach the person who has the authority to correct the problem. If your complaint is with a local business, address the letter to the owner or manager. If you're dealing with a local branch of a large corporation, you'll need to find out whether your complaint should be sent to the local branch or if the problem was created by policies set by a corporate office. It might take some detective work to find out who should receive your letter. If you can't find out by asking, try the company website, annual reports, or business directories in your local library.

- *Be courteous and professional.* Avoid sarcasm. No matter how angry you are, sending a rude, discourteous, inflammatory letter will not help you get the problem corrected.

- *Keep it short.* One page is all you need. A recipient is more likely to read and act on your letter if you keep it brief and to the point. No one has time or patience to wade through a six-page tome.

- *Be factual.* Identify the problem and outline the efforts you have made to correct the problem. Remember the questions journalists typically try to cover in their writing: Who, What, When, Where, and How.

- *Identify what you want.* You have a complaint. What will it take to make things right? Do you want your money refunded? The product exchanged? A service contract extended? An apology? Stipulate what you want, and you are more likely to get it.

- *Remember to date your letter and include full contact information,* including an email address and account numbers or any other information that the recipient might need to trace your problem.

- *State consequences only if previous letters have failed to get the problem corrected.* It is both unnecessary and ineffective to start out with threats of punitive action. Remember, other people dislike receiving threats as much as you do. But, when previous attempts have failed, it's time to state what you are prepared to do, and when.

Leaders regularly communicate through written correspondence to those outside of the organization. Equally important as writing letters to those outside the organization or team is learning effective strategies for writing other types of business documents, especially interoffice documents.

terms & definitions

Complaint letter a letter that expresses dissatisfaction with a product or service.

Write for Insight[33]

Sheila Lirio Marcelo, founder and chief executive of Care .com, gained valuable advice on how to become more mindful and skilled by doing something simple: write. As part of her own executive development program, Sheila hired an executive coach to enhance her leadership and communication skills.

When asked what the most valuable pieces of advice she received from her executive coach she replied, "The first thing she gave me advice on, and I give it to everybody, is to journal. Write things down. When you come out of a meeting, or you come out of an interview, or you just finished running a session, what's on your mind? How did it make you feel? How did you make people feel? What's going on? Again, it was raising my self-awareness around my management style. I think that was critical."[34]

To use this simple technique you don't need expensive equipment or the latest technological tools. Although you could record your observations on a blog, Facebook, or Twitter, you could be low-tech and just keep a notebook and pen handy to record thoughts and observations. Keeping a journal of your ideas and impressions can help you be more observant and thoughtful. It can also enhance your awareness of yourself and others.

When starting a journal your entries need not be lengthy or overly detailed. Just jot down observations about yourself, your feelings, moods, and ideas as well as your reflections about others. Making a conscious effort to write your thoughts and observations can be an effective way not only to increase your self-awareness (principle one), it can also enhance your writing skills as you practice describing what you observe and experience. Your writing skills improve as you continually work to develop your ability to write what you see, hear, and do. In this chapter we've emphasized the importance of how you write messages to others. Also consider the value of writing to yourself to sharpen your communication and leadership talents.

Writing Business Documents

As a leader, you will be responsible for organizing and developing a number of business documents, including memorandums (more commonly known as memos), progress and activity reports, sales proposals, and formal reports. This section outlines the basic components of each type of document, as well as considerations for their appropriate use. The sample documents provided are only guidelines; organizations may have their own procedures and formats for the various types of business documents.

Memos

A **memo** is a short and usually informal written communication to others within an organization. Memos are used as reminders or to pass along information. Memos can be as simple as a sentence written on a sticky note, but they are usually printed on company letterhead. An example of a memo appears in Figure 14.3. Although there is no standard format for memos, they should generally contain at least some form of each of the following elements:[35]

HEADING The heading should note the sender and the recipient, the date, and the subject. Ensure that all names of individuals who need to receive the memo are included following the word *TO*. If the subject of the memo is relevant to only one person, do not send the memo to the entire office. Also, be certain that material is not too sensitive to put in a memo; sometimes a face-to-face conversation or a phone call is preferable. For example, a memo is an inappropriate way to notify employees of a layoff. Memos are most effective when they communicate company or job objectives, such as a change in a standard procedure or a department reorganization.

BODY Although a memo's length can vary, depending on the content, a good rule is to keep it under one page. Many organizations have standard memo formats, so it's best to check with your organization first and follow established standards.

TRH Incorporated

TO: Kay Marquez, Service Manager
FROM: Stephanie Ramos, Local Store Marketer
DATE: May 17, 20XX
SUBJECT: Opportunity for local ad campaign

TRH has been offered an opportunity to participate in a local advertising campaign in conjunction with the Chamber of Commerce's "Local Tastes" program.

"Local Tastes" is an annual program featuring community restaurants and other businesses, including a two-week mailer campaign and events at local stores. This campaign culminates in a well-attended day-long event at the convention center featuring products from each participating business.

Participating businesses will be featured on a front page of the mailer, get a 30-second spot with a local news outlet, and be given a booth with banner at the "Local Tastes" event on July 3.

I think this would be an excellent opportunity to get the company recognized in the community and interact with the Chamber of Commerce as well as work with other businesses in the area.

Please respond by May 25 with a decision regarding participating in this event. I need to respond to the Chamber of Commerce and turn in a deposit by June 1.

cc: Juan Brown, Managing Partner

FIGURE 14.3 Sample Memo

CLOSING Most memos don't require the standard signature you would find in a letter or other correspondence. It is helpful, however, to include notation of any attachments and a list of people who received copies of the memo. When considering who within the organization should receive copies of your memo, keep in mind that in most companies this can be a highly political issue. Send copies only to those who need the information.

Progress and Activity Reports

A **progress report** gives updates on the status of a project. Figure 14.4 shows an example of a progress report. Most project reports are generated by a company that has been contracted to do a particular job or provide a service. In such cases, it is appropriate to submit project reports at regular intervals to communicate the project's status and keep all personnel on task.[36] Although the format for project reports varies depending on the project, the policies of the organization providing the report, and the requirements of the client or customer, all reports should maintain the same format for any particular project. Progress reports may contain information about whether a project is within budget. If you anticipate going over budget, mention that and discuss some possible reasons and solutions. A progress report should also include information about how the work is progressing—what has been completed as well as what is anticipated. If you expect you may not complete the work on schedule, discuss this in the progress report and explain what arrangements need to be made to complete the project.

terms & definitions

Progress report a report that outlines for a customer or a client the status of a project.

Date: August 17, 20XX
To: Juan Brown, Managing Partner, TRH Inc.
From: Mike Caro, NuSheen Services
Subject: Progress Report for July 1–29, 20XX

Dear Mr. Brown,

I am happy to say the parking lot and building refinishing project is on schedule. At this point we are somewhat over budget in terms of materials, but I am confident we will finish early enough to save you money in labor costs.

Costs: The truck rental went over cost by approximately $1700 because of two extra days' rental. The other materials are costing out at the price originally quoted to you.

Work Completed: The building has now been completely refinished. Work on the outside work area and parking lot still needs to be completed.

Work Schedule: With the addition of two crew members, we should be able to complete the work by August 30.

If you have any questions, please contact me.

FIGURE 14.4 Sample Progress Report

When communicating the status of a project within an organization, an activity report is most appropriate. An **activity report** is a document that communicates progress and achievements to others within an organization or on a team. Most activity reports give information on the status of one or several ongoing projects. If several departments are working on the same project, a manager may combine all the activity reports; the combined reports could be the basis for a progress report to send to a client. Activity reports are typically issued regularly (biweekly or monthly in most organizations) and normally do not require a formal structure because the material is familiar to the readers. Although progress reports and activity reports contain similar content, they differ in audience and often in tone. Progress reports are most often written to clients or an audience outside the organization, and they are more formal; an activity report is commonly an internal document, with a less formal structure and tone.

Sales Proposals

A **sales proposal** is a document intended to persuade possible clients of their need for your product or service. An effective sales proposal demonstrates to prospective clients that they have a problem and your product or service will help to solve that problem. The writer of a sales proposal must first determine the selling points, or the most attractive features of the product or service, and then construct a document that clearly illustrates these points. The proposal should highlight the specific benefits that customers will receive from the use of the product or service. For example, the owner of a landscaping business might notice that a local restaurant is surrounded by dry dead grass and overgrown shrubbery. In a proposal offering landscaping services, the business owner would try to persuade the restaurant manager of the appeal of a well-kept, lush, green exterior and convince him that landscaping could increase his bottom line.

Keep in mind that in many states, sales proposals are **legally binding documents,** which means that any incentives or benefits offered in the sales proposal must be reasonable

terms & definitions

Activity report a document that communicates progress on a project or achievements to others in an organization or on a team.

Sales proposal a document intended to persuade a possible client of his or her need for your product or service.

Legally binding documents documents that record an exchange of promises and are enforceable by law.

and must be delivered as promised.[37] It is not uncommon for organizations to be sued over failing to deliver on the promises offered in a persuasive sales proposal.[38]

If you choose to use a former client's testimony or image in a sales proposal, make sure you have permission to do so and that you have not fabricated the testimony. For example, if the landscaping business owner wanted to include comments from current or former customers about the quality of her company's landscaping work in her sales proposal, she would first need to get the customers' permission in writing to use the testimony or pictures of the work in the proposal. Following are some guidelines for creating an effective sales proposal that is adapted to the needs of the client.

OUTLINE THE PROBLEM Although you may have already discussed the problem with the client, a good sales proposal reminds the potential client of the problem and a need for some solution. Include any requirements the client has mentioned, such as for cost or procedure. Keep your message client focused, aligning yourself with the client's needs.

DISCUSS YOUR APPROACH Your sales proposal should discuss exactly what you suggest as an effective solution to the problem. Discuss what particularly needs to be done and how those actions will address the problem. Discuss as well why you and your organization are the best choice for implementing this solution. Mention any support and training you will provide (if necessary) and guarantees on your work or products. The landscaping company owner, for example, could discuss what type of vegetation she proposes to plant around the restaurant, how the plants might be combined and arranged, and possibly a contract for continuing maintenance to keep the outside looking well-cared for.

DESCRIBE THE BENEFITS Although they may seem obvious, it is a good idea to identify for the client the biggest benefits of your proposal. Indirect outcomes such as an increase in customer base or employee morale should be outlined. The landscaping business owner could describe what a well-maintained exterior communicates to customers and other business owners about the restaurant. Keep in mind, however, that this section should not promise anything that may not be within your power to fulfill. You can expose yourself and your organization to legal consequences if promised benefits are not realized.

MENTION SCHEDULE AND COSTS A sales proposal should outline a proposed schedule and cost estimate. These things will later be detailed more formally in a contract but should be discussed in a sales proposal so there will be no surprises later. The restaurant manager may expect the job to start tomorrow and be completed in two days; the landscaping company owner needs to communicate clearly about whether that timeline fits with her schedule. Most clients will not be willing to move on to the contract stage of the process without a clear outline of proposed costs and schedule.

Formal Reports

A **formal report** is a highly detailed and comprehensive report on an ongoing project or a completed project that is often coauthored by several writers. For example, if you were implementing new procedures in your organization over a twelve-month period, you might send out a status report midway through the implementation process to those affected by the changes. Once the implementation process was completed, you would send out a final report detailing the process and the effectiveness of the implementation. Reports are more strictly formatted than most other forms of business correspondence, and the format varies according to company policies. Reports are divided into three main parts: the front matter, the body, and the back matter. Each part contains several elements whose order and length vary according to company recommendations. Following are basic descriptions of the components of a formal report.[39]

FRONT MATTER **Front matter** consists of those aspects of a report that come at the beginning and serve to prepare the reader for the main information. The report title, the authors' names, lists of the report's contents, and a brief summary should all be a part of the front matter.

- *Title page.* A title page contains the full title of the report, a list of the writers' or researchers' names, date(s) of the report, the organizational affiliations of the writers, and the organization to which the report is being submitted.
- *Abstract.* An abstract is a summary (two or three paragraphs) that highlights the major points of the report.
- *Table of contents.* This should list all the major sections of the report along with page numbers.
- *List of figures and tables.*
- *Foreword or preface.* A foreword is an optional introductory statement about the report written by someone other than the authors; a preface is an introduction written by an author.

BODY The body of a formal report contains the main information in the report, including the reasons for researching the topic, how it was researched, and what was discovered.

- *Executive summary.* This summary provides a more complete overview than the abstract.
- *Introduction.* The introduction provides readers with the report's purpose and scope.
- *Text.* The text presents details on how the topic was researched.
- *Conclusions and recommendations.* This section discusses the findings of the research and consequent recommendations that are offered. Conclusions may be discussed in a separate section from recommendations.

BACK MATTER **Back matter** refers to those components of a report that traditionally come at the end of the report, after the main body, and that provide further detail and references.

- *Appendixes.* Any appendixes clarify or supplement information in the body of the report with information that is detailed or lengthy and is not necessarily relevant to all audiences.
- *Bibliography.* This is an alphabetical list of all the sources that were cited and consulted in researching the report.
- *Glossary.* This is an alphabetical list of terms and their definitions.
- *Index.* An index is an alphabetical list of all the major topics and subtopics discussed in a report, citing page numbers in the report where the reader can find those discussions.

If you work for an organization that requires you to write regular formal reports, it is a good idea to use a word-processing program style sheet to create a format for the report. You can then save it as a template and create future reports with the same format. You won't have to refigure font styles and sizes, margins, and the like.

Leaders have many opportunities to write various kinds of business documents. Letters are generally more formal and addressed to those outside the organization. Memos and activity reports are common interoffice communication forms. Progress reports, sales proposals, and formal reports are common business documents that most leaders will frequently compose or help to compose.

terms & definitions

Back matter the components of a report that traditionally come at the end, after the main body, and provide further detail and references.

Wrap-Up

Writing is a vital skill for business professionals, and learning to write well can be the key to an individual's success in the workplace. Professionals with effective, well-developed writing skills assist their leaders in fostering and maintaining an image of a competent organization with competent people. In addition, effective writing can lead to improved communication within an organization. To develop or enhance your basic writing skills, make sure to:

- Organize your document using paragraphs to identify the main ideas, and chunk your information.

- Use a writing style appropriate for the topic, audience, and occasion. Pay attention to the tone of the document.

- Write clear, concise messages to ensure understanding.

- Be sure to proofread the document for spelling and grammatical errors, which can damage your credibility. Do not rely on word-processing spell-check programs alone.

In our media-saturated workplace, we need to understand the importance of using technology effectively in written communication at work. Focus on using technology thoughtfully, selecting the correct medium for the message.

- Use media-rich channels for more emotional or personal messages.

- Use email thoughtfully, considering such details as spelling and grammar, tone, appropriateness of the message, and including a subject line.

Professionals at every level of the corporate ladder will likely find themselves writing letters. Even with the advent of new technology to assist us in the writing process, it remains important to understand the basics of standard business letters.

- When writing correspondence, take a moment to develop goodwill, deliver bad news tactfully, and develop or follow a standard format for all letters.

- Complaint letters are a specific form of business letter. Effective complaint letters often produce results. Make sure to ask for what you specifically want, and avoid being offensive in how you describe the problem.

Business professionals will also learn to write other forms of interorganization communication, including:

- Memorandums, or memos, are one of the more common types of interoffice communication.

- Progress and activity reports are effective for keeping all parties informed as a project develops.

- Sales proposals, when written effectively, can increase an organization's outcomes, such as number of clientele and profits.

- Formal reports use more structure and are often developed for clients, coworkers, supervisors, and stakeholders.

Reviewing Key Terms

Topic sentence *361*

Coherence *361*

Writing style *361*

Tone *361*

Biased messages *362*

Clarity *362*

Jargon *363*

Concise writing *363*

Telegraphic style *363*

Grammar *365*

Media richness *366*

Norms *368*

Correspondence *371*

Goodwill *371*

Complaint letter *373*

Memo *374*

Progress report *375*

Activity report *376*

Sales proposal *376*

Legally binding document *376*

Formal report *377*

Front matter *377*

Back matter *378*

The Principle Points

This chapter focuses on the technical and aesthetic skill of business writing. As business leaders place more emphasis on the writing abilities of their new hires, developing these skills remains vital. Writing focuses specifically on Principle Two, verbal messages, but the process of converting your thoughts into effective written documents requires making use of all five communication principles.

Principle One: Be aware of your communication with yourself and others.

- When writing business letters and memos, be aware of who will be reading the message and the level of detail and amount of background information that may be needed or expected.

- Be aware of the intended reader's expectations regarding the length, format, and style of the message.

Principle Two: Effectively use and interpret verbal messages.

- Use an appropriate written style (including tone and vocabulary) for memos or letters.

- Write clearly: Be concise, use appropriate subordination, avoid jargon and redundancy, and use appropriate grammar and accurate spelling.

- Express ideas briefly yet clearly; business and professional writing should get to the point yet provide enough detail to help the reader understand if any follow-up action is needed.

Principle Three: Effectively use and interpret nonverbal messages.

- The type of font used, placement of margins, and the number and style of headings and subheadings provide nonverbal information to complement the ideas you are communicating in writing.

- When appropriate, use images, color, or other visual information to make your written message clear, accurate, and interesting.

Principle Four: Listen and respond thoughtfully to others.

- Accurately listening for details and major ideas is important when you need to summarize spoken messages in writing.

- If you are uncertain about expectations regarding format or other aspects of written correspondence, ask others and then listen to their responses, which will guide you in preparing written messages.

Principle Five: Appropriately adapt messages to others.

- Adapt the format, structure, word choice, and style of a written message depending on the recipient and the function of the message.

- When composing a response to an email message, pay attention to cues in the original email and adapt your response accordingly. If your correspondent's email message was short, he or she may only expect a brief response; a longer, more detailed message may signal that he or she expects a more comprehensive response.

Applying Your Skills

1. Imagine you missed a class due to a family emergency. Write an imaginary email to your professor, informing her of the reason for your absence and requesting makeup work, information on what you missed, and so on. Consider the following: How long should the email be? What might you put for the subject line? What tone should you use? Make sure to proofread.

2. Rewrite each of the following phrases using concrete words:

   a. Sometime this summer

   b. A substantial saving

   c. A large number of people in attendance

   d. Increase efficiency

3. Rewrite the following messages so that they are more concise:

    a. We wanted to invite you to our Kids' Night special this Tuesday night. The kids will have a lot of fun as we will be having face painting, kids' games, and the kids can color. The kids eat free as well!

    b. We are sending this mailer to let you know that we are giving a free gift and music CD with every $50 you spend on gas at our gas station. The promotion is going on this weekend, July 18–20.

    c. The supervisor plans to go to the meeting that will be held on Monday evening at a little bit after 7 P.M. at night.

    d. Welcome. We are happy to have in this afternoon's meeting a guest, Mr. Paul Emerson. Mr. Emerson works at the local Chamber of Commerce and he is here to tell us a little bit about the "Local Tastes" program. If after this afternoon's meeting you still have more questions regarding the "Local Tastes" program, feel free to call Mr. Emerson at his office.

4. Think of a time when you were dissatisfied with either a service or a product. Draft a complaint letter, focusing on the suggestions for complaint letters mentioned in this chapter. Exchange letters with a classmate and critique each other's letters.

5. Examine the following messages. Considering the media richness continuum discussed in this chapter, identify a medium that would most suit each message. Give your reasons why. Which medium is least suited for each message? Why?

    -   A complaint about a customer service agent
    -   A meeting time has changed
    -   A report to the team leader about progress on a project
    -   A discussion with your supervisor about conflict with another employee
    -   A discount offer for services to select clients
    -   A notice of a potential layoff

Appendix
Managing Time: Managing Communication

appendix outline

After reading this appendix, you should be able to

- Write appropriately worded goals and objectives that are specific, measurable, attainable, and observable.

- Make a master list of work tasks and projects.

- Identify and implement strategies for prioritizing work.

- Develop strategies for managing work obstacles to achieve work goals and objectives.

- Take appropriate action to increase work efficiency on team projects.

It was Mark Twain who wrote, "Never put off until tomorrow what you can do the day after tomorrow." Based on the number of projects that many of us postpone and the piles of work that sometimes accumulate on our desks, many of us seem to agree with Mr. Twain. Few people in business and organizational settings claim to be underworked or to have too much time on their hands. Just the opposite is true. There never seems to be enough time to accomplish all of the tasks on our "to do" lists—that is, assuming we make "to do" lists. This chapter is about not only techniques for managing our "to do" lists but also some broad principles to help us manage our time. Time, it appears, is a precious commodity—there never seems to be enough of it. And research suggests we're filling more of our time with work. According to the federal Bureau of Labor Statistics, U.S. citizens worked five more hours per week in 2006 than they did just three years earlier in 2003.[1]

"I like work: it fascinates me. I can sit and look at it for hours."
—**Jerome K. Jerome**

Some people appear to accomplish more work than others. What is it they know that helps them enhance their efficiency and effectiveness? They understand how to manage time—or so it would appear. But is time really something that can be managed? We all have the same number of seconds, minutes, and hours in a day. Time is a fixed commodity. We believe that it's not *time* that needs to be managed, but something else. It probably won't surprise you that that "something else" is *communication*. As we noted in the early pages of this book, you spend more time communicating with others each day than you do in any other activity. We believe that the best way to enhance your work productivity is through a careful examination of how you communicate with others. How you manage incoming and outgoing messages is central to increasing work efficiency. Although this appendix draws on principles and practices of time management experts, it emphasizes the role of communication in overall work efficiency.

Time management is the use of techniques for analyzing and prioritizing goals and objectives in order to increase efficiency and productivity. By efficiently managing what you spend most of your time doing (communicating), you'll increase your productivity. And by increasing your productivity you will enhance your ability to lead others. Leaders who manage their time well are also better able to manage their communication with others. It takes time to manage the myriad of messages that leaders manage.

What are the essential time management/communication management competencies? Here's a preview of the essential time management/communication management strategies we will discuss:

- First, it's vital to identify your goals and objectives. Without a clear sense of what you wish to accomplish, it will be harder to manage your time and communication to attain those goals.

- Second, it's important to make a master list of the tasks you need to accomplish to achieve your goals.

- Third, it's not enough to compile a comprehensive list of your tasks; you need to develop priorities. Determining what you need to do first, second, third, and so on, is a key element in effectively managing your time and your communication.

- Fourth, life is punctuated with interruptions. Someone who effectively manages time anticipates potential interruptions and has developed a strategy for working through or around them.

- Finally, you can have goals, make lists, prioritize, and even anticipate interruptions, but unless you take action—turn your plans into behavior—you'll likely see little benefit. So the final task in effectively managing your time is to turn plans into action.

To emphasize the link between managing time and managing communication, we draw on our five familiar principles of communication to frame our discussion of specific strategies that can enhance your efficiency.

Being aware of your communication with yourself and others is an anchoring principle for increasing communication efficiency. Ineffective workers are oblivious to such problems as getting off task or getting distracted. By developing strategies to help you identify when you're off task and to increase awareness of your communication strengths, you can improve your ability to manage your time.

terms & definitions

Time management the use of techniques for analyzing and prioritizing goals and objectives in order to increase efficiency and productivity.

Principles two and three, effectively using and interpreting verbal and nonverbal messages, are also important in managing your time wisely. Your ability to make written lists and to prioritize the items on those lists are key verbal competencies that, if used wisely, can increase your productivity. Managing interruptions involves using several nonverbal communication behaviors so as to increase efficiency.

The fourth principle, being able to listen and thoughtfully respond, is critical to increasing your efficiency. There are many times when hearing a message accurately in the first place would have saved time, energy, and expense of redoing a project or task. Accurately interpreting what others say is directly linked with increased efficiency and goal achievement.

Finally, the fifth principle of appropriately adapting messages to others is key to managing time. Being able to assess situations and appropriately customize messages and behaviors to accomplish tasks are essential to both effective communication and achievement of goals.

Even without reading this appendix, you probably have a good sense of what a good time manager does, as well as what people do who are less skilled in efficiently managing their time. Table A.1 lists the results of a survey that identified the top ten time wasters. To help you get a sense of the time management issues that confront you, make a note of the behaviors on the list that you have found yourself doing. Note how many of the time wasters relate to how we communicate with others. Whether it's the phone, email, text messages, visitors, meetings, socializing, or explicitly poor communication, directly or indirectly most of those factors recognized as time wasters are linked to how we communicate with others. A first step to improving your response to those obstacles is being aware of those behaviors that decrease productivity.

Besides noting time wasters that you may be guilty of from time to time, another way to increase your awareness of your time management competence is to conduct a time audit. Take a moment to complete the time audit form in Rating Scale A.1. After each activity listed, estimate how much time (rounded off to quarter and half hours) you spend in a 24-hour period doing each activity. The scale indicates a target amount, which you may or may not agree with, but which gives you something to compare your own time estimates to. Once you've estimated how much time you spend performing each activity, review your estimates to determine if you're comfortable with the time you currently spend on these tasks. If you'd like to spend more time doing an activity (such as sleeping or pursuing a hobby) draw an arrow pointing up next to that activity. If you want to spend less time performing an activity (such as traveling or commuting to and from work or school), draw an arrow pointing down to indicate you'd rather spend less time doing this task. Your time management audit can begin to reveal how you'd like to spend your time on a typical day.

TABLE A.1	The Ten Biggest Time Wasters[2]
1.	Management by crisis
2.	Telephone/email interruptions
3.	Inadequate planning
4.	Attempting too much
5.	Drop-in visitors
6.	Ineffective delegation
7.	Personal disorganization
8.	Lack of self-discipline
9.	Inability to say no
10.	Procrastination

RATING SCALE A.1   Where Your Time Goes[3]

Daily Activity (Monday–Friday)	Number of Hours	
	Target	Actual
Utility Time		
Sleeping	8	_____
Bathing, Dressing	1/2	_____
Eating	1½	_____
Traveling	1½	_____
Total Utility Time	11½	_____
Employment Time/Academic Time		
Working/Studying/Attending Classes/Teaching	8	_____
Breaks	1/2	_____
Waiting	1/4	_____
Socializing	1/4	_____
Total Employment Time	9	_____
Discretionary (Leisure) Time		
Watching TV	1	_____
Athletic and Health Activities	1/2	_____
Hobbies, Housework	1	_____
Family and Social Activities	1	_____
Total Discretionary Time	3½	_____
Total	**24**	**24**

Develop Written Goals and Objectives

Without a map, directions, or a GPS system, it's difficult to navigate from one city to another or to find an unfamiliar address. Just as you need a map or a GPS to help you get where you're going, you also need a map of your work destinations. To manage your time well (and manage your communication, too), you need to establish goals and objectives to clearly identify where you want to go. Being able to develop clear and well-written goals and objectives is the first step in working and communicating more efficiently.[4]

Develop Goals

A **goal** is a clear statement that identifies what you'd like to accomplish in the future. Achieving a goal typically involves accomplishing several short-term tasks. Some time-management experts recommend that you develop a personal goal statement of your mission in life.[5] A personal goal statement prescribes outcomes you'd like to accomplish, such as earning a college degree, becoming more philanthropic, or becoming the chief executive officer of your company. Here are some examples of goal statements:

- Within the next two years I would like to complete my master's degree.

- Within the next four years I would like to have a major leadership position at a Fortune 500 company on the West Coast.

- By the end of the year, our department should have completed transferring our records from the old electronic filing system to the new Internet-based filing system.

Each of these goals articulates long-term outcomes that involve multiple steps and processes. Although it can be a challenge to clearly identify your long-term goals, it's worth the effort and thought. Taking time to become aware of your goals is one of your most important time/communication management tools.

Develop Objectives

An **objective**, like a goal, identifies what you'd like to achieve, but an objective is more immediate than a goal. Completing a specific task by the end of the day or week, making a purchase, and writing a report for your boss are examples of objectives.

A well-worded objective meets four criteria: it is specific, measurable, attainable, and observable.[6]

- *Specific:* An objective should precisely and clearly identify what you'd like to achieve.

- *Measurable:* Your objective should be able to be assessed or measured; you need to be able to determine whether the objective has been accomplished.

- *Attainable:* Appropriate objectives are realistic; they can be accomplished given the resources that you have or can obtain.

- *Observable:* A well-written objective should be stated in terms of an observable behavior, such as completing a report or project.

A key to developing well-worded objectives is to ensure that you use action verbs (*write, read, complete*) that clearly indicate what action you must take to accomplish your objective. Also, it helps to specify a time frame to indicate when you'd like to have the objective completed. Note the following examples:

- By the end of the week, I will finish writing the report about the proposed merger project.

- By the end of the month, I will make fifteen cold sales calls and follow up on each call with a letter to each potential customer.

- By the end of the year, I will complete sixty hours of required training to maintain my general education equivalent requirements.

Each of these objectives meets our four criteria (each is specific, measurable, attainable, and observable) and includes verbs that specify action steps (*write* a report, *make* sales calls, *complete* training).

Time management expert David Allen believes that the best way to begin accomplishing goals and objectives is to identify the next specific action step that you could take to implement the outcome you'd like to achieve.[7] For example, if you want to complete a report by the end of the week, what is the next precise action step you should take? Perhaps that action step is as simple as going to your computer, turning it on, and beginning to write. Or perhaps you need to make a phone call to a colleague to get data that you will include in the report. Whatever the next action step, that is the precise task you should identify. Making a written note of that next step may be just the prompt you need to take action.

terms & definitions

Goal a clear statement identifying something to be accomplished in the long term.

Objective a statement of something specific, measurable, attainable, and observable to be achieved in the short term.

Make a Master List

Once you have identified what you need to accomplish, combine all of your objectives into a comprehensive master list. If you only had one goal or objective to achieve you wouldn't need to make a list. But most of us have many tasks and projects to juggle. A written list helps you remain aware of what needs to be done.

Time management experts suggest a variety of ways to make and keep lists. Your list of action steps to achieve your goals and objectives can be as simple as a handwritten list on a piece of notebook paper. Some time management experts suggest using a day calendar that incorporates space to make lists as you keep your daily appointments.[8] We believe there is no single best system for making a list that works for everyone. Whether you make your list on sticky notes, store it in your computer, or write it on notebook paper, here's the key: *Have some system of tracking the various tasks and projects in an easy-to-use, easy-to-read format that you regularly review.* Develop a system that you will use. Here are other suggestions to help you make a master list of your tasks and projects.

- *Write it down.* What all time management experts seem to agree on is this: Your list of objectives and tasks should be a written list. It's not enough just to think about what you need to do. Again, the list needs to be in a format and system that works for you, whether you write it on paper or enter it into your computer or your personal digital assistant (PDA). Most cell phones permit you to make notes and lists and remind you of the projects and tasks on your "to do" list. The format doesn't matter as long as you have some system of tracking the various tasks on your list. Some suggest developing a list and then making a detailed analysis of each task by noting its overall importance, urgency, potential for delegation, and the key people you need to communicate with to accomplish each task.

- *Cross it off.* Whatever system you use for listing your tasks, it's important to be able to cross a task off the list once you've completed it.

- *Consolidate items when appropriate.* If you can bundle several related tasks together, you're more likely to tackle them. For example, if you have several phone calls to make, your list entry could read "Phone calls," followed by the names and numbers of those you need to call and a note on when to call them. The goal is not to make your master list lengthy, but to make it manageable. One way to make your list less daunting is to consolidate items. Make your list realistic.

- *Review your list.* It does no good to have a master list of your projects and tasks unless you look at it. One good habit is to look at your list at least twice: as you begin your workday and at the conclusion of your day. At the beginning of your day, note the projects and tasks that you want to make sure you achieve *that day*. Your "in basket" (whether it's in cyberspace or on your desk) is a good place to keep your master list. You are more likely to use your list if you keep it someplace where you can look at it frequently throughout the day.

- *Don't use your calendar as a substitute for your master list.* Because we've just suggested you keep your master list in or near your "in basket," you may think it's OK to keep several "to do" lists in your calendar. This is *not* a good strategy. Although you may use your calendar to remind yourself of important deadlines, some time management experts suggest it's better to keep your master list separate from your daily appointment calendar and to keep a single master list. An old Chinese proverb says, "A person who has two watches never knows the correct time." If you have more than one calendar or more than one list, you may lose track of something. The key to lists and calendars is having a consolidated, single place to show you when you need to be where (your calendar) and a single, comprehensive list of what needs to be done (your master list). You could make subcategories in your master list, but it's best not to have multiple lists in multiple places. One list, one place.

- *Schedule tasks on your list at your best times.* Are you a "morning person"? A morning person views the first half of the day as the best half and is at his or her best then. Or, maybe you work best late at night. Regardless of when your peak working hours are, schedule your work to correspond to those times to the extent possible.

Prioritize Your Work

Now that you have identified both your larger goals and your immediate objectives and you have a system for keeping track of your tasks by making a master list, determine your work priorities. Several time management experts suggest that one of the best ways to establish your priorities is to analyze the tasks on your list by asking yourself two questions:

1. How urgent is this task?

2. How important is this task?[9]

IS IT URGENT? Urgency is about time. Something is urgent if it is time sensitive. Urgent messages or urgent tasks are things that someone believes need to be accomplished sooner rather than later. One problem is that what other people may perceive as urgent may actually not be urgent to you. So your challenge as you review the many ways you could spend your time, is to decide how urgent a task is. Similarly, some things others may ask you to do are urgent but not important to you. That leads to the next key question.

IS IT IMPORTANT? What makes something important? A task is important if it helps you accomplish your goals and objectives. If you have not thought about your goals and objectives, then it will be difficult to determine what is important and what is not.

As shown in Figure A.1, you can sort any work task according to its urgency and importance. Is the task I'm planning to do (or being asked to do) urgent or not urgent? Is the task important or not important? Increasing your awareness of the tasks on your list as important or urgent can help you determine your work and communication priorities.

The use of technology to increase the speed at which we receive and send messages can create "unimportant urgency." This is not to say that technology can't help us increase our productivity—of course it can. But modern technology—email, cell phones, fax machines, iPads, BlackBerrys—can increase the speed and thus the *perceived* urgency of some messages that may not be urgent at all. Another factor that increases a sense of urgency is being

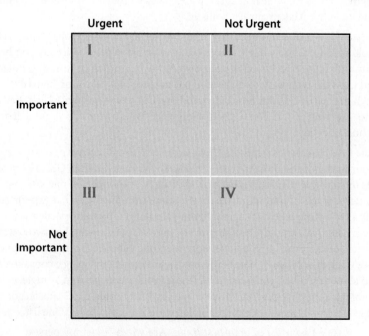

FIGURE A.1 Identifying What Is Urgent and Important

Source: Stephen Covey, A. Roger Merrill, and Rebecca R. Merrill, *First Things First* (New York: Fireside, 1996).

overbooked and making too many commitments to others that we can't keep. Overscheduling can make a small task seem daunting. We need to make some room in our schedules for those unexpected tasks that are simply part of our everyday life experiences. But if we've unwisely constructed a daily schedule that is chock full of tasks, projects, and mandatory events, we have no room for those things that emerge during the course of the day. That "one more thing" may not be all that time consuming, but it may be the task that induces greater stress and perceived urgency because we just can't fit it in.

URGENT AND IMPORTANT You probably don't have to worry about whether you will accomplish something that is both urgent and important. If you get an emergency call from your boss who asks you to help with an important project, you don't need to check a master list to determine if this task is something that you'll do. Given that the task is both time sensitive and important (because it comes from your immediate supervisor), you'll no doubt give it immediate attention.

IMPORTANT AND NOT URGENT Most of us also have a tendency to avoid important but not urgent tasks because there is no immediate need to complete the task. So one of the ways to increase your performance and work quality is to make a conscious effort to spend time on the important but not urgent tasks. Developing your goals and objectives and making a master list of your projects and tasks are examples of important yet not urgent tasks. What effective, productive leaders and managers know that unproductive people don't know is that you *must* spend time on important but nonurgent work. How do you do that? One way is to schedule time for it. Some important but nonurgent tasks not only affect your work, they also affect your health. Getting exercise, for example, is an example of an important but nonurgent task. To be more productive in the long run, identify those activities on your master list that are important but may not have an immediate deadline and budget time for them. Recreation activities and vacations are other examples of important yet nonurgent activities that we may postpone yet shouldn't.

URGENT AND NOT IMPORTANT The tricky part of managing your time and your communication comes when someone who is not your immediate supervisor views a task as urgent, but it's not important to you. Having a sense of what is important (based on your own goals and objectives rather than someone else's) will help you sort through whether you should take action on the task or not. You'll no doubt receive phone calls and email messages relating to tasks that someone else views as urgent and that must be accomplished soon, but that may not be all that important to you. A key in setting priorities is to sort through what is really important and what is really urgent, given all of the tasks on your master list.

NOT URGENT AND NOT IMPORTANT Finally, there are some things you do that are neither urgent nor important. These time wasters can include things like watching YouTube, mindlessly surfing the Internet, or playing computer Solitaire. We're not suggesting that you

leaders ON leadership

Take Time to Think

One well-known insurance company used the advertising slogan "Life comes at you fast." Life does indeed come at us at a fast clip. Sometimes so fast that there is little time just to think and reflect. *Reflection is one of your most powerful leadership tools.* To help slow down the pace of life, Cristobal Conde, president and CEO of SunGard, the world's leading software and technology services company, makes sure he has ample time just to think. Here's his advice:

> *I need an hour and a half once a day where I can go somewhere that doesn't have a PC or a phone, unless I choose to spend that hour and a half writing. But it's not just managing e-mails and stuff like that. I need an hour and a half to think. And it could be anything.*

Sometimes it gets cut short. But many topics or issues can only be dealt with in an uninterrupted format. I worry about our entry-level people—they're bombarded with information, and they never get to think.[10]

You don't have to be a company president and CEO to take time to think. It's one of those important but not urgent tasks that can make the difference between living life at a hurried, scatterbrained pace or being able to tackle projects in a thoughtful, systematic, mindful manner. The best way to have time to think and reflect about your work (and your life) is to schedule time for this important activity. Make a conscious effort to block out time just to think, prioritize your work, and make life plans for both your immediate and long-term future. Work smarter, not harder.

eliminate these activities—if they truly help you relax and recharge your mental and physical batteries, then by all means, enjoy them. The problem comes when we find ourselves engaging in activities that aren't, in the long run, edifying or helpful—they just waste time; those are the activities to remove from our daily routines.

Manage Interruptions

You now have a sense of the importance of having goals and objectives, making a master list, and then prioritizing your tasks. The next logical part of managing your time is simply to start accomplishing the high-priority items at the top of your list. But before you begin whittling down the tasks and projects on your master list, it's important to plan for the interruptions that are a normal part of our work and personal lives.

Stuff happens. As John Lennon noted in the lyrics to one of his songs, "Life is what happens to you when you're making other plans." Interruptions can range from a phone call, to a text message that you feel you need to check, to someone poking her head in your door to ask if you've got "a minute" to talk. In the daily course of doing your work these are normal and expected. The problem comes when you have not developed a plan to manage these interruptions. Unless your job is to answer the phone, you may not need to immediately take every phone call you receive. Unless your job is to serve as a receptionist, you may not need to accommodate everyone who stops by for information. Even the paperwork that streams across your desk can interrupt your work productivity.

People who are less productive have not developed a plan for managing the data, information, and messages that come their way. As we noted earlier, it's not time that we manage, but communication. Developing a system for managing the routine interruptions and distractions you encounter can help boost your productivity.

Manage Messages: Time Management Principles

Before we suggest tips for managing specific distractions and interruptions, let's some general time management principles that can help you process the volume of verbal and nonverbal messages that will come to your attention.

BATCH YOUR WORK To batch your work is to group your tasks so that you budget time to do one kind of thing at a time. For example, it's more efficient to respond to several email messages at a time—in one batch—than to respond to each email message as it arrives. Similarly, schedule a period in your workday to return phone calls rather than hopping from one task to another. Of course, if a phone call or email is both urgent and important (a call from your boss, for example), you should respond immediately. But many routine messages can wait and can be batched to be more efficiently managed.

DO YOUR WORK ONCE There are really only three options for handling any given task:

- *Do it*: Respond to the request for action or information.
- *Delegate it*: If you are a supervisor or have staff support, you could assign the task to others.
- *Delete it*: Some messages, such as some junk email messages, do not need a response.[11]

The most common but least efficient response to incoming work is to just stack it in a pile and assume that you'll get to it someday. Before you know it, you'll have a stack of "stuff" that can clutter up your work life. "Stuff," according to time management expert David Allen, is anything that is not related to any specific goal or action step.[12] It's best to make a decision about each work chore when it hits your in basket: do it, delegate it, or delete it.

ORGANIZE YOUR WORKSPACE Another way to increase your efficiency is to have everything you need to do your work at hand. The tools, supplies, sources of information, and anything else you need to do your work should be within easy grasp. If you have to hunt for paperclips, tape, notepads, a pen, or other resources that you typically use, you lose time.

USE A REMINDER FILE Instead of missing deadlines and being surprised by due dates, develop a reminder file or a system for tracking project due dates. One recommended system is to get a large file with multiple pockets, either five pockets for each day of the week, or (better yet), one with thirty pockets, one for each day of the month. If a task is routinely due on the 15th of each month, you simply look in the pocket marked "15th" for reminders you've placed in that pocket. Or, if you need to pay bills on a certain date each month, place the bills as they arrive in the file pocket corresponding to the day they are due (or the day when checks must be mailed or payment posted online). Just check the file each day to remind yourself of what needs to be accomplished that day. Another way to remind yourself is to make a note on your calendar of the due dates of major projects. In addition, most computers, cell phones, BlackBerrys, iPads, and other electronic tools can be programmed to remind you of deadlines. If a project is large and complex, you may want to provide update reminders several days or weeks before the project is due to remind yourself of what you should have accomplished by those dates in order to remain on schedule.

Manage Email

Email can dramatically increase your efficiency because it makes sending information, documents, or files to people who need them so easy and quick. But many people can find themselves buried by the avalanche of text messages and email messages that pour into their electronic in-boxes each day. If you miss a day of work, the next day you may find yourself overwhelmed by the email that you need to respond to.

SET ASIDE A SPECIFIC TIME OF THE DAY TO CHECK EMAIL Unless it's part of your job to immediately respond to email messages, use the principle of batching tasks that we mentioned earlier. For example, check your email first thing in the morning, at noon, and an hour before the end of your work day. We don't recommend setting your email program to notify you every time you receive an email; you may be tempted to see who just sent you a message rather than more efficiently processing your email in batches.

USE THE TWO-MINUTE RULE The email two-minute rule is this: If you can't respond to an email message in two minutes or less, wait to respond to it when you're responding to several email messages at the same time.[13] You can work more efficiently if you are working on the same kind of task (such as responding to email) than if you're checking email, deleting some messages, and then spending more than two minutes responding to others.

CREATE ACTION FILES If it takes more than two minutes to respond to or make a decision about what to do with an email message, create action files—files in your email system where you store messages to review later. At first it may sound as though we're encouraging procrastination, but we're actually encouraging more efficient management of your responses to messages. The simplest files to create are for action, for waiting, and for lengthy messages that simply need to be read. The action file can include all email messages that need more than two minutes in which to write a response. The waiting file is for email messages that don't need an immediate response but that you don't want to delete. Finally, the read file is for email that will take you longer than two minutes to read. By filing and batching your email, you'll work more efficiently.

Manage Paperwork

Email was supposed to eliminate paper and paperwork, and there are some organizations that have succeeded in stemming the rising tide of paper, but most workers still shuffle an ample amount of paper.

Some of the most common paperwork problems include indecision about what to do with incoming paperwork (so it gets handled more than once), procrastination, failure to delegate work to others, keeping or filing documents that you really don't need, or the complete lack of a system for managing the paper parade. Here are several strategies that can help overcome these problems.

READ SOMETHING ONCE AND HANDLE IT ONCE After you read a document, decide what you want to do with it. Keeping it on your desk or carrying it around in your briefcase only means you'll eventually have to figure out what to do with the document. Make the decision to file it, throw it away, or delegate it to someone else the first time you read it.

DISPOSE OF WHAT YOU DON'T NEED AGAIN AFTER YOU READ IT One time-management expert estimates that 80 percent of the daily flow of paperwork can be read and thrown away, yet the typical reader disposes of about 20 percent.[14] Decide whether you really need to keep what hits your in basket; it may improve your productivity if more of your paperwork hits your waste-basket.

DEVELOP A STRATEGY FOR FILING WHAT YOU NEED A reason some people are clogged with paperwork is because they file things they really don't need. Don't over-file—avoid placing things in a permanent, long-term file that don't need to be there. If you do develop a short-term holding file, make sure documents don't stack up there. Purge the file of outdated and unneeded documents periodically.

DON'T PAPER HOP Not only should you read something just once, you should also avoid starting to read one document, then stopping and switching to a different document so that you're hopping from one document to the other. You'll waste time. You work more efficiently if you stick to one task until you finish it. You may be praised for multitasking, but the more focused you are on one task, the more efficiently you'll work.

Manage the Telephone

A phone call is a classic example of an urgent but not important interruption. Obviously, some phone calls *are* important; and if your job requires you to answer the phone whenever you get a call, you should do so. But if your responsibilities give you some flexibility and freedom in responding to phone calls, you'll need to give careful thought to how you will manage incoming telephone calls. And you often have a choice of when you return phone calls; some return calls can be made at your convenience.

Among the most common telephone interruption problems are the lack of a system to screen calls, missing phone calls, and playing telephone tag. You may also find that you spend too much time on the phone, either in off-task conversation or because either you or the other person has difficulty ending the call. All of these problems are less about managing time and more about managing verbal and nonverbal communication.

Here are several strategies to help you manage telephone calls.[15]

RETURN NONURGENT CALLS IN BATCHES Rather than intermittently returning calls throughout the day, you'll work more efficiently if you set aside a time of the day to return phone calls.

COMMUNICATE YOUR PHONE AVAILABILITY TO OTHERS When you've called someone and the person you want to speak with is not available, in addition to leaving your name and phone number, indicate when it would be best for the person to call you. If someone takes phone messages for you, have that person find out the best time for you to return the call. Similarly, if you have voice mail or use an answering machine, make sure that the message callers hear asks them to indicate when it's best for you to return their call. You'll spend less time playing phone tag if you have information about when it's best to connect.

KNOW HOW TO END A PHONE CALL TACTFULLY It may seem to happen when you're at your busiest: Callers want to chat or prolong a phone call. You don't want to be rude, so you listen. And listening is both a virtue and a vital communication skill that we've emphasized throughout this book. But an equally important skill is to know how to politely and tactfully end a phone call that's neither important nor urgent. We can suggest three termination strategies:

- Identify your time limits when you begin the call. For example, say, "Frank, it's good to hear from you. I have about ten minutes right now; is that enough time for our conversation?" If the time frame you suggest isn't enough, you may need to schedule the call at another time.

- Signal that you'd like to end the call soon. You might say, "Roberta, before we end our visit, I have one more thing to say" or, "Before we conclude, do you have any more suggestions?"

- Be honest about your need to end the call. "Steve, I'm sorry, but I do have a meeting in a few minutes that I need to attend."

DEVELOP A PHONE CALL SCREENING SYSTEM This advice won't apply to you if your job is to be the phone screener (if you're a receptionist, for example), but if you don't have a way of screening your calls, develop one; you need some way of knowing who is calling so that you can make it your choice to answer the phone. If you have a receptionist, tell him or her when you're available for calls and when you're not. Many, if not most, phone systems include caller ID; use this information to decide whether to take a call or let your voice message system take it for you. If you're involved in writing a report, or in the middle of drafting a lengthy email message that needs your sustained concentration, you'll be more productive if you continue with your task rather than switching from your writing task to answer the phone. You may find it helpful to designate a "quiet hour" during part of each day in which you don't take calls (unless they are from your boss or customers). Of course, you'll have to customize our suggestions to fit your job and workplace culture, but the key to managing incoming calls is to be aware of the need to do so and then develop a system that works for you and your situation.

Manage Unscheduled Visitors

"Do you have a minute?" The person who pokes his head in your office or cubical probably needs more than a minute. These "minute" conversations can sap your time and energy and reduce your work productivity. Yet most jobs involve being available to respond to people who need your help. Rather than email or phone calls, it may be people who interrupt your work rhythm most frequently. People stop by because they need to see you in person. But if you always have an open door, you may find that it's difficult to balance responding to the immediate presence of someone who needs to speak with you and attending to the volume of work stacked on your desk or waiting for you in cyberspace.

One of the primary reasons drop-by visitors erode work efficiency is because no system has been developed for managing when or how to respond to visitors. Most of us like to be available to our colleagues and certainly to our customers and clients, yet if we set no limits on our availability it may be difficult to work efficiently and accomplish other tasks that are also important to our jobs. It may also be difficult to manage the flow of people who want to see you if:

- You're the boss and the people who report to you need access to you.
- You pride yourself on an open-door policy.
- You work in a cubical and have no door to open or close to signal when you're available.
- You have a boss or a colleague who frequently needs (or just wants) to visit.
- Your office is in a high-traffic area of the building; many people see you and stop to chat.

Again, it's not that you need to manage time, it's that you need to develop a system to manage communication. Here are some communication management strategies to help you balance the need for separateness and the need for connection that are integral to most jobs.

FIND A QUIET PLACE TO WORK ON TASKS THAT NEED YOUR FULL CONCENTRATION Rather than doing all of your work at your desk, consider finding a place where you can work independently, even if it's only for half an hour or an hour. Taking your laptop to a quiet corner in the company cafeteria, or finding an empty conference room where you can work undisturbed may let you reclaim the solitude that you need to accomplish a task that needs your uninterrupted concentration.

VERBALLY COMMUNICATE YOUR AVAILABILITY TO OTHERS Let your colleagues and customers know the best times for you to meet with them. Set specific time frames for communicating in person.

USE NONVERBAL CUES TO SIGNAL YOUR AVAILABILITY TO OTHERS If your office has a door, you may need to close it from time to time to express your desire not to be interrupted. If you work in a cubicle and have no door, if possible face away from the opening to your workspace. The more readily colleagues can establish eye contact with you, the more likely it is they will stop to visit. Some people without doors have posted signs to indicate when they are available and when they may not be available even though they are present in their workspace. (However, before implementing this strategy, consider the organizational culture of your workplace and whether it is formal or informal and how others may react to such signs.) The key is to make sure that you are in control of communication regulatory cues. Since it's often nonverbal cues that indicate whether or not we are available to communicate, monitor the nonverbal messages you and your office arrangement signal to others.

POLITELY BUT ASSERTIVELY END CONVERSATIONS OR LET OTHERS KNOW THAT YOU ARE BUSY When someone wants to see you, it can be hard not to be seen. A person's physical presence is a nonverbal cue of immediacy or urgency. But there are times when you may need to politely end a conversation or redirect your visitor to someone else. Here are some strategies to help limit or end conversations:

- When someone comes into your workspace, stand to greet the person. By remaining standing you signal that you're not inviting the person in for a long chat. Not everyone will pick up on this subtle cue, but by standing rather than sitting, you are indicating nonverbally that you expect the conversation to be short.

Communication Skills FOR A **Digital Age**

How Technology Can Help You Manage Time

You don't manage time, you manage what you do with your time: You manage your communication. Here are several software programs and applications that time management experts recommend to help you manage information and messages that you send and receive each day.[16]

- **Xobni <xobni.com>:** This free program helps you manage email messages and attachments.

- **MindManager <mindjet.com>:** This low-cost software program is based on the mind-mapping technique of making links between the ideas you develop. It provides tools to help you take notes and capture ideas while simultaneously helping you keep major projects in mind.

- **Evernote <evernote.com>:** If you currently use sticky notes or other methods to record ideas and information, this free software program can help you consolidate all of you scribbles in one place and also help you find what you've written.

- **RescueTime <rescuetime.com>** and **JournalLive <journalLive.com>:** These two free programs help you keep track of what you do with your time while on the computer.

- **Dropbox <getdropbox.com>:** This free software lets you sync files among several computers so you don't have to hunt for a file on your desktop computer that may be on your laptop.

- **Jott <jott.com>:** If you need to make a quick reminder note but don't have a pencil or pen handy, you simply call a phone number, leave a recorded message, and then later you'll receive an email message with your message now in text format.

- **FileCenter <lucion.com>:** This program is a document management system that permits you to scan large amounts of paperwork so you can easily track where you've electronically filed it.

- Meet people in their office or workspace rather than yours. If you are in someone else's office, you are less likely to get involved in a long conversation from which you can't escape. When the meeting is in your office, you have nowhere else to go; if you're visiting in a colleague's office you can keep the meeting short.

- Verbally communicate how much time you have for a visit. Let others know what your time limits are. You might say, "Janice, I'm due at a meeting in ten minutes, can we discuss this issue in that time?" We're not suggesting that you lie about meetings or other appointments to avoid conversations. But do honestly let others know of your time parameters.

- If you have an administrative assistant, ask him or her to announce when your next appointment is, which will help you signal the need to end a meeting.

- Verbally signal that your time is up. By saying, "Do you have any final observations before we conclude our visit?" you send a clear message that your time is limited. With some people you may need to be even more explicit: "Ken, I'm sorry, but I have to conclude our meeting."

Take Action

Having goals and objectives, making a master list, prioritizing your work, and managing interruptions won't be enough to achieve increased productivity unless you act. The final element in managing your time and managing communication in order to increase your efficiency is to turn your plans into action. One strategy that can help you take appropriate action to accomplish your goals and objectives is to use the power of reflection.

One of your most powerful time management/communication management tools is the power of reflection. When you reflect, you take time for an important but not urgent task: to review what you need to do next. As we emphasized at the beginning of this appendix, becoming aware of what keeps you from achieving your work goals and having clear goals and objectives is the starting place for taking concrete steps to working more efficiently.

terms & definitions

Xobni <xobni.com> program that assist in managing email messages and attachments.

MindManager <mindjet.com> software program that uses a mind-mapping technique to make links between ideas; it provides tools to take notes and capture ideas while keeping upcoming major projects in mind.

Evernote <evernote.com> software used to consolidate the user's notes and ideas. It also helps find entries that have been submitted.

RescueTime <rescurtime.com> and **JournalLive <journalLive.com)** program that helps keep track of how one spends time while on the computer.

Dropbox <getdropbox.com> file-syncing software that allows one to link files from several computers.

Jott <jott.com> system where one can simply call phone number, leave a message, and then receive an email message with the information in text format.

FileCenter <lucion.com> document management system that permits you to scan large amounts of paperwork to easily track its electronic filing.

The worksheet in Rating Scale A.2 lists common time/communication management problems. Review the list and identify the problems you need to address immediately. Once you have distilled what you perceive as the biggest obstacles to your success, review the material in this appendix and identify specific action steps that you can take to address these problems.

RATING SCALE A.2   Classifying Time Problems[17]

Study the list of time problems carefully. Place a check mark in the blank beside each one that is applicable to you.

Personal Habits and Attitudes

_____ Personal disorganization

_____ Lack of personal goals

_____ Lack of personal priorities

_____ Lack of personal deadlines

_____ Inability to delegate

_____ Over-commitment

_____ Procrastination

_____ Indecision

_____ Inability to say no

_____ Fatigue

_____ Lack of planning

_____ Perfectionism

_____ Other_____

_____

General Organizational Environment

_____ Too many meetings

_____ Too many classes

_____ Long meetings

_____ Lack of organizational goals

_____ Lack of organizational priorities

_____ Lack of organizational deadlines

_____ Unclear lines of responsibility or authority

_____ Poor information

_____ Lack of clear standards or expectations

_____ Poor records or filing system

_____ Red tape

_____ Poor communication

_____ Too much email

_____ Management by crisis

_____ Unwieldy paper flow

Types of Interruptions

_____ Phone/Texting

_____ Social drop-ins, clients, and other outsiders

_____ "Putting out fires"

_____ Questions from colleagues

_____ Questions from superiors

_____ Other _____

Look back over the items that you checked and circle each check mark that indicates a problem you could remedy—or at least markedly improve—by a change in your personal attitudes or behavior, given necessary knowledge and adequate motivation.

Now list below, in rank order, several of your most pressing time management problems. Then devise one action you can take this week that will contribute to the solution of these problems. Remember that time management is a continuing activity; one action will not magically change your whole environment. But one action makes a start.

My Biggest Problems	Action Needed
1. _____	1. _____
2. _____	2. _____
3. _____	3. _____
4. _____	4. _____
5. _____	5. _____

RECAP

Applying Time and Communication Management Principles

	How To Improve Individual Performance	How To Improve Team Performance
1. Set Goals	Write clear, measurable, attainable, and specific goals.	As a team, identify and discuss the team goals.
2. Make a Master List	Make a master list of all that you have to do.	As a team, list and describe the steps that need to be accomplished to achieve the team or project goals.
3. Prioritize	Identify the high-priority tasks. Determine what should be done first, second, and so on.	As a team, determine the priority of the steps or tasks and decide who should take responsibility for each task.
4. Manage Distractions	Identify what may keep you from accomplishing your goal and develop strategies to manage or eliminate the distractions (phone calls, interruptions, and the like).	As a team, identify the obstacles that may keep the team from achieving its goals. Identify strategies to overcome the obstacles.
5. Take Action	Identify what you need to do and then do it.	As a team, take action to achieve the goals of the project. Periodically meet to evaluate the plan and assess whether you are meeting your objectives.

Work Efficiently on Team Projects

You can apply the principles and strategies in this appendix to group and team projects. Although the only person you can really change is you, using these principles and strategies can help you develop a blueprint for working efficiently with others. To apply the time management principles to the work of a team, consider the following strategies:

- Make sure your team has clearly written, measurable, attainable, and specific work objectives.

- Before plunging in on a team task, make a master list of the key steps that the team needs to accomplish. Without a comprehensive list of the steps needed to do the work, it will be more difficult to develop clear team member roles and more challenging to divide and conquer the work objectives.

- Assess what the team priorities are. What is truly urgent and important? What needs to be accomplished first, second, and so on?

- Note obstacles that may keep the team from working efficiently. But do more than describe the obstacles—develop a plan to address the potential barriers that you identify.

- Take action by implementing the collaborative plan that the team has developed. Periodically take the time to assess how well the team is meeting its goals.

Wrap-Up

Rather than managing time, what we really manage is communication—the mounds of information that seek our attention throughout the day. To help manage the messages, information, and barrage of data that occupy much of our time, these five strategies can help you manage the messages that compete for your attention:

1. Identify your goals and objectives.

2. Make a master list of all of the tasks needed to accomplish your goals.

3. Prioritize your list; identify what's important and what's urgent.

4. Develop a strategy for managing the inevitable interruptions that may keep you from your tasks.

5. Take action to accomplish your goals.

Reviewing Key Terms

Time Management *383*

Goal *386*

Objective *386*

The Principle Points

Principle One: Be aware of your communication with yourself and others.

- Increase your efficiency by first becoming aware of how you currently use your time.
- Be cognizant of the goals and objectives you want to accomplish.
- Use the power of reflection to mindfully identify strategies for taking action.

Principle Two: Effectively use and interpret verbal messages.

- Develop written goals and objectives to significantly increase the likelihood that you will accomplish what you want to achieve.
- Make a written master list of all of your tasks, projects, and objectives to help increase both effectiveness and efficiency.

Principle Three: Effectively use and interpret nonverbal messages.

- Make sure that everything you need is within easy reach in your workspace to increase your efficiency.
- Minimize eye contact with people passing by your workspace to stay focused on your work and increase work efficiency.
- Develop nonverbal symbols, such as a closed door, to signal when you are not available to visit.

Principle Four: Listen and respond thoughtfully to others.

- Respond to the messages and responses of others to help you manage them with greater accuracy and effectiveness.

Principle Five: Appropriately adapt messages to others.

- Adapt your method of communicating to others (email, phone, in person) to help you work more effectively and efficiently; there may be no need to visit a colleague's office when a short email message will be just as effective in communicating a message.

Applying Your Skills

1. Make a list to help you identify important yet nonurgent tasks that you should spend more time on. (Examples: spend more time planning, reading, studying, preparing for class, building relationships with others)

2. What will you do to reorder your life to make time for these important but nonurgent tasks? (Examples: schedule time in my appointment book, develop a personal goal statement, make a master list)

Glossary

A

Accommodator someone who manages conflict by giving in rather than engaging in the conflict.

Activity report a document that communicates progress on a project or achievements to others in an organization or on a team.

Adaptive skills self-management skills that allow you to adjust to a variety of social situations.

Adult learners people who prefer to be given information they can use immediately, to be actively involved in the learning process, to connect their life experiences with the new information they learn, to know how the new information is relevant to their busy lives, to know how the information will solve a problem, and to receive information that is relevant to their needs.

Affirming message a message that reveals that you value and support another person.

Agenda a written list of issues, questions, information, or topics to be discussed or tasks to be completed in a meeting.

Amiable a social style characterized by high responsiveness and low assertiveness. People with this style are considered relationship specialists; they enjoy working in supportive and helpful roles.

Analogy a comparison between an unfamiliar idea, thing, or situation and something the audience already understands.

Analytical a social style characterized by low responsiveness and assertiveness. Individuals with this social style are considered technical specialists; they enjoy working in technical positions.

Appeal to misplaced authority using someone without the appropriate credentials or expertise to endorse an idea or product.

Appraisal interview an interview in which a supervisor shares information with an employee about his or her job performance; also known as a *performance review*.

Argumentativeness a tendency to advocate strongly for one's own position on an issue and criticize the positions of other people.

Articulation the enunciation of speech sounds.

Artifact a personal object used to communicate some part of one's identity.

Assertiveness an individual's capacity to make requests, actively disagree, express positive and negative personal feelings, and stand up for himself or herself without attacking another.

Asynchronous communication in which there is a time delay between when a message is sent and when it is received.

Attend to focus on a specific message.

Attention the first step of the motivated sequence involving capturing the audience's attention so that they will listen to the message.

Authoritarian leaders leaders who influence by giving orders and seeking to control others.

Avoider someone who manages conflict by steering clear of it.

B

Back channel cues nonverbal cues that signal to the other person that we are listening and wish for them to continue talking.

Back matter the components of a report that traditionally come at the end, after the main body, and provide further detail and references.

Bandwagon fallacy the argument that because everyone believes something or does something, the belief or behavior must be valid, accurate, or effective.

Bar graph a graph that uses bars of different lengths to represent statistical data.

Biased messages messages that include words or expressions that offend because they make inappropriate assumptions or repeat stereotypes about gender, ethnicity, physical or mental disability, age, or sexual orientation.

Boolean search an advanced web-searching technique that allows a user to narrow a key word search by specifying certain parameters.

Briefing a short talk that provides information to an audience.

C

Career-search information interview an interview in which you gather information about careers, jobs, and organizations and network with others so that you will have a job when you are ready for one.

Causal fallacy a faulty cause-and-effect connection between two things or events.

Causal reasoning reasoning that relates two or more events in such a way as to conclude that one or more of the events caused the others.

Cause-and-effect organization a strategy for identifying a situation and then discussing the resulting effects (cause-effect), or presenting a situation and then exploring its causes (effect-cause).

Central idea a one-sentence summary of your presentation; sometimes called a thesis sentence.

Centralized power cultures cultures that value a more concentrated or narrow distribution of power; power is held by one person or a select few.

Channel the means by which a message is expressed to the receiver.

Charisma a form of dynamism; a charismatic speaker possesses charm, talent, magnetism, and other qualities that make the person attractive.

Chronemics   the study of how people use and structure time.

Chronological organization   organization by sequential order, according to when each step or event occurred or should occur.

Clarity   the specificity of a message and how easily the reader can comprehend the information.

Classical approach to motivation   a leadership style that assumes that there is one best way to perform a specific task within an organization with maximum efficiency, and that a leader's job is to influence workers to behave in this way.

Classification   defining something by placing it in a group or category based on its qualities or characteristics.

Clique   a smaller group of people within a larger group who form a common bond among themselves.

Closed question   an interview question that limits the range of possible responses and requires a simple, direct, and brief answer.

Closure   a sense of being complete or "sounding finished" provided in the conclusion of a speech by finishing a story, answering a rhetorical question, or reminding the audience of a statistic presented in the introduction.

Coercive power   power stemming from the ability to punish others.

Cognitive dissonance   psychological discomfort experienced when a person is presented with information that is inconsistent with his or her current thinking or feelings.

Coherence   unity in writing created by common underlying concepts, logical organization, and clear, natural development of the content.

Cohesiveness   the degree of attraction that members of a group feel toward one another and the group.

Collaborator   someone who manages conflict by being willing to work with others to solve problems and make decisions.

Collectivistic cultures   cultures whose members value group or community interests over individual interests.

Communibiological perspective   an interdisciplinary approach to the study of human communication that makes connections between the fields of neurology, psychology, and communication.

Communication   the process of acting on information.

Communication apprehension (CA)   fear or anxiety associated with ongoing or anticipated communication with another person or persons.

Communication interaction pattern   communication pattern that emerges based on who talks to whom.

Communication trait   a label used to describe a person's communication behaviors.

Competence   the perception that a person is skilled, knowledgeable, and informed about the subject he or she is discussing.

Competitor   someone who manages conflict by being competitive and pushing ideas and solutions on others.

Complaint letter   a letter that expresses dissatisfaction with a product or service.

Complexity   arrangement of speech ideas from simple to complex.

Compromiser   someone who manages conflict by giving up part of what he or she wants in exchange for the other person's giving up part of what he or she wants.

Concise writing   writing that avoids unnecessary words and phrases.

Conclusion   the closing sentences of a speech, intended to summarize the speech, to reemphasize the main idea in a memorable way, to motivate the audience to respond, and to provide closure.

Concrete messages   referring to something you can experience with your senses.

Conditional statements   statements that qualify what is being said; they leave room for interpretation.

Confidentiality   the ethical principle that requires interviewers to keep information disclosed during an interview private.

Conflict phase   the second phase of group interaction, in which group members experience some disagreement about social issues and group tasks.

Conflict style   the way people are perceived to express and manage conflict.

Connotative meaning   the interpretation of a word based on personal experiences.

Consensus   group agreement that occurs when all group members support and are committed to a collective decision.

Content   the new information, ideas, or suggested actions that a speaker wishes to express.

Content dimension   the communication dimension that focuses on what is said; the verbal message.

Context   the physical, historical, and psychological environment in which communication occurs.

Conversational rituals   learned, routine scripts that people use when talking and responding to others.

Corrective feedback   communication feedback whose goal is to alter negative or inappropriate behavior.

Correspondence   business letters sent to customers, co-workers, superiors, and subordinates.

Cover letter   a document that accompanies a resume; a sales pitch that argues why you are the best candidate for a position.

Credibility   a listener's perception of a speaker as competent, trustworthy, and dynamic.

Cube   a small, modular office unit with no door and no floor-to-ceiling walls.

Cultural context   the nonverbal cues related to culture that surround and give meaning to messages.

Culture   a learned system of knowledge, behavior, attitudes, beliefs, values, and norms that is shared by a group of people.

D

Decentralized power cultures   cultures in which people value a broad distribution of power; the power belongs to the people, or the many, not to one person or group.

Decision making   the process of making a choice from among several alternatives.

Declarative statements   statements expressed as truths that leave no room for interpretation.

Decoding   the process of interpreting ideas, feelings, and thoughts that have been translated into a code.

Decorative font   a font designed to convey a feeling or tone.

Deductive reasoning   reasoning from a general statement or principle to reach a specific conclusion.

Definition   a brief explanation that identifies and clarifies what something is by classifying it or describing how it works.

Delegation   a manager's assignment of a specific task or project to an employee.

Delivery cues   notes a speaker uses to remind himself or herself of nonverbal behaviors to use while making a presentation.

Delivery outline   a condensed, abbreviated outline that provides the notes a speaker uses when presenting a speech.

Democratic leaders   leaders who consult with the group before issuing edicts.

Demographic information   statistics about audience characteristics such as age, gender, and cultural background.

Denotative meaning   the literal or dictionary definition of a word.

Derived credibility   the perception of a speaker's credibility that the audience forms as he or she presents a speech.

Description   a word picture; a detailed image that allows an audience to mentally see, hear, smell, touch, or taste whatever a speaker is describing.

Descriptive approach   an approach to team development that seeks to identify the typical ways teams behave in solving problems.

Devil's advocate   someone who criticizes or opposes something in order to provoke a discussion or an argument.

Dialect   a consistent style of pronunciation and articulation that is common to an ethnic group or a geographic region.

Downward communication   communication that flows from superiors to subordinates.

Driver   a social style characterized by high assertiveness and low responsiveness. Persons with this social style are considered control specialists; they often enjoy working in leadership and management positions.

Dropbox <getdropbox.com>   file-syncing software that allows one to link files from several computers.

Dynamism   an aspect of a speaker's credibility that reflects whether the speaker is perceived as energetic.

E

Either-or fallacy   the oversimplification of an issue into a choice between only two outcomes or possibilities.

Elaboration strategies   mental processing strategies that give information new meaning by organizing the information.

Emblem   a gesture that has a direct verbal translation and may substitute for a word or phrase.

Emergence phase   the third phase of group interaction, in which conflict or disagreement is managed and decisions are made.

Empathy   the emotion experienced by someone who feels what another is feeling.

Encoding   the process of translating ideas, feelings, and thoughts into a code.

Evernote <evernote.com>   software used to consolidate the user's notes and ideas. It also helps find entries that have been submitted.

Ethics   the beliefs, values, and moral principles by which we determine what is right and wrong.

Ethos   the credibility or ethical character of a speaker.

Evidence   the illustrations, definitions, statistics, and opinions presented as supporting material in persuasive speaking.

Exit interview   an interview in which an employer gathers information from an employee who is leaving the organization about his or her work experiences.

Expert power   power derived from having knowledge and expertise.

Expert testimony   an opinion offered by someone who is an authority on the subject under discussion.

Explanation   a statement of how something is done or why it exists in its present form or existed in its past form.

Expressive   a social style characterized by high assertiveness and responsiveness. Individuals with this social style are considered social specialists; they are able to use their communication skills to gain recognition and attention, and enjoy being noticed by others.

Extemporaneous speaking   speaking from a written or memorized speech outline without having memorized the exact wording of the speech.

F

Feed-forward messages   messages that inform others of how to process information from you.

Feedback   the response to a message.

Feminine cultures   cultures in which people have more of a social orientation and tend to value caring, sensitivity, and enhancing quality of life.

Figurative analogy   a comparison between two essentially unlike things or events that nevertheless share some feature.

FileCenter <lucion.com>   document management system that permits you to scan large amounts of paperwork to easily track its electronic filing.

Final summary   the final part of a speech, which restates a speaker's most important ideas.

Force field analysis   a tool that structures the analysis of a problem by identifying the driving forces that increase the probability that a goal will be achieved and the restraining forces that decrease that probability.

Formal report   a highly researched report on an ongoing project, often co-authored by several writers.

Forum presentation   a question-and-answer session that usually follows a presentation or a symposium.

Front matter   the components of a report that come at the beginning and prepare the reader for the main information.

Functional approach   an approach to leadership that suggests that leaders perform essential functions, tasks, and processes that help an organization or team achieve goals; an approach to team development that suggests that in order for a team to be effective, certain communication functions must occur.

Funnel sequence   a questioning sequence that begins with broad, open questions and proceeds toward more closed questions.

G

Gaps analysis   an analysis conducted by a supervisor of an identified gap between a performance standard and an employee's actual performance.

Gatekeeper   a person who controls the flow of communication within an organization.

Gender   the cultural and psychological characteristics that are associated with biological sex.

Goal   a clear statement identifying something to be accomplished in the long term.

Goodwill   a positive perception of an author on the part of the audience.

Government documents   published federal information on almost every subject, including records of official federal proceedings, pamphlets, special reports, and texts of speeches and debates.

Grammar   the study of the functions of words and the way they work together to form coherent language.

Group communication   verbal and nonverbal message transaction that occurs among from three to about fifteen people who share a common purpose or goal.

Group deviate   a team member who holds an opinion different from the rest of the group; group members may spend considerable talk time trying to change this person's opinion.

Grouphate   the loathing many people have for collaborating with others in groups and teams.

Groupthink   a faulty sense of agreement that occurs when team members seemingly agree but they primarily want to avoid conflict.

H

Haptics   the study of how we communicate through touch.

Hasty generalization   reaching a conclusion from too little evidence or nonexistent evidence.

Hearing   the physiological process of decoding sounds.

Hierarchy of needs   Abraham Maslow's classic theory that humans have five levels of needs and that lower-level needs must be met before people can be concerned about higher-level needs.

High-contact culture   a culture in which touching is seen as commonplace and appropriate.

High-context cultures   cultures in which nonverbal cues are extremely important in interpreting messages.

Horizontal communication   communication between peers.

Hostile environment sexual harassment   unwelcome conduct of a sexual nature that interferes with a person's ability to perform a job or gain an education and that creates a hostile or intimidating environment at the workplace.

Human communication   the process of making sense out of the world and sharing that sense with others by creating meaning through the use of verbal and nonverbal messages.

Human resources approach to motivation   an approach to leadership that views workers as resources who can be full partners in enhancing a team or organization.

Hygiene factors   basic aspects of a job that have to be there for a worker to feel satisfied about the work, including salary, working conditions, and supervision.

Hypothetical illustration   a description of something that has not actually occurred but that could happen.

Hypothetical question   a question that asks for an interviewee's reaction to an imaginary emotion-arousing or value-laden situation in order to gauge the person's likely response in a real situation.

I

Illustration   a story or anecdote about an idea, issue, or problem a speaker is discussing.

Illustrator   a gesture that illustrates or complements a verbal message.

Immediacy   a perception of psychological and physical closeness.

Impersonal communication   communication that occurs when people are treated as objects, or when others respond to people's roles rather than to who they are as unique people.

Impromptu speaking   delivering a speech without advance preparation.

Individual roles   behaviors that focus attention on an individual rather than the group.

Individualistic cultures   cultures whose members value individual interests over group interests.

Inductive reasoning   reasoning that arrives at a general conclusion from specific instances or examples.

Inflection   variation in vocal pitch.

Inform   to share information with others to enhance their knowledge or understanding of the information, concepts, or ideas presented.

Information-gathering interview   a focused, structured conversation whose goal is to seek out information from another person.

Information overload   the inability to effectively process information because there is too much of it.

Initial credibility   the impression of a speaker's credibility that listeners have before a speech begins.

Initial preview   the first statement of the main ideas of a presentation, usually presented in conjunction with or as part of the central idea.

Interaction   the give-and-take conversation that occurs when people collaborate.

Interest   a desire, need, concern, or fear that motivates one to take a particular position.

Internal previews   previews that introduce and outline ideas that will be developed as a speech progresses.

Internal summaries summaries that occur within and throughout a speech to help listeners keep ideas in mind as the speech progresses.

Interpersonal communication communication that occurs when two people interact to mutually influence each other, usually for the purpose of managing relationships.

Interview a form of oral interaction structured to achieve a goal; it often includes just two people (but can include more) who take turns speaking and listening.

Interview schedule a guide that lists all of the questions and follow-up probes to be used in an interview so that the interviewer can sequence questions.

Interview topic a standard theme that is explored with a particular category of questions that are asked during an interview.

Introduction the opening sentences of a speech, intended to get the audience's attention, introduce the topic, give the audience a reason to listen, establish the speaker's credibility, and preview the main ideas.

Inverted funnel sequence a questioning sequence that begins with closed questions and proceeds to more open questions.

J

Jargon language used by a particular group, profession, or culture that may not be understood or used by other people.

Job description a document outlining the specific skills required for and basic duties of a particular position.

Job interview a structured interview in which an interviewer assesses an interviewee's qualifications and skills for employment.

Job-related skills skills that are specific to a particular occupation.

Jott <jott.com> system where one can simply call a phone number, leave a message, and then receive an email message with the information in text format.

K

Kinesics the study of gestures, posture, and body movement.

L

Laissez-faire leaders leaders who take a hands-off, laid-back approach to influencing others.

Language a system of symbols (words) common to a community of people and structured by grammar (rules and standards) and syntax (patterns in the arrangement of words) that make it possible for people to understand and communicate with one another.

Lay testimony an opinion or a description offered by a nonexpert who has firsthand experience.

Leadership the process of influencing others to achieve goals through verbal and nonverbal messages.

Leading question a question that suggests either explicitly or implicitly the answer expected.

Legally binding documents documents that record an exchange of promises and that are enforceable by law.

Legitimate power power that stems from being elected or appointed to a specific position or office.

Line graph a graph that shows trends over time and relationships among variables.

Listening the process of receiving, constructing meaning from, and responding to verbal and nonverbal messages.

Literal analogy a comparison between two similar things.

Literary quotation an opinion or description by a writer, expressed in a memorable and often poetic way.

Logical fallacy false reasoning that occurs when someone attempts to persuade without adequate evidence or with arguments that are irrelevant or inappropriate.

Logos the use of logical arguments.

Low-contact culture a culture in which touching is uncommon.

Low-context cultures cultures in which people rely more on explicit language and words and use fewer contextual cues to send and interpret information.

M

Manager someone who has been appointed to coordinate and facilitate, to keep things organized and accomplish a task.

Manuscript speaking reading a speech from a written text.

Masculine cultures cultures in which people have a task orientation and tend to value achievement, heroism, material wealth, and more traditional roles for men and women.

Media richness the degree to which a channel of communication offers the possibility of immediate feedback; provides both verbal and nonverbal cues; allows the use of natural, informal language; and customizes messages to recipients.

Media richness theory theory that a communication medium is rich if it has (1) potential for instant feedback, (2) verbal and nonverbal cues that can be processed by senders and receivers, (3) natural language, and (4) a focus on individuals.

Meeting a structured conversation among a small group of people who gather to accomplish a specific task.

Memo a short, informal written communication within an organization.

Memorized speaking delivering a speech word-for-word from memory without using notes.

Message written, spoken, and unspoken elements of communication to which people assign meaning.

Message directness an indication of the extent to which a message expresses details clearly and leaves no doubt as to the intended meaning.

Metadiscussion discussion about discussion; comments that describe the discussion process rather than the topic under consideration.

Mindfulness awareness of your own and others' thoughts, actions, and motivations.

MindManager <mindjet.com> software program that uses mind-mapping technique to make links between ideas; it provides tools to take notes and capture ideas while keeping upcoming major projects in mind.

Mnemonic device   a short rhyme, phrase, or other mental technique that makes information easier to memorize.

Moderately structured interview   an interview that includes some scripted questions but allows the interviewer the flexibility to deviate from the script.

Monochronic cultures   cultures that stress a high degree of scheduling, concentration on one thing at a time, and promptness.

Motivated sequence   a five-step plan for organizing a persuasive message: attention, need, satisfaction, visualization, and action.

Motivation factors   aspects of a person's job that motivate the person to do better.

N

Need   the second step of the motivated sequence, involving establishing the rationale, problem, or need for a listener to make a change so that the listener will agree with the action requested by the speaker.

Negative visualization   a bleak picture of how terrible the future will be if nothing is done; a fear appeal used to motivate listeners to adopt a particular solution to a problem.

Negotiating strategy   the overall approach taken in an exchange of proposals and counterproposals during negotiation of a settlement to a conflict.

Negotiation   an exchange of proposals and counterproposals as a means of reaching a satisfactory settlement to a conflict.

Noise   interference, either literal or psychological, that hinders the accurate encoding or decoding of a message.

Nominal-group technique   a brainstorming method in which members work individually on ideas, rank suggested solutions, and then report their findings in a group discussion.

Non sequitur   Latin for "it does not follow"; an idea or conclusion that does not logically follow a previous idea or conclusion.

Nonverbal communication   any communication, other than written or spoken language, that creates meaning for someone.

Nonverbal messages   visual and audible symbols that do not rely on words but create meaning for the receiver.

Nonverbal transitions   nonverbal behaviors (facial expressions, pauses, changes in vocal pitch or speaking rate, or movement) that are used either alone or in combination with verbal transitions to show relationships among ideas in a speech.

Norms   general standards within an organization or a group that determine what is appropriate and inappropriate behavior.

O

Objective   a statement of something specific, measurable, attainable, and observable to be achieved in the short term.

Office romances   romances that develop between people who work for the same employer.

Offshoring   sending work to be done in other countries with lower labor costs.

Open question   an interview question that is broad and unstructured and allows the respondent considerable freedom to determine the amount and kind of information she or he will provide.

Operational definition   an explanation of how an item being defined works or what it does.

Oral citation   an oral statement of the source of information used in a speech.

Organizational culture   the learned pattern of beliefs, values, assumptions, rules, and norms that are shared by the people in an organization.

Orientation phase   the first phase of group interaction, in which members become adjusted to one another and to the group's task.

Other-oriented   focused on the needs, motives, desires, and goals of others in one's communication.

Outward communication   communication between a service provider and a customer.

P

Panel presentation   a presentation in which team members have a conversation with a moderator or a facilitator who manages the interaction.

Paradigm   a worldview; a way of thinking or a set of attitudes that guide your communication and behavior.

Paraphrasing   restating in your own words what you think another person is saying.

Parliamentary procedure   a comprehensive set of rules that prescribe how to take action on specific issues that come before a group. For a complete guide to parliamentary procedure, see *Robert's Rules of Order*.

Part-whole learning style   the style of a learner who prefers learning details first, before the big picture.

Pathos   the use of emotional appeals to move an audience.

Person-focused leader   a leader who places value on and makes a priority of getting to know people on a personal level.

Personal attack   attacking personal characteristics of someone connected with an idea, rather than addressing the idea itself.

Personality trait   any distinguishable, relatively enduring way in which one individual differs from another.

Persuade   to change or reinforce a person's attitudes, beliefs, values, or behavior.

Persuasive interview   a structured conversation intended to influence a person's attitudes, beliefs, or behaviors.

Physical attraction   the attraction we have toward others because of their appearance.

Pie graph   a circular graph that shows the distribution of data as a proportion of a total.

Pitch   how high or low a speaker's voice is.

Podcasts   A radio broadcast that uses the technology of an iPod through iTunes to share messages with others.

Polychronic cultures   cultures in which human relations and interactions are valued over arbitrary schedules or appointments.

Position   in a conflict, what each person wants to see in a negotiated outcome.

Positive visualization   a rosy word picture of how wonderful the future will be if your solution is implemented.

Power   the ability to influence others' behavior.

Powerful language   language that is stereotypically masculine: direct, assertive, task-oriented, and focused more on the content of a message.

Powerless language   language that is stereotypically feminine: indirect and focused more on the quality of a relationship than on the information being exchanged.

Preparation outline   a detailed outline of the central idea, main ideas, and supporting material for a speech; may also include the specific purpose, introduction, and conclusion.

Prescriptive approach   an approach to team development that assumes that team members need a specific sequence of steps and techniques in order to stay on task and be productive.

Presentation aid   any tangible item or image used to help communicate ideas to an audience.

Preview   a statement of what is to come in a speech.

Primacy   arrangement of ideas from most important or convincing to least important.

Primary tension   the tension that results from the uncertainty and discomfort people experience when they meet in a group for the first time.

Probing question   an interview question that encourages the interviewee to clarify or elaborate on partial or superficial responses and that usually directs the discussion in a particular direction.

Problem solving   a process of overcoming obstacles to achieve a goal.

Problem-and-solution organization   a strategy for organizing a persuasive speech that works best when a clearly evident problem can be documented and a solution or solutions proposed to deal with the problem.

Process functions   functions performed by leaders that help maintain a harmonious climate by encouraging amiable relationships among others.

Progress report   a report that outlines for a customer or a client the status of a project.

Proof   evidence and the conclusions you draw from it.

Proximity   the physical space and distance that we maintain in our communication with others.

Psychological information   listener attributes such as attitudes, beliefs, and values.

Public communication   communication that occurs when a speaker addresses a gathering of people with the intent to inform, persuade, or entertain them.

Public relations presentation   a presentation in which the speaker is specifically providing information to promote a positive public image for the person or organization the speaker is representing.

Q

Qualify   to learn as much as possible about a customer or an audience, such as backgrounds, likes, dislikes, interests, needs,

and goals; to identify whether a customer can afford a product or service and to learn how to best approach the customer.

Quid pro quo sexual harassment   actual or threatened use of rewards or punishments to gain sexual compliance from a subordinate.

R

Rapport talk   talk focused on sharing information about relationships.

Reasoning   the process of drawing conclusions from evidence.

Reasoning by analogy   a special kind of inductive reasoning that draws a comparison between two ideas, things, or situations that share some essential common feature.

Receiver   the person who interprets a message.

Recency   arrangement of ideas from least to most important, based on the principle that audiences remember best what they hear last.

Red herring   irrelevant facts or arguments used to distract someone from the issue under discussion.

Referent power   power that stems from being liked.

Refutation   an organizational strategy by which you identify objections to your proposition and then refute those objections with arguments and evidence.

Regulator   a nonverbal cue that helps control the interaction and flow of communication between two people.

Reinforcement phase   the fourth phase of group interaction, in which group members express positive feelings toward each other and toward the group.

Reiterating   restating information using different words.

Relational conflict   an expressed struggle between at least two interdependent individuals, each of whom perceives incompatible goals, scarce rewards and resources, and interference from the other person in achieving his or her goals.

Relational dimension   the dimension of communication that offers cues about the emotions, attitudes, and amount of power and control a speaker feels in relation to listeners; the communication dimension that focuses on how a message is said; the nonverbal message.

Relational goals   in an interview, using interpersonal skills so as to be perceived as attractive and credible.

Relational messages   messages that build rapport and are aimed at establishing relationships.

Relationship   an ongoing connection developed with another person through interpersonal communication.

Relevant messages   messages that others perceive to satisfy their own needs and goals.

Remember   to recall information from memory.

Repeating   restating information using the same words in the same order.

Report   a summary of what has been accomplished in the past or an update on a project.

Report talk   talk focused on sharing practical or statistical information.

RescueTime <rescuetime.com> and **JournalLive** <journalLive .com) program that helps keep track of how one spends time while on the computer.

Respond to let another person know whether you understood a message or to validate the other person.

Responsiveness an individual's capacity to be sensitive to the communication of others, be seen as a good listener, and to make others comfortable in communicating.

Resume a concise, well-organized, written description of your background, training, and qualifications for a job.

Reward power power arising from the ability to grant favors, money, or other rewards.

Rhetoric the process of discovering the available means of persuasion in a given communication situation.

Role the consistent way someone communicates with others in a team, based on the person's own expectations and what others on the team expect of the person.

S

Sales proposal a document intended to persuade a possible client of his or her need for your product or service.

Sans serif font a font without lines (serifs) at the tops and bottoms of letters and with letters of uniform thickness.

Satisfaction the third step of the motivated sequence, including telling the listener of a persuasive message how the proposed solution will meet or satisfy the need.

Schema a mental representation of knowledge.

Script font a font that imitates handwriting, but is precise and uniform.

Select to focus on one sound among all the sounds competing for attention.

Serif font a font that has lines (serifs) at the tops and bottoms of the letters.

Servant leadership a style of leadership in which the leader explicitly views himself or herself as being of service to the group or team.

Sex biological characteristics present from birth that identify an individual as male or female.

Sexual harassment deliberate and/or repeated sexual or sex-based behavior that is not welcome, not asked for, and not returned.

Signpost a verbal or nonverbal signal that a speaker is moving from one idea to another.

Situational leadership an approach that views leadership as an interactive process that links a particular style of leadership with such factors as culture, time limitations, group member personalities, and the work the group needs to do.

Small group a collection of from three to fifteen people who share a common purpose, feel a sense of belonging to the group, and exert influence on each other.

Small group communication the transactive process of creating meaning among from three to fifteen people who share a common purpose, feel a sense of belonging to the group, and exert influence on each other.

Social decentering the process of stepping away from your own thoughts and attempting to experience the feelings of another person.

Social roles behaviors that manage relationships and affect group climate; these roles help resolve conflict and enhance the flow of communication.

Social style a pattern of communication behaviors that others observe when you interact with them.

Source the originator of a thought or emotion, who puts it into a code that can be understood by a receiver.

Spatial organization organization based on location, position, or direction.

Specific purpose a concise statement of precisely what you want your listeners to be able to do, remember, or feel when you finish your speech. Your specific purpose statement indicates the *audience response* you seek.

Standard outline format numbered and lettered headings and subheadings arranged hierarchically to indicate relationships among main ideas, subpoints, and supporting material in a speech.

Statistics numerical data that summarize several examples.

Status an individual's importance and prestige.

Strategically ambiguous messages messages that may not convey all available information or may be unclear and are used purposely by the source to reach some goal.

Structure the way a group or team discussion is organized; provided by the agenda and by techniques that help a group stay focused on the task at hand.

Structured interview a scripted interview that uses a set of standard questions that are asked of every person who is interviewed.

Style flexing the process of adapting your communication to how others communicate.

Supporting material illustrations, explanations, descriptions, definitions, analogies, statistics, and opinions that clarify, amplify, and provide evidence to support the main ideas and the thesis of a presentation.

Supportive feedback communication feedback whose goal is to encourage desirable behavior.

Syllogism a three-part argument that has a major premise, a minor premise, and a conclusion.

Symbol a word, sound, visual image, gesture, or object that represents a thought, a concept, another object, or an experience.

Symposium presentation a presentation format that consists of a series of individual presentations without interaction or conversation; each person on the team gives a portion of the presentation.

Synchronous communication which is received and responded to in real time.

System any entity (such as an organization, a group, or a team) that is made up of many interconnected and interdependent pieces.

Systems approach an approach to leadership that views organizations and teams as complex interconnected sets of elements that are not easily influenced by simple techniques and tools.

T

Target audience　a specific segment of your audience that you most want to influence.

Task analysis　a detailed, step-by-step description of precisely what a trainee should do and know in order to perform a particular skill.

Task dimension　A form of content dimension in the workplace. Leaders, including managers, supervisors or those who take charge, communicate content messages to accomplish certain tasks.

Task-focused leader　a leader who believes that work takes priority over personal relationships.

Task functions　behaviors that help a team or organization get work done.

Task goals　in an interview, asking and answering questions in a clear, concise, and thoughtful manner in order to convey appropriate information.

Task messages　messages that focus on the content of an interview.

Task roles　behaviors that help a group achieve its goal and accomplish its work.

Team　a coordinated group of individuals who collaborate to achieve a specific common goal; usually more structured and organized than a group.

Team-based organization　an organization that has a flat structure rather than a hierarchical structure (one with many layers and levels of supervisors).

Team ground rules　explicit, agreed-on prescriptions for acceptable and appropriate behavior, which help the team organize routine tasks and procedures.

Team mission statement　a concise description of a team's goals or desired outcomes.

Telecommuting　working from somewhere other than an office using mobile technology.

Telegraphic style　a writing style that condenses the message by eliminating articles, pronouns, conjunctions, and transitions.

Terminal credibility　the perception of a speaker's credibility listeners have at the conclusion of a speech.

Theory X　a view of leadership that assumes that workers are generally lazy and that a leader's job is to reward good work and punish bad work.

Theory Y　a view of leadership that assumes that workers are self-motivated and inherently want to do a good job. If a leader treats people well and builds good relationships with them, they will work hard.

Theory Z　an approach to leadership that assumes that people have a long-term relationship with an organization and that the relationship is based on trust, collaboration, and a common organizational goal.

Time management　the use of techniques for analyzing and prioritizing goals and objectives in order to increase efficiency and productivity.

Time orientation　how members of a culture structure, organize, and use time.

Toast　a brief speech saluting a momentous occasion.

Tone　the attitude of the writer toward both the reader and the subject matter that is communicated in a written document.

Topic sentence　generally, the first sentence of a paragraph that states the main idea.

Topical organization　organization by natural divisions of a central idea presented according to primacy, recency, or complexity, or arbitrary arrangement of ideas that are equal in importance.

Touch avoidant　the tendency to avoid touch in interpersonal interactions.

Training　a type of informative speaking in which a trainer seeks to develop specific skills in listeners to help them perform a specific job or task more effectively.

Trait approach　an approach to leadership that focuses on the psychological and physical attributes or traits that make leaders effective.

Transactional　occurring simultaneously.

Transferable skills　skills that are useful in a variety of jobs and positions.

Transformational leadership　the process of influencing people to see the future in new ways.

Trustworthiness　the aspect of credibility that reflects whether a speaker is perceived as believable and honest.

Tunnel sequence　a questioning sequence that uses a combination of open and closed questions to gather a large amount of information in a short amount of time.

U

Uncertainty avoidance　a measure of how accepting a culture is of a lack of predictability.

Understand　to assign meaning to the verbal and nonverbal messages received.

Unstructured interview　an unscripted interview that is unique to the individual being questioned; it does not include a standard set of questions.

Upward communication　communication that flows from subordinate to superior.

V

Verbal messages　messages that use words to create meaning.

Verbal transitions　words or phrases that show relationships between ideas in a speech.

Vigilant thinkers　people who pay attention to the process of how work is done in teams rather than focusing only on techniques used to achieve a goal.

Virtual team　a team that interacts via a channel other than face-to-face communication but rather uses email, video conferences, or other technological tools.

Visualization　using words to create an image in audience members' minds.

Vocalics　the nonverbal aspects of the voice, including pitch, rate, and volume.

Vodcasts   an easy way to share video and audio messages to anyone around the world.

W

Web 2.0   the second generation of presenting and gathering information on the Internet using "read-write" technology.

Whole-part learning style   the style of a learner who prefers learning the big picture first, then the details.

Wiki   a web-based site that permits collaboration and access to edit and revise information.

Wikis   collaborative web-based sites that permit numerous people to share information with one another.

Willingness to communicate (WTC)   an individual's natural tendency to initiate communication with others.

Word pictures   lively descriptions that help listeners form a mental image by appealing to their senses (sight, taste, smell, sound, and touch).

Workplace bullying   an extreme, negative, and persistent form of emotional workplace abuse achieved primarily through verbal and nonverbal communication.

Writing style   the tone, language, voice, and overall viewpoint of the sentences in a piece of writing.

X

Xobni <xobni.com>   program that assists in managing email messages and attachments.

Endnotes

Chapter 1

1. E. Ross and Angus Holland, *100 Great Businesses and the Minds Behind Them* (Naperville, IL: Sourcebooks, 2006), 129.

2. A. Davidson and M. Bolmeijer, *1000 CEOs* (London: Korling Kindersley, 2009), 456; S. S. Smith, "Coffee Talk with Starbucks CEO Howard Schultz," *Entrepreneur*, n.d. Retrieved February 9, 2008, from http://findarticles.com/p/articles/mi_m0DTI/is_n5_v26/ai_20923860.

3. H. Schultz, *Pour Your Heart into It* (New York: Hyperion, 1997).

4. Schultz, *Pour Your Heart into It*, 116; B. Ardoin, "A Diffusion Analysis of H. Schultz's Pour Your Heart into It." Retrieved February 9, 2008, from http://www.start-at-zero.com/papers/schultz.htm.

5. Retrieved September 8, 2010, from http://wiki.answers.com/Q/How_many_Starbucks'_are_there_in_the_world.

6. As reported in D. Smith, "Managers Lack Proper Skills," *The Sunday Times* (September 14, 1997), 12; for a compendium of specific communication skills valued in the workplace, see *Skills for Today's Workplace*, retrieved October 26, 2010, http://www.khake.com/page3.html.

7. E. T. Klemmer and F. W. Snyder, "Measurement of Time Spent Communicating," *Journal of Communication* 20 (June 1972): 142; L. R. Barker et al., "An Investigation of Proportional Time Spent in Various Communication Activities of College Students," *Journal of Applied Communication Research* 8 (1981): 101–109; R. Emanuel, J. Adams, K. Baker, E. K. Daufin, C. Ellington, E. Fitts, J. Himsel, L. Holladay, and D. Okeowo, "How College Students Spend Their Time Communicating," *International Journal of Listening* 22 (2008): 12–28.

8. F. DiMeglio, "New Role for Business School Research," *Business Week Online* 14 (August 2007).

9. F DiMeglio, "New Role For Business School Research."

10. L. Alexander and S. Campbell, "Degrees and Skills Make for a Profitable Package," *The London Times* (June 29, 2006): 8; see also K. N. Kinnick and S. R. Parton, "Workplace Communication," *Business Communication Quarterly* 4 (2005): 429–456.

11. Casner-Lotto and Barrington, "Are They Really Ready to Work? Employers' Perspectives on the Basic Knowledge and Applied Skills of New Entrants to the 21st Century U.S. Workforce," *The Conference Board, Partnership for 21st Century Skills, Corporate Voices for Working Families, and Society for Human Resource Management*. October 2006. Retrieved February 9, 2008, from http://www.conference-board.org/publications/describe.cfm?id=1218.

12. Casner-Lotto and Barrington, "Are They Really Ready to Work?"

13. B. Goodwin, "Develop Business Skills to Survive Offshoring Challenge, IT Staff Urged," *Computer Weekly* (February 27, 2007): 17; also refer to "Improve Those Tech Skills," *Wall Street and Technology* (July 2007): 14–16.

14. As quoted from Granvillle N. Toogood, *The New Articulate Executive: Look, Act, and Sound Like a Leader* (New York: McGraw-Hill, 2010), 3.

15. Adapted from Toogood, *The New Articulate Executive*, 4.

16. See "Can Communicators Help Improve Business Performance?" *Business Communicator* 6 (December 2005/January 2006): 1–2; R. E. Riggio and S. J. Taylor, "Personality and Communication Skills as Predictors of Hospice Nurse Performance," *Journal of Business and Psychology* 15 (Winter 2000): 351–359; S. Jo and S. W. Shim, "Paradigm Shift of Employee Communication: The Effect of Management Communication on Trusting Relationships," *Public Relations Review* 31 (2005): 277–280; DiMeglio, "New Role for Business School Research." B. Palmer, M. Walls, Z. Burgess, and C. Stough, "Emotional Intelligence and Effective Leadership," *Leadership and Organizational Development Journal* 22 (2000): 5–10.

17. Associated Press, "JetBlue Didn't Break Any Guidelines by Keeping Passengers on Plane for Hours." February 16, 2007. Retrieved February 24, 2008, from http://www.foxnews.com/story/0,2933,252381,00.html; JetBlue's apology on YouTube. February 19, 2007. Retrieved February 24, 2008, from http://www.youtube.com/watch?v=-r_PIg7EAUw.

18. F. E. X. Dance and C. Larson, *Speech Communication: Concepts and Behavior* (New York: Holt, Rinehart & Winston, 1972).

19. Kip Tendell as quoted by Adam Bryant, "Corner Office: Three Good Hires? He'll Pay More for One Who's Great," *New York Times* (March 13, 2010).

20. S. A. Beebe, S. J. Beebe, and D. K. Ivy, *Communication: Principles for a Lifetime* (Boston: Allyn & Bacon, 2010).

21. P. Watzlawick, J. B. Bavelas, and D. D. Jackson, *Pragmatics of Human Communication* (New York: W.W. Norton, 1967).

22. Watzlawick, Bavelas, and Jackson, *Pragmatics of Human Communication*.

23. Ross and Holland, *100 Great Businesses and the Minds Behind Them*, 24–26.

24. James MacGregor Burns, *Leadership* (New York: Harper & Row, 1978).

25. A. Keith, as cited by J. Kouzes and B. Posner, *The Leadership Challenge* (San Francisco: Jossey-Bass, 2002).

26. A. Raes, U. Glunt, M. Heijltjes, and R. Roe, "Top Management Team and Middle Managers—Making Sense of Leadership," *Small Group Research* 38, no. 3 (2007): 360–386.

27. C. Mason and M. Griffin, "Group Task Satisfaction—The Group's Shared Attitude to Its Task and Work Environment," *Group & Organization Management* 30, no. 6 (2005): 625–652.

28. R. E. Kelly, *The Power of Followership: How to Create Leaders That People Want to Follow and Followers Who Lead Themselves* (New York: Doubleday/Currency, 1992).

29. Kouzes and Posner, *The Leadership Challenge*, 25.

30. M. S. Limon and B. La France, "Communication Traits and Leadership Emergence: Examining the Impact of Argumentativeness, Communication Apprehension, and Verbal Aggressiveness in Work Groups," *Southern Communication Journal* 70, no. 2 (2005): 123–133.

31. R. E. Kelly, *The Power of Followership*.

32. Kouzes and Posner, *The Leadership Challenge*, 25.

33. R. White and R. Lippitt, "Leader Behavior and Member Reaction in Three Social Climates," in *Group Dynamics*, 3rd ed., edited by D. Cartwright and A. Zander (New York: Harper & Row, 1968), 319.

34. For a description of situational leadership approaches, see F. Fiedler, *A Theory of Leadership Effectiveness* (New York: McGraw-Hill, 1967), 144; P. Hersey, K. H. Blanchard, and D. E. Johnson, *Management of Organizational Behavior: Leading Human Resources* (New Delhi: Prentice Hall of India, 2004), 175.

35. B. M. Bass and M. J. Avolio, "Transformational Leadership and Organizational Culture," *International Journal of Public Administration* 17 (1994): 541–554. Also see F. J. Yammarino and A. J. Dubinsky, "Transformational Leadership Theory: Using Levels of Analysis to Determine Boundary Conditions," *Personnel Psychology* 47 (1994): 787–809.

36. R. Piccolo and J. Colquitt, "Transformational Leadership and Job Behaviors: The Mediating Role of Core Job Characteristics," *Academy of Management Journal* 49, no. 2 (2006): 327–340; R. K. Greenleaf, The Servant as a Leader (Indianapolis, IN: Greenleaf Center), (2002): 4.

37. P. M. Senge, "The Leader's New Role: Building Learning Organizations," *Sloan Management Review* 32, no. 1 (1990).

38. For an excellent review of transformational leadership and its applications to cultural contexts, see A. Ergeneli, R. Gohar, and

Z. Temirbekova, "Transformational Leadership: Its Relationship to Culture Value Dimensions," *International Journal of Intercultural Relations 31* (2007): 703–724.

39. J. Barbuto, Jr., and D. Wheeler, "Scale Development and Construct Clarification of Servant Leadership," *Group & Organization Management 31*, no. 3 (2006): 300–326.

40. R. Piccolo and J. Colquitt, "Transformational Leadership and Job Behaviors"; R. K. Greenleaf, *The Servant as a Leader*, 4.

41. R. Rubin, D. Munz, and W. Bommer, "Leading from Within: The Effects of Emotion Recognition and Personality on Transformational Leadership Behavior," *Academy of Management Journal 48*, no. 5 (2005): 845–858; L. C. Spears, *Reflections on Leadership: How Robert K. Greenleaf's Theory of Servant-Leadership Influenced Today's Management Thinkers* (New York: Wiley).

42. The five fundamental principles are taken from our "sister" book: Beebe, Beebe, and Ivy, *Communication: Principles for a Lifetime*.

43. B. Berger, "Revolution at Whirlpool," *Internal Communication Focus* (November 1994); also see M. Loeb and S. Kindel, *Leadership for Dummies* (Indianapolis, IN: Wiley, 1999), 38.

44. S. Knorath, "Changes in Dispositional empathy in American College Students over Time: A Meta-Analysis." Paper presented at the annual meeting of the Association for Psychological Science, Boston, MA, 2010.

45. S. R. Covey, *The 7 Habits of Highly Effective People* (New York: Simon & Schuster, 1989); S. R. Covey, *The 8th Habit: From Effectiveness to Greatness* (New York: Free Press, 2004).

46. NCA Credo for Ethical Communication. Retrieved December 9, 2010, from http://www.natcom.org/Default.aspx?id=134&terms=ethical%20communication.

47. Our definition of "relationship" and our discussion of relating skills is based on information from S. A. Beebe, S. J. Beebe, and M. V. Redmond, *Interpersonal Communication: Relating to Others* (Boston: Allyn & Bacon, 2010).

48. For a discussion of media richness theory, see L. K. Trevino, R. L. Daft, and R. H. Lengel, "Understanding Managers' Media Choices: A Symbolic Interactions Perspective," in *Organizations and Communication Technology*, edited by J. Fulk and C. Steinfield (Newbury Park, CA: Sage, 1990), 71–74.

49. S. A. Beebe and J. T. Masterson, *Communicating in Small Groups: Principles and Practices* (Boston: Allyn & Bacon, 2012).

Chapter 2

1 "The World's 100 Most Powerful Women," *Forbes* magazine. Retrieved January 9, 2011, from http://www.forbes.com/wealth/power-women; "Fifty Most Powerful Women," *Fortune* magazine. Retrieved January 9, 2011, from http://money.cnn.com/galleries/2010/fortune/1009/gallery.most_powerful_women.fortune/index.html; "Women at the Top: The Ranking. New Directions. #1 Indra Nooyi, 55." *Financial Times*. Retrieved May 16, 2011, from http://womenatthetop.ft.com/articles/women-top/ca66b59e-ed92-11df-9085-00144feab49a. Quote on p. 10.

2. "Women at the Top," p. 10.

3. "Women at the Top," p. 10.

4. E. J. Langer, *The Power of Mindful Learning* (Reading, MA: Perseus Books, 1997); E. Ju-Lee, "When Placebic Information Differs from Real Information: Cognitive and Motivation Bases of Mindful Reactions to Information Social Influence," *Communication Research 32* (2005): 615–645.

5. D. W. Merrill and R. H. Reid, *Personal Styles and Effective Performance* (Radnor, PA: Chilton, 1981); R. Norton, *Communicator Style: Theory, Applications, and Measures* (Beverly Hills, CA: Sage, 1993); G. L. May and L. E. Gueldenzoph, "The Effect of Social Style on Peer Evaluation Ratings in Project Teams," *Journal of Business Communication 43* (2006): 4–20.

6. "*Letstalk* Annual Cell Phone Etiquette Survey: More People Find Cell Phone Use in Cars and Supermarkets Acceptable." Retrieved January 7,

2009, from http://www.letstalk.com/company/release_031406.htm; M. Haig, *Mobile Marketing: The Message Revolution* (London: Kogan Page, 2002); D. Reid and F. Reid, "Insights into the Social and Psychological Effects of SMS Text Messaging." Retrieved September 27, 2008, from www.160characters.org/documents/SocialEffectsOf TextMessaging.pdf.

7. Adapted from T. J. Lipscomb, J. W. Totten, R. A. Cook, and W. Lesch, "Cellular Phone Etiquette among College Students," *International Journal of Consumer Studies 31* (2005): 46–56; R. Wel and L. Leung, "Blurring Public and Private Behaviors in Public Space: Policy Challenges in the Use and Improper Use of the Cell Phone," *Telematics and Informatics 16* (1999): 11–26. "Letstalk Announces Cell Phone Etiquette Guidelines Based on 6 Years of Etiquette Research." Retrieved January 7, 2009, from http://www6.letstalk.com/company/release_031406.htm.

8. Adapted from C. A. Miller, "Communications of the ACM," *Special Issue: Human-Computer Etiquette 47* (2004): 30–61.

9. V. P. Richmond and J. C. McCroskey, *Communication: Apprehension, Avoidance, and Effectiveness*, 5th ed. (Boston: Allyn and Bacon, 1998); J. J. Teven, J. C. McCroskey, and V. P. Richmond, "Communication Correlates of Perceived Machiavellianism of Supervisors: Communication Orientations and Outcomes," *Communication Quarterly 54* (2006): 127–142.

10. Richmond and McCroskey, *Communication: Apprehension, Avoidance, and Effectiveness;* Teven, McCroskey, and Richmond, "Communication Correlates of Perceived Machiavellianism of Supervisors."

11. V. P. Richmond and J. C. McCroskey, *Organizational Communication for Survival* (Boston: Allyn & Bacon, 2008); K. W. Thomas, *Thomas-Kilmann Conflict Mode Instrument* (Mountain View, CA: CPP, 2002).

12. From Richmond and McCroskey, *Communication: Apprehension, Avoidance, and Effectiveness;* Teven, McCroskey, and Richmond, "Communication Correlates of Perceived Machiavellianism of Supervisors."

13. V. P. Richmond and J. C. McCroskey, *Communication: Apprehension, Avoidance, and Effectiveness* 5th ed. (Boston: Allyn and Bacon, 1998).

14. Adapted from R. Bolton and D. G. Bolton, *People Styles at Work;* May and Gueldenzoph, "The Effect of Social Style on Peer Evaluation Ratings in Project Teams."

15. Adapted from R. Bolton and D. G. Bolton, *People Styles at Work;* May and Gueldenzoph, "The Effect of Social Style on Peer Evaluation Ratings in Project Teams."

16. Frederick Taylor, *The Principles of Scientific Management* (New York: Harper & Row, 1911).

17. Max Weber, *Max Weber: The Theory of Social and Economic Organization,* translated by T. Parsons and A. Henderson (New York: Free Press, 1947).

18. Abraham H. Maslow, "A Theory of Human Motivation," in *Motivation and Personality* (New York: Harper & Row, 1954), Chapter 5.

19. F. J. Roethlisberger and W. J. Dickson, *Management and the Worker* (Cambridge, MA: Harvard University Press, 1939); E. Mayo, *The Social Problems of an Industrial Civilization* (Cambridge, MA: Harvard University Press, 1945).

20. F. Herzberg, *Work and the Nature of Man* (Cleveland, OH: World, 1966).

21. "Women at the Top," p. 10.

22. Robert Blake and Jane Mouton, *The New Managerial Grid* (London: Chartered Management Institute, 2005).

23. For excellent discussions of organizational culture, see K. Miller, *Organizational Communication: Approaches and Processes* (Belmont, CA: Thompson/Wadsworth, 2006); G. W. Driskil and A. L. Brenton, *Organizational Culture in Action: A Cultural Analysis Workbook* (Thousand Oaks, CA: Sage, 2005); J. Keyton, *Communication and Organizational Culture: A Key to Understanding Work Experiences* (Thousand Oaks, CA: Sage, 2005).

24. T. J. Peters and R. H. Waterman, Jr., *In Search of Excellence: Lessons from America's Best-Run Companies* (New York: Collins, 1982). An updated edition of Peters and Waterman's book was published in 2004.

25. J. Collins, *Good to Great: Why Some Companies Make the Leap . . . and Others Don't* (New York: HarperCollins, 2006).

26. See F. M. Jablin, "Organizational Entry, Assimilation, and Exit," in *The New Handbook of Organizational Communication*, edited by F. M. Jablin and L. L. Putnam (Thousand Oaks, CA: Sage, 2001): 732–881.

27. Quote by Lev Grossman, "Person of the Year 2010, Mark Zuckerberg," *Time*. Retrieved May 20, 2011, from http://www.time.com/time/specials/packages/article/0,28804,2036683_2037183,00.html.

28. J. Martin, *Organizational Culture: Mapping the Terrain* (Thousand Oaks, CA: Sage, 2002), 120.

29. Dan Rosenzweig as interviewed by Adam Bryant, "Remember to Thank Your Star Players," *New York Times* (July 10, 2010): B2.

30. E. Schein, *Organizational Culture and Leadership* (San Francisco: Jossey-Bass, 1992).

31. S. M. Davis, *Managing Corporate Culture* (Cambridge, MA: Ballinger, 1984), 7–8.

32. H. Wee, "Corporate Ethics: Right Makes Might," *Business Week*, April 11, 2002. Retrieved January 17, 2008, from http://www.businessweek.com/bwdaily/dnflash/apr2002/nf20020411_6350.htm?chan=search.

33. J. Bandler and N. Varchaver, "How Bernie Did It." CNNMoney.com. Retrieved February 25, 2011, from http://money.cnn.com/2009/04/24/news/newsmakers/madoff.fortune/index.htm.

34. L. Stern, "Bernie Madoff: Did He Steal Your Money Too?" *Newsweek Online*. Retrieved February 25, 2011, from http://www.newsweek.com/2008/12/16/did-bernie-madoff-steal-your-money.html.

35. B. Vlasic, "Toyota's Slow Awakening to a Deadly Problem." *New York Times*. Retrieved February 25, 2011, from http://www.nytimes.com/2010/02/01/business/01toyota.html. See also http://www.huffingtonpost.com/2010/01/21/toyota-recall-2010-more-t_n_432125.html.

36. A. G. Keane, "Toyota Put Profit before Customer Safety." *Bloomberg News Online*. Retrieved February 25, 2011, from http://www.bloomberg.com/apps/news?pid=newsarchive&sid=a3g5dmb3K8V4.

37. K. Thomas, "Toyota Recall Investigation Reports Cars Are Safe." From the Associated Press as reported in the online *Christian Science Monitor*. Retrieved May 20, 2011, from http://www.csmonitor.com/Business/Latest-News-Wires/2011/0208/Toyota-recall-investigation-reports-cars-are-safe.

38. The ideas on ethical challenges were adapted from M. Z. Hackman and C. E. Johnson, *Leadership: A Communication Perspective*, 4th ed. (Long Grove, IL: Waveland Press, 2004); C. E. Johnson, *Meeting the Ethical Challenges of Leadership: Casting Light or Shadow* (Thousand Oaks, CA: Sage, 2001).

39. This information was adapted from the George S. May International Company. Retrieved January 17, 2008, from http://ethics.georgesmay.com/check_yourself.htm.

40. A. G. Keane, "Toyota Put Profit before Customer Safety." *Bloomberg News Online*. Retrieved February 25, 2011, from http://www.bloomberg.com/apps/news?pid=newsarchive&sid=a3g5dmb3K8V4.

Chapter 3

1. C. Gallo, *The Presentation Secrets of Steve Jobs: How to Be Insanely Great in Front of Any Audience* (New York: McGraw-Hill, 2010). Also refer to http://www.cultofmac.com/the-secrets-of-steve-jobs-ipad-presentation-gallery/28799, retrieved January 3, 2011; P. Elmer-DeWitt, "How Big Was Apples' iPad Christmas?" *Fortune* magazine. Retrieved January 19, 2011, from http://tech.fortune.cnn.com/2010/12/30/how-big-was-apples-ipad-christmas/.

2. B. H. Spitzberg, "Methods of Interpersonal Skill Assessment," in *Handbook of Communication and Social Interaction Skills*, edited by J. O. Greene and B. R. Burleson (Mahwah, NJ: Erlbaum, 2003), 93–134.

3. D. R. Siebold, S. Kudsi, and M. Rude, "Does Communication Training Make a Difference? Evidence for the Effectiveness of a Presentation Skills Program," *Journal of Applied Communication Research* 21 (1993): 111–129.

4. J. M. Keller, "Motivational Design of Instruction," in *Instructional Design Theories: An Overview of Their Current Status*, edited by C. M. Reigeluth (Hillsdale, NJ: Erlbaum, 1983), 383–434.

5. J. Chesebro and M. Wanzer, "Instructional Message Variables," in *The Handbook of Instructional Communication: Rhetorical and Relational Perspectives*, edited by T. Mottet, V. P. Richmond, and J. C. McCroskey (Needham Heights, MA: Allyn & Bacon, 2006), 89–116.

6. J. Lamont, "Microblogging Eases into the Enterprise," *KM World 18*, no. 10 (2009):10–12; M. Breeding, "Social Networking Strategies for Professionals," *Computers in Libraries* 29, no. 9 (2009): 29–31.

7. C. G. Lynch, "Twitter for Business: Four Ways Companies Use Microblogging: Having a Good Dialogue with Users of Twitter, the Microblogging Service, Requires Being Personable and Avoiding Too Much Corporate Marketing Jargon." Retrieved May 22, 2011, from http://www.cio.com.au/article/303199/twitter_business_four_ways_companies_use_microblogging/?pp=2&rid=-154.

8. Ibid.

9. Lamont, "Microblogging Eases into the Enterprise."

10. Many of these ideas were adapted from M. Breeding, "Social Networking Strategies for Professionals," *Computers in Libraries* 29, no. 9 (2009): 29–31.

11. Ibid.

12. Adapted from Steven Covey's 7 Habits of Highly Effective People Signature Program, http://www.FranklinCovey.com.

13. K. Yamanouchi, "Delta Blasts Union for Nasty Attacks," Atlanta Business News. *The Atlanta Journal-Constitution*. Retrieved January 4, 2011, from http://www.ajc.com/business/delta-blasts-union-for-786362.html.

14. R. M. Guzley, "Organizational Climate and Communication Climate: Predictors of Commitment to the Organization," *Management Communication Quarterly* 5 (1992): 379–402. Also refer to B. Feng and J. Lee, "The Influence of Thinking Styles on Responses to Supportive Messages," *Communication Studies* 61 (2010), 224–238.

15. J. R. Gibb, "Defensive Communication," *Journal of Communication* 11 (1961): 141–148.

16. K. K. Sereno, M. Welch, and D. Braaten, "Interpersonal Conflict: Effects of Variations in Manner of Expressing Anger and Justifications for Anger upon Perceptions of Appropriateness, Competence, and Satisfaction," *Journal of Applied Communication Research* 15 (1987): 128–143.

17. J. R. Gibb, "Defensive Communication," *Journal of Communication* 11 (1961): 141–148.

18. A. Lenhart, S. Arafeh, A. Smith, and A. R. Macgill, *Writing, Technology, and Teens*. Pew/Internet & American Life Project, College Board: The National Commission on Writing. Retrieved September 28, 2008, from http://www.pewinternet.org/PPF/r/247/report_display.asp.

19. C. Thurlow and M. Poff, "The Language of Text-Messaging," in *Handbook of the Pragmatics*, edited by S. C. Herring, D. Stein, and T. Virtanen (New York: Mouton de Gruyter, 2009), 16.

20. Ibid.

21. A. Lenhart et al., *Writing, Technology, and Teens*.

22. Thurlow and Poff, "The Language of Text-Messaging."

23. Ibid.

24. Adapted from C. A. Miller, *Communications of the ACM* [Special issue]: *Human-Computer Etiquette* 47 (2004): 30–61.

25. N. Ambady and R. Rosenthal, "Half a Minute: Predicting Teacher Evaluations from Thin Slices of Nonverbal Behavior and Physical Attractiveness," *Journal of Personality and Social Psychology* 64 (1993): 431–441.

26. A. Mehrabian, *Nonverbal Communication* (Chicago: Aldine Atherton, 1972), 108.

27. D. Lapakko, "Three Cheers for Language: A Closer Examination of a Widely Cited Study of Nonverbal Communication," *Communication Education* 46 (1997): 63–67.

28. J. K. Burgoon and A. E. Bacue, "Nonverbal Communication Skills," in *Handbook of Communication and Social Interaction Skills*, edited by J. O. Greene and B. R. Burleson (Mahwah, NJ: Erlbaum, 2003), 179–219; B. H.

LaFrance, A. D. Heisel, and M. J. Beatty, "Is There Empirical Evidence for a Nonverbal Profile of Extraversion? A Meta-Analysis and Critique of the Literature," *Communication Monographs 71* (2004): 28–48.

29. P. Watzlawick, J. B. Bavelas, and D. D. Jackson, *Pragmatics of Human Communication* (New York: W. W. Norton, 1967).

30. M. L. Knapp, J. M. Wiemann, and J. A. Daly, "Nonverbal Communication: Issues and Appraisals," *Human Communication Research* 4 (1978): 271–280; J. K. Burgoon, "Nonverbal Signals," in *Handbook of Interpersonal Communication*, edited by M. L. Knapp and J. Daly (Thousand Oaks, CA: Sage, 2002), 240–299.

31. M. L. Knapp and J. A. Hall, *Nonverbal Communication in Human Interaction*, 6th ed. (Belmont, CA: Wadsworth, 2005).

32. "Building to Extremes," transcript from PBS Documentary, February 10, 2004. Retrieved February 21, 2008, from http://www.pbs.org/wnet/innovation/transcript_episode1.html.

33. M. J. Tews, K. Stafford, and J. Zhu, "Beauty Revisited: The Impact of Attractiveness, Ability, and Personality in the Assessment of Employment Suitability," *International Journal of Selection and Assessment* 17 (2009), 92–100; M. Hosoda, E. F. Stone-Romero, and G. Coats, "The Effects of Physical Attractiveness on Job-Related Outcomes: A Meta-Analysis of Experimental Studies," *Personnel Psychology* 56 (2003): 431–462. See also I. H. Frieze, J. E. Olson, and J. Russell, "Attractiveness and Income for Men and Women in Management," *Journal of Applied Social Psychology 21* (1991): 1039–1057.

34. Frieze, Olson, and Russell, "Attractiveness and Income."

35. M. Lynn and T. Simons, "Predictors of Male and Female Servers' Average Tip Earnings," *Journal of Applied Social Psychology 30* (2000): 241–252.

36. Quoted in J. Kita, "All to Be Tall," *Men's Health* (January–February 2004): 131–135. See also D. Elman, "Physical Characteristics and the Perception of Masculine Traits," *Journal of Social Psychology 103* (1977): 157–158.

37. J. H. Langlois, L. Kalakanis, A. J. Rubenstein, A. Larson, M. Hallam, and M. Smoot, "Maxims or Myths of Beauty? A Meta-Analytic and Theoretical Review," *Psychological Bulletin 126* (2000), 390–423; T. A. Judge, C. Hunt, and L. S. Simon, "Does It Pay to Be Smart, Attractive, or Confident?" *Journal of Applied Psychology 94* (2009): 742–755; See also J. Kita, "All to Be Tall."

38. K. J. Gross and J. Stone, *Chic Simple Dress Smart for Women: Wardrobes That Win in the Workplace* (New York: Warner Books, 2002). K. J. Gross and J. Stone, *Chic Simple Dress Smart for Men: Wardrobes That Win in the Workplace* (New York: Warner Books, 2002).

39. R. E. Bassett, A. Q. Stanton-Spicer, and J. L. Whitehead, "Effects of Attire and Judgments of Credibility," *Central States Speech Journal 30* (1979): 282–285. See also S. G. Lawrence and M. Watson, "Getting Others to Help: The Effectiveness of Professional Uniforms in Charitable Fundraising," *Journal of Applied Communication Research 19* (1991): 170–185; T. L. Morris, J. Gorham, S. H. Cohen, and D. Huffman, "Fashion in the Classroom: Effects of Attire on Student Perceptions of Instructors in College Classes," *Communication Education 45* (1996): 135–148.

40. S. Arnoult, "Dressed for Success," *Air Transport World* (June 2005): 58–60. See also K. Lovegrove, *Airline: Identity, Design, and Culture* (New York: teNeues, 2000); J. Schmeltzer, "McDonald's Lovin' Idea of Cool, New Threads," *Austin American Statesman* (July 6, 2005): D6.

41. Bassett, Stanton-Spicer, and Whitehead, "Effects of Attire and Judgments of Credibility." See also Lawrence and Watson "Getting Others to Help"; Morris, Gorham, Cohen, and Huffman, "Fashion in the Classroom."

42. Per T. Mottet, former in-flight service manager for Northwest Airlines.

43. M. C. Jenkins and T. V. Atkins, "Perceptions of Acceptable Dress by Corporate and Noncorporate Recruiters," *Journal of Human Behavior and Learning 7* (1990): 38–46.

44. J. S. Seiter and A. Sandry, "Pierced for Success? The Effects of Ear and Nose Piercing on Perceptions of Job Candidates' Credibility, Attractiveness, and Hirability," *Communication Research Reports 20* (2003): 287–298.

45. A. A. Acor, "Employers' Perceptions of Persons with Body Art and an Experimental Test Regarding Eyebrow Piercing," *Dissertation Abstracts International: Section B: The Sciences and Engineering*, Vol. 61 (7-B), (February 2001): 3885.

46. For a review of the research, see J. K. Burgoon, T. Birk, and M. Pfau, "Nonverbal Behaviors, Persuasion, and Credibility," *Human Communication Research 17* (1990): 140–169. Also see W. B. Pearce and F. Conklin, "Nonverbal Vocalic Communication and Perception of Speaker," *Speech Monographs 38* (1971): 235–241; R. L. Street, Jr., and R. M. Brady, "Speech Rate Acceptance Ranges as a Function of Evaluative Domain, Listener Speech Rate, and Communication Context," *Communication Monographs 49* (1982): 290–308.

47. L. L. Hinkle, "Perceptions of Supervisor Nonverbal Immediacy, Vocalics, and Subordinate Liking," *Communication Research Reports 18* (2001): 128–136. Also see Burgoon, Birk, and Pfau, "Nonverbal Behaviors, Persuasion, and Credibility."

48. Mehrabian, *Nonverbal Communication.*

49. W. G. Woodall and J. P. Folger, "Nonverbal Cue Context and Episodic Memory: On the Availability and Endurance of Nonverbal Behaviors as Retrieval Cues," *Communication Monographs 52* (1985): 320–333; A. A. Cohen and R. P. Harrison, "Intentionality in the Use of Hand Illustrators in Face-to-Face Communication Situations," *Journal of Personality and Social Psychology 28* (1973): 276–279; Knapp and Hall, *Nonverbal Communication in Human Interaction.*

50. S. Goldin-Meadow, H. Nussbaum, S. D. Kelly, and S. Wagner, "Gesture: Psychological Aspects," *Psychological Science 12* (2001): 516–522.

51. S. Duncan, "Some Signals and Rules for Turn Taking in Conversations," *Journal of Personality and Social Psychology 23* (1972): 283–292.

52. P. Ekman and W. V. Friesen, *Unmasking the Face* (Englewood Cliffs, NJ: Prentice-Hall, 1975).

53. A. R. Hochschild, *The Managed Heart: Commercialization of Human Feelings.* 20th anniversary ed. (Los Angeles: University of California Press, 2003).

54. J. Timmick, "How You Can Learn to Be Likeable, Confident, Socially Successful for Only the Cost of Your Present Education," *Psychology Today 16* (1982): 42–49.

55. M. Hickson III, D. W. Stacks, and N. J. Moore, *Nonverbal Communication: Studies and Applications* 4e (New York: Oxford University Press, 2004), 394.

56. S. A. Beebe, "Eye Contact: A Nonverbal Determinant of Speaker Credibility," *Speech Teacher 23* (1974): 21–25; J. M. Droney and C. I. Brooks, "Attributions of Self-Esteem as a Function of Duration of Eye Contact," *Journal of Social Psychology 133* (1993): 715–722; L. P. Napieralski, C. I. Brooks, and J. M. Droney, "The Effect of Duration of Eye Contact on American College Students' Attributions of State, Trait, and Test Anxiety," *Journal of Social Psychology 135* (1995): 273–280.

57. N. Gueguen and C. Jacob, "Direct Look versus Evasive Glance and Compliance with a Request," *Journal of Social Psychology 142* (2002): 393–396.

58. C. I. Brooks, M. A. Church, and L. Fraser, "Effects of Duration of Eye Contact on Judgments of Personality Characteristics," *Journal of Social Psychology 126* (1986): 71–78; G. Amalfitano and N. C. Kalt, "Effects of Eye Contact on Evaluation of Job Applicants," *Journal of Employment Counseling 14* (1977): 46–48; Burgoon, Birk, and Pfau, "Nonverbal Behaviors, Persuasion, and Credibility."

59. Jilly Stephens, executive director of City Harvest, New York City, as interviewed by Adam Bryant, "Rah-Rah Isn't for Everyone," *New York Times* (April 10, 2010): B2.

60. E. T. Hall, *The Hidden Dimension* (Garden City, NY: Anchor Books, 1966).

61. J. K. Burgoon and J. L. Hale, "Nonverbal Expectancy Violations: Model Elaboration and Application to Immediacy Behaviors," *Communication Monographs 55* (1988): 58–79.

62. J. K. Burgoon, "A Communication Model of Personal Space Violations: Explication and an Initial Test," *Human Communication*

Research 4 (1978): 129–142; J. K. Burgoon and S. B. Jones, "Toward a Theory of Personal Space Expectations and Their Violations," *Human Communication Research 2* (1976): 131–146.

63. N. M. Sussman and H. M. Rosenfeld, "Influence of Culture, Language, and Sex on Conversational Distance," *Journal of Personality and Social Psychology 42* (1982): 66–74; Hall, *The Hidden Dimension.*

64. L. Baxter and J. Ward, "Newsline," *Psychology Today 8* (1975): 28.

65. Hickson, Stacks, and Moore, *Nonverbal Communication.*

66. E. T. Hall, *The Dance of Life: The Other Dimension of Time* (New York: Anchor Books, 1984); E. T. Hall, *The Silent Language* (Garden City, NY: Anchor/Doubleday, 1959).

67. J. K. Burgoon, J. B. Walther, and E. J. Baesler, "Interpretations, Evaluations, and Consequences of Interpersonal Touch," *Human Communication Research 19* (1992): 237–263.

68. Hickson, Stacks, and Moore, *Nonverbal Communication*; P. A. Andersen, "Researching Sex Differences within Sex Similarities: The Evolutionary Consequences of Reproductive Differences," in *Sex Differences and Similarities in Communication*, edited by D. J. Canary and K. Dindia (Mahwah, NJ: Erlbaum, 1998), 83–100.

69. P. A. Andersen and K. Leibowitz, "The Development and Nature of the Construct Touch Avoidance," *Environmental Psychology and Nonverbal Behavior 3* (1978): 89–106.

70. M. S. Remland, T. S. Jones, and H. Brinkman, "Proxemics and Haptic Behavior in Three European Countries," *Journal of Nonverbal Behavior 15* (1991): 215–231; M. S. Remland, T. S. Jones, and H. Brinkman, "Interpersonal Distance, Body Orientation and Touch: Effect of Culture, Gender, and Age," *Journal of Social Psychology 135* (1995): 281–295.

71. Remland, Jones, and Brinkman, "Proxemics and Haptic Behavior in Three European Countries"; Remland, Jones, and Brinkman, "Interpersonal Distance, Body Orientation and Touch."

72. Hickson, Stacks, and Moore, *Nonverbal communication.*

73. S. L. Webb, "Sexual Harassment Should Be Defined Broadly," in *What Is Sexual Harassment?* edited by K. L. Swisher (San Diego, CA: Greenhaven Press, 1995), 10–18.

74. M. Salter and C. Bryden, "I Can See You: Harassment and Stalking on the Internet," Information *Technology Law 18* (2009): 99–122; S. Schenk, "Cyber-Sexual Harassment: The Development of the Cyber-Sexual Experiences Questionnaire," *McNair Scholars Journal 12* (2008), Article 8.

75. Webb, "Sexual Harassment Should Be *Defined* Broadly."

76. Ibid.

77. Ibid.

78. R. Paetzold and A. O'Leary-Kelly, "The Legal Context of Sexual Harassment," in *Sexual Harassment: Communication Implications,* edited by G. L. Kreps (Cresskill, NJ: Hampton Press, 1993), 63–77.

79. K. L. Scheppele, as quoted in E. Goodman, "The 'Reasonable Woman' Definition of Sexual Harassment Makes Sense," in *What Is Sexual Harassment?* edited by K. L. Swisher (San Diego, CA: Greenhaven Press, 1995), 25–27.

80. D. S. Dougherty, "Dialogue Through Standpoint: Understanding Women's and Men's Standpoints of Sexual Harassment," *Management Communication Quarterly 12* (1999): 436–468. Also see D. S. Dougherty, "Sexual Harassment as [Dys]functional Process: A Feminist Standpoint Analysis," *Journal of Applied Communication Research 29* (2001): 372–402; J. Keyton and S. C. Rhodes, "Organizational Sexual Harassment: Translating Research into Application," *Journal of Applied Communication Research 27* (1999): 158–173; B. A. Gutek, A. G. Cohen, and A. M. Konrad, "Predicting Social-Sexual Behaviors at Work: A Contact Hypothesis," *Academy of Management Journal 33* (1990): 560–577; J. W. Lee and L. K. Guerrero, "Types of Touch in Cross-Sex Relationships Between Co-Workers: Perceptions of Relational and Emotional Messages, Inappropriateness, and Sexual Harassment," *Journal of Applied Communication Research 29* (2001): 197–220.

81. M. Helft, "Jobs Takes Sick Leave at Apple Again, Stirring Questions." *New York Times Online.* Retrieved February 4, 2011, from http://www.nytimes.com/2011/01/18/technology/18apple.html.

82. Ibid.

83. Y. I. Kane and J. S. Lublin, "On Apple's Board, Fewer Independent Voices." WSJ.com. Retrieved February 4, 2011, from http://online.wsj.com/article/SB10001424052748704266504575141933921476048.html.

84. A. Satariano, "Apple is Right on Jobs Disclosure, Former SEC Chair Levitt Says." *Bloomberg News Online.* Retrieved February 4, 2011, from http://www.bloomberg.com/news/print/2011–01–20/apple-h.

Chapter 4

1. R. Ruggless, "Norman Brinker Hits the Comeback Trail." *Nation's Restaurant News.* Retrieved May 24, 2011, from http://www.fundinguniverse.com/company-histories/Brinker-International-Inc-Company-History.html.

2. S. Bell, Norm! *Food & Service* (January 1992); referenced in J. C. Maxwell, *Leadership Gold: Lessons Learned from a Lifetime of Leading* (Nashville, TN: Thomas Nelson, 2008).

3. Referenced in Maxwell, J.C. (2008). *Leadership gold: Lessons learned from a lifetime of leading.* Nashville, TN: Thomas Nelson, Inc. Also see W. Grimes, Norman Brinker, Casual Dining Innovator, Dies at 78. *New York Times.* December 25, 2010 from http://www.nytimes.com/2009/06/10/business/10brinker.html?scp=1&sq=norman%20brinker&st=cse

4. Ibid. Also see W. Grimes, "Norman Brinker, Casual Dining Innovator, Dies at 78. *New York Times.* December 25, 2010, from http://www.nytimes.com/2009/06/10/business/10brinker.html?scp=1&sq=norman%20brinker&st=cse.

5. A. D. Wolvin and C. G. Coakley, "Listening Education in the 21st Century," *International Journal of Listening 14* (2000): 143–152.

6. J. D. Weinrauch and R. Swanda, Jr., "Examining the Significance of Listening: An Exploratory Study of Contemporary Management," *Journal of Business Communication 13* (1975): 25–32; see also L. A. Janusik and A. D. Wolvin, "24 Hours in a Day: A Listening Update to the Time Studies," paper presented at the 2006 meeting of the International Listening Association, Salem, OR.

7. L. A. Janusik and A. D. Wolvin, "Listening Treatment in the Basic Communication Course Text," in *Basic Communication Course Annual,* edited by D. Sellnow (Boston: Academic Press, 2002).

8. National Association for Colleges and Employers, "Top Skills for Job Candidates." Naceweb.org. Retrieved February 17, 2011, from http://www.naceweb.org/Press/Releases/Top_Skills_for_Job_Candidates.aspx?referal=pressroom&menuid=273.

9. M. Rowh, "Listen Up!" *Career World* (May 2006), 22–25.

10. J. Foley, "Listen Up: Good Leaders Are All Ears," *The Globe and Mail* (Toronto, Canada) (March 8, 2008): C-1.

11. M. Meyer, "The Power of Listening," *Management Principles* (September 1, 2010): 35.

12. S. Banerji, "Report: Employers Say College Graduates Lack Essential Skills to Succeed in Today's Global Economy." *Diverse: Issues in Higher Education.* Retrieved February 17, 2011, from http://diverseeducation.com/article/6894.

13. International Listening Association, "An ILA Definition of Listening," *ILA Listening Post 53* (April 1995): 1, 4.

14. E. Raudsepp, "Listen Lessons: Poor Listening Habits Cost Qualified MBAs Job Offers and Promotions," *Minority MBA* (1993–94): 36–39; A. K. Robertson, *Listen for Success: A Guide to Effective Listening* (Burr Ridge, IL: Irwin Professional Publishing, 1994); R. Weiner, "Seven Rules for Effective Communication," *Public Relations Quarterly 52* (2007): 9–11.

15. L. R. Wheeless, "An Investigation of Receiver Apprehension and Social Context Dimensions of Communication Apprehension,"

The Speech Teacher 24 (1975): 263. K. L. Winiecki and J. Ayres, "Communication Apprehension and Receiver Apprehension in the Workplace," *Communication Quarterly* 47 (1999): 430–440; J. L. Chesebro, "Effects of Teacher Clarity and Nonverbal Immediacy on Student Learning, Receiver Apprehension and Affect," *Communication Education* 52 (2003): 135–147; J. L. Chesebro and J. C. McCroskey, "The Relationship Between Teacher Clarity and Immediacy on Students' Experiences with Receiver Apprehension When Listening to Teachers," *Communication Quarterly* 46 (1998): 446–456; C. V. Roberts, "A Validation of the Watson-Barker Listening Test," *Communication Research Reports* 3 (1986): 115–119.

16. J. Levy, H. Pashler, and E. Boer, "Central Interference in Driving: Is There Any Stopping the Psychological Refractory Period?" *Psychological Science* 17 (2006): 228–235; K. Woznicki, "Multi-Tasking Creates Health Problems," United Press International, August 6, 2001. Retrieved April 21, 2009, from http://www.umich.edu/-bcalab/articles/UPIArticle2001.html.

17. I. W. Johnson, C. G. Pearce, T. L. Tuten, and L. Sinclair, "Self-Imposed Silence and Perceived Listening Effectiveness," *Business Communication Quarterly* 66 (2003): 23–45.

18. Ibid.

19. These ideas were adapted from M. Booth-Butterfield, *Interpersonal Essentials* (Boston: Allyn & Bacon, 2002), 163.

20. R. Bierck, "How to Listen: Listening Is an Integral Part of Good Business Communication," *Harvard Management Communication Letter* (January 2001): 4–5.

21. Bierck, "How to Listen."

22. A. Sueyoshi and D. M. Hardison, "The Role of Gestures and Facial Cues in Second Language Listening Comprehension," *Language Learning* 55 (2005): 661–699; G. A. Mueller, "Visual Contextual Cues and Listening Comprehension: An Experiment," *Modern Language Journal* 64 (1980): 355–360.

23. T. P. Mottet, "Interactive Television Instructors' Perceptions of Students' Nonverbal Responsiveness and Their Influence on Distance Teaching," *Communication Education* 49 (2000): 146–164; Sueyoshi and Hardison, "The Role of Gestures and Facial Cues in Second Language Listening Comprehension."

24. A. Mehrabian, *Nonverbal Communication* (Chicago: Aldine-Transaction, 2007).

25. A. Mehrabian, *Silent Messages: Implicit Communication of Emotions and Attitudes,* 2nd ed. (Belmont, CA: Wadsworth, 1981), 2.

26. M. Gladwell, *Blink: The Power of Thinking Without Thinking* (New York: Little, Brown, 2005).

27. Gladwell, *Blink;* A. Damasio, *The Feeling of What Happens: Body and Emotion in the Making of Consciousness* (New York: Harcourt, 1999); J. K. Burgoon, "Nonverbal Signals," in *Handbook of Interpersonal Communication,* edited by M. L. Knapp and G. R. Miller (Thousand Oaks, CA: Sage, 1994), 229–285.

28. Mehrabian, *Silent Messages;* J. A. Russell and L. F. Barrett, "Core Affect, Prototypical Emotional Episodes, and Other Things Called Emotion: Dissecting the Elephant," *Journal of Personality and Social Psychology* 76 (1999): 805–819; J. A. Russell and A. Mehrabian, "Distinguishing Anger and Anxiety in Terms of Emotional Response Factors," *Journal of Consulting and Clinical Psychology* 42 (1974): 79–83.

29. Mehrabian, *Silent Messages;* V. P. Richmond, J. C. McCroskey, and A. Johnson, "Development of the Nonverbal Immediacy Scale (NIS): Measures of Self- and Other-Perceived Nonverbal Immediacy," *Communication Quarterly* 51 (2003): 504–517.

30. P. Andersen, *Nonverbal Communication: Forms and Functions* (Long Grove, IL: Waveland Press, 2007*).*

31. M. S. Mast and J. A. Hall, "Who Is the Boss and Who Is Not? Accuracy of Judging Status," *Journal of Nonverbal Behavior* 28 (2004): 145–165; M. Helweg-Larsen, S. J. Cunningham, A. Carrico, and A. M. Pergram, "To Nod or Not to Nod: An Observational Study of Nonverbal Communication and Status in Female and Male College Students," *Psychology of Women Quarterly* 28 (2004): 358–361; L. Z. Tiedens and

A. R. Fragale, "Power Moves: Complementarity in Dominant and Submissive Nonverbal Behavior," *Journal of Personality and Social Psychology* 84 (2003): 558–568; Mehrabian, *Silent Messages.*

32. P. Nicholas and K. Hennessey, "Shirley Sherrod Dismissal a Rash Decision." *Los Angeles Times.* Retrieved February 17, 2011, from http://articles.latimes.com/2010/oct/07/nation/la-na-sherrod-usda-20101008.

33. L. B. Resnick, "Cognition and Instruction: Recent Theories of Human Competence," in *Psychology and Learning: The Master Lecture Series,* Vol. 4, edited by B. L. Hammonds (Washington, DC: American Psychological Association, 1985), 127–186.

34. Resnick, "Cognition and Instruction."

35. R. G. Nichols and L. A. Stevens, "Listening to People," *Harvard Business Review* 35 (September–October 1957): 85–92.

36. A. King, "Autonomy and Question Asking: The Role of Personal Control in Guided Student-Generated Questioning," *Learning and Individual Differences* 6 (1994): 163–185.

37. M. Imhof, "How to Listen More Efficiently: Self-Monitoring Strategies in Listening," *International Journal of Listening* 15 (2001): 2–20.

38. King, "Autonomy and Question Asking."

39. R. E. Mayer, "Elaboration Techniques That Increase Meaningfulness of Technical Text. An Experimental Test of the Learning Strategy Hypothesis," *Journal of Educational Psychology* 72 (1980): 770–784; Imhof, "How to Listen More Efficiently."

40. C. G. Pearce, I. W. Johnson, and R. T. Barker, "Assessment of the Listening Styles Inventory," *Journal of Business & Technical Communication* 17 (2003): 84–113.

41. K. K. Halone and L. L. Pecchioni, "Relational Listening: A Grounded Theoretical Model," *Communication Reports* 14 (2001): 59–71.

42. Pearce, Johnson, and Barker, "Assessment of the Listening Styles Inventory."

43. Ibid.

44. Ibid.

45. P. Firestein, "The Art of Corporate Listening." *Bloomsburg Businessweek.* Retrieved December 25, 2010, from http://www.businessweek.com/managing/content/may2010/ca20100510_407452.htm. Also reference S. Vara, "Listening Marketing: Hearing Before We See," retrieved December 25, 2010, from http://kherize5.com/listening-marketing-hearing-before-we-see/.

46. Firestein, "The Art of Corporate Listening."

47. For a review of these awards, visit http://www.coca-colaindia.com/media/media_awards_csr.aspx.

48. Refer to "The Top 10 reasons to Monitor Your Brand in Social Media" and "The Next 10 Reasons: More Reasons to Monitor Your Brand in Social Media" authored by Radian6, an organization that provides software platforms to listen, measure, and engage in conversations across the social web. Retrieved December 25, 2010, from http://www.radian6.com/about/leadership-team/

49. Firestein, "The Art of Corporate Listening."

50. Adapted from Mottet, "Interactive Television Instructors' Perceptions of Students' Nonverbal Responsiveness."

51. M. Imhof, "What Makes a Good Listener? Listening Behavior in Instructional Settings," *International Journal of Listening* 12 (1998): 81–105; T. P. Mottet, S. A. Beebe, P. C. Raffeld, and A. L. Medlock, "The Effects of Student Verbal and Nonverbal Responsiveness on Teacher Self-Efficacy and Job Satisfaction," *Communication Education* 53 (2004): 150–163.

52. M. H. Immordino-Yang and A. Damasio, "We Feel, Therefore We Learn: The Relevance of Affective and Social Neuroscience to Education," *Mind, Brain, and Education,* 1 (2007): 3–10; K. Miller, "The Experience of Emotion in the Workplace: Professing in the Midst of Tragedy," *Management Communication Quarterly* 15 (2002): 571–600.

53. Reported in A. Kreamer, "Go Ahead—Cry at Work," *Time* (April 4 2011):52–55. Also reference A. Kreamer, *It's Always Personal* (New York: Random House, 2011).

54. O. Hargie, ed., *A Handbook of Communication Skills* (New York: Routledge, 2003); J. Authier, "Showing Warmth and Empathy," in *A*

Handbook of Communication Skills, edited by O. Hargie (New York: New York University Press, 1986), 441–464.

55. Refer to D. Tannen, "How Men and Women Use Language Differently in Their Lives and in the Classroom," *Education Digest 57* (1992): 3.

56. Sheila Lirio Marcelo as interviewed by Adam Bryant, "O.K., Team, It's Time to Switch Chairs," *New York Times* (August 7, 2010): B2.

57. Many of the ideas discussed in this section were adapted from J. C. Mc-Croskey and V. P. Richmond, eds., *Fundamentals of Human Communication: An Interpersonal Perspective* (Prospect Heights, IL: Waveland Press, 1996), 142–156; J. Chesebro, "Student Listening Behavior," in *Communication for Teachers*, edited by J. L. Chesebro and J. C. McCroskey (Boston: Allyn & Bacon, 2002), 8–18.

58. J. H. Gittell, *The Southwest Airlines Way: Using the Power of Relationships to Achieve High Performance* (New York: McGraw-Hill, 2003).

59. To learn more about how to use nonverbal responses to enhance receiver understanding, refer to T. P. Mottet and V. P. Richmond, "Student Nonverbal Communication and Its Influence on Teachers and Teaching," in *Communication for Teachers*, edited by J. L. Chesebro and J. C. McCroskey (Boston: Allyn & Bacon, 2002), 47–61.

60. R. C. Atkinson and R. M. Shiffrin, "Human Memory: A Proposed System and Its Control," in *The Psychology of Learning and Motivation: Advances in Research and Theory*, Vol. 2, edited by K. W. Spence (New York: Academic Press, 1968), 89–195; F. I. M. Craik and R. S. Lockhart, "Levels of Processing: A Framework for Memory Research," *Journal of Verbal Learning and Verbal Behavior 11* (1972): 671–684.

61. L. Wheeless, "An Investigation of Receiver Apprehension and Social Context Dimensions of Communication Apprehension," *The Speech Teacher 24* (1975): 261–268.

Chapter 5

1. Personal communication with Ms. Mitchell on April 11, 2011; also refer to http://www.mitchcommgroup.com/blog/. See also http://blog.prfirms.org/2011/04/public-relations-talent-imperative-fostering-diversity-and-inclusion/.

2. J. P. Guilford, *Personality* (New York: McGraw-Hill, 1959); D. C. Funder, *The Personality Puzzle* (New York: W. W. Norton, 1997).

3. D. A. Infante, A. S. Rancer, and D. F. Womack, eds. *Building Communication Theory*, 4th ed. (Prospect Heights, IL: Waveland Press, 2003).

4. J. C. McCroskey and V. P. Richmond, "Willingness to Communicate," *Communication and Personality: Trait Perspectives*, edited by J. C. McCroskey, J. A. Daly, M. M. Martin, and M. J. Beatty (Cresskill, NJ: Hampton Press, 1998), 119–131; K. B. Wright, L. Frey, and P. Sopory, "Willingness to Communicate About Health as an Underlying Trait of Patient Self-Advocacy," *Communication Studies 58* (2007): 35–51.

5. V. P. Richmond and J. C. McCroskey, *Communication: Apprehension, Avoidance, and Effectiveness*, 5th ed. (Boston: Allyn & Bacon, 1998).

6. V. P. Richmond and K. D. Roach, "Willingness to Communicate and Employee Success in U.S. Organizations," *Journal of Applied Communication Research* (1992): 95–115.

7. V. P. Richmond and J. C. McCroskey, *Organizational Communication for Survival: Making Work, Work*, 4th ed. (Boston: Allyn & Bacon, 2008); V. P. Richmond, "Implications for Quietness: Some Facts and Speculations," in *Avoiding Communication: Shyness, Reticence, and Communication Apprehension*, edited by J. A. Daly and J. C. McCroskey (Beverly Hills, CA: Sage, 1984), 145–156; V. P. Richmond and J. C. McCroskey, "Willingness to Communicate and Dysfunctional Communication Processes," in *Intrapersonal Communication Processes*, edited by C. V. Roberts and K. W. Watson (Scottsdale, AZ: Gorisuch Scarisbrick, 1989), 292–318.

8. B. Horwitz, *Communication Apprehension: Origins and Management* (New York: Singular, 2001).

9. J. C. McCroskey and V. A. Richmond, "Communication Apprehension and Small Group Communication," in *Small Group Communication: A Reader*, 5th ed., edited by R. S. Cathcart and L. A. Samovar (Dubuque, IA: William C. Brown, 1988), 405–420.

10. J. C. McCroskey, "Validity of the PRCA as an Index of Oral Communication Apprehension," *Communication Monographs 45* (1978): 192–203.

11. Richmond and McCroskey, *Communication: Apprehension, Avoidance, and Effectiveness*; C. B. Crawford and C. S. Strohkirch, "The Critical Role of Communication in Knowledge Organizations: Communication Apprehension as a Predictor of Knowledge Management." *Journal of Knowledge Management Practice 7*. Retrieved August 16, 2008, from http://www.tlainc.com/articl122.htm.

12. J. C. McCroskey and M. J. Beatty, "Communication Apprehension," *Communication and Personality: Trait Perspectives*, edited by J. C. McCroskey, J. A. Daly, M. M. Martin, and M. J. Beatty (Cresskill, NJ: Hampton Press, 1998), 215–231.

13. Richmond and McCroskey, *Communication: Apprehension, Avoidance, and Effectiveness*, 67–78; J. J. Teven, "Effects of Supervisor Social Influence, Nonverbal Immediacy, and Biological Sex on Subordinates' Perceptions of Job Satisfaction, Liking, and Supervisor Credibility," *Communication Quarterly 55* (2007): 155–177.

14. Richmond and McCroskey, *Communication: Apprehension, Avoidance, and Effectiveness*; see also M. Booth-Butterfield and S. Booth-Butterfield, *Communication Apprehension and Avoidance in the Classroom* (Edina, MN: Burgess Publishing, 1992); L. Kelly, "Skills Training as a Treatment for Communication Problems," in *Avoiding Communication: Shyness, Reticence, and Communication Apprehension*, edited by J. A. Daly, J. C. McCroskey, T. Ayres, T. Hopf, and D. M. Ayres (Cresskill, NJ: Hampton Press, 1997), 331–365; L. Kelly and J. A. Keaten, "Treating Communication Anxiety: Implications of the Communibiological Paradigm," *Communication Education 49* (2000): 45–57.

15. D. A. Infante and A. S. Rancer, "A Conceptualization and Measure of Argumentativeness," *Journal of Personality Assessment 46* (1982): 72–80.

16. Infante and Rancer, "A Conceptualization and Measure of Argumentativeness"; Rancer and Avtgis, *Argumentative and Aggressive Communication*.

17. A. S. Rancer, "Argumentativeness," in *Communication and Personality: Trait Perspectives*, edited by J. C. McCroskey, J. A. Daly, M. M. Martin, and M. J. Beatty (Cresskill, NJ: Hampton Press, 1998), 149–170.

18. D. A. Infante and W. I. Gorden, "Superior and Subordinate Communication Profiles: Implications for Independent-Mindedness and Upward Effectiveness," *Central States Speech Journal 38* (1987): 73–80; D. A. Infante and W. I. Gorden, "Argumentativeness and Affirming Communicator Style as Predictors of Satisfaction/Dissatisfaction with Subordinates," *Communication Quarterly 37* (1989): 81–89; D. A. Infante and W. I. Gorden, "How Employees See the Boss: Test of an Argumentative and Affirming Model of Superiors' Communicative Behavior," *Western Journal of Speech Communication 55* (1991): 294–304.

19. A. S. Rancer and T. A. Avtgis, *Argumentative and Aggressive Communication: Theory, Research, and Applications* (Thousand Oaks, CA: Sage, 2006).

20. Rancer and Avtgis, *Argumentative and Aggressive Communication*; Beatty, McCroskey, and Valencic, *The Biology of Communication*; Rancer, "Argumentativeness."

21. Susan Docherty as interviewed by Adam Bryant, "Now, Put Yourself in My Shoes," *New York Times* (February 6, 2010): B2.

22. A. G. Smith, ed. *Communication and Culture* (New York: Rinehart & Winston, 1966).

23. E. T. Hall, *Beyond Culture* (Garden City, NY: Doubleday, 1976).

24. For example, see A. V. Matveeve and P. E. Nelson, "Cross Cultural Competence and Multicultural Team Performance: Perceptions of American and Russian Managers," *International Journal of Cross Cultural Management 4* (2004): 253–270.

25. G. Hofstede, *Culture's Consequences: International Differences in Work-Related Values* (Beverly Hills, CA: Sage, 1980); G. Hofstede, *Cultures and Organizations: Software of the Mind* (London: McGraw-Hill, 1991).

26. Hofstede, *Culture's Consequences.*

27. S. Ohlemacher, "White Americans No Longer a Majority by 2042." Retrieved August 14, 2008, from http://abcnews.go.com/Politics/wireStory?id=5575766.

28. Hall, *Beyond Culture.*

29. L. A. Samovar, R. E. Porter, and L. A. Stefani, *Communication Between Cultures* (Belmont, CA: Wadsworth, 1998).

30. G. Hofstede and G. J. Hofstede, *Cultures and Organizations: Software of the Mind*, revised and expanded 2nd ed. (New York: McGraw-Hill, 2005).

31. E. Würtz, "A Cross-Cultural Analysis of Websites from High-Context Cultures and Low-Context Cultures," *Journal of Computer-Mediated Communication, 11,* no. 1 (2005): article 13.

32. Ibid.

33. H. Sun, "Building a Culturally Competent Corporate Website: An Exploratory Study of Cultural Markers in Multilingual Web Design," in Proceedings of Special Interest Group on Design of Communication (SIGDOC) of the Association for Computing Machinery SIGDOC, 95–102.

34. Sun, "Building a Culturally Competent Corporate Website."

35. Adapted from "Tips on Creating a Cross Cultural Website." 4C International Cross Communication Consultants. Retrieved April 18, 2011, from http://www.4cinternational.com/index.php?page=articles.

36. Hofstede, *Culture's Consequences*; Hofstede, *Cultures and Organizations.*

37. P. Salem, ed., *Organizational Communication and Change* (Cresskill, NJ: Hampton Press, 1999).

38. Hofstede, *Culture's Consequences*; Hofstede, *Cultures and Organizations.*

39. Ibid.

40. R. Vincent and K. Bensinger, "Toyota Works to Save Face. *Los Angeles Times.* Retrieved May 26, 2011, from http://articles.latimes.com/2010/feb/01/business/la-fi-toyota1-2010feb01.

41. G. Hofstede, *Culture's Consequences: Comparing Values, Behaviors, Institutions and Organizations Across Nations*, 2nd ed. (Thousand Oaks, CA: Sage, 2001).

42. Ibid.

43. G. Hofstede, "Cultural Dimensions in Management and Planning," *Asia Pacific Journal of Management* (January 1984): 81–98; Hofstede, *Cultures and Organizations.*

44. Hofstede, *Culture's Consequences: Comparing Values, Behaviors, Institutions and Organizations Across Nations.*

45. S. Romero, "Rescue May Redeem a Troubled Past for Chilean City." *New York Times.* Retrieved May 26, 2011, from http://www.nytimes.com/2010/10/15/world/americas/15copiapo.html?ref=chileminingaccident2010.

46. J. L. Chin, B. Lott, J. Rice, and J. Sanchez-Huckles, eds., *Women and Leadership: Transforming Visions and Diverse Voices* (Malden, MA: Blackwell); see also "Women in Leadership Roles: Report of Online Discussion," Division for the Advancement of Women, United Nations Department of Economic and Social Affairs, and Women Watch. Retrieved March 17, 2009, from www.un.org/womenwatch/feature/women_leadership_on-line_discussion_report_Women_in_Leadership_Roles.pdf.

47. Adapted from N. Payne, "Intercultural Communication Tips." Retrieved March 17, 2009, from http://ezinearticles.com/?Intercultural-Communication-Tips&id=254094.

48. H. Sirkin, J. Hemerling, and A. Bhattacharya, *Globality: Competing with Everyone from Everywhere for Everything* (New York: Business Plus, 2008).

49. D. Tannen, *You Just Don't Understand: Women and Men in Conversation* (New York: Morrow, 1990); D. Tannen, *Talking from 9 to 5: How Women's and Men's Conversational Styles Affect Who Gets Heard,* Who Gets Credit, and What Gets Done at Work (New York: Morrow, 1994).

50. D. J. Canary and K. Dindia, eds., *Sex Differences and Similarities in Communication: Critical Essays and Empirical Investigations of Sex and Gender in Interaction* (Mahwah, NJ: Erlbaum, 1998).

51. R. Lakoff, "Language and Woman's Place," *Language in Society 2* (1975): 45–80; R. Lakoff, *Language and Woman's Place* (New York: Harper & Row, 1975).

52. J. Wood, *Gendered Lives: Communication, Gender, and Culture.* 8th ed. (Belmont, CA: Wadsworth, 2008).

53. L. M. Timmerman, "Comparing the Production of Power in Language on the Basis of Sex," in *Interpersonal Communication Research: Advances Through Meta-Analysis,* edited by M. Allen, R. W. Preiss, B. M. Qayle, and N. Burrell (Mahwah, NJ: Erlbaum, 2002), 73–88.

54. K. Quina, J. A. Wingard, and H. G. Bates, "Language Style and Gender Stereotypes in Person Perception," *Psychology of Women Quarterly 11* (1987): 111–122; L. L. Haleta, "Student Perceptions of Teachers' Use of Language: The Effect of Powerful and Powerless Language on Impression Formation and Uncertainty," *Communication Education 45* (1996): 16–28.

55. M. Z. Hackman, M. J. Hills, T. J. Paterson, and A. H. Furniss, "Leaders' Gender-Role as a Correlate of Subordinates' Perceptions of Effectiveness and Satisfaction," *Perceptual and Motor Skills 77* (1993): 671–674; B. Q. Griffin, "Perceptions of Managers: Effects of Leadership Style and Gender." Paper presented at the annual meeting of the Southeastern Psychological Association, Knoxville, TN, March 1992.

56. N. A. Burrell and R. J. Koper, "The Efficacy of Powerful/Powerless Language on Attitudes nd Source Credibility," in *Persuasion: Advances Through Meta-Analysis,* edited by M. Allen and R. Preiss (Cresskill, NJ: Hampton, 1998), 203–216.

57. D. Tannen, "The Power of Talk: Who Gets Heard and Why," *Harvard Business Review 73* (September–October 1995): 138–148.

58. Tannen, "The Power of Talk"; Tannen, *Talking from 9 to 5.*

59. Tannen, "The Power of Talk."

60. Tannen, *Talking from 9 to 5.*

61. Tannen, *Talking from 9 to 5*; see also H. T. Reis, "Gender Differences in Intimacy and Related Behaviors: Context and Process," in *Sex Differences and Similarities in Communication,* edited by D. J. Canary and K. Dindia (Mahwah, NJ: Erlbaum, 1998), 203–231.

62. D. Geddes, "Sex Roles in Management: The Impact of Varying Power of Speech Style on Union Members' Perception of Satisfaction and Effectiveness," *Journal of Psychology 126* (1992): 589–607; Tannen, *Talking from 9 to 5*; Wood, *Gendered Lives*; K. Patterson, J. Grenny, R. McMillan, and A. Switzler, *Crucial Conversations: Tools for Talking When Stakes Are High* (New York: McGraw-Hill, 2002).

63. J. M. Twenge, "A Review of the Empirical Evidence on Generational Differences in Work Attitudes," *Journal of Business and Psychology 25* (2010): 201–210.

64. J. J. Deal, D. G. Altman, and S. G. Rogelberg, "Millennials at Work: What We Know and What We Need to Do (If Anything)," *Journal of Business and Psychology 25* (2010): 191–199.

65. Adapted from D. Durkin, "Youth Movement." *Communication World 25* (2008): 23–25.

66. L. Reynolds, E. C. Bush, and R. Geist, "The Gen Y Imperative." *Communication World 25* (2008): 19–22.

67. The following ideas were adapted from Durkin, "Youth Movement"; Reynolds, Bush, and Geist, "The Gen Y Imperative"; H. Havenstein, "Millennials Demand Changes in IT Strategy," *Computerworld 42* (2008): 12–13; G. Ross-Munro, "Cross-Generational Communication," *Woman Advocate 14* (2009): 3–5.

68. L. Gavett and R. Throckmorton, *Bridging the Generation Gap* (Franklin Lakes, NJ: Career Press, 2007). Results from this study were also reported in J. Klein, "Managing Across the Generation Gap." *Bloomberg Business Week.* Retrieved May 26, 2011, from http://www.businessweek.com/smallbiz/content/feb2007/sb20070212_399060.htm; G. Tonks, K. Dickenson, and L. Lindsay, "Misconceptions and Realities: The Working Relationships of Older Workers and Younger

Managers," *Research and Practice in Human Resource Management 17* (2009):36–54.

69. P. M. Arsenault, "Validating Generational Differences: A Legitimate Diversity and Leadership Issue," *Leadership & Organizational Development Journal 25* (2004): 124–141.

70. J. B. Davis, S. D. Pawlowski, and A. Houston, "Work Commitments of Baby Boomers and Gen-Xers in the IT profession: Generational Differences or Myth?" *Journal of Computer Information Systems 4* (2006): 43–49. Also refer to M. H. Collins, J. F. Hair, and T. S. Rocco, "The Older-Worker—Younger-Supervisor Dyad: A Test of the Reverse Pygmalion Effect," *Human Resource Development Quarterly 20* (2009): 21–41.

71. L. C. Lancaster and D. Stillman, *When Generations Collide* (New York: Harper Collins, 2003).

Chapter 6

1. G. Bethune, *From Worst to First: Behind the Scenes of Continental's Remarkable Comeback* (New York: Wiley, 1999).

2. A. Bryant, "Remember to Share the Stage. Interview with Gordon M. Bethune, the former chief executive of Continental Airlines." *New York Times.* Retrieved February 9, 2011, from http://www .nytimes.com/2010/01/03/business/03corner.html

3. J. Ott, "Gordon Bethune: Preaching the Gospel of Performance and Productivity," *Aviation Week.* Retrieved February 9, 2011, from www .aviationweek.com/media/pdf/spotlight_bethune.pdf.

4. A. Bryant, "Remember to Share the Stage."

5. S. Carey, "United-Continental Merger Closes." *Wall Street Journal.* Retrieved February 9, 2011, from http://online.wsj.com/article/SB1000 142405274870385920457552561138418 1790.html.

6. P. M. Sias, *Organizing Relationships: Traditional and Emerging Perspectives on Workplace Relationships* (Los Angeles: Sage, 2009); B. Fix and P. M. Sias, "Person-Centered Communication, Leader-Member Exchange, and Employee Satisfaction," *Communication Research Reports 23* (2006): 35–44.

7. R. Badowksi and R. Gittines, *Managing Up: How to Forge an Effective Relationship with Those Above You* (New York: Doubleday Business, 2004).

8. M. B. Wanzer, A. M. Wojtaszczyk, and J. Kelly, "Nurses' Perceptions of Physicians' Communication: The Relationship among Communication Practices, Satisfaction, and Collaboration," *Health Communication 24* (2009): 683–691; V. P. Richmond and J. C. McCroskey, "The Impact of Supervisor and Subordinate Immediacy on Relational and Organizational Outcomes," *Communication Monographs 67* (2000): 85–95.

9. L. K. Lewis, "Employee Perspectives on Implementation Communication as Predictors of Perceptions of Success," *Western Journal of Communication 70* (2006): 23–46; B. Kay and D. M. Christophel, "The Relationships among Manager Communication Openness, Nonverbal Immediacy, and Subordinate Motivation," *Communication Research Reports 12* (1995): 200–205; H. L. Walter, C. M. Anderson, and M. M. Martin, "How Subordinates' Machiavellianism and Motives Relate to Satisfaction with Superiors," *Communication Quarterly 53* (2005): 57–70; P. M. Sias, "Workplace Relationship Quality and Employee Information Experiences, *Communication Studies 56* (2005): 375–395.

10. Adams, "How to Manage up a Difficult Boss." Forbes Magazine Online. Retrieved April 21, 2010, from http://www.forbes .com/2010/01/19/manage-up-boss-leadership-careers-workplace .html; J. Owen, "Managing Your Boss," *Industrial and Commercial Training 39* (2007): 79–84; D. T. McAlister and J. R. Darling, "Upward Influence in Academic Organizations: A Behavioral Style Perspective," *Leadership and Organizational Development Journal 26* (2005): 558–573.

11. Stephen I. Sadove as interviewed by Adam Bryant, "For the Chief of Saks, It's Culture That Drives Result," *The New York Times* (May 29, 2010): B2

12. J. W. Koehler and G. Huber, "Effects of Upward Communication on Managerial Decision-Making," paper presented at the annual meeting of the International Communication Association, New Orleans, LA, May 1974.

13. Green and Knippen, "Breaking the Barrier to Upward Communication."

14. These reasons are reviewed in S. A. Myers and A. D. Johnson, "Perceived Solidarity, Self-Disclosure, and Trust in Organizational and Peer Relationships," *Communication Research Reports 21* (2004): 75–83; T. H. Feeley, J. Hwang, and G. A. Barnett, "Predicting Employee Turnover from Friendship Networks," *Journal of Applied Communication Research 36* (2008): 56–73.

15. B. Rose, "For Folks Like Us, It's Not a 9-to-5 World Anymore," *Austin American-Statesman* (June 2, 2005): C1, C3.

16. Bureau of Labor Statistics, United States Department of Labor, USDL 08-0859, June 25, 2008. Retrieved August 20, 2008, from http://www .bls.gov/news.release/atus.nr0.htm.

17. P. Lutgen-Sandvik, S. Riforgiate, and C. Fletcher, "Work as a Source of Positive Emotional Experiences and the Discourses Informing Positive Assessment," *Western Journal of Communication 75* (2011): 2–27; T. H. Feeley, J. Hwang, and G. A. Barnett, "Predicting Employee Turnover from Friendship Networks," *Journal of Applied Communication Research 36*, no. 1 (2008): 56–73. C. M. Riordan and R. W. Griffeth, "The Opportunity for Friendship in the Workplace: An Underexplored Construct," *Journal of Business and Psychology 10* (1995): 141–154; Myers and Johnson, "Perceived Solidarity, Self-Disclosure, and Trust in Organizational and Peer Relationships."

18. B. Carey, "Didya Hear the Latest? Gossip Has a Purpose," *Austin American-Statesman* (August 16, 2005): A1, A5.

19. M. Thatcher, "The Grapevine: Communication Tool or Thorn in Your Side?" *Strategic Communication Management 7* (2003): 30.

20. Ibid.

21. K. Davis, "Care and Cultivation of the Corporate Grapevine," *Dun's Review 102* (1973): 46.

22. N. Schultz, M. F. Hoffman, A. J. Fredman, and A. L. Bainbridge, "If Everyone Talked about Work all theTime, What Fun Is That? Building Bridges with Life-Talk at Work," paper presented at the annual meeting of the National Communication Association, San Francisco, CA, November 2010.

23. S. M. Horan and R. M. Chory, "When Work and Love Mix: Perceptions of Peers in Workplace Romances," *Western Journal of Communication 73* (2009): 349–369.

24. K. Riach and F. Wilson, "Don't Screw the Crew: Exploring the Rules of Engagement in Organizational Romance," *British Journal of Management 18* (2007): 79–92.

25. Horan and Chory, "When Work and Love Mix."

26. J. N. Cleveland, M. Stockdale, and K. R. Murphy, *Women and Men in Organizations: Sex and Gender Issues at Work* (Mahwah, NJ: Erlbaum, 2000); G. N. Powell and S. Foley, "Something to Talk About: Romantic Relationships in Organizational Settings," *Journal of Management 24* (1998): 421–448.

27. R. E. Quinn, "Coping with Cupid: The Formation, Impact, and Management of Romantic Relationships in Organizations," *Administrative Science Quarterly 22* (1977): 30–45.

28. These ideas were originally drafted by Sally Vogl-Bauer (University of Wisconsin-Whitewater) and appear in T. P. Mottet, S. Vogl-Bauer, and M. Houser, *Your Interpersonal Communication* (Boston: Pearson, 2012).

29. Horan and Chory, "When Work and Love Mix."

30. C. A. Pierce, H. Aguinis, and S. K. R. Adams, "Effects of a Dissolved Workplace Romance and Rater Characteristics on Responses to a Sexual Harassment Accusation," *Academy of Management Journal 43* (2000): 869–880.

31. N. Cole, "Workplace Romance: A Justice Analysis," *Journal of Business and Psychology 24* (2009): 363–372.

32. Powell and Foley, "Something to Talk About."

33. Horan and Chory, "When Work and Love Mix."

34. Cleveland, Stockdale, and Murphy, *Women and Men in Organizations.*

35. A. L. Darling and D. P. Dannels, "Practicing Engineers Talk About the Importance of Talk: A Report on the Role of Oral Communication

in the Workplace," *Communication Education* 52 (2003): 1–16; A. Vangelisti and J. A. Daly, "Correlates of Speaking Skills in the United States: A National Assessment," *Communication Education* 38 (1989): 132–143.

36. K. Ellis and P. Shockley-Zalabak, "Trust in Top Management and Immediate Supervisor: The Relationship to Satisfaction, Perceived Organizational Effectiveness, and Information Receiving," *Communication Quarterly* 49 (2001): 382–398; K. S. Cameron, *Positive Leadership: Strategies for Extraordinary Performance* (San Francisco: Berett-Koehler, 2008); L. Cockerell, *Creating Magic: 10 Common Sense Leadership Strategies from a Life at Disney* (New York: Doubleday, 2008).

37. C. Gomez, and B. Rosen, (2001). "The Leader-Member Exchange as a Link between Managerial Trust and Employee Empowerment," *Group and Organizational Management* 26 (2001): 53–69; K. G. Lamude, J. Scudder, D. Simmons, and P. Torres, "Organizational Newcomers: Temporary and Regular Employees, Same-Sex and Mixed-Sex Superior-Subordinate Dyads, Supervisor Influence Techniques, Subordinate Communication Satisfaction, and Leader-Member Exchange," *Communication Research Reports* 21 (2004): 60–67.

38. *Manager's Toolkit: The 13 Skills Managers Need to Succeed* (Boston: Harvard Business School Press, 2004).

39. Adapted from Franklin Covey, *The 7 Habits of Highly Effective People Signature Program*, Workbook, Version 3.0 (2005) p. 96; see also S. R. Covey, *The 7 Habits of Highly Effective People* (New York: Simon & Schuster, 1989); S. R. Covey, *The 8th Habit: From Effectiveness to Greatness* (New York: Free Press, 2004); Manager's Toolkit.

40. R. Goldman, "Sex Scandal Sheds Light on David Letterman's Love Life." ABC News Online. Retrieved April 12, 2011, from http://abcnews.go.com/Entertainment/sex-scandal-sheds-light-david-lettermans-love-life/story?id=8737083.

41. Annual CareerBuilder.com Valentine's Day Survey. Press Release. Retrieved April 12, 2011, from http://www.careerbuilder.com/share/aboutus/pressreleasesdetail.aspx?id=pr481&sd=2%2F10%2F2009&ed=12%2F31%2F2009.

42. J. A. Pearce, "What Execs Don't Get About Office Romance," *MIT Sloan Management Review* 51, no. 3 (Spring 2010): 37–44.

43. A. Marken, "Skills Training Is Becoming a Neverending Process." Office World News. Retrieved May 14, 2009, from http://yellowbrix.netbusiness.com.

44. W. S. Z. Ford, "Communication Practices of Professional Service Providers: Predicting Customer Satisfaction and Loyalty," *Journal of Applied Communication Research* 31 (2003): 189–211; C. Gallo, "How Disney Works to Win Repeat Customers," *Bloomberg Businessweek*. Retrieved March 26, 2011, from http://www.businessweek.com/smallbiz/content/nov2009/sb20091130_866423.htm.

45. Ford, "Communication Practices of Professional Service Providers"; W. S. Z. Ford, "Evaluation of the Indirect Influence of Courteous Service on Customer Discretionary Behavior," *Human Communication Research* 22 (1998): 65–89; W. S. Z. Ford, *Communicating with Customers: Service Approaches, Ethics, and Impact* (Cresskill, NJ: Hampton, 1998); W. S. Z. Ford, "Customer Expectations for Interactions with Service Providers: Relationship Versus Encounter Orientation and Personalized Service Communication," *Journal of Applied Communication Research* 29 (2001): 1–29; W. S. Z. Ford and C. N. Etiennne, "Can I Help You? A Framework for the Interdisciplinary Literature on Customer Service Encounters," *Management Communication Quarterly* 7 (1994): 413–441.

46. W. S. Z. Ford, "Communication and Customer Service," in *Communication Yearbook 22*, edited by M. E. Roloff (Thousand Oaks, CA: Sage, 1999), 341–375.

47. L. Cockerell, *Creating Magic* (New York: Doubleday, 2008); See also C. Gallo, "How Disney Works to Win Repeat Customers." *Bloomberg Businessweek*. Retrieved March 26, 2011, from http://www.businessweek.com/smallbiz/content/nov2009/sb20091130_866423.htm.

48. Adapted from Cockerell, *Creating Magic*,. pp. 127–128.

49. J. L. Hocker and W. W. Wilmot, *Interpersonal Conflict*, 7th ed. (New York: McGraw-Hill, 2005).

50. R. Kilmann and K. Thomas, "Interpersonal Conflict-Handling Behavior as Reflections of Jungian Personality Dimensions," *Psychological Reports* 37 (1975): 971–980; K. W. Thomas and R. H. Kilmann, *Thomas-Kilmann Conflict Mode Instrument* (Tuxedo, NY: XICOM, 1974); K. W. Thomas, "Conflict and Conflict Management: Reflections and Update," *Journal of Organizational Behavior* 13 (1992): 265–274.

51. K. W. Thomas, "Toward Multi-Dimensional Values in Teaching: The Example of Conflict Behaviors," *Academy of Management Review* 3 (1987): 487. R. S. Lulofs and D. D. Cahn, *Conflict: From Theory to Action*, 2nd ed. (Boston: Allyn and Bacon, 2000).

52. Reported in A. Kreamer, "Go Ahead—Cry at Work," *Time* (April 4, 2011), 52–55. Also reference A. Kreamer, *It's Always Personal* (New York: Random House, 2011).

53. Reported in Kreamer, *It's Always Personal*.

54. Ibid.

55. M. H. Immordino-Yang and A. Damasio, "We Feel, Therefore We Learn: The Relevance of Affective and Social Neuroscience to Education," *Mind, Brain, and Education* 1 (2007): 3–10.

56. Ibid.

57. E. Hatfield, J. T. Cacioppo, and R. L. Rapson, *Emotional Contagion* (New York: Cambridge University Press, 1994).

58. Ibid.

59. M. Booth-Butterfield, *Interpersonal Essentials* (Boston: Allyn & Bacon, 2002).

60. Ibid.

61. The idea for this model originated with the work of F. F. Fournies, *Coaching for Improved Work Performance* (New York: McGraw-Hill, 1995).

62. P. Lutgen-Sandvik, "Intensive Remedial Identity Work: Responses to Workplace Bullying Trauma and Stigmatization," *Organization* 15 (2008): 97–119.

63. Ibid. See also R. L. Cowan, "Yes, We Have an Anti-Bullying Policy, But . . .": HR Professionals' Understandings and Experiences with Workplace Bullying Policy," *Communication Studies*. In press.

64. Lutgen-Sandvik, "Intensive Remedial Identity Work."

65. J. Swartz, "More Small Businesses Use Twitter, Facebook to Promote." USA Today. Retrieved March 1, 2011, from http://blog.hubspot.com/blog/tabid/6307/bid/9134/Top-5-Things-Not-to-Do-on-Facebook.aspx.

66. Ibid.

67. Adapted from E. Mirman, "Top 5 Things Not to Do on Facebook." Retrieved February 19, 2011, from http://blog.hubspot.com/blog/tabid/6307/bid/9134/Top-5-Things-Not-to-Do-on-Facebook.aspx#ixzz1EyrpUszk Also see Facebook, "Statement of Rights and Responsibilities." Retrieved from http://www.facebook.com/terms.php.

68. L. L. Putnam, "Bargaining as Organizational Communication," in *Organizational Communication: Traditional Themes and New Directions*, edited by R. D. McPhee and P. K. Tompkins (Newbury Park, CA: Sage, 1985), 129.

69. A. Wrzesniewski and J. E. Dutton, "Crafting a Job: Revisioning Employees as Active Crafters of Their Work," *Academy of Management Review* 26 (2001): 179–201.

70. Covey, *The 7 Habits of Highly Effective People*; S. R. Covey, *Principle-Centered Leadership* (New York: Simon & Schuster, 1991).

71. Adapted from Franklin Covey, *The 7 Habits of Highly Effective People Signature Program, Participant Training Guide*, Version 3.0 (2005).

72. Fisher and Ury, *Getting to Yes*; M. E. Roloff, L. L. Putnam, and L. Anastasiou, "Negotiation Skills," in *Handbook of Communication and Social Skill Interaction*, edited by J. O. Greene and B. R. Burleson (Mahwah, NJ: Erlbaum, 2003), 801–833.

73. Fisher and Ury, *Getting to Yes*, 41.

Chapter 7

1. Anderson Cooper speaks at the Journalism School at Columbia University. Retrieved April 24, 2011, from http://blip.tv/file/1692934.

2. J. Van Meter, "Unanchored." *New York Magazine*. Retrieved May 9, 2011, from http://nymag.com/nymetro/news/features/14301/. Also

of interest is A. Kreamer, "Go Ahead—Cry at Work, *Time* (April 4, 2011): 52–55.

3. Van Meter, "Unanchored."

4. Ibid.

5. C. J. Stewart and W. B. Cash, Jr., *Interviewing: Principles and Practices*, 12th ed. (New York: McGraw-Hill, 2007).

6. B. F. Fitzgerald, "How to conduct an interview using Skype." TechRepublic Online. Retrieved May 17, 2011, from http://www.techrepublic.com/members/login?path=http%3A%2F%2Fwww.techrepublic.com%2Fwhitepapers%2Fhow-to-conduct-an-interview-using-skype%2F975889%2Fpost.

7. B. Kiviat, "How Skype Is Changing the Job Interview," *Time* magazine. Retrieved March 17, 2011, from http://www.time.com/time/business/article/0,8599,1930838,00.html#ixzz1MrF3fItT.

8. Stewart and Cash, *Interviewing: Principles and Practices.*

9. Bobbi Brown as interviewed by Adam Bryant, "High Heels? They Just Don't Fit," *The New York Times* (January 24, 2010): B2

10. T. W. Dougherty, D. B. Turban, and J. C. Callender, "Confirmatory First Impressions in the Employment Interview: A Field Study of Interviewer Behavior," *Journal of Applied Psychology 79* (1994): 659–665.

11. T. DeGroot and J. Gooty, "Can Nonverbal Cues Be Used to Make Meaningful Personality Attributions in Employment Interviews?" *Journal of BusinessPsychology 24* (2009): 179–192.

12. W. F. Chaplin, J. B. Phillips, J. D. Brown, N. R. Clanton, and J. L. Stein, "Handshaking, Gender, Personality, and First Impressions," *Journal of Personality and Social Psychology 79* (2000): 110–117.

13. Chaplin, Phillips, Brown, Clanton, and Stein, "Handshaking, Gender, Personality, and First Impressions."

14. D. Tannen, *You Just Don't Understand: Women and Men in Conversation* (New York: Morrow, 1990); D. Tannen, *Talking From 9 to 5: How Women's and Men's Conversational Styles Affect Who Gets Heard, Who Gets Credit, and What Gets Done at Work* (New York: Morrow, 1994).

15. D. Ifert Johnson and N. Lewis, "Perceptions of Swearing in the Work Setting: An Expectancy Violations Theory Perspective," *Communication Reports 23* (2010): 106–118.

16. M. Mino, "The Relative Effects of Content and Vocal Delivery During a Simulated Employment Interview," *Communication Research Reports 13* (1996): 225–238.

17. Stewart and Cash, *Interviewing: Principles and Practices*; D. B. Goodall and H. L. Goodall, "The Employment Interview: A Selective Review of the Literature with Implications for Communications Research," *Communication Quarterly 30* (1982): 116–123.

18. L. K. Thaler and R. Koval, *The Power of Nice: How to Conquer the Business World with Kindness* (New York: Currency, 2006).

19. M. McLoughlin, J. L. Sheler, and G. Witkin, "A Nation of Liars?" *U.S. News and World Report* (February 23, 1987): 54–61, See also J. S. O'Rourke, "The Ethics of Resumes and Recommendations: When Do Filler and Fluff Become Deception and Lies?" *Business Communication Quarterly 58* (1995): 54–56.

20. S. M. Ralston and W. G. Kirkwood, "Overcoming Managerial Bias in Employment Interviewing," *Journal of Applied Communication Research 23* (1995): 75–92.

21. R. L. Kahn and C. F. Cannell, *The Dynamics of Interviewing* (New York: John Wiley, 1964), 205.

22. "Manager's Toolkit: The 13 Skills Managers Need to Succeed," *Harvard Business Essential Series* (Boston: Harvard Business School Press, 2004), 295–298.

23. J. Schultz, "On Lying about Your Salary in Job Interviews." *New York Times*. Retrieved May 19, 2011, from http://bucks.blogs.nytimes.com/2010/06/16/on-lying-about-your-salary-in-job-interviews/?hp.

24. Ibid.

25. M. Mattson, M. Allen, D. J. Ryan, and V. Miller, "Considering Organizations as a Unique Interpersonal Context for Deception Detection: A Meta-Analytic Review," *Communication Research Reports 17* (2000): 148–160.

Chapter 8

1. M. Gunther, "How to Hire a Hotel Desk Clerk." Retrieved May 10, 2011, from http://www.marcgunther.com/2011/02/12/how-to-hire-a-hotel-desk-clerk/.

2. C. Conley, *Peak: How Great Companies Get Their Mojo from Maslow* (San Francisco: Jossey-Bass, 2007). See also http://www.chipconley.com/.

3. From interview with M. Gunther. Retrieved May 10, 2011, from http://www.marcgunther.com/2011/02/12/how-to-hire-a-hotel-desk-clerk/.

4. M. Farr, *Next Day Job Interview* (Indianapolis, IN: JIST Publishing, 2005).

5. M. S. Granovetter, "The Strength of Weak Ties," *American Journal of Sociology 78* (1973): 1360–1380. See also M. Kilduff and D. J. Brass, "Job Design: A Social Network Perspective," *Journal of Organizational Behavior 31* (2010), 309–318.

6. Granovetter, "The Strength of Weak Ties."

7. D. R. McKay, "Informational Interviews." Retrieved March 18, 2008, from About.com: Career Planning, http://careerplanning.about.com/cs/occupations/a/info_interviews.htm.

8. N. Carbone, "Suspicious Script: Is Inspirational Book *Three Cups of Tea* Inaccurate?" Time (April 16, 2011). Retrieved May 30, 2011, from http://newsfeed.time.com/2011/04/16/suspicious-script-is-inspirational-book-three-cups-of-tea-inaccurate/.

9. Reference http://www.ikat.org/, which is the website for the Central Asia Institute.

10. R. N. Bolles, *What Color Is Your Parachute?* (Berkeley, CA: Ten Speed Press, 2007).

11. Steve Hannah as interviewed by Adam Bryant, "If Plan B Fails, Go Through the Alphabet," *The New York Times* (May 15, 2010): B2

12. Farr, *Next Day Job Interview.*

13. Ibid.

14. The sample resume and our suggestions for developing a resume are based on information in the *2005 Texas State University Career Services Manual* (San Marcos, TX: Office of Career Services, 2005).

15. Bolles, *What Color Is Your Parachute?*

16. Farr, *Next Day Job Interview;* also see G. Crispin and M. Mehler, "Careerxroads 5th Annual Sources of Hire Survey." Retrieved May 14, 2009, from http://www.careerxroads.com/news/sourcesofhire05.pdf.

17. Crispin and Mehler, *Careerxroads 5th Annual Sources of Hire Survey.*

18. Farr, *Next Day Job Interview.*

19. Ibid.

20. Bolles, *What Color Is Your Parachute?*

21. M. Gladwell, *Blink: The Power of Thinking Without Thinking* (New York: Little, Brown, 2005).

22. R. Gifford, C. F. Ng, and M. Wilkinson, "Nonverbal Cues in the Employment Interview: Links Between Applicant Qualities and Interviewer Judgments," *Journal of Applied Psychology 70* (1985): 729–736. See also S. A. Devendorf and S. Highhouse, "Applicant-Employee Similarity and Attraction to an Employer," *Journal of Occupational and Organizational Psychology 81* (2008): 607–617.

23. D. Jones, "CEOs Say How You Treat a Waiter Can Predict a Lot About Character." USA Today. Retrieved May 14, 2009, from http://www.usatoday.com/money/companies/management/2006-04-14-ceos-waiter-rule_x.hym.

24. R. E. Riggio and B. Throckmorton, "The Relative Effects of Verbal and Nonverbal Behavior, Appearance, and Social Skills on Evaluations Made in Hiring Interviews," *Journal of Applied Social Psychology 18* (1988): 331–348; L. M. Watkins and L. Johnston, "Screening Job Applicants: The Impact of Physical Attractiveness and Application Quality," *International Journal of Selection and Assessment 8* (2000): 76–84.

25. C. J. Stewart and W. B. Cash, Jr., *Interviewing: Principles and Practices*, 12th ed. (New York: McGraw-Hill, 2007).

26. J. S. Seiter and A. Sandry, "Pierced for Success? The Effects of Ear and Nose Piercing on Perceptions of Job Candidates' Credibility, Attractiveness, and Hirability," *Communication Research Reports 20* (2003): 287–298.

27. K. Rodriguez, "Kids Can Find What Principals Can't on a Prospective Teacher's Character," *San Antonio Express-News* (February 4, 2007): B-1, B-3; see also T. Ferguson, "Want a Job? Clean up your Web Act." Retrieved March 30, 2007, from http://news.cnet.com/2100-1025-3-6171187.html; M. Goodman, "The Dumbest Online Job Hunt Blunders." Retrieved July 31, 2008, from http://abcnews.go.com/business/CareerManagement/story?id=5483048&page.

28. J. Hopkins, "Job Seekers Show Rather Than Tell," *USA Today* (April 25, 2007): 3B.

29. Ibid.

30. "Do's and Don'ts of Video Resumes." Retrieved March 25, 2009, from http://www.careerbuilder.com/JobSeeker/VideoResumes/DosDonts.aspx. For additional information, see Hopkins, "Job Seekers Show Rather Than Tell."

31. J. Ayres, T. Keereetaweep, P. Chen, and P. A. Edwards, "Communication Apprehension and Employment Interviews," *Communication Education* 47 (1998): 1–17.

32. Farr, *Next Day Job Interview;* see also Stewart and Cash, Interviewing: Principles and Practices, 12th ed.; Bolles, *What Color Is Your Parachute?*

33. T. DeGroot and S. J. Motowidlo, "Why Visual and Vocal Interview Cues Can Affect Interviewers' Judgments and Predict Job Performance," *Journal of Applied Psychology 84* (1999): 986–993.

34. Farr, *Next Day Job Interview.*

35. J. Perkins, "Questions Can Lead to Perfect-Fit Job," *Austin American Statesman* (October 29, 2006): D1; Bolles, What Color Is Your Parachute?, 87–88.

36. C. I. Hovland, I. L. Janis, and H. H. Kelley, *Communication and Persuasion* (New Haven, CT: Yale University Press, 1953).

37. Farr, *Next Day Job Interview,* 127–128.

38. S. E. Needleman, "Thx for the IView! I Wud © to Work 4 U!!" *Wall Street Journal* (July 29, 2008): D1, D4.

39. LinkedIn. Retrieved May 15, 2011, from http://press.linkedin.com/about/.

40. Adapted from A. Doyle, "Ten Tips to Enhance your Job Search on LinkedIn." Retrieved May 15, 2011, from http://blog.linkedin.com/2009/04/02/ten-tips-to-enhance-your-job-search-on-linkedin/. For more information on using LinkedIn for a job search, consult http://blog.guykawasaki.com/2009/02/10-ways-to-use.html#ixzz1MS09VERE.

41. H. Karp, "The Lost Art of Feedback," in 1987 *Annual: Developing Human Resources,* edited by J. W. Pfeiffer (San Diego, CA: University Associates, 1987), 14–24.

42. N. R. F. Maier, *The Appraisal Interview* (New York: John Wiley, 1958).

43. H. H. Meyer, "A Solution to the Performance Appraisal Feedback Enigma," *Academy of Management Executive 5* (1991): 68–76; J. L. Pearce and L. W. Porter, "Employee Responses to Formal Performance Appraisal Feedback," *Journal of Applied Psychology 71* (1986): 211–218.

44. D. Fandray, "The New Thinking in Performance Appraisals," *Workforce 80* (2001): 36–40. Retrieved March 27, 2009, from http://findarticles.com/p/articles/mi_mOFXS/is_5_80/ai_74886392; Meyer, "A Solution to the Performance Appraisal Feedback Enigma."

45. Fandray, "The New Thinking in Performance Appraisals"; Meyer, "A Solution to the Performance Appraisal Feedback Enigma."

46. G. Thornton, "Psychometric Properties of Self-Appraisals of Job Performance," *Personnel Psychology 33* (1980): 263–271.

47. "Manager's Toolkit: The 13 Skills Managers Need to Succeed," *Harvard Business Essentials Series* (Boston: Harvard Business School Press, 2004); also refer to G. Shepard, *How to Make Performance Evaluations Really Work* (Hoboken, NJ: John Wiley, 2005).

48. F. F. Fournies, *Why Employees Don't Do What They're Supposed to Do and What You Can Do About It* (New York: McGraw-Hill, 2007).

49. Meyer, "A Solution to the Performance Appraisal Feedback Enigma," 68–76; J. L. Pearce and L. W. Porter, "Employee Responses to Formal Performance Appraisal Feedback," *Journal of Applied Psychology 71* (1986): 211–218; Shepard, *How To Make Performance Evaluations Really Work.*

50. G. T. Fairhurst, "Dualism in Leadership Research," in *The New Handbook of Organizational Communication: Advances in |Theory, Research, and Methods,* edited by F. M. Jablin and L. L. Putnam (Thousand Oaks, CA: Sage, 2001), 379–439; L. P. Cusella, "Feedback, Motivation, and Performance," in *Handbook of Organizational Communication: An Interdisciplinary Perspective,* edited by F. M. Jablin, L. L. Putnam, K. H. Roberts, and L. W. Porter (Newbury Park, CA: Sage, 1987), 624–678.

51. FranklinCovey, *Latest FranklinCovey Research Reports Major Gaps in U.S. Workers' Focus and Execution on Top Organizational Priorities.* Retrieved March 27, 2009, from http://franklincovey.bg/news, 2003, 2, en.

52. A. N. Kluger and A. DeNisi, "Effects of Feedback Intervention on Performance: A Historical Review, a Meta-Analysis, and a Preliminary Feedback Intervention Theory," *Psychological Bulletin 119* (1996): 254–284.

53. B. Feng and E. L. MacGeorge, "Predicting Receptiveness to Advice: Characteristics of the Problem, the Advice-Giver, and the Recipient," *Southern Communication Journal 71* (2006): 67–85.

54. Meyer, "A Solution to the Performance Appraisal Feedback Enigma"; Pearce and Porter, "Employee Responses to Formal Performance Appraisal Feedback"; Shepard, *How to Make Performance Evaluations Really Work.*

55. Fournies, *Coaching for Improved Performance.*

56. E. Hatfield, J. T. Cacioppo, and R. L. Rapson, Emotional Contagion (New York: Cambridge University Press, 1994).

57. J. K. Burgoon, L. A. Stern, and L. Dillman, *Interaction Adaptation: Dyadic Interaction Patterns* (New York: Cambridge University Press, 1995).

58. K. Anderson, *Resolving Conflict Sooner: The Powerfully Simple 4-Step Method for Reaching Better Agreements More Easily in Everyday Life* (Berkeley, CA: Ten Speed Press, 1999); see also K. Anderson, "Handling Criticism with Honesty and Grace," *Public Management 82* (2000): 30–34.

59. Fournies, *Coaching for Improved Performance.*

60. B. F. Skinner, "The Science of Learning and the Art of Teaching," *Harvard Educational Journal 24* (1954): 86–97; see also B. F. Skinner, *Science and Human Behavior* (New York: Free Press, 1953).

61. Skinner, "The Science of Learning and the Art of Teaching."

62. Fairhurst, "Dualism in Leadership Research"; Cusella, "Feedback, Motivation, and Performance."

Chapter 9

1. The origins of Tupperware are described in E. Ross and A. Holland, *100 Great Businesses and the Minds Behind Them* (Naperville, IL: Sourcebooks, 2006), 308.

2. Ibid.

3. S. Sorensen, "Grouphate." Paper presented at the annual meeting of the International Communication Association, Minneapolis, MN, May 1981.

4. R. K. Mosvick and R. B. Nelson, *We've Got to Start Meeting Like This!* (Glenview, IL: Scott, Foresman, 1987); R. Y. Hirokawa, "Communication and Group Decision-Making Efficacy," in *Small Group Communication Theory and Practice: An Anthology,* edited by R. Y. Hirokawa, R. S. Cathcart, L. A. Samovar, and L. D. Henmann (New York: Oxford University Press, 2007), 125.

5. B. Harrington and G. A. Fine, "Where the Action Is," *Small Group Research 37,* no. 1 (2006): 4–19.

6. M. A. Hackman and C. E. Johnson, *Leadership: A Communication Perspective* (Prospect Heights, IL: Waveland Press, 2000).

7. T. Rapp and J. Mathieu, "Evaluating an Individually Self-Administered Generic Teamwork Skills Training Program Across Time and Levels," *Small Group Research 38,* no. 4 (2007): 532–552; E. Sales and J. A. Cannon-Bowers, "The Science of Training: A Decade of Progress," *Annual Review of Psychology 52* (2001): 471–499.

8. D. A. Romig, *Breakthrough Teamwork: Outstanding Results Using Structured Teamwork* (Chicago: Irwin, 1996), 41–42.

9. C. Klein, D. Diaz Granados, E. Salas, H. Le, C. S. Burke, R. Lyons, and G. F. Goodwin, "Does Team Building Work?," *Small Group Research* 40 (2009): 181–222; D. Strubler and K. York, "An Explanatory Study of the Team Characteristics Model Using Organizational Teams," *Small Group Research* 38, no. 6 (2007): 670–695.

10. See N. R. F. Maier, "Assets and Liabilities in Group Problem Solving: The Need for a Integrative Function," *Psychological Review* 74 (1967): 239–249; M. Argyle, *Cooperation: The Basics of Sociability* (London: Routledge, 1991); H. A. M. Wilke and R. W. Meertens, *Group Performance* (London: Routledge, 1994).

11. E. Stark, J. Shaw, and M. Duffy, "Preference for Group Work, Winning Orientation, and Social Loafing Behavior in Groups," *Group & Organization Management* 32, no. 6 (2007): 699–723.

12. Maier, "Assets and Liabilities in Group Problem Solving"; Argyle, *Cooperation*; Wilke and Meertens, *Group Performance*.

13. S. A. Beebe and J. T. Masterson, *Communicating in Small Groups: Principles and Practices* 9th ed. (Boston: Allyn and Bacon, 2009).

14. N. Katz and G. Koenig, "Sports Teams as a Model for Workplace Teams: Lessons and Liabilities," *Academy of Management Executive* 15 (2001): 56–67.

15. Our discussion of teams and teamwork is from Beebe and Masterson, *Communicating in Small Groups*; for an excellent review of teamwork theoretical models, see V. Rousseau, C. Aube, and A. Savoie, "Teamwork Behaviors—a Review and an Integration of Frameworks," *Small Group Research* 37, no. 5 (2006): 540–570.

16. See F. C. Broadbeck and T. Breitermeyer, "Effects of Individual Versus Mixed Individual and Group Experience in Rule Induction on Group Member Learning and Group Performance," *Journal of Experimental Social Psychology* 36 (2002): 621–648.

17. S. B. Shimanoff, *Communication Rules: Theory and Research* (Beverly Hills, CA: Sage, 1980).

18. M. Hoegl and K. P. Parboteeah, "Goal Setting and Team Performance in Innovative Projects: On the Moderating Role of Teamwork Quality," *Small Group Research* 34 (2003): 3–19.

19. H. Van Mierlo, C. Rutte, M. Kompier, and H. Kompier, "Self-Managing Teamwork and Psychological Well-Being: Review of a Multilevel Research Domain," *Group Organization Management* 30, no. 2 (2005): 211–235.

20. L. Erbert, G. Mearns, and S. Dean, "Perceptions of Turning Points and Dialectical Interpretations in Organizational Team Development," *Small Group Research* 36, no. 1 (2005): 21–58.

21. R. Y. Hirokawa and J. Keyton, "Perceived Facilitators and Inhibitors of Effectiveness in Organizational Work Teams," *Management Communication Quarterly* 8 (1995): 424–426.

22. D. J. Devine and J. L. Philips, "Do Smarter Teams Do Better? A Meta-Analysis of Cognitive Ability and Team Performance," *Small Group Research* 32 (2001): 507–535.

23. C. E. Larson and F. M. J. LaFasto, *Teamwork: What Must Go Right/ What Can Go Wrong* (Beverly Hills, CA: Sage, 1989).

24. Hoegl and Parboteeah, "Goal Setting and Team Performance in Innovative Projects."; D. Crown, "The Use of Group and Groupcentric Individual Goals for Culturally Heterogeneous and Homogeneous Task Groups," *Small Group Research* 38, no. 4 (2007): 489–508.

25. D. Crown, "The Use of Group and Groupcentric Individual Goals for Culturally Heterogeneous and Homogeneous Task Groups," *Small Group Research* 38, no. 4 (2007): 489–508.

26. M. A. Marks, J. E. Mathieu, and S. J. Zaccaro, "A Temporally Based Framework and Taxonomy of Team Processes," *Academy of Management Review* 26 (2001): 356–376.

27. S. Sonnentag and J. Volmer, "Individual-Level Predictors of Task-Related Teamwork Processes: The Role of Expertise and Self-Efficacy in Team Meetings," *Group & Organization Management* 34 (2009): 37–66.

28. Devine and Philips, "Do Smarter Teams Do Better?"

29. F. LaFasto and C. Larson, *When Teams Work Best* (Thousand Oaks, CA: Sage, 2001). Our discussion of the six characteristics of effective team members is based on information presented in Chapter 1.

30. F. A. Kennedy, M. L. Loughry, T. P. Klammer, and M. M. Beyerlein, "Effects of Organizational Support on Potency in Work Teams: The Mediating Role of Team Processes," *Small Group Research* 40 (2009): 72–93.

31. C. O. L. H. Porter, C. I. Gogus, and R. C. F. Yu, "When Does Teamwork Translate Into Improved Team Performance? A Resource Allocation Perspective," *Small Group Research* 41 (2010): 221–248.

32. "New Directions, Women at the Top: The Ranking," *Financial Times* (October 23, 2010): 10.

33. P. Balkundi and D. Harrison, "Ties, Leaders, and Time in Teams: Strong Inference about Network Structure's Effects on Team Viability and Performance," *Academy of Management Journal* 49, no. 1 (2006): 49–68.

34. P. Lencioni, *The Five Dysfunctions of a Team: A Leadership Fable* (New York: Jossey-Bass, 2002).

35. J. S. Prichard and M. J. Ashleigh, "The Effects of Team-Skills Training on Transactive Memory and Performance," *Small Group Research* 38 (2007): 696–726; T. L. Rapp and J. E. Mathieu, "Evaluating an Individually Self-Administered Genetic Teamwork Skills Training Program Across Time and Levels," *Small Group Research* 38 (2007): 532–555; E. Salas, D. R. Nichols, and J. E. Driskell, "Testing Three Team Training Strategies in Intact Teams: A Meta-Analysis," *Small Group Research* 38 (2007): 471–488.

36. M. Irvine, "E-Mail's No Longer Fast Enough." *Austin American-Statesman* (July 24, 2006): D3.

37. Susan Docherty as quoted by Adam Bryant, Corner Office: "Now, Put Yourself in My Shoes," *New York Times* (February 6, 2010).

38. For a discussion of the growth of virtual teams and a description of virtual team interaction processes, see M. M. Montoya, A. P. Massey, Y. C. Hung, and C. B. Crisp, "Can You Hear Me Now? Communication in Virtual Product Development Teams," *Journal of Product Innovation Management* 26 (2009): 139–155; also see Z. Wang, J. B. Walther, and J. T. Hancock, "Social Identification and Interpersonal Communication in Computer-Mediated Communication: What You Do Versus Who You Are in Virtual Groups," *Human Communication Research* 35 (2009): 59–85.

39. S. K. Johnson, K. Bettenhausen, and E. Gibbons, "Realities of Working in Virtual Teams: Affective and Attitudinal Outcomes of Using Computer-Mediated Communication," *Small Group Research* 40 (2009): 623–649.

40. C. M. McGrath, "The Pleasures of Text," *New York Times Magazine* (January 22, 2006): 15; Internet World Stats: Usage and Population Statistics. Retrieved October 3, 2011, from http://www.theyoungandthedigital.com/wp-content/uploads/2010/11/watkins_lee_facebookstudy-nov-18.pdf.

41. Y. Amichai-Hamburger, ed., *The Social Net: Human Behavior in Cyberspace* (New York: Oxford University Press, 2005), v; Retrieved September 3, 2010, from http://www.readwriteweb.com/archives/americans_sending_4x_as_many_texts_messages_as_bri.php.

42. S.C. Watkins and H.E. Lee, "Got Facebook: Investigating What's Social About Social Media," the University of Texas, Austin (accessed October 3, 2011) http://www.theyoungandthedigital.com/wp-conent/uploads/2010/11/watkins_lee_facebookstudy-nov-18.pdf.

43. M. Adkins and D. E. Brashers, "The Power of Language in Computer-Mediated Groups," *Management Communication Quarterly* 8 (1995): 289–322.

44. V. J. Dubrovsky, S. Kiesler, and B. N. Sethna, "The Equalization Phenomenon: Status Effects on Computer-Mediated and Face-to-Face Decision-Making Groups," *Human Computer Interaction* 6 (1991): 119–146.

45. N. S. Baron, *Always On: Language in an Online and Mobile World* (Oxford, UK: Oxford University Press, 2008).

46. J. Walsh and N. Maloney, "Collaboration Structure, Communication Media, and Problems in Scientific Work Teams," *Journal of Computer-Mediated Communication* 12 (2007): 712–732.

47. See the excellent review of the effect of technology on group decision making in M. S. Poole and G. DeSanctis, "Micro Level Structuration in

Computer-Supported Group Decision Making," *Human Communication Research* 19 (1992): 5–49.

48. R. E. Rice and G. Love, "Electronic Emotion: Socioemotional Context in a Computer-Mediated Communication Network," *Communication Research* 14 (February 1987): 85–108.

49. See J. B Walter, "Computer-Mediated Communication: Impersonal, Interpersonal, and Hyperpersonal Interaction," *Communication Research* 23 (1990): 3–43.

50. See R. Johansen, J. Vallee, and K. Spangler, *Electronic Meetings: Technical Alternatives and Social Choices* (Reading, MA: Addison-Wesley, 1979).

51. P. L. McLeon and J. K. Liker, "Electronic Meeting Systems: Evidence from a Low Structure Environment," *Information Systems Research* 3 (1992): 195–223.

52. M. Finley, "Welcome to the Electronic Meeting," *Training* (July 1991): 29–32. See also Poole and DeSanctis, "Micro Level Structuration."

53. J. B. Walther and R. U. Bunz, "The Rules of Virtual Groups Trust, Liking, and Performance in Computer-Mediated Communication," *Journal of Communication* 55, no. 4 (2005): 828–846.

54. D. S. Staples and J. Webster, "Exploring Traditional and Virtual Team Members' "Best Practices": A Social Cognitive Theory Perspective," *Small Group Research* 38 (2007): 60–97

55. C. Erik Timmerman and C. Scott, "Virtually Working: Communicative and Structural Predictors on Media Use and Key Outcomes in Virtual Work Teams," *Communication Monographs* 73, no. 1 (2006): 108–136.

56. T. Halfhill, E. Sundstrom, J. Lahner, W. Calderone, and T. Nielsen, "Group Personality Composition and Group Effectiveness—An Integrative Review of Empirical Research," *Small Group Research* 36, no. 1 (2005): 83–105.

57. K. D. Benne and P. Sheats, "Functional Roles of Group Members," *Journal of Social Issues* 4 (1948): 41–49. For a good review of role development in groups, see A. P. Hare, "Types of Roles in Small Groups: A Bit of History and a Current Perspective," *Small Group Research* 25 (1994): 433–438; A. J. Salazar, "An Analysis of the Development and Evolution of Roles in the Small Group," *Small Group Research* 27 (1996): 475–503.

58. R. F. Bales, *Interaction Process Analysis* (Chicago: University of Chicago Press, 1976).

59. A. Aritzeta, B. Senior, and S. Swailes, "Team Role Preference and Cognitive Styles—A Convergent Validity Study," *Small Group Research* 36, no. 4 (2005): 404–436.

60. M. Hogg and S. Reid, "Social Identity, Self-Categorization, and the Communication of Group Norms," *Communication Theory* 16 (2006): 7–30.

61. M. Shaw, *Group Dynamics: The Psychology of Small Group Behavior* (New York: McGraw-Hill, 1981), 281.

62. N. Katz, D. Lazer, H. Arrow, and N. Contractor, "Network Theory and Small Groups," *Small Group Research* 35 (2004): 307–332.

63. See D. A. Romig, *Side-by-Side Leadership* (Chicago: Irwin, 1997).

64. P. R. Scholtes, B. L. Joiner, and B. J. Streibel, *The Team Handbook*, 2nd ed. (Madison, WI: Joiner, 1996); J. R. Katzenbach and D. K. Smith, *The Wisdom of Teams: Creating the High-Performance Organization* (New York: HarperCollins, 1993).

65. C. Anderson, J. Beer, J. Chatman, S. Spataro, and S. Srivastava, "Knowing Your Place: Self-Perceptions of Status in Face-to-Face Groups," *Journal of Personality and Social Psychology* 91, no. 6 (2006): 1094–1110.

66. J. I. Hurwitz, A. F. Zander, and B. Hymovitch, "Some Effects of Power on the Relations Among Group Members," in *Group Dynamics: Research and Theory*, edited by D. Cartwright and A. Zander (New York: Harper & Row, 1953), 483–492; D. C. Barnlund and C. Harland, "Propinquity and Prestige as Determinants of Communication Networks," *Sociometry* 26 (1963): 467–479; G. C. Homans, *The Human Group* (New York: Harcourt Brace and World, 1992); H. H. Kelly, "Communication in Experimentally Created Hierarchies," *Human Relations* 4 (1951): 36–56.

67. For a discussion of how team leadership influences team power dynamics, see G. J. Galanes, "Dialectical Tensions of Small Group Leadership," *Communication Studies* 60 (2009): 409–425.

68. M. R. Singer, *Intercultural Communication: A Perceptual Approach* (Englewood Cliffs, NJ: Prentice-Hall, 1987), 118.

69. J. R. P. French and B. H. Raven, "The Bases of Social Power," in *Group Dynamics*, edited by D. Cartwright and A. Zander (Evanston, IL: Row, Peterson, 1962), 607–623.

70. Adapted from E. G. Bormann and N. C. Bormann, *Effective Small Group Communication* (Minneapolis: Burgess, 1980), 70–72.

71. For a review of how trust effects team cohesiveness and productivity B. A. De Jong and
T. Elfring, "How Does Trust Affect the Performance of Ongoing Teams? The Mediating Role of Reflexivity, Monitoring, and Effort," *Academy of Management Journal* 53 (2010): 535–549.

72. K. Jonas, P. Brazy, K. Sassenberg, and J. Shah, "Why Some Groups Just Feel Better: The Regulatory Fit of Group Power," *Journal of Personality and Social Psychology* 92, no. 2 (2007): 249–267; D. Mackie, E. Smith, and C. Seger, "Can Emotions Be Truly Group Level? Evidence Regarding Four Conceptual Criteria," *Journal of Personality and Social Psychology* 93, no. 3 (2007): 431–446.

73. M. Barrick, B. Bradley, and A. Colbert, "The Moderating Role of Top Management Team Interdependence: Implications for Real Teams and Working Groups," *Academy of Management Journal* 50, no. 3 (2007): 544–557.

74. J. Wellen and M. Neale, "Deviance, Self-Typicality, and Group Cohesion—the Corrosive Effects of the Bad Apples and the Barrel," *Small Group Research* 37, no. 2 (2006): 165–186.

75. S. Wheelan, B. Davidson, and E. Tilin, "Group Development Across Time: Reality or Illusion?" *Small Group Research* 334 (2003): 223–245; S. Furst, M. Reeves, B. Rosen, and R. S. Blackburn, "Managing the Life Cycle of Virtual Teams," *Academy of Management Executive* 18 (2004): 6–22.

76. B. A. Fisher, "Decision Emergence: Phases in Group Decision-Making," *Speech Monographs* 37 (1970): 60.

77. M. Burke, R. Kraut, and E. Joyce, "Membership Claims and Requests: Conversation-Level Newcomer Socialization Strategies in Online Groups," *Small Group Research* 41 (2010): 4–40.

78. For a discussion of primary tension and group phases, see E. Bormann, *Discussion and Group Methods* (New York: Harper & Row, 1975).

79. T. M. Scheidel and L. Crowell, "Ideas Development in Small Discussion Groups," *Quarterly Journal of Speech* 50 (1994): 140–145; C. J. Gersick, "Time and Transition in Work Teams: Toward a New Model of Group Development," *Academy of Management Journal* 32 (1989): 274–309; C. J. Gersick and J. R. Hackman, "Habitual Routines in Task-Performing Groups," *Organizational Behavior and Human Decision Processes* 47 (1990); A. Chang, P. Bordia, and J. Duck, "Punctuated Equilibrium and Linear Progression: Toward a New Understanding of Group Development," *Academy of Management Journal* 46 (2003): 106–117; M. S. Poole, "A Multisequence Model of Group Decision Development," *Communication Monographs* 50 (December 1983): 321–341.

80. R. Y. Hirokawa, "Discussion Procedures and Decision-Making Performance: A Test of a Functional Perspective," *Human Communication Research* 12 (1985): 203–224.

81. R. Y. Hirokawa, "Why Informed Groups Make Faulty Decisions: An Investigation of Possible Interaction-Based Explanations," *Small Group Research* 18 (1987): 3–29.

82. R. Y. Hirokawa and K. Rost, "Effective Group Decision-Making in Organizations: Field Test of the Vigilant Interaction Theory," *Management Communication Quarterly* 5 (1992): 267–288; Hirokawa, "Why Informed Groups Make Faulty Decisions"; R. Y. Hirokawa, "Group Communication and Decision-Making Performance: A Continued Test of the Functional Perspective," *Human Communication Research* 14 (1988): 487–515; M. O. Orlitzky and R. Y. Hirokawa, "To Err Is Human, to Correct for It Divine: A Meta-Analysis of Research Testing the Functional Theory of Group Decision-Making Effectiveness."

Paper presented at the meeting of the National Communication Association, Chicago, IL, November 1997.

83. Hirokawa, "Discussion Procedures and Decision-Making Performance."

84. We thank Dennis Romig, president of Side-by-Side and author of *Side-by-Side Leadership: Achieving Outstanding Results Together* (Marietta, GA: Bard Press, 2001), for this idea.

85. See R. Y. Hirokawa and R. Pace, "A Descriptive Investigation of the Possible Communication-Based Reasons for Effective and Ineffective Group Decision Making," *Communication Monographs 50* (December 1983): 363–379. The authors also wish to acknowledge D. A. Romig of Performance Resources, Inc., in Austin, Texas, for his contribution to the discussion.

86. D. G. Leathers, "Quality of Group Communication as a Determinant of Group Product," *Speech Monographs 39* (1972): 166–173; R. Y. Hirokawa and D. S. Gouran, "Facilitation of Group Communication: A Critique of Prior Research and an Agenda for Future Research," *Management Communication Quarterly 3* (August 1989): 71–92.

87. See F. J. Sabatine, "Rediscovering Creativity: Unlearning Old Habits," *Mid-American Journal of Business 4* (1989): 11–13.

88. Orlitzky and Hirokawa, "To Err Is Human, to Correct for It Divine."

Chapter 10

1. This example was freely adapted from E. Ross and A. Holland, *100 Great Businesses and the Minds Behind Them* (Naperville, IL: Sourcebooks, 2006), 94–98.

2. D. Barry, *Dave Barry's Guide to Life* (New York: Wings Books, 1991), 311.

3. "Survive Meetings with High-Tech Tools," *USA Today Online*, January 22, 1999, from http://www.usatoday.com.

4. Mosvick and Nelson, *We've Got to Start Meeting Like This!*; (Glenview, IL: Scott, Foresman, 1987). R. Y. Hirokawa, "Communication and Group Decision Making Efficacy," in *Small Group Communication Theory and Practice: An Anthology*, edited by R. Y. Hirokawa, R. S. Cathcart, L. A. Samovar, and L. D. Henmann (New York: Oxford University Press, 2007), 125.

5. Mosvick and Nelson, *We've Got to Start Meeting Like This!*

6. T. Ludwig and E. S. Geller, "Assigned Versus Participatory Goal Setting and Response Generalization: Managing Injury Control Among Professional Pizza Deliveries," *Journal of Applied Psychology 82* (1997): 253–61; for an excellent review of facilitation and collaboration leadership in teams and organizations, see D. A. Romig, *Side by Side Leadership* (Austin, TX: Bard, 2001) 9, 103–10.

7. D. W. Berg, "A Descriptive Analysis of the Distribution and Duration of Themes Discussed by Task-Oriented Small Groups," *Speech Monographs 34* (1967): 172–75; see also E. G. Bormann and N. C. Bormann, *Effective Small Group Communication* 2nd edition (Minneapolis: Burgess, 1970): 132; W.S. Poole, "Decision Development in Small Groups: A Multiple Sequence Model of Group Decision Development," *Communication Monographs 50* (1983): 321–41.

8. T. Hopthrow and L. Hulbert, "The Effect of Group Decision Making on Cooperation in Social Dilemmas," *Group Processes & Intergroup Relations 8*, no. 1 (2005): 89–100; J. Bonito, "A Longitudinal Social Relation Analysis of Participation in Small Groups," *Human Communication Research 32* (2006): 302–321.

9. R.F. Bales, *Interaction Process Analysis* (Chicago, IL: University of Chicago Press, 1976).

10. F. Niederman and R. J. Volkema, "The Effects of Facilitator Characteristics on Meeting Preparation, Set up, and Implementation," *Small Group Research 30* (1999): 330–60.

11. For a discussion of the role of goal clarification on team cohesion and performance, see F. Chiocchio and H. Essiembre, "Cohesion and Performance: A Meta-Analysis of Disparities Between Project Teams, Production Teams, and Service Teams," *Small Group Research 40* (2009): 382–420.

12. F. Brodbeck, R. Kerschreiter, A. Mojzisch, and S. Schulz-Hardt, "Group Decision Making Under Conditions of Distributed Knowledge: The Information Asymmetries Model," *Academy of Management Review 32*, no. 2 (2007): 459–479; T. Reimer, S. Kuendig, U. Hoffrage, E. Park, and V. Hinz, "Effects of the Information Environment on Group Discussions and Decisions in the Hidden-Profile Paradigm," *Communication Monographs 74*, no. 1 (2007): 1–28; R. de Vries, B. van den Hooff, and J. de Ridder, "Explaining Knowledge Sharing—The Role of Team Communication Styles, Job Satisfaction, and Performance Beliefs," *Communication Research 33*, no. 2 (2006): 115–135; D. Henningsen and M. Henningsen, "Do Groups Know What They Don't Know? Dealing with Missing Information in Decision-Making Groups," *Communication Research 34*, no. 5 (2007): 507–525; E. Dane and M. Pratt, "Exploring Intuition and Its Role in Managerial Decision Making," *Academy of Management Review 32*, no. 1 (2007): 33–54; T. Reimer, A. Reimer, and U. Czienskowski, "Decision-Making Groups Attenuate the Discussion Bias in Favor of Shared Information: A Meta-Analysis," *Communication Monographs 77* (2010): 121–142.

13. Susan Docherty as quoted by Adam Bryant, Corner Office: "Now, Put Yourself in My Shoes," *The New York Times*, February 6, 2010.

14. For an excellent review of collaborative leadership, see Dennis A. Romig, *Side by Side Leadership: Achieving Outstanding Results* (New York: Performance Research Press, 2006).

15. M. C. Roy, S. Gauvin, and M. Limayem, "Electronic Group Brainstorming: The Role of Feedback on Productivity," *Small Group Research 27* (1996): 21–47.

16. Mosvick and Nelson, *We've Got to Start Meeting Like This!*

17. A. Weitzel and P. Geist, "Parliamentary Procedure in a Community Group: Communication and Vigilant Decision Making," *Communication Monographs 65* (1998): 244–259.

18. We thank D. Romig for this observation. For additional information about structuring problem solving in teams, see D. A. Romig, *Breakthrough Teamwork: Outstanding Results Using Structured Teamwork* (New York: Irwin, 1996).

19. C. H. Kepner and B. B. Tregoe, *The Rational Manager* (New York: McGraw-Hill, 1965); see also G. Galanes and K. Adams, *Effective Group Discussion: Theory and Practice* (New York: McGraw-Hill, 2009).

20. B. J. Broome and L. Fulbright, "A Multistage Influence Model of Barriers to Group Problem Solving: A Participant-Generated Agenda for Small Group Research," *Small Group Research 26* (February 1995): 24–55.

21. See A. B. VanGundy, *Techniques of Structured Problem Solving* (New York: Van Nostrand Reinhold, 1981), 4.

22. VanGundy, *Techniques of Structured Problem Solving*, 4.

23. J. Dewey, *How We Think* (Boston: D. C. Heath, 1910).

24. This discussion of the Journalists' Six Questions is based on a discussion by J. E. Eitington, *The Winning Trainer* (Houston: Gulf Publishing, 1989), 157; also see R. Schwarz, *The Skilled Facilitator* (San Francisco, CA: Jossey-Bass, 2002).

25. Ross and Holland, *100 Great Businesses and the Minds Behind Them*, 112–115.

26. L. Gilson, C. Shalley, and T. Ruddy, "Creativity and Standardization: Complementary or Conflicting Drivers of Team Effectiveness?" *Academy of Management Journal 48*, no. 3 (2005): 521–531.

27. Ross and Holland, *100 Great Businesses and the Minds Behind Them*.

28. C. C. Miller and R. D. Ireland, "Intuition in Strategic Decision Making: Friend or Foe in the Fast-Paced 21st Century?" *Academy of Management Executive 19*, no. 1 (2005): 19–29; Brodbeck, Kerschreiter, Mojzisch, and Schulz-Hardt, "Group Decision Making Under Conditions of Distributed Knowledge."; F. Gino, L. Argote, E. Miron-Spektor, and G. Todorova, "First, Get Your Feet Wet: The Effects of Learning From Direct and Indirect Experience on Team Creativity," *Organizational Behavior and Human Decision Processes 111* (2010): 102–115.

29. S. Taggar, "Individual Creativity and Group Ability to Utilize Individual Creative Resources: A Multi-Level Model," *Academy of Management Journal 45* (April 2002): 315–330.

30. J. Kramer, G. P. Fleming, and S. M. Mannis, "Improving Face-to-Face Brainstorming Through Modeling and Facilitation," *Small Group Research 32*, no. 5 (2001): 533–557; S. Blomstrom, F. J. Boster, K. J. Levine, E. M. J. Butler, and S. L. Levine, "The Effects of Training on Brainstorming," *Journal of the Communication, Speech, & Theatre Association of North Dakota 21* (2008): 41–50.

31. E. Yasui, "Collaborative Idea Construction: The Repetition of Gestures and Talk During Brainstorming." Paper presented at the International Communication Association Conference, 2009.

32. A. F. Osborn, *Applied Imagination* (New York: Scribner's, 1962).

33. A. L. Delbecq, A. H. Van de Ven, and D. H. Gustafson, *Group Techniques for Program Planning: A Guide to Nominal-Group and Delphi Processes* (Glenview IL: Scott, Foresman, 1975), 7–16.

34. B. L. Smith, "Interpersonal Behaviors That Damage the Productivity of Creative Problem-Solving Groups," *Journal of Creative Behavior 27*, no. 3 (1993): 171–187.

35. G. Philipsen, M. Mulac, and D. Dietrich, "The Effects of Social Interaction on Group Generation of Ideas," *Communication Monographs 46* (June 1979): 119–125; F. M. Jablin, "Cultivating Imagination: Factors That Enhance and Inhibit Creativity in Brainstorming Groups," *Human Communication Research 7*, no. 3 (Spring 1981): 245–258; S. Jarboe, "A Comparison of Input-Output, Process-Output, and Input-Process Output Models of Small Group Problem-Solving Effectiveness," *Communication Monographs 55* (June 1988): 121–142. The idea of incorporating individual or silent brainstorming into the traditional brainstorming approach emerges from the nominal-group technique suggested by Delbecq, Van de Ven, and Gustafson, *Group Techniques for Program Planning*, 7–16; see also S. Jarboe, "Enhancing Creativity in Groups: Theoretical Boundaries and Pragmatic Limitations." Paper presented at the annual meeting of the Speech Communication Association, Atlanta, GA, November 1, 1991; F. M. Jablin and D. R. Seibold, "Implications for Problem-Solving Groups of Empirical Research on 'Brainstorming': A Critical Review of the Literature," *Southern Speech Communication Journal, 43* (1978): 324–356; Philipsen, Mulac, and Dietrich, "The Effects of Social Interaction"; VanGundy, *Techniques of Structured Problem Solving*; J. A. Goncalo and B. M. Staw, "Individualism-Collectivism and Group Creativity," *Organizational Behavior and Human Decision Processes 100* (2006): 96–109.

36. D. Stewart, C. Stewart, and J. Walden, "Self-Reference Effect and the Group-Reference Effect in the Recall of Shared and Unshared Information in Nominal Groups and Interacting Groups," *Group Processes & Intergroup Relations 10*, no. 3 (2007): 323–339.

37. E. Rietzschel, B. Nijstad, and W. Stroebe, "Productivity Is Not Enough: A Comparison of Interactive and Nominal Brainstorming Groups on Idea Generation and Selection," *Journal of Experimental Social Psychology 42* (2006): 244–251; J. Baruah and P. B. Paulus, "Effects of Training on Idea Generation in Groups," *Small Group Research 39* (2008): 523–541.

38. H. Barki and A. Pinsonneault, "Small Group Brainstorming and Idea Quality: Is Electronic Brainstorming the Most Effective Approach?" *Small Group Research 32*, no. 2 (2001): 158–205.

39. D. H. Gustafson, R. K. Shukla, A. Delbecq, and G. W. Walster, "A Comparative Study of Differences in Subjective Likelihood Estimates Made by Individuals, Interacting Groups, Delphi Groups and Nominal Groups," *Organizational Behavior and Human Performance 9* (1973): 280–291; VanGundy, *Techniques of Structural Problem Solving*; see also S. Beebe and J. Masterson, *Communicating in Small Groups: Principles and Practices,* 10th ed. (Boston: Allyn & Bacon, 2009).

40. Jarboe, "A Comparison of Input-Output, Process-Output, and Input-Process-Output Models"; Rietzschel, Nijstad, and Stroebe, "Productivity Is Not Enough."

41. Delbecq, Van de Ven, and Gustafson, *Group Techniques for Program Planning.*

42. M. C. Roy, S. Gauvin, and M. Limayam, "Electronic Group Brainstorming: The Role of Feedback on Productivity," *Small Group Research 27* (1996): 215–247.

43. Sosik, Avolio, and Kahai, "Inspiring Group Creativity"; W. H. Cooper, R. B. Gallupe, S. Pollard, and J. Cadsby, "Some Liberating Effects of Anonymous Electronic Brainstorming," *Small Group Research 29* (1998): 147–177.

44. M. C. Roy, S. Gauvin, and M. Limayam, "Electronic Group Brainstorming: The Role of Feedback on Productivity," *Small Group Research 27* (1996): 215–247; also see C. E. Timmerman and C. R. Scott, "Virtually Working: Communicative and Structural Predicators of Media Use and Key Outcomes in Virtual Work Teams," *Communication Monographs 73* (2006): 108–136.

45. Erich Witte, "Toward a Group Facilitation Technique for Project Teams," *Group Processes & Intergroup Relations 10*, no. 3 (2007): 299–309.

46. F. Niederman and R. J. Volkema, "The Effects of Facilitator Characteristics on Meeting Preparation, Set Up, and Implementation," *Small Group Research 30* (1990): 330–360.

47. U. Klocke, "How to Improve Decision Making in Small Groups—Effects of Dissent and Training Interventions," *Small Group Research 38*, no. 3 (2007): 437–468.

48. D. Matz and W. Wood, "Cognitive Dissonance in Groups: The Consequences of Disagreement," *Journal of Personality and Social Psychology 88*, no. 1 (2005): 22–37.

49. J. F. Veiga, "The Frequency of Self-Limiting Behavior in Groups: A Measure and an Explanation," *Human Relations 44* (1991): 877–895; S. Shulz-Hardt, F. C. Brodbeck, A. Mojzisch, R. Kerschreiter, and L. Frey, "Group Decision Making in Hidden Profile Situations: Dissent as a Facilitator for Decision Quality,' *Journal of Personality and Social Psychology 91*, no. 6 (2006): 1080–1093.

50. R. Y. Hirokawa, D. S. Gouran, and A. Martz, "Understanding the Sources of Faulty Group Decision Making: A Lesson from the *Challenger* Disaster," *Small Group Research 19*, no. 4 (November 1988): 411–433.

51. I. L. Janis, "Groupthink," *Psychology Today 5* (November 1971): 43–46, 74–76.

52. D. Seibold and R. Meyers, "Group Argument—A Structuration Perspective and Research Program," *Small Group Research 38*, no. 3 (2007): 312–336.

53. For a study exploring how group discussion influences consensus, see C. Pavitt and L. Aloia, "Factors Affecting the Relative Proportion of Reason and Preference Statements During Problem-Solving Group Discussion," *Communication Research Reports 26* (2009): 259–270.

54. B. Pan and H. Cho, "Subgroup Identification in Global Virtual Teams." Paper presented at the International Communication Association Conference, 2008.

55. Global Industry Analysts, Videoconferencing Global Strategic Business Report in Dennis Pamlin, *Virtual Meetings and Climate Innovation in the 21st Century* (Stockholm, Sweden: WWF, 2009), 16.

56. See www.zero-emission-meetings.com/content/examples. Also see Pamlin, *Virtual Meetings and Climate Innovation in the 21st Century*, 17.

57. See www.zero-emission-meetings.com/content/examples. Also see: Pamlin, *Virtual Meetings and Climate Innovation in the 21st Century*, 17.

58. Leslie Wolf, "How to Host an Effective Team Virtual Meeting." Retrieved December 3, 2010, from www.cdlib.org/cdlinfo/2010/10/13/how-to-host-an-effective-virtual-meeting/.

59. A. Gurtner, F. Tschan, N. Semmer, and C. Nagele, "Getting Groups to Develop Good Strategies: Effects of Reflexivity Interventions on Team Process, Team Performance, and Shared Mental Models," *Organizational Behavior and Human Decision Processes 102* (2007): 127–142.

60. K. Sager and J. Gastil, "The Origins and Consequences of Consensus Decision Making: A Test of the Social Consensus Model," *Southern Communication Journal 71*, no. 1 (2006): 1–24.

Chapter 11

1. E. Ross and A. Holland, "eBay," *100 Great Businesses and the Minds Behind Them* (Naperville, IL: Sourcebooks, 2006), 248–250.

2. T. Jeary, *Life Is a Series of Presentations* (New York: Simon & Schuster, 2004).

3. D. C. Bryant, "Rhetoric: Its Functions and Its Scope," *Quarterly Journal of Speech 39* (December 1953): 26.

4. Survey conducted by R. H. Bruskin and Associates, *Spectra 9* (December 1973): 4; D. Wallechinsky, I. Wallace, and A. Wallace, *The People's Almanac Presents the Books of Lists* (New York: Morrow, 1977).

5. S. B. Butterfield, "Instructional Interventions for Situational Anxiety and Avoidance," *Communication Education 37* (1988): 214–223; also see M. Motley, *Overcoming Your Fear of Public Speaking: A Proven Method* (New York: McGraw-Hill, 1995).

6. J. Ayres and T. S. Hopf, "The Long-Term Effect of Visualization in the Classroom: A Brief Research Report," *Communication Education 39* (1990): 75–78; J. Ayres and T. K. Wongprasert, "Measuring the Impact of Visualization on Mental Imagery: Comparing Prepared Versus Original Drawings," *Communication Research Reports 20* (Winter 2003): 45–53.

7. L. Fletcher, *How to Design & Deliver Speeches* (New York: Longman, 2001): 3.

8. M. Porhola, "Orientation Styles in a Public-Speaking Context," paper presented at the National Communication Association convention, Seattle, WA, November 2000; R. R. Behnke and M. J. Beatty, "A Cognitive-Physiological Model of Speech Anxiety," *Communication Monographs 48* (1981): 158–163; P. Addison, E. Clay, S. Xie, C. R. Sawyer, and R. R. Rehnke, "Worry as a Function of Public Speaking State Anxiety Type," *Communication Reports 16* (Summer 2003): 125–131.

9. Shannon C. McCullough, Shelly G. Russell, Ralph R. Behnke, Chris R. Sawyer, and Paul L. Witt, "Anticipatory Public Speaking State Anxiety as a Function of Body Sensations and State of Mind," *Communication Quarterly 54* (2006): 101–109.

10. A. M. Bippus and J. A. Daly, "What Do People Think Causes Stage Fright? Naïve Attribution About the Reasons for Public-Speaking Anxiety," *Communication Education 48* (1999): 63–72; also see D. C. Duff, T. R. Levine, M. J. Beatty, J. Woolbright, and H. Sun Park, "Testing Public Anxiety Treatments Against a Credible Placebo Control," *Communication Education 56* (January 2007): 72–88.

11. For an excellent review of communication apprehension research, see F. de Lima Osório, J. A. Crippa, and S. R. Loureiro, "Experimental Models for the Evaluation of Speech and Public Speaking Anxiety: A Critical Review of the Designs Adopted," *Journal of Speech and Language Pathology—Applied Behavior Analysis 2.4-3.1* (2008): 97–121; Graham D. Bodie, "A Racing Heart, Rattling Knees, and Ruminative Thoughts: Defining, Explaining, and Treating Public Speaking Anxiety," *Communication Education 59*, 1 (January 2010): 70–105; N. N. Vevea, J. C. Pearson, J. T. Child, and J. L. Semlak, "The Only Thing to Fear is . . . Public Speaking?: Exploring Predictors of Communication in the Public Speaking Classroom," *Journal of the Communication, Speech, and Theatre Association of North Dakota 22* (2009/2010): 1–8.

12. R. R. Behnke and Chris R. Sawyer, "Public-Speaking Procrastination as a Correlate of Public-Speaking Communication Apprehension and Self-Perceived Public-Speaking Competence," *Communication Research Reports 16* (1999): 40–47.

13. Desiree C. Duff, Timothy R. Levine, Michael J. Beatty, Jessica Woolbright, and Hee Sun Park, "Testing Public Anxiety Treatments Against a Credible Placebo Control," *Communication Education 56* (2007): 72–88.

14. P. D. MacIntyre and J. R. MacDonald, "Public-Speaking Anxiety: Perceived Competence and Audience Congeniality," *Communication Education 47* (October 1998): 359–365.

15. J. M. Honeycutt, C. W. Choi, and J. R. DeBerry, "Communication Apprehension and Imagined Interactions," *Communication Research Reports 26* (2009): 228–236.

16. J. Ayers and T. S. Hopf, "Visualization: A Means of Reducing Speech Anxiety," *Communication Education 34* (1985): 318–323; J. Ayres and B. L. Heuett, "An Examination of the Impact of Performance Visualization," *Communication Research Reports 16* (1999): 29–39.

17. Addison, Clay, Xie, Sawyer, and Behnke, "Worry as a Function of Public Speaking State Anxiety Type."

18. MacIntyre and MacDonald, "Public-Speaking Anxiety"; P. D. MacIntyre and K. A. Thivierge, "The Effects of Audience Pleasantness, Audience Familiarity, and Speaking Contexts on Public-Speaking Anxiety and Willingness to Speak," *Communication Quarterly 43* (1995): 456–466; P. D. MacIntyre, K. A. Thivierge, and J. Renee MacDonald, "The Effects of Audience Interest, Responsiveness, and Evaluation on Public-Speaking Anxiety and Related Variables," *Communication Research Reports 14* (1997): 457–468.

19. Chad Edwards and Suzanne Walker, "Using Public Speaking Learning Communities to Reduce Communication Apprehension," *Texas Speech Communication Journal 32* (2007): 65–71; also see Chia-Fang (Sandy) Hsu, "The Relationship of Trait Anxiety, Audience Nonverbal Feedbck, and Attributions to Public Speaking State Anxiety," *Communication Research Reports 26*, no. 3 (August 2009): 237–246.

20. MacIntyre and MacDonald, "Public-Speaking Anxiety"; R. B. Rubin, A. M. Rubin, and F. F. Jordan, "Effects of Instruction on Communication Apprehension and Communication Competence," *Communication Education 46* (1997): 104–114; Amber N. Finn, Chris R. Sawyer, and Paul Schrodt, "Examining the Effect of Exposure Therapy on Public Speaking State Anxiety," *Communication Education 58* (2009): 92–109; Amber N. Finn, Chris R. Sawyer, and Ralph R. Behnke, "A Model of Anxious Arousal for Public Speaking," *Communication Education 58* (2009): 417–432.

21. Joe Ayres, Terry Schliesman, and Debbie Ayres Sonandre, "Practice Makes Perfect but Does It Help Reduce Communication Apprehension?" *Communication Research Reports 15* (Spring 1998): 170–179.

22. The late W. Braden, longtime professor of speech communication at Louisiana State University, presented a memorable speech at the 1982 Florida Speech Communication Association in which he emphasized "the audience writes the speech" to indicate the importance and centrality of being an audience-centered speaker.

23. For an excellent discussion of how to adapt to specific audience situations, see J. Sprague and D. Stuart, *The Speaker's Handbook* (Belmont, CA: Thompson, 2007), 345.

24. T. Jeary, *Life Is a Series of Presentations* (New York: Simon & Schuster, 2004), 149.

25. F. E. X. Dance, *Speaking Your Mind: Private Thinking and Public Speaking* (Dubuque, IA: Kendall/Hunt, 1994).

26. T. Longaberger, "Leading," *Vital Speeches of the Day 73*, no. 8 (2007): 347–348.

27. S. Trujillo, "Now That the Dog Has Caught the Bus—What Next?" *Vital Speeches of the Day 72*, no. 20/21 (2006): 589–590.

28. J. C. Humes, *The Sir Winston Method: The Five Secrets of Speaking the Language of Leadership* (New York: William Morrow, 1991), 137.

29. N. Volkow, "Drug Addiction," *Vital Speeches of the Day 72*, no. 16/17 (2006): 505–508.

30. W. B. Harrison, Jr., "Challenges and Opportunities in a Globalizing World, " *Vital Speeches of the Day 72*, no. 13 (2006): 400–404.

31. E. Wolff, *Winning Orations 1994* (Mankato, MN: Interstate Oratorical Association, 1994), 67.

32. R. L. Weaver II, "Sticky Ideas," *Vital Speeches of the Day 73*, no. 8 (2007): 353–356.

33. G. Yash, "Beyond Wisdom: Business Dimensions of an Aging America," *Vital Speeches of the Day 76*, no. 2 (February 2010): 69–75.

34. Facebook press room website. Retrieved October 20, 2011, http://www.facebook.com/press/info.php?statistics.

35. As cited by G. Kolata, "Study Shows Why the Flue Likes Winter," *New York Times* (December 5, 2007): 1.

36. M. F. Curtin, "Media and the Degradation of Language," *Vital Speeches of the Day 72*, 20/21 (2006): 578–580.

37. M. Kushner, *Successful Presentations for Dummies: A Reference for the Rest of Us* (Foster City, CA: IDG Books, 1997), 66.

38. Guy Kawasaki as quoted by Adam Bryant, "Corner Office: Just Give Him 5 Sentences, Not 'War and Peace,'" *New York Times* (March 12, 2010).

39. Guy Kawasaki, "Corner Office," *New York Times*.

40. D. A. Lieberman, *Public Speaking in a Multicultural Environment*, Second Edition (Boston: Allyn and Bacon, 1997), 23.

41. Ibid.

42. Harrison, "Challenges and Opportunities in a Globalizing World."

43. G. Yash, "Beyond Wisdom: Business Dimensions of an Aging America," *Vital Speeches of the Day 76*, no. 2 (February 2010): 69–75.

44. A. Lincoln, "Gettysburg Address," delivered at Gettysburg, PA, November 19, 1863. Douglass Archives of American Public Address. Retrieved July 12, 1999, from http://www.gettysburg.com/bog/address.htm.

45. D. MacArthur, "Farewell to the Cadets," address delivered at West Point, May 12, 1962. Reprinted in *Contemporary American Speeches* 7e, edited by R. L. Johannesen, R. R. Allen, and W. A. Linkugel (Dubuque, IA: Kendall/Hunt, 1992), 393.

46. M. L. King, Jr., "I Have a Dream," delivered in Washington, DC, August 28, 1963. Reprinted in *Contemporary American Speeches*, edited by R. L. Johannesen, R. R. Allen, and W. A. Linkugel (Dubuque, IA: Kendall/Hunt, 1992), 369.

47. D. P. Starr, "Writing for the Web," *Vital Speeches of the Day 73*, no. 6 (2007): 269–270.

Chapter 12

1. Information about Oprah Winfrey was adapted from: E Ross and A. Holland, *100 Great Businesses and the Minds Behind Them* (Naperville, IL: Sourcebooks, 2006), 216–218.

2. H. Monroe, "Measurement and Analysis of Audience Reaction to Student Speakers' Studies in Attitude Changes," *Bulletin of Purdue University Studies in Higher Education 22* (1937). For an excellent discussion of the importance of speaker delivery as discussed by both classical and contemporary rhetoricians, see J. Fredal, "The Language of Delivery and the Presentation of Character: Rhetorical Action in Demosthenes' 'Against Medias,'" *Rhetoric Review 20* (2001): 251–267.

3. P. Heinbert, "Relationship of Content and Delivery to General Effectiveness," *Speech Monographs 30* (1963): 105–107.

4. J. C. Humes, *The Sir Winston Method: The Five Secrets of Speaking the Language of Leadership* (New York: William Morrow, 1991), 160.

5. Adapted from R. Ailes, *You Are the Message* (New York: Doubleday, 1989), 37–38.

6. Granville Toogood, *The New Articulate Executive: Look, Act, and Sound Like a Leader* (New York: McGraw-Hill, 2010), 96.

7. Humes, *The Sir Winston Method*.

8. Ibid.

9. S. A. Beebe, "Eye Contact: A Nonverbal Determinant of Speaker Credibility," *Speech Teacher 23* (1974): 21–25; S. A. Beebe, "Effects of Eye Contact, Posture, and Vocal Inflection Upon Credibility and Comprehension," *Australian Scan Journal of Nonverbal Communication 7–8* (1979–1980): 57–70; M. Cobin, "Response to Eye Contact," *Quarterly Journal of Speech 48* (1963): 415–419.

10. Beebe, "Eye Contact."

11. Ibid.

12. M. J. Beatty, "Some Effects of Posture on Speaker Credibility," library paper, Central Missouri State University, 1973.

13. P. Ekman, W. V. Friesen, and S. S. Tomkins, "Facial Affect Scoring Technique: A First Validity Study," *Semiotica 3* (1971).

14. P. Ekman and W. Friesen, *Unmasking the Face* (Englewood Cliffs, NJ: Prentice-Hall, 1975).

15. Ibid.

16. K. K. Sereno and G. J. Hawkins, "The Effects of Variations in Speakers' Nonfluency upon Audience Ratings of Attitude toward the Speech Topic and Speakers' Credibility," *Speech Monographs 34* (1967): 58–74; G. R. Miller and M. A. Hewgill, "The Effect of Variations in Nonfluency on Audience Ratings of Source Credibility," *Quarterly Journal of Speech 50* (1964): 36–44; A. Mehrabian and M. Williams, "Nonverbal Concomitants of Perceived and Intended Persuasiveness," *Journal of Personality and Social Psychology 13* (1969): 37–58.

17. Adapted from S. A. Beebe and S. J. Beebe, *Public Speaking: An Audience-Centered Approach* (Boston: Allyn & Bacon, 2012).

18. M. M. Gill, "Accent and Stereotypes: Their Effect on Perceptions of Teachers and Lecture Comprehension," *Journal of Applied Communication 22* (1994): 348–361.

19. J. W. Neuliep, *Intercultural Communication: A Contextual Approach* (Boston: Houghton Mifflin, 2000), 247.

20. O. Hargie and D. Dickson, *Skilled Interpersonal Communication: Research, Theory and Practice* (London: Routledge, 2004).

21. Robert W. Selander as quoted by Adam Bryant, Corner Office: "The X Factor When Hiring? Call it 'Presence,'" *New York Times*, June 26, 2010.

22. Selander, *New York Times*, June 26, 2010.

23. Eilene Zimmerman, "Staying Professional in Virtual Meetings," *New York Times* Business Section (September 26, 2010), 9.

24. B. Filson, *Executive Speeches: Tips on How to Write and Deliver Speeches from 51 CEOs* (New York: John Wiley, 1994).

25. Filson, *Executive Speeches*.

26. E. Ross and A. Holland, "Subway," *100 Greatest Businesses and the Minds Behind Them* (Naperville, IL: Sourcebooks, 2006): 388–391.

27. E. Bohn and D. Jabusch, "The Effect of Four Methods of Instruction on the Use of Visual Aids in Speeches," *The Western Journal of Speech Communication 46* (Summer 1982): 253–265; for an excellent review of advantages and disadvantages of PowerPoint, see M. R. Stoner, "PowerPoint in a New Key," *Communication Education 56* (2007): 354–381; also see D. Cyphert, "Presentation Technology in the Age of Electronic Eloquence: From Visual Aid to Visual Rhetoric," *Communication Education 56* (2007): 168–192; J. Mackiewicz, "Comparing PowerPoint Experts' and University Students' Opinions About PowerPoint Presentations," *Technical Writing and Communication 38* (2008): 149–165.

28. M. E. Patterson, D. F. Dansereau, and D. Newbern, "Effects of Communication Aids and Strategies on Cooperative Teaching," *Journal of Educational Psychology 84* (1992): 453–461.

29. Toogood, *The New Articulate Executive*, 96.

30. L. A. Burke and K. E. James, "PowerPoint-Based Lectures in Business Education: An Empirical Investigation of Student-Perceived Novelty and Effectiveness," *Business Communication Quarterly 71* (2008): 277–296.

31. Toogood, *The New Articulate Executive*, 96.

32. Ibid.

33. For a review of research and application about font size and use of capitalization see J. M. Adams, D. D. Faux and L. J. Rieber, *Printing Technology*. (Albany, NY: Delmar, 2001).

34. W. J. Earnest, "Developing Strategies to Evaluate the Effective Use of Electronic Presentation Software in Communication Education," unpublished dissertation, University of Texas at Austin (2003).

35. L. Mahin, "PowerPoint Pedagogy," *Business Communication Quarterly* (2004): 219–222; also see E. Brumberger, "Visual Communication in the Workplace: A Survey of Practice," *Technical Communication Quarterly 16* (2007): 369–395.

36. Dave Paradi, "What Annoys Audiences About PowerPoint Presentations?" Survey conducted in 2005, retrieved September 29, 2010, from www.thinkoutsidetheslide.com/pptresults2005.htm.

37. L. A. Burke and K. E. James, "PowerPoint-Based Lectures in Business Education: An Empirical Investigation of Student-Perceived Novelty and Effectiveness," *Business Communication Quarterly 71* (2008): 277–296.

38. J. Mackiewicz, "Comparing PowerPoint Experts' and University Students' Opinions About PowerPoint Presentations," *Technical Writing and Communication 38* (2008): 149–165.

39. Toogood. *The New Articulate Executive*, 103.

40. For an excellent discussion of how to time PowerPoint slides, see Toogood. *The New Articulate Executive*.

41. We acknowledge D. Cavanaugh's excellent supplement *Preparing Visual Aids for Presentations* (Boston: Allyn & Bacon/Longman, 2001) as a source for many of our tips and suggestions.

Chapter 13

1. E. Ross and Angus Holland, *100 Great Businesses and the Minds Behind Them* (Naperville, IL: Sourcebooks, 2006), 86.
2. "New Directions: Women at the Top: The Ranking," *Financial Times* (October 23, 2010), 13.
3. J. C. Humes, *The Sir Winston Method: The Five Secrets of Speaking the Language of Leadership* (New York: William Morrow, 1991), 58.
4. M. Knowles, *Self-Directed Learning* (Chicago: Follett, 1975).
5. R. E. Flax, "A Manner of Speaking," *Ambassador* (May–June 1991): 37.
6. R. J. Rivera and H. Paradise, "2006 State of the Industry Report," *American Society for Training & Development* (2007).
7. S. A. Beebe, T. P. Mottet, and K. D. Roach, *Training and Development: Enhancing Communication and Leadership Skills* (Boston: Pearson, 2013).
8. Ibid.
9. A. Maslow, "A Theory of Human Motivation," in *Motivation and Personality* (New York: Harper & Row, 1954), Chapter 5; D. A. Lieberman, *Public Speaking in the Multicultural Environment* 2e (Boston: Allyn & Bacon, 1997), 23.
10. See I. L. Janis and S. Feshback, "Effects of Fear Arousing Communications," *Journal of Abnormal and Social Psychology* 48 (January 1953): 78–92; F. A. Powell and G. R. Miller, "Social Approval and Disapproval Cues in Anxiety Arousing Situations," *Speech Monographs* 34 (June 1967): 152–159; K. L. Higbee, "Fifteen Years of Fear Arousal: Research on Threat Appeals, 1953–1968," *Psychological Bulletin* 72 (December 1969): 426–444; Bogeajis, "The Danger of Child Safety Seats: Why Aren't They Safe?" *Winning Orations 1996* (Mankato, MN: Interstate Oratorical Association, 1996), 10.
11. Aristotle, *The Art of Rhetoric*; D. Ehninger, B. E. Gonbeck, R. E. McKerrow, and A. H. Monroe, *Principles and Types of Speech Communication* (Glenview, IL: Scott, Foresman, 1986), 15.
12. D. A. Lieberman, *Public Speaking in the Multicultural Environment*, 2nd ed. (Boston: Allyn & Bacon, 1997), 23.
13. A. Bogeajis, "The Danger of Child Safety Seats: Why Aren't They Safe?" *Winning Orations 1996* (Mankato, MN: Interstate Oratorical Association, 1996), 10.
14. D. Ehninger, B. E. Gronbeck, R. e. McKerrow, and A. H. Monroe, *Principles and Types of Speech Communication* (Glenview, IL: Scott, Foresman, 1986), 10.
15. R. L. Kotcher, "Join the Conversation." *Vital Speeches of the Day 72*, no. 18/19 (2006): 541–543.
16. Kotcher, "Join the Conversation."
17. Ibid.
18. Ibid.
19. Ibid.
20. D. C. Bryant, "Rhetoric: Its Functions and Its Scope," *Quarterly Journal of Speech 39*, no. 4 (December 1953): 26.
21. For additional description of web-based methods of presenting information, see Beebe, Mottet, and Roach, *Training and Development*.
22. Posted by *The New Yorker*, http://www.newyorker.com/magazine/bios/the_new_yorker/search?contributorName=The%20New%20Yorker. Also, retrieved, September 30, 2010, from http://www.newyorker.com/online/blogs/ask/2010/09/malcolm-gladwell-twitter-social-media.html#ixzz10xOkeyLs.
23. E. Ross and A. Holland, "Red Bull: Taste Doesn't Always Matter," *100 Greatest Businesses and the Minds Behind Them* (Naperville, IL: Sourcebooks, 2006), 28–29.
24. Adapted from Granvillle N. Toogood, *The New Articulate Executive: Look, Act, and Sound Like a Leader* (New York: McGraw-Hill, 2010), 14.
25. In addition to using the motivated sequence, our suggestions for organizing a sales presentation are based on strategies discussed in D. DiResta, *Knockout Presentations: How to Deliver Your Message with Power, Punch, and Pizzazz* (Worcester, MA: Chandler House Press, 1998), 166–171.
26. Adapted from O. Hargie, D. Dickson, and D. Tourish, *Communication Skills for Effective Management* (New York: Palgrave MacMillan, 2004), 213.
27. Barbara J. Krumsiek as quoted by Adam Bryant, Corner Office: "It's Not a Career Ladder, It's an Obstacle Course," *New York Times* (May 22, 2010).
28. C. Pearlman, "Oscar Speeches: Statues in Their Hands, Feet in Their Mouths," *Austin American-Statesman 24* (March 1997): E8.
29. W. Faulkner, acceptance of the Nobel Prize for Literature, December 10, 1950, in *A Treasury of the World's Great Speeches*, edited by H. Peterson (New York: Simon & Schuster, 1965), 815.
30. "Slainte! Toasts, Blessings, and Sayings." Retrieved June 28, 1998, from http://zinnia.umfacad.maine.edu/~donaghue/toasts07.html.

Chapter 14

1. E. Brennan and E. Clarage, *Who's Who of Pulitzer Prize Winners* (Phoenix: The Oryx Press, 1999).
2. J. De Avila, "Many Workers Seen Lacking Skills for New Jobs." The WSJ Online. Retrieved April, 1 2011, from http://online.wsj.com/article/SB10001424052748704893604576200871243450518.html.
3. R. Ettison and J. Knowles, "Speaking in Tongues," *MIT Sloan Management Review 47* (2006): 99–108.
4. J. Gordon, "Best (Hiring) Practices." Business Week Online. Retrieved June 12, 2008, from http://www.businessweek.com/careers/content/aug2006/ca20060810_662254.htm.
5. G. J. Alred, C. T. Brusaw, and W. E. Oliu, *The Business Writer's Companion*, 4th ed. (Boston: Bedford/St. Martin's, 2005).
6. From *Cambridge Dictionaries* (New York: Cambridge University Press, 2008).
7. J. Gastil, "Generic Pronouns and Sexist Language: The Oxymoronic Character of Masculine Generics," *Sex Roles 23* (1990): 629–643; M. C. Hamilton, "Masculine Bias in the Attribution of Personhood: People = Male, Male = People," *Psychology of Women Quarterly 15* (1991): 393–402; J. Y. Switzer, "The Impact of Generic Word Choices: An Empirical Investigation of Age- and Sex-Related Differences," *Sex Roles 22* (1990): 69–82; W. Todd-Mancillas, "Masculine Generics—Sexist Language: A Review of Literature and Implications for Speech Communication Professionals," *Communication Quarterly 29* (1981): 107–115.
8. J. Wood, *Gendered Lives: Communication, Gender, and Culture*, 8th ed. (Belmont, CA: Wadsworth, 2008).
9. S. B. Gmelch, *Gender on Campus: Issues for College Women* (New Brunswick, NJ: Rutgers University Press, 1998); J. Wood, *Gendered Lives*.
10. I. Selvarajah, "Overusing Business Buzzwords." Generation Y Consultant. Retrieved from http://genyconsultant.com/2008/03/overusing-business-buzzwords.html.
11. Alred, Brusaw, and Oliu, *The Business Writer's Companion*.
12. J. H. Siess, "The Most Common Spelling Errors." Ezine Articles. Retrieved June 10, 2008, from http://ezinearticles.com/?The-Most-Common-Spelling-Errors&id=794024.
13. Alred, Brusaw, and Oliu, *The Business Writer's Companion*.
14. J. O'Malley, "Quiz—Are You Smarter Than a Spell-Checker?" Pongo Resume Online. Retrieved June 30, 2008, from http://www.pongoresume.com/blogPosts/146/quiz-are-you-smarter-than-a-spell-checker.
15. M. Richtel, "Growing up Digital, Wired for Distraction." New York Times. Retrieved April 1, 2011, from http://www.nytimes.com/2010/11/21/technology/21brain.html?pagewanted=1&_r=1.
16. K. Christoff, A. M. Gordon, J. Smallwood, R. Smith, and J. W. Schooler, "Experience Sampling during fMRI Reveals Default Network and Executive System Contributions to Mind Wandering," *Proceedings from the National Academy of Sciences (PNAS)*, February 9, 2009.
17. Taken from a report by comScore, "The US Digital Year in Review: 2010." Report available at http://www.comscore.com/Press_Events/Presentations_Whitepapers/2011/2010_US_Digital_Year_in_Review.

18. M. Mandel, "The Real Reason You're Working So Hard . . . and What You Can Do About It." *Business Week*. Retrieved February 5, 2008, from http://www.businessweek.com/magazine/content/05_40/b3953601.htm?chan=search.

19. R. H. Lengel and R. L. Daft, "The Selection of Communication Media as an Executive Skill," *Academy of Management Executive 2* (1988): 225–232.

20. Adapted from ibid.

21. Ibid. See also K. Stephens and T. P. Mottet, "Interactivity in a Web-Conferencing Learning Environment: Effects on Trainers and Trainees," *Communication Education 57* (2008): 88–104.

22. To learn more about how to match the message to the communication channel, read P. G. Clampitt, L. Berk, and M. L. Williams, "Leaders as Strategic Communicators." *Ivey Business Journal 66* (2002): 51–55; P. G. Clampitt and M. L. Williams, "Decision Downloading." *MIT Sloan Management Review 48* (2007): 77–82.

23. M. Memoli, "White House Apologizes to Fired USDA Worker." *Los Angeles Times*. Retrieved May 25, 2011, from http://articles.latimes.com/2010/jul/22/nation/la-na-white-house-usda-apology-20100722.

24. These ideas were taken from personal conversations with organizational communication scholar Phil Salem, Texas State University-San Marcos, January 17, 2008; also refer to P. Salem, *Organizational Communication and Change* (Cresskill, NJ: Hampton Press, 1996).

25. From a press release dated January 18, 2006, "We Don't Talk Anymore," discussing the results of a study conducted by an independent research firm that surveyed 150 senior executives at the nation's 1,000 largest companies sponsored by Office Team, a job search company. Retrieved February 7, 2008, from http://www.officeteam.com/portal/site/ot-us/template.

26. K. Stephens, "The Successive Use of Information and Communication Technologies at Work." *Communication Theory 17* (2007): 486–507.

27. S. A. Hewlett, "Is Your Blackberry Lowering your IQ?" Harvard Business Online. Retrieved February 13, 2008, from http://www.businessweek.com/managing/content/sep2007/ca20070920_461254.htm?chan=search.

28. L. Stack, "Use Proper Email Netiquette to Avoid Wasting Other's Time," ArticleCity. Retrieved February 15, 2008, from http://www.articlecity.com/articles/computers_and_internet/article_2117.shtml.

29. Ibid.

30. R. King, "Companies Want to Monitor Workers on Social Networks," *Bloomberg BusinessWeek*. Retrieved March 27, 2011, from http://www.businessweek.com/technology/technology_at_work/archives/2009/05/workers_social.html.

31. Ibid.

32. J. Bear and M. Bear, *Complaint Letters for Busy People* (Boston: Career Press, 2000).

33. Sheila Lirio Marcelo was interviewed by Adam Bryant, "O.K., Team, It's Time to Switch Chairs," *New York Times* (August 7, 2010), B2.

34. Ibid.

35. Alred, Brusaw, and Oliu, *The Business Writer's Companion*.

36. C. Bovee, J. Thill, and B. Schatzman, *Business Communication Today*, 7th ed. (Upper Saddle River, NJ: Prentice Hall, 2003).

37. D. Seibert, "Legal Precautions When Writing Proposals," The Siebert Group. Retrieved May 29, 2010, from http://www.persuasionselling.com/LegalPrecautions.htm.

38. Bovee, Thill, and Schatzman, *Business Communication Today*.

39. Alred, Brusaw, and Oliu, *The Business Writer's Companion*.

Appendix

1. For an analysis of increased work time, see Robert Pagliarini, *The Other 8 Hours* (New York: St. Martin's Press, 2010).

2. S. Winston, *The Organized Executive: The Classic Program for Productivity: New Ways to Manage Time, Paper, People, and the Digital Office* (New York: Warner Books, 2001).

3. A. McGee-Cooper, *Time Management for Unmanageable People* (New York: Bantam Books, 1994).

4. G. P. Latham and L. M. Saari, "The Importance of Union Acceptance for Productivity Improvement through Goal Setting," *Personnel Psychology 35*, no. 4 (1982): 781–787; G. P. Latham, T. R. Mitchell, and D. L. Dossett, "The Importance of Participative Goal Setting and Anticipated Rewards on Goal Difficulty and Job Performance," *Journal of Applied Psychology 62*, no. 2 (1978): 163–171; A. Tziner and R. Kopelman, "Effects of Rating Format on Goal-Setting Dimensions: A Field Experiment," *Journal of Applied Psychology 73*, no. 2 (1988): 323–326; A. Tziner and G. P. Latham, "The Effects of Appraisal Instrument, Feedback and Goal Setting on Worker Satisfaction and Commitment," *Journal of Organizational Behaviour 10*, no. 2 (1989): 145–153.

5. S. R. Covey, *The 7 Habits of Highly Effective People* (New York: Simon & Schuster, 1989).

6. S. Beebe, T. Mottet, and K. D. Roach, *Training and Development: Enhancing Communication and Leadership Skills* (Boston: Allyn & Bacon, 2004).

7. D. Allen, *Getting Things Done: The Art of Stress-Free Productivity* (New York: Viking, 2001).

8. S. Covey, A. R. Merrill, and R. R. Merrill, *First Things First* (New York: Fireside, 1996).

9. Covey, Merrill, and Merrill, *First Things First*.

10. Cristobal Conde, as quoted by Adam Bryant, "Corner Office: Structure? The Flatter, the Better," *New York Times*, January 17, 2010, B2.

11. Allen, Getting Things Done.

12. Ibid.

13. Ibid.

14. Ibid.

15. M. J. Cook, *Time Management: Proven Techniques for Making the Most of Your Valuable Time* (Holbrook, MA: Adams Media, 1998); R. Alexander, *Commonsense Time Management* (New York: AMACOM, 1992).

16. These software programs were suggested by Robert Pagliarini, *The Other 8 Hours*, (New York: St. Martin's Press, 2010), 57–59.

17. Alexander, *Commonsense Time Management*.

Index

Photo Credits